SSDI Solutions

Ideas to Strengthen the Social Security Disability Insurance Program

SSDI Solutions

Ideas to Strengthen the Social Security Disability Insurance Program

THE MCCRERY-POMEROY
SSDI SOLUTIONS INITIATIVE

A project of the Committee for a Responsible Federal Budget

INFINITY PUBLISHING

ISBN 978-1-4958-0956-9

Published March 2016

INFINITY PUBLISHING
1094 New DeHaven Street, Suite 100
West Conshohocken, PA 19428-2713
Toll-free (877) BUY BOOK
Local Phone (610) 941-9999
Fax (610) 941-9959
Info@buybooksontheweb.com
www.buybooksontheweb.com

TABLE OF CONTENTS

Preface ix

Advisory Council Members xi

Acknowledgments xiii

Foreword xv

Section I: Introduction 1

1. Seizing the Opportunity: Ideas for Improving Disability Programs
   Jim McCrery and Earl Pomeroy 3

2. An Overview of Social Security Disability Insurance (SSDI)
   Patricia Owens 25

Section II: Early Intervention 49

3. The Employment/Eligibility Service System: A New Gateway for Employment Supports and Social Security Disability Benefits
   David Stapleton, Yonatan Ben-Shalom, and David Mann 51

4. A Community-Focused Health & Work Service (HWS)
   Jennifer Christian, Thomas Wickizer, and A. Kim Burton 83

5. Using Transitional Jobs to Increase Employment of SSDI Applicants and Beneficiaries
   Julie Kerksick, David Riemer, and Conor Williams 113

Discussion of Early Intervention Proposals
Lisa D. Ekman 133

Section III: Program Administration 139

6. Data-Driven Solutions for Improving the Continuing Disability Review Process
Alexandra Constantin, Julia Porcino, John Collins, and Chunxiao Zhou 141

7. Social Security Disability Adjudicative Reform: Ending the Reconsideration Stage of SSDI Adjudication after Sixteen Years of Testing and Enhancing Initial Stage Record Development
Jon C. Dubin 177

8. Social Security: Restructuring Disability Adjudication
David W. Engel, Dale Glendening, and Jeffrey S. Wolfe 207

Discussion of Program Administration Proposals
Margaret Malone 235

Section IV: Interaction with Other Programs 239

9. Expanding Private Disability Insurance Coverage to Help the SSDI Program
David F. Babbel and Mark F. Meyer 241

10. Ensuring Access to Long-Term Services and Supports for People with Disabilities and Chronic Conditions
Mark Perriello 275

11. Improving the Interaction Between the SSDI and Workers' Compensation Programs
John F. Burton Jr. and Xuguang (Steve) Guo 293

Discussion of Interaction with Other Programs Proposals
David Wittenburg 331

Section V: Structural Reforms 337

12. Transitional Benefits for a Subset of the Social Security Disability Insurance Population
Kim Hildred, Pamela Mazerski, Harold J. Krent, and Jennifer Christian 339

13. Beyond All or Nothing: Reforming Social Security Disability Insurance to Encourage Work and Wealth
Jason J. Fichtner and Jason S. Seligman 357

14. Exploring an Alternative Social Security Definition of Disability
Neil Jacobson, Aya Aghabi, Barbara Butz, and Anita Aaron 389

Discussion of Structural Reform Proposals
Art Spencer 409

Section VI: International Comparisons and Long-Term Solvency 413

15. Approaches to Assisting Working-Aged People with Disabilities: Insights from Around the World
Robert Haveman 415

16. Options to Address SSDI's Financial Shortfall
Marc Goldwein and Edward Lorenzen 449

References 475

List of Contributors 525

About the Co-Chairs 529

PREFACE

The *McCrery-Pomeroy SSDI Solutions Initiative* is a project of the non-partisan Committee for a Responsible Federal Budget dedicated to identifying practical policy changes to improve the Social Security Disability Insurance (SSDI) program. These solutions are meant to help spur and contribute to a debate on how to ensure the SSDI program best serves those with disabilities, those who pay into the program, and the economy as a whole.

The SSDI program provides important support to millions of workers with disabilities and their families, helping many who are unable to work stay out of poverty. There are, however, a number of areas where the program could be improved to better serve workers with disabilities and others who are insured by the program. A number of experts, reviewers, and political leaders have found that improvements should be made to the determination process, program integrity, interactions between SSDI and other public and private programs, return to work incentives, and early interventions for workers with disabilities, to name just a few areas.

Rather than a top-down approach, the *SSDI Solutions Initiative* solicited ideas from experts who have been studying this program for years and even decades. Specifically, the *SSDI Solutions Initiative* issued a public "call for papers," allowing potential authors from different disciplines and ideological backgrounds to submit proposals. The project then selected the most promising ideas to be written into full papers; focusing on proposals encompassing a wide variety of areas within the program and placing an emphasis on proposals the inclusion of "intermediate steps" that could be enacted within the next few years.

Papers were written through an iterative process that included two formal peer reviews and ongoing feedback from the *SSDI Solutions Initiative* advisory council and staff. Papers were presented at the *SSDI Solutions Conference* held on August 4, 2015, where further feedback was offered by discussants and attendees.

The *SSDI Solutions Initiative* is co-chaired by former Congressmen and Ways & Means Social Security Subcommittee Chairmen Jim McCrery (R-LA) and Earl Pomeroy (D-ND) and guided by an advisory council of experts, advocates, and practitioners from across the ideological spectrum.

Advisory Council Members

G. Lawrence Atkins, Executive Director, Long-Term Quality Alliance. President, National Academy of Social Insurance.

Andrew G. Biggs, Resident Scholar, American Enterprise Institute. Former Principal Deputy Commissioner, Social Security Administration.

Barbara Butz, President & CEO, PolicyWorks.

Mary C. Daly, Senior Vice President & Associate Director of Research, Federal Reserve Bank of San Francisco.

Marty Ford, Senior Executive Officer for Public Policy, The Arc of the United States.

Steve Goss, Chief Actuary, Social Security Administration.

Ron Haskins, Senior Fellow & Co-Director of the Center on Children and Families, Brookings Institution.

Andrew Houtenville, Associate Professor of Economics & Research Director, University of New Hampshire Institute on Disability.

Andrew Imparato, Executive Director, Association of University Centers on Disabilities (AUCD).

Neil Jacobson, Founder & CEO, Abilicorp.

Stanford Ross, former Chair of the Social Security Advisory Board, former Commissioner of the Social Security Administration, and former Public Trustee, Social Security & Medicare Trust Funds.

Robert D. Reischauer, Distinguished Institute Fellow & President Emeritus, Urban Institute. Former and renominated Public Trustee, Social Security & Medicare Trust Funds.

C. Eugene Steuerle, Richard B. Fisher Chair, Urban Institute.

William Taylor, former Executive Director of the Office of Appellate Operations and Deputy Chair of the Appeals Council, and Deputy Associate Commissioner of the Office of Hearings and Appeals, Social Security Administration.

Rebecca Vallas, Director of Policy, Poverty to Prosperity Program, Center for American Progress.

ACKNOWLEDGMENTS

This volume could not have been written without the advice, feedback, support, and hard work of many individuals and organizations.

First and foremost, the *McCrery-Pomeroy SSDI Solutions Initiative* would like to acknowledge the members our advisory council: Larry Atkins, Andrew Biggs, Barbara Butz, Mary Daly, Marty Ford, Steve Goss, Ron Haskins, Andrew Houtenville, Andy Imparato, Neil Jacobson, Stan Ross, Bob Reischauer, Gene Steuerle, Bill Taylor, and Rebecca Vallas. These leading disability insurance experts generously donated their time to offer feedback throughout the project, assist us in selecting papers, review and comment on these papers, and help us develop the co-chairs' introductory chapter.

This project also would not be possible without the authors of each paper, who carefully crafted their proposals while integrating expert feedback along the way. A full list of contributors is available in the back of this book.

We would also like to recognize those who participated in our *SSDI Solutions Conference*: Senator Orrin Hatch, Bob Greenstein, Mark Warshawsky, Alan Cohen, Lisa Ekman, Art Spencer, Margaret Malone, and David Wittenburg.

In addition, we would like to thank the many Social Security experts who helped with this project by offering important advice and feedback, either by offering their assistance as a peer reviewer, presenting their thoughts on how to best improve the SSDI program, participating in one of our "listening sessions," or otherwise contributing to this project. Some of these individuals include: Henry Aaron, Michael Astrue, David Autor, Charles Blahous, Jonathan Breul, Kelly Buckland, Richard Burkhauser, Henry Claypool, Gina Clemons, Mark Duggan, Melissa Favreault, Joel Feinleib, Keith Fontenot, D. Randall Frye, Jagadeesh Gokhale, Thomas Golden, Claire Green, Rachel Greszler, Dorcas Hardy, David Hatfield, Jeffrey Hemmeter, Kevin Hollenbeck, David John, Jim Kessler, Paul Krawzak, Kate Lang, Jeffrey Liebman, Gina Livermore, Jeffrey Lubbers, Bryon MacDonald, Nicole Maestas, Joyce Manchester, Martin McGuinness, Jeanne

Morin, Ken Nibali, Web Phillips, Richard Pierce, Harold Pollack, Virginia Reno, Jon Schwabish, Ishita Sengupta, James Sherk, Jack Smalligan, Andrew Sperling, TJ Sutcliffe, Kate Thornton, David Walker, and Ethel Zelenske. Many others also provided us assistance, including numerous Congressional staffers and other federal government employees, especially those at the Social Security Administration and Social Security Advisory Board.

We would also like to acknowledge the staff of the Committee for a Responsible Federal Budget who ran this project – particularly current and former project staff members Mike Murphy, Alexandra de Filippo, Corbin Evans, Marc Goldwein, Erich Hartman, Walker Irving, Ed Lorenzen, Chris Towner, and expert consultant David Barnes.

Finally, we gratefully acknowledge the generous support of the Laura and John Arnold Foundation and the Lynde and Harry Bradley Foundation who provided funding for this project, as well as Charles River Associates, Community Advocates Public Policy Institute, Mathematica Policy Research, the National Institutes of Health, and the University of Pennsylvania who helped to fund specific papers.

Foreword

Mike Murphy, Project Director

When the *McCrery-Pomeroy SSDI Solution Initiative* was formed in 2014, the Social Security Disability Insurance (SSDI) trust fund was within two years of depleting its reserves. The need to prevent this trust fund depletion was clear, but it also offered an opportunity to further advance an important conversation over the future of the SSDI program. With this deadline in mind, the *SSDI Solutions Initiative* solicited, developed, and shared with lawmakers a number of ideas to improve the SSDI program as well as other services for individuals with disabilities.

In late 2015, lawmakers took action to delay the depletion of the SSDI trust fund. Specifically, the Bipartisan Budget Act of 2015 reallocated payroll tax revenue from the Old-Age and Survivors' Insurance (OASI) trust fund to the SSDI trust fund in order to extend the solvency of SSDI until 2021 or 2022. It accompanied this reallocation with several incremental improvements to the SSDI program, including several anti-fraud and program integrity measures, the renewal of (and reforms to) demonstration authority for the Social Security Administration, and the repeal of the Single Decision Maker pilot program.

The changes in the Bipartisan Budget Act—many in the spirit of the ideas we had been recommending and sharing with lawmakers—represent a small but important step forward. Yet much more must be done to truly improve the SSDI program.

A few chapters in this book have been written with the passage of the Bipartisan Budget Act in mind, and they reflect its passage. However, the text of the 12 proposals put forward in this book—chapters 3 through 14—were written before the Bipartisan Budget Act and have not been updated for its passage.

Despite not reflecting this new legislation, the 12 proposals in this book remain as relevant today as they were then. The proposals address a range of key issues not dealt with in the Bipartisan Budget Act, and they can help policymakers as they continue to grapple with not only how to extend the long-term health of the SSDI trust fund but also improve the lives of people with disabilities across the country.

Section I

INTRODUCTION

1

Seizing the Opportunity: Ideas for Improving Disability Programs

Jim McCrery and Earl Pomeroy

INTRODUCTION

Social Security Disability Insurance (SSDI) is a vital social insurance program that protects 150 million American workers against the loss of wages caused by a disability. Currently, nine million workers with disabilities and an additional two million family members receive and rely on SSDI benefits (SSA 2015a). For most, SSDI cash benefits are modest, averaging about $14,000 per year for current recipients and $15,000 for new recipients. But those benefits are also hugely important, representing the majority of personal income for eight out of 10 people who receive SSDI (Bailey and Hemmeter 2015). They also often lead to Medicare eligibility so that individuals with disabilities can get the health care treatments they need. For many, SSDI is the difference between being able to afford basic needs and living in poverty.

As former chairmen of the House Ways and Means Social Security Subcommittee, we may belong to different political parties, but we both believe strongly in the importance of the SSDI program. We also agree that much can be done to improve the program.

We started the *SSDI Solutions Initiative* in September of 2014 because the program faced a critical funding crisis. Without action, the program would have been unable to pay full benefits starting at the end of 2016. We believed that while the funding crisis needed to be addressed, it also presented an opportunity to improve SSDI and other services for people with disabilities.

Since then, Congress passed and the President signed the Bipartisan Budget Act of 2015, which temporarily averted the immediate funding crisis. The law made several small reforms to the program and reallocated a portion of the payroll tax for three years in order to fully fund the program until about 2022. Although this was a welcome development and a step in the right direction, it is not fundamentally a solution.

The previous 2016 deadline presented an opportunity to take steps to improve SSDI and other services for people with disabilities but little time to develop thoughtful and responsible actions. The new deadline of 2022 presents a similar opportunity with six years to develop good solutions. We cannot waste the opportunity by deluding ourselves into believing everything has been solved.

After working on this project for a year and a half, we have come to believe that, in order to preserve and protect SSDI, lawmakers need to follow three basic principles for action on the program:

1. **Begin to Test and Adance Programmatic Improvements Now**
2. **Improve the Effectiveness, Efficiency, and Integrity of the Current SSDI System**
3. **Support Work and Improve the Lives of Workers with Disabilities**

We discuss these in greater detail later in this chapter.

We are steadfast in our belief that this program can and should be improved upon and that policymakers should discuss and debate the many options to do so, without delay. This book—and the *SSDI Solutions Initiative*—is our contribution to that important conversation.

A Challenge and an Opportunity for Action

Although the SSDI trust fund has recently been extended, it continues to face a serious financial shortfall. The program has run cash deficits since 2005, and in 2014 it spent about $35 billion more than it took in. Prior to the Bipartisan Budget Act, the program's trust fund had been expected to run dry in the fourth quarter of 2016. That date has been extended to about 2022, when, absent legislative action, benefits for disabled workers and their families will need to be cut by about 15 percent.

The need to address SSDI's finances before the 2016 deadline sparked an important conversation on the future of the program. That's why we started this project—not as a budget-cutting exercise focused on achieving financial balance, but as a project to identify changes to the program that would improve the lives of those with disabilities along with those who pay into the program. Despite some positive changes in the Bipartisan Budget Act, the need for programmatic improvements remains. And we now have six years to do something about that. Failure to seize this opportunity and use this additional time to engage in the vital conversation of how to put forward such changes would represent a huge missed opportunity.

To begin the project, we formed an advisory council with some of the leading experts on disability policy and advocates in the disability community. They helped the initiative dig into the issues facing this program and better understand the challenges facing people with disabilities. They gave our project invaluable advice and feedback throughout the process. We then issued a call for papers, asking outside experts to submit their own ideas. The response was tremendous. Working with our advisory council, we reviewed dozens of proposals and selected 12 that we considered promising. They are a diverse set of ideas from a diverse group of authors.

We asked those authors to submit draft papers to explain the problems they wanted to address and their proposed solutions. Those drafts went through a rigorous review process that included feedback from our advisory council as well as our staff and expert consultants. They were also subject to two formal peer reviews. Authors presented their papers at our *SSDI Solutions Conference* on August 4, 2015 in Washington, DC, where they heard from leading experts and conference attendees about their proposals and received additional feedback from expert discussants.

Additionally, project staff have spent the past 18 months reading and studying dozens of proposals and papers, consulting regularly with the expert advisory council, and speaking with well over 100 experts, advocates, practitioners, and people with disabilities. This only strengthened our resolve to put forward ideas for improvements to the program. This book is the culmination of all that work. It presents what we believe are 12 thoughtful sets of proposals that could improve the SSDI program and other services to people with disabilities.

We firmly believe that with the right mix of creativity and resolve, the SSDI program can be improved so that it serves everyone—including applicants, beneficiaries, and the taxpayers—better. The determination process could be streamlined to reduce waiting times and improve accuracy. Fraud and improper payments could be reduced. Those who are already on the program could be given more support in efforts to return to work. And those not yet on the program could be given more opportunities to stay at work, so they can keep collecting a paycheck instead of a disability insurance check.

We believe policymakers must take advantage of this opportunity to enact improvements to the SSDI program that truly help those who are protected by it and rely on it, as well as society as a whole. Doing so will require the right mixture of research, creativity, and political will. It is our sincere hope that this book will help in that process.

OVERVIEW OF THE BOOK

The goal of the *SSDI Solutions Initiative* is to identify practical policy changes to improve the Social Security Disability Insurance program and other services to people with disabilities. The remainder of this book presents a number of these proposed policy ideas. Although these ideas are not exhaustive and we are not specifically endorsing them, we do believe each idea is worthy of consideration.

In this chapter, we have provided our own insights and put forward principles and recommendations for how policymakers should approach SSDI reform. Chapter 2, ***"An Overview of the Social Security Disability Insurance (SSDI) Program"*** by Patricia Owens, summarizes the SSDI program and many of the issues surrounding it and other services for individuals with disabilities.

Section II focuses on three sets of proposals to encourage early intervention in order to keep more workers in the workforce rather than on the program. Chapter 3 includes a proposal by David Stapleton, Yonatan Ben-Shalom, and David Mann titled ***"The Employment/Eligibility Service System: A New Gateway for Employment Supports and Social Security Disability Benefits."*** In Chapter 4, Jennifer Christian, Thomas Wickizer, and A. Kim Burton put forward a proposal for ***"A Community-Focused Health & Work Service (HWS)."*** And in Chapter 5, Julie Kerksick, David Riemer, and Conor Williams call for ***"Using Transitional Jobs to Increase Employment of SSDI Applicants and Beneficiaries."*** Following these chapters is a discussion of the proposals by Lisa Ekman, president of Ekman Advocates for Progress.

Section III includes three sets of proposals related to SSDI program administration. In Chapter 6, Alexandra Constantin, Julia Porcino, John Collins, and Chunxiao Zhou propose using ***"Data-Driven Solutions for Improving the Continuing Disability Review Process."*** Jon Dubin proposes changes to the process in Chapter 7 titled ***"Social Security Disability Adjudicative Reform: Ending the Reconsideration Stage of SSDI Adjudication after Sixteen Years of Testing and Enhancing Initial Stage Record Development."*** And in Chapter 8, David Engel, Dale Glendening, and Jeffrey Wolfe present their proposal ***"Social Security: Restructuring Disability Adjudication."*** Margaret Malone, former staff director of the Social Security Advisory Board, discusses these proposals at the end of this section.

Section IV presents proposals to improve interaction between SSDI and other programs. David Babbel and Mark Meyer present their proposal in Chapter 9 discussing ***"Expanding Private Disability Insurance Coverage to Help the SSDI Program."*** In Chapter 10, Mark Perriello presents his proposal around ***"Ensuring Access to LongTerm Services and Supports for People with Disabilities and Chronic Conditions."*** Next, John Burton and Steve Guo propose ***"Improving the Interaction Between the SSDI and Workers' Compensation Programs"*** in Chapter 11. At the end of this section, David Wittenburg, director of Health Research, Mathematica Policy Research, provides his thoughts on these proposals.

Section V presents three proposals for structural changes in the SSDI program. ***"Transitional Benefits for a Subset of the Social Security Disability Insurance Population"*** by Kim Hildred, Pam Mazerski, Harold Krent, and Jennifer Christian begins the section in Chapter 12. Following that, Jason Fichtner and Jason Seligman propose ***"Beyond All or Nothing: Reforming Social Security Disability Insurance to Encourage Work and Wealth"*** in Chapter 13. And finally, Neil Jacobson, Aya Aghabi, Barbara Butz, and Anita Aaron propose ***"Exploring an Alternative Social Security Definition of Disability"*** in Chapter 14. Former Social Security Administration Associate Commissioner Art Spencer follows these proposals with his thoughts at the end of this section.

Finally, Section VI includes two chapters meant to provide additional context around SSDI reform. In Chapter 15, ***"Approaches to Assisting Working-Aged People with Disabilities: Insights from Around the World,"*** Robert Haveman discusses disability insurance programs in other countries and how they have changed in recent years. And in Chapter 16, ***"Options to Address SSDI's Financial Shortfall,"*** Marc Goldwein and Edward Lorenzen (who are on the staff of the SSDI Solutions Initiative) lay out a number of options to improve the finances of the SSDI trust fund.

PRINCIPLES AND RECOMMENDATIONS

As our project gained insight from experts, advocates, and practitioners and pored over the literature, it became clear that many thoughtful ideas about how to improve the SSDI program already existed. Our initiative builds on this existing universe of ideas with 12 additional sets of proposals. These proposals cover a wide array of topics including strengthening work support and early intervention, reforming program administration, improving interaction between SSDI and other programs, and making structural reforms to the program.

Some of the ideas in this book represent major changes, while others are quite modest. Some would reduce trust fund spending, while others would add costs. Some would be carried out by the Social Security Administration (SSA), while others would need to involve other agencies or entities. But each proposal is intended to better the entire system of disability support in the United States.

Each of the proposals also includes intermediate steps leading to implementation. These include studies, pilots, and smaller scale changes to gather evidence of effectiveness. By offering intermediate steps, the authors show how to tackle large-scale problems in a cautious and responsible way.

Neither of us is endorsing any of the sets of proposals presented in this book. Nor is the Committee for a Responsible Federal Budget, the *SSDI Solutions Initiative* itself, or members of our advisory council. These proposals represent the work and ideas of their respective authors. These proposals were selected because we believe they are worthy of consideration, not necessarily because they are perfect or should be put into law as written.

Our hope is that lawmakers will carefully review, scrutinize, adjust, and then select from these and other existing ideas to develop meaningful programmatic improvements. We have three broad-based recommendations to guide congressional action, discussed below.

Recommendation #1: Begin Testing and Advancing Programmatic Improvements Now

The recently-enacted Bipartisan Budget Act extended the life of the SSDI trust fund for six years. As a result, the SSDI trust fund is on course to deplete its reserves by 2022, according to Social Security's Chief Actuary. At that time, the program would be bringing in enough revenue to pay for about 85 percent of program costs, necessitating an immediate cut to all beneficiaries of nearly one-sixth.

An abrupt reduction of that size would be devastating for many individuals with disabilities who count on the program. Nearly half of SSDI beneficiaries have family incomes of $30,000 per year or less, and almost one quarter have family incomes less than $15,000. SSDI keeps many of these families out of poverty and accounts for well over half of total family income for the average recipient (Bailey and Hemmeter 2015).

Our discussions with those in the disability community made it clear that, throughout 2015, the threat of an impending large benefit cut created much anxiety and fear among those who rely on the program. Although those anxieties and fears may have been relieved by passage of the Bipartisan Budget Act, that relief is temporary. Lawmakers waited too long to avoid trust fund depletion with any solution other than a temporary reallocation. In order to prevent that situation from recurring in 2022, action must be taken now.

Six years is certainly not a long time. But it should be enough time for policymakers in Congress, at the Social Security Administration, and in the White House to test and enact a variety of reforms to the SSDI program. Rather than waiting until the deadline approaches, lawmakers should act well in advance, building on the relatively modest reforms in the Bipartisan Budget Act to improve SSDI. Meanwhile, SSA should use the administrative tools at its disposal to do the same.

Some program improvements could be implemented quickly, but many others would benefit from testing and research to refine them and evaluate their effectiveness. To do so, pilots and demonstration projects should be undertaken with thorough and rigorous evaluation. This type of testing often takes a long time to produce results, which is why it should begin as soon as possible.

The Bipartisan Budget Act made some of this testing possible by restoring SSA's demonstration authority and specifically calling for a focus on projects "designed to promote attachment to the labor force." However, given the mixed results of past pilots, and given that many ideas worth testing would involve other agencies or organizations, a new mechanism for implementing pilots and demonstrations may be needed.

One option, proposed by our friends at the Bipartisan Policy Center (2015), would be to create a special office within SSA to implement pilots and an oversight committee to ensure effectiveness. Another option would be to establish an "innovation center" outside of SSA to test new ideas. A third option would be establishment of a formal inter-agency task force to coordinate new pilots and demonstrations across different parts of the government. Some pilots could be conducted at the state level.

Regardless of who is in charge, it is important to develop specific goals and quality metrics on which to base evaluations, with sound statistical practices and an adherence to the scientific method. The testing process must also be versatile and nimble. Pilots or demonstrations that aren't working should be shut down as soon as possible. Successful experiments should be expanded, and if success continues, they should ultimately be implemented nationwide.

Most importantly, policymakers must not wait another six years to take further action on improvements to SSDI and other programs and services for people with disabilities. Putting off action will only guarantee another hasty scramble to avert trust fund reserve depletion in 2022 without enough time to thoughtfully evaluate serious long-term solutions. This is not the time to take a six-year break from this vital work. The vital discussions on the future of SSDI must continue and new legislation, regulations, and administrative improvements must be enacted and implemented over the course of this six-year window of opportunity.

Recommendation #2: Improve the Effectiveness, Efficiency, and Integrity of the Current SSDI System

By and large, the SSDI program does what it is supposed to: it pays monthly checks to individuals with disabilities who are unable to engage in substantial work. But when it comes to putting and keeping the right people on the program in a timely manner with minimal complexity and without unnecessary hurdles, there is room for improvement.

Strengthen Program Integrity to Reduce Improper Payments

One common-sense principle is that the SSDI program should only pay benefits to individuals who are qualified to receive them. However, in some cases beneficiaries are improperly receiving benefits due to fraud, accidental overpayments, or because a person has recovered from their disability. Perfect payment accuracy can probably never be achieved, yet it is an important aspirational goal. Short of perfection, more could be done both to reduce fraud and overpayments (as well as underpayments) and to help SSA identify and discontinue benefits to those who are able to return to work.

Fraud is probably less common in the SSDI program than many believe. It is not a major cost driver for the program, and it is a mistake to exaggerate the size and scope of the problem. Depicting SSDI as rife with fraud and painting SSDI beneficiaries as fraudsters only undermines public support for the program and demonizes individuals with disabilities who rely on it.

But it would also be a mistake to ignore fraud altogether. Every dollar from the trust fund paid to someone cheating the system is a dollar unavailable for those truly in need. And every time a neighbor or colleague knows someone who is gaming the system, it also undermines support for the program.

Combating fraud is essential to the integrity of the program, and we should do everything we can to reduce fraud where it does exist. There are many bipartisan ideas in Congress and elsewhere for how to do so. These include: improved information technology; better data sharing and inter-agency cooperation; tougher penalties for fraud; more investigations of fraud allegations (including expansion of Cooperative Disability Investigations (CDIs)); and stricter standards for representatives, judges, and medical professionals who interact with the program. Many of these ideas were included in the Bipartisan Budget Act, and others should be included in subsequent legislation and policies to further combat fraud.

Importantly, many, and perhaps most, improper payments have nothing to do with fraud. They occur because beneficiaries no longer meet the program's definition of disabled but continue to receive benefits. Continuing Disability Reviews (CDRs) are designed to regularly review recipients for medical improvement or work and earnings above the levels allowed by the program and to stop payments when appropriate. Unfortunately, SSA faces a significant CDR backlog, and the agency may not be conducting CDRs as well as it could. Funding is a major issue (discussed later in this section), but more can be done to improve the CDR process. Some ideas others have recommended to improve CDRs include: strengthening and better applying exceptions to the Medical Improvement Review Standard (SSAB 2014; BPC 2015); conducting additional CDRs in cases for those awarded benefits by "Red Flag" administrative law judges (ALJs) with extremely high award rates (Lankford and Speier 2014); using new tools to acquire more accurate earnings information (Coburn 2014; President's budget 2015; BPC 2015; SSAB 2014); and providing more services and better communication of expectations to beneficiaries who are expected to improve (SSAB 2014; BPC 2015).

SSA could also improve the way it prioritizes CDRs. Currently, CDRs are scheduled based on whether the applicant is expected to improve, with workers put into one of three "diary" categories. In ***"Data-Driven Solutions for Improving the Continuing Disability Review Process"*** (Chapter 6), Constantin, Porcino, Collins, and Zhou propose to create a new information technology infrastructure that would leverage new and existing data sources and predictive modeling to create individualized diary entries that would help the agency target CDRs where there is the best chance of finding improvement.

In addition to reducing fraud and improving the CDR process, much could also be done to reduce accidental over- and under-payments by SSA, including leveraging new technologies and better data collection to more accurately track and more quickly react to wage earnings.

Improve Accuracy and Consistency, and Reduce Complexity of the Determination Process

To enroll in the SSDI program, individuals must often navigate a number of state and federal agencies over several months if not years. Eligibility is based on a relatively strict five-step evaluation process described in Chapter 2. This process is complicated, inconsistent, and plagued by subjectivity. We heard this over and over again from the people and groups we spoke with, and those complaints echo the finding of many studies for many years—including those from the Government Accountability Office (2004) and the Social Security Advisory Board (2006).

It can take months (or even longer in some cases) to get an initial decision on a disability claim. Each state has its own DDS agency to make these determinations. If a claim is denied, there is an incredibly long and complicated multistep appeal process to navigate. It starts (in most cases) with a reconsideration step that many believe is little more than a rubber stamp of the first decision.

If a claim is denied at reconsideration, the applicant can appeal by requesting a hearing before an ALJ—a procedure so intimidating that the vast majority of applicants hire a legal representative to handle their cases. It's a process that can take up to a year or more to complete, and it has rules-of-evidence procedures that are incomplete and complex. And, as at the earlier steps of adjudication, outcomes are widely variable and inconsistent.

Clearly, there is a trade-off between complexity and accuracy, and much of the complexity within the program is intended to ensure that the right benefits go to the right people. But it's difficult to see the benefits of this trade-off, and there is little evidence that all the complexity is producing correct outcomes. We believe that there may be room to both reduce complexity and improve accuracy and consistency by, for example, taking advantage of technology, streamlining and simplifying the determination and appeals process, and developing guidelines and training that prioritize consistency across actors in the process.

One frequently mentioned idea is to reduce the number of levels in the appeals process. In ***"Social Security Disability Adjudicative Reform: Ending the Reconsideration Stage of SSDI Adjudication after Sixteen Years of Testing and Enhancing Initial Stage Record Development"*** (Chapter 7), Dubin argues for eliminating the first level of appeal, known as reconsideration. He would divert those administrative resources toward improving the quality of the initial determination, including through enhanced case development. There are already 10 states with no reconsideration level.

We also heard many concerns about the current hearing process at the ALJ level. Some said ALJs have too little time to review each case, that they often have insufficient medical evidence, and that they lack clear of rules of procedure. There also appears to be considerable (albeit shrinking) decisional inconsistency among judges. In 2010, for example, one ALJ in Texas approved only 9 percent of applications for benefits while another in Tennessee approved 99 percent (SSA OIG 2012). Claimant representatives also appear to be playing an increasing role in the adjudication process, and in some cases they may be having an adverse effect on efficiency and outcomes.

In ***"Social Security: Restructuring Disability Adjudication"*** (Chapter 8), current ALJs Wolfe, Engel, and Glendening address some of these concerns. First, they propose that a government representative—or "present party" (PreP)—be a part of the hearing to advocate for a correct and timely ruling. Regardless of whether this proposal is adopted, they also propose that SSA establish formal rules of procedure such as evidentiary standards and rules for closing the record. They recommend reducing the Appeals Council's role in reviewing ALJ decisions. Finally, they propose to reform the way claimant representatives are paid so that they are not paid more when cases take more time and are no longer reimbursed for travel.

There are many other ideas to improve the determination and adjudication process, including expanding video hearings, streamlining and ramping up the ALJ hiring process, modifying various rules of evidence, changing the role of the Appeals Council, and establishing a corps or cadre of medical and vocational professionals to serve as expert consultants for disability cases. Some of these ideas will require testing, while others could be implemented relatively quickly.

Provide SSA Adequate Resources While Demanding Full Accountability

As improvements are made to the SSDI program, it is important to provide SSA with adequate resources to implement them. Unfortunately, SSA often appears to lack the funds to effectively administer the program, even in its current form. For example, the average beneficiary waits over three months to receive an initial decision, and almost two years if the case goes to an ALJ (SSA 2015b). And SSA currently issues about $1.6 billion per year in SSDI overpayments, largely because it cannot record and adjust fast enough to wage reporting with its current resources (SSA 2015c).

In some cases, lack of funds is not only creating hardship for recipients but is literally costing the trust fund money. Because of limited funding, there is a 726,000-case backlog of CDRs, which means SSA may be paying benefits to some people who are no longer disabled (SSA OIG 2015a). According to the Chief Actuary, the federal government saves between $8 and $12 for every $1 spent on CDRs (SSAB 2014, 21). Failing to fund these CDRs is essentially throwing money away.

A number of ideas exist for ensuring adequate agency funding. The Bipartisan Budget Act relied on one of those approaches to allow for increased near-term funding for CDRs and other program integrity measures through special adjustments to discretionary spending caps. This is certainly helpful, and we encourage appropriators to use these cap adjustments to ensure adequate funding. . Ultimately, Congress needs to give SSA the funding it needs to eliminate the CDR backlog, conduct timely reviews, and effectively administer other parts of the program. This could be achieved by continuing to rely on cap adjustments or by exploring other mechanisms to ensure a steady stream of future funding.

However, full funding must come with full accountability. SSA needs to show that it is using these additional funds in the most effective and efficient way possible.

SSA is in many ways a twentieth-century agency operating with outdated tools and an antiquated approach. SSA's technology, systems, and practices all must be updated and brought into the twenty-first century. This requires not only a significant financial investment, but also a culture change. Strong leadership at the top is essential to ensure that SSA is doing the best job it can to award (or deny) and pay (or discontinue) benefits in an accurate, timely, and user-friendly manner.

Accountability also means strong oversight of the agency, the DDSs, the ALJs, and various other parts of the program. SSA must do its job to self-evaluate, and its Office of the Inspector General has an essential role in doing so. Congress and the President must also do their jobs by using their own administrative and oversight authority. The Office of Management and Budget (OMB) and Government Accountability Office (GAO) also have parts to play here.

Recommendation #3: Support Work and Improve the Lives of Workers with Disabilities

The upcoming discussion should look beyond the goal of funding the current system and improving the SSDI program itself to identifying changes that will truly improve the lives of Americans with disabilities, as well as society at large. This means providing supports and incentives for workers to remain in or return to the workforce. And it means finding the right set of supports and incentives for each individual situation. In some cases, these supports and incentives may have little to do with SSDI. As a result, we need to look beyond today's SSDI cash benefit program to find other ways to support workers with disabilities, including through alternative national, local, and private programs.

Promote Work, Especially Through Early Intervention

One message we heard over and over again from disability experts, advocates, and practitioners is that early intervention is the key to helping individuals with disabilities work. For most Americans, including those with disabilities, work is an important foundation of adult life. Those who work are often happier, healthier, and certainly wealthier than those who do not. While work may not be an option for all people with disabilities, the advantages of working for those who are able to are substantial. For these individuals, the financial returns to work often far outweigh what can be offered from Social Security alone. From the standpoint of the SSDI program, more work means lower benefit costs and greater payroll tax revenue. And for the nation, more work means a larger economy with more production, consumption, and investment.

SSDI cash benefits are, and should continue to be, an important lifeline for individuals with disabilities who cannot work. For many others—including some current and potential SSDI beneficiaries—the right mix of incentives, supports, and accommodations can help to keep them in the labor force and improve their financial well-being.

In many ways, the current SSDI program discourages work because it generally does not allow people to stay on the program when they can consistently make more than $1,090 a month, or about $13,000 per year. The program does include a number of work incentives that encourage beneficiaries to work, but they are exceedingly complex. First, there is a Trial Work Period, where an individual can work on a short-term basis without losing benefits. If the individual is able to continue working and thus loses his or her benefits, there is an Extended Period of Eligibility where he or she can re-enter the program if his or her earnings fall. There is also a Ticket to Work program that gives SSDI recipients access to employment networks and vocational rehabilitation agencies to help them return to work.

There are many ideas for how to improve these work incentives. For example, instead of benefits ending completely if a beneficiary earns above the $1,090 threshold on a regular basis, there could be a "benefit offset" that reduces benefits gradually as earnings rise. A Benefit Offset National Demonstration (BOND) is already underway, and the Bipartisan Budget Act calls for testing and evaluating an alternative benefit offset design. Depending on the results, an offset could ultimately be expanded to all beneficiaries—though getting the details right would be extremely important. Improvements to the Ticket to Work program could also help, as could more oversight of vocational rehabilitation services. And SSA could set clearer expectations and develop better resources for recipients who may be able to return to work.

However, almost every expert we spoke with cautioned us about the limitations in getting people already on SSDI to return to work at a level necessary to exit the program. Once individuals leave the workforce and receive SSDI, they lose their connection to work, and it is difficult to reconnect them regardless of the incentives. The best opportunity to promote work is not by getting people off the program but by preventing (or delaying) them from needing to be on the program in the first place.

In ***"The Employment/Eligibility Service System: A New Gateway for Employment Supports and Social Security Disability Benefits"*** (Chapter 3),

Stapleton, Ben-Shalom, and Mann propose one such early intervention project, focused on providing work assistance when someone applies for SSDI rather than after they are approved. Under their proposal, states would create a new system that acts as a gateway to triage applicants into either SSDI or a system of work supports depending on an individual's needs and abilities.

In ***"A Community-Focused Health & Work Service (HWS)"*** (Chapter 4), Christian, Wickizer, and Burton propose an even earlier intervention to begin within the first 12 weeks of an onset of an illness or injury. Under their proposal, a nationwide HWS would coordinate services to workers right after they develop an impairment, leading to a faster recovery.

In ***"Using Transitional Jobs to Increase Employment of SSDI Applicants and Beneficiaries"*** (Chapter 5), Kerksick, Riemer, and Williams propose a different intervention. Their program would subsidize temporary employment in private businesses for people with disabilities and provide job counseling. This would allow employees to gain skills and get help finding permanent employment. They also propose an enhanced earned income tax credit for workers with disabilities.

Because these early intervention ideas are largely untested, all three papers propose pilot programs before implementation. Apart from these ideas, three other early intervention demonstration projects are called for in the President's budget: one to improve coordination of state DDSs, another to offer work supports to those with mental impairments, and one that test ways to encourage employers to retain workers who develop impairments.

One key question in designing early intervention projects is determining who will run them. SSA may be helpful in some areas, but most interventions must rely on a number of outside federal, state, local, and private entities to do much of the work. Another issue is timing, as acting early increases the chances of success, but may also require targeting a wider set of individuals and thus may be overly costly. Identifying the right people to assist at the lowest cost and highest potential gain will require thoughtful design that may take considerable testing to get right. For this reason, it is all the more important to begin now.

Address Interactions with Other Programs

SSDI is only one of many programs for workers with disabilities. Other programs that SSDI interacts with include Supplemental Security Income (SSI), Medicare, Workers' Compensation (WC), Medicaid, unemployment insurance, vocational rehabilitation services, private disability insurance, and many other federal, state, local, and private programs.

In ***"An Overview of the Social Security Disability Insurance (SSDI) Program"*** (Chapter 2), Owens discusses these interactions in more detail. Not surprisingly, interactions are seldom seamless. The process is often confusing and can cause work disincentives or cost shifting. The process can also result in unnecessary costs and poor support for workers with disabilities.

One idea that is often talked about, with supporters (and detractors) on both sides of the aisle, is to limit potential overlapping payments from unemployment insurance and disability insurance. A careful review of this and any other potential "double payments" is necessary, but policymakers should go beyond the legitimate concern about duplicative payments to make sure that systems of support for people with disabilities also function well together to create the intended incentives, offer the most effective support, and further the goal of encouraging work.

In ***"Expanding Private Disability Insurance Coverage to Help the SSDI Program"*** (Chapter 9), Babbel and Meyer take on the interaction between SSDI and private employer-sponsored disability insurance. They argue that because private disability insurance supports return-to-work through comprehensive disability management programs, it keeps many individuals from entering the SSDI system. They want to increase private disability insurance coverage by allowing employers to "auto-enroll" employees, requiring workers who do not want to participate in disability coverage to "opt-out."

In ***"Ensuring Access to Long-Term Services and Supports for People with Disabilities and Chronic Conditions"*** (Chapter 10), Perriello proposes addressing the connection between SSDI, health care, and long-term services and supports. Most SSDI beneficiaries currently have access to health insurance (Bailey and Hemmeter 2015). This may be from Medicare, Medicaid, employer-provided insurance or insurance obtained through an Affordable Care Act insurance exchange. But only Medicaid covers the specific costs people with disabilities incur when attempting to work, such as a personal attendant or durable medical equipment. Perriello proposes an expansion of Medicaid's Buy-In so that more workers with disabilities can access these services, along with new private "wrap-around" coverage for those with other types of insurance.

Finally in ***"Improving the Interaction Between the SSDI and Workers' Compensation Programs"*** (Chapter 11), Burton and Guo address many of the interactions between SSDI and the Workers' Compensation (WC) program. They propose reforming the existing WC-SSDI offset, which generally reduces SSDI benefits when total benefits would exceed 80 percent of prior income. They would eliminate the "reverse offset" in the 15 states that reduce WC instead of SSDI. They also propose requiring WC settlements to include a "set-aside" for future SSDI benefits (similar to the process used for Medicare benefits), creating national standards for state WC programs, and expanding WC "experience rating" to SSDI so that employers pay higher payroll taxes if more of their employees end up on the SSDI program and lower taxes if fewer do.

Addressing interactions between these and other programs is especially important because doing so can also be a form of early intervention. In examining these interactions and listening to many experts, it became clear to us that many individuals might not file for SSDI if they received better support from other programs. Therefore, one way to improve the lives of many workers with disabilities—and the long-term finances of the SSDI program—would be to strengthen other programs that are supposed to help people with disabilities work. In other words, improving vocational rehabilitation services, state mental health services, and other non-Social Security programs can be an important element of any effort to improve SSDI.

Examine Structural Reforms

Since its creation nearly 60 years ago, at least two fundamental features of the SSDI program have remained constant. First, the program is and always has been conditional on inability to work. It is designed to provide income replacement for those who cannot engage in substantial work. Second, the program is and always has been all-or-nothing. It provides benefits based on the binary criteria that an individual is either disabled or not disabled. Given the vital importance of SSDI as an income support program, policymakers should proceed extremely cautiously in pursuing major changes to either of these fundamentals. But with huge advances in medical and assistive technology, legislation strengthening rights and opportunities for people with disabilities, and changes in the structure of the economy over the past 60 years, it would be a mistake not to reexamine the program.

In ***"Transitional Benefits for a Subset of the Social Security Disability Insurance Population"*** (Chapter 12), Hildred, Mazerski, Krent, and Christian propose a modest structural change. For the small subset of SSDI recipients who are expected to medically improve, they recommend replacing traditional benefits with a temporary (but renewable) "transitional benefit," along with vocational supports and the removal of limits on earned income.

In ***"Beyond All Or Nothing: Reforming Social Security Disability Insurance To Encourage Work And Wealth"*** (Chapter 13), Fichtner and Seligman argue for a more significant change to ultimately offer a partial disability benefit. Certain workers with disabilities who are most likely to succeed in remaining attached to the workforce would receive a partial and temporary benefit payment (perhaps half, or some other fraction of their regular SSDI benefit), but would no longer be subject to an earnings limitation. Disability status and benefit amount would be reevaluated on a regular basis. In addition to this partial and essentially time-limited benefit, they also recommend engaging employers and creating a greater role for private disability insurance.

In ***"Exploring an Alternative Social Security Definition of Disability"*** (Chapter 14), Jacobson, Aghabi, Butz, and Aaron propose an even more significant change: a new SSDI definition of disability. Specifically, they would remove the requirement that an individual be unable to work in order to qualify. Instead, they would base eligibility on impairment and impediment to work. SSDI recipients would be allowed—and indeed encouraged and assisted—to work, and benefits would phase out slowly at higher incomes.

All three of these proposals have the potential to improve the lives of people with disabilities and encourage work among those who are able. But they all also come with risks and should be studied closely and tested carefully before being applied to the SSDI program.

CONCLUSION

There is no doubting the immense importance of SSDI in American society. The program provides millions of Americans with the income they need to maintain a basic standard of living, and it gives the majority of Americans peace of mind knowing that they are protected against the financial risks of becoming disabled. This is why lawmakers must protect and preserve the program. But it is also exactly why reform is necessary. Responsible changes have the potential to truly improve the lives of those with disabilities, workers who pay into the program, and society as a whole. And it can encourage economic growth in the process.

While many ideas to improve the program are featured in this book, others will come from the many legislators, think tanks, academics, practitioners, study panels, advocates, and benefit recipients who have thought carefully about what changes could be made to the program. Other countries' experiences, although their situations differ, can also provide lessons. In ***"Approaches to Assisting Working-Aged People with Disabilities: Insights from Around the World"*** (Chapter 15), Haveman presents a comparative analysis of how six Western nations approach disability policy, highlighting recently enacted reforms (like those in the Netherlands) and the overall effect of these policies on their populations.

Of course, public policy has its limits, and no silver bullet exists to "fix" the SSDI program or to improve it for everyone. For example, even with better support and accommodations, most SSDI recipients may never be able to engage in substantial work.

To the extent that any reforms might improve the finances of the trust fund, it seems unlikely that enough savings would appear by the time trust fund reserves are exhausted in about 6 years. That isn't the point of these ideas nor of this project. Over the long run, a number of these proposals would surely reduce program costs. But others would increase costs in order to provide better support to workers with disabilities. For many of the ideas, savings are possible but highly uncertain. And any significant savings are likely to only materialize well in the future.

This begs the question: what can we do now to address long-term funding? In ***"Options to Address SSDI's Financial Shortfall"*** (Chapter 16), Goldwein and Lorenzen put forward a number of options that could help close SSDI's long-term funding gap by bringing spending and revenue in line. As lawmakers consider these options and continue to identify ways to otherwise improve SSDI, they must recognize and consider the important trade-offs that they face. They should also pay close attention both to the incentives created by the current program and any incentives that might be created or changed by reform.

Ultimately, the long-term financing issues facing SSDI might be better dealt with in the context of comprehensive Social Security reform. The SSDI and OASI programs share a tax base and benefit formula, and they interact with each other in many ways. Comprehensive reform also offers the opportunity to consider a fuller range of options and trade-offs, though failure to act soon will cause this range of options to quickly narrow.

Over the last couple of years, the need to avoid trust fund depletion spurred interest in and outside of Washington in exploring program improvements to the SSDI program. The pressure and momentum that the nation felt to improve SSDI must be maintained, even after passage of the Bipartisan Budget Act. Not only because the next funding crisis is projected to occur in only a few years, but because so much more work needs to be done to improve and update the SSDI program for the 21st century. Regardless of when and how the program's financing issues are addressed, there is absolutely no reason to wait to begin enacting sensible improvements to the SSDI program and testing new ideas with the potential to offer more significant improvement over time. The Bipartisan Budget Act should not represent the end of the conversation about how to best support Americans with disabilities, but rather the beginning of the next chapter.

2

An Overview of Social Security Disability Insurance (SSDI)

Patricia Owens

The Social Security Disability Insurance (SSDI) program provides cash benefits for insured working-age individuals whose ability to work is compromised by one or more physical or mental impairments. The program was established in 1956 as an addition to the existing Social Security Old-Age and Survivors' Insurance (OASI) program and remains closely linked to the retirement program today.

Although the original definition of disability and criteria for receiving SSDI benefits has been modified over time, the program has and continues to cover only full disability as measured both by medical impairment and inability to engage in substantial work (Kearney 2005/2006). Specifically, to be awarded benefits a person must be unable to perform any substantial gainful activity (SGA) due to an impairment expected to last over a year or result in death. An individual must also meet the qualifications for "insured status," which are based primarily on one's work history.

Based on this criteria, roughly 9 million workers with disabilities received SSDI benefits in 2014, along with nearly 2 million spouses and children (Social Security Board of Trustees 2015). Among workers with disabilities, average benefits total about $15,000 per year for new recipients and $14,000 for existing recipients. SSDI benefit payments for 2014 cost about $142 billion, resulting in a total program cost of about $145 billion (Social Security Board of Trustees 2015, Table III.A2).

The cost of SSDI benefits is paid for mainly from a 1.8 percent payroll tax on an individual's first $118,500 of earnings in 2015. That tax is generally divided equally between employer and employee (or paid solely by the employee for self-employed workers), and the taxable maximum indexed to wage growth over time. Along with small amounts of income from the income taxation of SSDI benefits and interest on trust fund holdings, this tax generated about $115 billion last year (Social Security Board of Trustees 2015, Table III.A2).

Because program costs are currently well in excess of revenue, the SSDI trust fund has been projected to deplete its reserves in late 2016 absent legislative action such as a reallocation from the old-age trust fund (Social Security Board of Trustees 2015, 24). The need for such action sparked considerable interest in SSDI program. In late 2015, Congress passed and the President signed into law the Bipartisan Budget Act of 2015, which temporarily reallocates revenue for three years, delaying SSDI trust fund reserve depletion until approximately 2022 (Goss 2015).

This chapter provides an overview of many of the aspects of the SSDI program.

HOW IS BENEFIT ELIGIBILITY DETERMINED?

In order to receive SSDI benefits, a worker must both satisfy the rules for insured status and have an impairment which meets the SSDI definition of disability. The Social Security Administration (SSA) is responsible for issuing program guidelines, which carry out the legislative intent for making determinations of disability.

The Insured Status Requirement

Insured status is generally determined based on an individual's work history. Specifically, a worker must satisfy a duration-of-work test (fully insured) and a recency-of-work test (disability insured) based on past work in Social Security-covered employment. Credit for work is measured in quarters of coverage. Workers receive credit for one quarter of coverage for every $1,220 in earnings in 2015, to a maximum of four per year.

To be fully insured, a worker filing for SSDI must have at least as many quarters of coverage as the number of years between the year the worker turned age 21 and the year in which he or she became disabled. To be disability-insured, the work must have earned at least 20 quarters of coverage during the 40-quarter period that ended with the quarter he or she became disabled. The requirement is eased for those who become disabled before age 31, and there are special rules for individuals who had a previous period of disability (SSA 2015a).

The Disability Requirement

In addition to meeting the insured status requirement, a worker must also meet the statutory definition of disability: "be unable to perform any substantial gainful activity (SGA) by reason of a medically-determinable physical or mental impairment which can be expected to result in death or which has lasted or can be expected to last for a continuous period of not less than 12 months." To meet this definition, a person must not only be unable to perform his or her past work, but also unable to perform any other work that exists in significant numbers in the national economy.[1]

To determine whether an applicant meets this statutory disability requirement, SSA uses a five-step sequential evaluation process. The disability decision maker asks five questions in a specific sequence. If a finding of "disabled" or "not disabled" can be made at any step, the evaluation does not proceed with the remainder of the steps.[2]

The Work Test — The first question is whether the claimant is working and earning at the level of SGA as defined in Social Security regulations. SGA is remunerative work that is substantial as determined by the amount of money earned, the number of hours worked, and the nature of the work. Generally, work is considered SGA if the person earns $1,090 or more per month in 2015 (just over $13,000 per year), an amount that is indexed annually to increases in the average wage level (SSA 2015b). If the applicant is working at or above SGA, the claim is denied. Otherwise, the evaluation continues to the next step.

The Severity Test — The second question is whether the claimant has an impairment or combination of impairments that interferes with basic work activities (a "severe" impairment) and is expected to last at least 12 months or result in death. Over time, SSA's interpretation of the non-severe threshold and consideration of multiple non-severe impairments has been challenged. Judicial decisions and legislation have mandated clearer guidelines. The authority to deny based on medical evidence of non-severity alone remains, but adjudicators are cautioned if they are "unable to determine clearly the effect of an impairment or combination

---

1 See 42 U.S.C. § 423(d)(1)(A).

2 See 20 CFR Part 404, Subpart P.

of impairments on the individual's ability to do basic work activities, the sequential evaluation process should not end with the not severe evaluation step."[3]

The Medical Listings Test — The third question is whether the claimant's impairment either meets or is equal to the severity of SSA's Listings of Impairments. The Listings of Impairments describe, for each major body system, diseases and conditions considered severe enough to prevent an individual from performing substantial gainful activity. Listings have been revised periodically over the SSDI program's history. If the requirements in the Listings are met or equaled, the claimant is found disabled without further consideration. Otherwise, the evaluation continues to the next step.

The Previous Work Test — The fourth question is whether the claimant can do his or her past work considering the effects of the medical condition. This requires SSA to determine the person's residual functional capacity (RFC). RFC is a person's remaining mental and physical capabilities after considering the effects of his or her medical conditions. This is compared to the work demands of the person's past relevant work. If the claimant remains capable of past work, the claim is denied. Otherwise, the evaluation continues to the last step.

The Any Work Test — The final question is whether a person, despite being unable to perform past work, can perform other work that exists in the national economy. In Step 5, the burden of proof shifts to SSA to show that work, other than the individual's past work, exists in significant numbers in the national economy and to which the claimant can make an adjustment, considering the limiting effects of the individual's impairment, age, education, and work experience. If the person cannot perform other work, the claim is allowed.

---

3 Social Security Administration, Social Security Rulings 85-28: Titles II And XVI: Medical Impairments That Are Not Severe, SSR 85-28. https://www.socialsecurity.gov/OP_Home/rulings/di/01/SSR85-28-di-01.html Accessed September 1, 2015.

Figure 1 – The Disability Determination Process

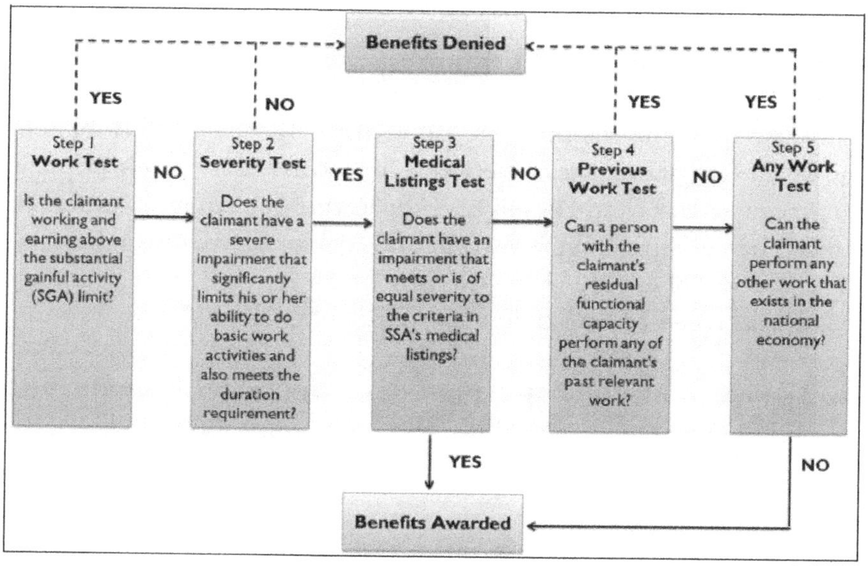

Graphic from Congressional Research Service Report 7-5700 (Morton 2014).

In order to expedite favorable decisions, SSA has two fast-track processes to identify cases involving the most severe disabilities. In the Compassionate Allowance process, SSA used expert input to identify a number of diseases and other medical conditions that almost invariably qualify under the Listing of Impairments and require a minimal amount of objective medical information. This allows Disability Determination Services (DDSs) to promptly allow claims of persons with those conditions. The Quick Disability Determination process employs a computer-based predictive model to screen initial applications and identify cases in which a favorable disability determination is highly likely and medical evidence is readily available so that such cases can be expedited (Rajnes 2012).

WHO RECEIVES SSDI BENEFITS?

Nearly 11 million Americans receive SSDI cash benefits, the vast majority being disabled worker beneficiaries who make up about nine million beneficiaries; the other two million beneficiaries are dependents of workers with disabilities (including spouses and children) or are disabled themselves and qualify for benefits under their spouse or parent (SSA 2015b, Table 2).

In addition to their differences in qualification, SSDI beneficiaries are also very diverse in geographic location, gender, age, and condition.

Beneficiaries by Geographic Location

While about 5 percent of the U.S. population receives SSDI benefits, the distribution among states varies between 3 percent of a state's population to almost 9 percent. Alaska and Hawaii have the lowest percentage of SSDI benefits, around that 3 percent mark; West Virginia and Alabama have the highest, hovering close to 9 percent. There are also a number of Americans in the U.S. territories and abroad who receive SSDI benefits (SSA 2014a, Table 9).

Figure 2 - Percentage of Population Receiving SSDI benefits, by State

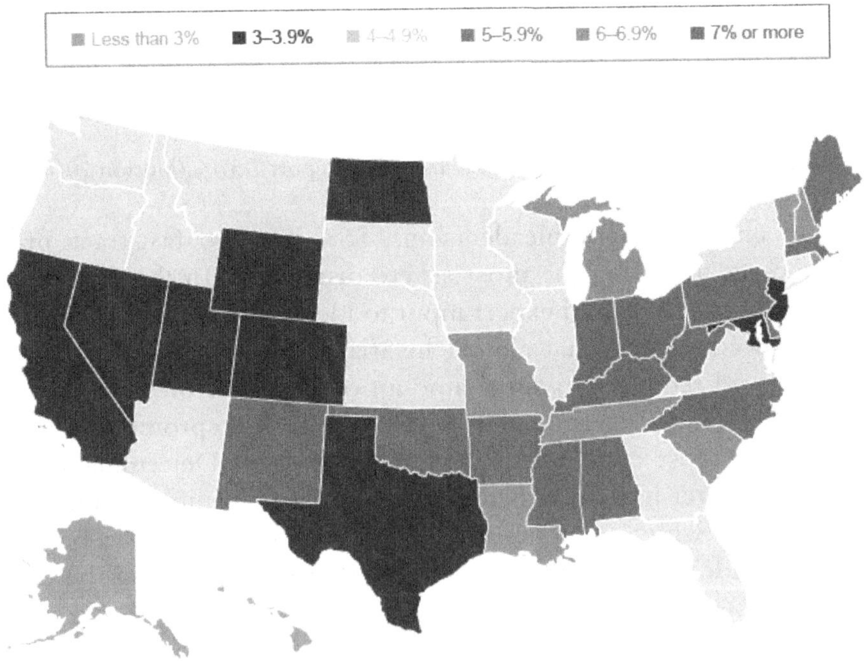

Graphic from the Annual Statistical Report on the Social Security Disability Insurance Program, 2013 (SSA 2014a).

Beneficiaries by Gender and Age

Over the life of the SSDI program, gender parity of beneficiaries has changed substantially, while the average age has mostly stayed the same. In 1960, about 22 percent of beneficiaries were women; today, that number is closer to half.

This change primarily reflects the evolution of the labor force over the last half-century (see section on program growth for more details). On the other hand, the average age of beneficiaries has only varied slightly around the current average age of 53 years (SSA 2014a, Table 19).

Beneficiaries by Condition

SSA classifies SSDI beneficiaries by the primary condition under which they qualify. The nature of each impairment varies greatly, but the most common primary conditions of SSDI beneficiaries are mental and intellectual disorders, accounting for about 35 percent of beneficiaries (split between 27 percent having mental disorders and 8 percent with intellectual disorders), and musculoskeletal and connective tissue disorders, accounting for about 28 percent of beneficiaries. Both men and women tend to experience these conditions at roughly the same rates. The breakdown of qualifying conditions can be seen in Figure 3 below.

Figure 3 – SSDI Beneficiaries by primary condition, 2013

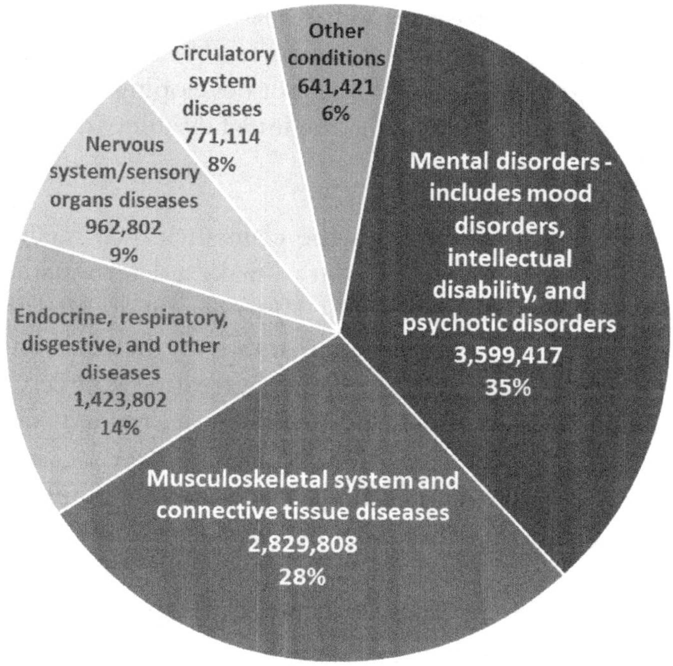

Source: Annual Statistical Report on the Social Security Disability Insurance Program, 2013 (SSA 2014a).

HOW ARE BENEFITS AWARDED?

In order to receive benefits, an individual must file an application and await a decision as to whether or not they meet the insured status requirement and satisfy the definition of disability. If an application is accepted at the initial level, a worker begins receiving monthly benefits and also can receive back payments for up to a year before the application was filed. If the initial application is denied, several levels of appeal are available.[4]

The Initial Decision

Applicants for disability benefits may apply in person at a field office or by telephone, mail, or online. The application and related forms ask for a description of the claimant's impairment(s), treatment sources, the date they became unable to work, and other information that relates to the disability.

The SSA field office is responsible for verifying non-medical eligibility requirements, which may include age, employment, marital status, or insured status. While the SSA field office is responsible for verifying necessary non-medical requirements, the disability evaluation is performed by a DDS, a state agency that is federally funded and applies federal rules for developing the necessary medical and vocational information and making the initial disability decision (Wixon and Strand 2013).

A DDS tries to obtain evidence from the claimant's own medical sources. If that evidence is unavailable or insufficient to make a determination, a DDS will arrange for a consultative examination (CE) to get the needed information. A DDS may purchase the CE from the claimant's own medical source, or from a qualified independent source if the claimant's treating source cannot provide one. After completing development of the evidence, trained staff at the DDS make the initial disability determination. Normally, after a case has been fully developed, a two-person team consisting of a disability examiner and a medical consultant (a physician or psychologist) makes the decision. SSA has also been testing an alternative Single Decision Maker program (SDM) for over a decade. The SDM program authorizes disability examiners to process some cases without

4 See 404.621 U.S. Social Security Administration Effective Filing Period of Application, What happens if I file after the first month I meet the requirements for benefits?, *Code of Federal Regulations*, title 20 (2014): 213-214, http://www.gpo.gov/fdsys/pkg/CFR-2014-title20-vol2/pdf/CFR-2014-title20-vol2-sec404-621.pdf

a medical consultant's involvement (SSAB 2015). However, a provision of the Bipartisan Budget Act of 2015 is expected to eliminate the SDM program in late 2016.[5]

The DDS then returns a completed case to the field office for appropriate action. If the DDS found that the claimant is disabled, SSA completes any outstanding non-disability determination work, computes the benefit amount, and triggers the benefit payment. If the claimant was found not disabled, the file is kept in the field office in case the claimant decides to appeal the determination.

The Appeals Process

If the applicant's claim for disability benefits is denied, he or she may appeal the decision. There are four potential levels of appeal: (1) reconsideration by the state DDS, (2) hearing by an administrative law judge (ALJ), (3) review by the Appeals Council, and (4) federal court review.

Generally, reconsideration is the first step in the appeals process, and a claimant has 60 days to request this review. Reconsideration is a case review similar to the initial determination except that the case is assigned to a different adjudication team at the DDS. The claimant is given the opportunity to present additional evidence, which is considered along with the evidence previously submitted. In 10 states, elimination of reconsideration is being tested and appeals are instead directed to the next level.

If the claim is denied at reconsideration (or at the initial level in states without reconsideration), the individual has 60 days to request a hearing before an SSA administrative law judge. ALJs are SSA employees tasked with hearing Social Security cases, the majority of which are disability appeals. The ALJ will hold a hearing unless the claimant requests that the decision be based on the existing written record. The ALJ is responsible for looking into all the issues and receives documentary evidence as well as the testimony of the claimant and witnesses. The ALJ will allow the claimant or the claimant's representative to present arguments and examine witnesses at the hearing. The ALJ then creates an entirely new decision evaluating the same criteria as the prior levels. Nearly a third of these cases are done by telecommunication (SSA 2015d).

---

5 See Sec. 832 of Public Law 114-74, https://www.congress.gov/bill/114th-congress/house-bill/1314/text?overview=closed#toc-H442FB118C81C4D91A92889A527AA9599

If a claim is denied at the ALJ level, the claimant may request (within 60 days of receiving the decision) that the Appeals Council (AC) review the case. The AC, made up of administrative appeals judges, may also motion to review a decision on its own. The AC considers the evidence of record, any additional evidence submitted by the claimant, and the ALJ's findings and conclusions. The AC may grant, deny, or dismiss a request for review. The AC may also uphold, modify, or reverse the ALJ's action, or it may remand it to the ALJ to hold another hearing and issue a new decision.

If denied or dismissed at the AC level, claimants may file a civil suit in a federal district court within 60 days after the date they receive notice of the AC's action. If the U.S. district court reviews the case record and does not find in favor of the claimant, the claimant can continue with the appellate process to the U.S. circuit court of appeals and beyond.[6]

According to the SSA, between 32 and 35 percent of applicants have been approved for benefits at the initial stage over the past five years. Of those who requested reconsideration, between 11 and 13 percent of initially denied applicants have been approved for benefits at this level. When it comes to further levels of appeal, the success rate has averaged between 45 and 62 percent at the ALJ level over the past five years, while success at the AC and federal court levels has averaged around 1 to 3 percent and 2 to 4 percent, respectively, though these appeals can also be remanded back to the ALJ level for additional consideration (SSA 2015e; SSA 2014b; SSA 2013; SSA 2012; SSA 2011).

HOW DO SSDI RECIPIENTS EXIT THE PROGRAM?

Once an individual is determined to qualify for benefits, he or she can generally continue to receive benefits until no longer considered disabled. Most beneficiaries remain on the program until they reach the Social Security normal retirement age (currently 66 and rising over the next few years to 67), at which point they convert onto the old-age program. However, some beneficiaries leave the program either due to death, because SSA determines them no longer eligible through a Continuing Disability Review (CDR), or because they choose to return to work—sometimes due to work incentives within the program.

[6] See 416.920 U.S. Social Security Administration Evaluation of Disability, Evaluation of disability of adults, in general, *Code of Federal Regulations*, title 20 (2014): 857-858, http://www.gpo.gov/fdsys/pkg/CFR-2014-title20-vol2/pdf/CFR-2014-title20-vol2-sec416-920.pdf

Continuing Disability Reviews

The Social Security Administration conducts regular CDRs to determine whether an individual remains eligible for the SSDI benefit based on medical disability and continued inability to work above SGA.

There are two types of CDRs—medical and work. For medical CDRs, cases are reviewed at certain intervals, depending on the likelihood of medical improvement. Cases deemed "Medical Improvement Expected" are supposed to undergo CDRs every six months to 1.5 years. Those deemed "Medical Improvement Possible" are supposed to undergo CDRs every three years. Those deemed "Medical Improvement Not Expected" are supposed to undergo CDRs every five to seven years. However, medical CDRs often run behind schedule, and currently there is a significant backlog. While medical CDRs are scheduled, work CDRs are only conducted if SSA is notified of a beneficiary returning to work.

Medical CDRs

When it is time to conduct a CDR, SSA uses a statistical modeling system using data from beneficiary records to rate a beneficiary's probability of having improved. This is a separate assessment from the evaluation of likelihood of medical improvement that is done when the claim was first approved. For individuals who have a high probability of having improved, the cases are sent to the state DDS for a full medical review. Individuals who have a lower probability of medical improvement receive a questionnaire—or "mailer CDR"—requesting updates on their impairments, medical treatment, and work activities. If the questionnaire indicates that there may have been medical improvement, the case is also sent to the DDS for a full medical review. Otherwise, the case is rescheduled for a later review based on the potential for improvement. CDRs are also processed when SSA receives a report of medical improvement from a beneficiary or third party (Colvin 2012).

If, as a result of a medical CDR, SSA decides that an individual's disability has ceased, the appeals process is similar that of initially unfavorable decisions. However, while most reconsideration of initial denials involves just a file review, a beneficiary who has been found no longer disabled can request an in-person meeting with a Social Security representative.

Work CDRs

A work CDR is a review generated by reported earnings from beneficiaries or third parties, systems alerts, or earnings posted to a beneficiary's record. The Continuing Disability Review Enforcement Operation uses Internal Revenue Service earnings data to identify possible work CDRs for SSDI beneficiaries. SSA receives about 600,000 alerts annually, and they generally prioritize alerts with the highest identified earnings. After an SSDI beneficiary completes a trial work period (TWP) and continues to work, SSA conducts a work CDR to determine if the beneficiary's earnings preclude entitlement to payment.

Work CDRs are conducted in SSA field offices and processing centers using an automated work processing program called eWork. This program collects data; prepares forms, notices, and work report receipts; incorporates policy and decision logic; and adjusts benefits. When a beneficiary works, the return to work incentive provisions such as TWP are taken into account.

Return to Work

Each year, a small number of SSDI beneficiaries are able and choose to go back to work, temporarily or permanently exiting the SSDI program. Although there are numerous obstacles to returning to work—from a "cash cliff," which can cause individuals to lose all benefits by earning above SGA, to the general loss of skill and attractiveness to employers for those who have spent a long time out of the labor force—SSDI includes a number of features meant to make it easier for individuals to return to work.

Many of these incentives revolve around allowing SSDI recipients to test out working and remain attached to the program during that period. These include: a nine-month TWP, during which recipients can receive earnings above SGA without experiencing reduced benefits; an extended period of eligibility (EPE), during which benefits are automatically restored if a worker makes below SGA within an additional three years; an immediate expedited reinstatement period, during which a former beneficiary can reapply and waive the waiting period for an additional two years beyond the EPE; and extended Medicare eligibility for that same time period (with a Medicare buy-in available thereafter) (SSA 2015f, 26-29).

In some cases, the program further encourages work by effectively letting recipients earn above SGA. For example, if work is subsidized or performed under special conditions, only the actual value of the work is considered in determining if the work is SGA. In addition, a worker may deduct impairment-related work expenses—the cost of certain impairment-related items and services that beneficiaries need to work—from their income in determining SGA.

In 1999, Congress established the Ticket to Work Program, a free and voluntary program designed to give beneficiaries greater access to and choice of rehabilitation and employment services and other support services to help them get or keep a job. The program established employment networks—often state vocational rehabilitation agencies—to provide these services. The program was coupled with the Work Incentives Improvement Program (WIPA) to provide community-based work incentives expertise to beneficiaries. Program evaluations have shown that these programs have had a positive but very limited effect on employment outcomes for those on the SSDI program (Livermore et al. 2013).

In addition to these programs, SSA has been testing a number of additional work incentives through various pilots and demonstrations. For example, the Benefit Offset National Demonstration (BOND) is currently testing a change in how SSDI benefits are offset when an individual receiving them works at above the SGA level. Currently, most individuals who work after the end of their trial work period receive no cash benefit in any month they perform SGA. This abrupt loss of benefits is commonly referred to as the "cash cliff." BOND tests a gradual reduction of benefits ($1 of benefit reduction for every $2 of earning above SGA). A completed pilot known as the Mental Health Treatment Study provided supported employment and systematic medication management services, coupled with the removal of some known programmatic disincentives, to SSDI beneficiaries with schizophrenia or an affective disorder. The results showed that employment supports, along with medical support and coordinated care, were successful in improving health, lowering hospitalizations, and increasing employment for SSDI beneficiaries with schizophrenia and other affective disorders. The Bipartisan Budget Act of 2015 includes a provision requiring SSA to conduct another demonstration project similar to BOND, but with the benefit offset starting at a lower earnings threshold.[7]

HOW IS SSDI FINANCED?

Most of SSDI's funding comes from a 1.8 percent payroll tax, split evenly between employees and employers (or paid entirely by a self-employed individual), on a

---

[7] See Sec. 823 of Public Law 114-74, https://www.congress.gov/bill/114th-congress/house-bill/1314/text?overview=closed#toc-H442FB118C81C4D91A92889A527AA9599

worker's first $118,500 in earnings in 2015 (this amount is indexed to average wage growth). A small amount of additional income comes from the partial income-taxation of benefits received by program recipients with high income, and from interest on the trust fund's reserves. In 2014, the program took in roughly $115 billion in revenue while incurring $145 billion in costs, primarily in the form of paid benefits. As a result, the program ran a $30 billion deficit—roughly 0.55 percent of payroll (Social Security Board of Trustees 2015).

Figure 4 – SSDI Revenue and Spending, 1970-2090

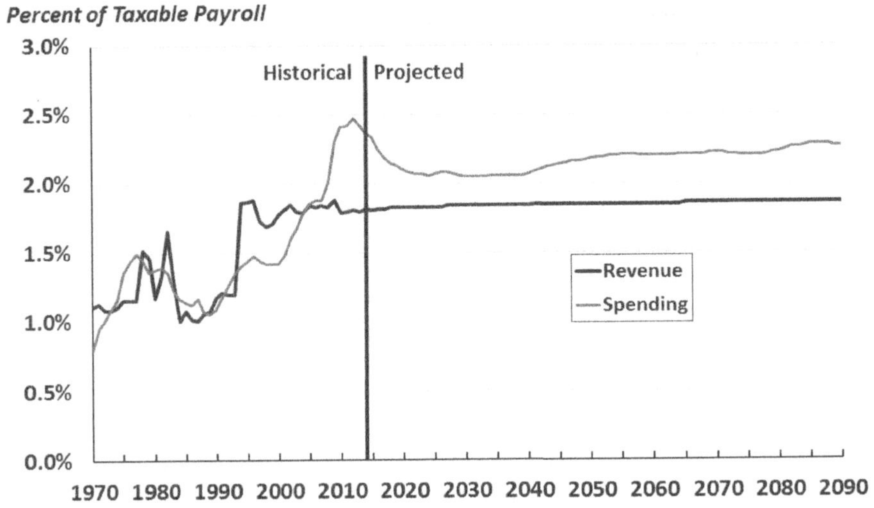

Source: 2015 Social Security Trustees' Report

Immediate and Long-Term Funding Needs

According to the 2015 Social Security Trustees' Report, the SSDI trust fund was projected to exhaust its reserves by the end of 2016. Without legislative changes, this depletion would have left the program with enough revenue to pay 81 percent of scheduled benefits. However, the Bipartisan Budget Act of 2015 delayed the depletion of the SSDI trust fund reserves until approximately 2022 by reallocating payroll tax revenue from the old-age trust fund to SSDI (Goss 2015).

Despite the immediate funding issue being temporarily resolved, the SSDI trust fund still faces a long-term funding gap as program costs continue to exceed revenue raised by the 1.8 percent payroll tax. The most recent Social Security Trustees report projected costs to decline over the next few years—from 2.4

percent of payroll in 2014 to 2.1 percent in the 2020s and 2030s, and then rise to 2.3 percent of payroll by 2090. It projected the 75-year actuarial shortfall of SSDI to be about 0.31 percent of payroll (Social Security Board of Trustees 2015); the Congressional Budget Office, meanwhile, projected a 0.7 percent shortfall (CBO 2015). Although the shortfall has been reduced somewhat by the temporary payroll tax reallocation and other Social Security provisions in the Bipartisan Budget Act of 2015, it has not been eliminated.

Ultimately, additional legislation will be required to close the entire shortfall. The gap between spending and revenue could be closed by reducing projected program costs, increasing dedicated taxes, diverting further revenue from other sources such as the OASI trust fund, or some combination of the three.

WHAT EXPLAINS THE GROWTH IN THE PROGRAM?

The cost of the SSDI program has grown considerably in recently years, from \$3.3 billion (0.81 percent of payroll) in 1970 to \$19.5 billion (1.14 percent of payroll) in 1985, \$56.8 billion (1.42 percent of payroll) in 2000, and \$145 billion (2.36 percent of payroll) in 2014 (Social Security Board of Trustees 2015, Table IV.B1 and Table VI.G8). This growth in part reflects continued increases in prices and wage growth (initial benefits grow each year with wages), but it also tracks a growth in the total number of recipients—from 2.6 million in 1970 to 11 million today (Social Security Board of Trustees 2015, Table IV.B3).

The incidence rate of working-age Americans receiving SSDI benefits has similarly increased. In the late 1970s, 2.2 percent of working-age Americans received SSDI; that share had risen to 3.5 percent leading up to the 2007-2009 recession, and was 4.6 percent in 2013 (Liebman 105, 123). In the late 1970s, 3.0 percent of working-age men received SSDI, increasing to 3.8 percent before the recession and 4.5 percent by 2013, while the corresponding SSDI receipt rates for women went from 1.4 percent, to 3.5 percent, and 4.3 percent, respectively (Liebman 2015, 128). Numerous explanations for the increase in the number of people receiving SSDI have been offered. There are three generally accepted drivers of increased costs:

- Population and demographic changes;
- Economic and labor market changes; and
- Program and policy changes.

It is difficult to attribute a specific proportion of the increase to each of those factors. Economists have used various techniques of factor analysis to help quantify the growth factors (Autor and Duggan 2003; Autor and Duggan 2006; Goss 2014; Ruffing 2014). As noted by one group of researchers, "[a]lthough researchers generally agree that a substantial portion of the SSDI program growth stems from demographic changes, . . . they disagree on the extent to which other, more difficult-to-quantify factors have played a role in SSDI program growth. . . ." (Livermore, Wittenberg and Neumark 2014, 2).

Population and Demographic Changes

One reason for the increase in the size of the SSDI program is the overall increase in working-age population and the corresponding increase in the number of people insured for SSDI. According to SSA, there were about 75 million individuals insured for SSDI in 1970. By 2014, that number had more than doubled to over 151 million (Social Security Board of Trustees 2015, Table IV.B3).

In addition, the age distribution of the working-age population also changed. Between 1970 and 1990, as the baby boomer generation (those born between 1946 and 1965) entered young adulthood, both employment and gross domestic product (GDP) rose more than SSDI cost as a result of the increase in the proportion of relatively young and healthy individuals in the workforce. However, from 1990 to 2010, the baby boomers moved to older working ages 45 to 64. The younger adult workers who followed them were from a generation with a lower birthrate, thus increasing the proportion of workers in disability-prone ages to the total population.

Another demographic factor has been the increase in the percentage of working-age women who have worked consistently enough to be disability-insured. Their number has nearly doubled since 1970 to 8.2 million. In addition, the incidence of disability among women has grown. In the late 1970s, 3 percent of working-age men received SSDI, but only 1.4 percent of working-age women did. Leading up to the 2007-2009 recession, the rate for working age men had gone up by less than a third to 3.8 percent, but the rate for women more than doubled to 3.5 percent. By 2013, the rates for men were 4.5 percent and for women, 4.3 percent (Liebman 2015, 127-128).

The increase in the Social Security full retirement age is another factor contributing to increased SSDI receipt. This contributed to the increase in the number and proportion of insured workers in their disability prone years, and also increased the total amount of SSDI benefits paid out to older workers before they are converted to retirement benefits at full retirement age. This change also increased the relative value of disability benefits compared to early retirement benefits, potentially increasing the rate of SSDI filing for duals age 62 and over (Morton 2014, 11). The effect of the rise in retirement age on SSDI awards has yet to be precisely calculated, but early research indicates that raising the retirement age would increase SSDI benefit eligibility (GAO 2010a). In addition to these causes, mortality and recovery rates must also be factored into any analysis of growth in incidence and duration (Liebman 2015).

As noted previously, there is general agreement that demographic changes in the U.S. population are an important factor in program growth; however, many disagree with the magnitude of its effect.

Program and Policy Changes

Legislative changes in the SSDI program since its inception in 1956 include a wide range of provisions: the addition of benefits for dependents, lowering of age for entitlement, liberalizing insured status requirements, and increases in benefit amounts. A quantifiable example of expansion is the effect of changing the definition of disability from an impairment that could be expected to last for a "long-continued and indefinite duration"—as defined in the 1965 amendments to the Social Security Act—to one that could be expected "to last for a period of 12 months or longer." It was estimated that upon enactment this new language allowed for immediate entitlement of 60,000 workers with disabilities. Among other actions which have added to cost growth are increased retroactivity of benefits, reducing the waiting period for application, and providing for Medicare benefits (Kearney 2005/2006).

The last major legislatively mandated changes were contained in the 1984 amendments to the Social Security Act and required that the listings for mental impairments and the methodology for assessing the impairment impact of chronic pain (frequently an issue when evaluating musculoskeletal disorders) be updated. These new procedures have been linked to more subjective decisions, which allow greater latitude in awarding benefits (particularly for those with mental and musculoskeletal disorders) and overall program liberalization (see, for example, Autor 2011). Others have questioned the significance of these changes (see, for example, Ruffing 2014). However, regardless of the cause, it is clear that the proportion of cases involving mental and musculoskeletal disorders has risen, while the share involving circulatory disorders and cancer has fallen (SSA

2014a, 63-64). Given that musculoskeletal and mental disorder are less likely to result in death than other impairments, "the growth in the share of beneficiaries with mental and musculoskeletal disorders likely increased the average duration of benefit receipt, as well as the total number of individuals on disability rolls" (Morton 2014, 11). The same law revised the standard for reviewing cases of continuing disability and mandated a new medical improvement standard, which tightened the criteria for stopping benefits and which may have contributed to fewer recipients being removed from the rolls.

Legislative changes outside of SSDI have also increased the size of the rolls to some degree. In particular, the increase in the normal retirement age from 65 to 66 (and headed to 67) has both extended the number of years a worker is eligible for and receives SSDI and increased the attractiveness of the SSDI benefit relative to the Social Security retirement benefit (CBO 2012).

Economic and Labor Market Changes

On the economic front, the Great Recession of 2008 resulted in lower GDP, making SSDI costs as a portion of GDP rise as GDP fell. Yet, the recession also appears to have increased costs, to some degree, in absolute terms. Historically, SSDI applications and awards have increased during economic downturns when unemployment rises (Rupp 2012). Jobs that are available for marginally disabled workers in good economic times may be much scarcer in bad times, and long spouts of unemployment likely further reduce skills and employability for many disabled workers. As a result, SSDI applications tend to increase significantly during recessions. And although award *rates* tend to go down to some degree as a response, total awards still go up.

Separate from the recession, other more structural changes to the economy may be increasing the number of individuals on SSDI. Changes in the labor market have eliminated many low-skilled jobs. This, along with more jobs requiring higher level skills, reduces the number of jobs available for unskilled workers in their disability-prone work years. And, coupled with the higher wage replacement ratios of benefits for lower wage earners, SSDI entitlement becomes more attractive to workers who might otherwise stay in the workforce.

One thing is certain: over time, many factors must be analyzed to understand the relationship between program growth and financing. Effective program improvements in design and administration require understanding the individual and interactive effects of a myriad of sometimes conflicting environmental impacts.

HOW DO OTHER PROGRAMS AND SERVICES AFFECT SSDI?

The relationships and interactions between SSDI and other benefit systems and services are important considerations in discussing the role of SSDI in the overall social insurance system. In many ways, SSDI and other programs at the federal, state, and local level as well as privately run ventures overlap and interact with each other.

At the same time, there is growing agreement about the need for coordination and integration of benefits and services for working-age persons with disability, especially in light of new and evolving concepts of disability (GAO 2010b). For example, GAO has reported there are more than 20 federal agencies and almost 200 programs that provide a wide range of assistance to people with disabilities, including employment-related services, medical care, and monetary support (GAO 2008). These programs provide help for working-age persons with disability and also assist in providing an adequate national labor force. There is a high cost to these programs. GAO later reported on 45 programs in support of employment for persons with disabilities. The programs administered by nine federal agencies were fragmented and often provided similar services to similar populations (GAO 2015).

Although agencies may be partnering on a case-by-case basis, agency officials and experts have cited a lack of communication and comprehensive coordination among the federal programs that serve individuals with disabilities. With increasing expenditures, a growing potential beneficiary population, and the number of programs providing assistance to individuals with disabilities, the importance of modernizing and effectively coordinating federal disability programs is constantly increasing.

An appendix including a detailed discussion of a number of SSDI program interactions is available on the McCrery-Pomeroy SSDI Solutions website at http://www.ssdisolutions.org/book. Below is a short discussion of some of the major interactions.

SSDI and OASI

Both OASI and SSDI are social insurance programs; one pays benefits upon death or retirement, while the other replaces income when a disability occurs before retirement. Benefits are calculated using intricate earnings- and age-based formulas which have evolved over time in consideration of economic and demographic alterations in the composition of the insured population.

To calculate benefits, a worker's Average Indexed Monthly Earnings (AIME) are converted to a Primary Insurance Amount (PIA). The AIME is the annual taxable earnings from covered wages or self-employment averaged and indexed over a period that encompasses most of the worker's adult years. The PIA is the monthly benefit payable to a worker upon initial entitlement at the full retirement age (FRA) or upon entitlement to disability benefits. The formula for computing the PIA from the AIME is progressive and thus provides a higher PIA-to-AIME ratio for workers with low earnings.

Disabled beneficiaries and persons retiring at the FRA are paid 100 percent of their PIA. If a worker applies for early retirement between age 62 and their FRA, they receive proportionally reduced benefits (reduced by up to 25 percent for people who retire when they first turn 62). When disability benefits are converted to retired-worker benefits at FRA, or at early retirement for recovered workers between the ages of 62 and FRA, the years of disability are disregarded to preserve insured status and the benefit level. Alternative methods of computing the PIA apply to workers who have low earnings but a steady work history.

If a disabled worker applies for early retirement and then becomes disabled before full retirement age, he or she could be eligible for a larger disability benefit, although that benefit would be reduced somewhat based on the period of time retirement benefits had already been received before incurring a disability. A worker at least age 62 who files for disability can receive a reduced retirement benefit while the SSDI claim is being processed and, if approved for SSDI, can receive retroactive payment for the difference between their reduced retirement benefit and their full SSDI benefit. Monthly benefits payable to the worker and family members or to the worker's survivors are limited to a maximum family benefit amount. Cost of living increases to benefits are legislatively mandated and calculated annually.

SSDI and Supplemental Security Income (SSI) Disability Benefits

SSI disability benefits are needs-based rather than coverage-based and require meeting a means test in addition to meeting the same definition of disability. SSI does not rely on a prior work qualification, and SSI beneficiaries are limited in the amount of earned and unearned income they can receive while receiving SSI, as well as how many assets they may own while receiving benefits. A person can have SSI benefits reduced or stopped because of income and/or resource ineligibility although they meet SSA disability criteria (Morton 2014). *SSDI is considered unearned income and thus reduces or can completely offset SSI cash benefits.* All but $20 of unearned income reduces SSI benefits.

The SSDI program has a five-month waiting period after the onset of categorical eligibility as disabled, but SSI benefits can start right after the month of application. Thus, a categorically disabled person may be eligible for SSI benefits during the SSDI waiting period. Some complexities arise because of different program rules regarding the date of disability onset and the date of application for disability benefits. SSDI has the potential for 12-month retroactivity in disability benefits. The SSI payment is payable in the month of application. If part or the entire SSDI waiting period occurred prior to application for SSDI, SSI benefit eligibility may be affected for the months of SSDI payment. State Medicaid benefits may be payable for SSI beneficiaries prior to or in coordination with eventual Medicare entitlement. State rules apply and vary.

SSDI and VA Benefits

Both the Department of Veterans Affairs (VA) and Department of Defense (DOD) pay disability benefits based on service-connected health conditions. The VA disability compensation program is for veterans with a disease or injury that incurred or was aggravated during active military service. Those benefits, unlike SSDI, are not contingent on whether the veteran is working. The amount of the monthly benefit is based on a rating of the severity of the medical condition, expressed as a percentage loss of normal function. The DOD disability retirement program is for active duty service members no longer fit for duty as a result of a service-connected health condition. The benefit amount is based, in part, on the same disability percentage rating as is used in the VA compensation program, although there are differences between how the ratings are made. VA and DOD disability benefits are paid separately from SSDI, and there is no SSDI offset. (The VA also administers the veterans pension program, which is a needs-based program for veterans totally and permanently disabled due to a non-service-connected medical condition and who have limited financial resources.)

A September 2014 GAO report on disability compensation showed that 59,251 individuals received concurrent payments from DOD disability retirement, VA disability compensation, and SSDI totaling over $3.5 billion in fiscal year 2013. Current law generally allows military personnel to receive concurrent disability compensation from DOD, VA, and SSDI. These concurrent payments ranged from $25,000 to $74,999 in total. As of January 2013, 48 percent of the individuals were age 60 or above. Eighty-one percent of individuals had a VA disability rating equal to or greater than 50 percent.

SSDI and State Workers' Compensation (WC)

WC benefits cover only disabilities arising out of and in the course of employment It is compulsory and is administered by states, with each state setting its own benefits rules, usually with a schedule of payment rates. Based on the principle that employers have responsibility for the health and safety of their employees, WC is fully funded by employers through purchase of insurance or self-funding. Costs may be influenced by incidence and duration of compensable accidents or illness. The *AMA Guides to the Evaluation of Permanent Impairment* (2008) are frequently used and translated into a percentage of loss of function, which is used to measure potential income loss and then converted to a monetary award amount. The benefit period is set based on the duration and severity of the worker's disability, with lump sum settlements possible.

Cash benefits are tax free and generally payable for lost work time after a three- to seven-day waiting period and in relationship to earnings. There are four cash payment categories. Temporary total disability cash payments are the most common, and are paid when a worker is precluded from work for a defined period of time. Temporary partial disability payments are made when workers return to work before they reach maximum medical improvement and at reduced responsibilities and a lower salary. Permanent total disability payments are made if a worker has severe permanent impairments after reaching maximum medical improvement. Permanent partial disability payments are made when a worker has permanent impairments that do not completely limit the worker's ability to work. The system for determining benefits in these cases is complex and varies across jurisdictions. WC also provides death and funeral benefits to workers' survivors.

An offset for WC was contained in the original 1956 disability program. It was eliminated in 1958 and reinstituted in 1965. The 1965 law, however, allowed states to reduce their benefits for a worker receiving SSDI, thus eliminating the SSDI offset for WC in those states. In 1981, PL 97-35 ended this "reverse offset" option (Reno, Williams, and Sengupta 2003/2004).

In all but 15 reverse-offset states, SSDI benefits including family benefits may be reduced to fully or partially offset a Workers' Compensation benefit. The reduction in a SSDI benefit (and family benefits) may be made if the total benefits payable *plus* Workers' Compensation plus any public disability benefits (if applicable) exceed the higher of 80 percent of average current earnings as determined before disability began or the family's total Social Security benefit (before the reduction) (SSA 2015g).

SSDI and Private Sector Disability Insurance

Protection against the risk of work disability not incurred in the course of employment (and thus not covered by Workers' Compensation) is offered by insurers, either directly to individuals or to employers. Employers may self-fund these benefits. Medium and large employers are most likely to provide such benefits.

Short-term disability (STD) programs cover workers' absences from their usual jobs because of illness and accidents not sustained in the course of employment. To receive benefits, employees must be out of work a certain number of days, usually five. The replacement rate is typically 50 percent of wages. Medical evidence is required. The benefits are generally paid for a set period of time based on the type of illness or injury and last no longer than six months.

Long-term disability (LTD) programs cover lengthy absences (after a six-month waiting period) caused by illnesses and accidents not sustained in the course of employment. Benefits are coordinated with sick pay or STD benefits. The norm is 60 percent wage replacement. The disability entitlement definition for the first six-12 months is inability to do the usual and customary occupation by reason of a medically determinable impairment. Most often, after one year, disability must cause inability to perform the functions of any occupation. Most LTD plans require that a person receive appropriate medical care.

LTD payments are generally offset by SSDI when the person becomes entitled to SSDI benefits. Insurers and employers maintain that this offset is important to the affordability of the coverage, since it covers disability of lesser severity and for longer periods of time. Insurers also make the argument that they reduce SSDI costs by their early intervention and return-to-work programs. There is a counter argument that employers and insurers may increase SSDI costs by requiring SSDI filing and providing legal representation during the claim and appeals process.

CONCLUSION

The SSDI program is a critical part of the lives of many persons with disabilities and their families. Many persons with severe disabilities cannot work even though they might want to. There is general agreement that there continues to be a need for wage replacement benefits for these workers.

At the same time, there is general agreement that the societal perspective on work disability has changed in light of the passage of the Americans with Disabilities Act, investments in adaptive technology, medical and technological advancements, and new perspectives driven in large part by the disability rights and independent living movements.

In many ways, disability policy is at a crossroads—facing two sometimes-competing goals of helping people with disabilities to enter or remain in the workforce while continuing to provide important support for the many people who will remain unable to work. These goals are in some ways in conflict under the current system, which generally sets inability to work as a criteria for receiving cash benefits and provides little support for those interested in remaining in the workforce.

Changes to the current program and how it interacts with other programs can improve this conflict on the margins and better optimize the existing program. In the future, perhaps, new approaches could be pursued in combination with SSDI to help maintain work function and increase the welfare and well-being of individuals with disabilities.

It is self-evident that disability policy initiatives should be balanced to protect those who really cannot work and provide avenues to work for those who can.

Section II

Early Intervention

3

The Employment/Eligibility Service System: A New Gateway for Employment Supports and Social Security Disability Benefits

David Stapleton, Yonatan Ben-Shalom, and David Mann

A NEW GATEWAY FOR SOCIAL SECURITY DISABILITY INSURANCE

We propose to modernize the gateway to the Social Security Disability Insurance (SSDI) program in a manner that addresses two major problems. First, workers with medical conditions that threaten their ability to continue to work frequently do not have access to timely supports, resulting in premature exit from the labor force and entry into SSDI. Second, the performance of the determination process for SSDI disability has been extremely problematic for decades. Both problems are fallout from the failure of the economic security system for such workers to keep up with changes in technology, medicine, the nature of work, and the conceptual understanding of "disability" in the decades since policymakers designed the SSDI program in the mid-1950s.

Any structural reforms to SSDI must address both gateway issues. The first could potentially be addressed by "early intervention" programs—those that deliver or incentivize timely support to workers and their employers once a work-threatening medical condition is recognized. Often overlooked, however, is the potential for using early intervention programs to address the second problem. As already is the case in other disability insurance contexts, the gateway to SSDI could integrate (1) the timely provision of work supports for those with significant medical conditions with (2) an eligibility determination process that immediately awards long-term income support to those with the most problematic circumstances, and to others only after a supported, good-faith work test is unsuccessful. A single integrated system is more efficient than two systems that separately provide work supports and perform eligibility determinations.

We propose the development, testing, and adoption of a nationwide system of integrated employment/eligibility services (EESs). This new SSDI gateway approach would be designed to improve the economic security of workers with significant medical conditions; reduce the rate at which they stop working and enter SSDI; slow the growth in federal expenditures to support such workers; and create an eligibility determination process that is equitable, effective, and efficient. The elements of our proposal are not all new, but our proposal includes greater emphasis on integrating SSDI eligibility determination within a system that also provides work supports. The proposal is consistent in many respects with early intervention demonstrations described in President Obama's 2015 budget proposal for the Social Security Administration (SSA) and the 2015 Omnibus Appropriations Bill (H.R.83, "Consolidated and Further Continuing Appropriations Act" 2015). This proposal, however, goes further—as described later, it would eventually result in changes to eligibility criteria and the determination process through the introduction of a supported work test in which a substantial subset of applicants would be required to engage before further consideration of their eligibility for SSDI benefits.

Nearly a decade after the Social Security Advisory Board (SSAB) called for research and development in this area (SSAB 2006), no serious effort has been launched even to pilot such an integrated system, perhaps because its development requires effective collaboration of multiple federal and state agencies as well as private organizations. Yet, the experience of private disability insurance (PDI) and workers' compensation (WC) carriers I n this country, as well as innovations in public disability insurance systems in other countries, demonstrate that EESs can address both the employment and eligibility determination problems our proposal aims to address. We take into account lessons from existing systems and apply them to the development of an effective EES system for SSDI. Adapting these ideas for the United States will take some effort, but it seems quite feasible to do so and simultaneously achieve several desirable policy goals.

Key features of the proposed EESs include effective outreach to targeted workers, employers, and health care providers; intake specialists who triage applicants into work supports, immediate SSDI entry, or no support; and narrow targeting of work supports to those for whom such supports will make a difference. Work supports will include elements the evidence base shows to have been beneficial in other contexts: coordinators to advise and facilitate communication between the worker, clinicians, the employer, and other service providers; a needs assessment and establishment of a work plan; time-limited cash benefits; tailored services; and requirements for demonstrating good-faith efforts, with SSDI entry if such efforts are unsuccessful. An EES system also will require a carefully developed appeals process.

We present options for rapid development and testing of EES models that would draw on the existing capabilities of both public and private entities under new organizational structures designed to ensure effective collaboration. Funding for EESs would come from redirecting other expenditures—such as those from SSA's administrative budget, the SSDI Trust Fund, other public programs, private health insurance, PDI, and WC—depending on each worker's circumstances. Importantly, the proposed system does not intend to place new burdens on employers, as such burdens are likely to discourage hiring or retaining workers at high risk for medical events. We thus avoid employer mandates, fees, or taxes as means to finance the system or increase employer incentives to retain workers.

In the second section, we document the problems addressed by our proposal and the success of similar systems. We describe the features of a generic EES gateway to SSDI in the third section, where we also outline the institutional infrastructure for a system of EESs. We analyze the likely effectiveness of such a system and its benefits and costs to various stakeholders in the fourth section; we outline a process for EES development, testing, and adoption in the fifth section; and we address the probable concerns of stakeholders in the sixth section. We provide our conclusions in the last section.

TWO PROBLEMS AND A SINGLE APPROACH TO A SOLUTION

In this section, we discuss the causes and consequences of premature SSDI entry and briefly review existing evidence that timely and appropriate assistance can prolong participation in the labor force. We then summarize the problems with the current disability determination process (including the outdated statutory definition of disability) and briefly review EESs that currently exist in PDI, WC, and other countries, comparing their contexts to that of SSDI.

Causes and Consequences of Premature SSDI Entry

Workers often fail to get the timely supports needed to continue working after a medical event, especially if the cause is not covered by WC or if the worker lacks PDI coverage, as is often the case. The result can be premature exit from the labor force and early entry into SSDI. Many factors contribute. Workers who experience a medical event often fall into the gap between employers with inadequate motivation to invest in retaining the worker and physicians who typically focus on diagnoses and treatment of the individual's medical condition, not on practices that might promote return to work (ACOEM 2006). For financial or other reasons, workers might not have access to the supports they need, and health care providers, state agencies, lawyers, private insurers, and others may benefit from encouraging application for SSDI (or Supplemental Security Income [SSI]) over pursuit of return to work (Mann and Stapleton 2011).[1]

A considerable number of workers exit the labor force because of medical conditions. In 2012, annual worker applications for SSDI benefits reached 2.8 million; allowances reached 976,000 by December 2012 (SSA 2014, Tables 60 and 39). Although some who enter SSDI might be capable of substantial work with support, fewer than one-quarter achieve that, and only about 6 percent earn enough to forego benefits for even a short period (Liu and Stapleton 2011; Ben-Shalom and Mamun 2013). Historically, about half of denied applicants return to work (von Wachter et al. 2011). Maestas at al. (2013) and French and Song (2014) have shown that substantial numbers of new SSDI entrants would be engaged in substantial gainful activity (SGA) two and three years, respectively, after entry if their applications had been denied.[2] We do not know how many more would work had they received timely assistance to stay in the labor force.

---

1 For example, health care providers benefit when their uninsured patients become eligible for Medicaid, and states benefit when Temporary Assistance for Needy Families (TANF) recipients obtain SSDI/SSI and Medicare/Medicaid. In fact, some states pay private companies to help move individuals on state welfare rolls into federal disability programs (Joffe-Walt 2013).

2 Maestas et al. (2013) estimate that in the absence of SSDI, the marginal entrant—belonging to the 23 percent of applicants whose ultimate outcome is estimated to depend on their initial examiner assignment—would be on average 18 percentage points more likely to engage in SGA (work with earnings above the annual equivalent of SGA) two years after the initial determination if the application had been denied. French and Song (2014) estimate that SSDI allowances reduced engagement in SGA by 16 percent three years after adjudication for applicants with marginal cases adjudicated by administrative law judges.

The consequences of work disability for workers and taxpayers are substantial. For workers and their families, a frequent consequence is a substantial reduction in their standard of living (Boden 2005; Schimmel and Stapleton 2012). From the taxpayer perspective, expenditures on SSDI, SSI, Medicare, Medicaid, and other federal and state programs are also large (Riley and Rupp 2015). For employers, the consequences of work disability are more complex. Many invest in return-to-work supports, presumably because they believe the benefits outweigh the costs, but employers are likely to replace the worker if this is the least expensive way to restore productivity (Ben-Shalom 2015). This probably helps to explain why such a large share of SSDI entrants have low skills and had most recently been employed by small and medium-sized firms (Stapleton et al. 2015).

Evidence on Supports to Prolong Labor Force Participation

Mounting rigorous evidence suggests that access to better work supports would delay the exit of workers from the labor force. In a systematic review of 10 work-based interventions designed to assist workers with musculoskeletal and other pain-related conditions, Franche et al. (2005) found strong evidence that interventions—including components of work accommodation and early contact between the workplace and health care providers—can reduce sick leave and work disability. Based on an extensive review of the evidence on various early intervention models, Waddell et al. (2008) concluded that the most effective ways to improve employment outcomes after a medical event involve intervening early—especially before the connection between worker and employer is severed—with coordinated health care and work supports. The evidence regarding one of the most common causes of work disability—low back pain—is especially compelling (Sullivan and Adams 2010). Wickizer et al. (2011) evaluated an intervention that provided financial incentives to physicians plus organizational support and care coordination aimed at reducing work disability among WC claimants in Washington State. The intervention led to reductions in disability days, labor force exit, and total costs; the number of WC claimants receiving cash benefits 12 months after filing was reduced by 21 percent. Recent evidence from the Netherlands on the 2002 introduction of employer-based employments supports is also quite strong. Hullegie and Koning (2014, Table 5) estimate that the Dutch reforms reduced the receipt of disability benefits by workers ages 40 to 58 who experienced an unscheduled hospitalization by 84 percent for men and 61 percent for women in the third year after the hospitalization, and by about 50 percent for younger workers of both sexes.

Problems with the Current Disability Determination Process

Problems with the SSDI disability determination process have persisted for decades, despite extensive investments to address them. Processing times are extremely long and the backlog is enormous; appeals of initial denials are high, as are the allowance rates on appeal;[3] and there appear to be inconsistencies in the application of eligibility criteria across states, between initial and appellate levels, and even across adjudicators within the same level (see, for example, GAO 2004; Autor et al. 2015). Furthermore, important decision rules are not supported by an evidence base—no evidence exists on how the "vocational factors" of age, education, and past work actually affect a worker's ability to learn a new job (GAO 2012; Mann et al. 2014). Finally, the disability determination process encourages applicants to demonstrate they are unable to engage in substantial work rather than encouraging them to attempt work as their application proceeds, thereby undermining their ability to work in the future (Autor et al. 2015).

A fundamental reason why these problems have proven intractable is the conceptual flaw in the Social Security Act's definition of disability—long-term inability "to engage in any substantial gainful activity because of a medically determinable physical or mental impairment." The current disability determination system is built on this definition, which focuses almost exclusively on medical conditions, with minimal regard for the many personal and environmental characteristics that affect whether an individual with a significant medical condition is able to work. The most important exception is the use of vocational factors for older workers, introduced in 1967 amendments to the Social Security Act. [4] Because

---

3 The hearings-level allowance rate for medical decisions for those who applied from 1992 through 2007 ranges from 70 to 73 percent, with no apparent trend (SSA 2014, Table 63). For more recent applicants, hearing allowance rates are notably lower (as low as 63 percent for 2010 applicants), but we do not know the extent to which these rates are affected by the many decisions pending for the applicant cohorts or the effect of the recession and slow recovery on applications, initial awards, and appeals.

4 SSA can also deny SSDI applications if the claimant fails to follow an evidence-based treatment prescribed by the applicant's own physician or use a prescribed orthotic or prosthetic device that would allow the applicant to engage in SGA. However, the agency does not deny applications on the basis of evidence-based treatments or devices that have not been prescribed; consider the use of major equipment such as motorized wheelchairs or scooters; or determine whether accommodations, whether provided by an employer or otherwise, would allow the applicant to engage in SGA. See: DI 23010.005: Failure to Follow Prescribed Treatment–Policies in SSA's Program Operations Manual System (available at https://secure.ssa.gov/poms.nsf/lnx/0423010005); and DI 34121.007 Musculoskeletal

the vocational factors are not backed by evidence (Mann et al. 2014), however, adjudicators often must rely on highly subjective information from vocational experts regarding the applicant's ability to perform previous work or other "work which exists in the national economy" (CFR 404.1566, "Work Which Exists in the National Economy").

The current approach to disability determination was appealing and practical at the 1956 inception of SSDI but is badly out of sync with health care, technology, social norms, and the nature of work in the 21st century. Major changes in all of these areas have increased the importance of personal and environmental factors in determining ability to work—as reflected in the International Classification of Functioning, Disability and Health (ICF), the framework for measuring health and disability adopted by the World Health Organization (2002). Although the Government Accountability Office (GAO) and SSAB have recommended incorporation of such factors in the disability determination process, little has been done (SSAB 2006; GAO 2012). One reason is the complexity it would add to the current determination process; another is that even if an SSDI applicant could continue to work with supports, he or she might not have access to them. A well-developed system of EESs would address these matters.

Existing EESs

EESs similar to the ones we propose already exist in other contexts. In 2014, 39 percent of U.S. private sector workers were covered by short-term PDI (typically for no more than six months), and 33 percent had long-term PDI (Monaco 2015). These programs generally assess eligibility for benefits and provide work supports, including time-limited cash benefits, while the worker is still employed (Autor et al. 2014). For medical events that are work-related and thus covered by WC, the WC carrier typically conducts eligibility determination and provides health care, work supports, and cash benefits (Burton 2007).[5] An important but seldom recognized feature in both PDI and WC programs is that the provided work supports essentially serve as a work test that can inform decisions about awarding long-term benefits.

Listings, Section J, Orthotic, prosthetic, or assistive devices (https://secure.ssa.gov/poms.nsf/lnx/0434121007).

5 Work supports are required in relatively few WC cases—the median number of days away from work due to nonfatal injuries and illnesses is eight days; most cases do not involve any lost days. In 2013, 917,000 private industry workers in the United States experienced at least one day away from work (BLS 2014).

In response to problems quite similar to those now confronting the United States, some countries have reformed their systems; EES systems are at the heart of reforms in the Netherlands, the United Kingdom, and Sweden (Burkhauser et al. 2014). Most notable is the Netherlands effort to address what became known in the 1990s as the "Dutch disease." That country's expenditures were the highest in the Organisation for Economic Co-operation and Development (OECD) as a percentage of the gross domestic product (GDP)—4.2 percent in 1990. From 2002 to 2010, after enactment of reforms to the DI program, the working-age population receiving DI benefits fell from nearly 8 percent to less than 6 percent. According to Hullegie and Koning (2014), a "gatekeeper protocol" that increased employers' sickness monitoring requirements is widely considered to have been the most effective element in that reform. The gatekeeper protocol instituted legal responsibilities for employers and sick-listed workers to cooperatively draft a "re-integration plan" soon after onset of a sickness period, leaving the Dutch social benefits administration as only a gatekeeper to DI. A DI benefit is awarded only after failure of "sufficient efforts to resume work," as demonstrated to the social benefits administration. If the administration determines that a worker did not make sufficient efforts, the employer is held responsible for additional months of sick pay.

In Sweden, rapid growth in disability receipt in the 1970s and 1980s led to lower replacement rates on sickness benefits, holding employers responsible for the first 14 days of sickness absence, and putting more emphasis on vocational factors (Burkhauser et al. 2014). Following renewed growth in the late 1990s, Sweden implemented additional reforms that focused on work supports rather than cash assistance. Most notably, standardized protocols for granting cash benefits helped promote return to work before offering cash benefits, and merging of the sickness and long-term disability programs led to triage sooner in the process. These changes were further reinforced in 2008 by rules that called for earlier and more frequent assessment of work capacity.

Differences between the contexts of the EESs described above and that of SSDI must be recognized in considering how such systems could be adapted to the latter. PDI and WC are financed through experience-rated premiums, giving the employer and insurer incentives to provide work supports. Workers with PDI coverage typically have relatively high skill levels, so their employers have a financial stake in their continued employment. WC is mandated for employers, covers at least some medical expenses, and often involves litigation over whether the medical event is due to work. Other countries that have introduced EES systems already had universal health coverage; short-term sickness benefits; more public support for working-age low-income individuals without disabilities; and, before enacting new systems, higher rates of participation in their public disability systems than occurs in the United States.[6]

Our goals for this paper are to describe (1) a comprehensive EES system for SSDI that is adapted to the U.S. context, and (2) how that system could be developed, building on what can be learned from other EES systems and the capabilities of existing public and private entities.

EMPLOYMENT/ELIGIBILITY SERVICES

To provide context for the description of the proposed gateway to employment supports and SSDI later in this section, we first briefly describe the current gateway to SSDI, along with the external employment support system, for comparison purposes. The new gateway will serve to integrate these systems.

The Current SSDI Gateway and Employment Support System

Currently, when workers become aware of a work-threatening medical condition, they face numerous options, as depicted on the left-hand side of Figure 1. They may choose to apply immediately for SSDI at an SSA field office (FO) or seek assistance from the private sector (e.g., from medical and rehabilitation providers) that might allow them to stay in the labor force, or the public sector (e.g., state American Job Centers and vocational rehabilitation [VR] agencies). Some may apply for benefits and seek assistance at the same time. Many workers will return to substantial work rather than enter SSDI, often with public or private supports, but others will not. Organizations that provide worker support may also help the worker apply for SSDI, or even insist that the worker apply (e.g., in the case of private long-term disability insurers or TANF agencies).

The SSA FO takes the initial application and, after determining that the worker meets the SSDI work history requirement, transfers it to a state Disability Determination Service (DDS), which is responsible for determining medical eligibility. The DDS collects medical evidence from the applicant's health care providers and, in some instances, orders a medical examination to collect additional

6 Though the SSDI participation rate has historically been lower than participation rates in the public disability systems in the European countries mentioned above, it has more than doubled since the mid-1980s and continues to rise even though the trend in self-reported health has been flat over this time period (Burkhauser et al. 2014).

information. The DDS returns its decision to the SSA FO. An SSA regional office reviews about half of the DDS allowances—those most problematic to adjudicate—and, in some instances, returns the case to the DDS for further development. If the claim is denied, the applicant may appeal the denial through a multileveled process (not shown). If the claim is allowed, SSA begins paying SSDI benefits.[7] At this point, SSA also offers financing for employment supports provided by prequalified public entities under the Ticket to Work program.[8] Thus, a feature of the current gateway is that it provides the worker with the option of entering SSDI without first attempting to continue to work using any available supports.

Figure 1. The current gateway to SSDI and the employment support system

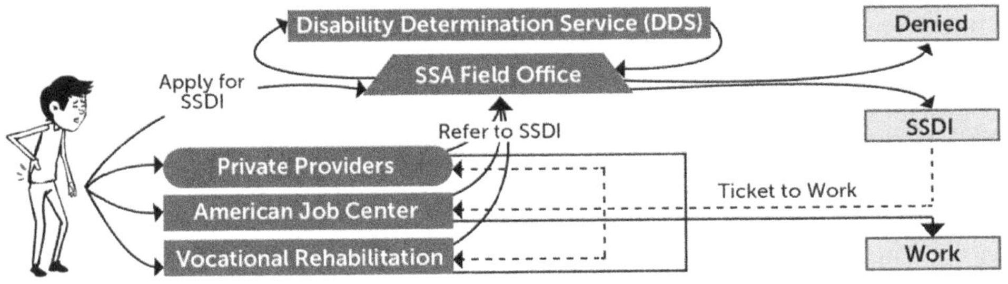

The EES

An EES, which could be established by a state or local government, would be an integrated gateway to both work supports and SSDI (Figure 2). To achieve its goal, the EES would have to (1) conduct effective outreach to all workers in the population; (2) identify and interact in a timely way with workers who experience a major medical event; (3) conduct triage—assess whether the worker should obtain SSDI benefits immediately, receive work supports, or receive no assistance at all; (4) design and manage the delivery of individualized work supports to workers determined eligible; (5) quickly award SSDI benefits, conditional on SSA review, to those determined to qualify for SSDI without a supported work attempt (analogous to what a DDS would do now), with benefits starting after

7 The new beneficiary is first entitled to benefits in the fifth month after the first month for which the applicant was not able to engage in SGA (as established by the DDS) and to Medicare 24 months later.

8 The beneficiary can use the Ticket—a performance-based voucher—to attempt to purchase employment services from a variety of prequalified public or private providers, or obtain such services from a state VR agency; in that case, SSA will reimburse the agency for costs, up to a limit, if the beneficiary engages in SGA for at least nine months.

the five-month waiting period; (6) award benefits to those who unsuccessfully attempt to continue to work with support (again conditional on SSA review); and (7) end work supports for those making no attempt to continue to work despite access to supports. Public and private entities external to the EES (not shown) would deliver many employment supports, but the EES would help manage and finance those supports. In contrast to the current SSDI gateway, the EES would funnel workers likely to be able to continue to work with supports toward available supports before SSDI entry. We consider EES functions in more detail in the next section.

Figure 2. The proposed gateway to employment support and SSDI

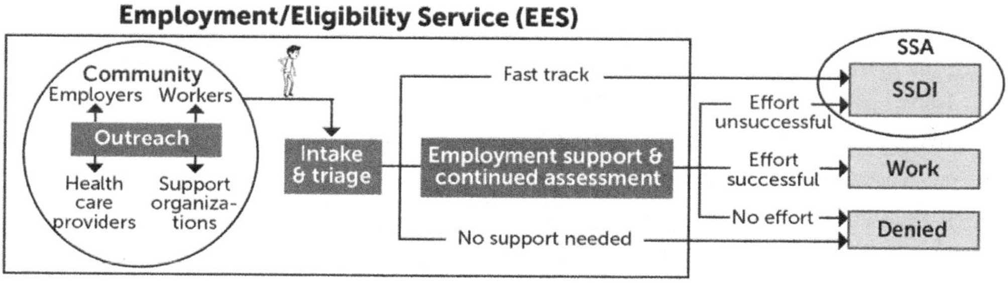

Outreach, entry, and triage

The EES would have to conduct direct outreach to workers and others—employers, health care providers, and advocacy and support organizations—likely to know when a worker experiences a serious medical condition that threatens work. All of these groups should be aware that the EES exists and is the gateway to economic security for such workers. Outreach would emphasize that workers or their representatives should contact the EES as soon as they become aware of a medical condition that threatens continuation of work, preferably before the worker loses his or her job, but the EES must also indicate that the door never closes. The EES would establish a "single door" to work supports and SSDI. Any covered worker with a work-threatening condition could seek public assistance—work supports or SSDI—through the EES. Workers would no longer have the option of applying directly to SSA for SSDI benefits.

The EES would conduct triage in three stages. First, the adjudicator would assess whether the worker meets work history requirements for SSDI benefits. If not, the EES would refer him or her to whatever supports are available outside of the

EES.[9] Second, for those meeting the work history requirement, the adjudicator would determine whether the consequences of the condition are of sufficient severity and duration to warrant any support at all, given the worker's personal characteristics and supports already available. The conceptual criterion would be "unlikely to be able to engage in SGA within a fixed period (e.g., 24 months) with or without work support"—comparable in stringency to current medical criteria. Those who meet this test would become EES clients and qualify for support of some sort, to be determined at stage three. Anyone not qualifying would be notified and provided information on appeal rights.

At the third stage, the adjudicator would determine whether there is a sufficiently high probability that the worker could return to substantial work within a specified period, given available supports. The decision would be based on the worker's medical condition; personal characteristics, including age, skills, and current employment status; and the availability of work supports known to be effective for similar medical conditions and circumstances. If the decision was affirmative, the worker would be offered employment supports, referred to an employment support specialist, and notified of the right to appeal for immediate SSDI entry. Should the worker decline the offer of employment supports, the worker's only remaining avenue to SSDI would be via an appeal to SSA. If the decision was negative, the adjudicator would award SSDI benefits, conditional only on a review by SSA. Our expectation is that these two groups—those awarded employment supports and those awarded SSDI—would each include large shares of those workers awarded support at stage two, but it is not possible to predict what their shares would be. Those awarded SSDI would be allowed to opt into work supports if appropriate supports are available at a cost less than that of their projected benefits.

Initially, assessment of the prospects for continued SGA with supports should be based on available evidence about the characteristics of workers most likely to continue SGA if they have supports (such as those with lower back pain or affective disorders and those who could potentially return to their current or most recent job with support) and who have not already received evidence-based supports financed by their health care, workers' compensation, or private

9 This criterion would exclude individuals who might be eligible for SSI but not SSDI, reflecting our intent to focus on SSDI and those already in the workforce. As discussed later, the EESs' functions could be expanded to cover SSI eligibility determinations.

disability insurers.[10] The criteria should also reflect the expected costs of the work supports relative to the expected benefits. The new system will increase public outlays if support costs routinely exceed expected benefit savings. Life expectancy is a final consideration, with those having substantially limited life expectance because of medical conditions not being required to engage in a supported work test. As success is achieved and capacity developed, the criteria for requiring a supported work test could be broadened—perhaps over decades—to the point where all applicants currently allowed under vocational factors or at the hearings level, plus some of those now allowed on the basis of SSA's current Listing of Impairments (the Listings), could not enter SSDI without taking a supported work test. Fast-track SSDI awards would then go only to those with a low probability of engaging in SGA within a specified period, even with available supports, or those with a remaining life expectancy below an established threshold. Many (but not all) applicants who meet or equal the Listings would be allowed on this track.

To complete the initial assessment, the adjudicator would collect medical evidence from health care providers and, in some instances, order a medical examination (as state DDSs do now) on behalf of SSA. Except in cases where it might be harmful to the worker, the EES could also collect information from the worker's employer pertaining to the nature of the job and options for accommodating the worker's condition or otherwise helping him or her return to the same job. This information also would be used to support development of work plans and conditional SSDI awards.

Work supports

EESs are expected to deliver evidence-based services only; services for which there is no evidence of substantially improved work continuation for targeted workers would not be considered.[11] EESs would assign a well-trained case coordinator to each eligible client; this coordinator would be someone other than

---

10 Regulations will likely be needed to discourage insurers from shifting costs for certain services to the government.

11 By implication, workers meeting the severity criteria normally would not be eligible for work supports if evidence-based services for workers with their condition and circumstances are unavailable. It will be important for the government to support research activities that improve the evidence base over time, and EESs should play an important role. Such research can ultimately improve outcomes and reduce costs both by improving the targeting of work supports to those most likely to benefit and improving the outcomes of those eligible for supports.

the adjudicator, with a different set of skills and expertise.[12] The coordinator would work with the client and, as appropriate, the employer, health care provider, and others, to develop a work plan, including a timetable and milestones. Work plans would include elements related to health care, rehabilitation, accommodations, assistive technologies, transportation assistance, personal assistance, trial work or gradual return to work, employer incentives, and cash assistance. Services would commonly be purchased from other organizations and, in some instances, paid for by other parties (e.g., health care by the worker's health insurance plan if the worker has coverage); the EES would be the payer of last resort. The EES would provide time-limited cash assistance only if the worker has used up all medical leave and short-term disability benefits and is ineligible for cash assistance from another source.

The work plan should provide clear expectations for worker adherence to the plan, inform him or her about the consequences of failure to adhere, and advise what to do if adherence becomes problematic.[13] The plan should also set expectations for performance of other parties regarding the plan; performance incentives should be incorporated when warranted and feasible. As the parties execute the work plan, the coordinator would facilitate communication between them, provide advice when needed, monitor progress relative to milestones, record information about activities and results, and work with all parties to adjust the plan when needed. If the client persistently failed to attain milestones despite adherence to the plan, the coordinator could recommend to a supervisor that the EES terminate work supports and proceed with a conditional SSDI award. If the coordinator attributed persistent failure to achieve milestones to the client's ongoing and inexcusable lack of adherence, the coordinator would recommend service termination without recommending an SSDI award. If the supervisor accepted the coordinator's decision, the EES would inform the client of the decision and the right to appeal. Otherwise, the supervisor would advise a

12 One reviewer of an earlier draft noted a similarity between SSA's Disability Claims Manager (DCM) test, completed in the early 2000s, and the EES: the consolidation of the functions of the SSA FO and the DDS into a single office. There is an important structural difference, however; whereas the DCM test assigned a single person (the DCM) to perform all major process functions for an individual applicant, with some support from expert consultants, we envision a combination of staff, each specialized in outreach, triage, or planning and management of employment supports, perhaps with subspecialists among the latter—again with support from expert consultants.

13 Muijzer et al. (2010) provide a review of how several European systems have implemented work requirements.

suitable course of action, such as a change to the recommendation or adjustment of supports and further pursuit of work continuation.

Conditional SSDI allowances

Upon conditional award of SSDI benefits, the EES would provide a documented rationale to SSA on the basis of information already gathered. For clients found ineligible for work supports, the rationale essentially would be the same as that for which DDS examiners search now. For clients who receive work supports, however, the rationale for the recommendation would use evidence from the client's supported return-to-work efforts. In such cases, the EES would argue that it has tested the client's capability to engage in SGA with available support and has determined the client cannot do so due to a combination of his or her medical condition and other circumstances.

SSA's own role in adjudication of conditional SSDI allowances would be limited to reviewing the rationale for the recommendation (or denial) and the evidence submitted to support it. This is the same role SSA currently plays in conducting pre-effectuation reviews of at least 50 percent of all medical decisions made by DDS examiners.[14] The actual review differs in the case of EES clients with an unsuccessful work test because the content of the EES's recommended allowance would include evidence pertaining to the test. In effect, the application would already have passed through an initial determination process before it reaches SSA.

Workers would have the right to appeal major decisions made by EES adjudicators, case coordinators, and their supervisors. Each EES would be required to establish an internal appeal process and provide timely decisions. In addition, the federal government would establish a second, external level of appeals for workers dissatisfied with the outcome of their first appeal.

The EES's environment

The success of EESs in achieving policy objectives will also require reshaping critical aspects of the external environment via legislation, regulations, and changes in the administrative functions and processes of existing agencies. We

[14] If the SSA reviewer is not convinced that the information provided by the DDS warrants an allowance, the reviewer will typically ask the DDS examiner to provide additional evidence before SSA effectuates the allowance.

begin by discussing how private organizations and state agencies might interact with or be engaged by EESs. We then discuss financing, federal oversight, and quality improvement activities.

The private sector

The relationship between EESs and employers will be important to the success of the EES. To succeed, the EES must be a useful resource to employers—one that helps them retain workers without imposing new costs—while not displacing work support efforts that employers would otherwise undertake themselves. Ideally, employers would cooperate with the efforts of the EES, but the need for the EES reflects the fact that employers currently stand to gain little from providing work support to low-skill, easily replaced workers—the sorts of workers who predominate among SSDI entrants (Ben-Shalom 2015).[15] Hence, employers of such workers will have little incentive to cooperate unless the EES offers a participation incentive, such as time-limited monthly payments while the worker is returning to work (Stapleton et al. 2009). A possible way to incentivize employer cooperation with the EES would be to consider such cooperation *prima facie* evidence of compliance with the Americans with Disabilities Act (ADA). This approach would be especially helpful for firms not large or prosperous enough to have well-trained human resource specialists with expertise in ADA compliance.

In many cases, employer-financed work supports are delivered by PDI and WC carriers and vendors that specialize in disability management. One way to limit displacement of currently available services is to require PDI and WC carriers to become EESs. They already carry out the basic functions of an EES for covered workers except for making conditional SSDI allowances and documenting their rationale in a manner that meets SSA requirements. The regulations and federal oversight required to ensure the performance of carriers acting as EESs and address conflict of interest (COI) issues would impose new costs on the carriers and, by extension, employers. It would be reasonable to offer financial incentives

---

[15] Many employers already make substantial investments in work-continuation supports, and the cost to the public of funding the EES would be inflated to whatever extent it displaces those efforts, presumably with little impact on work continuation. Many larger employers and employers of any size that must invest in their workers' capabilities already provide work-continuation support after a significant medical event occurs, and because of WC, almost all employers have some incentive to do so when the medical event is an occupational injury or illness.

that address COI and are commensurate with benefits to SSA and new costs for carriers.[16]

State agencies

We anticipate that most states will establish their own EESs using the capabilities of state agencies that already perform some EES function. A few states may choose to leverage private sector capabilities. The state's DDS is likely to be fully incorporated into the EES because of its vital role in the current gateway to SSDI.

State VR agencies provide work supports to people with disabilities who are trying to work, or in some cases already working, and many VR clients enter SSDI while receiving VR services or shortly thereafter. These agencies presumably could develop the capability to intervene earlier, as they are explicitly authorized, but not required to do under the 2014 Workforce Innovation and Opportunity Act (WIOA).[17] American Job Centers (AJCs), under the aegis of state workforce development agencies, could also play a role. They provide assistance to all job seekers, including administering unemployment benefits, supporting job search, and delivering employment and training services. The federal government has invested significant funds to make AJC services available to workers with disabilities.

Some states might leverage their WC responsibilities to help the EESs. Washington State provides an example of such assistance.[18] Five states have mandatory short-term disability insurance (STDI) programs. In some of these states, some

---

16 The benefits to SSA stem from the fact that the EESs' conditional SSDI allowances will displace direct applications to SSA and the initial determinations that follow. Further gains to SSDI might be achieved by partially replacing the implicit SSDI subsidy of long-term PDI benefits with an explicit payment to support the carrier's EES activities (Stapleton et al. 2009). The implicit subsidy stems from the private insurer reducing its own long-term benefit payment to the client by one dollar for every dollar of SSDI benefits a client receives. When a private carrier acts as an EES, the government could require the carrier to pay all of the benefit for some period (for example, 12 or 24 months) and compensate the carrier via a commensurate direct payment.

17 In fact, the WIOA mandate for VR agencies to first serve their most severely disabled applicants significantly limits available funds, and SSA payments to VR agencies for services provided to SSDI and SSI beneficiaries have the effect of encouraging VR agencies to serve such workers last (Mann and Stapleton 2011).

18 Washington's Department of Labor & Industries has established an innovative system to offer timely work-continuation support to all WC claimants covered by the public fund. There is rigorous evidence that the supports have hastened return to work and reduced WC

employers purchase private coverage and others get coverage through a public fund. To our knowledge, none of these programs provides work supports to their claimants. Nevertheless, states could use the programs as a way to quickly identify those workers who experience major medical events and bring them in to the EES. Other state or local agencies that have capabilities of potential value to an EES include, but are not limited to, Medicaid agencies, state and municipal hospitals and health clinics (including mental health providers), transportation agencies, and community colleges.

Financing

A large share of the funding for administering an EES and for much of the work support would come from existing federal, state, and private funding streams. SSA would gradually convert funding for administering the current SSDI gateway to funding the new gateway as EESs replace/subsume DDSs and the role of SSA's field offices in the disability determination process diminishes. SSA financing of work supports for beneficiaries under Ticket to Work and Work Incentive Planning and Assistance could be partially redirected to supports for EES clients as EESs slow the flow of workers into SSDI. Similarly, VR, workforce development, Medicaid, and other state agencies already provide some support to those who would be EES clients. We expect a large majority of these clients to have private health coverage or Medicaid; the latter would pay for medical services incorporated into work-continuation plans. One role of the EES would be to encourage health providers to follow best practices and encourage carriers to pay for them. We expect that many EES clients would initially be eligible for medical leave pay, short-term disability benefits (especially in states with mandatory STDI), or unemployment benefits. States that choose to develop EESs can be expected to draw on these resources in the process. Employers should be required to maintain their own efforts via PDI and WC coverage. We recommend against requiring employers to pay more, however, because one goal is to make it more economically attractive for employers to hire and retain those workers at risk of a medical event and retain those who experience one.

Ultimately, additional funding will be needed to pay for work supports not currently offered to prospective EES clients. One option could be to draw on the SSDI Trust Fund, with the expectation that EES-generated reductions in SSDI benefit costs will exceed the marginal costs of the work supports. Given

costs by more than the system's cost (Wickizer et al. 2011). In principle, the same services could be made available to workers who experience medical events that are not job related.

the long-term imbalance of the Trust Fund, however, it would be more prudent to rely on discretionary revenues until the EESs actually start to reduce benefit payments. This is one of many reasons to start with small tests of EESs and then expand EES funding commensurate with the evidence that emerges (see section on "Development, Testing, and Establishment of an EES System").

Federal role

SSA would no longer take applications for SSDI directly from workers, but SSA and federal partner agencies will need to have strong roles in the oversight of EESs. Also, the EES could rely on SSA to determine whether an applicant meets the SSDI work history requirement—a process that requires IRS data and that SSA could perform quickly at a central location.

The federal government must provide strong oversight of EESs beyond SSA's review of allowances because the EESs will have conflicts of interest that involve federal funding (see section on "Analysis of the Proposal"). Many precedents exist for the extent and nature of federal oversight required. Because the DDSs currently have similar COIs, SSA provides oversight through a complex system that includes regulations, rules, technical assistance, financial incentives, quality reviews, pre-effectuation reviews of the 50 percent of DDS allowances deemed most likely to contain decision errors, and a federal appeals process. Similar tools are used by other federal agencies for oversight of state-run programs that rely to a large degree on federal funding.[19] The federal government also uses the private sector to administer other major benefit programs—most notably Medicare.

We envision the establishment of a multiagency EES office tasked with leading the effort to improve the economic security—through a combination of employment, income, and in-kind supports—of workers who experience medical events. SSA would play a lead role within that office, as would the Department of Health and Human Services (HHS); the Department of Labor (DOL) and Department of Education (ED). Because of its multiagency nature, reports prepared by the office and submitted to the president and Congress would be signed by the leaders of each agency involved. SSA would continue to have final authority to allow SSDI applications after review of an EES recommendation and return cases to the EES for further development when warranted.

---

[19] To ensure a certain degree of uniformity across states, the federal monitoring process for EESs could incorporate a testing system designed to assess uniformity and support efforts to address excessive variation.

Other oversight elements would include (1) regulations and rules that govern the EES assessment process (including workers' medical and other personal and environmental characteristics that make them good candidates for work supports); (2) contractual arrangements between the EESs, the federal government, and subordinate entities, including performance incentives; (3) decision criteria and standards for supporting conditional award submissions; (4) description of the work supports the EESs are expected to use; (5) requirements for internal appeals; (6) the external appeals process; (7) a management information system and data requirements, including the interface with SSA systems; (8) privacy protection and data security; (9) provisions for use of data analytics to support operations and quality improvement;[20] (10) performance measurement and data collection and reporting; (11) auditing;[21] and (12) technical assistance.

The external federal appeals process for EES decisions would be a reformulated version of the SSDI/SSI appeals process currently operated by SSA's Office of Disability Adjudication and Review. Workers dissatisfied with an EES decision could appeal it to the external process only after denial of an initial appeal to the EES. In the external process, administrative law judges (ALJs) would adjudicate cases. A possible option for future consideration is for the EES to be represented in the appeals process because its decisions will typically be based on factors that go well beyond the medical condition of the client, such as the individual's other characteristics and circumstances, the evidence base for work supports, and the availability of supports.[22]

ANALYSIS OF THE PROPOSAL

We begin this section with a discussion of how the proposed system of EESs simultaneously expands early intervention for workers at risk of SSDI entry and improves on the current disability determination process. We then analyze the potential benefits and costs of the proposed system—from multiple

20 For example, rapid-cycle evaluation (Cody and Asher 2014) could be used to quickly compare and prioritize between alternative approaches to the targeting of work supports as well as the types of supports provided to the targeted individuals.

21 Predictive analytic techniques (Cody and Asher 2014) could be used to identity potentially fraudulent EES cases and effectively triage fraud prevention efforts.

22 This option would be an important departure from current practice. The DDS currently is not represented in external appeals, and the ALJ must represent SSA as well as serve as an independent adjudicator (see Bloch et al. 2014). Having the ALJ take on this dual role would be even more challenging when the interactions of many nonmedical factors with the worker's medical condition play a greater role in determining eligibility.

perspectives—and briefly discuss potential financial and administrative challenges to implementing such a system. We conclude with a discussion of how the rest of the public disability support system could adapt to this new gateway for SSDI.

Effective Expansion of Early Intervention Supports

The proposed EES system addresses the limited availability and use of early intervention work supports. Workers, employers, health care providers, and other relevant parties would know where to seek assistance when a worker experiences a medical event, regardless of whether the condition is work related. Workers would be evaluated for work supports and potentially required to make good-faith efforts to continue to work before they could enter SSDI. Timely and effective targeting would ensure supports are provided to those for whom they would make a difference while they are still connected to the labor force. Others would either receive SSDI benefits with minimal delay or immediately learn they were ineligible for any supports. Trained service coordinators would advise and facilitate communication between the worker, clinicians, the employer, and other service providers. This approach would maximize the worker's chances of retaining his or her current position, or transitioning to a more suitable job with the same or a different employer. Time-limited cash benefits would provide economic security as well as an incentive to return to work.

Improvements to the Disability Determination Process

The EES triage process will incorporate nonmedical information, including personal and job characteristics, in a manner consistent with today's conceptual understanding of disability. This process will assess ability to work with full consideration of worker medical and nonmedical characteristics and the worker's environment, including the availability of work supports. It will stand in stark contrast to the current process, which encourages workers to demonstrate they cannot engage in SGA solely because of their medical condition. The work supports provided by the EES serve two purposes: increasing employment security and providing a test of work capability (with appropriate supports), rather than inability, in the determination process. The test changes the eligibility determination in a fundamental way. Instead of passively comparing known medical and vocational information about the applicant to criteria that at best approximate whether the worker can engage in SGA in any jobs available in the economy, with limited regard for available work supports, the adjudicator observes how the applicant performs in an active effort to stay in the workforce using available supports.

Potential Benefits and Costs

From a national economic perspective, the potential benefits of an EES system that effectively reduces labor force exit and SSDI entry are many and likely to be large, but their size cannot be predicted with reasonable confidence. Potential benefits include increased growth in GDP, employment, wages, personal income, and tax revenues; reduced growth in federal and state expenditures; reduction in the federal deficit; and an eligibility determination process that will restore public trust in the program's integrity. The costs include investments in work supports above and beyond those already being made.

In an appendix (available on the SSDI Solutions website), we analyze the likely long-term benefits and costs from the perspectives of workers, employers, the federal government, state and local governments, service providers, and the general public. We also consider transition costs. Economically, the greatest beneficiaries of the new system will be those workers able to continue to engage in SGA with supports they currently do not receive. Employers may or may not benefit; our intent is to build a system that does not impose new burdens on employers and, if anything, makes it more attractive for them to hire and retain workers at risk for work-threatening medical problems.

Our expectation is that this system will eventually reduce annual federal outlays from all programs by a large amount and increase revenues by a comparatively small amount. Although it is not possible to predict these amounts with any degree of confidence, our calculations suggest that federal savings on the order of $25 billion per year are certainly plausible. These include gross savings to SSDI of $20 billion, plus another $12 billion for Medicare, SSI, and Medicaid, partially offset by additional work support expenditures of $7 billion. Higher administrative costs are likely to offset the savings somewhat, but we expect them to be small because of the potential for gains in efficiency—perhaps $0.5 billion. Comparatively small revenue gains could also be achieved: perhaps on the order of $3 billion for income tax revenue, the SSDI Trust Fund, and the Medicare Trust Fund, combined. These annual outlay savings and incremental revenues would be realized well into the future, however, and only after a sustained period of annual investments, perhaps on the order of $1 billion to $2 billion per year. After that, savings will start to increase toward the projected long-run annual savings, as SSDI beneficiaries who entered under the existing SSDI gateway leave the rolls. The extent of savings and the speed with which they are realized will depend critically on how this time period is managed and what is learned in the process.

Although state governments play an important role in the proposed system, the financial implications for them will be small and largely positive: new, skilled and federally financed jobs in the public and private sectors and positive impacts on revenues. The new gateway will offer substantial opportunities to private insurers and other organizations in a position to contribute to its development, but some of those opportunities will be accompanied by regulatory changes to counteract shifting of costs from the private to the public sector. There are many reasons for voters to support the new system, beginning with better economic security of workers, more efficient use of taxpayer dollars, and improvements in program integrity accompanying adoption of a modern definition of disability and a gateway to support that makes more economic sense.

Challenges

Many important topics must be considered in the establishment of any EES system. For example: the length of time the EES and case coordinator follow clients as part of the work test (which may depend on client characteristics); what happens if beneficiaries need ongoing support, such as personal assistant services; and program design features to encourage early application to the EES well before all other forms of assistance have been exhausted.

Strong federal oversight (see previous section) is vital. Without it, many of the state or private organizations that lead the EESs might be inclined to use federal funds for purposes other than increasing the extent to which workers who experience medical events stay in the workforce. Without oversight, there could be many opportunities for EESs to use new federal funding to pay for services or supports that otherwise would have been financed by the state or the private sector or, in the case of the latter, to increase profits.[23]

Although the potential for reduced growth of federal expenditures net of revenues is high, there is also potential for increased growth. We expect EESs to reduce SSDI entry, but the number of workers who become EES clients might exceed the number of SSDI entrants under current law. For this reason, it is imperative to create safeguards against delivery of ineffective or excessively

---

[23] The challenges of federal oversight are illustrated by those SSA currently encounters in providing oversight of DDSs. For instance, even though SSA fully finances DDS operations, states make critical human resource decisions for all of their employees, including hiring, transferring across agencies, and setting salary scales; those decisions are not always in the best interest of the determination process.

expensive services, displacing private sector services, and shifting state costs to the federal government. New operational systems can build on the best of existing systems, but oversight and appeals processes will be challenging to implement successfully. It is possible that administrative savings will be realized, but the system might instead require an increase in administrative resources that is more than the modest increase we would expect. The higher administrative costs will be economically justifiable if they more than pay for themselves through better economic outcomes for workers and lower program benefits, but there is a risk they could become excessively high.

Adaptation of the Public Disability Support System to the New SSDI Gateway

The establishment of an EES system would provide the opportunity to make improvements in other aspects of the disability support system. Such changes could potentially improve the well-being of the target population and achieve considerable efficiencies by integrating support system components and shifting resources toward high-return investments to help this population make use of its work capacity, along the lines described in Mann and Stapleton (2011).

The program most obviously affected by the change in the SSDI gateway is SSI, because the two programs have common medical eligibility criteria and the current SSDI gateway is also the gateway to SSI. Those meeting the SSDI work history requirements who become eligible for SSI as a supplement to SSDI benefits could enter through the proposed gateway without modification. The gateway could be expanded to accommodate those meeting the SSI means test but not meeting the SSDI work history requirements, including many children. To be consistent with the modernized definition of disability, the triage process would result in immediate awards to some applicants, appropriate employment supports to others, and no support for the rest.[24]

The change in the SSDI gateway would offer opportunities to improve the work incentives currently offered to SSDI beneficiaries. Compared to today, presumably a far smaller share of SSDI beneficiaries would be able or willing to

---

24 Based on current evidence and research in progress, it might be reasonable to require applicants as young as 14 to participate in supported work tests, although the tests would be of very long duration. See Fraker et al. (April 2015) for a summary of the findings from SSA's Youth Transition Demonstration and Fraker et al. (June 2014) for the design report on the multiagency Promoting Readiness of Minors in SSI (PROMISE) demonstration.

pursue work after SSDI entry because they would have had the opportunity to use employment supports before they entered SSDI. Nonetheless, three groups of beneficiaries might benefit from work incentives and employment supports. The first has been mentioned previously: those who meet the fast-track criteria but choose to opt for employment supports.[25] The second is composed of those who entered SSDI before the new gateway was fully in place; they could be offered the opportunity to use the same work supports and give up their benefits if successful, while not being required to do so. The third group would be those who could work productively but would be economically worse off if they gave up their benefits for work. The new SSDI gateway could be used to identify such individuals and potentially provide them with variants of SSDI benefits not available today, such as a partial benefit, a benefit offset, or an allowance for work supports. The resulting support system would be much more tailored to the individual's work capacity and other circumstances than the current system.

The new gateway also offers the opportunity to improve employment supports to workers with medical conditions, including some who would not be eligible for SSDI under current criteria or are not seeking SSDI benefits, whether or not they are eligible. The EES could be the gateway to employment supports for all workers with medical conditions, regardless of interest in or possible eligibility for SSDI, including those currently offered by state VR agencies, AJCs, and other state agencies. Consistent with the goals of the WIOA, integration of the gateways to these supports would presumably make it easier for workers to access the most appropriate supports and also improve cooperation and coordination among agencies.

The scenarios described above are the most obvious opportunities for the larger disability support system to leverage the new SSDI gateway. There are likely to be others involving other programs that support this population—Medicaid, Medicare, mental health services, developmental disability services, special education, the Supplemental Nutrition Assistance Program, housing, and various others. The EES system could catalyze changes in the public disability support system that would take better advantage of modern medicine, technologies, and the work capacity of the target population. Of course, it is also possible that it could catalyze undesirable adaptation to the system. How to ensure desirable

[25] Also, special conditions could be placed on the SSDI awards of those expected to be in this group, requiring reassessment for employment supports rather than continuation of SSDI benefits after a reasonable period.

rather than undesirable adaption should be a critical consideration in efforts to develop, test, and establish an EES system.

DEVELOPMENT, TESTING, AND ESTABLISHMENT OF AN EMPLOYMENT/ELIGIBILITY SERVICES SYSTEM

Considerable time and investment would be required to develop, test, and establish a system of EESs. Current policymakers could leave to future leaders the decision of whether and when to commit to replacing the current gateway to SSDI with an EES system, and simply enact legislation that supports pilot tests and larger demonstrations. The goal would be to gradually develop the evidence base and external infrastructure necessary to support such a system. Alternatively, policymakers could enact legislation that commits to replacing the current gateway with an EES gateway in the future, giving the SSA commissioner and leaders of other relevant agencies authority to plan and start testing, develop infrastructure, and gradually scale up to a full system under the watchful eyes of policymakers and advocates over a lengthy period. In either case, the legislation would include a statement of objectives, an aspirational timetable, guidance on measuring progress toward objectives, and reporting requirements. We focus on the latter approach, which is more challenging, and potentially more risky, but would put the government more squarely on a path toward a new gateway for SSDI and better economic security for workers. Policymakers could scale back to a less ambitious initiative without a firm commitment to eventually replace the SSDI gateway with an EES gateway.

Legislation that commits to changing the SSDI gateway would amend the Social Security Act in several ways and might require amendments to acts that authorize other programs. Because of the latter, congressional leaders would likely need to convene special committees including representatives from the committees responsible for the relevant agencies and programs.

Perhaps the most important amendment to the Social Security Act would change the definition of disability for purposes of SSDI and SSI eligibility in a manner that recognizes all factors affecting a person's ability to engage in SGA and is conditional on the availability of work supports. Such an amendment would signal to all stakeholders that the federal government is launching a determined effort to modernize the economic security system for people with disabilities. It would not, however, immediately change the current disability determination criteria or process. Instead, it would specify that work supports be considered only if, according to the evidence, supports that are likely to allow the worker to engage in SGA are available to the applicant. The legislation would also instruct SSA's commissioner to continue using the existing criteria and determination process pending successful design and testing of EESs and establishment of an EES system. The legislation would define "success" as increasing the economic security of workers after they experience major medical events while reducing growth in total federal expenditures for their support.

Equally important, the legislation would establish a multiagency office, perhaps a Center for Employment and Eligibility Integration (CEEI), to efficiently improve the economic security of workers via directing the testing and development of a new gateway system for SSDI and, once success is achieved, oversee its gradual implementation and subsequent performance. SSA would be well represented in this office, as would those agencies with substantial responsibility for programs that currently finance supports for the same target population—most notably HHS, DOL, and ED.[26]

The legislation should direct the CEEI to focus initially on supporting tests of EES models. Such tests are needed to learn more about (1) how best to structure EESs and how they can screen workers into evidence-based supports without excessive costs, and without providing supports to large numbers of workers unlikely to benefit; (2) the types of workers most likely to work and not enter SSDI without supports; (3) the costs of providing supports relative to the cost of awarding SSDI benefits; and (4) how outcomes of providing supports vary with worker age and other characteristics. The legislation would have to grant the participating agencies the necessary waiver authority. In addition, legislation should direct the CEEI to start developing the federal and state infrastructure required to oversee EESs along the lines described in the previous section. Components of the infrastructure could be incorporated in some tests and then refined.

The CEEI would invite applications for grants to establish and test EESs from states, PDI and WC carriers, and perhaps others. The solicitation should specify a substantial set of grant conditions (e.g., the purpose and functions of an EES, the types of workers to be targeted for work supports, the scope of supports to be provided, the objectives and scale of the initial tests, and requirements to support

[26] Because of the multiagency nature of the operation, the CEEI must be permanent to provide ongoing oversight to the new gateway once it is established. As the guardian of the SSDI Trust Fund, SSA would still have sole responsibility for awarding SSDI benefits by approving conditional allowances made by EESs and via external appeals.

rigorous evaluation). It would invite grantees to be creative in proposing the details, encouraging them to take maximum advantage of existing capabilities. To reduce risk to workers and federal financing, initial tests would target workers for whom the evidence on the effectiveness of work supports is especially strong.[27] As confidence in the system's integrity and success grows, and relying on the evidence base, the CEEI would allow test EESs to broaden the definition of the group targeted for work supports.

The CEEI would lead the effort to evaluate the new systems, using rapid-cycle methods that rely heavily on administrative data and inform decision makers and others about findings as quickly as feasible (Cody and Asher 2014). The CEEI would also promote dissemination and discussion of new information as it emerges.

The legislation could also charge the CEEI with measuring annual federal and state expenditures to support workers who experience medical events at the state level under the various programs that fall within the agencies' purview, including 10-year projections. Such accounting would provide a yardstick for policymakers to assess how efforts to improve economic security are affecting expenditure growth (Mann and Stapleton 2011).

Finally, the legislation should establish an aspirational timetable and milestones, including conditions under which the CEEI can order full transition to an EES system. To proceed with a full transition, the office would first have to present an evidence-based transition plan to policymakers and the public. The office would also identify any additional legislation that might be required to support the full transition, incorporating what has been learned during the testing and development process. The legislation could specify that Congress and the president must formally accept the plan before the CEEI and its constituent agencies can proceed further.

Congress should also consider expanding the scope of the CEEI beyond that specified above. The CEEI could lead a national effort to modernize the disability support system around the new gateway to employment supports and SSDI. Such an expansion would support pursuit of the potential for improvements in those

---

27 Evidence cited in "Two Problems and a Single Approach to a Solution" suggests that many workers with chronic musculoskeletal issues, such as low back strains, would be good candidates. In 2013, the primary impairment of 36 percent of SSDI entrants was musculoskeletal (SSA 2014, Table 40).

components of the disability support system most directly related to the new gateway to SSDI, as outlined earlier.

LIKELY OBJECTIONS TO BUILDING A NEW GATEWAY FOR SSDI

Some groups will probably have major concerns about any change to the SSDI gateway. Advocates may fear that existing beneficiaries will be harmed, early intervention will discourage employers from hiring workers at high risk for a medical event, or state and local governments or the private sector will co-opt funds intended to help workers. Labor unions and others may object that workers will be denied benefits to which they are currently entitled. Federal and state agency leaders and employee unions might oppose this approach because it infringes on systems they currently operate. Some groups might object to EESs that give a major role to the private sector; others may object to a larger role for states. Many will likely be concerned that the costs will outweigh the benefits for some or all stakeholders. Finally, policymakers may fear that a costly testing program will ultimately fail to deliver an effective system in the near future, if ever.

Several features of this proposal are responsive to these concerns and objections. First, it would actually expand worker eligibility for support—either employment support or SSDI. Notably, many workers whose applications would be denied under current law would be eligible for timely support, including temporary cash benefits in some cases. Second, existing evidence demonstrates that early intervention can improve outcomes for well-targeted worker groups and pay for itself through reductions in benefit expenditure. Third, the proposed system focuses solely on non-beneficiaries and does not reassess current ones. Fourth, the system should make it *more attractive* for employers to hire and retain workers at risk for a medical event; it does not include an employer mandate to support such services, or fees or penalties when their workers use services or enter SSDI. Fifth, the proposal allows for state variation in preferences for public versus private roles.

Finally, and perhaps most important, the legislation should lead to full system deployment only after test results demonstrate that the new system will improve economic security for workers and meet fiscal objectives. The tests are much more likely to be successful than past demonstration efforts because they will start with interventions that have proven successful in other contexts and apply only to a small share of potential SSDI applicants—those with limited current access to supports and likely to succeed at work when supports are provided. To further ensure success, the tests would invite bottom-up innovation by administrators and professionals who already engage in similar efforts in other contexts. The initiative would collectively test many variants simultaneously and use a rapid-cycle, collaborative learning process, leading to abandonment of ineffective efforts and improvement and scaling up of effective ones.

CONCLUSION

We propose the development, testing, and adoption of a nationwide system of employment/eligibility services. Many of the ideas incorporated in the proposal are not new; some of them have been around at least since the inception of SSDI.[28] Our contribution is to blend and develop these ideas in a way compelling to today's policymakers as they grapple with addressing the many problems of the current disability support system. Specifically, these include the labor force exit and SSDI entry of workers who could continue to work if they had access to evidence-based supports and the long-intransigent problems of the SSDI determination process. The broader goal is to modernize the disability support system, gradually rebuilding it around a modern definition of disability and resulting in better opportunities for people with disabilities and more efficient delivery of support.

The proposed EES system would replace the current gateway to SSDI with one leading to work supports or SSDI and, in so doing, efficiently enhance the economic security of workers with work-threatening medical conditions. EESs would be responsible for outreach to targeted workers, employers, and health care providers; triage of applicants into work supports, immediate SSDI entry, or no support; and narrow targeting of evidence-based work supports to those for whom they will make a difference.

---

28 Before establishing SSDI, Congress debated various ways of integrating vocational rehabilitation and SSDI but ultimately created separate programs. Some of the ideas are also reflected to some extent in Project NetWork, a 1991 SSA demonstration project that offered supports to SSI applicant volunteers as well as SSDI and SSI beneficiary volunteers, but not to SSDI applicants or any workers who had not already applied for SSDI benefits. In the early 2000s, SSA designed, but did not implement, an early intervention test for SSDI applicant volunteers meeting certain criteria, but that design did not include enrollment of workers before SSDI entry or dual use of supported employment as a work test for SSDI eligibility. Many of the features of the system we proposed have also appeared more recently in less specific conceptual proposals by the Social Security Advisory Board (2006), MacDonald and O'Neil (2006), Stapleton and Mann (2011), Stapleton (2012), and Liebman and Smalligan (2013).

We propose legislation to support the testing and development of EESs that would put the United States on track to adopt a new, common gateway to employment supports and SSDI once sufficient evidence is available to ensure the system will meet its goals. Development and testing of EES models would draw on the substantial existing capabilities of both public and private entities under organizational structures designed to ensure effective collaboration. Employers must necessarily play a role, and our intent is to make it less expensive for them to retain such workers and more attractive to hire and retain those at high risk for major medical problems, not impose new burdens on them. The new gateway could be the first major step in system reforms that will ultimately yield better economic opportunities for people with challenging physical and mental conditions, thereby both reducing their reliance on government support and fulfilling the promise of the Americans with Disabilities Act.

4

A Community-Focused Health & Work Service (HWS)

Jennifer Christian, Thomas Wickizer, and A. Kim Burton

INTRODUCTION

Science is now confirming what the Greek physician Galen wrote in AD 172: "Employment is nature's physician, and is essential to human happiness." Recent reviews of the evidence are documenting how work promotes positive physical, mental, family, and social wellbeing for all of us, including those with chronic health conditions (Waddell and Burton 2006)—and how worklessness does the opposite (Waddell and Burton 2006; Strully 2009). Thus, in addition to supporting entry into employment of people with longstanding disabilities, a major focus of public policy should be to help working-age people with health problems keep their jobs or promptly find new ones.

We recommend establishment of a community-focused Health & Work Service (HWS) dedicated to responding rapidly to new health-related work absence among working people due to potentially disabling conditions. The first few days and weeks after onset are an especially critical period during which the likelihood of a good long-term outcome is being influenced, either favorably or unfavorably, by some simple things that either do or do not happen during that interval (Bowling 2000; Cornelius et al. 2011; Franklin et al. 2013; Loisel and Anema 2013; Nicholas et al. 2011; Shaw et al. 2013; Waddell and Burton 2004; Waddell, Burton, and Main 2001). It is the optimal window of opportunity to improve outcomes by simultaneously attending to the worker's basic needs and concerns (Shaw et al. 2013) as well as coordinating the medical, functional restoration, and occupational aspects of the situation in a coordinated fashion (Wickizer et al. 2011).

The best opportunity for basic intervention appears to last about 12 weeks or three months (DeWitt 1995; Franklin et al. 2013; Hashemi et al. 1997; Johnson and Fry 2002; Loisel and Anema 2013; Turner et al. 2008) although some data shows it ending by 6 months (Rumack 1987; Waddell and Burton 2004). A modest set of simple services—that embody an immediate, systematic, pro-active, integrated, and multidimensional approach—can mitigate the potentially destructive impact of common injuries, illnesses, and chronic conditions on quality of life among the working population (Burton et al. 2013; Hill et al. 2010; Iles, Wyatt, and Pransky 2012; Kendall et al. 2009; Lagerveld et al. 2012; Loisel and Anema 2013; McLaren, Reville, and Seabury 2010; Mitchell 2012; Nicholas et al. 2011; Shaw et al. 2013; Sullivan et al. 2005; Turner et al. 2008; Waddell and Burton 2004; Wickizer et al. 2011).

This new approach will allow people to avoid the kind of adverse secondary consequences of medical conditions that they too often experience today (Institute of Medicine 2001; Dartmouth 2008; Franklin and Mueller 2015). Those consequences are not usually obvious until months or years later, after unfortunate things have happened. The unlucky ones have received sub-optimal health care, been left with undertreated or iatrogenic impairment, become dependent on opioids, found themselves socially isolated, lost their jobs, withdrawn from the workforce, lost economic independence, and ended up on long-term disability benefits programs or SSDI in order to survive (Darlow 2011; Franklin et al. 2008; Franklin et al. 2014; Franklin and Mueller 2015; Habeck, Hunt, and VanTol 1998; Nguyen et al. 2011). Anticipatory programs that ensure the right things happen from the start and include early identification of those needing extra support are the simplest and most effective way to prevent later adverse secondary consequences of these conditions.

We envision the HWS building strong collaborative relationships with referral sources in local communities: treating physicians, employers, and benefits payers. We predict that service delivery in individual cases can be largely telephonic and internet-based because these technologies are proving to be as or more effective than face-to-face care delivery (Burton 2013). The quadruple goal is to maximize service quality, optimize outcomes, minimize logistical challenges, and control costs. After a series of steps including design, prototyping, development, and field-testing in different geographies, followed by a large randomized controlled trial, the HWS can gradually roll out across large geographic areas.

The HWS will provide services that are generally not available today, particularly to lower-wage workers and those who work for small firms. It will: (a) get referrals from affected individuals, local treating physicians, employers, benefits payers and others when work absence has lasted or is expected to last more than four weeks; (b) champion the stay-at-work and return-to-work (SAW/RTW) process from the time of referral through the end of the immediate response period (usually 12 weeks post onset); (c) quickly evaluate the individual's situation, screen for known risks for poor outcomes, help them make a SAW/RTW plan and support them in carrying it out; (d) facilitate communications among all involved parties as needed to get everyone on the same page and driving towards the best possible outcome.; (e) expedite and coordinate external medical, rehabilitative and other kinds of helping services, including referrals for specialized services as needed to address remediable obstacles in a variety of life domains; (f) take a problem-solving approach with affected individuals , treating physicians, employers, and payers.

Key Distinctions:

Readers should be aware of several critical distinctions that are important to understand in reading this paper—and some similar-sounding terms with quite different meanings.

- **Disability vs. Work Disability**

  According to the ADA, ***disabilities*** are impairments affecting major life functions (such as work). In the world of employment and commercial insurance, ***work disability*** is absence from or lack of work attributed to a health condition. Having a disability need not result in work disability, a core concept embodied in the Americans with Disabilities Act, and the main theme of this paper. Similarly, having symptoms or a diagnosis need not (and usually does not) result in work disability.

- **Medical Recovery vs. Functional Restoration**

  Medical recovery refers to the resolution (disappearance or remission) of the underlying pathological process. ***Functional restoration*** refers to reestablishing the usual rhythm of participation in everyday life including the ability to go about one's regular daily business: performing necessary tasks and enjoyable activities at home and work, and participating fully in society. Functional restoration does not necessarily require medical recovery. It can be achieved through rehabilitation (broadly defined), and can include the successful use of assistive technology, adaptive equipment, and/or reasonable accommodation in the workplace.

- **Early Intervention vs. Immediate Response**

  To our knowledge, the triggering event for HWS is different in kind than all prior SSA projects. The need for ***immediate response*** by HWS begins the first day the affected individual stays home from work or admits to difficulty working due to a health problem – because that starts the period of life disruption and uncertainty. We expect the HWS will usually get involved within the first few days and up to six or eight weeks after onset at the latest. This triggering event (and timeline) is different than the ***early intervention*** used in most Social Security-related proposals and programs. In general, those programs have used some interaction with SSA as the triggering event, which usually mean about six months after work disability onset. In that setting, the intervention looked "early" from in SSA's eyes, not the affected individual's.

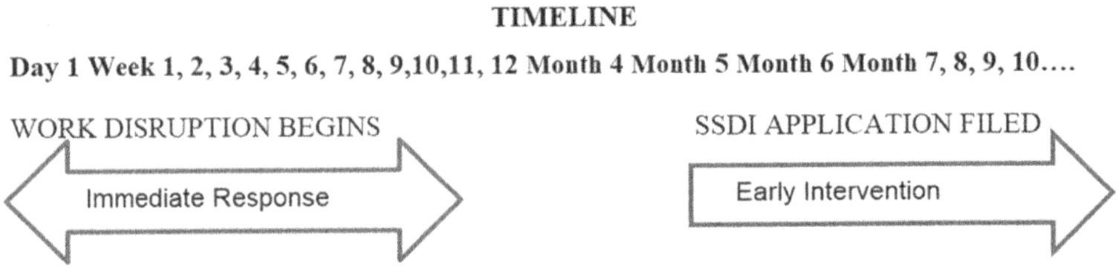

THE PROBLEM

The Committee for a Responsible Federal Budget (CRFB) initiative of which this proposal is part is being conducted because growing numbers of Americans are withdrawing permanently from the labor force for health reasons (Autor 2011). Since they were able to work before and now are not, something has changed: most often a newly acquired impairment but sometimes a worsening of a longstanding one.

Opportunity: Help People Avoid Adverse Consequences of Common Health Problems

Our proposal is especially designed to respond to the large and growing fraction of SSDI awards being made to people deemed totally unable to work due to conditions that are among the most common health problems in America and the world, but which only rarely cause permanent withdrawal from the workforce. Low back pain and other chronic musculoskeletal conditions (MSK), and common mood disorders (CMD)—particularly depression and anxiety—are the most prominent conditions in this category.

One might assume that the people on SSDI due to these common health problems have the worst (most severe) form of their particular MSK or CMD from a biological/pathological perspective, and that nothing could have prevented their entry into SSDI. While undoubtedly true in many cases, the evidence underlying this paper has revealed otherwise for a significant group. Some people lose their footing in the world of work and end up on SSDI because of events that occurred in response to their health condition—not the condition itself. Their lives fell apart due to a cascade of adverse secondary consequences of the initial medical problem, and after a time SSDI became the best option for survival. The standard medical care process is not sufficient to help people like this avoid poor life outcomes. What is needed is coordinated activity during a fleeting opportunity to address and resolve a set of pivotal issues (both medical and non-medical) around the time the condition starts interfering with work—because that will set the situation off onto the right or wrong path.

What Factors Predict Poor Outcomes, Remediability, and Avoidability

At the time when the common health problems of this subgroup of SSDI recipients first started, they would often have looked very similar to other patients with the same diagnosis and objective clinical findings—but who then experienced good recoveries. This is because the factors that predict poor outcomes (serious impairment and prolonged work disability) as a consequence of MSK, especially low back pain, are **not** tightly related to either the specific diagnosis or the extent of the pathology (Caruso 2013; Franklin et al. 2014; Franklin and Mueller 2015; Habeck, Hunt, and VanTol 1998; Harris et al. 2008; Johnson and Fry 2002; Mahmud et al. 2000; Nicholas et al. 2011). Although less research has been done on factors that predict poor outcomes in CMD, and diagnosis does play a more significant role, there are other important non-medical factors (Ahrends 2014; Cornelius et al. 2011; Loisel and Anema 2013).

Some of the factors that predict poor outcomes are immutable (such as age, past medical history, work history, and geographic location). But other factors are potentially remediable (such as elapsed time out of work (ACOEM 2010; McLaren, Reville, and Seabury 2010; Loisel and Anema 2013; Wickizer et al. 2011), uncertainty and distrust due to lack of communication or information (Bowling 2000; Loisel and Anema 2013), uncoordinated or inappropriate medical care and advice (Abásolo et al. 2000; Franklin et al. 2014), low expectations of recovery (Cornelius et al. 2011; Sullivan et al. 2005), excessive vigilance, catastrophic thinking, false beliefs, fear of movement, self-limitation, perceived injustice (Sullivan et al. 2005), and lack of employer support (Cornelius et al. 2011). Today, those who handle these situations do not typically look for any of these remediable problems and address them. None of the professionals involved has been trained to feel responsible for driving the situation forwards towards a good outcome (ACOEM 2006).

The way the episode unfolds over time in all dimensions—biological, psychological, social, and economic—can have a big impact on the outcome. Events that occur can either mitigate or aggravate existing risk factors in the situation, leading to better or worse outcomes. There are usually many opportunities to actively influence the course of events immediately after onset of a health problem (and many fewer opportunities later on), but today there are few resources devoted to finding and exercising these opportunities. Most of the current attempts to steer situations to a better outcome are made long after the best opportunities have passed by.

Most People with Common Health Conditions Do Not Leave the Workforce

The leading causes of disability in both America and the world are common back pain and depression (US Burden 2013; Global 2015). They are also among the most frequent conditions in the US population. But in most cases these conditions do not necessitate permanent workforce withdrawal. These diagnoses and impairments frequently **do** create severe impairment and reduce the quality of everyday life, but only very rarely bring it to a long-term standstill.

Each year, about 10 percent of the US population experiences chronic low back pain lasting at least three months and regularly impairing daily function (Martin et al. 2009). The US workforce is 154 million adults. If 10 percent of working adults have a long-lasting chronic low back pain episode each year, that is 15.4 million cases. Yet the intake each year onto SSDI of people with musculoskeletal conditions—which combines backs with knees, shoulders, hands, and so on—is only about 300,000. So at the very most 2 percent of those 15.4 million with a chronic back pain episode fail to recover, and probably many fewer.

The gold standard for objective evidence of back problems is the MRI of the spine. But a series of studies have confirmed that asymptomatic volunteers, working people with no pain or symptoms whatever, often have the exact same horrible-looking MRIs as people who are incapacitated by back pain (Boos et al.

1995; Deyo 2013). This buttresses our assertion that diagnosis and impairment are often not what determines whether someone will be able to continue working.

Likewise, 4.5 percent of the adult population (roughly 10.4 million people) experienced a major depressive episode with severe impairment lasting at least two weeks in 2012. A similar number (4.1 percent) experienced a severe anxiety disorder (NIMH 2015). If we assume 100 percent overlap between these two conditions, 10 million people have severe impairment due to these two CMD each year. Roughly 68 percent or 10 million people with some amount of depression are estimated to be employed (Charbonneau et al. 2005). Fewer than 500,000 people per year are being awarded SSDI for these two diagnoses. That is only 5 percent of all people with severe cases of these CMD (500,000 out of 10 million). This confirms that the overwhelming majority of people who develop these conditions do not end up on SSDI.

Growing Numbers on SSDI with MSK and CMD Reveals Need for Secondary Prevention

Ending up on SSDI for a low back problem, depression, or anxiety may be unusual for people with those diagnoses, but it has become more frequent. The fraction of all SSDI awards made for MSK conditions has been steadily rising each year for several decades, accounting for 36 percent of awards in 2013. Of the 868,965 people awarded SSDI in 2013, exactly 312,133 received benefits for impairments due to MSK conditions, many for low back pain. More than 50 percent of awards are now based on either MSK or CMD (largely depression and anxiety) as primary impairments. The three are related: depression and anxiety increase pain symptoms and vice versa (Kroenke et al. 2011). Helping people to avoid getting derailed by their symptoms and find a way to stay productively engaged in life and work will protect the overall quality of their lives in the future—and reduce the heavy cost burden on the SSDI program.

The "Classic Disabilities" vs. the Overlooked Other Half

We observe that spokespersons for people with disabilities tend to be people with "classic disabilities": noticeable, severe, and immutable impairments, often present from birth or longstanding, or the result of genetic disorders, or devastating injuries or diseases. They have impairments due to losses so obviously irrevocable that the idea of trying to reverse them is nonsensical—an impossible dream given the current state of knowledge.

Among the population with classic disabilities are a small number so disabled that they are unable to do anything productive such as those with extremely low IQs, constant seizures, in comas or persistent vegetative states.

The majority of individuals with classic disabilities including amputations, blindness, deafness, and low intellectual ability feel entirely well and are often raring to go. Those who appear in marketing campaigns to promote inclusion and employment of people with disabilities see themselves as healthy and fit enough to participate fully in society and work despite their impairments, often with support and accommodation.

Although most of the nation's programs devoted to serving persons with disabilities envision individuals like these as their target population, these classic disabilities now comprise less than half of new SSDI awardees annually, a fraction that continues to shrink. In 2013, awards for injuries—such as traumatic spinal cord injuries and amputations—were only 3.2 percent of all awards, and awards for intellectual disability accounted for 1.2 percent of the total. (SSA 2013)

Although by definition people on SSDI for common health conditions have severe impairments (since they have met SSA criteria), they are different in some important ways from many in the classic group. For one example, most SSDI beneficiaries with chronic musculoskeletal problems suffer from persistent pain and those with mood disorders do not feel good. They have come to see themselves as too uncomfortable, too sick, or too fragile to participate fully in life and work. They may be unaware that the intensity of their symptoms, their functional limitations, and their current low level of participation in life could conceivably have been avoided and might still be remediable—because those things are often the result of unfortunate interactions between their condition, the connection between their mind and body, the care and assistance they received, choices and decisions that were made, the overall context in which those things occurred, and the unfolding of subsequent events. If some of those things had been different, the outcome could have been better—and might still be if something important has been missed.

There is a big opportunity here to conserve resources for people with classic disabilities by stemming the inflow onto SSDI of people with iatrogenic impairment and over-disability due to MSK and CMD. This is a win-win because the way to divert people from SSDI is to help them get their lives back on track, stay productively engaged in life and economically self-sufficient.

What Creates These Unfortunate Outcomes? How Can They Be Prevented?

The people whose lives fall apart due to common health problems started out looking like their peers, but then their paths diverged. One may reasonably ask what was different about that small group of people or about their situations that caused them to end up on SSDI. Researchers have asked these questions and come up with many answers (Franklin and Mueller 2015; Franklin et al. 2008; Habeck, Hunt, and VanTol 1998; Krause and Ragland 1994; Lötters and Burdorf 2006). Sometimes it is a quality of the person (low education, traumatic childhood history); sometimes a feature of the environment (high unemployment rate or a hostile workplace). Sometimes it is lack of medical care, ineffective medical care or even harmful medical care (Dartmouth 2008; Franklin et al. 2014; Mahmud et al. 2000; Nguyen et al. 2011; Steinbrecher et al. 2011). Economic influences are involved. Most often it is some combination. (Caruso 2013; Loisel and Anema 2013).

Researchers have also showed that small things like a few careless words or administrative issues or being taught you are a powerless nobody early on can make a big difference (Aurbach 2014). Cases can get on the wrong path because the right things didn't happen (Nicholas et al. 2011; Wickizer et al. 2004). Reasonable questions were never answered. Voicemails were not returned. Delays created a lot of time to worry. No one from work picked up the phone and said "How's it going, how can I help?" No one listened for an unstated concern or worry. No one offered education or suggested how to solve a problem. No-one helped find a good doctor and get an appointment promptly (Bowling 2000). Or the doctor said "Avoid anything that makes you hurt or causes stress," which led to less and less activity. Or the doctor signed a form describing what the worker couldn't do, and the boss said he didn't have work for him and let him go. Or the doctor said "You're never going to be able to work again." (Darlow et al. 2011)

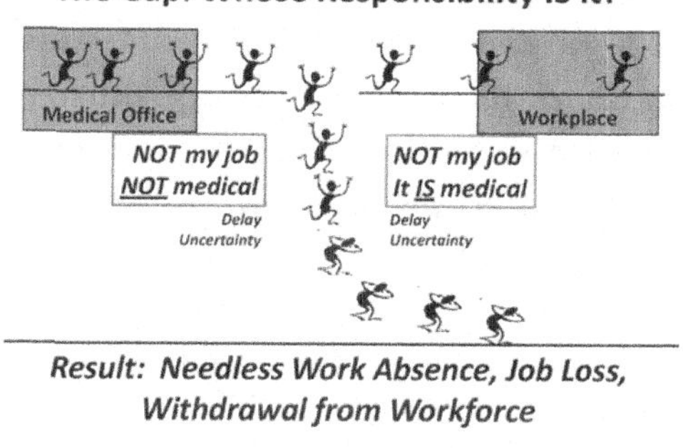

The gap in our social fabric through which people are falling out of work and onto benefit programs is longstanding. It is caused by the current structure of our society, and in particular the lack of dialogue and collaboration between the employment and health care sectors when a working person develops health problems that affect work ability. In that case, four professionals (the employer, the doctor, the health payer and a commercial disability benefits administrator) may all start responding to the situation—but separately, not in concert.

The backdrop is complex: Each of those four professionals is operating within an organization that has its own priorities, culture, policies and procedures and operates under its own laws and regulations. In addition to these structural challenges, the organizations are all potentially fallible human systems. Both organizations and the professionals who work in them vary in capability and commitment, mistakes are made, and things fall through the cracks every day. As a result, people fall through the gap and onto SSDI—the failures of our country's work disability prevention system.

Sometimes one of the professionals involved has a commitment to driving the situation towards a good overall outcome and takes a collaborative and pro-active approach to stay-at-work and return-to-work communications between the health care and employment sectors. But as things go today, no one usually does it. (See Optional On-line Appendix 2 – Gaps in Social Fabric for more specific information about where the gaps are along with examples of how the chain of events for lucky people differs from unlucky ones. Available on the SSDI Solutions website.)

National leadership is urgently required to address this issue. Free market forces perpetuate it. On a national basis, the aggregate social cost and economic burden of this avoidable work disability (to both government and the private sector) is enormous: hundreds of millions of lost work days and forfeited productivity per year (Martin et al. 2009; US Burden of Disease Collaborators 2013).

The good news is that long-term work disability can often be averted. The right professional doing the right things can help working individuals with newly acquired common health conditions avoid prolonged work disability, job loss (Bowling 2000; ACOEM 2010; McLaren, Reville, and Seabury 2010; Waddell, Burton, and Aylward 2008; Wickizer et al. 2004; Wickizer et al. 2011), and entry onto SSDI (Wickizer et al. 2014). For maximum effect, the services must be applied systematically very early, in concert with initial medical care and while the person is still employed—long before an injured person applies for SSDI (Waddell and Burton 2004).

For at least the past decade, the common-sense and humane logic of the work disability prevention model which focuses on the "front end" of episodes (Christian 2009; ACOEM 2006) has gained considerable traction in the private sector among proactive employers and insurance companies. Many large and sophisticated employers have put in place proactive (and effective) programs to reduce needless absence and work disability (DMEC 2015; McLaren, Reville, and Seabury 2010). However, many smaller employers and insurers have neither heard of nor bought into the idea. This concept is still largely unknown in the federal arena.

The solution demands an overarching (national) strategy and oversight, even though service delivery may end up outsourced and occurring at the local level in order to adapt to the wide variability in the health care and human services delivery landscape as well as the nature of local employment opportunities in communities across the United States.

We realize that "quick fixes" to shore up SSDI in the short run are very attractive, but one of the largest opportunities for longer term positive impact lies in this untapped area. There is mounting evidence that as many as a quarter to a third of the people with common health conditions now coming onto SSDI could have avoided that outcome if they had received the right kind of support and guidance in dealing with their life predicament from the outset (Waddell, Burton, and Aylward 2008; Franklin et al. 2014).

The next section outlines our proposal for a nationwide strategy and approach based on public health and preventive medicine principles coupled with the best available evidence which shows that responding quickly and doing some simple but important things expertly can prevent needless work disability and help people stay employed.

The economic case for investment in building capacity for systematic immediate response at the community level and then doing the simple things that can help people with newly acquired disabilities keep their jobs is compelling. Each person who leaves the workforce unnecessarily is a double hit to the vitality of our nation: the loss of a self-sustaining and productive contributor to the economy, and the gain of another person dependent on taxpayer dollars for their sustenance. The financial implications of <u>both</u> sides of this equation should be considered in evaluating the return on public investment in all interventions.

We urge Congress to show its commitment to taking a public health approach to prevention of work disability by declaring an intention to do so and funding the initial steps we propose here.

PROPOSAL

We propose that a Health & Work Service (HWS) be gradually developed and deployed across the nation. The goal is to build a nationwide capability to deliver secondary work disability prevention services to respond immediately when working people with new health problems or impairments are having difficulty coping with the impact on their work.

Thus, the HWS will insert someone with expertise into the gap displayed in the diagram above. They will drive the situation forward towards the best practicable outcome under the circumstances: by facilitating communications and problem-solving among the key parties; identifying issues that require attention; referring outside for special expertise or outside resources; coordinating care and services as needed; and providing positive support for the affected individuals, guiding them towards functional restoration so they can stay at or return to work.

The specific details of this proposal for a HWS are a logical outgrowth of a relatively simple evidence-based conceptualization of the problem of avoidable work disability (Schultz et al. 2007; Waddell and Burton 2004; Waddell, Burton, and Aylward 2008; Waddell, Burton, and Main 2001). The main precepts are as follows:

- Work is good for people's health and wellbeing; prolonged worklessness is detrimental.
- Preserving people's ability to function and work is an important health care outcome.
- Helping people with medical problems stay at work or return to work in a timely manner is beneficial for them and their families and advantageous for society.
- The longer people are away from the workplace for a medical reason, the less likely they are to return and the more likely they are to become permanently work disabled.
- Unnecessary work disability due to common health problems should be avoided.
- Most prolonged work disability is due to common health problems, which is both harmful and costly.
- There is good scientific evidence about the obstacles to work participation for people with a health problem, and about what helps them return to work.

- A medical threat to one's ability to work often causes a life crisis that must be addressed, that most people have not experienced before, for which most people are unprepared, and which will exceed some people's coping abilities.
- For most medical conditions associated with work disability, the medical condition itself does not require withdrawal from work.
- Non-medical factors in the person's situation are often responsible for work disability, and are often remediable with appropriate help.
- For many acquired medical conditions, especially common health problems, work disability can often be prevented if appropriate help is delivered within the first few days or weeks of onset.
- When work disruption begins, it is both effective and cost-beneficial to have a coordinator assist the treating doctor with communications, as well as make plans for functional restoration and return to work.
- Implementation of novel structures and methods to build capacity for service delivery is an urgent priority.

The specific types of services the HWS will deliver in the first 12 weeks of disabling health episodes are evidence-based (Burton et al. 2013; Hill et al. 2010; Iles, Wyatt, and Pransky 2012; Lagerveld et al. 2012; Loisel et al. 1997; Nicholas et al. 2011; Shaw et al. 2013; Turner et al. 2008; Waddell and Burton 2004; Wickizer et al. 2001; Wickizer et al. 2004; Wickizer et al. 2011). Most of them were initially developed by employers and insurance companies in the workers' compensation industry, but are now spreading to the disability benefits industry. These techniques are now commonly used to improve outcomes and avoid work disability in selected private sector environments around the United States (generally by large and sophisticated employers and forward thinking workers' compensation and disability insurance companies).

Here are some examples: Tyson Foods was able to reduce the number of employees going onto long-term disability by putting into place an actively managed short-term disability program (Unum 2015). Navistar was able to simultaneously reduce absenteeism, disability, workers' compensation, and health care costs (despite marketplace rises) through a tightly integrated, proactive approach (IBI 2015). For another, the RAND corporation surveyed 20 large corporations with return to work (RTW) programs and found that their employees returned to work 1.4 times faster than those in companies without such programs, and that employees with more severe injuries with permanent impairment benefitted most by returning to work more than four months earlier (McLaren, Reville, and Seabury 2010). At the Disability Management Employer Coalition annual conference, employer-speakers teach each other about the latest absence and disability management innovations (DMEC 2015).

Description of the Health & Work Service

The HWS will be staffed, equipped, and funded:

- To respond immediately when asked to assist a working-age person who:
    - has very recently developed work problems due a common everyday health problem and/or a common functional impairment;
    - is dealing with typical obstacles to medical recovery, functional restoration, and work retention (most of which are not medical in nature);
- To accept referrals directly from affected individuals, or indirectly from their treating physicians, employers, insurance companies, managed care providers and governmental agencies any time between Day 1 (the date the problem started) to 12 weeks later.
- To intervene directly in situations and directly provide a limited set of multidimensional helping services of limited duration, scope, and cost to facilitate the functional restoration and stay-at-work or return-to-work (SAW/RTW) processes.
- To refer people whose predicaments require capabilities beyond those available in the HWS to other appropriate private or governmental resources;
- To coordinate care and services to fulfill a SAW/RTW plan for no longer than 12 weeks on a routine basis, and to 26 weeks by exception.

In its role as an immediate responder, the HWS will not be prepared to handle all comers and every situation. HWS will develop relationships with other organizations equipped to manage medical recovery and functional restoration from catastrophic or profoundly disabling clinical conditions and/or provide rehabilitative solutions involving technically complex or expensive equipment. HWS will make referrals and collaborate with those organizations as appropriate.

It is premature to offer a fully detailed design for HWS, but we offer some broad design features here. (There is a more detailed discussion of the specific aspects of the design in the On-line Optional Appendix 1: Important Details. Available on the SSDI Solutions website.)

- The HWS will be community-focused with clearly defined geographic service areas
- The HWS will be positioned as an innovative state of the art center of excellence within its area of expertise, committed to outperforming "usual care" by delivering higher patient satisfaction and achieving better outcomes for its specified target population.
- The HWS will be available as soon as a working person who has a new medical problem that has compromised their ability to work needs a little extra help to get life back to normal and get back to work—no matter what benefits system or payer is involved as long as their doctor is affiliated with the HWS.
- It is likely that the vast majority of patients will have common health conditions, but the service will be open to anyone with any new health-related disruption of work, whether or not it has been identified as an acquired disability.
- The HWS will be delivered by professionals with training, experience, and expertise in conducting the kind of low-cost and simple yet individualized, integrated, and multidimensional situation management activities known to minimize the destructive impact of injury, illness and acquired disability and lead to positive outcomes: medical recovery, restoration of function and the normal rhythm of life, timely return to work and preservation of jobs.
- The HWS will primarily use telephonic and electronic channels (internet, email, etc.) to enable focused, high quality, and efficient delivery of these services at acceptable cost. (Burton et al. 2013)
- A stepped care model will be used which requires the simplest and lowest cost solutions to be employed first, employs screening processes (Melloh et al. 2009) that allow escalation to more expert professionals and more intensive (expensive) levels of service based on protocols and clear criteria.
- The service will be time-limited to 12 weeks from onset of work problems, with occasional extension to 26 weeks for cases meeting certain criteria. Cases not responding to the integrated, multidimensional interventions offered will be closed or referred elsewhere.
- All treating physicians, employers, workers' compensation, and disability benefits claims payers in the geographic service area will be invited to affiliate with the HWS and refer their patients / employees / claimants that meet certain criteria.
- The HWS will operate in a multi-system / multi-payer environment, accepting referrals of employed patients with disability benefits coverage,

workers' compensation claims, health care insurance, Medicaid, Medicare, or no benefits at all.

- The HWS will only enter a new geographic area after determining there is sufficient local demand for its services and that local stakeholders are willing to support it.
- Once the HWS does enter, it will be funded entirely by federal or state agencies during the start-up period and early operations. After the HWS has had a chance to demonstrate its value to local employers and claims payers, it will switch to a partial fee-for-service model. However, government, NGOs, or charitable organizations will probably need to continue long-term partial subsidies of operating costs to cover services to working people who have no, or inadequate, benefits coverage.

Undertaking and executing this strategy will eliminate a good fraction of avoidable work disability, reduce demand for SSDI benefit payments—probably substantially—and deliver much better life outcomes for the individuals involved. This is why the proposed service is such an important opportunity.

ANALYSIS OF PROPOSAL

This is a public health initiative aimed at creating access to specific services hitherto unavailable to most Americans due to the fragmentation and poorly aligned incentives of the nation's existing private and public sector programs, systems, and the safety net. The purpose is to augment the nation's system of care by building the capacity to:

- Increase the likelihood that all patients receive practical and effective assistance with restoration of function and staying at or returning to work when life is disrupted by a health condition.
- Decrease the use of certain types of medical services (such as early MRI imaging, opioid medications, spine fusion surgery and prolonged ineffective psychotherapy) that evidence has shown can cause excessive impairment, foster over-disablement, and result in job loss (Bernacki, Tao, and Yuspeh 2010; Darlow et al. 2011; Dartmouth 2008; Franklin et al. 2008; Franklin and Mueller 2015; IOM 2001; Nguyen et al. 2011)
- Increase the likelihood that employers will cooperate with timely and effective efforts to help employees with newly acquired disabilities stay productive during recovery and keep their jobs.

By caring for and helping individuals keep their jobs, this program will help employers retain valuable employees; stem inflow of applicants onto publicly funded health care, social welfare, and disability programs; and when benefits are needed, maximize the individual's economic self-sufficiency and productive contribution to society.

The proposed HWS aligns well with the public purpose of the employment provisions of the ADA. It meets the particularly time-sensitive critical needs of adults with newly acquired disabilities who want and need to protect their jobs and livelihoods.

This new strategy also brings to the fore the large subset of all persons with disability due to common health conditions which has historically been overlooked by disability-related government programs and advocacy groups. The traditional disability-focused organizations tend to emphasize more the perspectives, concerns, and practical needs of people with longstanding disabilities and those who are more visibly and severely impaired.

In order to bring this into being, a broad consensus must be built among policymakers, lawmakers, regulators, insurers, employers and others:

- that worklessness is a poor health outcome;
- that work disability can often be avoided by the right early management;
- that we cannot afford as a nation to continue the entry onto SSDI disability rolls of so many people with avoidable disability due to common health conditions;
- that the best scientific evidence available in a variety of disciplines should continuously guide our efforts at improvement, even as it continues to evolve;
- and that it is important to muster the resources and support needed to implement the HWS.

(For a draft list of other potential messages that stakeholders need to hear, see On-line Optional Appendix 1, Important Details. Available on the SSDI Solutions website.)

Trailblazer Examples: United Kingdom and Washington State

The features of the HWS we recommend here are adapted and combined from two existing programs that have served as models: Washington State's COHE program, and the United Kingdom's Fit For Work Service. These are large-scale community-focused initiatives that have created new structures housed within the local health care ecosystem. They are charged with intervening nearly immediately to help people with health problems get life back on track and stay in the workforce. The two initiatives provide useful real-world information that validates both the value and practicality of adopting the strategy we recommend and then implementing an HWS service nationwide as we propose. A very brief summary of each of them appears below. (More information about them appears in the Optional On-line Appendix 3: UK and COHE. There is an overview followed by a more detailed description of the background and history of each one. Available on the SSDI Solutions website.)

The interventions they employ are multidimensional and reflect a bio-psycho-socio-economic (BPSE) approach to managing these situations. (See more information about multi-dimensional interventions and the BSPE approach in the Optional On-line Appendix 1 – Important Details. Available on the SSDI Solutions website.)

In summary, over the past decade, the United Kingdom has fundamentally revamped its approach to long-term work disability. Based on what it learned from a long and broad series of events, ancillary initiatives and pilot projects, the government decided to put in place a national Fit For Work Service that embodies many features similar to the HWS proposal. Fit For Work is being operated by a vendor in England, Ireland, and Wales, and directly by the government in Scotland. Fit For Work began to slowly roll out its services to individuals just four months ago—in March 2015.

The Washington State workers' compensation insurance fund began a pilot project called Centers for Occupational Health & Education (COHE) in 2001. From the start, it proved highly successful at improving medical as well as return-to-work outcomes while reducing costs (Wickizer et al. 2004). The number of pilot sites increased and the program remained so successful (Wickizer et al. 2008; Wickizer et al. 2011) that a 2011 state law (SB 5801) made the COHE program both permanent and statewide.

The COHEs are separate entities, housed within health care delivery organizations, with community physicians as members. The program is defined by contract and emphasizes the use of proven best practices to improve outcomes of work-related injuries. The staff of the COHE serves as communications hubs, medical care coordinators, and SAW/RTW coordinators for all new work-related injuries being treated by member physicians. Doctor-members of the COHE are encouraged to perform a well-defined set of simple best practices such as reporting new episodes immediately, developing an activity prescription that includes delivery of key messages to injured workers, communicating directly with COHE staff or employers about SAW/RTW plans, assessing the reasons when recovery appears delayed, and participating in team conferences as necessary.

The COHE project has been studied at intervals for more than a decade. To date, those evaluations of the pilot programs have not focused on the costs to deliver the service, so return on investment is not known. Part of the purpose of the pilots was to discover the level of service intensity required and the extent to which treating providers would respond to financial incentives to adopt prescribed best practices. Fees charged by the COHEs have become progressively more standardized and were increased recently to increase the economic sustainability of the COHE organizations (personal communications). They now receive an administrative fee of $43 for every new injury treated by a COHE member physician. Those fees are intended to cover overhead costs. COHE coordinators bill for a prescribed set of services at $84 per hour, with a maximum of eight hours allowed on any case. Separately, COHE member physicians use specially created medical billing codes to document delivery and bill for a short list of specific best practices. Together, these are the system costs added by the COHE program.

Results are known for the first cohort of workers to be treated in the COHE program. That group has been followed for eight years. Total combined medical and wage replacement costs per injury episode were reduced by approximately 17 percent or $510 (Wickizer et al. 2011). Time away from work was reduced at the rate of 66,327 disability days per 10,000 treated injured workers. That translates into 182 years of work disability avoided, which also meant 182 years of productive contribution available to employers (Wickizer et al. 2014). And that first cohort of injured workers was 26 percent less likely to transition onto SSDI (2.5 percent of those managed by the COHE, compared to 3.4 percent of the controls) (Franklin et al. 2014).

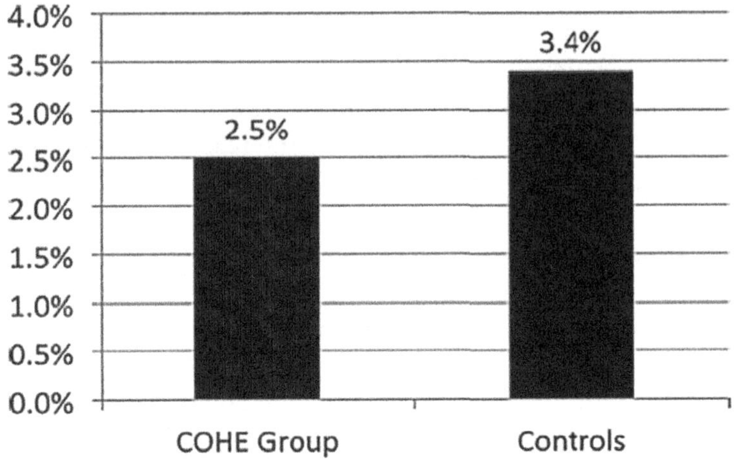

P < .001

FIGURE 2. Reduction in risk of transitioning to Social Security Disability Insurance, 8 years of follow-up from 2002 to 2010 for original COHE cohort.

Franklin GM, Wickizer TM, et al. Workers' Compensation: Poor Quality Health Care and the Growing Disability Problem in the United States. Am J Ind Med 58: 245-251. 2014. DOI 10.1002/ajim.22399 p4

The detailed histories of the successful Washington and UK initiatives reveal how essential it is to spend time, energy, and money building a foundation of widespread shared understanding of both the problem and its potential solution and collective will for change—particularly to garner support for an unfamiliar, slow, and challenging initiative which attacks fundamental problems with enough power to actually deliver substantial results. Their stories of prolonged effort also challenge the United States to find shortcuts so we can move faster, given the looming financial exigencies with which this country is faced.

Our Proposal: Develop and Launch the HWS

Something must be done about the preventable over-disablement and avoidable work disability among adults with chronic health conditions. It is accelerating workforce withdrawal, reducing income for individuals and their families, creating costs for employers and many different disability-related programs in different silos, layers, and sectors of society—workers compensation insurers, commercial and public short- and long-term disability programs, large employers who are self-insured for these benefits, auto liability insurers, and, as the final stop for many of those programs, SSDI and its sister federally funded programs including Medicare, SSI, and Medicaid. They are all sustaining higher benefit payouts than are necessary because of unaddressed causes of avoidable work disability. Some are catastrophically affected, notably SSDI, which is facing impending insolvency.

The overall benefit of having a HWS available to Americans and improving functional outcomes for many individuals should be clear: healthier, happier individuals and their families; increased economic vitality; more people contributing to the economy; and fewer people living on tax dollars instead of earned income.

In our view, it is time for Congress to move in a new direction that will promote the public's health and well-being in a very practical way. We propose that the Congress:

(a) Commit in principle to taking a public health approach to upstream prevention of work disability.
(b) Fund initial planning, development, and proof-of-concept testing of the HWS concept, followed by iterative refinement, revision and repeated pilot testing over several years until it definitively demonstrates its value (or not). The concept needs enough funding and time to mature and prove itself.
(c) Make funding for a national launch contingent on the HWS performing as intended.

This will be the first time these features and services are applied at such a large scale, over such wide geography, and in such a complex multi-payer/multi-system environment. Since this is admittedly a bold new effort and will require time, creativity and commitment to develop and implement widely, we further recommend that the foundational work should begin as soon as possible: administration, organization, project and budget planning and development of the business plan.

After that, the effort should begin with the orderly design, development, prototyping and feasibility testing of the services to be delivered by HWS and of the program as a whole. Most likely, the basic model will consist of centralized call centers plus geographically disperse staff responsible for building and maintaining relationships with local referral sources, payer sources, community resources, vendor partners and contracted providers as needed for occasional face-to-face encounters. Some mistakes, miscalculations and change are naturally to be expected as the initiative moves through the development process. Enough time and development money must be available to allow cycles of trial, revision, bug-fixing and adaptation before proceeding with the major investment required for in a national rollout. These cycles are intended to assure that the design is modified as necessary to assure that the service succeeds in accomplishing its purpose.

Next, a randomized controlled multisite trial should be conducted that is still flexible enough to allow minor ongoing refinements to adapt to local variation and maximize effectiveness. If HWS proves ineffective, cease development. If it proves promising but flawed, revise as necessary. Follow that with gradual rollout of the national community-oriented service in a manner that continues to acknowledge variability among the states and allows for considerable local adaptation. We predict it will take about seven years from the date the decision is made to embark on this strategy to successful delivery. But immediate cost is a paramount concern for all. All participants already feel they are paying more than they can or should, yet these new services will generate new costs. The COHE experience is reassuring since the cost to deliver the service has been more than offset by the economic benefits it is creating—for the payer, for employers, and for workers and their families. And as mentioned above, during that same period it reduced entry onto SSDI by 26 percent.

The UK experience points out the possibility of finding creative funding solutions: There it was found that a tax credit for small employers with high absenteeism rate had been creating a perverse incentive for employers not to encourage attendance. By cancelling the tax credit, the money thus saved was available to fund the FFW service. An analogous trade-off might be possible in the United States.

The services the HWS will deliver are relatively simple, and the process of delivering them is relatively straightforward as already demonstrated by the COHE, the FFW pilots and existing SAW/RTW programs now operated by private sector United States employers. The evidence base is good (not perfect), and the trailblazing by Washington State and United Kingdom have already revealed some of the operational challenges and how to manage them. We can follow their lead on staffing with respect to required prior training, work experience (and perhaps most importantly, the temperament and the "soft" listening and human relationship skills needed). There are sample templates available for some of the detailed tools staffers will need to work with and the information system will become clear as the process evolves. The day-to-day work is neither highly complex nor technical nor difficult—except interpersonally because communication and problem-solving skills are essential.

The challenges of making the HWS a success lie more in practical issues: creating a strong expert steering group to ensure that the HWS relies on best available evidence in its methods and techniques in all aspects of its operations; operational execution; selection and development of information systems; the financial/business model; deciding where to house it organizationally; planning marketing communications and how to position the HWS with health care providers, employers, legislators, regulators, and the public; building relationships and generating an on-going stream of referrals for services from the many organizations touched; how to pay for HWS services and fairly reflect benefits received; how to share necessary information efficiently among the many parties; how to ensure that the many parties affected are willing, able, and capable of playing as team members rather than isolated actors; and so on. (For a more detailed list of the specific success factors for the HWS initiative as a whole, as a nationwide enterprise, and especially on the local level, see Optional Online Appendix 1 – Important Details. Available on the SSDI Solutions website.)

There are a number of economic and funding considerations, with these prominent among them:

- Costs for development, feasibility, and demonstration projects will need to be funded by either the federal or state governments or the charitable sector, alone or in partnership.
- Local entities must be engaged and cooperating with the HWS in order for it to receive a good volume of referrals and successfully achieve its purpose of helping a substantial number of people to stay at work, return to work, or promptly find new employment.
- Once in full operation, HWS should be partially self-sustaining with multiple revenue sources, but may require some ongoing operational subsidy or other type of financial support from government and/or charities.
- Some public and private economic participation at both the state and local level should probably be required as a condition of contract award. This will limit the extent of federal subsidy.

INTERMEDIATE STEPS

We also recommend that the detailed planning work for this initiative begin immediately. It will take an estimated seven years to get through everything that stands between "here" and "there:" the launch of an effective and well-managed HWS.

Designing, building and delivering a HWS service will require sustained attention and budgetary commitment from Congress. In order to speed development time, the default option should be to proceed straight from phase to phase, which anticipates iterative revision and refinement of the design followed by re-testing. However, there must be a caveat: if the program fails to perform as intended due to fatal flaws in the design discovered at any point in the development process, it should be re-thought and if the flaws are not correctable, scrapped. Funding for the national launch must be contingent on the HWS producing the expected results.

Elements of the Initiative and Timeline of Development

Because this service does not yet exist, the anticipated amount of learning and number of required revisions in early phases is predicted to be very high. Thus, the plan for the initiative should be designed to allow it to proceed at a measured pace initially. The pace can accelerate after a series of small-scale pilot tests are complete and their implications understood.

As much as possible, the elements of the initiative should be managed so they overlap on the overall project timeline (see graphic later in this chapter) in order to minimize delays and ensure uninterrupted transitions from one phase to another.

A. Year 1 – Legislative/regulatory authority, funding, appointing lead agency and staffing it, appointing scientific advisory panel to oversee best evidence synthesis reports, development of conceptual design, financial models and business plan.
B. Year 2 - Procurement: RFP, bid process, and contracting with winning vendor.
C. Years 3 and 4 – Public awareness and communication campaign begins and continues through all years. Design, prototyping, "garage testing" of core/ key intellectual material and IT system takes two years.

D. Years 5, 6, 7 – Continue development of other necessary components, small pilots in different places, ending with randomized assignment test at significant volume. Sequence will take three years.

E. Year 7 – Finish random assignment trial (and assuming all went well) start preparing for gradual nationwide rollout.

ELEMENT	Y 1	Y2	Y 3	Y 4	Y 5	Y 6	Y 7
A – Legislation, Regulation, $$, Leadership							
B – Vendor Contracting		For C-1 and C-2	For D-1	For D-2		For E	
C -1. Foundation Work – Public Awareness							
C -2. Foundation Work – Design							
D -1. Prototyping and Small Pilot Tests							
D -2 Large scale Randomized Test							
E. Gradual National Roll-out Begins							

(More details about the specific issues and activities that comprise each of these Elements can be found in Optional Online Appendix 1 – Important Details. Available on the SSDI Solutions website.)

QUESTIONS OR CONCERNS

In this section we briefly explore several questions or concerns that a proposal such as this might reasonably engender. They include:

A. What agency should be responsible for this initiative?

B. Who will be the HWS service operator?

C. Is there a workforce prepared to deliver this service?

D. What are the costs and funding implications?

A. Responsible Agency

In the near term, it may be better to find a temporary federal government home for these efforts and wait a year or two to find a permanent one, rather than have no progress made until a perfect solution can be found.

Though services may end up being provided by contractors, the HWS must be overseen by a federal agency. The oversight entity should have as its charter the prevention of harmful secondary consequences of illness, injury, aging, and the progression of chronic conditions on the quality of life for the working age population, including avoidable work disability and withdrawal from full social participation.

Because the focus of the HWS is on delivery of services at the intersection of the workplace and health care, and because it will be employing a BPSE model and delivering multi-dimensional services, either a real working collaboration between two existing agencies or an entirely new fully integrated entity seems to be required. The best solution for the long-term is probably to set up a new and fully integrated organization. Ironically, the problem it is charged with solving exists mainly because it is so difficult today to collaborate across professional disciplines, organizational silos, sectors, and government agencies.

To get started, it would be most logical for the departments of Health and Human Services (HHS) and Labor (DOL) to partner. One possibility might be the office of the Assistant Secretary for Planning and Evaluation within HHS and an analogous office within the Employment and Training Administration of DOL.

Housing this fledgling initiative at SSA would not be our first choice despite the large benefit HWS is expected to provide to the SSDI program. In our view, SSA is ill-equipped to oversee a program of the type described here. But Congress may decide to house it at SSA on an interim basis. If so, we recommend that the HWS be established as a new and separate organizational unit with its own funding stream, autonomy, strong clinical and operational leadership and ability to staff afresh—so it has the flexibility of a startup organization and is easy to spin off later. This unit will need the kind of expertise required to build something from nothing, to understand the key issues and provide appropriate direction to construct this kind of fast-moving clinical/workplace communications exchange and problem-solving operation. For example, one of the first tasks should be to appoint a Scientific Advisory Panel to oversee development of the updated best evidence reviews that will serve as the foundation for the social marketing/ communications campaign as well as the detailed design of the HWS.

B. HWS Service Operator

In planning the service, an early decision must be whether the service should be centrally driven or delegated to the states. In either case, we strongly recommend that the federal agency with responsibility for secondary prevention of work disability have the authority to hold the organization(s) actually delivering the service accountable for meeting core service and performance specifications and delivering the intended outcomes. That federal agency should be reporting to Congress how the service performs, no matter who operates it.

It is conceivable that a single organization could operate the entire nationwide HWS because that is often the fastest way to build capacity. The advantage of a single solution is consistency of delivery and simple accountability. However, the United States is much larger than the United Kingdom and the situations we are talking about occur in local communities with local players. Thus, a single design is likely to be a poor fit for many locations. But 50 separate operations create a different kind of added complexity and may increase costs.

After that the next decision will be a "make-buy" analysis to decide whether to have this service delivered by government employees or contract it out to vendor(s). In general, since this project will conceivably span all 50 states, it will be a very large undertaking for a government which has no experience doing this kind of thing. If it is decided to use vendors, there are companies accustomed to delivering health care and social services to hundreds of thousands or millions of people, such as the Employee Assistance Programs, SSDI Consultative and Veterans Disability Exams, and so on.

C. Workforce

There is a workforce available to staff a national HWS service. There is an enormous amount of pertinent know-how in the nation's health care and rehabilitation professionals, albeit scattered, under-mobilized, and currently frustrated by the lack of opportunities to use their talent, skill and professional commitment to helping people get their lives back on track.

(Instead of paying them to focus their creative professional energy on the collaborative teamwork required to restore function and prevent or end work disability, the traditional systems today tend to pay most professionals to spend their time diagnosing and treating medical problems, and then certifying, justifying, determining the extent of impairment or work capacity, and predicting the length of work absence, and for vocational counselors only, documenting the availability of jobs in the local economy.)

There are several different kinds of helping professionals with training and expertise in occupational settings, for example occupational medicine physicians, disability management specialists, vocational rehabilitation counselors, social workers, occupational health nurses, occupational and physical therapists, health psychologists, and so on. At least one program in the United Kingdom found that professions from the information and referral sector can also be very effective in the role of recovery coordinator.

D. Costs and Funding Requirements

Of course, an HWS operating nationwide will require a substantial budget. We cannot even make a wild guess at the routine operating cost of the national HWS because neither the design nor the accompanying business models have been designed and financially modelled, much less tested.

The total cost to operate, and the share that must be borne by government will depend in major part on what is discovered about the business model when the service is pilot tested: whether state and local agencies and private sector organizations (employers and insurers) decide to help subsidize the service on an annual basis, pay market value for services one-by-one, or decline to participate. However, at this point we predict that several sources of revenue will be possible that should grow over time and partially offset outlays. And, it remains to be seen whether the various payers see the value they get from the services as more than offsetting the contributions to operating costs that the HWS requires of them.

Cost of getting started – Element B

A rough estimate of the cost of all sub-projects in Element B would be in the range of $2 million per year for the first two years for a total of $4 million:

- One million dollars should be devoted to "Element B-1. Build a Foundation of Support" to get the best-evidence synthesis reviews completed and written up prior to commencement of other activities in this long-lived Element.
- The rest of the funds would go toward Element B-2: Create the wherewithal: Pay for the design, development and refinement of the essential core of the materiel that will later be incorporated into C-1. Based on the actual design, estimates for subsequent elements can be corrected/revised.

Data points re: future costs

Two pieces of financial information may be valuable in building financial models of the HSW during launch and operations. Washington State has no doubt developed some initial impressions of the cost-benefit of the COHE program since it has kept expanding it. Whether that analysis will be formally corroborated and reported by researchers, or might be obtained informally from the agency, a key difference is important to take into consideration. COHE includes all new injuries starting from day one, even trivial ones with a single visit to the doctor and return to work on the same day, with no action required by the COHE. Thus, per capita costs will be expected to rise somewhat if the HWS is limited to referrals for cases that do require active response by HWS staff. Cost control will be facilitated by (a) carefully delineating the scope of services the HWS provides, (b) creating defined "packages" of services delivered for a flat fee instead of open-ended referrals for services, and (c) capturing data that allows evaluation of overall performance of vendors across all cases, which will assist with holding everyone accountable for delivering the intended outcomes, not just services.

The second piece of financial information is the ceiling amount that the United Kingdom was willing to pay its vendor for the first five years of the FFW. The fee was based on a very slow geographical rollout across England, Ireland and Wales (Scotland has a separate budget/program). In a personal conversation in late April 2015, the physician leading the vendor's implementation said the contract reflected an expectation that the product design will be substantially revised and adjusted frequently, almost like a "keep-developing-while-delivering" model. The amount shown in the tender document (RFP) was £170 million, or approximately $255 million.

CONCLUSION

We are confident that the orderly sequence of projects like that laid out here will confirm the feasibility and delivered value of establishing a community-focused Health and Work Service, and then allow it to become a nationwide reality. There is a strong evidence base for this type of service, which uses a holistic approach linking healthcare with the workplace to overcome obstacles to work participation for people with work-relevant health problems. There is also a strong evidence base for helping people avoid adverse secondary consequences and unnecessary time away from work due to common health problems—because it is good for their health and well-being.

Similar services have already been shown to improve life outcomes and reduce long-term disability for people with workers' compensation injuries in Washington State, and for people with medical problems due to any cause in Ireland, Scotland, and England.

Once established, the HWS is likely to be well-utilized given the number of people who need help and the lack of anything like it today here in the US. The service will create a practical channel through which to more consistently prevent avoidable work disability in a timely manner.

We acknowledge that bringing the HWS to life and realizing its benefits will take longer and cost more than some other proposed fixes for the SSDI program's problems. However, we think it is going to be far more powerful, will improve the lives of many more people and reduce the drain on a wider array of taxpayer-funded health and disability-related programs than other solutions.

Assuming that the development process proves successful, we believe that systematically making services available to working individuals to prevent the harmful secondary consequences of illness, injury or the effects of age on their lives and livelihoods will prove to be a very wise investment.

5

Using Transitional Jobs to Increase Employment of SSDI Applicants and Beneficiaries

Julie Kerksick, David Riemer, and Conor Williams

INTRODUCTION/SUMMARY

We propose providing access to Transitional Jobs and an expanded earnings supplement to individuals whose ability to work has been affected by a medical condition. Transitional Jobs are subsidized, wage-paying jobs, typically in the private-for-profit or not-for-profit sectors. We describe how these subsidized jobs would be designed and administered, and propose a pre-pilot to test the viability of this approach. The pre-pilot, if successful, would be followed by a demonstration project in which a statistically valid number of Social Security Disability Insurance (SSDI) beneficiaries, denied applicants, and applicants would be randomly assigned to a control group or an experimental group to determine the effect on SSDI enrollment and costs, employment and earnings, income and poverty, and other measurable impacts.

We also include access to work incentive counselors to help individuals currently receiving SSDI obtain accurate information about how part-time and full-time work affect their benefits and medical coverage. This would ensure that all the current earnings offsets and other incentives are used in helping individuals receiving SSDI to manage a transition back into the workforce.

This proposal focuses on ways to bolster employment outcomes for individuals living with a disability or medical condition that affects their ability to work. It builds on the existing efforts of Ticket to Work and the Enhanced Work

Incentive Counselor model now being evaluated as part of the Benefits Offset National Demonstration (BOND).

Our proposal would provide access to work that can accommodate the individual's work capacities, while ensuring, through expanded tax credits, that work will pay more than the SSDI benefit. It is an approach that recognizes the limitations of local job markets, and offers individuals opportunities to remain in the workforce, or return to the workforce. This proposal reflects our values as a society, both to ensure an income for those who cannot work and to encourage those who can work to find appropriate work.

THE PROBLEM

In the 2010 National Beneficiary Survey of all beneficiaries of Supplemental Security Income (SSI) and SSDI, 41 percent of respondents indicated having work goals or saw themselves working for pay within the next five years (Wright et al. 2012, 18). Yet in the same survey, only about 15 percent were employed, were actively seeking employment, or had worked during the previous calendar year (Wright et al. 2012, 18). Among those who were NOT working, the overwhelming majority said they could not work due to physical or mental conditions. But of the respondents receiving both SSI and SSDI, a substantial minority said they were not working because they were discouraged by previous attempts, or others did not believe they could work, or they could not find a job accessible to those with their disabilities (Wright et al. 2012, 32).

The bottom lines for SSDI beneficiaries: Very few are able to do substantial work and just 3.9 percent earned more than $10,000 during the year (Mamun et al. 2011, 16). And less than half of one percent are able to return to work at levels that result in reducing their benefit to zero (Maestas et al. 2010).

The above citations show that while individuals may indicate a desire to continue working or return to work, most SSDI beneficiaries and claimants will not likely return to work. Yet we believe that the number who can and do return to work could be higher, through a combination of making work available and making work pay.

Our proposal aims to target current beneficiaries, individuals who have been denied benefits, and those applying for benefits for intervention through a Transitional Job and Enhanced Earned Income Tax Credit.

Current Beneficiaries

A lesson from current and past efforts to encourage work is that not all beneficiaries are equally likely to respond to work incentives. In a program that has strict eligibility rules,[1] it should not be surprising that if someone qualifies for SSDI, he or she is not likely to be able to work. Yet work incentives have helped some beneficiaries return to work, and it is worth understanding more about who does utilize the Trial Work Period, and whose benefits are suspended or terminated because of earnings beyond the threshold of Sustainable Gainful Activity (SGA). Yonatan Ben-Shalom and Arif Mamun have just published a paper on "Return to Work Outcomes Among Social Security Disability Insurance Program Beneficiaries" (2015).

Here is a summary from the Abstract:

> We found that younger beneficiaries are more likely than are older beneficiaries to achieve the milestones [starting, completing Trial Work Period and a return to work] and that there exists substantial variation across impairment types. In addition, the probability of achieving the milestones is higher for individuals with more years of education, for blacks, and for individuals residing in states with low unemployment rates at the time of the award. It is lower for beneficiaries with a high DI benefit amount at award, an award decision made at a higher adjudicative level, and/or Supplemental Security Income or Medicare benefits at the time of DI award.

Rebecca Vallas and Shawn Fremstad recently published a brief, "Social Security Disability Insurance: A Bedrock of Security for American Workers" (2015). They point out the importance of the disability insurance program in keeping individuals and families from economic hardship. Still, they note that:

> The amount a qualifying worker receives in benefits is based on his or her prior earnings. Benefits are modest, typically replacing about half or less of a worker's earnings. The average benefit is about $1,165 per month—not far above the federal poverty line. For more than 80 percent of beneficiaries, disability insurance is their main source of income. For one-third, it is their only

---

1 According to the Organization for Economic Cooperation and Development (2010), the United States has relatively strict eligibility rules in comparison to other countries.

> source of income. Benefits are so modest that many beneficiaries struggle to make ends meet; nearly one in five, or about 1.6 million, disabled-worker beneficiaries live in poverty (Vallas and Fremstad 2015, 3).
>
> Before turning to Social Security, most disabled-worker beneficiaries worked at "unskilled" or "semiskilled" physically demanding jobs. About half—53 percent—of disabled workers who receive disability insurance have a high school diploma or less. About one-third completed some college, and the remaining 18 percent completed four years of college or have further higher education (Vallas and Fremstad 2015, 6).

SSDI beneficiaries are a diverse group. But the above statistics indicate that many beneficiaries, even if they are able to work, may lack the educational credentials to compete for higher paying jobs in today's economy. And if their previous jobs were physically demanding, they will only be able to return to work if they are able to find new kinds of work to do.

We do not know how many current recipients would respond to the offer of subsidized employment and the enhanced earnings supplement, but we would target outreach to those who would most likely see a significant increase in monthly income in combining work and the earnings supplement, those under 40, and those who have been receiving SSDI for less than five years. Of course, we would not deny the offer to any current beneficiaries, but rather we would invest more in reaching out to the above categories of constituents.

Denied Applicants

Currently, more than four out of 10 applicants are denied, even after appeals. Even denied applicants exhibit very limited work capacity. Results suggest that among those living to age 65, those who applied for SSDI/SSI benefits and had their applications denied fared as poorly (if not more so) in old age as those deemed eligible for disability benefits (McGarry and Skinner 2012, 1). If we can help such individuals remain in or return to the labor market, we can help them improve their economic outcomes and possibly reduce some of the workload of the eligibility determination systems.

Applicants

Researchers and policy experts in disability insurance have noted that there is a contradiction in policies that incentivize work only after someone has demonstrated that he is not able to work. We would like to test the waters of offering immediate employment and earnings supplements to applicants.

We anticipate that we would reach out to applicants and those who have been denied through a variety of methods. These might include contacting the organizations and attorneys who specialize in assisting individuals who are applying for SSDI, as well as a cooperative effort with the Wisconsin Disability Determination Bureau to send out letters to individuals informing them of our alternative offer.

LARGER CONTEXT OF OUR PROPOSAL: THE LABOR MARKET AS OPPORTUNITY AND PROBLEM

For most working-age adults, working at a job (or more than one) is the way they take care of themselves and their dependents. Becoming unable to work due to illness or injury, whether for the short-term or the long-term, creates multiple crises. They must simultaneously address their medical condition(s), find a way to replace lost income, deal with the stresses of unpaid bills and uncertainty about their future, and handle the emotional pressures brought on by all of the above.

In some cases, some of the medical issues are related to the loss of a job itself. The stresses_arising from the job loss may be compounded in situations where an entire industry is in decline or the individual's community is experiencing the disappearance of a large numbers of jobs.

At the same time, there have been seismic shifts in the U.S. economy over the past 30 years. Many low-skilled jobs that paid living wages have been eliminated. The *New York Times* headline from August 2012 was blunt: "Majority of New Jobs Pay Low Wages, Study Finds." The study showed that lower-wage occupations accounted for 21 percent of recession losses, but 58 percent of recovery growth, while mid-wage occupations saw 60 percent of recession losses but only 22 percent of recovery growth (NELP 2012, 1). The larger challenges of making jobs available, and making work pay for all workers, affect the ability of SSDI beneficiaries to return to work—and applicants to remain in the workforce.

Even as the nation has moved out of the recession and into a more sustained recovery over the past two years, there are still approximately twice as many unemployed workers as there are jobs available.[2] The New Hope Project evidence strongly suggests that creating time-limited but widely available Transitional Jobs is critical to ensuring that paid employment is available to all who want to work (Huston et al. 2003).

The severe economic downturn in 2008-2010 provided experience in the use of Transitional jobs with broad populations and the provision of larger numbers of such jobs. The 2009 Recovery Act created a $5 billion fund over two years for Temporary Assistance to Needy Families (TANF)-eligible families to address growing needs. The funds could be used for any of three categories: basic assistance; non-recurring, short-term assistance; and subsidized employment.

As Pavetti, Schott and Lower-Basch reported in their 2011 paper, "Creating Subsidized Employment Opportunities for Low-Income Parents":

> Some 39 states, the District of Columbia, Puerto Rico, the Virgin Islands, and eight tribal TANF programs received approval to use $1.3 billion from the fund to create new subsidized employment programs, or expand existing ones. [These jobs programs] placed more than 260,000 low-income adults and youth in paid jobs during a time of high unemployment.

The 39 states were led by governors from both parties, including governors of Mississippi and Wisconsin who were initially skeptical of the idea but became strong supporters after seeing that Transitional Jobs were embraced by the private sector. Currently, 22 states offer some kind of Transitional Jobs program (as illustrated in the map below from the National Transitional Jobs Network website).

---

2 In January 2015, the Bureau of Labor Statistics estimated the number of unemployed 16 years and older to be 8.979 million. In the same month, the number of U.S. nonfarm job openings was estimated to be 4.998 million. See: Bureau of Labor Statistics, "*Labor Force Statistics from the Current Population Survey: Unemployed persons by age, sex, and marital status, seasonally adjusted*" Table A-9, http://www.bls.gov/web/empsit/cpseea09.pdf, and "*Job Openings and Labor Turnover Survey,*" http://data.bls.gov/timeseries/JTS00000000JOL, data extracted on April 1, 2015.

State Support of Transitional Jobs

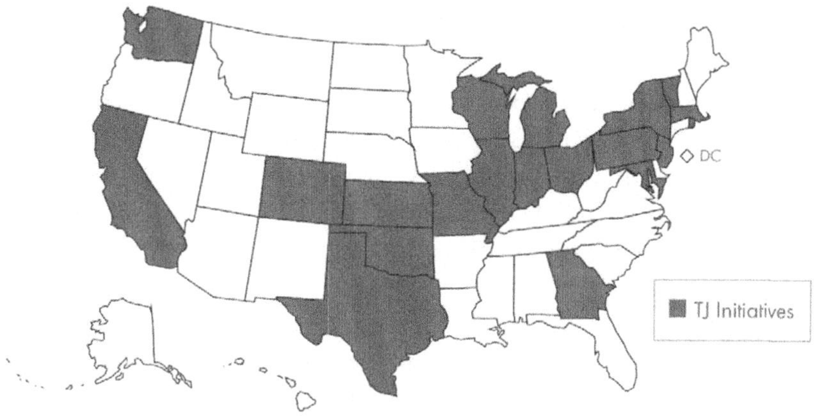

The premise of this proposal is that Transitional Jobs may be particularly effective in assisting individuals with disabilities to stay in or rejoin the labor market.

All jobseekers and under-employed workers face these challenges in the labor market:

- As noted above, there are frequently not enough jobs available for all those who want to work;
- Even when the overall number of jobseekers roughly approximates the supply of job openings, there are often spatial mismatches that result in large numbers of unemployed individuals clustered in geographic areas of few jobs;
- There are also skills mismatches that result in too many jobseekers who lack the skills or experiences that are in demand by employers;
- Full-time work is not always available, due to business models that rely on part-time and flexible scheduling;
- Not all full-time jobs provide wages high enough to meet basic needs.

The data brings all this home: a very large number of those who are poor in this country are looking for a job or already working, whether part-time or full-time. According to the Census Bureau, in 2013, in addition to millions of poor adults (ages 18-64) who were unemployed, a total of 8 million adults below the poverty line worked part-time, and another 2.8 million adults in poverty worked full-time (DeNavas-Walt and Proctor 2014, 13).

OUR PROPOSED POLICY PACKAGE

Transitional Jobs

Against the backdrop of a labor market that features periodic job shortages, spatial and skills mismatches, unstable hours, and low wages, Transitional Jobs can serve as an effective tool to help all workers (Roder and Elliott 2013, 51). For those with disabilities, they can help them remain in—or return to—the labor market by creating new work opportunities that can also accommodate individual needs.

Transitional Jobs (TJs) are subsidized, wage-paying jobs, typically in the private for-profit or not-for-profit sectors. They can be full- or part-time jobs, but individuals perform real work and are held to the work rules of the employer. These are jobs of last resort, and should be viewed as a way to help individuals who cannot find work, or who need to identify new kinds of work after an injury or illness.

Our proposed Transitional Jobs program would be administered through an intermediary responsible for developing a variety of Transitional Jobs that can accommodate a wide range of disabilities, as well as recruiting and coaching individuals who wish to apply for work through the TJ program.

The intermediary would be the "Employer of Record," and the individual businesses or organizations that host a TJ worker the "TJ Host Sites." The intermediary would be responsible for paying payroll taxes, unemployment insurance taxes and Workers' Compensation premiums. This design would make the Transitional Jobs program more attractive to businesses and organizations considering hosting a TJ worker, because it would reduce costs and risks associated with adding employees to their payroll who may be temporary. Small businesses, in particular, have noted that they are more willing to give a worker a chance if they do not have to incur the full costs of Workers' Compensation and unemployment insurance until they know that they can add a position more permanently, or that they will hire the TJ worker permanently. Businesses could have a worker on full subsidy for no more than six months, to protect against exploitation of the individual worker or the program.

The wage subsidy for these jobs would be up to $10 per hour. Individuals would be covered by Workers' Compensation and unemployment insurance. Host site employers could choose to "top up the wage," but that would not be required.

TJ workers' wages would be subject to normal payroll taxation. The wages would be treated like all others for income tax purposes, and could be used to claim the federal Earned Income Tax Credit and the Child Tax Credit.

The jobs would be available to individuals who have been out of work for four weeks or longer. For the purposes of this proposal, Transitional Jobs would be targeted to individuals who are (A) currently receiving SSDI, (B) have been denied benefits; or (C) are applying for SSDI.

The Transitional Jobs would be structured to be available for up to six months, or 1,040 hours. Individuals would work closely with a jobs counselor throughout that period. If the work experience was successful, the counselor would help the TJ worker find unsubsidized work. Sometimes that would occur naturally, through the decision of the Transitional Jobs host site to hire the individual on a permanent basis. In most cases, the TJ worker would look for work elsewhere. If, after four weeks, the individual had not found unsubsidized work, she would be eligible for a new Transitional Job. If the work experience had not been productive, or shown that the individual is not able to work consistently, the individual would continue on the SSDI path.

Each host site would sign a contract with the intermediary spelling out what services the intermediary would provide, what rules would govern host sites' participation, and the rights and responsibilities of all parties. Transitional Jobs host sites would not be allowed to use transitional workers to replace workers in any labor dispute, nor to displace workers in their regular workforce. They would have to provide a job description and ongoing supervision of the TJ employee. They could terminate the TJ employee, using the same disciplinary processes they use for their regular workforce.

TJ employees would be paid only for hours worked. If an individual had concerns about safety or working conditions, she could request a meeting with both the TJ host site and the intermediary's staff person assigned to that company. If such a step did not resolve the concerns, the TJ worker could request access to a different Transitional Job. TJ workers would receive regular feedback on attendance, punctuality, job skills and collaboration.

The intermediary would be responsible for staffing both the ongoing contact with the Transitional Jobs host sites and the Transitional Jobs employees. This would include regular site visits, occasional three-way meetings to discuss performance issues or work place concerns, and regular contact with the TJ worker to assess how she is responding to the job duties and hours.

The intermediary would also be responsible for developing transitional jobs. Recent experience in Wisconsin attests to the wide variety of jobs that can become available in a well-structured TJ program. A report to the Wisconsin state legislature listed 225 different types of jobs filled by TJ workers at 814 businesses and organizations that participated as TJ host sites (Wisconsin Department of Children and Families 2013). Although the barriers to employment are different for SSDI beneficiaries than for the population served by the Wisconsin Transitional Jobs Demonstration Project, there are still a great many opportunities compatible with the work capabilities of SSDI beneficiaries.

Enhanced Earned Income Tax Credit

Making work available through Transitional Jobs is the first necessity if we are to help people with disabilities stay in the labor market or return to work. But it is also critical to make work pay—both to create a powerful incentive to pursue employment and stay in a job, and to ensure that employees obtain through their work enough income to pay the rent, buy food, pay the electric bill, and meet other basic necessities.

Since the 1970s, the Earned Income Tax Credit (EITC) has emerged as the primary U.S. vehicle for making work pay. Supported and increased by every president since Gerald Ford, the EITC was famously praised by President Ronald Reagan as "the best antipoverty, the best pro-family, the best job creation measure to come out of Congress." (Donosky 1986)

There are two major shortcomings with the EITC, however, that particularly reduce its effectiveness as a tool for incentivizing and rewarding work for people with disabilities. First, many people with disabilities do not have dependent children, and as a result can claim only a very small EITC. (The maximum credit for workers without dependent children in 2014 was $496, compared to a maximum of $3,305 for a worker with one dependent child, $5,460 for those with two children, and $6,143 for those with three or more children) (IRS 2014).

The second shortcoming of the EITC is that, for many workers who do have dependent children, it imposes a large "marriage penalty" if they wed. The credit is based on the *total* earnings of the tax-filing unit as reported on Form 1040, the federal individual income tax return. Two unmarried workers who live together, and want to get married, may see a sharp drop in their EITC—thus, their disposable income—if, instead of filing two separate returns of which one is low enough to leverage a very large EITC, they decide to get married. That's because, in order to claim the EITC at all, the new married couple must file a "married and filing jointly" return. On the joint return, they must combine their earnings, which could push down their EITC to very little or even nothing. In short, in some cases, the rules governing the EITC may cause marriage *not* to pay.

To fix these two shortcomings of the EITC, we propose to model an enhanced EITC that (A) substantially increases the value of the EITC for workers without dependent children, and (B) nearly eliminates the marriage penalty. These changes will substantially increase the incentive to work—and rewards from working—for persons with disabilities. They also would get rid of the marriage penalty that may discourage some workers with disabilities from getting married (or, in extreme cases, contribute to divorce).

The average benefit of this enhanced EITC works out to approximately $4,500 per recipient as detailed in the Urban Institute's report. (Lippold 2015, Table B5).

The specific formula we propose to model is to provide participating workers with the difference between the current federal EITC and the following:

Revised EITC Formula for Unmarried Individuals

The following table shows the proposed credit parameters for taxpayers who are not "married filing jointly" (i.e., either "single" or "head of household" for tax purposes).[3] The credit parameters would be indexed for inflation.

[3] Please note that, while the current EITC for unmarried individuals increases the credit phase-in rate and maximum when the number of qualifying children increases from two to three or more, the proposed EITC for unmarried individuals uses the *same* credit phase-in rate and maximum for *both* the two children category and the three or more children category. Thus, for unmarried individuals, the unique category of "Three or More Qualifying Children" is gone. Despite this, the EITC would deliver (compared to today) larger credit amounts for unmarried individuals with three or more children.

Earned Income Tax Credit Parameters for Unmarried Individuals

Group and Parameter	Proposal
No qualifying children	
Phase-in rate	50%
Phase-in ends	$10,000
Maximum credit	$ 5,000
Phase-out begins	$10,000
Phase-out rate	24%
One qualifying child	
Phase-in rate	70%
Phase-in ends	$10,000
Maximum credit	$ 7,000
Phase-out begins	$10,000
Phase-out rate	24%
Two or more qualifying children	
Phase-in rate	90%
Phase-in ends	$10,000
Maximum credit	$ 9,000
Phase-out begins	$10,000
Phase-out rate	25.5%

Revised EITC Formula for Married Individuals

In order to largely eliminate the marriage penalty that is embedded in the current EITC, the proposed policy would make several changes to the EITC for married couples (i.e., "married filing jointly").

Each married individual would be able to claim a separate EITC based on his or her *individual* earnings. In the computation of each spouse's EITC, individuals would first compute their separate credits without children; the spouse with the higher childless EITC would then claim any qualifying children, resulting in an enhancement—based on *that spouse's* individual earnings—of that spouse's separate EITC that increases with the number of children. When the computation is complete, the two separate credits would be added together.[4] Another policy

[4] For example, in the case of a married couple with two children where one spouse has $30,000 of earnings and the other has $15,000 in earnings, the family would claim a combined EITC equal to (1) one EITC figured with the $30,000 amount, plus (2) one EITC figured with the $15,000 amount. Since the childless EITC is higher at $15,000 of earnings than at $30,000, the spouse earning $15,000 would compute his or her credit using the parameters for two children, while the other spouse would use the childless parameters.

aimed at eliminating the marriage penalty would allow married couples to claim a larger EITC if they have three, or four-or-more, children.

The following table shows the proposed credit parameters for married taxpayers who file as "married filing jointly." The credit parameters would be indexed for inflation.

Earned Income Tax Credit Parameters for Married Individuals

Group and Parameter	Proposal
No qualifying children	
Phase-in rate	50%
Phase-in ends	$10,000
Maximum credit	$ 5,000
Phase-out begins	$10,000
Phase-out rate	24%
One qualifying child	
Phase-in rate	70%
Phase-in ends	$10,000
Maximum credit	$ 7,000
Phase-out begins	$10,000
Phase-out rate	24%
Two qualifying children	
Phase-in rate	90%
Phase-in ends	$10,000
Maximum credit	$ 9,000
Phase-out begins	$10,000
Phase-out rate	25.5%
Three qualifying children	
Phase-in rate	110%
Phase-in ends	$10,000
Maximum credit	$11,000
Phase-out begins	$10,000
Phase-out rate	27%
Four or more qualifying children	
Phase-in rate	130%
Phase-in ends	$10,000
Maximum credit	$13,000
Phase-out begins	$10,000
Phase-out rate	28.5%

Access to Enhanced Work Incentive Counseling

The third component of our proposed policy package would ensure that current and potential SSDI beneficiaries have regular access to a knowledgeable work incentive counselor. There are policies that have been put into place in order to encourage SSDI beneficiaries to consider returning to work. These include, but are not limited to, the Trial Work Period, the Extended Period of Eligibility and Medicaid Buy-In.

However, researchers have learned that individuals often are not aware of these, or do not understand how they apply to their individual circumstances.

Because of the complex factors that drive an individual's decision making about SSDI and work, we believe that the Transitional Job and enhanced Earned Income Tax Credit policies would benefit from an Enhanced Work Incentive Counseling component. It is critical to be able to address individuals' questions about how working above the SGA will affect their eligibility, and their receipt of benefits. This would also include the impact of the enhanced Earned Income Tax Credit.

In addition to ensuring that SSDI beneficiaries understand how working in a Transitional Job would affect their benefits, the Enhanced Work Incentive Counseling model can provide a good deal more support for the individual seeking to return to work. In the current Benefit Offset National Demonstration (BOND), running in 10 states, one of the interventions includes Enhanced Work Incentive Counseling (EWIC). In contrast to existing policy with Work Incentive Counseling, EWIC involves more proactive and intensive outreach and counseling with SSDI beneficiaries in one of the BOND treatment groups. EWIC providers administer assessments and use online tools to match skills to occupational requirements. They help develop vocational goals and create a plan that tailors services to overcome barriers. They provide referrals for employments services, and follow up with providers and beneficiaries. Finally, the counselors follow up with the beneficiary and employer after the beneficiary starts a job (CSDP 2015).

Stephen Bell reported that the Enhanced Work Incentive Counseling resulted in a very substantial increase in engagement and enrollment in employment activities, and that both Work Incentive Counselors and EWIC resulted in increased employment effects, compared to the control group. However, the enhanced counseling had not shown impacts relative to the regular work incentive counseling—at least not to date. We would expect that the pre-pilot would utilize the enhanced model, because initial engagement is critical to understanding not just who takes up the TJ offer, but why people do or don't follow through. The enhanced model is more likely to provide more in the way of explanations for follow through—or lack of it.

If, however, in the intervening time between making this proposal and actually setting up the pre-pilot there is more conclusive evidence about one versus the other, we would be open to changing our approach.

In our proposal, the counselors would be part of the intermediary's staff and work with all participants, whether they were applicants for SSDI or current beneficiaries.

INTERMEDIATE STEP: TESTING THE VIABILITY OF THE PROPOSED POLICIES THROUGH A PRE-PILOT

We propose that a sponsor test the viability of the proposed policies through a pre-pilot of two sites with 500 participants over an 18-month period. If the pre-pilot shows that the proposed policies can be implemented, and participants are responsive to the offers, then we would propose a large national demonstration project.

The authors believe a pre-pilot is necessary before any randomized control study to ensure that the policies can be delivered as intended. When promising ideas are studied, or best practice models are evaluated using random assignment, it can be difficult to distinguish whether any disappointing results are the result of the policies not producing rigorous results, or poor implementation.

The proposed policies are straightforward, and yet implementing them would require working through multiple challenges. They would be working laboratories to test the viability of implementing the proposal, and getting information on how these policies could be used to address the complex interaction of work and SSDI.

Questions/Challenges of This Model

The challenges of using this model with SSDI applicants and beneficiaries include (but are not limited to):

- Understanding and adapting to the existing rules for determining eligibility, as well as the current work incentives in place for current beneficiaries;
- Creating sufficient numbers of Transitional Jobs appropriate for a wide range of disabling medical conditions;
- Creating sufficient numbers of Transitional Jobs in rural areas;
- Integrating the periodic payment of our enhanced Earned Income Tax Credit with the IRS and SSDI systems;
- Executing memoranda of understanding with appropriate federal agencies (Social Security Administration and Treasury, for example);
- Developing sufficient staff capacity to deliver this model;
- Measuring the costs and benefits of the model.

Understanding and Adapting to Existing Rules

For the most part, the incentives provided for applicants would overlap with those for persons currently receiving SSDI benefits. But there would be some crucial differences.

Applicants would likely be in greater need of immediate income, but also would be more wary of trying work while they await a decision on their application. Our proposal is rooted in the belief that the best way to reduce the growth in SSDI is to slow down the rate of new applicants. We do not wish to accomplish this by changing eligibility rules to make it harder to qualify; we are hoping to accomplish it by helping people find alternative ways to work that accommodate their medical condition. But we need to actually see what happens when we offer the combination of the Transitional Job and enhanced Earned Income Tax Credit. If potential applicants do NOT respond, why? If their lack of response is due to the fact that it is likely to work against their chances of being approved for SSDI, what could we do to address this? Would we be able to work out an agreement to treat their efforts to work in ways that would not lead to automatic denial of their SSDI claim, if they were not successful in finding work they could do?

Under the SSDI program's work rules, current beneficiaries are permitted and encouraged to work if they are able.[5] They may earn an unlimited amount for

---

5 Additionally, SSDI beneficiaries remain eligible for Medicare for seven years, no matter how much they work and whether or not they continue to receive cash benefits through SSDI. For a full discussion of SSDI work rules, see U.S. Social Security Administration, "The Red Book – A Guide to Work Incentives," available at http://www.ssa.gov/ redbook/eng/ ssdi-only-employment-supports.htm#a0=3.

up to 12 months with no impact on their benefits. Those who earn above the SGA level ($1,090 per month for 2015) for more than 12 months enter a nearly three-year "extended period of eligibility" (EPE) during which they receive an SSDI benefit only in months when they earn less than SGA. After the EPE ends, if at any time in the next five years their health declines and they are no longer able to continue working above SGA, they can return to SSDI through "expedited reinstatement." These work incentives and protections provide a valuable platform for SSDI beneficiaries to test their ability to return to work through a Transitional Job.

Creating Sufficient Numbers of Transitional Jobs

One obvious challenge is the need to create Transitional Jobs that can accommodate a wide range of participants' medical conditions. In some cases, the intermediary will be working with someone whose disabling condition is obvious, and therefore the TJ host site will be aware of the situation and be able to determine whether there are ways to adapt the job or environment to the individual's situation.

In other cases, where the condition is not visible or apparent in casual contact, the intermediary will have to balance the need to identify accommodations against the concern that too much information will result in pre-judgment about someone's ability to be a productive worker. Many SSDI applicants and beneficiaries live with mental illness. Our goal is to provide them with the opportunity to try different kinds of work and environments in order to potentially find a good fit.

Some advisors to our proposal have said they fear this would lead to sheltered workshops. However, Transitional Jobs will pay at least $10 per hour, and the individual will have some choice about the job. Generally, to mirror the actual labor market, we would have individuals apply and interview for the jobs. The intermediary would get feedback from both the TJ host site supervisor and the worker.

It would also be critical to test the model in a rural area, as the regular job market is generally more limited there.

Multiple Transitional Jobs programs have succeeded in developing large numbers of jobs—in the thousands. Indeed, recent efforts created more than 260,000 TJs nationwide using federal funds appropriated under the American Recovery and Reinvestment Act (Pavetti, Schott, and Lower-Basch 2011, 6). We believe it can be done, but acknowledge that it would be breaking new ground to work exclusively with the SSDI population.

Integrating the Periodic Payment of the Earned Income Tax Credit

We are proposing both an enhanced Earned Income Tax Credit, and a periodic payment of it. The enhanced EITC is crucial to the model; one of our guiding principles is that work and the EITC should make one substantially better off than the SSDI benefit. It is also crucial to understand that the EITC is connected directly to work effort. We have structured the proposed enhancement to reward work, and to avoid income cliffs, such as the current SSDI cliff.

But the current delivery system has reduced the connection to work effort by only paying the EITC once a year, at tax time. People understand that they have to work in order to qualify for the EITC (among other requirements). However, the link to the policy goal of using the tax credit to make up the difference between one's monthly earnings and one's monthly expenses has been weakened. There is currently no way to get any of the EITC on a periodic basis, when it might be most useful in meeting ongoing needs. Instead, it comes as a windfall once a year.

While there were good reasons for eliminating the Advanced Earned Income Tax Credit, we believe that we would need to develop a periodic payment option for this model. We have experience in doing this, as the original New Hope Project paid out its earnings supplement on a monthly basis. We would likely adapt the periodic payment model currently being tested in Chicago (Marzahl and Bellisle 2014, 2). We could explore doing this through the IRS, which would require working out a memorandum of understanding (and the negotiation that would entail), or we could run the periodic payment as a separate, stand-alone function handled by the intermediary. For the pre-pilot, we would most likely run it as a function of the intermediary, and use the experience to test the waters with the IRS if a larger demonstration went forward.

Developing Sufficient Staff Capacity

As noted above, one of the critical pieces of our proposal is to ensure that participants and would-be participants have access to work incentive counselors who have solid knowledge of how work interacts with SSDI rules, and have skills to help guide job exploration.

Many times, new programs or interventions are designed and implemented without sufficient thought about how to hire people with the right skills or aptitudes, or how to provide ongoing training to ensure that staff turnover is managed as well as possible. Small pilot sites would be ideal for working this through.

We anticipate that the staff would work for the intermediary, but they might be situated at another organization, such as a disability services organization or vocational rehabilitation office. We expect that staff members would have caseloads of 50-75 active participants, with additional participants who may be sporadically active, for a total caseload of approximately 100 at any time. Again, this would be assessed during the pre-pilot.

The Cost of Implementing and Running the Pre-Pilot

Transitional Jobs models vary in how they build their budgets. We are basing our estimate on the average costs per job in the Wisconsin Transitional Jobs Demonstration, which ran from 2010-13. (The program's successor continues on a somewhat reduced scale, but is recommended for additional funding in the governor's current Wisconsin state budget proposal.)

Under that program, the cost of a yearly Transitional Job slot is $10,000, which includes the intermediary's operating costs (Davis and Rupisnky 2013, Tables A5 & A6). We add $500 per participant per year for the Enhanced Work Incentive Counseling.

Our estimate for the enhanced EITC is $4,500 per household, per Kye Lippold's report.

Therefore, the cost of implementing this proposal is estimated at $15,000 per participant, assuming full-time work and qualifying for the enhanced EITC. Even if 500 individuals accepted the offer, we know that not all would work full time or for more than six months. For the purpose of this proposal, we estimate that we would utilize full funding for 250 individuals.

There would also be costs associated with setting up and running the pre-pilot. We estimate costs in the range of $500,000 to $700,000 for setting up and administering the pre-pilot, depending upon where the pre-pilot would take place. That would cover staffing, contracting (including an evaluation firm to document the outcomes and lessons learned in the pilots), operating costs, and travel.

Budget Estimate for the Pre-Pilot of up to 500 Individuals

Program Expenses	
Transitional Jobs – wages, taxes and costs of staffing the intermediary:	$2,500,000
Enhanced Earned Income Tax Credit	1,125,000
Enhanced Work Incentive Counselors	125,000
Subtotal Program Expenses	$3,750,000
Administering the Pilot – range of $500,000 to $700,000	

Acknowledgements

The authors wish to acknowledge the assistance of Joelle Brouner and Karen Ferrington of the Colorado Department of Human Services, Division of Vocational Rehabilitation; Peter Pike of the Colorado Disability Benefits Support Program; Tom Gautier of Adonai Employment Services; and Kasaundra Brown, Community Advocates.

Discussion of Early Intervention Proposals

Lisa D. Ekman

This discussion is a summary of the comments made by the discussant at the SSDI Solutions Conference on August 4, 2015, before chapters were made final.

Workers with chronic conditions that affect functional capacity to work and who have significant disabilities can often stay at work or return to work when they receive affordable medical care and access to the services and supports they need to live independently and work. Unfortunately, many workers currently lack timely access to affordable medical care and work-based services and supports. For some workers with disabilities, this lack of access can hasten both their departure from work and application for Social Security Disability Insurance (SSDI). In addition, the programs and systems we have in the United States designed to support workers with disabilities are underfunded, have waiting lists, or impose eligibility rules that often exclude the workers who need them (based on resources, income, or severity of disability).[1] The papers in this section advance proposals to provide better access to services and supports to workers with disabilities and chronic conditions that create functional impairments.

---

1 For information on Medicaid waiting lists, see Terence Eng et al., Medicaid Home and Community-Based Services Programs: 2011 Data Update, Kaiser Family Foundation, table 14, December 22, 2014, available at http://kff.org/report-section/medicaid-home-and-community-based-services-programs-2011-data-update-eligibility-and-cost-containment-policies-used-in-medicaid-hcbs-programsFor information on State Vocational Rehabilitation services, see University of New Hampshire Institute on Disability, Annual Disability Statistics Compendium, Table 12.7: Vocational Rehabilitation—State Agencies on Order of Selection: 2008 through 2012, December 2014, available at http://disabilitycompendium.org/compendium-statistics/vocational-rehabilitation/12-7-vocational-rehabilitation-state-agencies-on-order-of-selection.

What is clear to me from all three papers in this section is that there is neither completed research nor an evidence base upon which to enact nationwide early intervention or work support programs. Additional study and evaluation will be needed to generate this evidence; certainly before making changes to the SSDI program. Where examples of early invention do exist, it is also not clear how applicable they are to those who would otherwise receive SSDI benefits. For example, "The Employment/Eligibility Service System: A New Gateway for Employment Supports and Social Security Disability Benefits" by Stapleton, Ben-Shalom, and Mann points to private disability insurance's stay-at-work efforts which, for a number of reasons (including differences in educational attainment, skill levels, types of work performed) between individuals covered by private insurance and workers who generally end up on SSDI, do not appear likely to me to be translatable to SSDI. Given the lack of an evidence base, most disability advocates support piloting new ideas to gather evidence rather than making substantial changes based on a presupposition that pilots will prove effective.

As another note of caution, several of the papers in this section point to the experiences of other countries without fully recognizing many important differences that limit the transferability of policy choices. For example, the Netherlands, which is referred to in "The Employment/Eligibility Service System," has universal health coverage and very different relationships between employers and employees.[2]

Finally, I believe it is important that as the proposals for early intervention and work support contained in this section are piloted, no Social Security Trust Fund dollars should be used for any purpose other than administering and paying benefits to people already determined eligible for benefits by the Social Security Administration. While providing work supports and medical care to workers is extremely important, the link between these services and avoided entry into the program is unproven and too indirect, in my view, to justify using Trust Fund dollars for pilots for non-beneficiaries.

Beyond these general principles, I have a number of questions and concerns regarding "The Employment/Eligibility Service System: A New Gateway for

---

[2] See Elaine Fultz, Disability Insurance in the Netherlands: A Blueprint for U.S. Reform?, September 16, 2015, Center on Budget and Policy Priorities available at http://www.cbpp.org/research/retirement-security/disability-insurance-in-the-netherlands-a-blueprint-for-us-reform for a fuller discussion of the differences.

Employment Supports and Social Security Disability Benefits." To begin with, the paper essentially proposes a new definition of disability and an additional process before workers with disabilities would be able to access benefits. Despite advances in civil rights, technology, and medical care for individuals with disabilities, there is a strong case that the current definition and process remains appropriate for the purpose of replacing wages for individuals with significant impairments that prevent substantial work. I, along with most disability advocates, believe that creating additional hurdles to entry is unfair and unwarranted given SSDI benefits are paid for and earned by workers through payroll tax contributions.

The cost and savings estimates in this paper also appear extremely optimistic. Given severe underfunding of current disability employment support programs, establishing EES services in each state would likely require a significant increase in administrative spending, not to mention income support payments. As a result, it is quite possible that this new system would greatly increase spending in both the short and long run—particularly if the availability of the EES and new work support services led to significant increases in SSDI applications.[3]

The authors also fail to present any convincing evidence that return to work—and therefore SSDI savings – is possible at the magnitude they suggest. Past demonstrations and pilots, although they have improved quality of life, have not resulted in significant numbers of individuals leaving the SSDI rolls and going to work.[4] The authors' assertion that a 15-percent reduction in SSDI applicants of all ages is plausible vastly exceeds past results, especially when it comes to the above-40 population which is highly unlikely to return to work. Assuming instead that 15 percent of applicants under 40 went back to work (which is still probably too high by a large margin based on past research findings) and there

---

[3] For example, individuals with significant disabilities who are working but underemployed and earning less than substantial gainful activity, or individuals on waiting lists for VR or Medicaid waiver services who have not applied for SSDI might apply for work support through the EES.

[4] See for example, the Mental Health Treatment Study, https://socialsecurity.gov/disabilityresearch/documents/MHTS_Final_Report_508.pdf, and the Youth Transition Demonstration, http://www.ssa.gov/disabilityresearch/documents/YTD%20Final%20Report%20508%20Compliant%2012-29-2014.pdf. While both showed increases in work of participants, neither resulted in significant numbers of participants performing self-supporting work, and both cost more per beneficiary. See also the Ticket to Work program evaluation, http://www.ssa.gov/policy/docs/ssb/v71n3/v71n3p105.pdf

was no significant change for older beneficiaries, the proposal would result in only about 2.2 percent of new awardees not receiving benefits.[5]

"A Community-Focused Health & Work Service (HWS)" by Christian, Wickizer, and Burton proposes to create a national health and work service (HWS) that would provide telephonic counseling, communication assistance, referrals to services, and coordination of services for people within 12 weeks of the onset of a newly diagnosed condition that could lead to impairments that prevent work. Providing access to assistance directly after a health incident is a promising idea. However, rather than piloting it to figure out how to best implement it nationalwide, further testing and piloting would likely be needed first to determine *if* it should be expanded nationwide.

The authors' examples of other programs, though encouraging, reflect situations that are quite dissimilar to those of most workers who end up receiving SSDI benefits. With regards to the authors' first example of Washington State's Workers' Compensation program, it is important to note that a distinct event or incident signifies the beginning of the development of an individual's disability. In SSDI, on the other hand, conditions often develop over time without any particular trigger incident. In this case as well as the authors' second example—a similar program in the United Kingdom—a third party is responsible for the costs of health care, vocational rehabilitation, and other services (universal health care in the United Kingdom and employer responsibility in the case of Workers' Compensation). Meanwhile, many workers in the United States still lack health insurance (one in seven in 2014)[6] and might not have access to or the ability to

---

5 In 2013, 14.9 percent of men awarded benefits and 15.7 percent of women were under age 40. If approximately 15 percent of new awardees are under 40 based on 2013 awards (and that might be high because only 10.5 percent of male beneficiaries and 10 percent of female beneficiaries in 2013 were under 40) and they are the most likely to go to work, a much lower percentage of people would successfully achieve self-supporting employment. For example, there were 868,965 disabled workers awarded benefits in 2013. If 15 percent of them would become employed by receiving EES work supports, 130,344 would be working instead of receiving benefits. However, if only applicants under 40 were counted, there were 131,931 in 2013. If 15 percent of them went back to work, EES work supports would only have assisted 19,790 workers or 2.2 percent of awardees to work instead of receiving SSDI benefits. All data is from the Social Security Administration, Annual Statistical Supplement to the Social Security Bulletin 2014, available at https://www.socialsecurity.gov/policy/docs/statcomps/supplement/

6 See United States Department of Health and Human Services, Centers for Disease Control and Prevention, Center for Health Statistics, "Health Insurance Coverage: Early Release of

pay for any additional services or rehabilitation needed to remain on the job. This proposal does not provide the additional access that would be necessary, and as such there may be little change in the number of people applying for or receiving SSDI as a result.

"Using Transitional Jobs to Increase Employment of SSDI Applicants and Beneficiaries" by Kerksick, Riemer, and Williams proposes to provide access to subsidized jobs and an earnings supplement to individuals with medical conditions that affect their ability to work. The idea of providing access to transitional jobs with an enhanced earned income tax credit (EITC) is a promising one worth testing—though policymakers should be wary of using trust fund dollars for reasons described above. In addition to the enhanced EITC, perhaps the project could test other tax improvements such as converting the deductions for impairment-related work expenses into a refundable credit and making it refundable. If the pilot proves successful after a number of years of testing, this proposal could be expanded and transitional jobs made available more broadly.

Estimates From the National Health Interview Survey, 2014" June 2015, available at http://www.cdc.gov/nchs/data/nhis/earlyrelease/insur201506.pdf

Section III

PROGRAM ADMINISTRATION

6

Data-Driven Solutions for Improving the Continuing Disability Review Process

Alexandra Constantin, Julia Porcino, John Collins, and Chunxiao Zhou

INTRODUCTION

The Social Security Disability Insurance (SSDI) and Supplemental Security Income (SSI) programs are the largest federal income programs for individuals with disabilities. In 2014, these programs paid out $175 billion to 15 million beneficiaries (House Committee on Oversight and Government Reform Subcommittee on Energy Policy, Health Care and Entitlements 2014). To ensure that only those who remain disabled stay on the rolls, the Social Security Administration (SSA) is required by law[1] to conduct medical continuing disability reviews (CDRs) on all disability insurance beneficiaries, some SSI recipients,[2] and all SSI children.[3] The law requires that CDRs be conducted every three

1 Section 221(i) of the Social Security Act (SSA 2011).

2 Section 1614(a)(4) of the Act gives SSA discretionary authority to conduct periodic CDRs of SSI recipients. (SSA 2011).

3 Public Law 104-193 required SSA to redetermine the eligibility of all SSI child recipients who attain age 18 based on the adult initial eligibility criteria. This law also required that SSA perform a CDR: 1) at least once every three years for SSI recipients under age 18 who are eligible by reason of an impairment that is likely to improve; and 2) not later than 12 months after birth for recipients whose low birth weight is a contributing factor material to the determination of their disability. Since SSA has no backlog for the for the age 18 redetermination process, this paper will address only those benefit categories with CDR backlogs (SSA 2011).

years for SSDI beneficiaries with potentially non-permanent disabilities, while beneficiaries with permanent disabilities are to be reviewed at such times as the SSA Commissioner determines to be appropriate. Since the inception of the SSDI program, Congress has emphasized the importance of CDRs as a way to preserve the social safety net for disabled individuals. In fact, when the SSDI program was established in 1956, Congress created a provision to allow SSA to monitor a beneficiary's continued eligibility for disability benefits. Periodic medical reviews are one of the most cost-effective provisions available to SSA to improve program integrity. However, in recent years the backlog of CDRs that need to be completed has grown to over 1.3 million cases. While completion of CDRs is often limited by funding and resources, the process is also hampered by a lack of access to and availability of medical or functional data, as well as a fragmented system that is slow to adapt and make the most of modern technological advances. To address the CDR backlog and improve the overall efficiency of the CDR process, we propose four main strategies: investment in information technology for collecting and leveraging data; acquiring new and additional data; use of data analytics and predictive modeling for discovering insights, informing policy, and optimizing business processes; and creation of a dynamic CDR case prioritization queue ordered by expected lifetime savings. The scope and direction of these initiatives would have positive agency-wide implications by increasing the productivity and consistency of handling all SSA claims, not just CDRs.

BACKGROUND

When a decision is made that an applicant is, or continues to be, disabled, SSA sets a medical diary, which classifies beneficiaries into three categories: medical improvement not expected (MINE), medical improvement possible (MIP), and medical improvement expected (MIE). Medical diary designations are based on rules developed in the early 1990s that have not been updated. The MINE rules were developed in a data-driven fashion using historical SSA decisions. The MIE rules were based on a medical literature review. The MIP category includes everyone not in the MIE or MINE groups, and consists of roughly 60 percent of SSA beneficiaries. Approximately 35 percent of beneficiaries are designated as MINE and the remaining 5 percent are designated MIE (SSAB 2014). SSA intends to review cases every five to seven years, every three years, or every six to 18 months, depending on the respective diary designation.

SSA conducts two types of medical CDRs: full medical reviews and mailers. A statistical profiling model (the CDR predictive model) is applied to cases every year to assign scores that reflect the likelihood of cessation were a full medical CDR to be conducted. The CDR predictive model uses SSA program data including age, impairments, length of time in disability status, basis for the original determination, data on prior CDRs, and recent earnings as variables for its estimations (SSA 2012). The predictive model is used to determine which cases with medical diaries due that year should be given a full medical CDR. Cases are assigned to low, medium, or high likelihood of cessation groups based on the model's predictions. Cases in the low group are typically sent a short-form mailer and those in the high group are given a full medical review. Beneficiaries in the medium group may be sent a mailer or undergo a full medical CDR depending upon other factors such as the CDR budget for that fiscal year.

The mailer is a questionnaire designed to obtain additional information about a beneficiary's impairments, treatment, and earnings. This information is then used to determine if a full medical review should be initiated. Only about 2.5 percent of beneficiaries who return the completed mailer are referred for full medical CDR based on the information received. A full CDR involves development by SSA of a complete medical history covering the most recent 12 months. The goal of the case development for a full CDR is to obtain sufficient medical evidence for a comparison point decision of the status of the beneficiary's impairments under the Medical Improvement Review Standard (MIRS), which differs from initial determination criteria since the CDR is looking to establish whether there is any change in the beneficiary's function and ability to return to work.

The CDR process consistently yields a favorable ratio of savings-to-costs. SSA estimates that the CDR process yielded a savings-to-costs ratio averaging $10 to $1 for fiscal years 1996 through 2011, and a savings-to-costs ratio of $14.6 to $1 for fiscal year 2012 (SSA 2014). In January 2014, SSA reported that it had accumulated a backlog of 1.3 million CDRs (GAO 2014). SSA has cited resource limitations and a greater emphasis on processing initial claims as reasons for falling behind on the number of CDRs conducted despite the consistently favorable ratio of savings-to-costs generated by these reviews. When CDRs are not conducted as scheduled, the potential for improper payments increases as some recipients receive benefits for which they are no longer eligible. In the March 2010 OIG report entitled "Full Medical CDRs," SSA estimated that between 2005 and 2010 the agency will have made benefit payments of between $1.3 billion and $2.6 billion that could have been avoided if SSA had conducted the 1.5 million full medical CDRs that were in the backlog during that time as soon as they became due (SSA OIG 2010).

While the current CDR process is very cost effective, it is possible to significantly improve it by increasing productivity and accuracy in the handling of cases, better targeting cases for full medical review, and guaranteeing sufficient funding of the CDR program. With the use of the CDR predictive model, about 6 percent of full medical CDRs result in disability program cessation (SSAB 2014). While this level of cessations still makes the program cost effective, there is room for improvement. The most significant limitations of both the CDR predictive model and the overall accuracy and efficiency of the CDR process stem from lack of access, use, or acquisition of accurate and reliable medical data and inefficient use of electronic business processes that mimic antiquated paper-based processes and do not take full advantage of automatic data entry and collection.

The following sections give detailed descriptions of our proposed solutions for addressing these issues and improving the CDR process, including implementation challenges, interim steps, and critical success factors.

INVESTMENT IN INFORMATION TECHNOLOGY FOR DATA ACQUISITION, ACCESS, CONSISTENCY, AND INTEGRITY

The Problem

The most significant limitations to SSA data-driven tools such as the CDR predictive model are access to, and availability of, the most relevant data related to measuring a beneficiary's medical improvement. The inability to quickly access the right data can lead to poorly informed decisions. SSA's existing information technology (IT) infrastructure was not designed to process today's magnitude, complexity, or workload of data. SSA's IT system is fragmented amongst its departments and programs and across each stage of the disability adjudication process. To access all relevant information for one beneficiary, one needs to query many databases and make use of many applications. This creates problems regarding data consistency and duplication. Moreover, access to these data sources is limited even within the agency, making these data difficult to use for analytics purposes. For example, a beneficiary's electronic health record contains the most pertinent evidence related to her conditions and the possibility of medical improvement. However, the database housing that data was set up in such a way that it cannot be directly queried to extract records in bulk by most SSA personnel. Previously, we obtained access to a small sample of electronic medical records for research purposes by writing a program that uses SSA's eView system (an application created to allow adjudicators to view case evidence) and automatically clicks on all relevant links to download the files of interest.[4] We were unable to identify a way to more efficiently download medical evidence in bulk. The problem of being unable to download data in bulk from databases is not limited to medical evidence. This is a major impediment to all initiatives to make data-driven decisions and policy changes.

The data analysis of medical evidence to improve the accuracy and consistency of SSA processes is hampered by the lack of medical and functional evidence stored in structured format, even though this evidence is routinely generated as part of SSA business processes. These processes mimic a paper-based system where SSA staff fill out various forms and templates and then save them as TIFF[5] images, which prevents these forms from being searched automatically or their contents included in a structured database. The development of a modern system for capturing this information and automatically sending it to structured databases would allow SSA to use data analytics to improve its processes, would increase program consistency, and would reduce costs. For example, a 2007 Government Accountability Office report found that between fiscal years 1995 and 2005, the number of disability appeals reviewed by the federal district courts increased, as did the proportion of decisions that were remanded (GAO 2007). More disability claims were remanded than affirmed, reversed, or dismissed over this period, and the proportion of total decisions remanded ranged from 36 percent to 62 percent with an average of 50 percent (GAO 2007). SSA has addressed the need to reduce remands, and in 2006, along with other initiatives, introduced new decision-writing templates to improve efficiency and reduce errors. SSA has made additional efforts to improve efficiency and consistency of decisions with the development of the electronic Claims Analysis Tool (eCAT) system, a web-based application designed to document the disability determination rationale of a disability examiner and to ensure that SSA policies are adhered to during claims adjudication. This application facilitates the standardization of state disability determination practices. The eCAT automatically captures case characteristics, functional information, and examiner actions. However, eCAT addresses only a small part of the disability determination process and is built on top of the SSA legacy system. The system is not yet being used for the CDR process. Additionally, SSA still relies heavily upon Microsoft Word templates that

4 This research was supported by the Intramural Research Program of the National Institutes of Health, Clinical Research Center and through an interagency agreement with the US Social Security Administration.

5 Tagged Image File Format for storing images, which is common with scanned or faxed images, but has a large amount of variability

can be edited manually. The standardization and modernization of this process is necessary in order to make full use of data to improve business processes and policy.

Investment in information technology has yielded great success for SSA in the past. Some of the agency's very successful investments in technology include the CDR predictive model; iClaim, an online system for applying for disability, retirement, and Medicare; mySocialSecurity, a personalized online portal that individuals can use to view detailed information on benefits received, get a benefit verification letter, start or change direct deposit information, and change their address; the Access to Financial Institutions program, which allows SSA employees to automatically and electronically gather SSI recipients' financial account information directly from financial institutions; the SSI Telephone Wage Reporting System, an automated toll-free number that allows SSI recipients to update the wage information on their records and a mobile wage-reporting application; and, the Continuing Disability Review Enforcement Operations Predictive Model, which identified DI beneficiaries who appear to have substantial earnings after disability onset through an automated matching of the current DI beneficiaries with earnings reported to the Internal Revenue Service (IRS). Many other agencies including the Department of Veterans Affairs (VA), Department of Defense (DOD), and Centers for Medicare & Medicaid Services (CMS) achieved their most successful reductions in backlogged cases by maximizing the use of technology and the corresponding data it can put at their disposal. For example, in the VA's 2013 Strategic Plan to Eliminate the Compensation Claims Backlog, the department anticipated that over 40 percent of their backlog cases would be removed with implementation of new and additional technology (Veterans Benefits Administration 2013). All these agencies have introduced methods for electronic filing and management of claims and cases as both a strategy for reducing backlog and for improving their systems overall. The VA, DOD and CMS have introduced online portals, which are used not only for electronically submitting claims, but also for keeping claimants appraised of the status of cases and for storing data that claimants and the agency may need now or in the future. The CMS portal also allows professionals involved in claimants' cases, such as attorneys and insurance carriers, to directly enter case information into the portal, which reduces cost and time spent following up with these sources (Centers for Medicare & Medicaid Services 2013). And with the shift toward electronic filings, the agencies can now ensure that all necessary information is collected before a case progresses, reducing the need for claims to be returned due to insufficient case development. While SSA has made some great strides in using information technology to handle the CDR backlog, the agency needs to make greater use of data and technology in order to truly improve the CDR and the overall adjudication processes.

Recommendations

Below, we describe investments in information technology that would allow SSA to efficiently acquire and leverage medical and functional data, thus addressing the issues outlined above.

1. Data modernization and integration through an Enterprise Data Environment (EDE) with the following components (described later in this section)
   - Integrated master data repository
   - Operational business intelligence repositories
   - Unstructured data repository
   - Enterprise metadata and services repository
   - Enterprise data services and enterprise business services
   - Demonstration environment
2. IT infrastructure modernization

These recommendations are informed by CMS's plan for "Modernizing CMS Computer and Data Systems to Support Improvements in Care Delivery," released in 2010 (Centers for Medicare & Medicaid Services IT Modernization Program 2010). Indeed, CMS faced a lot of the same challenges SSA is currently facing. CMS's detailed plan to modernize its systems and put data at the core of its operations can serve as a model for SSA's modernization effort and provide insight into overcoming implementation challenges and lessons learned. Below is a more detailed description of the recommendations.

SSA needs to create an EDE to stand at the core of its data and IT infrastructure modernization efforts. An EDE is an integrated, modular environment for managing enterprise data and optimizing data-driven applications and decision making over its lifetime. This environment needs to be created from a global, agency-level perspective, and not be broken up into silos artificially created by the agency's departments and programs. The essence of the enterprise data environment core design should be to improve the integration, completeness, quality, timeliness, and accessibility of SSA data. SSA should treat data as an enterprise asset and should focus on collecting and storing data necessary to identify opportunities to improve business processes and policies, and not just data required for applications that lead to operational expedience. The EDE should provide timely access to authoritative data sources at all levels within the agency, empower collaboration, automate and simplify operations, and support enterprise growth. This initiative should result in improved security through implementation of privacy controls to ensure protection of sensitive data via roles, policies, and business processes.

SSA needs accurate, timely, complete, and authoritative information about its applicants and beneficiaries. This is vital to maintaining core program operations and program integrity, and to evaluate the effectiveness and performance of new and existing initiatives. This data is also necessary to hold programs, states, and adjudicators accountable, promote transparency, and support agency research and data-driven decision-making needs. The EDE should provide an overarching plan for managing SSA's data using best practices from Master Data Management (MDM), the discipline in which IT specialists engage business experts in the development and maintenance of consistent and accurate lists of an enterprise's most critical information. MDM methodology focuses on eliminating redundancy, inconsistency, and fragmentation by having a single, synchronized, comprehensive, authoritative source of master information.

The integrated master data repository should contain all structured information pertinent to an applicant. It should be structured as a relational database and it should uniquely identify beneficiaries, claims, cases, providers, and representatives. Data should be stored in a format that permits partial updates (e.g. an applicant's address changes but all other fields remain unchanged) and a variable number of fields (e.g. current SSA systems only allow for two impairment codes even though there are applicants with as many as 11 impairments). The master data repository should serve as the authoritative source of information for the entire agency. It should support both operational and research and demonstration needs. The operational business intelligence repositories will serve as the authoritative source of near-real-time and/or historic data for individual SSA programs and components. Whereas the master data repository is SSA's enterprise solution for creating highly integrated information products, the operational business intelligence repositories will allow for timelier, more consistent, and greater dedicated operational support. Only one extract of the operational business intelligence repositories will be sent to the master data repository for integration. The unstructured data repository should include the millions of unstructured documents that SSA receives or produces every year. This unstructured data includes medical evidence, SSA forms, SSA reports, and SSA decision documentation. The business processes associated with the generation and processing of these documents are manual, time-consuming, and inefficient.

Unstructured data objects are ultimately stored by the agency as TIFF images, making them difficult to use to gain insight or create work- and time-saving applications. Unstructured data should be saved in its native format and classified through unified classification schemes. When storing this data, the agency should take into account the requirements for capacity, latency, access, security, cost, persistence, flexibility, and application awareness for both business operations and research and demonstration initiatives. The agency should explore using NoSQL (Pokorny 2011) databases for unstructured data. The enterprise metadata and services repository should manage and store all information about SSA data, such as data models, data exchange layouts, data definitions, data lineage, data integrity rules, operational metrics, and data services under configuration management. It should support application developers by providing detailed information about SSA data. It should support data analysts by providing a better understanding of historical analytics and by enabling traceability of information. SSA should also manage a library of reusable software building blocks that can be combined in ways specific to each applications' needs. Enterprise data services should be technically oriented services that interact with the databases directly and can be aggregated or combined to support the specific needs of the organization. Enterprise business services are business-oriented services that can be used across the enterprise or services provided by off-the-shelf products.

The flexibility of the EDE infrastructure should offer the potential for reconfiguration in novel ways—sometimes using EDE production data and systems "as is" and sometimes using a demonstration environment or sandbox where experimentation can take place without impacting the production environment. Dedicated IT infrastructure should exist to support prototypes, demonstrations, and simulations for a wide variety of administrative and research innovations. The demonstration environment should have access to the entire range of data and services offered by the EDE.

In order to implement the vision of a modern enterprise data environment, SSA needs to also invest in its IT infrastructure. The agency should create a sound plan for implementation of a robust, secure architecture to support the EDE. This would include support for a virtual data center providing improved security, modern network capabilities, required capacity, and high availability for critical information and business continuity. SSA should carefully establish system requirements, keeping in mind both business operations and research and demonstration needs. It should consider a combination of technologies that together meet all of the system requirements, rather than trying to invest in a one-size-fits-all solution. It should consider all approaches, including virtualization or shared services such as Cloud Computing and Infrastructure.

Implementation

The data and information technology projects outlined above are very ambitious and present numerous challenges. The EDE would reach across all SSA departments and programs and require a major overhaul of both data management and storage solutions and all applications requiring access to these data. A list of major challenges is presented below.

Major challenges:

- Fragmented, unsynchronized data
- Outdated data systems that can only be accessed and supported by a limited number of technicians
- Poor documentation of legacy systems
- Stressed data processing capacity
- Limited capabilities to accept and process clinical data for automated decision support, workflow management, and knowledge discovery
- Lack of an authoritative data source
- Lack of enterprise services that facilitate easy access to SSA systems and data
- Monolithic, closed systems that were created with a single purpose in mind and have contributed to an inflexible architecture
- Degree of manual manipulation required before data can be used for analyses
- Communication challenges caused by fragmented agency operations and leadership
- Transition to data-driven enterprise-level decision making and policy changes

Strong management is critical to ensure the establishment and adoption of the EDE by the entire SSA organization. At a minimum, data management should address standards, organizational readiness, budgetary capitalization of shared enterprise data assets, enterprise data engineering and planning, and business transformation. SSA should build its shared, integrated data and service model in incremental steps. It should maintain its existing systems to continue its day-to-day business operations while preparing them for the new environment. The agency should employ a coordinated approach that includes short-term investments to sustain the existing systems and longer-term business change that utilizes authoritative data and new analytical techniques. The new IT and data storage infrastructure should be developed independently of SSA legacy systems and deployed incrementally to ensure a smooth transition.

Implementation of the EDE involves a series of phased, highly interdependent initiatives to achieve data improvement, business process modernization, enhanced security and privacy, best practice standards, and enterprise data center enhancements. A list of possible interim steps is described below.

Interim Steps

- Identify all SSA data stores that need to be integrated into the EDE.
- Identify new data to be acquired and stored in the EDE.
- Create conceptual architectural design for collecting, organizing, and integrating SSA data stored in the enterprise data repository.
- Create detailed system requirements for all phases
- Build the enterprise infrastructure capability to enable the needed scalability, agility, and flexibility to handle all SSA processes and big data analytics
- Build a case processing and workflow management architecture that can address all requirements and disability processing levels and steps, enable automatic data acquisition during case processing, be flexible to policy changes and regional differences (without requiring the purchase of additional software or database systems). Successful implementation involves agility and cooperation between SSA components and alignment within departments and regions to develop an enterprise-wide vision.
- Agile Cycles through multiple Plan, Do, Study, Act cycles (Highsmith 2004)
- Incremental cost-benefit analyses as components of the system are tested and deployment is performed on a small scale at first
- Incremental retirement of legacy applications

Creating and implementing a complex data and IT modernization plan is a challenging undertaking that requires an incredible communication effort. Previous successful and failed IT initiatives can help in identifying some critical success factors.

Critical Success Factors

- Solid executive and business sponsorship
- Centralized guidance with an agency-wide vision for initiatives

- Incrementally retiring legacy applications
- Acceptance of an SSA-wide information-centric approach
- Agile response to new business demands
- Comprehensive planning
- Aggressive risk management
- Adequate engagement of users in the entire process
- Adequate sharing of risks with vendors and creating contracts that properly align incentives
- Quality-driven procurement options
- Clear performance metrics established during the planning phase
- Sound fiscal and project management
- Good communication and involvement of stakeholders throughout the process
- Updated security and privacy regulations
- Adequate alignment of incentives and sharing of risks, responsibilities, and credit for successes with those involved in approval processes
- Good interagency coordination and communication
- Willingness to focus on long-term gains rather than short-term solutions

While the upfront cost would be high, a complete modernization of SSA IT and data storage infrastructure to a system capable of leveraging data is cost-effective in the long run because of the relative high cost of creating new IT applications on top of fragmented, antiquated legacy systems. This would also protect SSA from the hidden costs of smaller IT initiatives. Organizations often sprout small, independent data initiatives throughout their departments. This disparate, small-scale approach often costs more, takes longer, and delivers meager results. Below is a list of potential cost savings or cost avoidance that could be generated by the EDE.

Cost Savings

- Reduced risk of systemic failure due to overly complex, customized systems
- Simplified infrastructure through the retirement of hardware, applications, and databases
- Retirement of legacy systems will reduce the burden of maintaining product licenses and support costs (monitoring, upgrades, and patches) of retired systems
- Reduced labor activities related to the legacy hardware, applications, and databases (acquisition, storage, analysis, enhancement, maintenance, troubleshooting, archival, and distribution)

- Negotiation of better rates for resources that do not require domain knowledge or expertise that is presently required for the complicated infrastructure of legacy assets
- Significant administrative savings once the core infrastructure capabilities are established; other more modest administrative savings as the enterprise technology systems are integrated and the data services mature during the initial phases
- Enhanced program integrity
- Optimization of business processes and workflows
- Easy two-way information sharing with other government agencies
- Ensure complete, timely, and accurate data across the agency

NEW DATA ACQUISITION

The Problem

The effectiveness of the CDR predictive model is determined by the timeliness of the data used in its predictions. Therefore, the inability to quickly access the right data poses significant limitations to the CDR predictive model and can lead to poorly informed decisions. Even if existing data access and consistency issues were addressed, the lack of medical and functional data collected between full medical reviews would still be a severe limitation to the CDR process. At the time a decision is made whether to perform a full medical CDR, most of the data available is from the beneficiary's last review, thus typically collected at least three years prior to the CDR. While SSA has invested in applications to automatically collect financial information and to allow applicants to report changes in their financial circumstances, the agency has not made significant strides to collect medical and functional data or to allow applicants to report changes in their disability status between reviews of their case. According to the 2014 Office of Inspector General (OIG) report "Full Medical Continuing Disability Review Cessations Reversed at the Reconsideration Level of Appeal," 80 of every 100 cases reversed at the reconsideration level were reversed because there was new documentary evidence or testimony at the reconsideration level that was not available during the initial CDR (SSA OIG 2014a). Allowing beneficiaries to easily provide this evidence early in the CDR review process would likely result in cost savings, an increase in efficiency, and a reduction in the emotional burden on disabled beneficiaries.

Recommendations

We recommend that SSA explore three new functional and data collection initiatives to address the issues outlined above:

1. Acquisition of periodic Work Disability Functional Assessment Battery (WD-FAB) scores to precisely measure capacity across the full continuum of human functioning, in areas such as mobility, cognition, interpersonal interaction, communication, self-care, and general tasks and demands
2. Development of a web-based application that would enable claimants and their representatives to view their cases and upload their recent medical evidence
3. Automatic collection and leveraging of electronic medical records such as Medicare and Medicaid data, data from other health insurers, and electronic health records from providers and pharmacies

Implementation

Here are the steps through which the three data-acquisition recommendations can be implemented incrementally, and in parallel with each other. It should be noted that while the automatic collection of electronic medical records does not depend upon first having a functional version of the web-based application for their upload, the two initiatives synergize well once both are operational. Also, the same web-based application could eventually be used to both collect WD-FAB scores and to allow for the upload of medical records.

Acquisition of periodic WD-FAB scores

The Work Disability Functional Assessment Battery (WD-FAB) is currently being developed for use in the SSA data collection and disability evaluation processes.[6] In order to understand distinct factors influencing work, individual capabilities as well as workplace demands and critical features of the workplace environment must be captured. This modern concept of function has been embraced by the global community and is rooted in the World Health Organization's International Classification of Function, Disability and Health (ICF).

---

[6] The development of the WD-FAB tool was supported by the Intramural Research Program of the National Institutes of Health, Clinical Research Center and through an interagency agreement with the Social Security Administration.

The WD-FAB uses Computer Adaptive Testing (CAT) coupled with Item Response Theory (IRT) to precisely measure capacity across the full continuum of human functioning. IRT-CAT represents a simple form of artificial intelligence software requiring a computer for administration. These assessment instruments will cover all the major ICF areas that are highly related to work, such as basic mobility, cognition, interpersonal interaction, communication, self-care, and general tasks and demands. The National Institutes of Health (NIH) is working with researchers from Boston University on IRT-CAT development. The utilization of IRT-CAT technology could potentially allow the SSA to collect more relevant, comprehensive, and precise data about human functioning in a much more efficient fashion. This could promote simplification of the determination process, reduce processing time and cost, strengthen medical evidence resulting in more accurate and consistent decisions, and allow the SSA to collect data at points in the process when it proves most useful for decision making.

Major Challenges

- WD-FAB will require pilot testing within SSA
- Adoption of WD-FAB will require integration into SSA's business process

Interim Steps

- WD-FAB domain calibration, item replenishment, and methods to counter "cheating" or malingering
- Validation of WD-FAB scores through comparison to legacy instruments, test-retest comparisons, and SSA determination outcomes
- User simulation demonstration projects at state Disability Determination Services (DDS) offices for SSA and NIH to examine how best to include WD-FAB data collection into the existing business practice
- Usability support for the WD-FAB through multiple methods to connect scores to outcomes from SSA business practices
- Development of web-based, in-office, and phone-based applications for the collection of WD- FAB scores from claimants online, at DDS or hearings offices, or by phone
- Capstone demonstration project to compare SSA determination process to an augmented process that collects and uses WD-FAB data
- Progressive rollout of the WD-FAB to SSA regions to allow for comparison of business processes and to make adaptations from insights received from the field offices and DDS centers

Boston University is, as of June 2015, in the final stages of a study to calibrate the Learning and Applying Knowledge and Daily Activity domains of the WD-FAB. The other two domains of Interpersonal Interactions and Physical Function have already been calibrated and are undergoing item replenishment in this study, which is where new items are considered for inclusion and older items may be dropped to improve the overall quality of the instrument. Item replenishment is a continual process through which the WD-FAB can take advantage of improvements in the science of functional measurement or changes in functioning of the population. The instrument is being developed through the methods of Item Response Theory, which is the methodology used for the SAT, GRE, and other modern computerized tests that are able to analyze response patterns to automatically detect discrepancies. The implementation of WD-FAB as a computerized adaptive test allows it to detect malingering by comparing a claimant's combinations of response patterns to existing patterns of response from earlier users who had alleged similar impairing conditions.

Validation of the WD-FAB is done at several levels of specificity. These efforts include an ongoing predictive validity study of SSDI claimants to be completed in 2016 in which the WD- FAB scores of those who are approved or denied for benefits as of their most recent determination date will be compared. One user simulation demonstration has already been conducted at four field offices in the New England and Mid-Atlantic regions in which case workers read the items to claimants and filled in their responses on a computer. Caseworkers reported almost unanimously that the administration of the WD-FAB was straightforward and understandable to them and rarely took more than 30 minutes of their time. Finally, the WD-FAB has already been developed as a program that can run on any modern operating system. The decision on how to implement it within SSA's network should be decided by SSA's systems divisions, but NIH will cooperate with them as needed and can make the code for the program available.

Critical Success Factors

- The proposed changes in SSA policies to require the collection and use of WD-FAB data are implemented
- Adjudicator use of WD-FAB to provide a systematic summary of functioning that helps guide their development of the medical evidence
- Making WD-FAB scores interpretable to SSA adjudicators, administrators, and researchers

The acquisition of periodic WD-FAB scores (by phone, through an online application, or through eCAT) early in the adjudicative process would allow SSA to paint a full picture of applicants' and beneficiaries' functional status over time. The WD-FAB scores could be collected at times that SSA is already collecting beneficiary data, such as acquiring the WD-FAB in addition to the mailer, which would then provide more relevant function information for deciding whom to target for a full medical CDR while keeping administrative costs low. Acquiring these data periodically, such as every year, would allow SSA to set more flexible individualized diary dates, identify new rules for setting diary types, and more accurately target cases for full medical reviews.

Cost Savings

- Change (or lack thereof) in WD-FAB scores can be used to detect changes in functioning status between initial determination and CDR
- Improved timeliness of adjudication by identifying claimant's functional domains of greatest impairment
- Detection of unexpected functional improvement between diary dates

Web-based self-service application for uploading recent medical evidence

The development of a web-based application for claimants and their representatives can expand upon existing SSA efforts to support electronic rather than paper claims submissions. SSA applicants and beneficiaries should be permitted to upload medical evidence while their cases are not actively under review. Once an adjudicator "checks out" a case to begin actively working on it, the system would temporarily restrict applicants' and beneficiaries' ability to upload new evidence. At the beginning of the process, applicants should be informed that the timely upload of information is advised, and that their ability to make uploads will be temporarily suspended while the case is actively under review. When uploading medical evidence, users should be required to provide the date of service and to select what type of document they are uploading (e.g. doctor's notes, radiology report, laboratory findings, etc.) to mimic SSA's current process of labeling files. The options may change according to the information provided, such as impairments, body systems affected, etc. Statistical models can be used to identify potentially missing types of information and to request that users upload it or provide an explanation as to why it is not available.

Major Challenges

- Changes to operational structure are needed in order to take advantage of frequent and "real time" updating of claimant records
- Integration with existing databases and SSA efforts

Interim Steps

- Assess the feasibility of expanding the existing online disability application system to allow uploads of medical evidence in an effort to reduce duplication
- Identify key stakeholders and engage them throughout the process
- Create a strategy for labeling documents based on body systems and impairments
- Identify the application requirements for the back end and for the user interface. Allow flexibility for later adding the collection of WD-FAB and the use of statistical models to identify potentially missing information.
- Develop the application (using Agile project management techniques (Highsmith 2004)) and perform quality testing before rollout
- Deploy the application in beta mode and allow time to fix issues before using the information collected in the adjudication process
- Start using uploaded data in the adjudication process
- Build and test statistical models of medical evidence necessary based on case characteristics and add corresponding functionality to the online application

Critical Success Factors

- Engaging key stakeholders to determine how to best make use of uploaded medical information in the adjudication process
- Maintaining the trust of claimants in the security of their data and its use by SSA.

The automatic collection of medical and functional evidence in structured format through efficient IT applications would enable automatic integrity checks, a speedier grasp of medical evidence that could lead to faster, more efficient decisions, and the development of data analytics projects for finding patterns in the medical evidence. These projects could lead to faster, less costly, and more consistent decisions for specific subsets of applicants, as in the example of the Compassionate Allowances. The implementation of an application to allow beneficiaries and their representatives to upload their own medical information and keep their files current would allow an improved targeting of cases for full medical review and a faster, cheaper case development process. Having this medical evidence would make the full medical development of a case less costly and time consuming.

Cost Savings

- Improvements to CDR decision timeliness and accuracy
- Enhanced decision-making for full medical CDR targeting in advance of claimant diary dates

Automatic collection of electronic medical records and administrative data

Automatic collection and leveraging of electronic medical records such as Medicare and Medicaid data, data from other health insurers, and electronic medical records from providers and pharmacies could help SSA more accurately target CDR cases for full medical reviews, to corroborate information submitted by beneficiaries, and to monitor adherence to prescribed treatment. SSA is already partnering with CMS to obtain CMS data and use it to take people out of the CDR full medical review queue if their administrative claims data shows evidence of continued impairments. CMS has been going through an extensive IT modernization process that should allow real-time information sharing with SSA in the future. SSA should continue to make efforts to gain access to provider electronic health records and to drive the policy changes necessary for the standardization of these records and for the ensured seamless communication and information transfer between electronic health record systems.

Major Challenges

- Under the current agreement, CMS data can only be used by SSA to support continuances
- Real-time downloading from CMS and provider databases requires compatible structures and careful coordination
- Multitude of health care providers need to be convinced to participate in automatic data-sharing agreements
- The transfer of information between different types of electronic health record systems is sometimes difficult or impossible.

Interim Steps

- Organize presentation to SSA stakeholders by CMS representatives on recent database changes that allowed improved access and use of CMS data by researchers
- Pilot efforts to expand existing SSA-CMS coordination on sharing of Medicare health records
- Use lessons from the CMS partnership to inform planning by SSA stakeholders in designing a web portal that facilitates the transfer of claimant medical records from insurers and health professionals

Critical Success Factors

- Partnership with CMS at a higher level to facilitate timely transfer of data to SSA
- Applying lessons from CMS to data-sharing agreements with other insurers and providers
- Coordinated modernization of SSA IT systems

DATA ANALYTICS AND PREDICTIVE MODELING TO IMPROVE ASPECTS OF THE CDR PROCESS

The Problem

SSA administers a very complicated and compartmentalized adjudication system which relies on many rules and policies that are not evidence-based and that have not been updated in a long time. The creation of this system was necessary at the inception of the SSI and SSDI programs. However, advances in technology have changed how organizations are run. Our world today is marked by an overabundance of information. Powerful big data analytics solutions are now being used to analyze this explosion of information and to fundamentally change the way organizations manage their daily operation. The advantages that can be gained from data analytics are substantial. Insights from big data analytics have helped organizations differentiate themselves from their competition and gain a stronger foothold in their market. SSA could benefit tremendously from integrating big data and analytics into its business processes and using them to inform policies. The agency should analyze the tremendous amount of data it collects and generates to discover new insights and previously hidden correlations. These new insights can be used to reduce latency in decision-making and to increase the consistency of decisions and the efficiency of the disability adjudication processes.

Recommendations

Areas of the CDR process where data analytics can have a strong impact are outlined below.

1. Using data and text mining to improve medical diary designations (MIE/MIP/MINE designations)
2. Setting individualized diary dates using periodic scores and historical CDR decisions
3. Checking for adherence to prescribed treatment using CMS and other electronic claims data

Data and text mining to improve medical diary designations

Medical diary designations are based on rules developed in the early 1990s that have not been updated. The MINE rules were developed in a data-driven fashion, using historical SSA decisions. The MIE rules were based on a medical literature review. The MIP category includes everyone not in the MIE or MINE groups, and consists of roughly 60 percent of SSA beneficiaries. Recent medical advances have made new treatments, medications, medical equipment, and assistive devices readily available to individuals with disabilities. Regular updates of medical diary designation rules are thus necessary in order to keep the rules relevant. Furthermore, since there is usually a multiyear period between two CDRs for the same beneficiary, medical advances may change that individual's diary designation before their case matures. Being able to reclassify individuals' diary designations periodically, between consecutive CDRs, in order to take into account medical advances and individual functional and medical data available since the last review may lead to significant improvements in the CDR process.

We recommend using data analytics to devise new rules for setting the diary type by leveraging functional and medical evidence, medical literature, and current SSA compassionate allowance and medical listings data. This process can be done incrementally, based on the types of functional and medical evidence available. We also recommend automatic periodic updates to individual diary designations by collecting and utilizing new data sources and by accounting for medical advances. A predictive model for individual medical diary designations could be created if enough of the relevant functional and medical evidence were collected or extracted. In addition, the periodic collection of Work Disability Functional Assessment Battery (WD-FAB) scores would allow for creation of a functional decline or improvement curve that would help measure the expectation of medical improvement and thus assist in the setting of the diary. The optimal periodicity for collecting WD-FAB scores and updating individual medical diary designations should be evaluated in a data-driven fashion. Performing these updates yearly will likely lead to optimal results. Below is a description of how various types of data can be used to improve MIE/MIP/MINE rules and individual medical diary designations. Note, though, that any changes to medical diary designation rules identified using data analytics methods should be evaluated and confirmed by medical experts.

Medical Diary Designation Rules

1. Medical listings, impairments, and historic CDR decisions

The SSA medical listings (including compassionate allowances), impairments, and relevant beneficiary characteristics (such as age and education) could be used in conjunction with historical CDR decisions to create new MINE rules. Medical listings and compassionate allowances allow SSA to target the most obviously disabled individuals for allowances based on objective medical information that can be obtained quickly. Presumably, individuals who meet the medical listings are also some of the least likely to improve because they have some of the most disabling impairments. Therefore, we propose using data analytics to identify combinations of characteristics of beneficiaries (met medical listings, impairments, etc.) that, according to death records and historical CDR decisions, indicate benefits are never or almost never ceased. A description of pattern recognition methodology that could be used to create new rules is provided in Appendix A. An issue of concern regarding this model is the availability of an accurately labeled dataset representative of the distribution of CDR cases. Theoretically, if all CDRs were performed accurately and on time, this dataset would be available. However, the limitations introduced by the delays in performing CDRs and the decision to revert to mailers more in some years than others need to be evaluated.

2. Medical and functional information extracted from beneficiaries' electronic folder

Medical information extracted from beneficiaries' electronic folders could be used to find additional MINE rules by expanding the set of individual characteristics or variables used in the method described above.

Medical evidence can also be used to find possible medical advances, and thus to eliminate old MINE rules or identify new MIE rules. Natural language processing methods can be used to extract relevant information from unstructured text. Such information includes a complete list of the beneficiary's impairments, symptoms, medications, procedures, and laboratory tests, as well as the frequency of different types of doctors' visits and procedures. While information extraction will never be 100 percent accurate, it can be very useful in identifying previously unknown associations. Information extracted from medical records can be used to estimate the distribution of disability benefits applications and determination decisions given specific case characteristics.

Changes in the distribution of recent applications for disability benefits can be used to identify medical advances and, potentially, to eliminate old MINE rules. Similarly, decreases in approval rates for cases with certain characteristics can also signal medical advances.

It may also be possible to identify changes in treatment by comparing the medical records of beneficiaries with similar impairments and case characteristics using natural language processing methods.

3. Work Disability Functional Assessment Battery scores

The acquisition of yearly WD-FAB scores would eventually lead to creation of a dataset that could be used to identify better medical diary designation rules. The timeliness and frequency of full medical CDRs and the lack of functional information during the period in between full medical reviews pose significant statistical challenges to using Residual Functional Capacity (RFC) forms or historical CDR decisions to mine for medical diary designation rules. Thus, a gold standard on individuals' medical improvement does not exist in the current SSA data. Administering the WD-FAB annually would provide the gold standard "labels" necessary to mine for medical diary rules or to create a medical diary predictive model without the high cost of conducting full medical reviews often and on all individuals. These scores would be similar in cost to the CDR mailer, but they would provide a far better picture of a person's functional abilities and changes in these abilities over time. Learning about these changes is necessary to more accurately predict medical improvement at the time of adjudication.

4. Medical claims records

Medicare, Medicaid, and other health insurance claims records offer structured data that could be used to identify medical advances. This data can be used to identify new medication, devices, and treatment options, and link these advances to changes in survival rate or changes in the number of applications for disability benefits.

Automatic Individual Diary Designations

Data analytics can be used to update medical diary designation rules and to create new rules. However, it is also necessary to understand which subgroups of current beneficiaries are affected by these changes. For example, when identifying medical advances, it is important to be able to identify which subgroups of SSA beneficiaries could benefit from these medical advances and to update the probability of their MINE/MIP/MIE designation. This can be done by comparing the medical records of beneficiaries to those of people who benefited from new medical advances. Other techniques include using a more comprehensive, web-based version of the mailer that includes the acquisition of WD-FAB scores and also asks questions pertinent to medical advances to those individuals to whom the medical advances might apply. It is important to note that environmental factors may make medical advances and assistive devices inaccessible to some claimants. All pertinent factors should be taken into account when determining continuing disability status. The automatic individual medical diary designation should only be used to determine the likelihood of medical improvement and the frequency of review.

The change in an individual's functional ability measures is the most relevant information related to the medical diary designation. If functional ability were measured over time, it would be possible to estimate a mapping between CDR cessation decisions and changes in functional ability. The yearly acquisition of WD-FAB scores could be used to estimate functional improvement or decline curves and to set the optimal functional thresholds for performing full medical CDRs. Medical advances, WD-FAB scores, mailer information, medical records uploaded online, and administrative health records from insurers can be used to update individual diary designations annually, with small additional costs.

An updated, improved, and possibly more detailed medical diary designation based on medical evidence collected between full medical reviews, at very low costs, would constitute a highly predictive input variable for the CDR predictive model.

Individualized diary dates

Diary dates indicate when cases become due for CDRs, and thus the frequency of CDRs. SSA intends to review cases every five to seven years, every three years, or every six to 18 months depending on the medical diary designation. These time periods are selected from a programmatic perspective and are not tightly linked to evidence related to medical improvement. If cases are reviewed too early, SSA incurs unnecessary administrative costs and beneficiaries have to go through the emotional hurdle of unnecessary full medical reviews. On the other hand, if cases are reviewed too late, SSA may make unnecessary payments to beneficiaries who no longer meet program eligibility requirements. Individualized diary dates could be set to find the optimal functional threshold to perform a full medical CDR, provided that periodic functional information such as WD-FAB scores was acquired. As individualized diary dates would be determined by a predictive model, this would also result in more consistent and equitable treatment of claimants and beneficiaries by removing the examiner-level variation in setting of diary dates.

Checking adherence to prescribed treatment

One other area where data analytics could be used to identify individuals who may benefit from special interventions is in automatically checking for adherence to treatment. We propose using administrative data and electronic health records to track adherence to treatment and to identify beneficiaries who are not following their prescribed treatments. Early intervention and support given through an SSA program could help these beneficiaries to improve their health faster.

If beneficiaries are unwilling to follow prescribed treatment that may improve their functional abilities, these individuals should undergo a thorough full medical review. SSA needs to determine if the treatment is prescribed by the treating source, is expected to restore ability to work, and whether it is justifiable not to follow the treatment. If these conditions are not met, SSA policy dictates that these individuals' benefits should be ceased. Estimating if a treatment has the potential to improve functioning can be done by examining whether there are a significant number of SSA beneficiaries with similar case characteristics who followed the prescribed treatment and whose function improved.

In its May 2014 audit report, "Medical Improvement Review Standard During Continuing Disability Reviews," the OIG found that in 2012, the DDSs used MIRS exceptions in 9,517 cases of the 39,660 cases where benefits were ceased.

Of those 9,517 cases where MIRS exceptions were used, the Group II exception "failure to follow prescribed treatment" was used in only 22 (SSA OIG 2014b). Further investigation is necessary to determine whether this exception is underutilized or whether there are very few instances of this exception actually occurring. If the exception is underutilized because of lack of relevant data or a lack of instructions on how to make such a determination, then a data analytics solution may be helpful.

Implementation

Data analytics can have a tremendous impact on the efficiency and consistency of the CDR pro- gram. However, the success of the analytics efforts described above depends on the acquisition and ease of access to functional and medical data of good quality. A set of major challenges is provided below.

Major Challenges

- Lack of structured medical and functional information
- Structured data lying in silos across the organization
- Difficulty accessing scanned medical evidence in bulk
- Dependence on legacy systems for data processing and management
- Lack of IT infrastructure for "big data" predictive analytics
- Lack of IT infrastructure dedicated to IT demonstration projects
- Difficulty identifying and engaging stakeholders and users early in the process
- Developing strong but flexible security policies and guidelines that allow the use of open source software and other technologies prevalent in industry

The implementation of data analytics to improve medical diary designations and dates and to check adherence to prescribed treatment should follow a phased approach, with more sources of data being built in at every stage. To ensure the success and validity of these methods, they need to be implemented in an environment where their performance can be monitored and incremental updates and improvements can be made over time. A list of interim steps for deploying such applications is presented below.

Interim Steps

- Identify key stakeholders and put together a comprehensive list of assumptions, existing practices, goals, requirements, and measures of success
- Retrieve relevant historical data; start with existing data to achieve near-term results and build in new data through phased approach
- Implement method prototypes and test on simulation data, historical data, and possibly new data
- Perform cost-benefit analysis based on prototype and historical data
- Dedicate IT infrastructure environment for testing/demonstration of promising methods
- Implement method inside SSA IT infrastructure; try to automate data access
- Perform demonstration study (e.g. use the method for one DDS, one program, or in con- junction with current method, etc.); ensure validation sample is available and demonstration is performed in such a way that performance can be evaluated
- Perform cost-benefit analysis based on demonstration
- Document a detailed project plan for mitigating pilot into production
- Deploy application globally; ensure validation samples are available and deployment is per- formed in a way that facilitates performance evaluation
- Integrate model with other applications or models
- Train and engage users
- Refine, improve, and monitor the validity of models over time
- Quantify returns of investment

The success of the data analytics methods suggested is dependent on the willingness to make changes to the current workflow. Without a strong desire for change, the adoption of these methods will be deterred by inflexible workflows and the benefits will be marginal. Below, we identified some critical success factors.

Critical Success Factors

- Trust in and understanding of the methodologies and their applications from users
- Sufficient data
- Well-defined performance metrics
- Applying Agile project management methodology (Highsmith 2004) to allow for a sufficient level of interactions between users and developers

- Adoption by users
- Strong model life-cycle management
- Deployment platform that allows regular model validation and testing

While highly cost-effective, the current CDR predictive model results in an average cessation rate of only 6 percent (SSAB 2014). If the model had 100 percent accuracy, then only cases leading to benefit cessations would undergo full medical reviews. An accurate model would be advantageous to all. It would allow SSA to cut the costs of unnecessary reviews and it would save beneficiaries the stress of undergoing a full medical CDR. Due to the lack of availability and access to medical and functional data, the current CDR predictive model uses very little medical evidence, even though this evidence is the most relevant when it comes to medical improvement. The current model uses only program data such as age, impairments, length of time in disability status, basis for the original determination, data on prior CDRs, and recent earnings as the variables for its estimations (SSA 2012). Thus, any of the steps described above are likely to increase the accuracy of the model significantly. This would result in substantial savings to SSA. As an exercise, let's assume that SSA performs 280,000 full medical reviews per year and that the rate of cessation is 6 percent. Let's assume that a full medical review costs $914, and a mailer costs $24. Let's also assume that the number of cessations remains the same (16,800), but that the predictive model gets better at identifying these cases. If the cessation rate for the CDR predictive model were 25 percent, 50 percent, or 75 percent, that would result in administrative savings of $190 million, $220 million, or $230 million, respectively. Below is a list of cost savings that would be generated from the use of data analytics to extract information from medical evidence.

Cost Savings

- Lower administrative costs through more accurate targeting of cases for full medical review
- Identification of insights that can lead to listings-type rules that reduce processing time and backlogs
- Enhancements to program integrity by improving the consistency of the CDR process.

DYNAMIC PRIORITIZATION QUEUE FOR OPTIMIZING THE PROCESSING OF NEW AND BACKLOGGED CDR CASES UNDER FUNDING CONSTRAINTS

The Problem

In recent years, SSA has cited resource limitations, a greater emphasis on processing initial claims, and requests for hearings appeals as challenges for conducting large numbers of CDRs despite the consistently favorable ratio of savings-to-costs generated by these reviews. According to OIG estimates, performing full medical reviews in a timely manner could save SSA billions of dollars per year (SSA OIG 2010). Without a mechanism to provide annual designated CDR funding, SSA is having difficulty performing full medical reviews when they become due. Given this reality, an optimal strategy for setting the order in which due and past due medical reviews are performed is necessary in order to maximize efficient use of resources. Furthermore, current SSA business processes are unable to reclassify cases in the backlog in light of new evidence before they are reviewed, other than through the yearly reclassifications of the CDR predictive model. As the predictive model does not incorporate medical records or functional information directly, this may result in wasted resources performing reviews that are no longer likely to result in cessations. Additionally, the desired frequency of CDR reviews (every six to 18 months, three years, or five to seven years) determined at the setting of the medical diary setting is chosen without the guidance of any scientific evidence to ensure consistent and accurate entry.

Recommendations

In order to efficiently make use of limited CDR funding, we recommend that SSA:

1. Prioritize CDR workload assignments according to their probability of cessation and expected lifetime savings
2. Update the priority queue yearly at the end of each fiscal cycle to support budgetary decisions on CDR funding levels
3. Reprioritize cases in the queue biannually or quarterly in light of any new data sources obtained, as described earlier in this paper

The SSA's Office of the Chief Actuary currently estimates the average cost-benefits of performing CDRs each year. These recommendations propose to take this office's work further by estimating individual, rather than aggregate, cost-benefits and then making use of these statistics to improve cost efficiency of the business process. The accumulated expertise and insight of the office of the Chief Actuary will be invaluable when developing the proposed individualized expected lifetime savings model.

Implementation

The proposed changes in the current CDR business processes pose significant organizational challenges. This proposal involves the use of a model for setting individualized diary dates, the creation of an automated CDR case queue, and the automation of the current CDR workload assignment process. Automating CDR case assignments would mean that cases at the front of the queue would be assigned to an adjudicator who could not open new CDR cases until the ones initially assigned are closed. While these steps are likely to result in organizational hurdles, we believe they are necessary for optimizing the use of resources and maximizing savings. Issues of fairness may be raised regarding the ordering of the queue according to expected lifetime savings if insufficient funding for CDRs is available to prevent a backlog in the queue forming from year to year. While we believe that a resource optimization strategy is justified, the queue could be ordered according to alternative measures, such as the likelihood of cessation.

Major Challenges

- Necessary changes in business processes could be challenging and time consuming
- Current IT infrastructure may not allow for implementation of a queue-based CDR case assignment strategy
- Ability of the queue to optimize CDR spending depends upon quality of CDR predictive model and estimate of lifetime savings

The expected lifetime savings for a case is the product of the likelihood of cessation and the lifetime savings generated by a cessation. The CDR predictive model will provide the expected likelihood of cessation initially. The lifetime savings generated by a cessation needs to be estimated, and will take into account the monthly payout, the cost of associated expenses such as Medicare, the likelihood of return to the rolls in the future, and time until retirement age. The queue will order cases by estimated lifetime savings. When a beneficiary's diary has matured, their case will be adjudicated at that time if the expected savings would place them at the front of the queue. Set up that way, the queue need only be determined once a year as it can include any backlogged cases as well as all those coming due that fiscal year. The use of the queue would ensure that cases are always processed according to their current expected savings, thus resulting in the most efficient use of resources regardless of the amount of CDR funding available. Once implemented, these steps will result in a more efficient business process and greater program savings.

If an extended version of the CDR predictive model was developed that included functional or more detailed medical information, its predictions of the likelihood of cessation could replace those of the existing CDR model at that time. Once the extended model was developed and validated, its implementation in the queue would be straightforward. To minimize disruptions to business practices, it is recommended that the extended version not be used to determine queue size and order until the start of the following fiscal year. Similarly, once the model for individualized diary dates has been created and validated, its diary date determinations can be incorporated into the queue without changing how the queue itself is set up.

Interim Steps

- Estimate expected lifetime savings using existing CDR predictive model
- Create the queue using current diary dates and expected cost-benefits
- Develop models as described in the previous section to implement extensions of the CDR predictive model or individualized diary dates
- Use the updated CDR predictive model and/or individualized diary dates to improve the queue
- Perform cost-benefit analysis of changing business processes to include queue-based workload assignment
- If indicated, create the infrastructure necessary for the queue-based workload assignment, test, and deploy it using a phased approach and sound project management techniques.

Critical Success Factors

- Acquiring large quantities of functional data on claimants through WD-FAB or suitable medical records to inform an improved CDR predictive model
- Modernized IT system that allows for automatic workload assignments
- Willingness to rethink and optimize business processes, not just make the minimal changes necessary.

Through determination of queue size and expected cost-benefits of those in the queue, SSA and Congress would have a valuable tool in future discussions of the CDR budget. As the first cases in the queue would be the most cost-effective, if insufficient funding was available to prevent a backlog in a given year the queue would support the efficient allocation of funds. The queue would also aid in clarifying the short-term CDR funding versus long-term program solvency tradeoffs by enabling estimation of the cost of not performing CDRs on those cases that may be backlogged for a year in absence of funding for clearing the queue.

Cost Savings

- Computation time to update predictions and sort into the queue is not expensive or lengthy
- Optimizes money spent on CDRs in years when there is insufficient funding to complete all cases coming due
- No additional expenses in years SSA has funding to clear any CDR backlog and all cases coming due

SUMMARY

Our proposals for improving the medical continuing disability review process have been developed and presented in such a way that we hope emphasizes not only the need for greater system consensus, but also the importance of having a strong technology foundation in order to build up specific program initiatives. These recommendations are meant to work seamlessly and in support of each other. The Enterprise Data Environment would be the backbone of SSA's data and technology systems, allowing for the easy storage and retrieval of data as would be necessary for the optimal use of data acquisition and analytics proposed in our second and third recommendations. For the CDR program specifically, once SSA has a comprehensive and flexible IT infrastructure, it will be possible to collect, store, and analyze data that can then be used to build and update the predictive models that generate the queue for processing CDRs. The connections among the recommendations are underscored by the fact that often the major challenges and critical success factors of one solution are addressed by the ones that come before it. To see the specific connections, we can think through the proposals in reverse order of suggestion. The three recommendations made for establishing a queue for optimizing CDR case processing are all initiatives that can be started right away. These recommendations fit into the business practice as it exists now, but they would be more effective with additional changes, most notably with the addition of predictive analytics. The data analytics recommended above would provide more accurate probabilities of cessation, which would improve the ordering of the queue. But these data analytics also rely on access to the most relevant and up-to-date medical and functional evidence, which is best collected periodically and stored in data environments that allow for easy access for adjudicators and researchers alike. The following is a possible course of immediate next steps, which can be taken either sequentially or concurrently:

Immediate Next Steps

- Conduct study of current diary designation system and history to evaluate its accuracy
- Identify key stakeholders in each initiative and ensure the relevant participants are engaged throughout the process
- Update SSA regulations on medical CDR diary designations to allow for more flexible and individualized diary dates
- Use WD-FAB validation studies to determine optimal use of WD-FAB scores with SSA business practices, which may include CDR-specific uses such as collecting scores with the current mailer or more program-wide uses such as collecting scores at time of initial application
- Designate medical and policy experts to review MINE/MIP/MIE designation rules and compare them with other SSA medical listings to check for disparities
- Begin collection of historical data relevant for comparison in order to update MINE/MIP/MIE designation rules
- Introduce a case processing queue to the current CDR processing system that will be updated annually
- Work with the Office of the SSA Chief Actuary to collect accurate figures for shifting current CDR predictive model to order cases in the queue by expected lifetime savings
- Develop an automated system to deliver CDR cases to adjudicators that will only release the next case when the file is closed
- Investigate data-mining techniques for pulling from SSA's electronic folders system evidence that could be relevant to medical diary designations
- Assess the feasibility of expanding the existing online disability application system to allow electronic completion of SSA forms and the uploading of medical evidence
- Open dialogue with CMS about improved access, exchange, and use of data

In addition to improving the CDR process and handling the backlog, these strategies for improving information technology, data collection, and analytics are also critical to supporting other SSA programs and initiatives. Having a more comprehensive IT infrastructure with access to data that are then available for analytics will increase the overall efficiency of any type of case processing and will eliminate most need for repetition or rework. Most of the proposed methods or applications are flexible enough that they could be adapted to other areas. For example, the queue could be expanded to handle initial claims cases in addition to CDR cases. This might be an eventual application that would also address the issue of CDRs being overlooked in order to work more initial cases. Systems that centralize information to both ensure consistency and remove duplication are also key for fraud detection and prevention. In a special report from September 2014, the OIG pointed to both the disparity of the DDS systems and the lack of a comprehensive records profile and search system as significant vulnerabilities that leave the agency at a disadvantage for detecting or preventing fraudulent activity (SSA OIG 2014c). Both of these are issues that the recommendations provided in this paper will naturally address and correct.

CONCLUSION

In this paper, we proposed modernizing SSA IT infrastructure to better support business processes, automatically store data generated through these processes, and integrate analytics-optimized systems and insights into the agency's adjudication process. We believe that a large-scale approach to data storage and IT infrastructure designed to handle the magnitude and complexity of the agency's data is the most cost-effective long-term solution. This type of approach can dramatically increase the efficiency, consistency, and timeliness of the SSA adjudication process in general, and the CDR process in particular. We proposed specific data analytics projects that could improve parts of the CDR process and result in considerable savings to the agency while being advantageous for its disability beneficiaries. Some details and implementation challenges of these proposals remain to be worked out. However, we believe that this paper serves as a good starting point for an open discussion about SSA's IT modernization efforts and how the agency might benefit from large-scale big-data analytics projects.

Pattern Recognition Methodology for Identifying New MINE Rules

Assume we have a labeled dataset, where the data points correspond to an individual's characteristics (met a specific medical listing, impairments, age, education, etc.), and an associated label, seven-year-cessation, which is a binary variable that is true if the beneficiary had his or her benefits ceased within seven years of the previous decision, and false if the beneficiary either died within seven years of the previous decision or had a CDR and their benefits were not ceased. We are using the seven-year mark because MINE cases are supposed to be reviewed every seven years. However, if the historical data show that these cases are generally reviewed less often, this threshold can be adjusted. Given this labeled dataset, an ensemble of decision trees can be used to identify case characteristics associated with a low probability of seven-year-cessation. A decision tree is a predictive model that maps observations about an item to conclusions about that item's label. In a decision tree, leaves represent class labels and branches represent conjunctions of features that lead to those class labels. The goal is to predict the label based on several input variables. A tree can be learned by iteratively splitting the data into subsets based on variable value tests. This process is repeated on each derived subset in a recursive manner, until the subset at a node has all the same value of the target variable or splitting any further no longer adds value to the prediction. The splitting variable at each step is usually selected as the variable that best reduces the "impurity" of the labels in the resulting subsets. In a decision tree, all paths from the root node to a leaf node proceed by way of conjunctions. If the leaf contains data with a very low probability of seven-year-cessation, then these conjunctions can be used to form a MINE rule. In order to maximize the chance of identifying MINE rules, we can search over a set of decision trees by using a randomized procedure to select splitting variables at each node.

Acknowledgement

We thank Dr. Xuan Che for his assistance compiling a list of cost estimates related to the CDR process.

7

Social Security Disability Adjudicative Reform: Ending the Reconsideration Stage of SSDI Adjudication after Sixteen Years of Testing and Enhancing Initial Stage Record Development

Jon C. Dubin

INTRODUCTION

The Social Security Administration's (SSA) system of administrative adjudication of disability claims has been referred to as "the largest adjudicative agency in the western world" (Mashaw et al. 1978). It processes nearly three million new claims and issues over four million decisions at its various stages each year (SSA 2015b, 143). SSA system contains a four-stage adjudication process. The first two stages are an initial application and reconsideration stage before the state disability determination services agencies (DDS). The latter two stages are hearings and appeals at SSA Office of Disability Adjudication and Review's (ODAR) hearing offices and Appeals Council, respectively.

The vast majority of agency decision-making is done at the first two levels of adjudication before the state (DDS) agencies. Whereas over 3.5 million claims are processed annually at the first two levels—most at the initial stage—less than one million are handled at the latter two hearings and appeals stages (SSA 2015b, 143). Thus, to avert the common criticism that debates about SSA adjudicative process have "an instinct for the capillary" by focusing largely on reform of the more newsworthy hearings and appeals stages rather than the largely "invisible" yet far more numerically significant DDS stages (Mashaw et al. 1984, 19), this paper will focus on the earlier two stages.

Of the approximately 750,000 claims handled at the reconsideration stage each year, only approximately 11 percent obtain a different outcome than at the first or initial stage of the process. This compares with a claimant success rate at the initial stage of approximately 32 percent, and a 45 percent rate of change or claim approval at the Administrative Law Judge (ALJ) stage (SSA 2015b, 143). For over 30 years, the agency, at Congress's urging, has itself formally questioned the efficacy and efficiency of continuing the reconsideration step, at least in its current form; it has piloted alterations or eliminations of reconsideration since 1984.[1] SSA is currently testing an elimination of reconsideration in 10states with an initially announced goal of eliminating the reconsideration stage nationally.[2] That goal has not been realized and the testing, while continuing at least through the Fall 2015 and likely thereafter,[3] was proposed for a reduction in scope by the most recently confirmed SSA commissioner (SSA 2010a, 13), thus calling into question SSA's present policy direction on this issue.

This paper argues that SSA is well overdue for eliminating the reconsideration stage once and for all and streamlining the adjudicative process from four stages to three.[4] The reasons provided for not acting on the initial plan to abolish the

1 See Pub. L. No. 98-860, § 6(d), (e), 98 Stat. 1794, 1802-03 (Oct. 9, 1984).

2 Process Re-engineering Program; Disability Reengineering Project Plan, 59 Fed. Reg. 47,887 (Sept. 14, 1994); Modifications to the Disability Determination Procedures; Disability Claims Process Redesign Prototype, 64 Fed. Reg. 47,218, 47,219 (Aug. 20, 1999); New Disability Claims Process, 66 Fed. Reg. 5494 (Jan. 19, 2001).

3 *See* 79 Fed. Reg. 39,453 (July 10, 2014).

4 Some studies have also questioned the continued need for and utility of the Appeals Council. *See, e.g.,* Koch and Koplow (1990). The Appeals Council has a remand rate of only 14 percent and a reversal rate of only 1 percent (SSA 2016b, 143). This has led to proposals and pilot projects for the elimination of this fourth adjudicative stage as well. *See, e.g.,* Administrative Review Process, Testing Elimination of the Fourth Step of Administrative Review in the Disability Claims Process (Request for Review by the Appeals Council), 62 Fed. Reg. 49,598 (Sept. 23, 1997); see also 59 Fed. Reg. 47,887, 47,917-18 (Sept. 19, 1994). However, the Appeals Council provides a different and potentially more policy-oriented agency review stage to observe trends and make policy decisions about the handling of types or patterns of cases and issues before those cases enter the federal courts for judicial review. See SSA HALLEX II-5-0-1, 2003 WL 25498917, at *1 ("The Appeals Council is admirably well-suited and well-situated to serve a major role in promoting policy integrity. The Appeals Council is the only unit in SSA which regularly receives and adjudicates a broad run of

reconsideration process provide insufficient policy justification and perhaps even questionable legal rationale for continuing this highly inefficient stage.[5]

In addition, during the same greater than 30-year period that SSA has experimented with altering reconsideration, it has also, at the direction of Congress, experimented with ways to promote greater record development at the initial determination stage to enhance the decisional value of this stage.[6] While some limited progress has been made in this area, this paper also includes a series of recommendations to make the initial stage more meaningful to promote greater decisional fairness, consistency, efficiency and integrity in lieu of and with a diversion of focus, resources and person power from the largely superfluous, rubber stamp reconsideration stage. These measures seek to promote fuller record development at the initial stage to better mirror well-developed administrative records adjudicated at the third (ALJ hearing) adjudication stage in order to reach more accurate decisions earlier in the process.[7]

---

ordinary and extraordinary cases."). As such, the Appeals Council furthers more classical administrative exhaustion functions than what is essentially a do-over of the initial stage through the reconsideration process. See generally McCarthy (1992) describing purposes of the administrative exhaustion doctrine such as protecting agency autonomy and promoting judicial efficiency. Thus, whatever can be argued about the utility and efficacy of the Appeals Council stage, stronger and more obvious rationale is manifest for eliminating the largely repetitive and duplicative reconsideration process.

5 See *infra* text accompanying note 17-18, 80 (discussing the potential for creating excessive and unreasonable delay in contravention of 42 U.S.C. § 405(b) and the Due Process Clause and the potential legal issues raised by bureaucratic disentitlement).

6 See Pub. L. No. 98-860, § 6(d), (e), 98 Stat. 1794, 1802-03 (Oct. 9, 1984)

7 This is not to imply that all hearing stage cases have well-developed records but only that the ALJs possess tools and a culture established to promote greater development through, face-to-face inquiry, identification of evidentiary lapses, subpoena power to order evidence, and the ability to procure the testimony of medical advisors and vocational experts. See Dubin and Rains (2012), 113-14. As such, fuller record development than what occurs at the DDS is the norm. Nevertheless, federal case law is replete with examples of inadequate record development at the ALJ stage necessitating court remands for additional development, particularly in cases where claimants lack attorney representation. See Kubitschek and Dubin (2015), §§ 6:8, 6:9, 6:11, 6:12, 6:17 (collecting cases); see also Sims (2000) noting that a large and significant number of claimants either lack attorney representation or any representation in SSA hearings.

THE PROBLEM

Discussion: Reconsideration Structure

The Social Security Administration (SSA) utilizes a four- stage administrative adjudicative process for the disposition of claims under the Social Security Disability Insurance (SSDI) and Supplemental Security Income Disability (SSID) programs. A claimant initiates the process by filing an application online using SSA website or at one of SSA's district or branch offices.[8] SSA district office determines financial or non-disability eligibility and, if such eligibility is found, forwards the claim to a state agency operating as the state's federally funded Disability Determination Service (DDS) pursuant to SSA regulations (SSA 2015a).[9]

The state's DDS proceeds to develop the claim by seeking medical records and reports from the claimants' treating sources, hospitals, and clinics. If those records or documents are unavailable or insufficient to make a determination, "the DDS will arrange for a consultative examination (CE) to obtain the additional information needed" (SSA 2015a). Although SSA regulations designate the claimant's treating physician as the preferred source for the CE,[10] the DDS rarely obtains the CE from treating sources (Wittenberg et al. 2012, 26).[11] After completing its development of the evidence, the DDS then usually employs a two-person team consisting of an internal medical or psychological consultant and a disability examiner to determine the DDS's initial disability decision (SSA 2015d).

After rendering its decision, the DDS returns the case to SSA field office for appropriate action. If the DDS found that the claimant is disabled, SSA completes any outstanding non-disability development, computes the benefit amount, and begins paying benefits. If the claimant was found not to be disabled, the file is

8 See 20 C.F.R. §§ 404.611, 404.614, 422.505(a) (2015). While claims under the SSI program utilize the same process, only the regulations pertaining to the SSDI program will be referenced henceforth.

9 20 C.F.R. § 404.1620 (2015).

10 See 20 C.F.R. §§ 404.1519h (2015); 416.919h (2015).

11 Aa study of CE evaluations found that in less than 5 percent of the cases were treating sources even requested to perform a needed CE evaluation and that none of the CEs in the study were ultimately performed by treating sources.

kept in the field office in case the claimant decides to appeal the determination to the next stage to obtain reconsideration.

The reconsideration stage is handled under the identical procedures as the initial application stage except that different personnel within the respective DDS offices make the reconsidered decisions.[12] The claimant can submit additional evidence at the reconsideration stage although is neither required to do so nor is informed of specific evidence that was lacking or ways to remedy those deficiencies through additional evidence. Nor is the DDS mandated to solicit additional evidence to address identified deficiencies at the initial stage, and additional development is largely focused on obtaining evidence only in the relatively limited situations where there is significant worsening in condition, new ailments (or allegations of the same) or newly developed evidence (SSA 2014).[13] With the exception of a pilot project conducted during the mid-1980s,[14] the claimant ordinarily does not appear in person before SSA or DDS decision makers during reconsideration of initial applications.

Evidence that Outlines or Quantifies the Problem

Although the number of applications to the disability programs appears to have crested and is on the decline, dropping from 3,391,000 initial disability claims in fiscal year 2011 to 3,207,000 in FY 2012 to 2,998,000 in FY 2013 to 2,862,000 in FY 2014 (SSA 2015c, 10), the present load is still considerable. In FY 2014, 32

---

12 See generally (SSA 2014) (noting the requirement of a different two-person DDS team than that used for the initial determination); (SSA 2013) (noting that the process is essentially the same for reconsideration as in initial application determinations except when there is a continuing disability review (CDR) in the case of a benefits termination decision which triggers resort to a DDS hearing examiner at the reconsideration stage).

13 "2. Case development at reconsideration. Once a reconsideration case on an initial claim has been received from the FO, the disability examiner is responsible for reviewing the case *to determine if additional development is warranted. If further case development is warranted*, the disability examiner:
Obtains additional information needed to document *new* allegations or *a worsening* of the claimant's condition (*e.g.*, SSA-3373 Function Report).
Contacts all medical sources from which the claimant received examination or treatment *since the initial determination* for any medical evidence they may be able to provide."
(emphasis added).

14 See, e.g., 54 Fed. Reg 54,533 (1993) (describing the 1984-87 Personal Appearance Demonstration (PAD) Pilot).

percent of initial claims were granted (SSA 2015b, 143). The average processing time from application to notification in 2014 was 110 days.

In the past year, 761,772 claimants appealed denial of their initial applications to the reconsideration stage. Eleven percent of the 744,336 reconsideration decisions were favorable and the other 89 percent were affirmed (SSA 2015b, 143). The average processing time at the reconsideration level was 108 days (SSA 2015c, 10). This reflects a significant increase over reconsideration processing times in prior decades (Bertoni 2007, 20).[15] To put this 108-day average reconsideration processing time in context, SSA has acknowledged before the United States Supreme Court, (*Heckler v. Day* 1983, 111)[16] and a lower court has ruled, (*Barnett v. Bowen* 1987)[17] that a reconsideration processing time in excess of 90 days is excessive and violates the Social Security Act's requirement in 42 U.S.C. § 405(b) that SSA agency action not be unreasonably delayed. Furthermore, the extended reconsideration processing times exacerbate a four-stage process with significant delays and time lapses at each of the other stages. Adjudicative delays at the other stages are also substantial. For example, the median adjudicative delay at the third (ALJ hearing) stage is up to 422 days from request to decision (SSA 2015c, 10).

Thus, by largely duplicating the initial application stage, the reconsideration stage is not designed to produce meaningful additional adjudicative benefits or results beyond those achieved at the prior stage. Its limited alteration rate is an inevitable byproduct of its limited design. As such, the reconsideration stage lacks meaningful or sound public policy justification. It mandates devotion of agency resources for an entire additional adjudicative stage with attendant personnel and administrative costs for three quarter of a million annual reconsideration decisions, imposes significant delays in adjudicative results for the vast majority of claims initially denied, and produces limited tangible adjudicative benefits.

---

15 Noting that the process from request for reconsideration to reconsidered decision had increased by 50 percent over the previous decade and had risen to 72 days by 2007.

16 SSA concedes before the U.S. Supreme Court that a 90-day or greater period between reconsideration request and reconsideration decision violates the Social Security Act's requirement in 42 U.S.C. § 405(b) that SSA agency action not be unreasonably delayed.

17 The court finds that excessive delays in reconsideration and hearing determinations defined, in the context of reconsideration determinations, as decisions exceeding greater than 90 days from reconsideration request, violate § 405(b) and it orders various forms of injunctive relief on behalf of delayed claimants.

Past Initiatives aimed at Addressing the Problem

For many years, SSA has experimented with eliminating or altering the reconsideration stage due to its limited benefits, and SSA is still testing the elimination of reconsideration at least until September 2015. In the Social Security Disability Benefits Reform Act of 1984 (DBRA), Congress mandated that SSA initiate demonstration projects in at least five states that would alter the process at the state DDS stages.[18] The Administrative Conference of the United States (ACUS) issued a report in 1987 discussing the rationale for and structure of the 1984 pilot project initiated pursuant to Congress's direction in the Act; ACUS interpreted the Act as a mandate for select DDS offices "to try a one-step proceeding, allowing a personal interview *but eliminating the reconsideration step*."[19] It noted that SSA's adjudicative process "has been subject to criticism" because, among other reasons, "the current system with its four tiers of successive reviews often results in the replacement of one decision maker's determination with that of the next, but without necessarily improving the quality of any of the actual decisions."[20] In that regard, it observed that the reconsideration stage was "*essentially a repeat of the initial determination process*."[21] Although SSA was required to report the project results to the House Ways and Means Committee no later than December 31, 1986, the agency" issued no final report" and "made no definitive findings" (Carrow 1994, 297).[22]

Then, in 1993, SSA proposed to test five models for altering the DDS stages of adjudication in order to: "provide assistance to the disability applicant by making the filing of a disability claim simpler, more responsive and more compassionate; promote fairness in each disability determination by ensuring that each disability applicant is given an opportunity to provide all the necessary information to complete the claim and is aware of his/her rights under the program; and ensure that the Agency's determination is both inclusive and equitable."[23] One model entitled "the reconsideration elimination model" was "designed to test whether

---

18 Pub.L. 98-860, § 6(d), (e), 98 Stat. 1794, 1802-03 (Oct. 9, 1984).

19 Administrative Conference of the United States, State Level Determinations in Social Security Disability Cases, ACUS No. 87-6 (Dec. 17, 1987), 52 Fed. Reg. 49,142 (Dec. 30, 1987) (emphasis added).

20 Ibid. (emphasis added).

21 Ibid. (emphasis added).

22 See 58 Fed. Reg. 54,533 (Oct. 22, 1993).

23 See Testing Modifications to the Disability Determination Procedures, 58 Fed. Reg. 54,532, 54,533 (Oct. 22, 1993).

the disability process is improved by the elimination of the reconsideration step."[24] Under this model, if a claimant was not satisfied with the initial determination, he or she could proceed directly to request a hearing before an ALJ.[25]

Just one year later, in 1994, the agency announced the more far-reaching Process Reengineering Program—Disability Reengineering Project Plan.[26] In the agency's words: "[t]he Process Reengineering Program essentially asks the question, 'If SSA had the opportunity today to design its processes, what would they look like?' In other words, 'how would we design a process if we were starting over?'"[27] The program's "objective is to fundamentally rethink and radically redesign SSA's processes to achieve dramatic improvements in critical measures of performance such as quality of service, speed and efficiency."[28] A component of the Reengineering Project Plan was the elimination of the reconsideration step which was planned to commence with further testing and then be "fully implemented nationwide" by FY 1998.[29] The agency noted that of all the proposed process and substantive changes to the disability determination process recommended in the Reengineering Project, the "most popular concept" reflected in the most frequently mentioned comments received during the agency's notice and comment period was the proposal to eliminate the reconsideration stage.[30]

After a few years of testing various aspects of the Reengineering Plan on a smaller scale,[31] SSA announced in 1999 that it was selecting 10 states, representing approximately 20 percent of all disability benefits applicants, for more focused testing of three aspects of the disability redesign process.[32] It noted that "several tests have been conducted" and as a result, the agency is "now announcing a prototype that incorporates multiple modifications to the disability determination procedures employed by State Disability Determination Services (DDS) which

24 Ibid. at 54,535.

25 Ibid.

26 Process Re-engineering Program; Disability Reengineering Project Plan, 59 Fed. Reg. 47,887 (Sept. 14, 1994).

27 Ibid.

28 Ibid.

29 Ibid. at 47, 923.

30 Ibid. at 47, 940.

31 See, e.g., 60 Fed. Reg. 20,023 (April 24, 1995); 60 Fed. Reg. 47, 469 (Sept. 13, 1995); 62 Fed. Reg 16,209 (April 4, 1997); 62 Fed. Reg. 41,457 (Aug. 1, 1997); 63 Fed. Reg. 40,946 (July 31, 1998); 63 Fed. Reg. 58444 (Oct. 30, 1998).

32 Modifications to the Disability Determination Procedures; Disability Claims Process Redesign Prototype, 64 Fed. Reg. 47,218, 47,219 (Aug. 20, 1999).

have been shown to be effective in earlier tests."[33] The four changes shown to be effective by "improv[ing] the initial disability determination process" and therefore included in the 10-state prototype included: "providing greater decisional authority to the disability examiner and more effective use of the expertise of the medical consultant; ensuring appropriate development and explanation of key issues; increasing opportunities for claimant interaction with the decision maker before a determination is made; and simplifying the appeals process by eliminating the reconsideration step."[34]

Finally, in 2001, SSA issued a notice of proposed rulemaking indicating its intent to apply three of these process modifications nationally over the next year until they were implemented in every state with a "projected completion date" no later than 2003.[35] It stated:

> 1. We are proposing to change our rules for how State agencies make disability determinations for us. The change would allow State agency adjudicators, called "disability examiners," to decide whether input from a medical or psychological consultant is needed to make a disability determination. The medical or psychological consultant would not be responsible for the determination; i.e., would not be an adjudicator of the claim.
>
> 2. We are proposing to add rules providing that disability examiners will offer claimants an opportunity for an informal conference whenever it appears that the evidence does not support a fully favorable determination.[36]
>
> 3. We are proposing to eliminate the reconsideration step of our administrative review process.[37]

---

33 Ibid. at 47,218.

34 Ibid.

35 New Disability Claims Process, 66 Fed. Reg. 5494 (Jan. 19, 2001).

36 The conferencing aspect of the prototype was time-consuming and was discontinued in 2002. *See* Modifications to the Disability Determination Procedures; Extension of Testing of Some Disability Redesign Features, 67 Fed. Reg. 42594 (June 24, 2002); *See also* (Robinson 2002a, 16) (noting initial decisions in prototype with claimant conferences took approximately 14 days longer).

37 Ibid.

The agency then supplied the rationale for making these changes permanent based on its analysis of the costs and benefits from the years of testing. It stated:

> We found that these actions resulted in better determinations at the initial level, with more allowances of claims that should have been allowed. We believe that many claims that would have been allowed only after appeal under the old process were allowed at the initial step under the new process. These claimants were able to receive benefits months sooner than they otherwise would have, an important protection for individuals who are unable to work. By eliminating the reconsideration step, claimants who appealed reached the hearing level an average of 2 months sooner than claimants who went through the reconsideration step and therefore had an opportunity to receive their hearing decisions sooner. Also, the quality of our determinations improved. Reviews of disability determinations from the FPM by SSA's Office of Quality Assessment indicated that the new process improved the accuracy of initial decisions to deny claims from 92.6 percent to 94.8 percent. If implemented nationally, this would translate to approximately 34,000 fewer disabled claimants being erroneously denied benefits and facing the prospect of a lengthy appeal. **We believe that these positive results were due to a number of factors. For example, we know that removing the reconsideration step permitted the State agencies to redirect their resources so that the individuals who formerly worked on reconsideration claims could work on initial claims. This permitted increased contact with the claimants and improved documentation of the disability determinations.**[38]

The agency had earlier concluded that: "Although the prototype is continuing and we continue to gather information and gain operational experience, we believe that we now have sufficient information to propose changes to our regulations."[39] Accordingly, further comments received on these proposed changes will assist only to the extent of "fine-tuning" these changes."[40]

---

38 Ibid. at 5495 (emphasis added).

39 Ibid. at 5394.

40 Ibid.

However, rather than moving toward the promised national implementation, on May 1, 2001, a mere five months later, SSA Associate Commissioner for Disability Kenneth Nibali issued DDS Administrators' Letter No. 566 explaining that because "preliminary data from the prototypes have raised questions about the program costs of national implementation final decision about rollout will be reserved until more complete data are available," which was expected by the end of the year. The letter explained in somewhat ambiguous language that significant additional program costs for national rollout were anticipated "since some of the people we are paying at the DDS level would not have appealed and been paid by OHA [now ODAR] under the old process."

From 2001 to 2005, the agency continued the prototype in the 10 selected states. Then, in 2005 and 2006, the agency proposed and partially implemented yet another new process reform program entitled Disability Service Improvement (DSI) process.[41] Among other process changes proposed in DSI, the agency called for eliminating the reconsideration step but replacing it with review by a federal reviewing officer (FRO).[42] A claimant denied at the initial stage would be required to seek review by the FRO, who would then issue a decision on that request for review.[43] Failure to seek FRO review would preclude access to an ALJ hearing.[44] The FRO would work outside the DDS and would possess some evidence-gathering capabilities beyond that exercised by the DDS on reconsideration, such as the ability to develop the evidence in the file, issue subpoenas, and consult with experts through a new Medical and Vocational Expert System (MVES) operated within a newly created federal Office of Medical and Vocational Expertise (OMVE). The FRO could then issue decisions based on the evidence.[45] Nevertheless, even among prominent proponents of DSI, a significant critique of the proposed FRO process was the likelihood that the structure would simply replicate reconsideration and supply yet an additional barrier with attendant delays and insufficient countervailing benefits to justify its existence.[46]

---

41 Administrative Review Process for Adjudicating Initial Disability Claims, 70 Fed. Reg. 43,590 (proposed July 27, 2005); Administrative Review Process for Adjudicating Initial Disability Claims, 71 Fed. Reg. 16,424 (to be codified at 20 C.F.R., pts. 404,405, 416 & 422).

42 See Ibid.

43 See Ibid.

44 See Ibid.

45 See Ibid.; *See generally* BLOCH ON SOCIAL SECURITY § 1:11 (2015) (describing DSI).

46 See, *e.g.*, (Bloch, Lubbers and Verkuil 2007, 237) ("The concern remains, however, that authorizing the FRO to issue a decision to deny benefits will excessively formalize this stage

SSA implemented DSI only in one of its smallest regions (Boston).[47] While it proceeded to national implementation with one aspect of DSI that it determined was working effectively–a process for quick disability determinations (QDD) for certain types of obvious claims[48]–it ultimately suspended the FRO and much of the rest of DSI in 2008 citing budgetary constraints.[49] In describing its rationale for suspending FRO, the agency cited overwhelming support for eliminating FRO in public comments and offered its response to those comments:

> All but one of the commenters specifically expressed support for the suspension of new claims to the FedRO and MVES/OMVE. Several of these commenters discussed concerns over the processing time for claims and the claimant's or the representative's ability to contact the FedRO. One commenter also discussed concerns over FedRO case development and the quality of FedRO decisions.
>
> Response: The primary reason for the processing time and service issues raised in the comments is the staffing levels of the OFedRO and MVES/OMVE. The staffing levels for these organizations have been approximately 50 percent of the levels we believed would be needed to handle the Boston region workload. . . . Accordingly, we staffed the OFedRO and MVES/OMVE to the greatest extent possible while also focusing our scarce resources on the backlog of disability hearings.[50]

With the end of the FRO stage of DSI, the agency restored reconsideration in the Boston region states with the exception of New Hampshire which, as one

---

of the process, canceling out the streamlining provided by eliminating the reconsideration stage."); *cf.* (Rains 2007, 250) ("[I]t is hard to see how use of a federal reviewing official (FedRO) will be a significant improvement over the reconsideration stage. . . . Rather than add the FedRO, SSA should put more resources into the initial determination process and the ODAR in order to encourage full and timely development of the record at these two critical stages.").

47 71 Fed. Reg. at 16440. The Boston Region is Region I and includes (Connecticut, Massachusetts, Maine, New Hampshire Rhode Island and Vermont). *See Ibid.*

48 Amendments to the Quick Disability Determination Process, 72 Fed. Reg. 51,173 (Sept. 6, 2007).

49 See, e.g., Suspension of New Claims to the Federal Reviewing Official Review Level, 73 Fed. Reg. 2411 (Jan. 15, 2008).

50 Ibid. at 2412.

of the10 prototype states testing elimination of reconsideration, was restored to that ongoing test.[51]

On April 27, 2010, SSA Commissioner Michael J. Astrue signaled a potential change in policy direction on the elimination of reconsideration. In testimony before the House Ways and Means Committee during a hearing on the backlog of hearing-stage cases, Commissioner Astrue revealed that one way the agency was evaluating possible improvements in the disability process and hearing backlog was to take a "new look" at the disability caseloads in prototype states which have been testing elimination of reconsideration (SSA 2010b, 3). As a function of that new look, the commissioner proposed reducing the testing by two states by removing Michigan and perhaps Colorado from the tests. He observed:

> We expected that eliminating the reconsideration step in the prototype states would result in earlier decisions and reduced waiting times for claimants; however, we have found the opposite is true. In 1998, prior to the start of the prototype test, the proportion of initial decisions that ended up at the hearings level was 1.4 percentage points higher in the prototype states than in the non-prototype states. By 2007, that difference between prototype and non-prototype states had grown to 7.5 percentage points. . . .
>
> In Michigan, an economically hard-hit state, we have concluded that too many cases are needlessly going to the hearings level from the DDSs. Therefore, we plan to reinstate reconsideration in Michigan next fiscal year. Of all the prototype states, Michigan has the highest percentage of hearing requests, not to mention some of the most backlogged hearing offices in the country. Reinstating reconsideration would allow a significant number of cases to be allowed at reconsideration, resulting in earlier payment to those claimants and a reduction in the number of hearing requests. Moreover, those cases that do go to hearing would be more thoroughly developed, having already been through the reconsideration step. . . . In addition to Michigan, we are also looking at reinstating reconsideration in Colorado[.]

---

51 Modifications to the Disability Determination Procedures; Reinstatement of "Prototype" and "Single Decisionmaker" Tests in States in the Boston Region, 73 Fed. Reg. 12,495 (March 7, 2008).

Although the president's FY 2011 budget called for curtailing of the elimination of reconsideration testing with the removal of Michigan (SSA 2010a, 13), SSA nevertheless chose to continue testing unabated and to retain Michigan and Colorado in the prototype program. Although the agency has indicated that the tests of elimination of reconsideration were supposed to end by 2009 unless extended,[52] notwithstanding the former commissioner's announced misgivings and apparent attempted change of policy direction, the tests have been extended each year and are fully operative until at least September 2015 and likely thereafter.[53]

DETAILED PROPOSAL

For many years, Congress, ACUS, Social Security disability scholars, and the agency itself have urged improvement of SSA's massive disability adjudicative system by focusing on streamlining and consolidating resources at the DDS levels—where the vast majority of decision-making occurs—through elimination of reconsideration and strengthening of record development at the initial application stage. An unbroken series of initiatives commencing with the congressionally mandated demonstration projects in the 1984 DBRA, through the 1994 Reengineering Project and even including aspects of the 2006 Disability Service Improvements and the continuation of the prototype testing thereafter and to the present, effect this policy priority.

Nationwide Elimination of Reconsideration

This paper suggests that more than 16 years of testing with no end in sight is sufficient. It proposes as a first process recommendation that SSA finally make permanent the nationwide elimination of reconsideration. Undoubtedly SSA could study and test reconsideration elimination for another 16 years and the most recent 16-year period of focused testing appears to have been continued indefinitely. However, the agency has supplied no indication of what it seeks to gain from further extended testing of reconsideration elimination that it has been unable to observe or obtain in the past 16 years, or why it has taken 16 years to identify the deficiencies of its current testing protocols. Nor has the agency indicated what it would do differently through further extended testing and how different testing protocols or results would likely lead to different public policy conclusions or options.

---

52 Modifications to the Disability Determination Procedures; Extension of Testing of Some Disability Redesign Features, 71 Fed. Reg. 45,890 (Aug. 3, 2006).

53 79 Fed. Reg. 39, 453 (July 10, 2014).

Initial Stage Modifications to Promote Better Record Development

A significant criticism of SSA adjudicative process is the relatively high, albeit diminishing, approval rates by the ALJs (Pierce 2011). ALJs currently approve 45 percent of decisions, down from 63 percent six years ago (SSA 2015b).[54] Rather than necessarily suggestive of adjudicative inconsistency and reversals of the DDS, these still relatively significant ALJ approval rates are explainable in part by the utilization of significantly different and more developed medical and evidentiary records at the entirely *de novo* ALJ stage than at the initial application stage (Dubin and Rains 2012, 113-14).[55] ALJs possess tools and a culture established to promote greater development through, face-to-face inquiry and conferencing with the claimant, identification of evidentiary lapses and subpoena power to procure evidence from treating sources and order evidence, and the ability to obtain the testimony of medical advisors and vocational experts.[56] The development of medical and evidentiary records at the initial stage which are closer to the ultimate records developed at the ALJ stage would not only promote greater inter-stage consistency but also more accurate decision-making earlier in the process—a major objective of the past thirty years of the SSA's adjudicative process reform proposals. Accordingly, the second process recommendation in this paper is to divert DDS resources and personnel liberated from assignment to processing three quarters of a million annual reconsideration claims to work on enhancing record development at the initial stage. As a start, the agency should adopt the prototype changes it is already utilizing and has evaluated on multiple occasions as more productive of decisional accuracy and quality than initial determinations in non-prototype states. This includes the components of the prototype that have also been tested since 1999.[57]

In addition, since the existing prototype does not focus significantly on enhancing initial stage evidentiary development, beyond freeing up time for development through the use of a single decision maker model (SSAB 2015, 4),[58] other

---

54 (Office of Disability Program Management information) FY 2009, FY 2010, FY 2011, FY 2012, FY 2013, and FY 2014.

55 It is also explainable in part by the claimants' age and the fact that their conditions sometimes deteriorate between the DDS and hearing stages. See Ibid.

56 Ibid.

57 See supra notes 38-39 and accompanying text.

58 The prototype's single decision maker (SDM) model significantly reduces initial decision time and was projected to shave eleven days off of initial decision time if the SDM model were implemented nationally.

recommendations for greater initial stage steps to develop initial stage records closer to those developed at the hearing stage should include:

1) Developing and providing questionnaires and forms that track SSA listing criteria and listing equivalency considerations and residual functional capacity relevant criteria, including assessing the full range of vocationally relevant medical restrictions that vocational experts rely upon in assessing ability to make an adjustment to work other than jobs performed in the past, as reflected in agency Social Security Rulings and relevant vocational source materials;
2) Providing such forms to both treating and consulting physicians in the process and, where needed, explanation and training to them, to advance firmer and more supportable rationales for decision-making earlier in the process and ensuring the medical sources responses are appropriately supported and not mere box-checking as is often present in DDS internal agency physician form and questionnaire evaluations.[59]

With respect to those first two recommendations, SSA personnel sometimes assert the position that because SSA decision makers are responsible for determining residual functional capacity (RFC), meeting or equaling listings, and the ultimate determination of disability and these matters are "reserved to the Commissioner" under agency regulations,[60] they should not be seeking treating medical opinions on, and should give no weight to, treating findings and opinions that are components of RFC and listings. This is in error. SSA regulations also mandate that as a general matter significant and sometimes controlling weight be given to treating physician findings and opinions noting:

> Generally, we give more weight to opinions from your treating sources, since these sources are likely the medical professionals most able to provide a detailed, longitudinal picture of [the

---

59 See, e.g., (*Frey v. Bowen* 1986, 515) ("In comparison with the objective tests and measurements described by [claimant's treating physicians'] report in this regard consists solely of boxes checked on the secretary's form to indicate his conclusion of no limitation on right arm use."); (*Laird v. Stidwell* 1997, 1193) ("plaintiffs point out that the check-box type forms the DDS consultants use to prepare the RFCs are of limited value in assessing a claimant's vocational abilities."); see also (*Mason v. Shalala* 1993, 1065) ("In contrast to the other two medical reports, the report from the New Jersey Division of Vocational Rehabilitation is but a two-page form, entitled 'General Basic Medical Examination,' that requires the physician only to check boxes and briefly to fill in the blanks.").

60 See 20 C.F.R. § 404.1527(d) (2015).

> claimant's] medical impairment(s) and may bring a unique perspective to the medical evidence that cannot be obtained from the objective medical findings alone or from reports of individual examinations, such as consultative examinations or brief hospitalizations.[61]

Accordingly, the courts reconcile SSA adjudicators' responsibility for rendering the ultimate legal decision of disability reserved to the commissioner with the generally substantial solicitude accorded treating physician evidence under the regulations by explaining that it is the underlying treating medical findings and medical opinions that must be accorded great and sometimes "controlling weight" under agency regulations; not the ultimate legal determination of disability, RFC or listing status.[62] As the United States Court of Appeals for the Tenth Circuit recently elaborated, medical findings as to work-related limitations would, if accepted, always "impact the ALJ's determination of RFC—they always do, because that is what they are for—but that does not make the medical findings an impermissible opinion on RFC itself. If doctors could only give opinions on matters that could not affect RFC, medical opinions would be inherently useless in disability determinations" (*Krauser v. Astrue* 2011, 1330). Thus, for example, a treating physician finding that a claimant's clinically and diagnostically well-supported severe spinal impairment limited the claimant to ten pounds of lifting, two hours standing and walking and six hours of sitting—the exertional medical components of sedentary work[63] — may be entitled to great or controlling weight under SSA's regulations. However, a treating opinion indicating merely that a claimant was "disabled" or limited to "sedentary work" would not warrant the same consideration. Accordingly, DDS personnel should attempt to acquire treating physician findings and opinions on listing and RFC components earlier in the process. Indeed, as discussed above, SSA regulations further acknowledge the importance of treating physician evaluation by expressing a preference that treating sources supply needed consultative evaluations (CEs) at all levels of adjudication.[64] As also discussed above, despite SSA's express regulatory preference, treating physician CEs are exceedingly rare (Wittenberg et al. 2012, 26).

---

61 20 C.F.R. § 404.1527(c)(2)(2015).

62 See, e.g., (*Ralph v. Colvin* 2015, 16) (collecting cases and authority on this point).

63 20 C.F.R. 404.1567(a) (2015); SSR 83-10.

64 See 20 C.F.R. § 404.1519h; 416.916h (2015).

3) Employing vocational sources to provide "step-five" work assessments to guide decisions at the fifth substantive stage of SSA's five-step regulatory sequential evaluation process involving the issue of a claimant's ability to make a work adjustment to other work (not previously performed) based on the claimant's age, education, past relevant work experience and residual functional capacity (RFC);[65]
4) Providing greater identification of and assistance to mentally challenged and language-challenged claimants earlier in the process though the use of interpreters and adjudicative staff to avert impediments to record development attributable to those barriers;
5) Publication and effective enforcement of minimal quality standards for the conduct of consultative examinations (CEs); and
6) More comprehensive training to state agency adjudicators on the many important evaluative rules which, the author's multi-decade clinical practice and consultation with disability advocates and claimant organizations reveal, are often, perhaps systematically (*Laird v. Stidwell* 1997),[66] disregarded at the DDS stages including: a) application of the standards and factors for assessing impairment symptomology;[67] b) assessing listing equivalency;[68] c)weighing medical evidence including treating physician evidence and applying the criteria and factors in the medical evidence regulations for so doing[69] and; d) proper application of vocational considerations in cases involving non-exertional limitations or otherwise not resolvable solely through direct and conclusive application of SSA's medical-vocational guidelines or "grid" regulations.[70]

With respect to the above recommendations of "step-five" consultations with vocational sources and training on and proper application of vocational considerations (#3 and #6d, above), it is of course, manifest that SSA develop an acceptable, empirically supported and non-obsolete occupational taxonomy to permit meaningful and accurate development of step-five medical-vocational

65 See 20 C.F.R. § 404.1520(g) (2015).

66 The court grants partial summary judgment finding that the DDS in Iowa systematically failed to apply proper application of subjective symptomology and pain regulations in initial and reconsideration stage determinations.

67 See 20 C.F.R. § 404.1529 et seq. (2015); Social Security Ruling 96-7p.

68 See 20 C.F.R. § 404.1526 (2015).

69 See 20 C.F.R. § 404.1527 et seq. (2015); Social Security Ruling 96-2p.

70 See Social Security Rulings 96-9p; 83-14; 85-15; 82-41; 83-10; 83-11; 83-12.

"other work" conclusions by vocational sources at the initial level and other levels of adjudication (Dubin 2011). The courts,[71] the U.S. Department of Labor (DOL),[72] and U.S. General Accounting Office (GAO) (Robinson 2002b, 23)[73] have each found that the present occupational classification system, DOL's Dictionary of Occupational Titles ["DOT"] (1991) is "obsolete" as it has not been updated in nearly 25 years and is based largely on data from a fundamentally different 1960's labor market and American economy (Traver 2009, § 1403.1).[74] Furthermore, the DOL's current labor market classification system, the O*NET, is inadequate for disability determination purposes due to its failure to classify jobs by RFC (Tippins and Hilton 2010, 159-70). In addition, the courts have increasingly rejected step-five assessments based on questionable job incidence data as the DOT never supplied information on the number of occupations or jobs defined in its classification system and their location, and there is no apparent

---

71 See, e.g., (*Browning v. Colvin* 2014, 709) ("A further problem is that the job descriptions used by the Social Security Administration come from a 23–year–old edition of the *Dictionary of Occupational Titles*, [DOT] which is no longer published, and mainly moreover from information from 1977—37 years ago. No doubt many of the jobs have changed and some have disappeared. We have no idea how vocational experts and administrative law judges deal with this problem."); (*Cunningham v. Astrue* 2010, 614-16) ("[C]ommon sense dictates that when such [DOT] descriptions appear obsolete, a more recent source of information should be consulted. . . . [W]e conclude that the VE's dependence on the DOT listings alone does not warrant a presumption of reliability."); (*Abbott v. Astrue* 2010, 559) (referencing "the now-defunct DOT").

72 Letter from Dixie Somers, Assistant Commissioner, U.S. Department of Labor, Office of Occupational Statistics, to David Lowery (Nov. 26, 2007) (noting that DOL's Bureau of Labor Statistics (BLS) regards the DOT as "obsolete since much of the information contained in the most recent [1991]version is based on research conducted at least two decades [earlier than 1991].").

73 "Labor has not updated DOT since 1991 and does not plan to do so. . . . Meanwhile, as new jobs and job requirements evolve in the national economy, SSA's reliance upon an outdated database further distances the agency from the current market place."

74 "The Social Security Administration figures the DOT and its related data are 'better than nothing.' But 'better than nothing' is not a reliable basis to award or deny life-sustaining benefits to the disabled and disadvantaged."); *see* (DOL 1991) (noting SSA's continuing reliance on the DOT and related data that derives from a time "when the Beatles ruled the AM pop charts, and Elvis was still the king"). Indeed, SSA regulations acknowledge that occupational information more than 15 years old is assumed unreliable because: "A gradual change occurs in most jobs so that after 15 years it is no longer realistic to expect that skills and abilities acquired in a job done then continue to apply." 20 C.F.R. §§ 404.1565(a); 416.965(a) (2015).

current data source collecting numerical job data linked to DOT codes and occupational titles, even assuming DOT job classifications were not obsolete.[75]

Thus, at a minimum, SSA must pursue three steps to restore integrity to non-grid (Dubin 2011, 63-64),[76] step-five, adjudications:

> i) It must develop or obtain, with DOL, a valid, updated occupational taxonomy that includes residual functional capacity (RFC) and exertional and non-exertional impairment SSA medical criteria in occupational classifications so that this system can be employed in disability determinations;
>
> ii) After completion of a proper occupational taxonomy, it should develop or obtain (also likely with DOL/BLS) a data source to determine the incidence and location of such accurately classified occupations in order to inform decision-making under the statutory criteria that looks to whether claimants unable to perform their past relevant work can adjust to "work which exists in significant numbers either in the region where such individual lives or in several regions of the country;"[77] and

---

75 See, e.g. (*Voigt v. Colvin* 2015, 879) ("There is no official source of number of jobs for each job classification in the *Dictionary of Occupational Titles*, and while there are unofficial estimates of jobs in some categories, the vocational experts do not in general, and the vocational expert in this case did not, indicate what those data sources are or vouch for their accuracy."); (*Herrmann v. Colvin* 2014, 1113-14) ("Asked at oral argument, the government lawyers in both social security disability cases argued before us on October 28 confessed ignorance of the source and accuracy of such statistics. . . . We do not know how the vocational expert in this case calculated the numbers to which he testified. Nothing in the record enables us to verify those numbers, which the administrative law judge accepted."); (*Browning v. Colvin 2014, 709)* (We also have no idea what the source or accuracy of the number of jobs that vocational experts (including the one in this case, whose estimates the administrative law judge accepted without comment) claim the plaintiff could perform that exist in the plaintiff's area, the region, or the nation . . . vocational experts do not in general, and the vocational expert in this case did not, indicate what those data sources are or vouch for their accuracy.").

76 As I have previously argued, since the grid regulations are based in large part on the now-obsolete DOT classifications, its provisions must also eventually be updated as consistent with the newly developed occupational taxonomy and valid job incidence and locational data related thereto.

77 42 U.S.C. § 423(d)(2)(A).

iii) Finally, because any such new labor market classification systems and data sources will become obsolete in a dynamic and fluid labor market, SSA (again most likely in collaboration with DOL) should establish a mechanism for mandatory periodic revisions that account for the inevitable and foreseeable labor market evolution.

SSA appears to have finally accepted recommendations to discontinue its own recently unsuccessful solo project (the Occupational Information Disability Advisory Panel "OIDAP")[78] and is currently collaborating with the U.S. Department of Labor, Bureau of Labor Statistics (BLS) in an effort to create a taxonomy useful for both for DOL employment placement and SSA adjudicative needs, which it also plans to update regularly (SSA 2015e). The success of this effort will be an essential first step to restoring integrity to SSA step-five adjudications, regardless of whatever process improvements and efficiencies are adopted. However, this work alone as currently described will not be enough. As an additional recommendation beyond SSA and DOL's current joint project, these agencies must also develop a regularly updateable data source for job incidence and job location information based on any new post-DOT occupational taxonomy created.

ANALYSIS OF PROPOSAL

The only public rationale supplied for not nationally eliminating reconsideration stems from concerns raised by the associate commissioner for disability in his May 2001 DDS Administrators' Letter 566 and from the former commissioner's 2010 testimony to Congress. However, a closer look at those statements and the rationales supplied for retaining the reconsideration stage and the status quo approach to initial determinations demonstrates that they lack sufficiently supportable public justification.

First, the May 2001 DDS Administrators' Letter did not attempt to reconcile the somewhat cryptic and unelaborated "anticipation" that significant new net program costs would be generated from the prototype with the agency's extensive contrary prior findings and glowing accounts of prototype successes in the notice of proposed rulemaking issued just five months earlier in January 2001 based on the results of several years of testing. Nor did the letter explain

[78] See (Dubin 2011, 63) (recommending SSA abandon OIDAP and collaborate with DOL on a new occupational taxonomy).

how the administrative costs of additional hearings for the small percentage of claimants who would have been granted benefits under the non-prototype system at reconsideration, were now calculated to significantly exceed the costs of devoting personnel, resources and time for a full reconsideration process for the large percentage of persons whose reconsideration would amount to little more than a rubber-stamp denial of the initial stage.

Perhaps the DDS Administrators' Letter's ambiguous language also meant to suggest that the agency could further escape the additional costs from hearings and eventual benefit awards in prototype states attributable to otherwise eligible claimants improperly denied at the initial stage, who, in non-prototype states, would also be denied benefits at both the initial and reconsideration stages and then become frustrated with the process after a second improper denial and decline to pursue a meritorious appeal to a hearing. However, an administrative process principally justified by its ability to produce "bureaucratic disentitlement" of otherwise eligible claimants produces neither cost-effective decisional accuracy nor fairness, is contrary to public policy (Lipsky 1984), and calls into question statutory and constitutional prohibitions against unjustified, excessive or unreasonable delay in Social Security adjudication.[79]

Moreover, one month after the DDS Administrators' Letter, on June 25, 2001, SSA's Management Information and Evaluation Workgroup issued a Draft Disability Prototype Interim Report that listed successes and challenges identified by mid-2001. It stated:

Overview of Successes

Perhaps the most significant observation regarding successful aspects of the Prototype at this time is that generally there is a consensus among DDS managers and staff that the new process results in better initial determinations. A common

[79] See, e.g. (*Heckler v. Day* 1983, 111) (SSA concedes before the U.S Supreme Court that a 90-day or greater period between reconsideration request and reconsideration decision violates the Social Security Act's requirement in 42 U.S.C. § 405(b) that SSA agency action not be unreasonably delayed); (*Barnett v. Bowen* 1987) (excessive delays in reconsideration and hearing determinations defined, in the context of reconsideration determinations, as decisions exceeding greater than 90 days from reconsideration request, violates § 405(b) and entitles delayed claimants to various forms of injunctive relief); (*White v. Mathews* 1976, 1259-61) (excessive delays in SSA hearing decision times violate both the Fifth Amendment's Due Process Clause and the Social Security Act, 42 U.S.C. § 405(b)); *see generally* (Blasi 1988)

theme in Prototype discussions is the comment that the new process is 'the right way to do business.'

- One of the goals of the Prototype is to allow claimants who should be allowed as early as possible in the process. The increased allowances in the DDSs under the Prototype are meeting that goal by processing as many allowances in one step as these States did in two steps under the old process. In addition, some claimants may be allowed under the process who might have been denied under the old but would never be allowed because of their not appealing to a higher level.
- Quality Review data indicate that allowances being made under the Prototype are appropriate. Prototype accuracy is better than the historical accuracy in Prototype sites.
- Customer survey data indicate that claimants are better satisfied with a process that offers a claimant conference and increased contact with the adjudicators who decide their claims.
- For those claimants who appeal for a hearing, it is clear that their cases reach OHA considerably faster under the new process.

Areas of Challenge

The major challenge is meeting the demands of the new process with current resources. Most managers and adjudicators agree that the process needs to be refined particularly in the areas of documents and the claimant conference to make the process less resource intensive.[80]

Thus, whatever could be determined about the public policy desirability of the prototype by the middle of 2001 after issuance of DDS Letter 566, the quantified benefits in terms of increased initial decisional quality and accuracy, significant reduction in unjustified delays for those proceeding to hearing, and increased customer satisfaction appeared to outweigh any serious identified countervailing detriments.

Second, with respect to the commissioner's 2010 congressional testimony, the agency again failed to reconcile its new conclusion on the waiting times for decision in prototype states with the agency's earlier statistical and empirical findings and contrary conclusions after years of testing in the 2001 NPRM or

[80] SSA Management Information and Evaluation Workgroup, Disability Prototype Interim Report, June 25, 2001, p.26 (emphasis in original) (copy on file with author).

conclusions in the Interim Prototype Report. Nor did the commissioner supply a basis for the conclusion that the mere 11-14 percent reconsideration reversal rate would result in earlier payment to a sufficiently significant number of claimants to justify the delays and administrative costs of continuing reconsideration for the 86-89 percent of claimants who would experience a rubber stamp of the initial denial decision from a reconsideration process and a delay from that process to an ultimate administrative decision.

Indeed, at the same April 27, 2010 hearing (on hearing level delays and backlog), at which the former SSA commissioner testified, SSA's inspector general (IG), Patrick P. O'Carroll Jr., explained the delay issues alluded to by the commissioner through the elimination of reconsideration. O'Carroll noted that SSA had reassessed its policy on reconsideration elimination since commencing the prototype in 1999, then in 2010 "believing that reinstating this process will get benefits to deserving beneficiaries more quickly than an administrative hearing." The IG assessed four scenarios from the planned reinstatement of reconsideration in Michigan in FY 2011, finding that: "[i]f SSA reinstates and fully funds the reconsideration process in Michigan, Initial claims will take 123 days; Reconsideration claims will take 276 days; and Claims requiring hearings will take 915 days." However, "[i]f SSA does not reinstate the reconsideration process in Michigan, and there is no additional funding: Initial claims will take 123 days; and Claims requiring hearings will take 762 days."

The IG then discussed the administrative opportunity costs or savings from reconsideration elimination by noting that: "[i]f SSA does not reinstate the reconsideration process in Michigan, and the funding that would be used for reconsideration is instead devoted to processing initial claims: The DDS could process 25,300 additional claims." Similarly, "[i]f SSA does not reinstate the reconsideration process in Michigan, and the funding that would be used for reconsiderations is instead devoted to processing hearings: ODAR could process 17,600 additional hearings per year."

The IG concluded:

> In summary, by reinstating the reconsideration step, some individuals who appeal will get an allowance decision sooner and some would get an allowance decision later. For example, if SSA reinstates the reconsideration step in Michigan, the claimant denied at the initial level could get an allowance decision in 276 days, which is 486 days sooner than if they had to appeal to

> ODAR without going through the reconsideration step. However, if the claimant is denied at the reconsideration level and appeals to ODAR, it would take 915 cumulative days for a decision, which is 153 days longer than the current processing time (762 days) for cases that go to ODAR without a reconsideration step (SSA 2010c, 3).

As described above there are eight to nine times as many claimants denied at the reconsideration level than approved and therefore potentially subject to the latter delays, in comparison to the much smaller percentage benefited with a quicker final decision from the very low reconsideration approval rate.[81] Accordingly, it is hard to determine how or why the commissioner quantified the delay factor as supporting the imposition of reconsideration based on the IG's data and conclusions.

Furthermore, the increase in the rate of hearing requests in prototype states which the Commissioner also identified in his testimony as a justification supporting the reconsideration stage, is explainable in part by the likelihood that most of those whose claims would have been approved at reconsideration stage (persons in the 11-14 percent reconsideration approval rate) would request a hearing and become additional hearing appellants in prototype states. It is also likely that some persons, including those with meritorious claims, would have become discouraged and surrendered their pursuit of benefits when forced to endure the long delays culminating in yet another administrative denial decision at the reconsideration stage in non-prototype states. In addition, because of the only 60-day appeal or limitations period for challenging decisions between each level, it is also likely that some claimants, perhaps understandably preoccupied with serious medical and

---

[81] An argument could be made that the delays in successful hearing decision receipt attributable to the reconsideration stage relative to those in prototype states where reconsideration has been eliminated may be somewhat overstated because the reduction of the 11 percent of cases in which benefits are awarded at the reconsideration stage also reduces the flow of cases and hearing backlog in such states relative to prototype states. However, the GAO found that the approval rate in one stage (initial) in prototype jurisdictions (40.4 percent) was actually slightly higher than the approval rate after two stages (initial and reconsideration), in non-prototype jurisdictions (39.8 percent) (Robinson 2002a, 16). Therefore, the increases in hearing requests in the prototype states are less likely attributable to claimants who otherwise would have prevailed earlier at reconsideration in non-prototype states and more likely due to the lesser attrition of claimants who would otherwise have been discouraged from appealing further due to the frustration of receiving two administrative denials if rejected at reconsideration.

mental health concerns or financial hardships and exigencies, would have simply failed to complete an appeal in that relatively short time-frame through this additional step and would therefore be barred from proceeding to the hearing stage in non-prototype states. In short, none of these likely explanations for an increased hearing rate in prototype states suggest end results or meaningful public policy justifications for continuing the reconsideration stage.

Finally, the Commissioner's only other suggestion of tangible benefit for continuing the reconsideration stage is the unexplained suggestion that cases which have proceeded to hearing "would be more thoroughly developed having been through the reconsideration step" (SSA 2010b, 3). However, this conclusion is questionable on two grounds: 1) the reconsideration process does not generally compel meaningfully additional case development, but only a similar claim reevaluation by a different DDS team;[82] and 2) SSA has on multiple occasions determined that prototype DDS's are diverting resources and personnel from the eliminated reconsideration stage to case development tasks at the initial stage to produce ultimately better developed, more accurate and higher quality decisions in the one-stage DDS process than in the two-stage process in non-prototype cases.

Summary of Costs and Benefits

In short, SSA has offered no meaningful public justification for failing to implement the elimination of reconsideration nationally after multiple decades of experimentation and testing. The benefits from the combination of the above process recommendations, as described in SSA's 2001 NPRM, the prototype interim report, and SSA Inspector General's testimony to Congress, include greater decisional accuracy, lesser delays for more claimants, earlier final decisions, greater customer satisfaction, and opportunity savings at other adjudicative levels from the diversion of resources from reconsideration to the initial and/ or hearing levels. The costs appear to be somewhat greater benefits outlays due to slightly greater approval rates in the prototype attributable to more accurate decisions and greater appeal rates in prototype states.[83] These costs also seem

---

82 See note 14 *supra* and accompanying text.

83 SSA has not made generally available to the public granular cost data regarding the prototype costs attributable to reconsideration elimination or its projections for reconsideration elimination costs if the prototype went national as originally projected 16 years ago. The agency's chief actuary, Stephen C. Goss, has indicated in a letter to Senator Tom Coburn that nationwide reconsideration would increase the actuarial deficit by 0.02 percent of taxable payroll and in the same letter has characterized other potential agency measures which would

understandable and justified since lower grant rates would be expected in cases with less record development as underdeveloped cases produce benefit denials in otherwise meritorious claims.

Other largely unavoidable costs include an increased burden on the hearing process, especially at the initial point when a decision is made to transition appeals from initial stage denials to the hearing stage without the historic reconsideration-stage buffer. While the hearing backlog and unprecedented and growing level of applications in 2010 led the commissioner to suggest that reconsideration elimination would have overly adverse consequences on hearing delay times, as indicated above, the application wave has crested now and is in decline and the commissioner has also reduced the hearing backlog somewhat in that time period. In addition, as indicated in the inspector general's testimony, perhaps the agency could consider diverting some of the considerable administrative resources saved from the elimination of three quarters of a million annual reconsideration evaluations and decisions, to the processing of hearings if this problem were to reach similar levels in the future.

INTERMEDIATE STEPS

Fortunately, many decades of experimentation and testing should have prepared the agency with intermediate protocols for a national rollout of the prototype. However, apart from reconsideration elimination which can be extended nationally now after 16 years of testing, the aspects of the recommendation for enhanced initial stage record development utilized in conjunction with current prototype initial stage modifications such as the SDM Model, would benefit from testing and a more gradual roll-out to refine their application based on experience and evaluation and to permit an extended period of analysis.

With respect to the SDM modification at the initial stage, the Social Security Advisory Board has recently found that SSA's 16 years of testing of the SDM

reduce the deficit by less than 0.005 percent of taxable payroll as a "negligible amount." Letter from Stephen C. Goss to the Honorable Tom Coburn, United States Senate, July18, 2011 (copy on file with the author). I have requested from Chief Actuary Goss more granular data on these costs including the specific administrative savings from the elimination of the 750,000 annual reconsideration evaluations and decisions and additional expenses including the costs from projected additional benefit outlays to claimants who would prevail at the hearing or appeal stage who would have abandoned pursuit of benefits and not appealed if denied at the reconsideration stage. That data or information has not been supplied as of the date of this writing.

model, both employed in the prototype and in separate tests outside of the prototype, supplied neither a "well-considered research design" nor a "data collection plan with tight administration over the past 16 years" (SSAB 2015, 2). It recommended a better-considered research plan with tighter state-to-state administration to more confidently permit acting on the agency's positive conclusions that the SDM had helped decrease processing time adjudicative delays while slightly improving both accuracy and allowance rates (8-10). Obviously, if the data and research design can be realistically improved, an appropriate intermediate measure would be to take better steps to produce higher quality data on the SDM as SSAB has recommended.

However, it merits comment that 16 years is a long time for testing without being able to meaningfully evaluate and act on those test results, and it is not clear from SSAB report whether some of the data sought can be produced or significantly improved. For example, the report suggests that there should be a basis for isolating the specific reasons why the SDM model slightly increases the initial stage allowance rates (SSAB 2015, 9). However, there simply might not be a way to definitively isolate those reasons. It may be that since multiple decisions makers (MDMs) take and require more decision time, (4, 5) there is more pressure on MDMs to work more promptly than is comfortable sometimes, and when stressed and in doubt they are more likely to issue a potentially incorrect denial. By law, SSA must review 50 percent of all state agency approval decisions but there is no such requirement for denials. [84]Accordingly, there are incentives to err on the side of benefit denial to avert scrutiny. As former SSAB Chairman Sylvester J. Schieber explained on April 23, 2008 to the House Ways and Means Committee:

> [A] quality review process that targets almost exclusively allowance decisions sends an unintended message. Only a small fraction of denied cases are selected for quality review. The chance of an insufficiently documented denial determination slipping through the system unchecked cannot be discounted. There may be many reasons why there has been a steady decline in allowance rates in the DDS, but it certainly seems likely that inadequate investment which has led to a 'start and stop' type of work environment is a major factor. This is not about a culture of denial but about human nature. When faced with pressure to clear cases quickly,

---

[84] See 42 U.S.C. § 42 USC 421(c)(3)(A).

> adjudicators may take shortcuts and those shortcuts can lead to unintended consequences (SSAB 2008, 3).[85]

This suggestion is a theory and possible explanation for higher SDM allowance rates, but there may simply be no definitive protocol to prove it. It would not be a desirable result if the agency pursued another 16 years of testing with no significant initial stage improvements extended nationally, due to the pursuit of facts or data that simply might not be definitively proven or obtainable. On the other hand, other SSAB cited data deficiencies, such as not controlling for adjudicator tenure and experience, (SSAB 2015, 9) could presumably be corrected more promptly and definitively.

QUESTIONS OR CONCERNS

It is inevitable that observations and conclusions during the many years of testing about issues and problems that have arisen in the prototype should be fully evaluated and ongoing consideration provided to consistently fine-tuning and upgrading initial stage case development under the modifications implemented. Similarly, as additional modifications are implemented, further evaluation should guide additional fine-tuning to assure maximal benefit from these process recommendations. In addition, granular cost data should be made available and examined to permit consideration of greater efficiencies and to identify obstacles to implementation and subsequent rationale for modification or abandonment of aspects of this initiative.

CONCLUSION

More than 20 years ago, the former director of the National Center for Administrative Justice, Milton Carrow, observed that "reforms recommended by congressional committees, the GAO, the Administrative Conference of the United States, the Advisory Committee to the Commissioner of Social Security, and the studies of responsible organizations such as the American Bar Association," (304) all propose the elimination of reconsideration and steps

---

[85] See also (*Bowen v. City of New York* 1986, 474-75 n.5) (a unanimous Supreme Court affirms and relies on lower court finding that DDS physicians in MDM teams "were pressured to reach 'conclusions' contrary to their own professional beliefs in cases where they felt, at the very least, that additional evidence needed to be gathered in the form of a realistic work assessment.").

to enhance initial-stage record development (302).[86] Carrow decried the slow pace towards implementing these needed and obvious reforms and argued that further proposed testing was unnecessary as it was time for these changes simply and finally to be enacted (304). He concluded that SSA "has been dilatory in implementing sound recommendations" and that it "is unconscionable to delay further." Certainly with respect to the elimination of the reconsideration stage, Director Carrow's observations hold obviously greater force more than two decades later after additional experimentation and focused testing has further demonstrated the benefits of the proposed reforms.

A version of this paper will appear in Volume 23 of the Georgetown Journal of Poverty Law & Policy in 2016 with the express permission and consent of the Committee for a Responsible Federal Budget. In turn, this version of the paper is reproduced herein with the permission and consent of the Georgetown Journal of Poverty Law & Policy.

86 "The studies recommend eliminating the entire reconsideration stage of the initial claims process"; *see also* 297-301 (describing and summarizing those studies and reports). Indeed, as Professor Gay Gellhorn has observed, although one might have expected ALJs facing a hearing case backlog and pressures to adjudicate cases more rapidly, to express opposition to "the removal of a buffer between them and disappointed claimants, in fact the National Conference of Administrative Law Judges favor[ed] abolition of Reconsideration." (Gellhorn 1995, 989); see also (Carrow 1994, n.150) (citing a former SSA ALJ's article, also recommending elimination of reconsideration which had reasoned that "under the present system, DDS is simply doing half the job, but doing it twice." Quoting (Moore 1994, 43).

8

Social Security: Restructuring Disability Adjudication

David W. Engel, Dale Glendening, and Jeffrey S. Wolfe[87]

INTRODUCTION

This paper proposes a restructuring of the Social Security Administration's formal disability decision-making process so that it more closely functions similar to American courts (Kessler and Finkelstein 1988, 577).[88] By doing so, the current adjudicatory system will gain a significant measure of heretofore unattainable flexibility, enabling early resolution of claims by means other than hearing.

It is important at the outset to note that while the authors are keenly aware of the need for systemic reform in the fundamental definition of what it means to be "disabled," that issue is beyond the scope of this proposal, which focuses on procedural/regulatory reform affecting the decision of disability claims appealed to federal administrative law judges (ALJs) within the Social Security Administration.

---

87 The opinions and views expressed are those of the authors and do not represent any view, position, policy or policy statement, or finding of the U.S. Government or the Social Security Administration or any of its components.

88 The authors note the emergence of the courthouse as a multi-functional institution, focused not on litigation *per se*, but upon dispute resolution by a number of means:
"Professor Frank E. A. Sander of Harvard Law School first articulated the multi-door courthouse concept in April 1976 at a conference convened by Chief Justice Warren Burger to address the problems faced by judges in the administration of justice. Professor Sander envisioned the courthouse of the future as a dispute resolution center offering an array of options for the resolution of legal disputes. Litigation would be one option among many including conciliation, mediation, arbitration, and ombudspeople." *(Citations omitted.)*

The initial part advanced in the proposal seeks transformation of the role of the Social Security Administration (the Agency) from that of an uninvolved non-party in the hearings and appeals process, to that of a "party," directly represented and engaged in individual disability hearings before ALJs. Doing so would fundamentally reform the hearings and appeals process, opening now-closed lines of communication to both the Agency and claimant's representative. These lines of communication enable early resolution of claims, either foregoing a hearing altogether or limiting the issues to be decided, streamlining the hearings process.

The second part of the proposal continues in the same vein as the first part proposing that the Agency be represented by counsel[89] operating out of the Office of General Counsel (OGC); a logical result given that OGC represents the Agency in appeals of these very decisions before the U.S. courts.

The third part of the proposal further builds on the first two calling for adoption of formal rules of disability practice and procedure before ALJs, thus filling a critical gap in caseload management and adjudication. The objective for the disability adjudicatory process should be as voiced by Rule 1 of the Federal Rules of Civil Procedure (FRCP),[90] recognizing in Rule 1: "the affirmative duty of the court to exercise the authority conferred by these rules to ensure that civil litigation is resolved not only fairly, but also without undue cost or delay" (Coquillette 2014).

Next, we propose that the role of the Appeals Council (AC) of the Social Security Administration (SSA) be refocused consistent with recommendations of the Administrative Conference of the United States (ACUS). The role of the AC should be that of a limited appellate body, hearing appeals only where the decision raises significant issues of public policy or statutory/regulatory interpretation.

We then question the efficacy of rewarding representatives for delayed decision making. Under the current system, attorney fees are calculated as a percentage (25 percent) of the award of "past due" benefits. The longer the wait, the greater the attorney's fee. Unfortunately, absent enforceable rules of practice and procedure,

---

89 "Counsel" is inclusive of licensed attorneys as well as certified non-lawyer representatives—those who have taken the Social Security Certification Examination.

90 FRCP Rule 1 provides: "These rules govern the procedure in all civil actions and proceedings in the United States district courts, except as stated in Rule 81. They should be construed and, administered, and employed by the court and the parties to secure the just, speedy, and inexpensive determination of every action and proceeding."

it is all too easy to engender delay. This practice runs contrary to the public policy that seeks to minimize delay, calling into question the efficacy of the current attorney's fee calculation.

The last part of the proposal examines the now-antiquated and costly practice of reimbursing representatives for travel, including airfare, car rental, and lodging. Though there may once have been an understandable rationale for such reimbursements when there were only a few representatives who did this work, that day has come and gone. One need only survey the Internet to discover that disability representatives may literally be found throughout the United States. Should not a representative's travel to represent his or her client be a business expense, borne by the representative and not the American people? Travel reimbursement encourages questionable practices, including the inability to meet with the claimant in advance of the hearing, as representatives travel a "circuit," often appearing in multiple states in as many days, with little time to meet with a claimant before a hearing and resulting in unnecessary delay.

Finally, we lay out some Key Facts relating to this issue. An Appendix is also available on the SSDI Solutions website.

PROPOSAL

Recognition and Treatment of the Social Security Administration as a Formal "Present Party" to Administrative Adjudications before the Office of Disability Adjudication and Review

The Social Security Administration should be made an actual "party" to the formal disability hearing. This is a critical first step in the creation of a flexible system of formal disability adjudication and decision making—one which contemplates resolution of pending hearings by means other than a full hearing. Current formal adjudication before an ALJ generally involves only an individual "party" who has received a reconsidered determination by the Agency.[91] No Agency or government representative appears. However, any other person may be made a "party" if he/she shows "in writing that his or her rights may be adversely affected by the hearing." [92] The Agency is not, by definition a "party" and chooses not to appear. As discussed, *infra,* its failure to do so significantly erodes the potential to resolve a pending hearing other than by a hearing, a result

[91] See 20 CFR Part 404.

[92] Ibid.

at odds with the practice in virtually every other court system in the United States, where the overwhelming majority of pending cases are resolved without hearing or trial.

By definition, the Agency's existing system of formal adjudication is solely designed to hear and decide cases, with only very limited opportunities to resolve appeals by other means. The adjudicatory process possesses little "flex" to function otherwise. That this is so is obvious from the current single-party configuration. No representative appears for the Agency, the only government entity present being the judge—who by virtue of his/her role as a neutral is not a party, though an argument can be made that (s)he is asked to engage in activity which mimics party status (Verkuil 1978, 258-329). Without the presence of the Agency as a party to the disability hearing, the adjudicatory system will remain rigidly committed to resolving the vast majority of pending hearings only by hearing. Except for a small percentage of pending hearings decided without hearing by senior attorney adjudicators (SAAs) and a relatively few "on-the-record" decisions by ALJs, the pending hearing must be held before the ALJ, as there is no other voice of the Agency present and able to intervene at any earlier point (SSA OIG 2011).[93]

---

[93] The report succinctly points out that pending hearings before the Office of Disability Adjudication and Review (ODAR) are resolved by decision or dismissal in only three ways: by decision of an administrative law judge; by decision of a senior attorney adjudicator; or by dismissal.

The following is an excerpt from Table 1 of the cited OIG report, titled, *Pending Hearings Backlog Projections (Based on FY 2012 Budget).* Senior attorney adjudicator dispositions are shown for Fiscal Year 2010, with projections declining slightly through FY 2013. However, despite the small decline, the number is fairly consistent over time, decisions by SAAs representing the only other alternative by which to decide a pending hearing before an administrative law judge.

The OIG report further points out that SAA decisions represent less than 10 percent of case decisions, making it clear that the overwhelming majority of pending hearings must proceed in lockstep toward a hearing, with no other alternative for decision: "In FY 2010, SAAs issued 54,186 OTR [on the record, meaning, without hearing] decisions, representing about 7.3 percent of all dispositions."

Workloads/Staffing	FY 2010 Actual	FY 2011 Projected	FY 2012 Projected	FY 2013 Projected
SAA Dispositions	54,186	53,200	49,200	48,600

That this is so is evident from the full Table, shown below. Case dispositions occur only by decisions by two ODAR actors: administrative law judges, who, by reason of the rigid single-track hearings procedure, may only decide a pending hearing by holding a hearing; or by senior attorney adjudicators who may only decide cases without a hearing, and then

The only other mechanism for resolution of a pending hearing is a "dismissal," and while a dismissal is not a decision, *per se*, such action nevertheless accounts for 15 percent of pending hearings resolved by ALJs.[94]

In contrast, a "flexible" decision-making system contemplates resolution of a significant number of pending hearings by more than one means, often much earlier. Such has been the evolution of the state and federal courts, termed the "multi-door courthouse." The benefit and the rationale supportive of the

---

may only decide a pending hearing favorably. *See also,* Social Security Administration, Office of Inspector General: "Effects of the Senior Attorney Adjudicator Program on Hearing Workloads." Report No. A-12-13-23002 (June 2013). An adverse decision may only be made by an administrative law judge, which, as noted, requires a hearing.

Table 1: OIG Pending Hearings Backlog Projections (Based on FY 2012 Budget)

Workloads/ Staffing	FY 2010 Actual	FY 2011 Projected	FY 2012 Projected	FY 2013 Projected
Beginning Balance[1]	722,822	705,367	668,104	595,691
Projected Receipts[2]	720,161	777,300	751,700	682,600
ALJs Available[3]	1,154	1,285	1,319	1,313
ALJ Productivity[4]	2.38	2.37	2.35	2.34
Total ALJ Dispositions[5]	683,430	761,363	774,913	768,105
SAA Dispositions[6]	54,186	53,200	49,200	48,600
Total Dispositions[7]	737,616	814,563	830,708	826,553
Year-End Pending[8]	705,367	668,104	595,691	461,586

This number does not include dismissals of the *Request for Hearing,* where the claimant withdraws or abandons his/her *Request* or passes away. More precisely, "[i]n FY 2011, ODAR issued over 793,000 dispositions, of which approximately 740,000 were issued by ALJs and over 53,000 were issued by Attorney Adjudicators . . . Of the 740,000 dispositions issued by ALJs, approximately 629,000 dispositions resulted in an allowance or denial decision and the remaining 111,000 dispositions were dismissals of the hearing request. A hearing request can be dismissed for a variety of reasons, including failure of the claimant to appear at the hearing, the claimant choosing to withdraw the hearing request, or death of the claimant." *See* 20 CFR Parts 404.957, 416.1457: *Dismissal of a Request for a Hearing Before an Administrative Law Judge* (2015). *See also,* Social Security Administration Office of the Inspector General: "The Social Security Administration's Review of Administrative Law Judges' Decisions." Report No. A-07-12-21234 (March 2012). *See further still* Social Security Administration Office of the Inspector General: "Hearing Request Dismissals." Report No. A-07-10-21049 (July 2010).

94 In calendar year 2011, per the 2012 OIG report, *supra*, note 6, administrative law judges disposed of 740,000 pending hearings; of which 111,000 were dismissals. Thus, of the total number of pending hearings resolved by administrative law judges, 15 percent were by reason of dismissal, that is, [744,000/111,000 = 15 percent] and the balance of 629,000 were decided only after a hearing. This means that only 23 percent of pending hearings were resolved by other than a hearing, such that SAA decisions = 7.3 percent; and dismissals = 15 percent. This stands in marked contrast with the cases resolved other than by trial in the United States courts (70 percent).

"multi-door courthouse" are immediately apparent and equally applicable to disability decision making. As Judge Kessler, then Supervising Judge, Superior Court of Multi-Door Dispute Resolution Program, District of Columbia, cogently observed (1988):

> "For the court, accessible and workable alternatives would mean a reduction in the number of bench and jury trials and less congestion on court calendars. Certain cases would be processed more quickly, providing judges with more time to devote to the cases that require their attention and intervention."

The first room in the "multi-door courthouse" is generally said to be a screening room, examining "the nature of the dispute, the parties' relationship, the amount in dispute, the cost of each [alternative dispute resolution] process, and the speed of each process," thereby "fitting the forum to the fuss" (Hedeen 2011, 941). Termed "differentiated case management" or "triage" (*Id.*), the purpose is to advance the case towards early resolution by pairing the dispute with the most efficacious decision-making/dispute-resolution process. The principle is equally applicable to Social Security disability decision making, were there to be a "present party" in person of the Social Security Administration.

The concept of the *"present party"* (hereafter, the *PreP*) contemplates *two parties* to every disability hearing: the claimant who seeks an award of benefits and the *PreP*, representing the Agency. This straightforward adjustment to the disability juridical paradigm has the effect of returning the administrative law judge to his/her traditional role as an American judge, at all times a passive, neutral decision maker—longstanding traditional hallmarks of Anglo-American adversarial jurisprudence. However direct this seems, this result does not end the discussion. Why? Because the presence of the Agency in the disability hearing sets the stage for flexibility in judicial decision making, enabling a significant number of pending hearings to be decided by ALJs without hearing, or, with a limited hearing, and likely well before they might otherwise have been resolved. Apart from a relatively few on-the-record (OTR) decisions, the administrative law judge makes no decision absent a hearing (keeping in mind, a dismissal is not a decision).[95]

The near-exponential rise in the filing of new disability claims, with attendant increases in the number of hearings pending, serves to spotlight the inherent

---

95 See 20 CFR Part 404.957, 416.1457.

rigidity or lack of flexibility of the current system of hearings and appeals. The *PreP* heralds a fundamental change in the currently rigid disability system of hearings and appeals, bringing to it the heretofore-absent ability to "flex." In taking his/her place on stage, the Agency's representative ends the conveyor-belt jurisprudence reminiscent of the *I Love Lucy* skit in which Lucy and Ethel find themselves working at a chocolate conveyor belt on which masses of chocolates proceed implacably faster and ever-faster still, overwhelming the two friends in a smeared chocolaty deluge.

Put another way, the presence of the *PreP* is the difference between a 1954 Schwinn bicycle cruiser *Wasp* and a 2015 Schwinn bicycle racer *Fastback 2 Mens*. Faced with an uphill climb, the 1954 *Wasp* depends solely on increased effort from the rider, the single chain-driven gear offering no other options. The steeper the grade, the harder the rider must work, and the slower (s)he proceeds. The only other choice is to dismount the bike and walk, ensuring even greater delay. The 2015 *Fastback 2 Mens*, on the other hand, employs variable gearing ratios, maximizing the rider's effort, ensuring a constant rate of climb, negating the adversity of the steeper grade, and allowing the rider to maintain his/her pace with the same relative effort, despite the rising road. The improved functioning in the more recent model is analogous to the nature of the proposal made here.

PROPOSAL TWO

The "Flexible" Role of the *Present Party*: Agency Representation by Counsel Attached to the Office of General Counsel

The addition of the Agency representative or *PreP* might appear in its configuration to be simply another expression of an adversarial system—this time in the context of disability decision making—criticized by many because of the image of potentially ill claimants "cross-examined" by prosecutorial-like government lawyers bent solely on winning. Nothing could be further from the truth, taking into account the history and conceptual underpinnings upon which the Social Security Administration was constructed. The *PreP* is the evolutionary successor to the referee/hearing examiner/ALJ, charged, as were his/her predecessors, to implement the goals, purposes and policies of the Agency, and indirectly, of Congress and the American people. In this, the *PreP* looks not to the heritage of the Anglo-American adversarial system, but to the uniquely conceived "procedural innovations" which birthed "the concept of the administrator as benign inquisitor" (Wolfe 2009, 29), a concept which found its way to the Social Security hearings process and which, as here proposed, is now bequeathed to the

Agency representative or "present party." In essence, the *PreP's* role is to promote administrative justice for all parties in a disability proceeding.

Verkuil, in a 1978 law review citing his earlier 1940 work, pointed to the then "new rationale for the role of decision maker in the hearing process." He points out: "the Board discussed the values to be achieved in an administrative hearing in terms of 'simplicity and informality' as well as 'accuracy and fairness.' It referred to a Social Security decision maker as a 'referee' or 'social agent.' This concept of the administrator as an agent for the public (working to ensure that the program goals are fulfilled) is different from the roles assigned to the common-law judge. The Social Security 'referee' thus emerges with a role that is independent of the judicial one" (Verkuil, 1978, 258-329).

In adopting this new role, "[t]he decision model proposed by the Social Security Board was designed to make an enormously complex program work at low cost and with substantial public satisfaction. The scope of the inquisitorial solution was not intended to be carried over to the civil or criminal process. But it did signal the kind of innovative thinking about administrative procedure that would ultimately lead to the emergence of an independent procedural model for administrative law" (Verkuil 1978).

> The jurisprudential foundation underpinning this new administrative procedure called for a decision maker who was to make decisions designed to implement programmatic policy instead of one whose role was to administer "justice" as that term is recognized in traditional Anglo-American jurisprudence.

It is this history that colors the role of the Agency representative. The *PreP* or "present party" represents the Social Security Administration and in doing so does not undertake the role of an advocate whose charge is to "win," charged instead as the Agency's representative to ensure that the congressional mandate manifested in the Social Security Act be carried out. It is this responsibility which motivates and circumscribes the representative's actions in his/her role as the "present party" to the disability hearing.[96] The representative advocates

---

[96] Some might argue that this places the Agency representative or "present party" in an untenable role, as the Social Security Administration has previously denied benefits at both the initial and reconsideration determination stages. Two factors mitigate against such a conclusion. First, the task of reviewing the evidence at the initial and reconsideration stages is generally undertaken by the state disability determination service (DDS), under contract

for the correct result, urging the grant of benefits as may be appropriate given the evidentiary record; or argues for affirmation of a previous denial, again, in accord with the evidentiary record. In any given appeal, the claimant might find a "present party" an ally or a skeptic, but in either case one who is nevertheless bound to fully develop the record, having inherited the duty of inquiry from the administrative law judge. In exercising such duty, the "present party" strives for the correct and just result in accord with Social Security Act.

In 1982, the Social Security Administration gave notice of proposed rulemaking to establish the "Social Security Representation Project." While seemingly similar, it was not, viewing the "representative" as an adjunct to the ALJ and not an independent actor/party. The 1982 program did *not* envision the Agency as a party to the disability hearing. The failed history of the program is well documented and need not be revisited here. For the reasons cited, herein, the proposal for an Agency representative in the form of a "present party" is a timely, essential step in addressing the pervasive ills that plague the disability program.

If, as one might argue, this is yet but another variation on the adversarial model, it is nevertheless a variation tempered by the history from which it arises. A "present party" is able to interact with the ALJ as an advocate for the correct result. In this role, the *PreP* argues for the Agency as an advocate of the Agency's social and policy mandate under the Social Security Act, its implementing regulations, and corresponding policy interpretations. This role does not conjure up inherently negative visions as some have argued, though it does move the process to more closely resemble the adversarial model. Still, this is not an undesirable result. Consider the words of legal philosopher Professor Lon Fuller (1971):

> Despite its flaws, the adversarial model is preferable to the inquisitorial model. The inquisitorial model places on judges the potentially conflicting roles of fact finder and decision maker. This burden unavoidably allows biases and prejudicial influences to unfairly prejudice results. The wisdom of the adversary process

---

with the Social Security Administration. These early administrative determinations are thus not, strictly speaking, undertaken by the Agency itself. Second, it is well-settled that the passage of time generates new evidence; and the call of the "present party" or Agency representative is not to defend the Agency's earlier determination, but to ensure on appeal to the administrative law judge that (s)he has fulfilled his/her duty to fully inquire, considering the question of the claimant's entitlement in light of the most recent evidentiary record developed before the administrative law judge.

> is in placing potentially conflicting tasks on the participants best suited to their discharge [footnotes omitted].

In a study designed to test this very hypothesis, Thibaut, Walker, & Linds (1972, 393) constructed an experimental system designed to replicate both the adversarial and inquisitorial models. They conclude that "the most important result of the experiment is some empirical support for the general claim advanced by Fuller that an adversary presentation significantly counteracts decision-maker bias. The overall significant effect on final judgments exercised by the biasing experience lays the substructure for this empirical result." They further concluded:

> In the adversary mode, the choice alternatives are given a special salience through their physical separation and embodiment in the counterpoised adversary roles. The decision maker is presented with a clear opposition of viewpoints that dramatizes the act of choosing. In the inquisitorial mode, the act of choosing may be less clear. The decision maker may be influenced unobtrusively without ever being fully aware that choices are being foreclosed to him.

The Agency representative in the form of the "present party" or *PreP*, restores balance to the jurisprudential equation by ensuring a neutral, passive decision maker in the ALJ, while concurrently maintaining the duty to develop the record (a duty of inquiry) in the *PreP*. The benefits of the *PreP* as a flexible actor are several fold, outlined in *Table 1*. To maximize this flexibility the current attorney's fee, presently contingent on "past due" benefits, should be revised so that a fee agreement rewards *early* hearing and/or resolution of the case.[97] Failure to effect this key change will adversely affect the flexible role of the *PreP*. The significance of much of this flexibility within the hearings process is that it need not be dependent on the ALJ, but occurs between counsel independently per the operation of (yet-to-be-adopted) rules of disability hearing procedure, much as now occurs in the state and federal courts.

---

97 As discussed in greater detail, *infra*, instead of being contingent on the award of "past due benefits"—thus, rewarding delay—a graduated fee should be instituted which is higher the earlier the case is presented. Alternately, a fee petition examining expertise, difficulty etc., should always be an option.

Table 1

Flexible Roles of the *PreP* Upon a Request for Hearing	Duty of Inquiry	Duty of Representation	Hearing Advocacy	Case Resolution
	Early case management	Joint Case Management Order	Inquiry of claimant	Agreed Upon Decision before hearing with or without amended onset.
	Early evidentiary discovery	Assessment of outstanding issues	Inquiry of expert(s)	Agreed Upon Decision after hearing with or without amended onset.
	Early assessment for consultative examination (s).	Assessment for early disposition; nature and type of hearing, if a hearing is necessary.	Argument to the ALJ	Disputed Decision – Favorable to Claimant with no appeal permitted (after hearings) Disputed Decision – Favorable to Claimant with appeal permitted (after hearing) Disputed Decision – Unfavorable, No appeal permitted. Disputed Decision – Unfavorable, appeal permitted.

Thus, the benefit of the Agency representative or "*PreP*" in a disability hearing includes:

- Early case management with or without input from the judge;[98]
- Improved evidentiary development through early production of documentary evidence and addressing requests for consultative examination(s);
- Early review of the evidence for the purpose of determining the nature and type of hearing that will be needed, the estimated time needed for hearing, the need for expert or other witnesses;
- Potential for stipulation as to facts and legal issues to include amendments to alleged onset date and transferable skills from work history resulting in agreed-upon decision(s);
- Concurrence of parties as to readiness of case for hearing.
- Parties submitting proposed decision with recitation of issues, facts, findings and conclusion in accordance with established format to facilitate drafting a final decision.

98 Which necessarily requires early assignment of the case to the judge, contrary to current case assignment procedures in which cases are not generally assigned to judges except when a hearing docket has been set. As a result, under present processes, there is little time before the hearing for the judge to engage in any meaningful "case management."

At bottom, the Agency representative or "present party" benefits the claimant, enabling a range of activities designed to expedite hearings and appeals; and, where possible, to reach early decisions in substantial numbers of cases, leaving only those claims where there is a significant question, for hearing. With consideration for the mandates of the Administrative Procedure Act (APA)[99] and due process, the Agency representative or *PreP* should be attached to a Social Security Administration component outside of ODAR, ideally the Office of General Counsel, a uniquely qualified entity within the Social Security Administration, responsible for appeals to the federal courts, among other activities. This is consistent with OGC's mission statement, and role as representative of the Agency in the United States courts.[100]

Adoption of Formal Rules of Procedure

Conspicuously absent from the current Social Security disability hearing process are formal rules of practice and procedure governing the adjudication of disability claims. Adoption of formal rules of practice and procedure will prove beneficial both to the claimant and the Agency, establishing, among other things, clearly delineated paths to resolution of pending hearings by means other than hearing. Formal rules also include ascertainable deadlines governing both pre-hearing and hearing activity, including deadlines for the submission of evidence and for closing the record after hearing. Long delays plague the current hearings procedure, which lacks certitude and predictability with endemic delay.

Formal rules of practice and procedure promote efficiency and economy of resources. Procedural mechanisms must be in place that enable the parties to pursue flexible outcomes, not formally acknowledged under existing Social

---

99 The Administrative Procedure Act (APA) defines the scope of its reach as regards administrative adjudications when it provides at U.S. Code, Title 5, Section 554(a) that the act is applicable "in every case of adjudication required by statute to be determined on the record after opportunity for an Agency hearing."

100 The Social Security General Counsel Mission Statement provides, in-part:
The Office of the General Counsel advises the Commissioner on legal matters, is responsible for providing all legal advice to the Commissioner, Deputy Commissioner, and all subordinate organizational components (except OIG) of SSA in connection with the operation and administration of SSA. Responsible for the policy formulation and decision making related to the collection, access, and disclosure of such information in the records of the Social Security Administration; and processing of Freedom of Information requests and appeals (under the Freedom of Information and Privacy Acts.

Security regulations. According to Professor Kevin Clermont (2009), the "nature of civil procedure," is that it "observes both outcome and process values in establishing a process to resolve factual and legal disputes."[101] It is precisely the absence of codified process values as expressed in a comprehensive body of procedural rules that now plagues the disability adjudicatory system.

In the context of disability hearings and appeals, it might be said that "civil procedure concerns society's process for submitting and resolving factual and legal disputes over entitlement to the award of disability benefits under the Social Security Act and its implementing regulations." Like Professor Clermont's analysis, the "shapers" contemplate and "observe both outcome and process values." At present, few if any procedural mechanisms permit, much less, envision, pro-active, early, party-driven resolution of either the disability claim generally, or intermediate issues, specifically. Indeed, under the current system, statistics show that only 7.3 percent of all pending hearings are decided without hearing (SSA OIG 2011).

Practice and procedural mechanisms can be divided into the following broad categories, which, in turn, give rise to a framework for promulgation and organization of specific procedural and practice rules to be adopted for use in Social Security disability hearings.[102]

1. *Pre-Hearing*: adoption of comprehensive rules governing the following pre-hearing actions:
   a. *Case Management* – requiring/enabling the parties to meet/confer within a defined time period after the filing of the initial *Request for Hearing*, for the purpose of:

      i. Narrowing and/or establishing the scope of the claim;
      ii. Establishing a reasonable period for discovery/production of existing treatment and/or other medical and nonmedical records;

---

101 Professor Clermont's comments are clear: to carry into effect the substantive law, rules of practice and procedure governing the hearings process must echo these selfsame principles.

102 The *Procedural Rules for Disability Hearings* (PRDH) should be guided, as are the Federal Rules of Civil Procedure, by Rule 1 of the FRCP:
"These rules govern the procedure in all civil actions and proceedings in the United States district courts, except as stated in Rule 81. They should be construed and administered to secure the just, speedy, and inexpensive determination of every action and proceeding."

   iii. Establishing the need for case development, as in consultative examinations.

   b. Authorizing voluntary prehearing conferences between counsel for the purpose narrowing the issues and/or early resolution.
   c. Authorizing prehearing conference by the administrative law judge for the purpose of ascertaining case readiness, discovery, or any other issue affecting hearing.

2. *Discovery and Case Development:* establishing a defined period, based on the nature of the claim, for production/submission of existing evidence as well as case development, including consultative examination(s).
   a. *Experts.* Provision for written interrogatories to medical and vocational experts following submission of medical and/or other evidence.

3. *Early Resolution Prehearing:* authorizing prehearing conferences between counsel without the ALJ for the purpose of resolution of the claim without hearing;
   a. Provision for submission of an agreed-decision for approval by the ALJ.
   b. Provision for review by the ALJ, who may accept or reject the proposed decision.

4. *Resolution Post Hearing:* authorizing submission of an agreed-decision post-hearing.
   a. Provision for review by the ALJ, who may accept or reject the proposed decision.

5. *Hearing Procedure:* establishing rules governing the nature, course and order of hearing proceedings.
   a. Authorizing direct and cross-examination;
   b. Authorizing the objection to evidence, whether it is testimonial, documentary, electronic or otherwise, based on minimum standards of reliability and validity.

6. *Evidentiary Standards:* establishing minimum standards of reliability and validity of evidentiary submissions in disability hearings (including limiting and/or defining the use of forms not prepared by the Social Security Administration)

a. The *Federal Rules of Evidence* serve as a guide, but do not govern the submission of evidence, whether testimonial, documentary, electronic or otherwise.
b. Provision for minimum standards of materiality.
c. Provision for standardized forms and/or criteria for forms used in assessment of a claimant's residual functional capacity, further ensuring uniform application of regulations. This should not foreclose opinion expressed in medical/treatment records or other submissions generated solely by the treating source.
d. Requiring parties to submit evidentiary documents in accordance with enforceable formatting and submissions standards.

7. *Closing the Record:* authorizing the administrative law judge to close the record within a defined period following conclusion of the hearing and prior to issuance of the decision.

Adoption of standardized *Rules of Practice and Procedure for Disability Hearings* (PRDH) would ensure predictability of proceedings, establish a clear structure within which the parties may act and interact, and foster a procedural environment conducive to effective case management and readiness as well as for early decision.

Refocusing the Role of the Appeals Council Consistent with Recommendations of the Administrative Conference of the United States

ACUS (1987) issued its recommendation concerning the role of the Appeals. In particular, ACUS recommended that "[t]he Social Security Administration (SSA) should, as soon as feasible, restructure the Appeals Council in a fashion that redirects the institution's goals and operation from an exclusive focus on processing the stream of individual cases and toward an emphasis on improved organizational effectiveness."

Toward this end, ACUS recommended various substantive and procedural changes; but notably emphasized the need for the Appeals Council to reduce its caseload in "order to fulfill its responsibility to develop, and to encourage utilization of, sound decisional principles and practices throughout SSA." ACUS further recommended that "the Appeals Council must be empowered to exercise its review sparingly, so that it may concentrate its attention on types of cases identified in advance by the Appeals Council."

Procedural reform necessarily includes close review of the right of appeal. In the proposed restructured disability hearings jurisprudence, the addition of an Agency representative or *PreP* acting for the Social Security Administration, triggers an additional appeals right currently, in effect, held by the Appeals Council via "own motion review."[103] The presence of the Agency representative or "present party" extends the rebalanced juridical equation to the Appeals Council, such that an appeal of a decision favorable to the claimant may also be appealed by the Agency when the Agency believes the judge has erred—but only in highly circumscribed cases. Thus, a favorable decision may only may be appealed by the Agency (through the offices of the *PreP*) where significant issues of public policy or statutory/regulatory interpretation are implicated. Absent such a showing, as in a case turning on credibility—a purely factual question—any appeal not meeting this standard must be dismissed.

This is consistent with the ACUS recommendation, limiting Appeals Council review of otherwise routine disability decisions in favor of a heightened leadership/policymaking role.

A similar standard should also govern appeals taken by claimants. A denial decision by an ALJ may be appealed only under the same standard—where there is a showing that the decision implicates significant public policy or statutory/regulatory construction and/or interpretation. As a result, the Appeals Council is limited in its review, effectively accepting the decision of the ALJ, except as noted above—in those cases where "significant public policy or statutory / regulatory interpretation" is implicated.[104]

This standard is intended as a high bar, and a decision reviewed under this standard should be reversed or remanded only where there is a finding that the ALJ's decision was *clearly erroneous or contrary to law*. Limiting review by the Appeals Council recognizes the simple legal fact that individual disability decisions are not precedential and do not act in their resolution to establish Agency policy. Thus,

---

[103] See 20 CFR Part 404.

[104] This effectively echoes the ACUS recommendation, which further provided: "[T]he Secretary should direct the Appeals Council to design a new review process, subject to the Secretary's approval, that would continue to be part of the available administrative remedy for a claimant dissatisfied with an [ALJ's] initial decision, but that would enable the Appeals Council to deny a petition for review if the issues it sought to raise are deemed inappropriate for the Appeals Council's attention. If a petition for review is denied, the ALJ's decision should be deemed to be final Agency action" (ACUS 1987).

review is appropriate only in those cases which significantly depart from Agency policy or which depart from or contravene accepted statutory and/or regulatory interpretation.

Enabling appeals by the Agency through the office of the "present party" or *PreP* acts to "check" a judge's award where, as has been alleged in various congressional forums, incorrect decisions have been made in aid of the so-called practice of "paying down the backlog." The ability to appeal a judge's decision in a favorable case presently only exists in the Appeals Council regulatory right of "own motion review." This proposed right of appeal broadens the potential for such review where, as noted, there has been a significant departure from Agency policy and/or statutory and/or regulatory interpretation.

Limiting Appeals Council review as first suggested by ACUS would further reduce the backlog, ensuring that cases do not simply circulate between the ALJ and the Appeals Council, thereby adding to cost and delay. The Office of the Inspector General (OIG) takes note of the present increasing workloads for the Appeals Council:

> "If dissatisfied with the ALJ decision, claimants can appeal. Since FY 2007, the number of appealed cases to the AC was greater than dispositions, resulting in a tripling of pending cases. The AC pending levels grew from about 53,000 to about 157,000 cases by the end of FY 2013. The increase in pending claims also resulted in longer average processing times on appeals. Claimants waited about 364 days for an AC action in FY 2013, up from 227 days in FY 2007" (SSA OIG 2014).

Figure 1 shows 2013 ALJ decisional allowance rates, reflecting an average of 56 percent nationally. Close review reveals an essentially bell-shaped curve, indicating relative uniformity of decision making by the overwhelming majority of ALJs. Limiting appeals to decisions implicating "significant public policy or statutory/regulatory interpretation" will have little effect on current decisional outcomes.

Figure 1

Figure A-2: FY 2013 ALJ Decisional Allowance Rates(Relates to 1,477 ALJs with at least 200 dispositions)

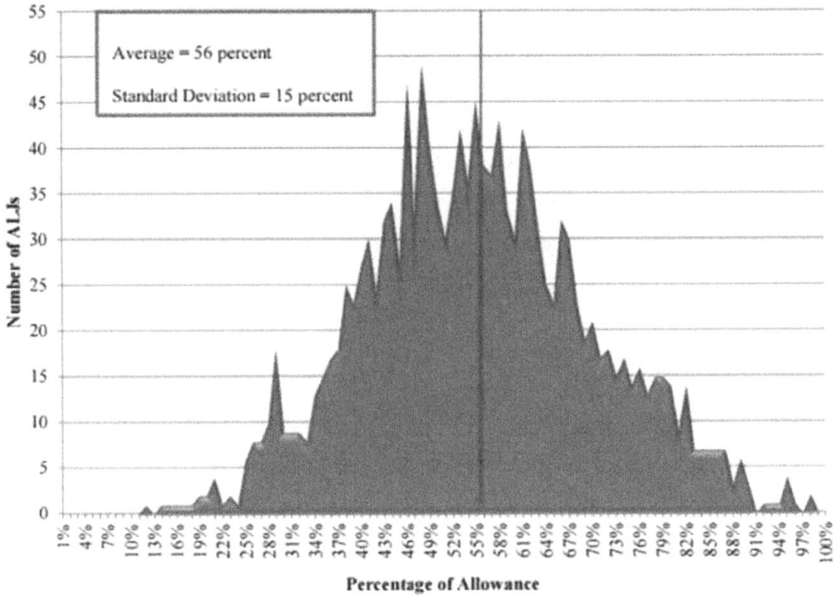

Source: Social Security Administration Office of the Inspector General Report No. A-12-13-13084.

Assess Attorney's Fees on the Value of Services Rendered or as a Flat Rate, Foreclosing Fees Based on Past-Due Benefits

For the Agency representative or *PreP* to be effective in seeking early disposition in disability hearings, the current basis for the award of fees as a function of "past-due benefits" in accord with a signed "fee agreement" must end.[105]

[105] Attorney fees awarded by United States District Court under the authority of the Equal Access to Justice Act (EAJA) are not here discussed. *See,* Social Security Administration: Hearings, Appeals and Litigation Law Manual (HALLEX), ¶ I-1-2-91 (2015), provides in part:

> The Equal Access to Justice Act (EAJA), United States Code, Title 28, Section 2412: "authorizes an attorney to obtain reimbursement of expenses incurred (*e.g.*, legal fees, expert witness fees, etc.) in the course of representing a litigant in a court action and certain administrative proceedings involving a government Agency; stipulates that reimbursement of legal fees and other expenses applies only with respect to proceedings in which the party prevails against the Agency, and only if the court finds that the position of the government was not substantially justified;

Where the claimant has signed a fee agreement that comports with federal statute and regulation, Social Security provides that a fee shall not exceed the lesser of:

- o 25 percent of the claimant's *past-due benefits* **OR**
- o $4,000 if the fee agreement was approved before February 1, 2002.
- o $5,300 if the fee agreement was approved on or after February 1, 2002, but before June 22, 2009.
- o $6,000 if the fee agreement was approved on or after June 22, 2009.

Applicable regulations also alternately provide for payment of a fee, determined as a result of a "fee petition," considering:[106]

(i) The extent and type of services the representative performed;
(ii) The complexity of the case;
(iii) The level of skill and competence required of the representative in giving the services;
(iv) The amount of time the representative spent on the case;
(v) The results the representative achieved;
(vi) The level of review to which the claim was taken and the level of the review at which the representative became your representative; and
(vii) The amount of fee the representative requests for his or her services, including any amount authorized or requested before, but not including the amount of any expenses he or she incurred.

For the vast majority of representatives, the fee agreement has become the norm, whereas the fee petition is generally utilized where more than one attorney/representative has rendered services. No issue is raised by use of a fee petition, as this generally results in an assessment of fee as a question of skill.

At issue is the use of a fee agreement where the calculation is not based on skill or effort, but simply on "25 percent of past-due benefits or $6,000, whichever is less" (SSA 2015). The problem is immediately apparent: a fee that increases with the passage of time is a direct *disincentive* to early case management and

---

and provides that when a representative received fees for the same work under both section 206(b) of the Social Security Act [U.S. Code, Title 42, Section 406(b)] and EAJA, the representative must refund to the claimant the amount of the smaller fee."

106 See 20 CFR Part 404.

disposition. There is no good reason, other than ease of calculation, to maintain such a corrosive disincentive,

Past-due benefits are defined as those "that result from a favorable determination or decision (hereafter 'decision') and are the amount of benefits for all beneficiaries under title II of the Act that have accumulated because of a favorable administrative decision, up to but not including the month the Social Security Administration (SSA) effectuates the decision. Therefore, for most fully favorable decisions, the end date of the past-due benefits period is the month before the month SSA effectuates the decision." *The net effect:* the longer a case is pending, the greater the attorney's fee, with a current ceiling (when signing a fee agreement) of $6,000. The obvious conclusion is that, regardless whether or not intended, there is a built-in incentive for delay.

Given that some 80 percent of claimants are now represented, there is an inherent reward for those who delay, whether intentional or otherwise (SSA OIG 2007).[107] This circumstance stands in direct contravention to ongoing congressional concern over the current backlog, continuing endemic delay and the simple plea by claimants who are in need assistance at the earliest opportunity (Fahrenthold 2014).[108]

---

107 Based on this September 2007 report by SSA's OIG, which shows that of the 559,000 claims heard by ALJs in FY 2006, 439,000 were represented by attorney and non-attorney representatives, representing claimants in almost 80 percent of all claims appealed. Examined another way, the OIG notes, "[i]n FY 2006, approximately 26,000 attorneys and 5,000 non-attorneys represented claimants before ODAR." The number of persons is likely higher now as may be inferred from recent statistics showing an increase in the number of representatives now appearing at the initial stages of the disability applications process. Government Accountability Office. GAO Report No. 15-62, "Social Security Disability Benefits, Agency Could Improve Oversight of Representatives Providing Disability Advocacy Services." GAO Report No. 15-62 (December 2014).

108 Mr. Fahrenthold observes in his October 2014 Washington Post article that there is "a queue of waiting Americans larger than the populations of six different states. It is bigger even than the infamous backups at the U.S. Department of Veterans' Affairs (VA), where 526,000 people are waiting in line, and the patent office, where 606,000 applications are pending", further stating:

> "When . . . [ALJs] . . . make a [disability] ruling, they must decide whether someone is truly unable to hold any job. That is slow work, made slower by a pileup of outdated rules and oddball procedures. The judges' official list of jobs, for instance, is a Depression-era relic last updated in 1991. It still includes "telegram messenger" and "horse-and-wagon driver"—not exactly growth industries. It doesn't mention the Internet at all." *Id.*

Employing representatives who are only paid if they win, and whose pay is calculated as a function of past-due benefits creates an essential imbalance in the jurisprudential paradigm of today's disability hearing. Furthermore, a contingent fee encourages increased filings for benefits as representatives advertise for clients and encourage pursuit of disability, which is in effect pursuit of a fee (Paletta and Searcey 2011).[109] A contingent fee based on past-due benefits encourages delay because the greater the delay, the larger the attorney fee.

Equally significant, "*Pay-for-delay*" creates an inherent conflict between the representative, who benefits from delay, and his client, who seeks an early resolution of his claim for benefits. There are a number of alternatives to the current *pay-for-delay* contingent fee" (Wolfe and Engel 2013, 46).

A flat fee: One example is a flat fee.[110] Upon award, an attorney or representative would be entitled to an established fee, regardless of the amount of past-due benefits or the amount of time spent preparing the case. Instead, the fee amount would be established by the complexity of the case, much as is the case now with a fee petition. Adopting the current maximum fee of $6,000, the judge would determine whether counsel would receive one-third of the maximum ($2,000), two-thirds of the maximum ($4,000), or the maximum fee ($6,000), dependent upon the complexity of the case. No appeal could be taken from this administrative judicial determination. Fee petitions would be precluded, in effect replaced by a simpler calculation. The fee would be taken from a claimant's past-due benefits or, if this amount were insufficient, the balance would be paid by the government to counsel. The amount advanced by the government would be deducted from the claimant's monthly benefit in $100 or other increments (as appropriate to the claimant's circumstances) until the government was repaid.

---

109 Paletta and Searcey wrote:

> "Lawyers Harry and Charles Binder began representing applicants for Social Security disability benefits in the 1970s, when the field was a professional backwater. Last year, their firm collected $88 million in fees for guiding clients through the system, government data indicate, making it the nation's largest Social Security disability advocate by far. . . . The Social Security Administration figured cases would move through the pipeline faster if more claimants were guided by experts. So in 2004 the Agency and Congress relaxed rules governing representation, making it easier for non-lawyer advocates to get paid. Binder swiftly hired lower-paid non-lawyers to handle cases, ramped up advertising and began processing far greater numbers of clients."

110 See, generally, Government Accountability Office, Report No. 15-62, 2014, concerning the application of flat fees.

No hardship rules would apply. This alternative has some appeal for it allows administrative law judges, who have no ability to institute sanctions, to redress poor representation or other conduct by means of a fee adjustment.

Reverse-Time Dependent Fees: Alternately, in direct response to the pending backlog, attorney fees could be reverse-time-dependent. A hearing within six months of filing the *Request for Hearing* would result in payment of the maximum fee of $6,000. Holding a hearing within 12 months would result in payment of $4,000 (two-thirds of the maximum), whereas a hearing held after 12 months would result in a fee of $2,000 (one-third of the maximum). The same rules for payment would apply as outlined earlier, including the disallowance of fee petitions. Time-dependent resolution would encourage counsel to proceed with the case, thereby benefitting the claimant, who, as noted, has an interest in a timely decision. Where delay was occasioned by factors outside the representative's control, the judge would have the discretion to "bump'" to the next earlier fee category.

Hybrid Fees: The two foregoing scenarios could be combined in a *hybrid* scenario, such that the primary determining factor would be time, and upon motion of counsel the administrative law judge could increase an otherwise lower fee, recognizing that delay was caused by complexity and not foot-dragging. "Elimination of the current pay-for-delay contingent fee ends the incentive for delay by the representative and at the same time re-incentivizes counsel to proceed apace, all to the benefit of the claimant. Realignment of the fee structure accomplishes a positive realignment of both the claimant's and the representative's interests" (GAO 2014).

Curtailment of Travel Reimbursements to Attorneys/Representatives.

The Social Security Administration currently pays travel fees to attorneys and non-attorney representatives who travel to represent a claimant.[111] Social Security provides for reimbursement for travel for "[y]ou, [the claimant] your representative, and all unsubpoenaed witnesses we or the State Agency determines to be reasonably necessary who attend disability hearings." The Code of Federal Regulations, Title 20, Section 404.999c, details what travel costs are reimbursed:

"(a) Reimbursement for ordinary travel expenses is limited—

---

[111] See 20 CFR Part 404.

(1) To the cost of travel by the most economical and expeditious means of transportation available and appropriate to the individual's condition of health as determined by the State Agency or by us, considering the available means in the following order—

(i) Common carrier (air, rail, or bus);

(ii) Privately owned vehicles;

(iii) Commercially rented vehicles and other special conveyances."

Amazingly, travel costs also include reimbursement for "unusual travel expenses," provided they are approved in advance. These include:

> "Unusual expenses that may be covered in connection with travel include, but are not limited to—
> (1) Ambulance services;
> (2) Attendant services;
> (3) Meals;
> (4) Lodging; and
> (5) Taxicabs."

The rationale for such payment is no longer applicable. In an era when at least 80 percent of claimants are represented, there appears to be little or no justification for such payments. In effect, the government is subsidizing private enterprise, with little or no rationale. So pervasive is Social Security's disability program nationally, no formal data is required to conclude that lawyers and non-lawyer representatives who represent claimants can literally be found in every municipality in the United States.

Given the number of annual hearings, discussed *supra*, travel costs across some 150 ODAR offices potentially amounts to millions of dollars each year. The Office of Inspector General cites an ACUS in-house study to the effect that "SSA video hearings could save ODAR an estimated $59 million, annually" (SSA OIG 2012a). So-called national law firms and non-lawyer disability advocates advertise in most major U.S. media markets, seeking out-of-state claimants despite the often thriving practices of local counsel and non-lawyer representatives. Foreclosing travel subsidies for private firms would return the cost of such travel to the private sector, where it belongs. Indeed, then-Senator Tom Coburn, of Oklahoma, introduced Senate Bill 3003, "Protecting Social Security Disability Act of 2014" that, among other things, would "prohibit a representative from being reimbursed by the Social Security Administration for travel expenses related to a case."

In an earlier era when few attorneys or non-lawyer representatives were available to represent claimants, there may have been some justification for reimbursing travel expenses. Such justification no longer exists. Expending public monies to support private practice simply makes no sense. The cost of travel should simply be, as with any other private enterprise, a cost of doing business and should not be, as it is now, an all-but-hidden public subsidy. This is not, however, simply a question of appropriate expenditures of ever decreasing public monies; *it is also a question of hearing efficiencies.* Frequently, out-of-state lawyers/representatives never meet with their clients until the day of the hearing. This results in missing documents, failed communication, and hearing postponements.

These practices, enabled by the Agency's travel reimbursement policy, frequently have an unintended adverse effect on claimants. Because lawyers and non-lawyer representatives are, by definition, traveling (not uncommonly, from a state different than that of the claimant's residence) there is no person-to-person meeting between the claimant and the representative before the day of the hearing. Anecdotal stories abound, describing the traveling lawyer/representative searching the lobby, photo in hand, asking one person after another, if they are "the client"—often less than an hour before the hearing is to begin.

That such travel fees have become common practice is readily apparent. It is not uncommon for a representative to schedule travel to one locale for a hearing Monday morning, then board a plane for a neighboring state for a hearing on Tuesday, generally meeting the claimant shortly before the scheduled hearing. It is not unusual in such cases to find two, three, and in some cases more than five different representatives who have at one time or another been designated by the claimant to represent his or her interests, only to be succeeded by a different member of the same firm because of varying travel schedules or postponements.

Is there any valid reason why the federal government should incentivize hearing inefficiencies by paying for representatives' airfare and other travel, when local counsel are almost always available to handle such cases without the need for such subsidies?

There is not. Legislation should be enacted ending lawyer and non-lawyer subsidies as an ill-conceived use of scarce public funds.

KEY FACTS

The Hearings Process

The Social Security Administration has not altered its adjudicatory model for more than 50 years. Given the shortcomings of earlier "solutions," the persistent and growing *hearings pending* backlog and concerns for errant ALJ decisions augurs for a change. When first devised, the hearings process was conceived as non-adversarial, adopting an inquisitorial jurisprudence akin to that of judicial systems in continental Europe, this in light of the fact that few persons were represented. Professor Viles published his study of the Social Security disability system in 1968. He describes, in the words of one [then] hearing examiner [now an administrative law judge], the 1968 hearing procedure, still followed today. Rather than act at all times as a neutral, the hearing examiner mimics, in part, each of the parties, acting to develop the evidence favorable to the claimant, as well as that for the government. (S)he is then to return to the neutral position, and despite having just searched the evidence for evidence both for and against the claimant, render an impartial decision (Viles 1968).

With one telling exception, this 47-year-old description of the 1968 disability hearings process reflects precisely the same hearings procedures in effect today. In other words, despite the passage of time and notwithstanding the addition of new technology (*e.g.,* video hearings), the disability hearing of 2015 resembles, with little exception, the disability hearing before a Social Security hearing examiner in 1968.

The telling exception? The presence of lawyers and non-lawyer advocates as claimant's representatives. Contrary to the 1968 hearing examiner's observation, at least 80 percent of claimants are now represented. This is not a new figure, but has gradually increased over time. Social Security noted in a September 2007 report by its OIG that in fiscal year 2006, 439,000 of the 559,000 claims heard by administrative law judges were represented by attorney and non-attorney advocates, representing claimants in almost 80 percent of claims appealed. The OIG noted: "[i]n FY 2006, approximately 26,000 attorneys and 5,000 non-attorneys represented claimants before ODAR" (SSA OIG 2007).

The Pending Hearings Backlog

The backlog is not, new, but is, instead, the product of an ongoing, flawed adjudicative appeals process which embraces an antiquated, outdated jurisprudence—a holdover from a time when few claimants were represented by either counsel or non-lawyer advocates. **Figure 2** reflects not only the distribution of appeals pending hearing by their age, but also the total numbers of appeals annually. Even a quick glance demonstrates a backlog growing since 2008. Adding the number cases pending less than 270 days with those pending greater than 270 days reveals a rapid increase in the number of pending hearings, growing from 760,813 in 2008 to 1,010,729 in 2015, the numbers representing an overall increase of more than a quarter million hearings pending in less than seven years. Examined as a percentage of pending hearings, the backlog has increased in this short period by almost 25 percent (24.73 percent).

Figure 2

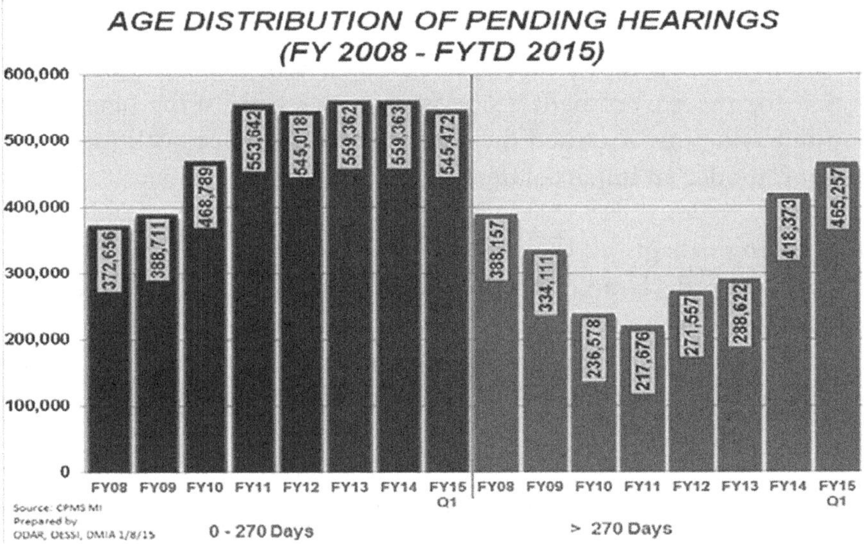

Social Security Administration Official Website, accessed September 2015

National Hearing Decisions by ALJs

The Social Security Administration Office of the Inspector General observes that "SSA has experienced a growing hearing backlog and increasing case processing times in recent years, causing the public to wait longer for decisions. SSA's pending hearing backlog grew from about 694,000 cases at the end of June 2010 to approximately 955,000 at the end of June 2014. Average processing time on hearings has also increased from 415 days in June 2010 to 437 days in June 2014. Annual appeals hearings before federal administrative law judges continue to rise in response to rising numbers of applications" (SSA OIG 2015a).

Despite significant increases in the number of hearings held by administrative law judges, there remains a growing backlog of undecided appeals, a fact which starkly highlights the impending insolvency of the Social Security Disability Insurance (SSDI) program. See **Figure 3**.

Figure 3

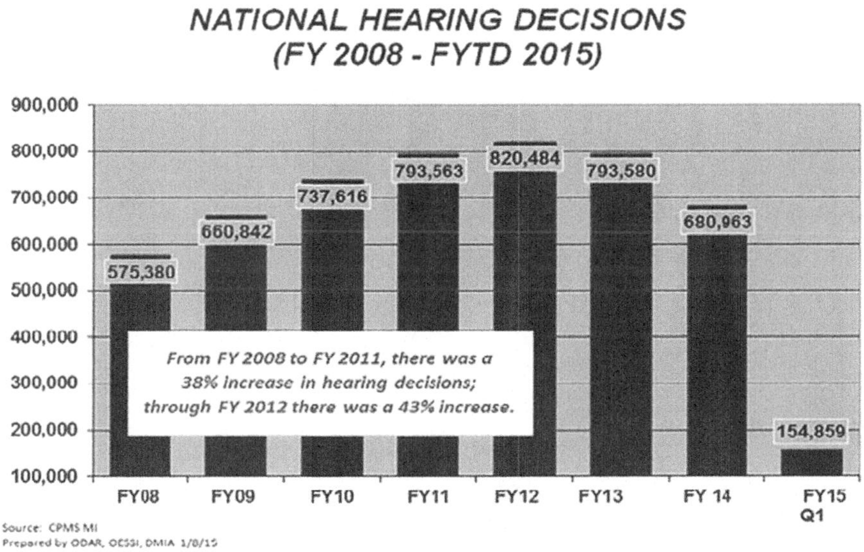

Social Security Administration Official Website, accessed September 2015

Discussion of Program Administration Proposals

Margaret Malone

This discussion is a summary of the comments made by the discussant at the SSDI Solutions Conference on August 4, 2015 before chapters were made final.

The three papers in this section address a number of important issues among the many that the Social Security disability system faces today—and, unfortunately, that it has been facing for decades.

The first paper, *Social Security Disability Adjudicative Reform: Ending the Reconsideration Stage of SSDI Adjudication after Sixteen Years of Testing and Enhancing Initial Stage Record Development*, is by Jon Dubin. It is a well-researched and well-argued paper that proposes ending the reconsideration stage of Social Security Disability Insurance (SSDI) adjudication. The paper reminds us of arguments that have been made since at least the 1990s, and yet the agency has kept testing and maintaining uncertainty as to the future. I am sympathetic to Professor Dubin's proposal to end reconsideration, but I believe that change would be less likely to face negative consequences if the initial decision stage would first be made stronger. I think that making the following changes should be a high priority:

(1) undertaking a vigorous ongoing national training program for Disability Determination Services (DDS) staff in all states that would improve the quality, consistency and the fairness of decision making throughout the country;

(2) setting standards and providing ongoing training for all medical and vocational experts and medical consultants;

(3) working to improve the quality of written decisions, so that claimants will understand the bases for negative decisions and judges will understand the reasoning of the DDS decision maker; (When I was special advisor to the

commissioner for disability, I asked the quality office to share with me a random sample of DDS denial notices that had been sent to claimants. Almost universally, these notices provided no rationale that might persuade the claimant that the case had been carefully examined and considered. No wonder the claimant chooses to appeal!)

(4) giving decision makers the tools they need to make sound decisions; (Creating a new and well-crafted Dictionary of Occupational Titles is a proposal that Professor Dubin wisely emphasizes in his paper. This is an improvement that the Social Security Administration (SSA) has worked on for a good number of years. It is past time to bring this effort to fruition.)

(5) requiring SSA reviewers and analysts to make full use of the agency's Policy Feedback System to identify and correct errors in decision making—both allowances and denials.

In summary, by improving the first level of decision making I think we can acquire the positive information needed to convince policymakers and participants in the process that reconsideration can safely be eliminated. And that—I believe—will be the time to make the change.

Jeffery Wolfe, Dale Glendening, and David Engel's paper, *Social Security: Restructuring Disability Adjudication*, also proposes a change that is worthy of consideration. They propose that each hearing office have what they refer to as a "referee," or "PreP," whose role would be to promote administrative justice for all parties in a disability proceeding. This proposal builds on previous proposals that called for establishing an adversarial procedure in the hearing office. There is merit in this proposal, but I believe it raises issues that need to be resolved. I would suggest that SSA solicit and analyze the views of judges and Hearing Office attorneys throughout the country. This could be done by holding teleconferences, requesting written views, or perhaps by holding regional meetings. But certainly those who have experience in the field should be involved in developing a plan for precisely how this would be implemented. And before a plan is put in place, it should be carefully tested and evaluated—perhaps in 15 or 20 offices in locations around the country.

Among the issues that need to be addressed is what the proposal would require in terms of additional funding, hiring, and training. The role of the PreP that they propose needs to be defined precisely. And, since this proposal specifies that the PreP should be part of the Office of General Counsel rather than the

Hearing Office, it raises the issue of who will oversee the work of the PreP in each hearing office, and what would be the relationship of the PreP to the judge. Questions such as these are important to the efficient and effective operation of this proposed new configuration of the hearing procedure.

The *Data-Driven Solutions for Improving the Continuing Disability Review Process* paper was written by experts from the National Institutes of Health, Alex Constantin, Chunxiao Zhou, John Collins, and Julia Porcino. The paper emphasizes the value of enhancing decisions for purposes of the Continuing Disability Review (CDR) process, but the authors make clear that their detailed and carefully considered proposals for change in SSA's data infrastructure and review process would strengthen decision making at all levels—an important enhancement to the disability decision process.

By improving the CDR process, as the authors of the paper propose, SSA would also promote the movement of disabled individuals into employment, an objective that is of great interest to a number of members of Congress as well as many others. I would suggest that SSA also develop a program to provide employment assistance to those who are expected to be or who are terminated through the CDR process. In addition, this would be an appropriate time to amend the budget process to provide that savings from performing CDRs be allocated to SSA on an annual basis to be used to cover CDR and related administrative costs.

There is another issue I consider to be of the highest priority, and which so far has not been discussed. After consulting with many of the agency's ablest DDS and Hearing Office experts over the years, I am convinced that the most valuable improvement the agency could make is to improve the disability program policy. When I was working as a disability advisor to the Commissioner some years ago, and after extensive study and discussion among agency experts, we found broad agreement that there were many areas in which disability policy should be clarified, and regulatory language and operational procedures should be improved and made less confusing and subjective. In order to accomplish this objective, we proposed a new policy body. We referred to it as a Decision Review Board. I think that a variation of this proposal should be considered now. For example, I think the Commissioner should appoint a new review body composed of outstanding and experienced employees—representatives of DDSs, administrative law judges, administrative appeals judges, and attorneys with the Office of General Counsel who, together, will report directly to the Commissioner. They should serve on a rotational basis, with terms of two to three years or more in order to have time to consider and address issues that are causing inconsistency and error throughout the system.

Section IV

Interaction with Other Programs

9

Expanding Private Disability Insurance Coverage to Help the SSDI Program

David F. Babbel and Mark F. Meyer

INTRODUCTION

For working Americans facing a disabling illness or injury, private group long-term disability insurance (hereafter "group disability") provides a crucial supplement to Social Security Disability Insurance (SSDI) benefits. Approximately one-third of Americans working in the private sector have disability income-protection coverage, most often through group policies sponsored by their employers (BLS 2014, under "Private Industry Workers" Table 16). Three primary benefits characterize group disability insurance for employees: it replaces a significant proportion of pre-disability income; it typically starts paying income protection benefits three or six months after disability onset (with short-term disability plans typically covering payments during the first three to six months); and it provides affected employees access to return-to-work expertise and assistance. Group disability coverage also benefits sponsoring employers by facilitating a quicker return to the job after a disabling incident and better retention of employees. While these direct benefits are the primary motivation for employers and workers to purchase private disability coverage, recent research has demonstrated and quantified federal budget savings arising from group disability coverage. We maintain that an expansion of the number of employees covered by private group disability insurance can and should play a significant and positive role in bolstering the long-term solvency of the SSDI program.

This paper proposes extending group disability income protection to a greater proportion of working Americans by encouraging employers to adopt automatic enrollment or "opt-out" arrangements under employer-sponsored group disability plans. Increasing the number of employees with group disability coverage will reduce the number of workers receiving SSDI benefits, since more workers affected by a disability will benefit from the income protection and return-to-work features of group disability coverage. Recent experience with a similar approach to boosting participation in employer-sponsored retirement savings plans has shown that opt-out arrangements can have a powerful and significant positive effect on employee participation in employer-sponsored benefit plans. Implementing opt-out arrangements in group disability plans should increase employee participation and facilitate more employers offering such benefits to their workers. We complement the opt-out arrangement proposal by proposing that the federal government facilitate education and outreach efforts to help working Americans and their employers understand the risk of disabling illness and injury, the financial implications of work disability, and what they can do to mitigate and protect against the risks of disability. This proposed education effort would amplify the efforts that group disability providers and employers would carry out to explain the workings of the new opt-out arrangements and group disability coverage.

To explain the fiscal benefits of group disability coverage to the SSDI program, this paper first quantifies the number of working Americans who have either avoided dependence on SSDI or reduced their time on the program's rolls as a direct consequence of group disability provider financial support and return-to-work assistance. Our analysis estimates that group disability insurance, at the current proportion of the U.S. workforce with coverage, will save the federal treasury at least $25 billion over the next 10 years—at least $10 billion in SSDI benefits and approximately $15 billion in other federal programs.

Based on current research, our analysis then sets forth attainable figures for the expansion of private income protection coverage arising from opt-out arrangements and calculates the resulting additional savings to the SSDI program. Our calculations indicate that for each 10 percentage point increase in the proportion of workers that have group disability coverage, 20,000 to 25,000 workers affected by a disabling condition would either avoid SSDI or spend less time receiving SSDI benefits. This would increase the savings that group disability coverage brings to the SSDI program by between $280 million and $350 million per year, or $2.8 billion to $3.5 billion over a 10-year period. The benefits to the SSDI program come from the higher overall return-to-work rates for workers with group disability coverage. Much of this return-to-work advantage comes in the first few months after disability onset—before affected individuals would receive SSDI benefits—and is therefore not recorded in available SSDI statistics. Absent group disability coverage, however, some number of affected individuals would decline in physical function and financial resources and therefore eventually need to apply for SSDI.

The benefits of expanded group disability coverage can reduce the burden on the SSDI program at minimal cost to the federal budget. The SSDI program itself would incur no costs. There may be some reduction in tax revenue if group disability premiums are paid with pre-tax dollars, but that would be at least partially offset by taxes on the benefit payments. The costs of the public education and outreach program would not be high, and would be at the discretion of budget authorities. The low cost of implementing this proposal to the federal government means that the benefit-to-cost ratio would be favorable, even recognizing the uncertainty and variability regarding participation rates and socio-economic characteristics of the additional population covered by group disability insurance. Also, the benefits to the SSDI program from implementation of this proposal are independent of, and in addition to, most SSDI program-specific proposals suggested elsewhere.

STATEMENT OF THE PROBLEM

SSDI provides crucial financial assistance to millions of families where a wage earner has experienced a disability of sufficient severity and duration to prevent him or her from working (SSA 2014). The current and longstanding orientation of the SSDI program, however, provides little support helping affected individuals get back to work.[1] Individuals receiving, or in the process of applying for, SSDI benefits largely must look elsewhere for supporting resources (Bardos, Burak, and Ben-Shalom 2015, 1-2).

Group disability plans, however, focus on getting affected individuals back to work when that is feasible and appropriate. The key insight into group disability plans is that they get to affected individuals early and with substantially more focused return-to-work effort than is possible through the SSDI program. Group disability coverage benefits the SSDI program primarily through two groups of affected individuals—those who avoid the SSDI program entirely and those who leave the SSDI program sooner than otherwise would happen.

1 The "Ticket to Work" program is an exception to this statement. It will be discussed more fully later in this paper.

Before discussing and quantifying the number of individuals avoiding or exiting the SSDI program as a consequence of group disability coverage, it is useful to highlight the differences between the SSDI and private group disability approaches, and what this implies for affected individuals.

Comparing SSDI and Group Disability Financial Support

There is a distinct difference in the level of financial benefits provided by SSDI and group disability programs. In 2013, SSDI payments to disabled workers averaged $13,757 per year, and most received less than $20,000 per year (SSA 2014, 21 & 122).[2] On average, SSDI benefits replace less than 35 percent of average pre-disability income, and that percentage declines as pre-disability income increases.[3] Group disability benefits are determined by the contract between the employer and the insurer. In 2013, 64 percent of private industry workers covered by group disability contracts had benefits equal to 60 percent of pre-disability annual earnings (BLS 2014, private industry worker Table 30).[4] For a worker earning $50,000 per year, a 60 percent replacement rate on pre-disability salary yields $30,000 in annual benefits. A worker earning $80,000 per year would obtain $48,000 per year in benefits at a 60 percent income replacement rate. Workers earning more than approximately $23,000 per year will obtain more income from group disability insurance at a 60 percent income replacement rate than the average SSDI benefit payment to disabled workers. Importantly, if the group disability premiums are paid with "after tax" dollars (i.e., not deducted from salary before the federal tax is computed), the amounts paid to beneficiaries are not taxable (Internal Revenue Service 2015; GenRe Research 2012, 50).

Key differences also exist between when SSDI and group disability coverage benefits commence. Under SSDI, eligibility for monthly cash benefits begins

---

2 The average monthly benefit for all disabled workers was $1,222.34, and only 10.5 percent of beneficiaries received monthly benefits of $2,000 or more (SSA 2014, 122 Table 45).

3 The average monthly SSDI payment for disabled beneficiaries between the ages of 30 and 34 is $839.61. The median weekly earnings of workers between the ages of 25 and 34 are $701. For this age group, therefore, SSDI replaces 29.9 percent of median weekly earnings. Monthly SSDI payments to disabled beneficiaries between the ages of 50 and 54 average $1,113.52. The median weekly earnings of workers between the ages of 45 and 54 are $884. For this age group, therefore, SSDI replaces 31.5 percent of median weekly earnings (SSA 2014, 22 and BLS January 22, 2014, Table 3).

4 Twenty-four percent had benefits less than 60 percent (generally between 50 percent and 60 percent) and 12 percent had benefits exceeding 60 percent but no more than 67 percent (BLS 2014, private industry worker Table 30).

for most applicants five months after disability onset (SSA 2014, 3). But the five-month period is not the only timing consideration SSDI applicants face. In fiscal 2014, the average processing time for initial disability claims was 110 days, or about three and two-thirds months (SSA 2015a, 108). If the affected individual does not apply for SSDI benefits within the first two months of disability onset, the claimant will likely have to wait more than five months for benefits to start. In fiscal 2014, 68 percent of initial disability claims were denied (SSA 2015a, 143.) For the three-fourths of claims denials issued in states with a reconsideration phase, those individuals faced on average another 108 days for a determination on reconsideration in fiscal 2014—another almost three and two-thirds months (SSA 2015a, 108). Eighty-nine percent of appeals for reconsideration were denied in fiscal 2014 (SSA 2015a, 143). Another level of determination, an appeal to an administrative law judge, is available. In fiscal 2014, the average time for a decision at that level was 422 days—more than 14 months (SSA 2015a, 108). So the time from disability onset to receipt of SSDI benefits can be significant, even if the SSDI claim application is ultimately approved.

Though policies vary, under group disability plans it is common for long-term disability income benefits to begin three months or six months after disability onset. More employees are covered by short-term disability plans that provide income benefits soon after disability onset (a week in some cases) than are covered by long-term disability plans (BLS 2014, private industry workers Table 16). In most cases, the short-term and long-term group disability coverages are coordinated so that the affected individual experiences an integrated process of financial and return-to-work support during the initial months of the disability. This process contrasts sharply with the typical situation faced by SSDI applicants not also covered by group disability programs. The availability of the short-term coverage in conjunction with coordinated group disability coverage means that the financial situation of the families with these benefits is substantially superior to families without group disability benefits.

Return-to-Work Efforts of Group Disability Coverage Providers and SSDI

Return-to-work efforts, one of the key elements of group disability coverage, have been implemented and systematized in *comprehensive disability management* programs administered by private group disability insurers. There are a number of available product features and almost all group disability insurers offer reasonable accommodation benefits, rehabilitation, and return-to-work incentives (GenRe Research 2012, 52). These programs work with the employee, the employer and the employee's physician to align interests and expectations and thereby encourage the return to work of an employee experiencing a disability. They rely on timely communication with the involved parties to establish appropriate expectations regarding reemployment, establishment of a return-to-work plan, ongoing support and motivation, and the application of procedures appropriate to each return-to-work effort.

The steps involved in developing a return-to-work plan can include:

- Regular telephone contact with the employee experiencing a disability by a rehabilitation counselor or claim professional;
- A detailed job analysis of the tasks the employee was performing before the disability episode;
- A functional capacity evaluation to understand the tasks the employee is capable of performing subsequent to the disabling condition;
- Medical record review and return-to-work planning discussions with the employee's treating medical provider(s); and
- Partnering with federal and state job placement and vocational assistance programs.

Each return-to-work support plan is customized to the situation of the individual employee and might include the following services:

- Coordination with the employer to help the employee return to work;
- Identification of adaptive equipment or job accommodations that could enable the employee to resume job duties;
- A vocational evaluation to determine how the employee's disability may affect his or her employment options;
- Job placement services;
- Resume preparation; and
- Job-seeking skills training.

Early intervention and timely communications are crucial to successful return-to-work outcomes. Insurer vocational rehabilitation professionals engage in collaborative dialogues with employees experiencing disabling conditions to build a supportive relationship with the common goal of helping the employee recover and return to work (Bardos, Burak, and Ben-Shalom 2015, 4).

The SSDI program also offers employment support provisions. The "trial work period" allows a beneficiary to work and earn without losing benefits for up to nine months. The "extended period of eligibility" backstops work earnings with

SSDI and Medicare benefits for up to 36 months. Finally, the "Ticket to Work" program provides beneficiaries the opportunity to obtain vocational rehabilitation services (SSA 2014, 6; Ben-Shalom and Mamun 2015, 2).

Costs to Employees and Employers

Together, private sector employees and employers pay an amount equal to 1.8 percent of salary (0.9 percent each) on up to $118,500 in earnings in 2015 to fund SSDI (Social Security and Medicare Boards of Trustees 2015, 13; SSA 2015b). An employee making $50,000 per year, therefore, has $900 in annual payroll tax designated for SSDI, while an employee making $118,500 or more per year in salary has $2,133 in annual payroll tax for SSDI. Since 2003, payments from the SSDI trust fund have exceeded the SSDI payroll tax receipts, and the trust fund is currently projected to be completely depleted in 2016 (Social Security and Medicare Boards of Trustees 2015, 9-10).[5] This indicates that the 1.8 percent payroll tax has yielded less than the actuarial cost of the program for at least the past decade.

Group disability premiums are paid by the employee, employer, or some combination. GenRe Research reported average group disability premiums of $245 per covered employee per year in 2013, while average new group disability sales premiums were $226 per covered employee annually (GenRe Research 2014, 7). The Council for Disability Awareness notes, "A traditional employer-sponsored long-term disability insurance plan tends to cost about $250 to $400 a year. Premiums are often fully or partially picked up by the employer" (Council for Disability Awareness 2014b, 7). Given that group disability coverage is not legally mandated, but provided as part of an overall compensation package, group disability providers succeed only when their services are perceived to offer higher value than that same money used elsewhere in the compensation package.

Implications

Group disability coverage offers both financial and return-to-work support. As a consequence, a significant number of affected individuals (quantified later) avoid deterioration in functional and financial circumstances and therefore avoid receiving SSDI benefits. These individuals do not show up on SSDI rolls and may not even apply for SSDI benefits. Nevertheless, the SSDI program benefits

---

[5] This chapter was written prior to the enactment of the Bipartisan Budget Act of 2015, which pushed depletion to 2022.

substantially from the efforts of group disability providers to get thousands of employees each year back to work.

For more severely affected individuals who receive SSDI benefits, group disability coverage continues to support them financially and with work reengagement programs. For claimants identified as having the potential to return to work, group disability insurers work with the disabled employee to get him or her back to work, perhaps with accommodations identified and financed by the group disability providers. Here again we see a direct benefit to the SSDI program, as individuals exit SSDI rolls sooner than would be the case if the group disability coverage was not available.

DETAILED PROPOSAL

To harness the ability of private group disability programs to reduce the number of people receiving SSDI benefits, we propose: (1) enactment of legislation to make clear that opt-out arrangements under disability income plans are permitted (but not mandated) under federal law and (2) that the federal government undertake education and outreach to provide working Americans with information and resources regarding disability income security.

Increase Group Disability Coverage of Working Americans by Encouraging Employers to Adopt "Opt-out" Arrangements for Employer-Sponsored Income Protection Plans

Employers are not required to offer group disability as a component of their compensation package and not all employees elect group disability coverage when their employers offer the coverage. According to data reported by the Bureau of Labor Statistics, 34 percent of surveyed private industry workers have access to employer-sponsored group disability insurance and 97 percent of those workers sign up for the coverage when available. Consequently, about one-third of all private industry workers are covered by group disability insurance (BLS 2014, private industry workers Table 16). Industry research, however, indicates a lower employee participation rate when employees pay all or part of the premiums, which suggests that the 97 percent figure in the survey reflects a high portion of responses pertaining to 100 percent employer-paid plans When employees pay all or part of the premiums, participation rates fall in the 30 to 50 percent range—higher as the portion the employer pays increases and as age decreases (GenRe Research 2012, 64-5; LIMRA 2015, Table 2).

Some employers sponsor income protection plans on an opt-out basis, but most do not. One reason is that employers are unsure that such arrangements comport fully with state payroll laws requiring employee consent prior to payroll reductions. The U.S. Department of Labor has provided guidance indicating that certain employer-sponsored benefits are not subject to state payroll law provisions that would frustrate opt-out arrangements, but the department has not specifically addressed the application of these laws to disability income protection opt-out arrangements. Case law has not clarified the issue. Congressional action to confirm the permissibility of opt-out arrangements within income protection plans would eliminate uncertainties and send a strong signal of the importance of disability income protection coverage.

There are any number of reasons—inertia, distraction, uncertainty, or procrastination—an employee is more likely to fail to act in his or her long-term interests when plan enrollment requires a timely affirmative action in the face of competing demands and insufficient information. Opt-out arrangements change the default outcome to enrollment, and therefore make plan participation much more likely.

Increase Employer Sponsorship of Group Disability Insurance Coverage and Employee Plan Participation through Education and Outreach

To complement the implementation of the opt-out proposal outlined earlier, the federal government should undertake a concerted and sustained education and outreach campaign to encourage workers and employers to face the key disability income security and workforce productivity issues. As up to two-thirds of private sector American workers are not covered by employer-sponsored disability income insurance against the loss of income due to illness or injury, there is clearly much outreach to do. More than half of American workers indicate that they know little—or nothing at all—about disability income insurance (Consumer Federation of America 2012, 3).

Lack of understanding about important disability income security issues has been a stubborn problem despite the educational and marketing efforts of the private providers. The federal government could help address this by facilitating dissemination of information about the risk of disabling illness and injury; the financial implications of work disability; and what working Americans can do to protect income security against the risk of work disability. This would be an especially helpful resource for working Americans presented with a need to consider income protection coverage under plans with opt-out enrollment arrangements.

Employers, too, would benefit from information regarding the role of group disability coverage in maintaining workforce productivity and helping ill or injured employees return to work. Such information, with the *imprimatur* of the federal government, could do a great deal to raise the profile of disability income security issues for employers and employees. The public education and outreach efforts, in conjunction with the opt-out arrangement and private provider education and marketing, would facilitate greater participation in group disability coverage.

ANALYSIS OF THE PROPOSAL

The essential premise of this proposal is that group disability coverage, particularly through return-to-work programs, helps affected workers avoid or spend less time on SSDI status. In this section we summarize the research supporting and quantifying the number of workers helped by group disability coverage, the estimated savings to the SSDI program arising from the reduction in beneficiaries, the additional benefits arising to the federal government from group disability coverage, and the evidence from another federal policy that provides support for the efficacy of the automatic enrollment proposal. Similar to the approach taken in Bardos, Burak, and Ben-Shalom (2015), we pull together various strands of research that demonstrate empirical support for the efficacy of group disability financial support and return-to-work programs.[6]

---

[6] To conduct a rigorous and comprehensive study of disability, recovery, and reemployment, we would ideally like to be able to determine whether and when the condition of the worker with a disability improves to the point where he or she is once again employable both in the absence and the presence of group disability coverage and SSDI status.
In theory, one could design a study where a portion of the employees with disabilities covered by group disability insurance received disability management services and another "control group" did not. The difference in recovery and return-to-work profiles, incorporating the appropriate statistical controls, could then be observed in the resulting data. This type of study is commonly used to evaluate the effectiveness of medications or medical procedures. Such a study, however, would not be feasible in the case of group disability insurance. First, withholding disability management services to covered employees for the sake of this sort of information would not be fair to the control group. Such a study protocol would require withholding assistance from individuals who would benefit from the assistance. Second, withholding such services would also be costly for the insurer. The insurer would have to keep paying benefits instead of helping the individual to recover and become employed. Third, the nature of the services means that the study cannot be conducted in a "double blind" fashion. Therefore, the pure scientific value of such a study protocol cannot measure

The Effect of More Timely Support

One way the benefit of group disability coverage shows up is the mere fact of substantial and coordinated financial support for the affected family provided shortly after the onset of a disability results in a higher probability that the affected individual will reenter the job market. An academic working paper examining experience in the SSDI program calculated the probabilities for the ability of affected individuals to reengage in work as a function of the time spent waiting for a SSDI determination (Autor et al. 2011). This paper starts by observing "that SSDI applicants must engage in a prolonged period of labor force nonparticipation while they seek [SSDI] benefits." It then proceeded to note the following:

> If applicants' employment potential deteriorates while they are out of the labor force, then the observed, post-application labor supply of denied and allowed applicants may understate their employment potential at the time of SSDI application. Moreover, if either the rate of deterioration or average SSDI determination time differs between allowed and denied applicants, a comparison of their post-SSDI determination labor supply may not identify the pure effect of the SSDI award on employment outcomes. (Autor et al. 2011, 1)

Using data from all initial SSDI medical determinations in 2005, this study econometrically tested the hypothesis that the rate of post-disability employment was lower the longer the "time to decision." The authors determined the effect of the time lapse from initial SSDI application until determination on employment and earnings two, three and four years after the application—i.e., in 2007, 2008 and 2009. The data set consisted of more than 1.1 million observations, one-third where the application was approved on initial submission and two-thirds where the application was initially denied (Autor et al. 2011, 25). Figure 1 graphically summarizes results from this study.

---

up to the scientific research "gold standard" and may be subject to criticism and dismissal, which would decrease the motivation for attempting to conduct such a study in the first place. Because it is not feasible to conduct a direct experiment comparing a randomly selected group with access to group disability insurance and disability management programs to a control group without those benefits, this study quantifies the benefits of group disability insurance indirectly using publicly available data that are sparse, aggregated, and often challenging to interpret. We nevertheless believe that the evidence below supports the efficacy of group disability insurance coverage in reducing the SSDI rolls.

Figure 1: Effect of Delay on Employment of SSDI Applicants

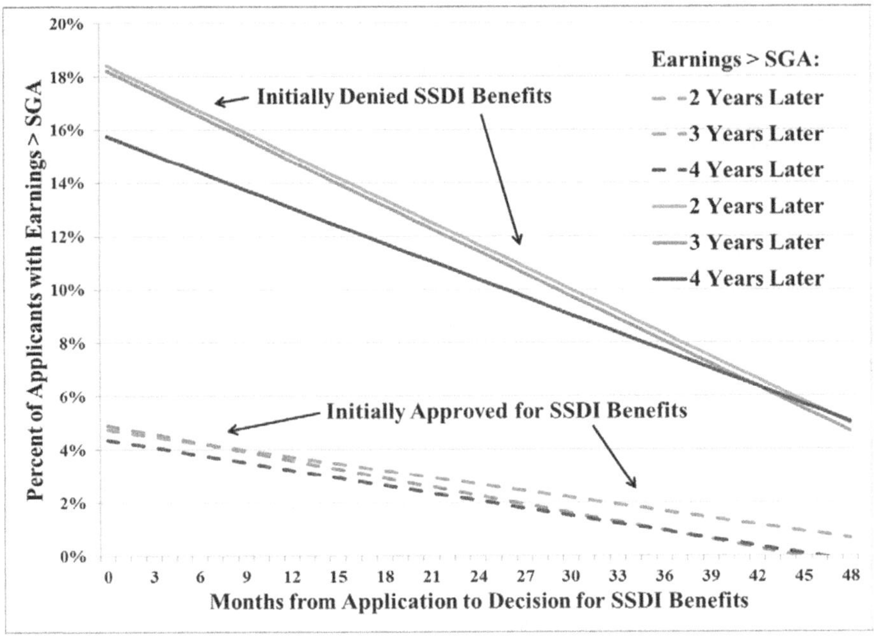

Source: Calculated from regression results presented in Autor et al. 2011, 30 Table 6.

The horizontal axis in Figure 1 shows elapsed time, in months, from the application for SSDI benefits until a final determination of SSDI status was made. The vertical axis shows the percentage of the SSDI applicants who experienced earnings in excess of the Substantial Gainful Activity (SGA) threshold—approximately $12,000 per year (SSA 2014, 2). The important conclusion of the study as summarized in Figure 1 is captured in the downward slope of all the lines. The longer it took for an SSDI applicant to receive a decision—whether approval or denial, upon initial review or reconsideration or appeal—the lower the percentage of applicants who had earnings in excess of SGA. The Autor et al. study documents the proposition that the time involved in getting an SSDI decision, with no other services provided, affects post-disability employment prospects.[7] Delay in determining SSDI status alone reduces substantially the likelihood of the individual being reemployed after a disability episode.

7 The Autor et al. study is rigorous, comprehensive, and sophisticated in its empirical protocols. The paper presents a number of alternative specifications, some of which have arguably superior statistical properties to the specifications underlying the relationships exhibited in Figure 1. The regressions represented in Figure 1 were chosen because: (1) they are based

A subsequent study by three of the four authors of the Autor et al. study directly examined the effect of SSDI benefits on employment of SSDI applicants. That study found that employment would have been 28 percentage points higher for the roughly one-quarter of SSDI beneficiaries "on the margin of program entry" had they not received SSDI benefits. The effect, understandably, varies substantially depending on the severity of the impairment. Employment rates for those with less severe disabilities would be 50 percentage points higher in the absence of SSDI benefits (Maestas, Mullen, and Strand 2013). We suggest that these are SSDI beneficiaries that could have returned to work had they received appropriate support—support that group disability insurers are motivated and able to supply. In their evaluation of the Maestas, Mullen and Strand (2013) article, Bardos, Burak, and Ben-Shalom write, "with just modest assistance, more than 120,000 [SSDI recipients] could have returned to work but did not." (Bardos, Burak, and Ben-Shalom 2015, 2).

These studies support the proposition that private group disability coverage can increase post-disability employment rates due to the financial and return-to-work support provided. This is because the affected families with private disability insurance have substantial support early in the disability episode, which leads to higher overall employment rates for those workers experiencing a disability episode. Importantly, many individuals successfully helped by group disability coverage would be invisible to analysts investigating SSDI termination results. The return-to-work benefits of group disability coverage occurred before the individuals would join the SSDI beneficiary rolls.

Return-to-Work Program Effects

A second way group disability coverage helps individuals suffering from a disability to reengage in the labor market arises from specific return-to-work efforts. Once again, direct evidence for the efficacy of return-to-work programs comes from an examination of efforts within the SSDI program. In addition, there is indirect evidence that the return-to-work efforts of group disability insurers help a substantial number of affected individuals reengage the labor market.

---

on the largest number of observations, (2) they split the observations into groupings that are pertinent to the goals of this study, and (3) the empirical results are close to those represented in other, arguably statistically superior specifications. See the Autor et al. study for more details.

Evidence supporting the effectiveness of a return-to-work element on increasing the likelihood of post-disability employment comes from studies of the experience of SSDI recipients. The Ticket to Work "provides disabled beneficiaries with a voucher they may use to obtain vocational rehabilitation services, employment services, and other support services from an employment network of their choice." (SSA 2014, 2) One study, summarized in Table 1 below, found that the Ticket to Work participants experienced a substantially higher rate of success finding employment than SSDI beneficiaries not enrolled in the Ticket to Work program.

The "success rate" measured in Table 1, however, is modest—the first incidence of a suspension (not the termination)[8] of SSDI benefits. The facially important conclusion from this study summarized in Table 1 is that the Ticket to Work program yielded from well over double to over 10 times the likelihood of some level of post-disability employment compared to the cohort of SSDI recipients who did not participate in the program.

Table 1: Employment by Participation in Ticket to Work Programs

Social Security Disability Insurance Recipients	Percentage of all SSDI beneficiaries experiencing first STW (suspension or termination of benefits for work) event				
	2002	2003	2004	2005	2006
Ticket-to-Work participants	2.58%	3.76%	4.11%	4.54%	3.84%
Milestone-outcome	3.66%	5.73%	5.04%	6.08%	4.71%
Outcome-only	4.23%	9.69%	9.43%	8.48%	6.57%
Traditional	2.33%	3.22%	3.79%	4.21%	3.64%
Nonparticipants	0.87%	0.83%	0.77%	0.77%	0.65%

Source: Schimmel and Stapleton 2011, 87. In this study, Ticket to Work participants were placed into one of three different programs: Milestone-outcome, Outcome-only and Traditional. As reported in the table above, the programs had different rates of "beneficiaries experiencing first STW event."

O'Neill et al. (2015) "examined the progression to substantial employment milestones for DI beneficiaries over a 10-year period beginning with their entry

[8] Before SSDI benefits can be terminated, they are generally suspended. SSDI payments are terminated for those beneficiaries when their SGA on a monthly basis exceeds certain thresholds after the exhaustion of the mandated "trial work period" and "extended period of eligibility." (SSA 2014, 6)

into the DI program (1)." They found that SSDI recipients who enrolled in state vocational rehabilitation agency services had "substantially better" return-to-work experience than those not enrolled in such programs. More specifically, O'Neill et al. found that SSDI recipients who participated in state vocational rehabilitation programs experienced a 46 percent to 100 percent increase in the rate of suspension or termination from the SSDI program due to work, relative to a matched comparison group (8).

There are at least two limitations when applying Ticket to Work program results to group disability insurance. First, the measure of post-disability employment used in the Ticket to Work studies is below that considered successful for private group disability coverage—the return of the affected individual to his or her employer.[9] Second, self-selection permeates participation in the Ticket to Work program. This means that the Ticket to Work results have only limited applicability to private group disability return-to-work programs. Nevertheless, this line of research also supports the proposition that intentional efforts to help individuals with disabilities reenter the workplace do result in higher post-disability employment rates.[10]

Data on return-to-work outcomes consistently shows that a significantly higher proportion of group disability claimants return to the workforce than the proportion of SSDI beneficiaries who have benefits terminated for income above the Substantial Gainful Activity" limits.[11] As reported in Table 2 below, only about

---

9 Many policies have an "own job" provision for the first two years of group disability coverage, thereafter switching to an "any job" provision.

10 A companion study of the Ticket to Work program, using a longitudinal approach, found that 3.7 percent of those individuals made eligible for SSDI benefits were off the SSDI rolls by December 2006 after participating in the Ticket to Work program. (Liu and Stapleton 2011).

11 The limits for Substantial Gainful Activity in 2013 entailed income from employment in excess of $1,040 per month for individuals able to see, and $1,740 per month for a person experiencing blindness (SSA 2014, 2).
SSDI payments are terminated for beneficiaries whose SGA on a monthly basis exceeds certain thresholds after the exhaustion of the mandated "trial work period" and "extended period of eligibility." "Disabled beneficiaries are encouraged to return to work by providing a trial work period (TWP) and an extended period of eligibility (EPE). During the TWP, earnings are allowed to exceed the SGA dollar amount for nine months. During the three-year EPE that follows the TWP, benefits are withheld only for those months in which earnings exceed the SGA amount. After the end of the EPE, monthly benefits are terminated when earnings exceed the SGA amount. . . . Even if cash benefits are withheld, Medicare and Medicaid coverage can continue" (SSA 2014, 6).

one-half of one percent of SSDI beneficiaries stop receiving benefits in any year by returning to work. In contrast, the return-to-work outcomes for private group disability beneficiaries are considerably better—a return-to-work rate of 1.5 percent to 2.0 percent annually.

Table 2: SSDI Aggregate Termination for Work and Group Disability Insured Recovery Rate

Year	1997	1998	1999	2000	2001	2002	2003	2004	2005	2006	2007	2008	2009	2010	2011	2012	2013
SSDI	*N/A*	*N/A*	*N/A*	*N/A*	0.55%	0.53%	0.48%	0.46%	0.56%	0.53%	0.47%	0.51%	0.42%	0.50%	0.46%	0.43%	0.35%
GLTD	1.64%	1.65%	1.83%	1.89%	2.02%	1.97%	1.89%	1.84%	1.84%	1.83%	*N/A*	*N/A*	*N/A*	*N/A*	*N/A*	*N/A*	*N/A*

Sources: SSDI row: O'Leary, Livermore, and Stapleton 2011, Table 2 for years from 2001 to 2009; SSA 2014, "Work Above SGA" for workers in Table 50 divided by "Workers" in Table 1 for 2010 through 2013; GLTD, group disability, row is derived from Society of Actuaries 2011, Pivot Table.

Note that the 1.57 percent figure for the average over 1997 through 2006 is not directly comparable to the 0.5 percent figure for the SSDI program, as it includes recipients who recovered from their disability condition in less time than it would take someone applying for SSDI benefits to be approved for eligibility. Excluding from the calculations those workers who "recovered" in less than six months, the overall group disability claimant recovery rate was 1.14 percent. Excluding those experiencing a disability who recovered in less than 12 months yields a 0.72 percent recovery rate. From Table 2 and the information in the Schimmel and Stapleton (2011) and O'Neill et al. (2015) studies, the available data support the proposition that those SSDI recipients receiving return-to-work support reenter the work force at 50 percent to 100 percent higher rates than those receiving only SSDI benefit payments.

Additional materials in the Society of Actuaries *2008 Long-Term Disability Study Report* reveal that recovery rates in the 1997 to 2006 period improved over expectations based on the experience of prior years. Figure 2 summarizes this information. The Society of Actuaries' Long Term Disability Experience Study Committee compared the results derived from the new data against that available from the *1995 Long Term Disability Experience Study* (Society of Actuaries 2009, 10). Notably, the recovery experience in the 2008 table for 1997 and 1998 comports quite closely to the experience predicted from the 1995 table. There are differences by duration from disability episode grouping, but 1997 and 1998 look to average out fairly closely to what would have been projected using the older experience table (98 percent and 102 percent of expectations, respectively).

Starting in 1999 and continuing through 2006, however, the actual recovery experience exceeded that projected from the 1995 table. While claim durations of four to 12 months improved by approximately 20 percent from 1997 to 2006 relative to what the 1995 experience table would project, for other claim durations the improvement in recovery was considerably higher. Reviewing Figure 2 and the associated data, disability claims with a duration of 13 to 24 months had a 40 percent higher recovery rate in 2006 than projected by the 1995 experience table. Disability claims with a duration of 25 to 36 months experienced almost double the recovery rate by 2006 than that projected by the 1995 experience table. After first declining relative to the 1995 experience, disability claims with a duration of 37 to 60 months ended up about 20 percent higher in 2006 compared to expectations. Disability claims with a duration of more than 60 months first experienced a strong recovery rate relative to the 1995 table, and then ended up about 20 percent higher by 2006.

Figure 2: Recovery Rate Experience by Year and Claim Duration Compared to 1995 Group Disability Experience Study

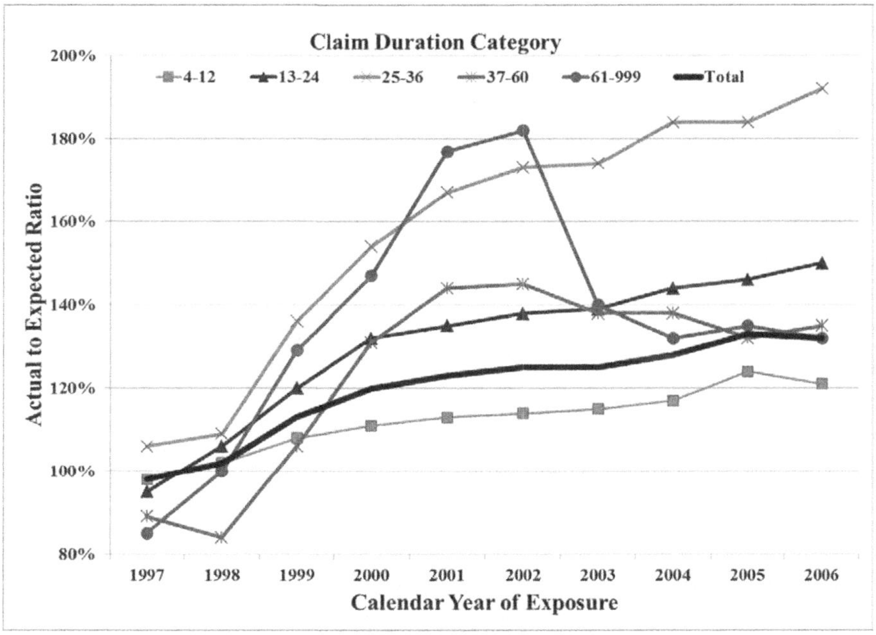

Source: Society of Actuaries 2009, 24, Table 3.1.A.

Figure 3 presents another look at the 2008 experience table compared against the 1995 table supporting the position that focused recovery efforts lead to higher post-disability employment. In Figure 3, the disability insurers are combined into four groups by "similar patterns of death and recovery A/E [actual 2008 study data to expectation based on the 1995 table] results." (Society of Actuaries 2009, 69). While it is clear that this was a period of substantial progress in medical technology, the patterns exhibited in Figure 3 suggest that some insurers experienced much better recovery rates than others over the entire period. Group 1 insurers, for example, averaged 50 percent higher than expected recovery rates over the entire duration span, and in some durations exhibited over 100 percent higher than expected recovery rates. This is in sharp contrast to the Group 4 insurers, whose overall experience in the 1997 through 2006 data was not substantially different from that projected using the 1995 experience table.

Taken together, the phenomena portrayed in Figures 2 and 3 support the proposition that private sector group disability coverage enhances post-disability employment.

Figure 3: Recovery Rate Experience by Company Group

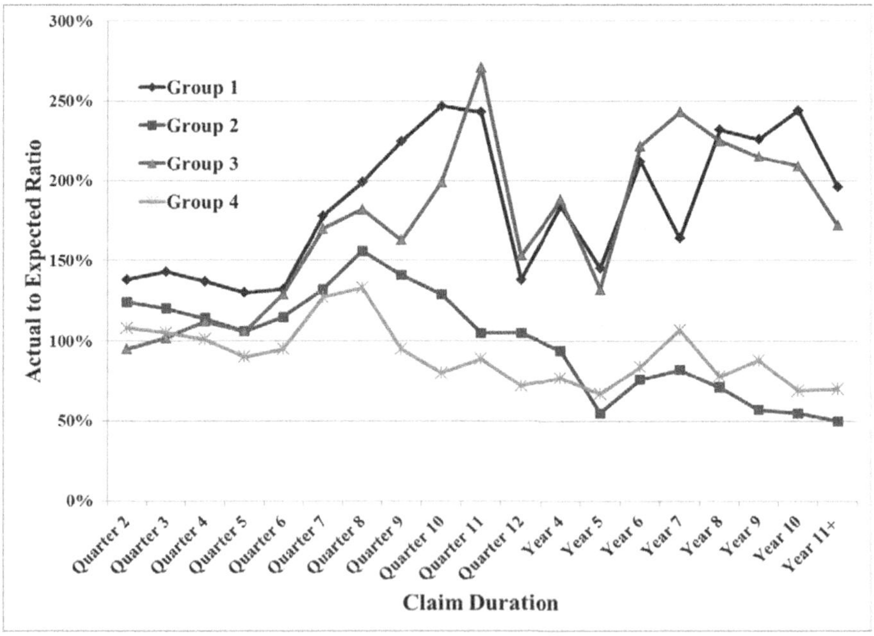

Source: Society of Actuaries 2009, 70-71, Chart 10.1.B and Table 10.1.A.

While neither the SSDI nor group disability studies provide direct quantification of the reduction in SSDI rolls as a consequence of group disability coverage, they all support the proposition that the existence of group disability coverage and associated disability management processes do result in higher post-disability employment rates. The range of observed improved re-employment is substantial—a minimum of 20 percent up to double or even triple. Consequently, we estimate that there are tens of thousands of individuals working today who would be on the rolls of SSDI and other federal programs if they had not had group disability coverage.

Research on the Number of Workers Avoiding SSDI because of Group Disability Coverage

With the proposition now established that group disability coverage can and does get affected individuals reengaged in the labor market, the next task is estimating the number of individuals who experienced a disability and then avoided or exited federal programs as a consequence of group disability coverage and its attendant comprehensive disability management programs.

There are two groupings of individuals who have avoided SSDI status as a consequence of group disability coverage. First, there are those where the worker with a disability received group disability benefits and payments and *subsequently returned to work*, but in the absence of the group disability benefits and payments would have eventually needed SSDI. Second, there are those where the worker with a disability received group disability benefits and payments and *never returned to work*, but in the absence of the group disability benefits and services would have eventually become eligible for SSDI. These workers also *"avoided"* SSDI status completely. While individuals in both of these groups avoided SSDI status, only the first group can be considered a successful return-to-work situation for the group disability provider. People in the second group are not capable of returning to work, but are not impaired enough to qualify for SSDI.

There are also two groupings of individuals who have exited SSDI status as a consequence of group disability coverage. First, there are those where the worker with a disability received SSDI benefits, but also received group disability benefits and payments and, as a consequence, returned to work. These workers *would have remained* on SSDI status until retirement or death in the absence of group disability coverage. These workers *"exited"* SSDI status. Second, there are those where the worker with a disability received SSDI benefits but also received group disability benefits and payments and, as a consequence, *returned to work faster* than in the absence of the group disability benefits and payments. These workers would have eventually exited SSDI, but the group disability coverage accelerated their exit. These workers *reduced their time* in SSDI status.

For purposes of this paper, the situations can be summarized along two dimensions – (1) whether the worker with a disability was ever eligible for SSDI and (2) whether the worker with a disability recovered enough to reengage in work. Table 3 depicts the situations along these two dimensions.[12]

Table 3: Taxonomy of Situations by Recovery and SSDI Status

		Recovery Status	
		Not Working	Working
SSDI Status	Eligible	*Receiving SSDI.*	**Exited or reduced time on SSDI status.**
	Not Eligible	**Avoided SSDI status.**	**Avoided SSDI status.**

Babbel and Meyer (2013) undertook a detailed examination of the available information to provide figures for the cells in Table 3. Solid figures pertaining to the "Not Working" column are available from information provided by the private disability insurers and compiled by the Council for Disability Awareness, the nonprofit organization whose supporting members include many of the major private disability insurers. There were approximately 653,000 individuals receiving long-term disability benefit payments from insurers in 2013, and 72 percent of these (approximately 470,000) were also eligible for SSDI. This means that 28 percent of those receiving private long-term disability payments (approximately 183,000) were not eligible for SSDI at that time (Council for Disability Awareness 2014a, 3-4). We can use this information to provide figures for the left column in Table 3, the "Not Working" column.

We can calculate the number of individuals in the right columns using information from the *2008 Long Term Disability Experience Table Report*. We know that in the 10 years from 1997 through 2006, companies participating in the *2008 Group Long Term Disability* study experienced 1.2 million disability claims (Society of Actuaries 2011, 3). This is an average of 120,000 new private disability claims per year. We

[12] Note the situation depicted in the shaded, upper left cell of Table 3. This represents those unemployed workers with disabilities receiving private disability insurance payments as well as SSDI benefits. These individuals are not the focus of this study as they have not avoided or reduced their time on SSDI. The workers with disabilities in this situation form part of the population investigated in Babbel et al. 2011. That study found that these workers with disabilities benefited substantially from private disability insurance as it prevented them from becoming impoverished. This, in turn, benefits the federal government by reducing demand on federal programs such as Temporary Assistance to Needy Families, Supplemental Nutrition Assistance Program, Medicare, Medicaid, housing subsidies, etc.

also know that in the years from 2008 through 2012, the companies participating in the Council for Disability Awareness *Disability Claims Review* approved more than 150,000 new disability claims in each year (Council for Disability Awareness 2014a, 2). Consequently, in every year since 1997 there have been at least 100,000 (actually, most likely somewhere between 120,000 and 150,000) new disability claims extending for at least six months after the disability incident in each year. Applying the monthly recovery rates for each quarter or year after disability, we find that each 100,000 claims yield over 5,000 recoveries from the point six months after the onset of the disability through Year 11.

The 5,000 recoveries per 100,000 claims is a figure derived from an annual number of new group disability claims. Each year for more than two decades now, there have been at least 100,000 new group disability claims. The benefit to the federal government would come from cumulating each year's new disability claim recoveries into a number of recoveries over all available years of disability claims. Five thousand recoveries over 20 years yields 100,000 total recovered employees. Over the course of 20 years, a portion of the formerly disabled employees would either retire or die, removing them from the current number of those not currently on SSDI due to the previous group disability benefits. Applying the appropriate mortality and retirement rates results in at least 50,000 individuals currently working who experienced disabilities at some point in the past 20 years.

The evidence from the SSDI and private group disability programs previously discussed indicate that a focused return-to-work effort results in at least a 50 percent improvement in getting individuals suffering from a disability back to work. It is conservative, therefore, to posit that between one-quarter and one-third of the approximately 183,000 individuals receiving group disability benefits (but not SSDI benefits) and not working would likely receive SSDI benefits in the absence of their group disability coverage. Similarly, approximately one-third of the 50,000 employees who received group disability benefits, but who are now working, would receive SSDI benefits had they not had the benefit of group disability coverage. Table 4 summarizes the figures on the estimated number of individuals avoiding, exiting or reducing time on SSDI as a consequence of group disability coverage.[13] The figures reported in Table 4 are the current best

[13] For presentation purposes, the figures have been rounded—one-quarter of ~183,000 is 45,750, one-third of 183,000 is 61,000, and one-third of at least 50,000 is 16,667. Combining these and rounding again yields approximately 50,000 and 15,000, hence the "at least 65,000"

estimates based on the application of parameter estimates incorporating cautious and conservative assumptions.

Table 4: Estimating the Number of Individuals Avoiding Federal Programs Due to Private Sector Disability Insurance Programs

Not on SSDI Due to Group Disability Insurance		Recovery Status	
		Not Working	Working
SSDI Status	Eligible	None	At least 15,000
	Not Eligible	~50,000	

Source: Authors' calculations.

Savings to SSDI Due to Group Disability Coverage

SSDI pays most worker beneficiaries less than $20,000 per year (SSA 2014, 18). In 2013, about 8.9 million SSDI worker beneficiaries received an average annual benefit of $13,757 (SSA 2014, 21). The 65,000 individuals not now on SSDI because of their access to group disability coverage means that approximately $900 million per year in SSDI payments are avoided due to the past return-to-work efforts on the part of group disability insurers.

The Social Security Disability Insurance Trust Fund, the funding mechanism for SSDI, held $90.4 billion in reported total asset reserves as of December 31, 2013 (Social Security and Medicare Boards of Trustees 2015, 2). Absent the comprehensive disability management programs of group coverage providers, fewer workers with disabilities would have returned to work, more workers with disabilities would be receiving SSDI benefits, and SSDI alone would have had to pay an additional $10 billion to $15 billion in benefits over the past two decades. This means that the Disability Insurance Trust Fund would have approximately 10 percent to 15 percent fewer assets than those reported at the end of 2013.

Additional Benefits to the Federal Government from Group Disability Coverage

SSDI is not the only federal program available to the families affected by the disability of a wage earner. The average annual cost for each of the 4 million nonelderly individuals with disabilities benefiting from the Supplemental Nutrition

figure. These figures are likely underestimated, as there have been more than 100,000 private disability claims annually over the past 20 years.

Assistance Program in FY 2013 was $2,450 (U.S. Department of Agriculture 2014, 19).[14] In 2012, the 9.7 million individuals with disabilities enrolled in Medicaid averaged $17,255 in medical expenditures (U.S. Department of Health and Human Services 2013, 13).[15] If a worker with a disability accessed just those two programs at their average amounts reported for the most recent years, he or she would require approximately $15,000 to $20,000 in annual expenditures. This assumes, of course, that those programs are the only ones accessed by the hypothetical worker with a disability. Average expenditures will be higher to the extent that workers with disabilities access other federal or state programs.

Given the information available, it appears that each worker with a disability who did not require assistance from public programs by virtue of private disability coverage saves the federal government at least $30,000 each year. This $30,000 figure results from assuming that the individuals would receive average SSDI benefits and lower-than-average SNAP and Medicare/Medicaid payments for individuals with disabilities. If the individual with a disability is eligible for SSDI and SNAP payments that are higher than average, plus substantial medical expenses, the annual cost to the federal government could be higher. The available information supports an average savings to the federal government of $30,000 per year for each worker that experiences a disability but is not on federal programs due to the disability management programs of private disability insurers. In their examination, Bardos, Burak, and Ben-Shalom identify fiscal benefits to taxpayers ranging from $160,000 to $290,000 as a consequence of getting a disabled employee back to work within a year of disability onset. These are "almost entirely due to foregone government benefits that would be received by the worker with a disability if he or she were unable to return to work," cumulated over the remainder of the employee's work career (Bardos, Burak, and Ben-Shalom 2015, 34-35).

---

14 Average monthly SNAP benefits for nonelderly individuals with disabilities were $204. Those living alone received an average monthly SNAP benefit of $119 ($119/person) while those not living alone received an average monthly SNAP benefit of $331 ($103/person). The $204 per month average figure covers both individuals living alone and those living with others. To the extent that the nonelderly individual with a disability receiving SNAP benefits lives with more than one other eligible person, the benefit figure increases by approximately $100 per month per person. So a family of four would receive, on average, about $430 per month (U.S. Department of Agriculture 2014, 19).

15 A 2011 study using 2005 data found SSDI recipients look to have required an average of $13,999 in expenditures for Medicaid, $4,599 in expenditures for Medicare, and $22,728 in expenditures for "dual eligible" (Autor, Chandra, and Duggan 2011, 5-6).

Above and beyond the reduction in federal expenditures for SSDI outlined earlier, the federal government would also benefit from higher tax revenues as workers with disabilities become reemployed. Incremental federal income and payroll tax revenue arising from reemployment is a function of the post-disability income. If the reemployed group disability insurance beneficiary averages $50,000 per year, which is approximately the average for nondisabled workers,[16] incremental Social Security and Medicare taxes would be approximately $7,650 per year, while additional federal income taxes on that amount would be around $3,000 per year. So the incremental federal tax revenue arising from reemployment would be about $10,000 per year per worker covered by group disability insurance if the post-disability salary was $50,000.

Summing the results from all the relevant situations, the federal government benefits by at least $2 billion per year from workers who experienced a disabling condition but whose group disability coverage facilitated reemployment. As this analytical effort was conservative when selecting responses from the range of responses observed in the data—conservative in the sense of using figures leading to a lower effect—the $2 billion per year estimate is likely below that experienced in the current (and future) environment. At an average annual SSDI benefit payment of $13,757, SSDI savings alone amount to almost $900 million per year. Given foreseeable demographic trends and projected inflation rates, group disability insurance as currently configured will save the federal treasury at least $25 billion over the next 10 years—at least $10 billion in SSDI benefits and approximately $15 billion in other federal programs.

Looking to a future with an opt-out enrollment program entails projecting the responses of employers and employees to such a change. For now, note that for each 10 percentage point increase in the proportion of workers that have group disability coverage (e.g., from 33 percent to 43 percent), the methodology employed above calculates that ultimately between 20,000 to 25,000 additional workers affected by a disabling condition either would avoid or spend less time on SSDI status because of group disability coverage. These additional 20,000 to 25,000 reemployed workers would increase the savings that group disability brings to the SSDI program by between $280 million and $350 million per year, or $2.8 billion to $3.5 billion over a 10-year period.

---

16 The estimated median household income in 2012 was $51,017 (DeNavas-Walt, Proctor, and Smith 2013, 6 Table 1).

Supporting Evidence from the Opt-out Arrangement for Participation in 401(k) Defined Contribution Programs

The Pension Protection Act (PPA) of 2006 facilitated mechanisms for employers to adopt opt-out enrollment features in their 401(k) retirement savings programs (Employee Benefit Research Institute 2009, 191).[17] Since passage, the opportunity for opt-out enrollment in 401(k) defined contribution plans has substantially increased as summarized in Figure 4.

Figure 4: Growth in 401(k) Plans and Participants Using Opt out Enrollment

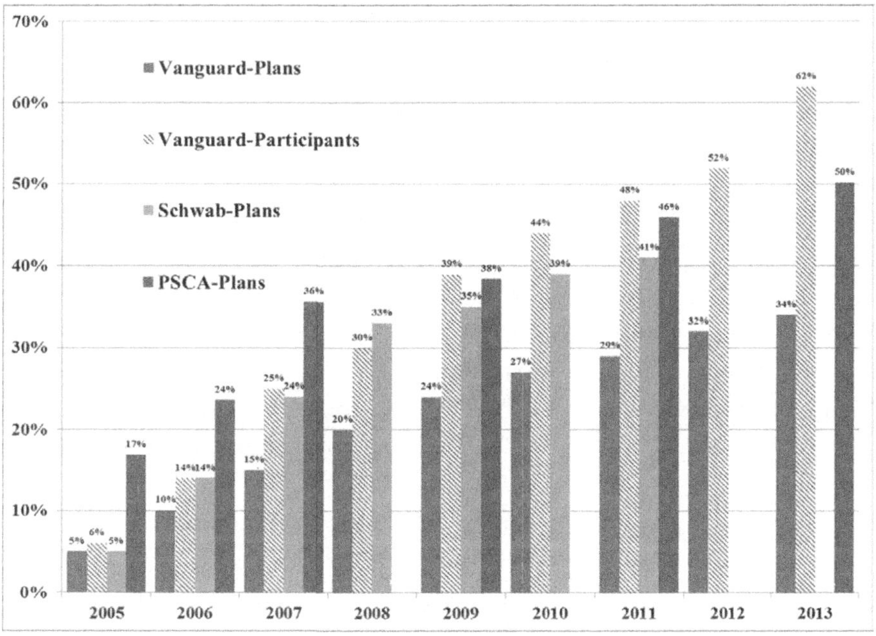

Sources: Plan Sponsor Council of America 2014, 66; PSCA 2012, 50; PSCA 2010, 56; and PSCA 2008, 40; Vanguard 2014, 19 for plans and 20 for participants; Society for Human Resource Management 2011 for Schwab figures.

Before passage of the PPA, the Plan Sponsor Council of America (PSCA) reported that 17 percent of surveyed 401(k) plans had opt-out enrollment features in 2005. The most recent PSCA survey reported that 50 percent of surveyed 401(k) plans had auto-enrollment in 2013. 401(k) plans administered by the Vanguard Group grew opt-out enrollment from 5 percent in 2005 to

[17] The incentives cited included preemption of state laws that might inhibit the adoption of automatic enrollment and additional nondiscrimination safe harbor protections.

34 percent in 2013. Because larger employers have adopted opt out at a higher rate than smaller employers, over 60 percent of employees in 401(k) plans with Vanguard had opt-out enrollment by 2013. The portion of Charles Schwab & Co. 401(k) plans with opt-out enrollment increased from 5 percent in 2005 to 41 percent in 2011. Clearly, the PPA encouraged substantial plan sponsor adoption of the opt-out enrollment feature. The goal of the group disability plan opt out is parallel—to increase the number of employers offering disability income protection on an opt-out basis.

The opt-out enrollment feature of 401(k) programs has also resulted in higher participation by employees whose employers have sponsored such programs. Figure 5 shows that for retirement plans surveyed by the PSCA in 2013, the opt-out enrollment feature resulted in a 10 percent to over 20 percent increase in the number of employees participating in their firms' 401(k) programs. This increase in participation occurred across all plan sizes. As another set of data in 2013, employees with 401(k) plans handled by Vanguard exhibited an 82 percent participation rate under an opt-out enrollment program compared to a 65 percent participation rate when participation was not available under an opt-out enrollment situation. Across all demographic dimensions the Vanguard data showed higher employee 401(k) participation rates were associated with opt-out enrollment plans. In particular, 401(k) participation rates in opt-out enrollment programs were more than double those without opt-out enrollment for the lowest income, youngest, and lowest job tenure categories (Vanguard 2014, 25).

Figure 5: Additional 401(k) Participation from Opt out Enrollment by Plan Size

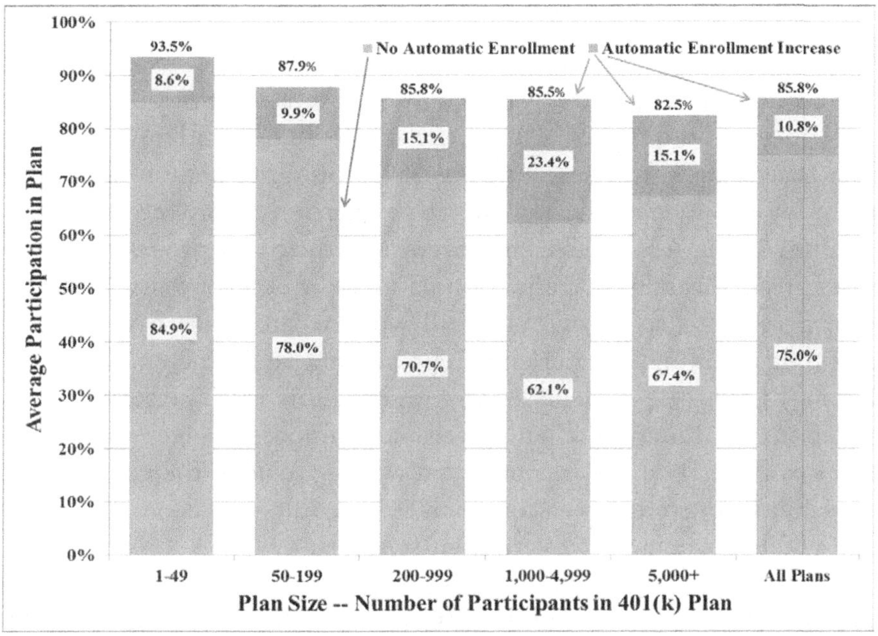

Source: Plan Sponsor Council of America 2014, 69.

This experience suggests that a 20 percentage point increase in the number of private sector employees covered by group disability (e.g., from the current 33 percent to 53 percent) is attainable. Group disability premiums are small fractions of meaningful 401(k) contributions—$250 to $400 per year (Council for Disability Awareness 2014b, 7) compared to the multiple thousands. Moreover, group disability income protection benefits are significant—estimated at $20 to $60 in expected economic welfare for each dollar of premium (Babbel et al. 2011, 1-4).

DISCUSSION

Several concerns regarding the feasibility of the proposal or the operations of group disability coverage have been raised.

The Difference in Covered Populations

SSDI currently covers more than three times as many private sector workers as group insurance. The population covered under private group disability and the population covered only by SSDI differ in their socioeconomic characteristics.

Those currently with group disability coverage generally have higher wages and are more likely to work in service and professional industries (BLS 2014, private industry workers Table 16).

The difference between the group disability-covered population and the SSDI-only population, however, does not imply that extending group disability coverage to working Americans in the SSDI-only population is not feasible. Nor does this difference indicate that such expansion of private coverage would not benefit working Americans, employers, and the SSDI program. Though the SSDI and group disability-covered populations differ, group disability coverage has been present to some degree in all worker categories covered by SSDI, and private insurers have experience representing all segments of the working population (BLS 2014, private industry workers Table 16). The current difference in populations is a function of employer and employee choices regarding group disability coverage. The opt-out proposal would facilitate the expansion of the group disability-covered population, thereby extending the economic benefits of group disability coverage to government significantly.

Are Group Disability Beneficiaries Inappropriately Shifted to SSDI?

The practice of reducing group disability payments by the amount of a claimant's SSDI benefit has been cited as a motive for insurers to shift affected individuals to SSDI inappropriately. Benefit coordination of this type, however, has the advantage of keeping group disability coverage more affordable for employers and employees. One study showed that such coordination lowers the cost of group disability coverage by about 40 percent (Milliman 2005).

Group disability insurers generally do encourage and assist their claimants who suffer long-term disabilities to claim their rights under the SSDI program, and this increases the number of applications for SSDI to the extent that some applicants otherwise would not have applied. Insurers assist their claimants in the application process because most private disability claimants are, in fact, determined to be eligible for SSDI benefits. In recent years, 72 percent of long-term group disability beneficiaries, or about 470,000 individuals in 2013, also received SSDI benefit payments (Council for Disability Awareness 2014a, 3-4). The 470,000 individuals receiving both group disability and SSDI benefits in 2013 constituted 5.3 percent of the 8.9 million workers receiving SSDI payments in 2013 (SSA 2014, 17). By definition then, with the possible exception of SSA error, these disabled workers are appropriately on the SSDI rolls. Helping disabled individuals to access SSDI benefits in timely fashion also confers important additional benefits. These include additional income benefits for a spouse and/or dependents and eligibility for Medicare benefits after a period of 24 months.

Although a still significant proportion of group disability claimants do not become eligible for SSDI benefits, it is generally still in their best interest to apply. Only the SSA—not group disability insurers—can determine eligibility for SSDI benefits. Moreover, it is not possible to determine in advance of the SSDI process whether or not an individual will qualify for SSDI benefits. One key reason is that an individual's health and functional capacity change over time.

The assistance that group disability insurers provide in the application process reduces the administrative burden on the SSA by improving the quality and completeness of applications, shortening the time required for consideration, and often avoiding the latter steps of the application process. This is very much in keeping with the SSA goal of getting to the right benefit decision as quickly as possible.

Group disability insurers are not alone in encouraging people to apply for SSDI benefits. Public entities such as the Federal Employee Retirement System require disabled beneficiaries to file for SSDI benefits. Many states' workers' compensation systems, as well as public employee retirement systems, also require beneficiaries to apply for SSDI benefits.

There is scant evidence to support the contention that group disability insurers have inappropriately shifted individuals onto the SSDI program. Group disability coverage may accelerate SSDI benefit awards to some number of affected workers who would have eventually attained SSDI beneficiary status. This does not increase total SSDI benefits paid, since benefits are paid retroactively to the onset of disability regardless of when they are awarded. The cumulative effect of this number, however, is a fraction of the number of affected workers kept off, or minimizing their time on, SSDI rolls because of the financial support and return-to-work efforts by group disability insurers. The relatively small number of disability claimants who apply for—but are not awarded—SSDI benefits, combined with SSA's longstanding "open door" policy for applications, confirms that group disability insurers are not imposing undue costs on the SSA by encouraging and assisting claimants to apply for SSDI benefits.

The Effect on Employee Compensation

Basic economic theory teaches that the total compensation (wages, benefits, taxes, etc.) of workers is determined by the marginal revenue product of the employees working in the firm and total cost of employing the worker. This means that if, for example, taxes or the cost of benefits for workers increase without a change in the revenue product of the workforce from greater productivity, there will be a change in the composition of the total compensation of the employees—taxes or benefit costs will be a larger portion of total compensation with a smaller part going to the remainder.

An opt-out enrollment program for group disability plans would, in the aggregate, increase the amount of employee compensation going to this element. Holding all else constant, other parts of employee compensation would either be reduced or grow more slowly.

We know, however, that group disability premiums are relatively low, generally falling in the range of $225 to $400 per employee per year (GenRe 2014, 7 and Council for Disability Awareness 2014b, 7). In addition, research has demonstrated that employees receive large economic welfare benefits from disability insurance coverage—$20 to $60 for each dollar of premiums paid (Babbel et al. 2011). Employees' welfare in the situation where an adverse event occurs is vastly higher with private disability insurance than without it. Therefore, although automatic enrollment into group disability coverage might displace other aspects of compensation, the overall expected economic welfare of the worker is improved.

The Capacity of Private Sector Disability Insurers

If the proposal is successfully implemented, the number of workers covered by group disability programs could increase from the current one-third of private sector employees to possibly one-half or even more. This would be a significant increase in the number of sponsoring employers, covered employees, and beneficiary recipients. Could the industry cope with this substantial increase in demand?

There are two crucial inputs for expanding group disability insurer capacity—capital and personnel, particularly therapeutic and rehabilitation personnel. Current providers of disability insurance include a number of large, well known, and well regarded insurers: Aetna, AIG, Ameritas, Guardian, The Hartford, Lincoln Financial Group, MassMutual, MetLife, Principal Financial, Prudential,

Sun Life, UnitedHealthcare, and Unum to name a few (Council for Disability Awareness 2014a, 14). Given the ramp-up time involved in opt-out enrollment programs, as well as the current borrower-friendly interest rate environment, access to capital should not be a problem. Expanding the supply of personnel focused on return-to-work is more involved, but is also ultimately solvable. In that regard it is notable that the job growth for physical therapists, occupational therapists, athletic trainers and exercise physiologists, and occupational therapy assistants and aides, among others, are projected to either be "faster than average" or "much faster than average" by the Bureau of Labor Statistics through at least 2022 (BLS March 2015).

CONCLUSION

Group disability coverage provides working Americans and their families with crucial income security when disabling illness or injury strikes. Private income protection insurers also possess unique expertise and capacity to work with employees, employers and physicians to help disabled workers return to work when that is feasible, safe and timely. A significant byproduct of the assistance that group disability insurers provide takes the form of federal budget savings from the reduction of the burden on public programs that provide assistance to disabled Americans. One of the programs that benefits from savings arising out of private market coverage is SSDI. Our analysis has identified savings to the SSDI program, from current levels of group disability coverage, of $900 million annually, shortly to rise to $1 billion. SSDI program savings, and savings to other federal programs, would increase if more working Americans enjoyed private market coverage.

Approximately one-third of Americans working in private industry now have group disability coverage. The federal government could play an active and effective role in increasing this proportion by implementing policies to encourage more employers to adopt opt-out enrollment arrangements under employer-sponsored group disability plans. Specifically, we propose the enactment of legislation to make it clear to employers that opt-out enrollment is permissible under current law. This would address legal uncertainties that are holding employers back from putting in place opt-out enrollment within group disability plans and would send a strong signal of the importance of income protection coverage. Our nation's recent experience with the Pension Protection Act of 2006 shows that opt-out enrollment arrangements can have a significant positive impact in helping working Americans overcome inertia, distraction and procrastination to act in their long-term self-interest.

We further propose that the federal government undertake education and outreach to working Americans and their employers to empower them with information and resources regarding key disability income security issues. This education and outreach program, especially when combined with the group disability insurers' education and marketing efforts, could also help working Americans and employers understand and make decisions regarding disability income plans and opt-out arrangements.

Expanding the proportion of working Americans with disability income protection coverage would bring greater financial security to many more employees. It would also produce savings in the SSDI program through improved overall return-to-work outcomes, and would bolster the long-term financial stability of the Social Security Disability Insurance Trust Fund. Expanded private income protection would also increase the likelihood of labor force participation for employees facing work impairment, thereby improving the overall economy and increasing government revenue.

For each 10 percentage point increase in the proportion of workers with long-term group disability coverage (e.g., from the current 33 percent to 43 percent), we estimate that ultimately between 20,000 and 25,000 additional workers affected by a disabling condition would either avoid or spend less time on SSDI status. Those 20,000 to 25,000 workers would increase the savings that group disability brings to the SSDI program by between $280 million and $350 million per year, or between $2.8 billion and $3.5 billion over 10 years. If participation in group disability coverage by private sector employees increased to just over 50 percent, an attainable participation rate if the experience of 401(k) opt-out plans are a reasonable guide, the additional savings figures would double—to additional annual savings in excess of $500 million up to $700 million per year and additional ten-year cumulative savings of $5 billion to $7 billion. The federal government also benefits from group disability coverage even when a return-to-work is not achieved, since group disability income protection benefits keeps many households from dependence on other federal programs (e.g., TANF, SNAP, SSI, etc.).

These benefits to the SSDI program would come at minimal cost to the government, so the net savings to the federal government would be substantial. Finally, there is a clear benefit to adopting these proposals, even if other, more SSDI program-specific proposals are also implemented.

This paper was prepared and submitted at the request of, and with funding by, America's Health Insurance Plans (AHIP) and the American Council of Life Insurers (ACLI). The authors of this paper are employees of Charles River Associates (CRA) and the views expressed herein are the views and opinions of the authors only and do not reflect or represent the views of CRA, AHIP, ACLI or any other organization. The authors, CRA, AHIP, and ACLI disclaim all liability of any kind whatsoever to any party arising in connection with this paper.

10

Ensuring Access to Long-Term Services and Supports for People with Disabilities and Chronic Conditions

Mark Perriello

INTRODUCTION

Gaps in the Support System for Workers with Disabilities

The United States does not currently have adequate programs and policies to provide affordable access to services and supports to working individuals with disabilities and chronic conditions that cause functional limitations. The passage of the Affordable Care Act (ACA) and its requirement that people with disabilities and chronic conditions be able to purchase insurance irrespective of preexisting conditions, without paying more for it, has created new opportunities for people with disabilities and chronic conditions to participate more fully in the workforce. Likewise, for people with mental health conditions, the ACA's expanded requirements for parity between physical and mental health coverage, which built upon the requirements of the Mental Health and Addiction Equity Act of 2008, increases the availability of screening and treatment for people with mental health conditions. Despite the progress made through the ACA and other recent legislation, there still exist significant gaps in programs and services to assist workers with chronic conditions and disabilities who want to continue working when their chronic conditions progress and their functional limitations increase. Some of these health care and long-term services and supports (LTSS) gaps include:

- Affordable access to ongoing behavioral treatments and supports, such as evidence-based peer support models;
- Access to LTSS such as personal assistance services, especially employment based. Virtually no commercial health care insurance provides access to personal assistance services;
- Adequate coverage of durable medical equipment and assistive technologies;
- Affordable access to prescription drug coverage;
- Access to certain rehabilitation and habilitation services; and
- Access to employment-related transportation.

The United States needs to establish or expand programs that support workers with disabilities and chronic conditions without requiring them to first leave the labor force to gain access to those services and supports, or to impoverish themselves in order to qualify and remain poor to maintain eligibility. Establishing these programs is critical, as people with disabilities and chronic conditions are more likely to experience lower socioeconomic status compared with other Americans. This leads to poorer health and a lower quality of life (APA 2015).

Social Security Disability Benefits Easiest Way to Access LTSS

Unfortunately, people with chronic conditions and disabilities who have service and support needs, and who also have work capacity, are often required to apply for income support benefits through the Social Security Act programs in order to access the very services and supports that might allow them to continue working. The federal-state Medicaid program is currently the only program through which the vast majority of people with functional limitations can access the assistance they need. Private long-term care insurance is simply unavailable or, if available, unaffordable to people who already need services or are at high risk of needing to use it. State Medicaid Buy-In (MBI) programs provide some access to needed LTSS to working individuals with disabilities, but unrealistic income and asset limits, uneven access to services and supports (insufficient in scope and quantity in many states), insufficient grace periods for unemployment, and lack of portability from state to state, among other reasons, make current MBI programs inadequate. Working individuals with disabilities and chronic conditions in need of LTSS require a program different from the traditional Medicaid program that would provide access to comprehensive coverage, including certain LTSS, without having to impoverish themselves or access income support benefits first.

Creating a Seamless System for Accessing LTSS

The proposals in this paper argue for creating a comprehensive, seamless system of access to LTSS for working individuals with disabilities and chronic conditions. The system would involve three main parts: a national MBI program, improved tax provisions for individuals who pay for LTSS out of pocket, and additional research into creating a new program to wrap around commercial health care insurance to fill in coverage gaps and provide LTSS. The system would be designed to provide affordable coverage to people with disabilities and chronic conditions across income and asset levels with no interruption in affordable access to the LTSS needed to obtain and maintain employment. The three parts of the system are:

1. A national Medicaid Buy-In program, which would have:
   a. Standard minimum asset and earnings limits across the states, providing coverage to all workers with increasing cost sharing and premiums as income increases, and which allow enrollees to save for emergencies, large purchases, and retirement;
   b. A standard set of services and supports with generous scope and quantity;
   c. A mandatory minimum grace period for periods of unemployment;
   d. Reciprocity for assets accumulated during participation in an MBI program in a state with more generous asset limits when an individual moves to another state to take a new job;
   e. A strong definition of employment; and
   f. A functional assessment for eligibility.

2. Improvement of tax provisions for the purchase of LTSS: Current tax provisions designed to assist individuals with disabilities and chronic conditions are inadequate to make LTSS affordable, except to those with the highest incomes. The tax assistance available to individuals who pay out of pocket for LTSS could be improved by allowing lower- and middle-income individuals to take a tax credit rather than a deduction, as well as making disability-related expenses necessary for work that occurs outside of the workplace allowable expenses. That would help working individuals with disabilities and chronic conditions afford needed LTSS if the individual chose not to participate in the MBI program, or if the individual still had out-ofpocket costs despite being enrolled in the MBI program.

3. Study the creation of a program to provide wraparound coverage, including LTSS: The paper proposes to study creation of a program providing LTSS coverage to working individuals with disabilities and chronic conditions that wraps around private health care insurance. This wraparound coverage would fill gaps in coverage for people with disabilities and chronic conditions that exist in private insurance—such as coverage of durable medical equipment and assistive devices, prescription drugs, and personal assistance needs—and provide additional cost-sharing protections. The study should look at requiring workers to take advantage of insurance offered by their employers or purchase it through the marketplace to be eligible. This program would be designed to ensure working individuals get the coverage, services, and supports they need, while limiting the cost to states and the federal government to only the cost of those additional services and supports not covered by private plans. Some features of the new program could include:
    a. Individuals would pay premiums to purchase this wraparound coverage and copayments for services could apply;
    b. There would no asset limits for participation; and
    c. Services and supports would be available based on functional need and functional assessment.

Additional study is needed to determine exact program design, whether the program should be public, private or a public/private partnership, and how it would interact with the ACA and Medicaid.

STATEMENT OF THE PROBLEM

Lack of a Support System for Workers with Disabilities: Access to Affordable Home and Community-Based Services and Supports

People with disabilities and chronic conditions that cause significant functional limitations have very low participation in the labor force. Only about 20 percent of people over age 16 with disabilities participate in the labor force, compared to just under 70 percent of people without disabilities (BLS 2015). The unemployment rate among people with disabilities who are participating in the labor force is also twice as high as the unemployment rate for people without disabilities, currently just under 12 percent (BLS 2015). In addition, the percentage of people with disabilities living in poverty is 28.7 percent, also twice the rate for people without disabilities (StatsRRTC 2014a).

The United States has made significant progress in many areas to allow people with disabilities to live in the community independently. The passage of the Americans with Disabilities Act (ADA) created the expectation that people with disabilities be integrated in all aspects of life, including employment.[1] The Individuals with Disabilities Education Act ensures that children with disabilities receive a free and appropriate education. However, the disappointing statistics regarding employment and poverty among people with disabilities persist despite the passage of these landmark laws and the evolution of attitudes regarding the abilities of people with disabilities.

The lack of progress in improving the economic status of people with disabilities can be attributed in large part to the failure of the United States to establish programs and policies that support workers with disabilities and chronic conditions and allow them to keep working when their chronic condition progresses or functional limitations progress (Vallas, Fremstad, and Ekman 2015). This is especially the case when a worker with a chronic condition or disability requires access to assistance that is not generally available through standard commercial health care insurance and that an employer is not required to provide under the ADA, as discussed in the introduction. In fact, it is estimated that one in five adults with disabilities living in a community setting has unmet LTSS needs (CRS 2013). The nature of the services and supports will vary depending on the nature of the person's disability or chronic condition, level of educational attainment, and current job and job skills.

This paper focuses on the need to improve access to services and supports for working individuals with disabilities and chronic conditions, but it is important to note that this is only one of the gaps in the current support system (CRS 2013). Working individuals also lack adequate access to vocational rehabilitation and job retraining when the functional limitations created by their chronic condition or disability increase and create the possibility that the worker might not be able to continue to do their current job in the future. State vocational rehabilitation programs provide these services to people with disabilities, but with their limited resources must focus on the unemployed and people with the most significant disabilities, and they lack sufficient resources to even serve all currently eligible individuals in many states (StatsRRTC 2014b).

---

1 Americans with Disabilities Act of 1990 (ADA), 42 U.S.C. §§ 12101-12213 (2000).

THE CURRENT SYSTEM

The Social Security Disability Insurance (SSDI) program was created in 1956 (Kearney 2005/2006) to provide income replacement to workers over the age of 50 who could not continue working until they reached retirement age due to a disability or chronic condition. As originally conceived, it was essentially a medical retirement program for workers who could not work until the retirement age. Although the age for eligibility was later lowered, it was never intended to support workers with disabilities, but rather to replace earnings for people with severe disabilities who no longer had the capacity to support themselves through work. SSDI performs that function very well and provides income replacement to more than 9 million workers with disabilities and their families, many of whom would be destitute without it. The SSDI program is vital for the people who receive its benefits, providing more than 75 percent of the income to one in three families that receive it and more than 90 percent of the household income of one in five families that benefit (Favreault, Johnson, and Smith 2013). SSDI has never provided (nor was it designed to) any type of support to the tens of millions of individuals with disabilities who can work. SSDI will always be needed to provide support to individuals whose disabilities and chronic conditions prevent them from supporting themselves, and the current definition of disability is appropriate for an income-replacement program. Rather than trying to adapt this very successful income-replacement program to support workers with disabilities, it would be more effective for the United States to expand or alter other existing programs already designed to support workers with disabilities.

Current Medicaid Options are Insufficient

As mentioned in the introduction, it is difficult for people with disabilities who need LTSS, such as personal attendant care, to access those services while working. For an individual with a disability or chronic condition, Medicaid is the only option for gaining access to those services and supports. Private long-term care insurance is either unaffordable or unavailable due to preexisting conditions, and paying out of pocket for needed services is not possible for any but the highest earners (UMass 2010).

Getting affordable access to needed services and supports is vital for people with disabilities and essential for becoming and remaining employed and independent. Medicaid is generally the only way to access affordable LTSS for most people with significant disabilities, and it is far from ideal. The services and supports available through Medicaid vary by state, services are often provided through a waiver, enrollment in those waiver programs is often capped with waiting lists, and eligibility is restricted to individuals with very low income and assets. In addition, receiving a disability determination from the Social Security Administration (SSA) is the easiest way to become eligible to receive the services and supports that can allow an individual with significant disabilities to continue to work. Unfortunately, being found eligible for disability benefits from SSA requires the individual to not be working at any significant level, and therefore blocks access to these vital services and supports. It is vital that automatic eligibility for health care coverage for SSDI and SSI beneficiaries (Medicare and Medicaid respectively) be maintained. This paper does not argue for changing that in any way. Rather, this paper is arguing for improving the ability of workers with disabilities to access the supports and services they need without having to apply for Social Security disability benefits.

As previously referenced, Congress gave states the option to create MBI programs in recognition of the fact that many working people with disabilities need access to services and supports to allow them to enter and remain in the workforce (Kehn, Croake, and Schimmel 2010). Forty-four states currently allow working individuals with disabilities and chronic conditions that cause functional limitations to buy in to Medicaid when they earn or have more resources than is allowed for regular Medicaid eligibility (NCD 2015). Unfortunately, these MBI programs vary significantly in eligibility requirements (from no income or resource limit in Massachusetts down to income under 80 percent of the federal poverty level and standard Medicaid resource limits in Virginia as of 2010), as well as the services and supports available and the scope of those services and supports (NCD 2015). This variability limits the ability of people with disabilities to work up to their full potential or maximize their independence, and often prohibits people from moving to another state to take a new job. Surveys and studies show that people with disabilities limit their work and earnings to ensure continued access to the services and supports they need to live and work independently, accessed through the MBI program (Gavin, McCoy-Roth, and Gidugu 2011). In particular, limits on assets and earnings for eligibility purposes causes workers to adjust work behavior to maintain eligibility (Gavin, McCoy-Roth, and Gidugu 2011). This leaves workers with disabilities or chronic conditions that progress with very few options: leave the workforce to get the services they need, apply for SSDI, or impoverish themselves to become eligible. No other affordable options currently exist to assist workers with disabilities in meeting their service and support needs, except for the highest earners who can pay out of pocket.

Current Tax Provisions are Inadequate

Workers with disabilities and chronic conditions who are not eligible for Medicaid but have LTSS needs and pay for them out of pocket can deduct certain expenses from their taxable income through the impairment-related work expense (IRWE) deduction. Eligible workers with disabilities can deduct expenses that "are ordinary and necessary business expenses for attendant care services at your place of work and other expenses in connection with your place of work that are necessary for you to be able to work" (IRS 2014, 13). Several features of the current tax provision limit its usefulness for workers with disabilities. First, it does not help many workers with disabilities with low or moderate earnings because it is a deduction from taxable income rather than a credit against taxes owed. Second, it excludes expenses an individual incurs that are necessary for work but are not incurred at the place of work (personal attendant care at home to get ready for work, for example).

Capitalizing on the ACA

Workers with chronic conditions and disabilities are now able to purchase commercial health care insurance for the first time though the marketplaces created by the ACA. This coverage expansion creates the opportunity to consider how a new program could be designed to wrap around that insurance to fill the coverage gaps identified earlier in this paper. Medicaid will still be the right program for some workers, irrespective of the historic opportunity created by the private market reforms required by the ACA. However, more study regarding how a new program might be created to help meet the needs of working individuals with chronic conditions and disabilities should be undertaken.

DETAILED PROPOSALS

Creating a Seamless System of Affordable Access to Services and Supports for Workers with Chronic Conditions and Disabilities

As discussed in the previous two sections of this paper, current programs and policies in the United States do not adequately support working individuals with chronic conditions and disabilities with expensive LTSS needs. Ensuring that people with disabilities and chronic conditions have uninterrupted affordable access to any needed LTSS could allow more people with disabilities to work and live independently without ever having to access income support benefits or delay application for income support. This paper proposes to design that system by creating a national MBI program and completely delinking eligibility for the MBI program from the Social Security definition of disability, and by improving and expanding current tax provisions available to people who pay out of pocket for LTSS. In addition, research should be conducted into ways of offering wraparound coverage to commercial health care insurance that would fill coverage gaps people with disabilities and chronic conditions experience, including LTSS.

A National Medicaid Buy-In

The first component of a seamless system of providing access to services and supports is ensuring that individuals have affordable uninterrupted access to LTSS through an improved and uniform MBI program throughout the United States. The national MBI program proposed here would be designed to address the problems identified in the current state MBI programs in the introduction to this paper. The national MBI program would include the following components:

- *Uniform income eligibility requirements:* Income limits for the MBI program should never limit the amount a person works in order to maintain eligibility and access to LTSS. Unlimited income for eligibility purposes with increasing cost sharing and premiums as income increases should be considered as a potential program design. At a minimum, people with incomes up to at least 400 percent of the federal poverty level for the applicable family size should be eligible to participate in the program. States should be allowed and encouraged to retain higher income eligibility limits if the current MBI program in the state allows participation by people with incomes over the national minimum.
- *Uniform resource eligibility limits:* People enrolled in the program should be encouraged to save for large purchases and emergencies, as well as retirement. The national MBI program could be modeled after the expansion of Medicaid in the ACA and have no limits on resources for eligibility. If a limit on resources must be placed, enrollees should be able to save at least $100,000 and remain eligible. Retirement savings should not be counted against that limit. Any resources accumulated during participation in an MBI program should also be excluded from eligibility determinations for other Medicaid categories in the future should the individual no longer be able to work.
- *Definition of work:* The inability to define work for the purposes of eligibility has been raised by states as an issue related to their program design and decisions not to expand eligibility in their MBI programs. A number of

different definitions of work could be employed in the national MBI program to limit participation to people who are not otherwise eligible for LTSS. Eligibility could be limited to individuals working a certain minimum number of hours per week (such as 20 or 30). Earning enough to qualify for a quarter of coverage for the purposes of Social Security eligibility during a three-month period could be another approach. Finally, a minimum amount of monthly earnings could be required for eligibility.

- *Reciprocity between states:* If the national program has income or resource limits, an individual participating in an MBI program that has higher income or asset limits than required by the national program must be allowed to enroll in the MBI program in a new state if their income or resources exceed the eligibility limits in the new state, provided the individual would still be eligible in the original state.
- *Standardized services and supports:* The national MBI program would detail the services and supports states would be required to provide to eligible individuals, both in terms of type and minimum scope of services available. Services that could be included are: adaptive aids (general and vehicle); care/case management (including assessment and case planning); communication aids/interpreter services; community support program; consumer education and training; counseling and therapeutic resources; home modifications; housing counseling; personal emergency response system services; durable medical equipment and supplies for long-term duration, except for hearing aids; home health; mental health services, except those provided by a physician or on an inpatient basis; relocation services; residential care apartment complex (RCAC); community-based residential facility (CBRF); respite care (for caregivers in non-institutional settings); supported employment (including individualized placement and support model); supportive home care; vocational futures planning; nursing services (including respiratory care, intermittent and private duty nursing); personal care (home- and employment-based); specialized medical supplies; transportation (non-Medicaid covered transportation services and Medicaid-covered services except ambulance and transportation by common carrier).
    - *Eligibility based on functional assessment:* Eligibility to participate in the national MBI program would not be tied to meeting the Social Security definition of disability, except for the income or asset limitation (as is currently the case), but rather would be based on a functional assessment documenting the need for the services offered through the MBI program. States already do functional assessments

for the need for services that could be adapted for this purpose (MACPAC 2014).

- o *Grace Period for Unemployment:* Participants in the MBI program would have a grace period of at least one year (with state options for more generous grace periods) in which they could continue to be enrolled in the program when they are not working for any reason, provided they continued to pay premiums if applicable.
- o *Sliding scale premiums and cost sharing:* The MBI program would set out a basic premium and cost-sharing structure and contain protections for low-income workers with disabilities.

The creation of a national MBI program would not have a significant administrative impact. There would be no real impact on the Centers for Medicare and Medicaid Services at the federal level. Most states already have MBI programs and already complete functional assessments for eligibility for LTSS in existing MBI or 1915 waiver programs, so additional administrative burden at the state level would be minimal.

Improving Tax Provisions to Support Workers with Disabilities

As discussed in Section 2, the main tax provision currently available to workers with disabilities and chronic conditions that cause functional limitations is the IRWE deduction, and the current design limits its usefulness for many workers with disabilities. The IRWE deduction should:

- *Be changed to a credit for low- and moderate-income individuals:* Because deductions are often not helpful to low and moderate-income individuals, the IRWE deduction should be changed to a credit for individuals with incomes under $100,000. The credit should be refundable for individuals with incomes up to 400 percent of the federal poverty level with a limit on the amount of the refund. Individuals with earnings over $100,000 would remain eligible for the IRWE deduction.
- *Be expanded to allow for the inclusion of expenses related to the disability or chronic condition that are necessary to work but not incurred at the work site:* Individuals with disabilities have many expenses incurred at home or away from their work site related to their disability or chronic condition and necessary for work, but that are not allowable expenses under the current IRWE deduction. Expenses related to an individual's disability or chronic condition that are necessary for the individual to go to work but do

not occur at the workplace (such as homebased personal attendant care) should be allowable expenses in the IRWE credit/deduction.

Wraparound Coverage Program

Additional study should be undertaken regarding the creation of a new program to provide wraparound coverage to commercial health care insurance to cover LTSS, as well as fill coverage gaps identified in the introduction. Individuals participating in the new program would need to have insurance either provided by an employer or purchased through the health insurance marketplaces created by the ACA. Research should be conducted regarding the following features of the program:

- *Public, private, or public/private partnership:* How could such a program be structured so that workers with disabilities have access to the LTSS and comprehensive coverage they need and take advantage of the options for acute health care coverage available through employer-sponsored plans or plans purchased through the ACA marketplace? Should it be a stand-alone program or build on an existing one?
- *Financing structure:* Should the program be a federal program or a state/federal partnership similar to Medicaid? Is a social insurance model appropriate?
- *Cost sharing and premium structure:* How should participants contribute to the cost of the program and the services and supports they receive through it?

ANALYSIS OF THE PROPOSALS

Analysis of the National MBI Program Proposal

The national MBI program would provide working individuals with disabilities and chronic conditions that cause functional limitations affordable access to the service and supports necessary to work and live independently in the community. By removing income and asset limits as eligibility criteria, the fear of loss of LTSS, or the inability to access LTSS while working in the first place, would no longer limit the work activity of individuals with disabilities and chronic conditions. As previously stated, individuals have noted in surveys that the fear of loss of health and LTSS coverage through Medicaid causes them to limit their work activity. This directly addresses the problem described in Section 2.

The improved access to LTSS and comprehensive health coverage while working should also delay or prevent some workers with disabilities and chronic conditions from applying for Social Security disability benefits (Chapman, Hall, and Moore 2013). Results from the Demonstration to Maintain Independence and Employment offers some evidence that providing working individuals at risk of applying for Social Security disability benefits with access to comprehensive health coverage can delay or prevent application for disability benefits (Whalen et al. 2012). However, the results were mixed and the intervention in this demonstration did not provide access to the full array of LTSS that would be available to individuals enrolled in the new national MBI program (Whalen et al. 2012). The extent of the impact the national MBI program would have on SSDI applications is therefore difficult to estimate. No in-depth economic or statistical analysis of the national MBI program proposed in this paper has been completed.

Expanding access to LTSS through the national MBI program proposed in this paper would have costs at both the state and federal levels. Assessing how much it will cost is difficult for a number of reasons. To begin with, the number of working individuals with disabilities and chronic conditions who are not currently eligible for any Medicaid coverage and have unmet LTSS needs is unknown and hard to estimate. Some individuals currently enrolled in state MBI programs would not be eligible for the new national MBI program due to the new stricter definition of work, although the extent of that population of workers is not known because the exact definition of work that would be contained in the new MBI program is not known. There are also a number of cost control levers contained in the proposal that could be adjusted to change the cost of the national MBI (such as income and resource limits, premium structure and cost sharing, required services, etc.).

Evaluating this proposal based on near-term cost, however, is counterproductive. Adequately supporting workers with disabilities and chronic conditions that cause functional limitations by providing affordable access to LTSS and comprehensive health care coverage is a necessary step toward continuing the progress that people with disabilities have made toward full integration into community living and employment. People with disabilities need to be certain that their work activity will not jeopardize access to health care and the services and supports they require to maximize their work activity and work up to their capacity. Making this investment in working people with disabilities is the right thing to do and results in many nonfinancial positive benefits—increased economic self-sufficiency, better quality of life, and better health for individuals with disabilities.

Analysis of the IRWE Tax Deduction Proposal

The IRWE tax deduction improvements suggested in this paper would contribute to the economic well-being and self-sufficiency of workers with disabilities who have long-term care needs. This proposal might have no impact on applications for Social Security disability benefits on its own. However, in combination with the national MBI program, the improvements suggested here should allow some workers with disabilities and chronic conditions to maintain their attachment to the workforce longer than they otherwise would be able to, and delay or prevent them from needing Social Security disability benefits.

The cost of this proposal is difficult to estimate. Data is not publicly available regarding the current utilization of the deduction. Lacking baseline data makes it hard to determine what impact the changes outlined in this paper would have. And, as previously discussed, unmet need for LTSS among working individuals with disabilities is also not readily quantifiable. No formal analysis has been completed on the cost of the improvements to the IRWE deduction proposed in this paper and completing one is beyond the scope of this paper.

This proposal would not have a significant administrative impact. The changes to the IRWE deduction would not require significant additional effort by the Internal Revenue Service or any other administrative agency. There should not be additional administrative cost from this proposal.

INTERMEDIATE STEPS

The concepts and ideas presented in this paper remain in the early stages of development. Law and policy makers interested in pursuing these ideas must take up further study of these proposals in order to determine the extent of their impact on SSDI and the programs' fiscal viability overall.

One challenge that any policymaker is sure to face is the ability to accurately calculate the true cost of expanding and improving these programs, while offsetting any savings to SSDI as a result of more Americans with disabilities and chronic conditions entering and remaining in the workforce. Current scoring methodologies are unlikely to consider potential savings or any increased revenue as a result of an expanded pool of taxpayers. Nevertheless, this remains among likely next steps.

In order to determine true costs and savings, policymakers should consider a range of outstanding questions, such as:

1. What is the cost-per-person for these proposals?
2. Regarding the recommended changes to the tax code, should an existing framework such as the child care credit be utilized?
3. What should be the federal/state split? Should the federal government pick up 100 percent of the costs?
4. Should the wraparound benefit be part of the buy-in, or should there be a different structure altogether? How different would the matching rates be? What would the premium charges be?
5. What are the exact eligibility criteria?

As these questions demonstrate, additional research and discussion must take place in order to fully realize the potential of the proposals in this paper.

QUESTIONS AND CONCERNS

The proposals in this paper argue for expansion and improvement of two existing programs/provisions. This section will lay out questions and raise some areas for additional examination.

Questions Regarding National MBI Program

Political Feasibility?

The national MBI program proposed in this paper would represents an expansion of the states' obligations under the Medicaid program. The current Congress seems unlikely to be supportive of increasing the obligations of states and creating more mandates on states related to coverage. Both the House and Senate budget proposals for fiscal year 2016 contain proposals to block-grant the Medicaid program. The approach of the current Congress toward Medicaid and the rejection by many states of the Medicaid expansion contained in the ACA raises significant questions regarding the feasibility of getting a national MBI program passed into law and implemented at this time.

Enhanced Matching Rate?

Another question in designing a national MBI program is what percentage of the costs should be the responsibility of the federal government and what should be paid by the states. Congress has chosen to enhance the matching rate paid to states to encourage them to take up certain options to improve access to LTSS, especially home- and community-based services. Congress also created an enhanced match for the expanded coverage of single individuals required under the ACA—providing 100 percent federal funding for the first year, then gradually decreasing to a permanent federal share of 90 percent. Increasing the share of the expense of the national MBI program paid by the federal government should be considered, up to and including having the federal government pay 100 percent.

Cost Estimate?

As mentioned in the Analysis section and the Intermediate Steps section, it is difficult to estimate the take-up rate of working individuals with unmet need for coverage and what the national MBI program will cost. The overall cost will also depend on the premium and cost-sharing structure created for the national program.

Questions Regarding Improving the IRWE Deduction

The proposal to expand and improve the IRWE deduction does not raise significant questions or concerns. As this is a longstanding provision of the tax code, there are not likely to be unintended consequences or implementation challenges with making the changes to the IRWE deduction proposed in this paper.

CONCLUSION

The current programs and policies designed to support workers with disabilities and chronic conditions that cause functional limitations leave large gaps in what workers need. These gaps include, but are not limited to, access to affordable and accessible transportation and housing, paid leave and sick time, a permanent wage supplement for individuals who can only work part time or sporadically due to their disability, and affordable access to long-term services and supports. This paper proposes solutions to address only the final gap: the lack of affordable access to services and supports and fill coverage gaps in commercial health insurance.

This paper proposes several actions to ensure working individuals with disabilities and chronic conditions that cause functional limitations have access to LTSS and adequate health care coverage. First, the current option available to states to provide Medicaid coverage to working individuals with disabilities through the MBI program should be a mandatory eligibility category and should have a federal floor for income and assets and standardized services. Current issues with the MBI programs would be addressed so that an individual would never need to leave the workforce to gain access to needed LTSS coverage and the more comprehensive health care coverage provided through Medicaid. Individuals with disabilities would also be able to earn up to their capacity, take raises and promotions, and move to a new state to accept a job offer without concern regarding losing access to the very service and supports that enable the individual to work in the first place.

Second, the paper proposes to improve the IRWE deduction available to workers with disabilities who have high out-of-pocket costs for expenses related to their disability or chronic condition necessary for work, whether or not the individual participates in an MBI program.

Finally, the paper proposes taking a look at how the new options created by the ACA for the purchase of commercial health care insurance by people with disabilities and chronic condition can be built upon. More research should be undertaken to study the design of a program to provide wraparound coverage to commercial health care insurance in order to provide LTSS and fill in coverage gaps that exist for people with disabilities and chronic conditions in virtually all commercial health care insurance plans.

The proposals in this paper attempt to address only one area in which the current support system for workers with disabilities is inadequate. As discussed, it is difficult to estimate the impact that these changes will have on the number of people with disabilities applying for or receiving SSDI because the course of an individual's disability or chronic condition is impossible to predict, and whether an individual with a disability can continue to work is dependent on a variety of factors including the individual's health. Ensuring that access to needed services and supports does not limit an individual's work effort or earnings necessarily means spending more at both the federal and state levels on the Medicaid program and at the federal level on the tax code. It can cost more to support an individual with a significant disability to work than it would to provide them with income support through the SSDI or SSI program.

Supporting work by people with significant disabilities is the right thing to do, irrespective of whether doing so costs or saves money. Studies show that individuals with disabilities who work experience improved health, economic security, and quality of life, and the United States should invest to achieve those outcomes.

11

Improving the Interaction Between the SSDI and Workers' Compensation Programs

John F. Burton Jr. and Xuguang (Steve) Guo

INTRODUCTION

Social Security Disability Insurance (SSDI) is the largest source of cash benefits for disabled workers and their families with $140.1 billion paid in 2013. Workers' compensation (WC) is the second-largest source of cash benefits for these workers and their families, paying $32.0 billion in 2013 (Sengupta and Baldwin 2015). WC benefits are limited to workers whose disabilities are the result of work-related injuries and diseases,[1] while SSDI benefits are paid regardless of the source of the disability. Although there are other differences between the programs in coverage and eligibility rules, many workers actually or potentially qualify for both sources of benefits.

In the next three sections, we provide a primer on SSDI, Medicare, and WC, examine the retrenchments in WC since 1990, and review evidence suggesting there is cost shifting from WC to SSDI. We then devote four sections to proposals that could reduce the extent of cost shifting. The final section provides our conclusions and recapitulates our suggestions for the initial implementation of the proposals.

---

1 We use "injuries" to include "injuries and diseases" in this study.

A PRIMER ON SSDI, MEDICARE, AND WORKERS' COMPENSATION

The primer provides only a brief discussion of the SSDI program, on the assumption that most readers are reasonably familiar with the program. The discussions of Medicare and the medical components of WC are also brief since the main focus of this chapter is cash benefits.

SSDI and Medicare Benefits

SSDI benefits are paid to workers who become disabled and unable to work prior to the normal retirement age. SSDI benefits are available to workers with disabilities, whether or not their disabilities result from work injuries. However, SSDI benefits are paid only to workers who meet the definition of disability in the Social Security Act: "the inability to engage in any substantial gainful activity (SGA) by reason of any medically determinable physical or mental impairment(s) which can be expected to result in death or which has lasted or can be expected to last for a continuous period of not less than 12 months."

Workers must have a substantial history of contributions to the Social Security system in order to be eligible for SSDI benefits, which begin after a five-month waiting period. Workers who qualify for SSDI benefits can lose their benefits if they subsequently have enough earnings to indicate they are capable of SGA. However, most workers who qualify for SSDI benefits continue to receive benefits until they die or until they are old enough to qualify for old age benefits in the Social Security program.

Medicare pays health care costs for persons who receive SSDI benefits after an additional 24-month waiting period (or 29 months after the onset of disability).

Workers' Compensation Benefits

WC benefits are paid to workers who become disabled or who require medical treatment as a result of work-related injuries. Workers are eligible for benefits from the first day of employment. WC provides medical benefits, which begin the day of the injury. In most jurisdictions, the medical benefits are provided without limits on duration or dollar amount, and there are no deductibles or co-insurance payments for the medical care.

Seventy-five percent of WC cases involve only medical benefits (Sengupta and Baldwin 2015, 7), while cases including cash benefits (almost always in addition to medical benefits) account for the other 25 percent. Most WC claims that pay cash benefits are for temporary total disability (TTD), which means the disability temporarily precludes a person from performing the pre-injury job or another job at the employer that the worker could have performed prior to the injury. In most states, TTD benefits have a waiting period of from three to seven days and continue until the worker is able to return to work, is determined to have a permanent disability, or reaches a statutory limit on the duration of TTD benefits.

While most WC cases involving cash benefits involve only TTD benefits, most payments of cash benefits go to workers who receive permanent total disability (PTD) or permanent partial disability (PPD) benefits. Those are the categories of cash benefits most likely to involve workers who also qualify for SSDI benefits because of the serious nature of the injuries. (O'Leary et al. 2012, Chart 5).

Permanent total disability benefits are paid to those with disabilities that preclude material levels of employment. PTD benefits account for only 0.3 percent of the WC cases paying cash benefits, but accounted for 7.1 percent of all cash benefit payments in 2009 (Sengupta, Baldwin, and Reno 2014, Figure 4). Burton (2012, 53) estimated there were about 13,200 PTD cases nationally in 2009. PTD benefits are paid for the duration of the period of total disability or for life in 38 states (Tanabe 2014, Table 5). In the other 13 jurisdictions, the duration or dollar amount of PTD benefits is limited.

PPD benefits involve disabilities that are permanent but that do not completely limit a person's ability to work. In almost all PPD cases, the duration of the benefits is determined after the date of maximum medical improvement.[2] Once the duration is determined (e.g., 100 weeks), the worker receives benefits for that duration, even if he or she returns to work at full preinjury wages prior to 100 weeks. Conversely, PPD benefits stop after 100 weeks, even if the worker is

---

[2] Burton (2005) identified three operational approaches to PPD benefits: the impairment approach (which determines the duration of the PPD benefits by rating the worker's medical condition); the loss-of-earning-capacity approach (which determines the duration of PPD benefits by rating the worker's loss of earning capacity based on the worker's medical conditions as well as factors including age, education, and prior work experience); and the actual-wage-loss approach (which determines the duration of PPD benefits by the period in which the worker experiences loss of earnings due to the work injury). The actual-wage-loss approach is used in only a few states, and those states are likely to limit the duration of PPD benefits.

continuing to experience a loss of earnings due to the work-related injury. PPD benefits accounted for 37.7 percent of cases paying cash benefits and for 62.0 percent of cash benefits payments in 2009 (Sengupta, Baldwin, and Reno 2014, Figure 4). Burton (2012, 53) estimated there were about 468,000 PPD cases nationally in 2009.

The Adequacy of WC Permanent Disability Benefits.

One approach to assessing the adequacy of WC benefits relies on wage-loss studies that compare the WC benefits received by a sample of injured workers to the actual wage losses experienced by those workers. Wage losses are calculated by comparing the workers' post-injury wages with estimates of the wages the workers would have received if they had not been injured. (Non-injured workers in jobs similar to the injured workers are used as a control group to produce estimates of potential wages.) One issue in the wage-loss studies is the value of the replacement rate (benefits divided by earnings losses) that is considered adequate. The National Commission on State Workmen's Compensation Laws (1972, 18-20) indicated that replacement of two-thirds of lost earnings was the appropriate standard for TTD, PTD and death benefits, but did not specify an adequacy standard for PPD benefits. A study panel of the National Academy of Social Insurance, while acknowledging the decision was somewhat arbitrary, endorsed "the historical standard of replacing two-thirds of gross wages as a measure of benefit adequacy" for PPD benefits (Hunt 2004, 128). In recent decades, there have been a series of wage-loss studies of PPD benefits, which are summarized by Boden, Reville and Biddle (2005, Table 3.4). The studies indicate that replacement rates for the 10 years after injury were 46 percent in New Mexico, 41 percent in Washington, 37 percent in California, 36 percent in Oregon and 30 percent in Wisconsin. The authors concluded (at 60) the "replacement rates do not approach the benchmark for adequacy."

Financing of SSDI and Workers' Compensation

The SSDI program is financed by employer and employee contributions of 0.9 percent each up to an annual taxable maximum of earnings (currently $118,500). The contribution rates do not vary depending on prior benefit payments made by the employer.

The WC program is largely financed by insurance premiums paid by employers.[3] (With the exceptions of a few states, workers do not pay WC premiums.) The premiums vary among employers based on previous benefit payments attributable to the firm or similar employers. (More information on experience rating is provided in proposal 3.)

DEVELOPMENTS IN WORKERS' COMPENSATION CASH BENEFITS SINCE 1980

Cash Benefits Increased until the early 1990s and then Decreased

Payments per $100 of covered payroll for WC cash benefits from 1980 to 2013 are shown in Figure 1. (The figure also includes information on SSDI benefits per $100 of payroll, which will be discussed in the next section.) WC cash benefits increased from $0.68 per $100 of payroll in 1980 to a peak of $0.99 per $100 of payroll in 1991. Cash benefits then declined in most subsequent years until reaching $0.50 per $100 of payroll in 2013, tying four other recent years for the lowest figure since 1980.

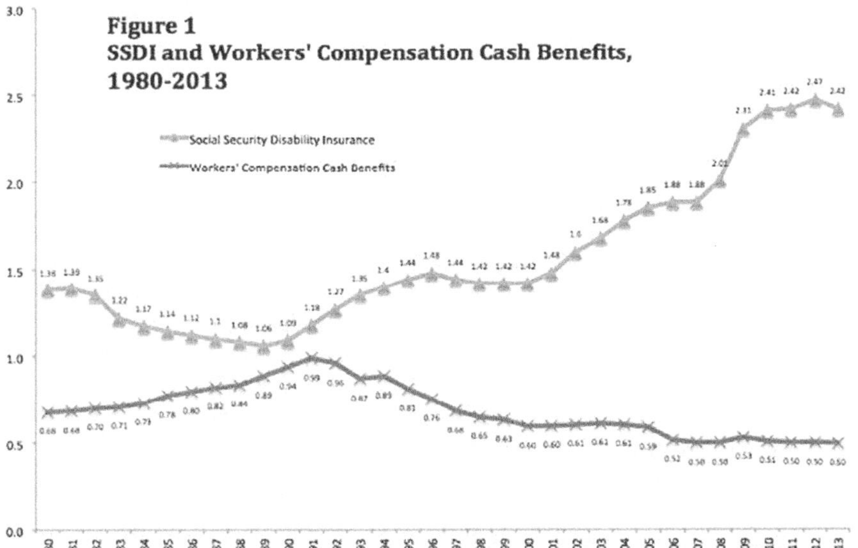

Figure 1
SSDI and Workers' Compensation Cash Benefits, 1980-2013

3 In most states, employers can self-insure their workers' compensation obligations, which constitutes perfect experience rating (although many self-insuring employers reinsure some of their risks).

Explanation of the Increase and Subsequent Decline in Cash Benefits

The National Council on Compensation Insurance (NCCI) publishes information on countrywide changes in workers' compensation premium levels, which are divided into two primary components: (1) experience change, which is largely "based on analyses of state premium and benefit cost data," and (2) benefit changes [which we describe as changes in statutory benefits], which reflect changes in cash benefits "adopted by various state legislatures, as well as medical fee and hospital rate changes" (NCCI 2015, Exhibit 1).

Figure 2 shows the benefit changes for sub-periods (most involve five-year intervals) from 1959 to 2014. Workers' compensation statutory benefits increased significantly during the 1960s, substantially between 1970 and 1985, and modestly between 1985 and 1990. Then statutory benefits declined in the decades of the 1990s and the 2000s, before increasing by 1 percent between 2010 and 2014.[4]

Figure 2
Workers Compendsation Statutory Benefits Changes
Percentage Changes in Sub-periods, 1959-2014

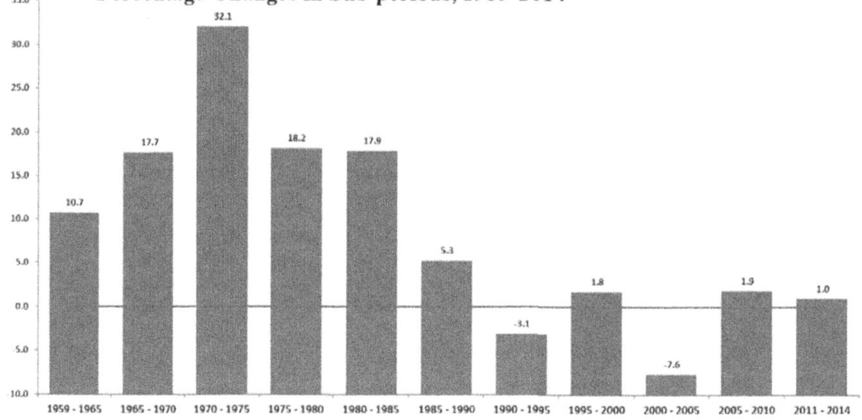

Source: Calculations by John Burton based on NCCI (2015 and earlier editions)

There are only a few published studies that attempted to determine the sources of declining payment of WC cash benefits since the early 1990s. Spieler and Burton (2012) provide a qualitative analysis examining changes in state WC statutes and court decisions that reduced the durations of cash benefits and, of even more importance, changed the compensability rules in many states. Some

---

4 The NCCI reported a 0.8 percent national increase in statutory benefits in 2014, including a 24.1 percent decline in cash benefits in Oklahoma and a 16.2 percent decline in Tennessee (NCCI 2015, Exhibits 1 and 3).

of the changes include limits on the ability of workers to qualify for benefits when their work injuries aggravated preexisting conditions; restrictions on benefits for certain diseases, including stress-related mental disorders and carpel tunnel syndrome; requirements that disorders must be proven by "objective" medical evidence; and higher standards of proof so a claimant must prove the case by "clear and convincing evidence" rather than by the "preponderance of the evidence." Guo and Burton (2010) conducted a quantitative analysis of the determinants of cash benefits relying on annual observations for 46 jurisdictions (including the District of Columbia).[5] They found that part of the decline in cash benefits between 1990 and 1999 was due to a drop in the work-related injury rate, but that a larger share of the decline was caused by a combination of (1) more stringent administrative practices, rules, and decisions by state courts, (2) tightening of eligibility rules in state statutes, and (3) the declining share of WC cases that qualified for permanent partial disability benefits.

Recent Developments Affecting WC Cash Benefits

A recent example of the effort to tighten compensability rules involved Illinois, where Gov. Bruce Rauner proposed in 2015 a change in the causation standard used to determine if a worker qualifies for WC benefits:

> The causation standard should be raised from an "any cause" standard to a "major contributing cause" standard. The accident at work must be more than 50 percent responsible for the injury compared to all other causes.

The governor's discussion of this proposed standard indicates that Missouri, Kansas, Oklahoma, and Tennessee have recently passed laws requiring the workplace to be "the *primary* cause for workers' compensation to be compensable," and indicates that "Florida's major contributing cause standard is identical to the one we are proposing." The major contributing cause (MCC) requirement contrasts with the traditional approach in WC, in which a worker is eligible for benefits so long as the work-related injury is a nontrivial source of his or her disability. An example of how restricting eligibility affects workers is provided in Oregon, where Thomason and Burton (2001) estimate that a series of legislative changes, including adopting the MCC provision, resulted in benefits (and costs) about 25 percent below the amounts they would have been without the more restrictive eligibility standards.

---

5 Additional information on Guo and Burton (2010) is provided in proposal four.

In addition to reductions in the duration and weekly amounts of cash benefits and the constriction of compensability rules, there is a nascent movement to reduce the mandatory coverage of workers by state WC laws. The most significant recent development concerning mandatory coverage was Oklahoma's adoption of an employer opt-out provision that applies to injuries sustained after January 1, 2014. Robinson (2013, 154-55) distinguishes the Oklahoma approach from the long-standing provision in Texas that allows employers to be "non-subscribers" to the state's workers' compensation law, and thus subject themselves to tort suits. (Many Texas employers have, however, voluntarily established disability plans that provide some protection to injured workers). The Oklahoma law allows employers the choice of (1) remaining with the "traditional" workers' compensation act or (2) establishing a written benefit plan that provides "for payment of the same form of benefits" that are at least equal to or greater than those under the state's WC law. The advantage to an employer is that the benefit plan they adopt may qualify as an Employee Retirement Income Security Act plan, which could mean that a dispute involving the benefit plan would be resolved in federal courts rather than by the Oklahoma Workers' Compensation Commission or Oklahoma state courts. It is too soon to assess the extent to which the 2013 Oklahoma law will result in significantly reduced WC coverage for the state's workers, but several commentators, including Torrey (2015, 10-11), have expressed concern about the opt-out provision.

Although the decline in WC benefits shown in Figures 1 and 2 that were examined by Spieler and Burton (2012) and Guo and Burton (2010) began in the early 1990s, the rate of constriction in coverage and benefits may have accelerated in the past 10 years. Grabell and Berkes (2015) report that "Since 2003, legislators in 33 states have passed workers' compensation laws that reduce benefits or make it more difficult for those with certain injuries and diseases to qualify for them."

THE POSSIBLE SHIFTING OF COSTS OF WORKPLACE INJURIES AND DISEASES FROM WORKERS' COMPENSATION TO SSDI

Payments per $100 of covered payroll for WC cash benefits and for SSDI benefits from 1980 to 2013 are shown in Figure 1. As previously discussed, WC cash benefits per $100 of covered payroll increased from 1980 until 1991, and then declined in most subsequent years. In contrast, SSDI benefits declined during most of the 1980s, but increased significantly in subsequent years. WC cash benefits were only slightly less expensive than SSDI benefits in the early 1990s, but by 2013, SSDI benefits were almost five times WC cash benefits as a percent of covered payroll. The divergent trends in SSDI and WC since 1980 caused the National Academy of Social Insurance to "raise the question of whether retrenchments in one program increase demands placed on the other" (Sengupta, Reno, and Burton 2011, 45).

Coordination of SSDI and WC Benefits

The Social Security Act was amended in 1965 to require that the total of SSDI and WC benefits, and certain other public disability plans (PDB) operated by most states, not exceed the "applicable limit," which for most workers is 80 percent of the worker's average current earnings (ACE) prior to qualifying for SSDI benefits (Altomare 2009). In most states, the offset provision requires SSDI benefits to be reduced if necessary to achieve the 80 percent limit if the worker is receiving benefits from both programs. For example, if the ACE is $4,000 per month, then the "applicable limit" is $3,200. If the WC monthly cash benefit is $2,800, and the SSDI benefit would have been $1,800 without the offset provision, then the application of the offset provision requires the SSDI monthly benefit to be limited to $400. However, in 15 states with reverse-offset laws, WC benefits are reduced to achieve the 80 percent limit. Using the figures in the prior example, SSDI benefits would be $1,800 and WC cash benefits would be $1,400 after application of the reverse offset provision. In short, in this example, the use of the reverse-offset provision in place of the offset provision used in most states results in a $1,400 increase in SSDI benefits. (The offset topic is examined in more depth in the next section.)

Cost Sharing by WC and SSDI

Some workers receive WC cash benefits that meet the adequacy standard for the WC program (replacement of two-thirds of lost wags resulting from a work-related injury or disease) and also receive SSDI benefits. This can happen for a variety of reasons, such as the worker experiencing a work-related injury, which is compensated by the WC program, and a non-work-related injury (such as an auto accident), which results in SSDI benefits. Or the worker may receive WC cash benefits that replace two-thirds of lost wages plus SSDI benefits that bring the total of WC and SSDI benefits up to the limit of 80 percent of ACE. We classify such cases as cost sharing rather than cost shifting, even though there are SSDI benefits paid in addition to the WC benefits, because the objective of adequate WC benefits is met.

Cost Shifting from WC to SSDI

There are at least four types of shifting of costs of work-related injuries and diseases from WC to SSDI. First, some of the costs of work-related injuries and diseases can be shifted from WC to SSDI by the offset provision if workers receiving both SSDI and WC benefits are receiving weekly WC benefits that are inadequate. While the cost shifting may not be the intent of the offset provision, that is the effect because SSDI benefits are higher than they would be if WC benefits were adequate to bring the total of SSDI and WC benefits to the 80 percent limit.[6]

Second, cost shifting from WC to SSDI can occur if WC benefits terminate while the loss of wages due to the work-related injury persists. In this case, all of the disability benefits must be provided by the SSDI program after WC benefits cease.

Third, cost shifting can occur if some workers with work-related injuries never receive WC benefits, either because WC claims are never filed or the WC claims are denied because of restrictive compensability rules. In this case, all disability benefits are provided by SSDI.

Fourth, while the offset provision in a majority of states requires SSDI benefits to be reduced if total benefits exceed the applicable limit (80 percent of ACE), in 15 states the offset provision allows the states to reduce WC benefits in cases that exceed the maximum. In those states, the offset provision shifts some of the costs of work-related injuries from WC to SSDI.

Social Security Administration Data on the Overlap of SSDI and WC

There is a substantial overlap between SSDI and WC (or PDB) beneficiaries whose benefits from the two programs are coordinated as required by the offset provision in the Social Security Act (Sengupta and Baldwin 2015, Table 19). As of 2013, Social Security Administration (SSA) data indicate that 492,000 (5.5 percent) of workers receiving SSDI benefits were currently affected by the offset

[6] The example in the *Coordination of SSDI and WC benefits* subsection assumed that the ACE is $4,000 a month, the "applicable limit" is $3,200, the WC monthly benefit is $2,800, and the SSDI monthly benefit would have been $1,800 without the offset provision. But because of the offset provision, the actual SSDI monthly benefit is $400. However, if the WC benefit is not $2,800 (assumed to adequate) but instead is $1,500 (not adequate), the actual SSDI monthly benefit will be $1,700 (not $400).

provisions. However, it is impossible to distinguish between cases involving cost sharing and cases involving the first type of cost shifting. In addition, there were 549,802 workers for whom SSDI benefits were previously offset by WC benefits. However, it is not possible to distinguish between cases involving cost sharing and cases involving the second type of cost shifting. Finally, 43,817 workers (or 0.5 percent of all workers receiving SSDI benefits) were currently receiving SSDI and WC benefits in reverse-offset states, which represents the fourth type of cost shifting. While studies discussed in the next section suggest that the workers eligible for both SSDI and WC benefits are undercounted in the SSA data in this paragraph, these data are not particularly useful in identifying the extent of cost shifting from WC to SSDI. To demonstrate cost shifting, other types of evidence are available.

Evidence of Cost Shifting from WC to SSDI

One source of evidence uses data from national surveys. An example of this approach is the analysis by Reville and Schoeni (2004/2004) of the 1992 Health and Retirement Study (HRS), a nationally representative study of the U.S. population aged 51-61. Among the disabled who reported that their health condition was caused by their work, 29 percent were enrolled in the SSDI program at the time of the survey but just 12.3 percent had ever received WC benefits (Reville and Schoeni 2003/2004, Table 6). For the workers whose health condition was caused by work but who never receive WC benefits, this represents the third type of cost shifting.

A second source of evidence relies on data from secondary sources compiled by organizations concerned with the costs of occupational injuries and illnesses. An example is the study by Leigh and Marcin (2012), who relied on data from several sources including the National Council on Compensation Insurance and the Bureau of Labor Statistics to estimate that the total costs of workplace injuries and illnesses in 2007 were $249.64 billion.[7] The authors estimated that the amounts and percentages of the total costs accounted for by the various payers were workers' compensation ($51.725 billion or 20.72 percent)[8], out-of-pocket

---

7 Leigh and Marcin (2012) estimated that the total cost of workplace injuries and illnesses in 2007 was $249.64 billion, with $67.09 billion attributed to medical costs and $182.54 billion to indirect costs. Indirect costs consisted of (1) lost earnings ($110.02 billion), (2) lost fringe benefits ($29.03 billion), and (3) lost home production ($43.49 billion).

8 Leigh and Marcin (2012, Table 3) estimated that workers' compensation benefits in 2007 were $51.725 billion, compared to the National Academy of Social Insurance estimate of

costs absorbed by the families ($124.88 billion or 50.02 percent), private health insurance ($32.92 billion or 13.19 percent), the federal government ($26.76 billion or 10.72 percent), and state and local governments ($13.35 billion or 5.35 percent) (Leigh and Marcin 2012, Table 4). The costs for the federal government included $12.51 billion for medical care and $14.25 billion for indirect costs, which includes *inter alia* the costs of SSDI benefits paid for workplace injuries and diseases. The essence of this study is that the federal government payments for cash benefits and medical care for workplace injuries and diseases are roughly half the amount paid by the WC program. This evidence involves examples of the first three types of cost shifting.

A third source of evidence relies on administrative data for individual WC recipients matched with administrative data for those individuals maintained by SSA. An example of this approach is the study of recipients of WC beneficiaries in New Mexico conducted by O'Leary et al. (2012). The results indicate that some workers who received WC benefits subsequently received SSDI benefits, and some portion of those SSDI benefits were due to the lingering effects of work-related injuries (O'Leary et al. 2012, Chart 5). For example, about 30 percent of workers who received PTD benefits from the WC program received SSDI benefits within 15 years after the date of their work-related injuries, and more than 20 percent of workers who received PPD benefits from the WC program received SSDI benefits within 15 years of their injuries. (These percentages refer to the excess number of SSDI cases compared to workers who receive only WC medical benefits). Even workers who only received WC temporary disability benefits for less than eight weeks were more likely to receive SSDI benefits than similar workers who received only WC medical benefits. The results indicate that some losses of earnings resulting from workplace injuries are only partially compensated by WC benefits, which is evidence of the first and second types of cost shifting

A fourth source of evidence uses state-level data on WC programs matched with state-level data on the SSDI program compiled by SSA. A particular issue that has been examined using this approach is whether the costs of work-related disability have been shifted from WC to SSDI as a result of the changes in WC statutes in recent decades that reduced cash benefits and constricted eligibility rules. While there is clear evidence that WC coverage and benefits have declined in recent decades, only a few studies have tested whether the costs have been shifted from WC to SSDI, and the results of these studies are mixed. Using

---

$55.4 billion.

state-level data on WC and SSDI activity, McInerney and Simon (2012) examined whether PTD or PPD weekly benefits provided by WC state programs were negatively associated with SSDI applications or allowances in those states. That is, in states where WC rules were less generous were applications or awards for SSDI benefits higher? They concluded "it is unlikely that state workers' compensation changes were a meaningful factor in explaining the rise in DI during our study period of 1986 to 2001." A different conclusion was reached by Guo and Burton (2012), who examined state-level data on SSDI applications in approximately 45 jurisdictions between 1981 and 1999. We found that population aging, increasing female labor force participation, changes in the unemployment rate, and the DI replacement rate (DI benefits/lost earnings) explained most of the changes in SSDI benefits between the 1980s and the 1990s. Nonetheless, changes in WC permanent disability statutory benefits and WC eligibility rules had a small but statistically significant and positive effect on increasing SSDI applications in the 1990s (explaining about 3 to 4 percent), which is evidence of the first three types of cost shifting. Additional research is needed to determine if the extent of cost shifting from WC to SSDI has increased in recent years. One research project we recommend be initiated as soon as feasible is a national survey with the same questions contained in the 1992 HRS to see if the results reported by Reville and Schoeni (2003/2004) have changed.

For the balance of this paper, we assume that the evidence is clear that a significant proportion of the cost of work-related injuries is paid by the SSDI program rather than by the WC program, even if evidence demonstrating that of cost shifting has recently increased is sparse.

PROPOSAL ONE: IMPROVE THE DESIGN AND IMPLEMENTATION OF THE OFFSET PROVISION

History and Reasons for the Offset Provision

Coordination of SSDI and WC benefits has an interesting history (Larson 2015, §157.03(1): "When disability benefits were first added to the Social Security Act in 1956, a rather crude offset provision was included, generally reducing [disability] benefits by the amount of compensation from other systems. In . . . 1958, the entire offset provision was quietly repealed." The Act was amended in 1965 to require that the total of SSDI and WC benefits and certain other public disability plans (PDB) not exceed 80 percent of the worker's prior earnings. In most states, SSDI benefits are reduced if necessary to achieve the 80 percent limit when the worker is receiving benefits from both programs. However, in 15 states with reverse-offset laws enacted before 1965, WC benefits are reduced to achieve the 80 percent limit.

We believe there are two reasons for an offset provision that limits the total amount of WC and SSDI benefits relative to a worker's income prior to disability. The first reason is to directly limit the total amount of SSDI and WC benefits in order to reduce the total costs of these programs to employers and workers. The second reason for the offset is to decrease the incentives for disabled workers to extend their period of disability after they qualify for SSDI and WC benefits[9]

We believe there also are reasons why the offset should result in a reduction of SSDI benefits rather than WC benefits. First, as discussed in proposal three, WC premiums are experience rated, which is designed to encourage employers to improve workplace safety. If WC benefits are reduced through the offset provision, the safety incentives in WC are reduced with no offsetting increase in safety incentives through higher SSDI benefits, since SSDI taxes are not experience rated. Second, the history of the offset provision suggests that Congress intended the offset to reduce WC benefits not SSDI benefits.[10]

Problems with the Current Offset Provision

Defective Design

The provision in the 1965 amendments to the Social Security Act that allows 15 states to operate reverse-offset laws is not a rational design decision consistent with the original formulation of SSDI benefits. Although the 15 states with reverse-offset rules are 30 percent of the states, they probably account for more than 30 percent of all WC benefits nationally, since the 15 states include California, New York, Florida, Illinois, New Jersey, and Washington, six of the seven states with the greatest amounts of WC benefit payments in 2013 (Sengupta and Baldwin 2015, Table 8).

Defective Implementation

---

9 Three incentives for workers that occur when WC benefits are increased are discussed in proposal one. Similar incentives occur when SSDI benefits are increased.

10 The United States Supreme Court upheld the constitutionality of the offset in *Richardson v. Belcher*, 404 U.S. 78 (1971). Larson (2015, 157.03[2] observed "As to which program should apply the offset, the Court noted the judgment of Congress that the duplication of benefits may lead to the erosion of the workers' compensation systems."

These reasons for the offset provision are only fulfilled, however, if SSDI and WC effectively coordinate their benefits. This requires, for example, that SSA uses accurate information about the amount of WC benefits to calculate SSDI benefits after the application of the offset provision.

The limitations of the verification process for the amount of WC benefits were documented in a report by the Government Accounting Office (2001), which compared WC records from Virginia with SSA beneficiary records. The examination showed that SSA was unaware that about 26 percent of Virginia disability insurance beneficiaries concurrently received WC benefits for at least a month. Among these unrecognized concurrent benefit cases, about 6 percent had received WC benefits for periods of six months to seven years (Government Accounting Office 2001, 3). The Government Accounting Office report also indicated that the SSA review indicated that more than 50 percent of SSDI beneficiaries whose benefits were being offset had been paid inaccurately, often leading to lower SSDI benefits than the beneficiaries were entitled to, because reductions in WC benefits had not been reported. The Government Accounting Office (2001, 4) recommended that SSA take several actions to test the viability of a voluntary reporting process on WC benefits with WC insurers.

A subsequent study by O'Leary et al. (2012, 4) suggests that the Social Security Administration (SSA) has not developed an effective verification process to determine the number of workers receiving both WC and SSDI benefits, and the amounts of WC benefits:

> SSA maintains some information on workers' compensation claims to manage the offset provision. However, the workers' compensation benefits data maintained by SSA are self-reported, and there are no existing automated data matches with states. For reported workers' compensation benefits, SSA individually verifies the type and amount with the workers' compensation providers before adjusting DI payment, but there are no means for SSA to check for unreported workers' compensation claims.

The ongoing deficiencies of the verification process for implementation of the offset provision were verified by a 2015 report by the GAO (now the Government Accountability Office) of the concurrent receipt by federal employees of SSDI and Federal Employees' Compensation Act (FECA) benefits. The GAO study involved workers who received concurrent benefits from both programs in at least one month between July 2011 and June 2014. The GAO found that

SSA successfully detected the concurrent payments to about 52 percent of the workers, but did not detect concurrent payments in about 13 percent of the cases. The GAO could not tell if SSA detected concurrent benefits for about 35 percent of the workers who received both SSDI and FECA benefits. In a small sample of 20 individuals whose concurrent receipt of SSDI and FECA benefits SSA had not recognized, the GAO found that potential overpayments to seven individuals had lasted more than a decade and resulted in potential overpayments of more than $100,000 to each person. GAO indicates that SSA reported making an estimated $371.5 million in SSDI overpayments stemming from FECA benefits from FY 2009 to FY 2013 (about $75 million per year), but that SSA was unable to determine how much of those funds SSA had recovered.

One of the recommendations by the GAO (2015, 25) is that SSA compare the costs of benefits of SSA's current approach to reducing the potential overpayment of SSDI benefits—which relies on SSDI beneficiaries to self-report any FECA benefits they receive—with the costs and benefits of alternative approaches including routinely matching FECA and SSDI program data to detect potential SSDI overpayments.

Description and Advantages of the Proposal to Revise the Design and Implementation of the Offset Provision

We propose that the offset provision used to coordinate SSDI and WC be modified in two ways in order to encourage workplace safety and reduce SSDI financial woes:

(1) The reverse-offset provisions in 15 states should be eliminated. The reverse-offset provision is inequitable (applying to only a few favored states) and shifts some of the costs of workplace injuries to the SSDI program, aggravating the financial difficulties of the Disability Insurance Trust Fund and reducing incentives for employers to improve workplace safety.

(2) All states workers' compensation programs should be required to provide SSA with electronic data for all cases that pay cash benefits. SSA should use that data to identify all cases in which workers are concurrently receiving SSDI and WC benefits and to reduce the SSDI benefits to achieve the 80 percent limit for the combined benefits.

Concerns about the Proposal and Responses to the Concerns

1) Employers, legislators, and WC administrators in the 15 states and their allies will object. A compelling response is that the depleted Disability Insurance Trust Fund is in such dire condition that special treatment of these states needs to be eliminated, even if the provision is 50 years old.

2) Implementation of the proposal to collect more data from the states and to effectively use the data will place additional burdens on SSA and state WC agency staffs. A response is that additional resources used to hire additional personnel will result in reduced payments of SSDI benefits and a more appropriate allocation of the costs of workplace injuries, which should improve workplace safety. We are encouraged that the FY 2016 budget overview prepared by the SSA Acting Commissioner proposes to "improve program integrity by requiring states, local governments and private insurers that administer WC and PDB to provide [WC benefit payments] information to SSA" (Colvin 2015, 22-23).

Implementation of the Proposal: Initial and Ultimate

(1) The initial implementation could involve a multiyear phased-in increase in benefits paid by the WC programs in the 15 states with reverse-offset provisions. However, we recommend immediate elimination of the reverse-offset provision in order to avoid confusions during a transition period and to expedite financial relief for the Disability Insurance Trust Fund.

(2) The initial implementation to collect data from the states could involve a coordinated effort of SSA and National Institute for Occupational Safety and Health (NIOSH), which sponsors a program to collect benefit data from state workers' compensation programs.[11] The ultimate implementation should also coordinate data collection efforts with the Centers for Medicare and Medical Services (CMS) in order to collect data on cash and medical benefits in WC settlements, as discussed in the next section. The ultimate implementation could involve collecting and analyzing data from a larger set of states than those involved in the NIOSH project.

---

[11] The NIOSH Center for Workers' Compensation Studies (NIOSH 2014, 3) has a current project to "Analyze existing state-level workers' compensation data and use results to identify research and intervention priorities" in order to improve workplace health. "A number of states have been collecting a series of occupational health indicators, including certain WC data" and NISOH intends to commit up to $5.4 million in new money to add additional states.

PROPOSAL TWO: REQUIRE WORKERS' COMPENSATION SETTLEMENTS TO COVER FUTURE CASH BENEFITS

The Current Status of Workers' Compensation Settlements

WC Benefits and Compromise and Release Agreements

One common feature of the claims resolution process in WC cases providing PPD or PTD benefits is the closing of cases both administratively and financially by compromise-and-release (C&R) agreements. These agreements are allowed in 43 states (Torrey 2007, Tables 1 and 2, 457-461). A C&R agreement usually involves three elements (National Commission 1972, 109): (1) a compromise on the amount of benefits that falls between the employer's previous offer and the worker's demand, which is likely to be based in part on what the worker would potentially have received from an administrative law judge's award of continuing indemnity payments; (2) payment of the benefits in a single, lump-sum payment rather than on an ongoing basis; and (3) release of the employer from further liability for cash benefits (in all cases) and for medical benefits (in some, but not all, C&R agreements). An injured worker who accepts a C&R agreement waives any subsequent cash benefits for the work-related injury involved in the settlement and, if applicable, to any subsequent medical benefits for the case settled by the C&R.

Views differ over the relative merits of C&R agreements (Savych 2012, 7; Thomason and Burton 1993, S10-S11). Proponents argue that C&R agreements reduce administrative costs in the WC delivery system as well as providing fair resolution of "doubtful" cases that would otherwise result in extensive litigation. Another supporting argument, referred to as the closure effect, asserts that receipt of a settlement may encourage workers to return to work or to start a new career rather than prolonging the duration of disability in the hopes of increasing the amount of WC benefits received. The settlements also eliminate uncertainty for workers, insurers, and state WC agencies about the ultimate benefit payments in a case.

Critics of C&R agreements *inter alia* allege that the injured worker's interests may be subordinated to those of other participants in the WC program. C&R agreements are considered beneficial to: 1) carriers (who pay out less in cash benefits than they otherwise would, and who no longer accrue administrative costs associated with processing a still-open claim); 2) claimants' attorneys (who typically receive a large, up-front payment that is a percentage of the lump-sum award, rather than receiving legal fees in smaller increments over time if the worker is paid benefits on a continuing basis); and 3) state WC agencies (which permanently clear their dockets of the claims closed by C&R agreements).

There have been only a few studies of the consequences for workers who accept C&R agreements. A common finding is that C&Rs typically pay out less than the injured worker would have received had he or she continued to receive ongoing cash benefits. Thomason and Burton (1993, S10-12) reviewed several previous studies, including those involving workers from Michigan, California, and Texas. Their conclusion (1993, S12) was that:

> Past research indicates that injured workers who settle with a compromise and release agreement receive an amount that is less than the benefits they would have received had the case been adjudicated.

Thomason and Burton (1993) examined lump-sum settlements of PPD claims in New York and found evidence that (1) insurer adjustment activities, such as appealing initial awards for workers, increased the probability that cases were settled with lump-sum settlements; (2) a 24-25 percent discount rate was required to equate the lump sum settlements with the present value of the benefits stream paid in adjudicated awards, even though there were no disputes over liability in these New York cases involving lump-sum settlements; (3) use of attorneys increased the probability of lump-sum settlements; (4) use of attorneys reduced the amount of benefits in the lump sum settlements that were voluntarily agreed to by the parties; and (5) use of attorneys had no statistically significant effect on the size of litigated awards.

Potential Cost Shifting from WC to SSDI and Medicare

The widespread use of C&R agreements that terminate further cash and often additional medical benefits has resulted in inadequate cash benefits and possibly insufficient medical benefits in many state WC programs. One likely consequence is that some of the costs of work-related disabilities are shifted to SSDI and Medicare.

The Medicare as a Secondary Payer Act

The concern that state WC programs may be inappropriately shifting portions of the costs of work-related disabilities to SSDI and Medicare cannot be described as nascent. The *Medicare as a Secondary Payer Act* enacted in 1984 established the principle that if medical expenses could be covered under either WC or Medicare, then WC not Medicare should pay for the care. WC's primary responsibility for medical expenses resulting from work-related disability was strengthened by the *Medicare, Medicaid, and SCHIP Extension Act of 2007*. These laws are administered within the Department of Health and Human Services by the CMS.[12] Prior to completing a WC settlement in excess of a specified amount, the parties to the settlement must obtain confirmation from the CMS that sufficient funds have been set aside to cover all outstanding and prospective medical expenses resulting from the workplace injury or disease.

Description and Analysis of the Proposal to Require Workers' Compensation Settlements to Cover Future Cash Benefits

We propose that SSA establish a procedure to ensure that WC C&R agreements include enough resources to cover future cash benefits, which would be similar to the current procedure used by the CMS to ensure that WC settlements include enough resources to cover future medical benefits. The settlement review procedure would consist of several elements:

(1) In a WC case in which the work-related tests have been clearly established, the cash benefit component of a C&R agreement would have to be no less than the present value of PPD and PTD benefits unpaid at the time of the settlement, taking account of the weekly benefits and the duration of PPD or PTD benefits included in the applicable state's WC statute.[13]

(2) The SSA settlement review procedure for WC cash benefits should be combined with the CMS settlement review procedure for WC medical benefits and jointly administered by SSA and CMS. The participation of SSA will ensure that the allocation of the settlement between cash and medical benefits is

---

12 The 120 pages of instructions for approving proposed Workers' Compensation Medicare Set-Aside Arrangements (WCMSA) amounts are contained in the CMS Reference Guide (CMS 2015).

13 The present value of future benefits can be calculated by using an interest rate no greater than the rate on 10-year US Treasury bonds as of the date of the settlement plus 2 percent.

appropriate and that the present value of the cash benefits has been calculated appropriately.

The offset provision for SSDI and WC cash benefits discussed earlier and the *Medicare as a Secondary Payer Act* both tend to increase the proportion of WC settlements that are devoted to medical benefits as opposed to cash benefits.[14] The proposal to require WC settlements to cover future cash benefits should increase the proportion of WC settlements devoted to cash benefits, thereby reducing the shifting of the costs of work-related disability from WC to SSDI. The proposal may also result in an increase in the size of WC settlements, which may also reduce the shifting of the costs from WC to both SSDI and Medicare.

Concerns about the Proposal and Responses to the Concerns

The current policy requiring CMS approval of the amount of future medical benefits provided in WC settlements is controversial and opposed by many practitioners, including employers, insurance carriers, applicants' attorneys, and state administrators.[15] Adding a review of future cash benefits is likely to induce elevated ire among these participants in the WC delivery system. A partial response is that the combination of the current policy on future medical care and

---

14 The incentives to increase the share of a WC settlement devoted to medical benefits instead of cash benefits can be illustrated by a three-step example. In step one, the worker (typically with the assistance of his attorney) and the employer (typically with the assistance of the insurer and a lawyer) negotiate a C&R agreement for $100,000 to cover medical and cash benefits. The parties agree that $80,000 of the settlement is for cash benefits and $20,000 is for medical benefits. In step two, assume the offset provision discussed in proposal one is introduced. The parties may now agree to allocate $60,000 of the settlement to cash benefits and $40,000 to medical benefits. The employer is indifferent to the reallocation since the total amount of the settlement has not changed. The worker prefers the reallocation because the amount of SSDI benefits received by the worker after application of the offset provision will be higher if the WC cash benefits are $60,000 than if the WC cash benefits were $80,000. In step three, assume that the Medicare as a Secondary Payer Act is enacted and the CMS decides that $50,000 needs to be set aside for future medical care, thus reducing the amount of the $100,000 settlement devoted to WC cash benefits to $50,000, which means that the SSDI benefits may have be further increased to bring the total of WC and SSDI benefits up to the 80 percent limit of prior earnings included in the offset provision.

15 A coalition of organizations concerned with the Medicare secondary payer rules have drafted the *Medicare Secondary Payer and Workers' Compensation Settlement Agreements Act of 2015*. The organizations include UWC Strategic Services on Unemployment and Workers' Compensation and the Workers' Injury Law & Advocacy Group.

the proposed policy for future cash benefits is likely to reduce the use of C&R agreements, which is a desirable outcome.

Implementation of the Proposal: Initial and Ultimate

Initial implementation should involve a task force—including representatives of CMS, SSA, NIOSH, the important interest groups in WC, and researchers—to develop a plan to require prior approval of both the cash and medical benefits components of WC settlements. The task force would be asked *inter alia* to prepare a plan for full implementation of the proposal.

PROPOSAL THREE: EXPERIENCE RATE THE SSDI PROGRAM

Financing Social Insurance Programs

The SSDI program is financed by employer and employee contributions. Each contributes 0.9 percent of taxable earnings up to an annual maximum of earnings (currently $118,500). The contribution rates do not vary depending on benefit payments made to former employees of the employer.

Most other U.S. social insurance programs rely on experience rating, in which the employer is the sole or primary source of funding for the program and the employer's contribution rate depends at least in part on benefit payments to current or former employees. Both unemployment insurance (UI) and workers' compensation (WC) rely on experience rating, although there are important differences between the experience rating formulas in those programs.

Experience Rating in the UI Program[16]

The annual taxable wage base in UI is at least $7,000 (as required by federal law since 1983). Most states have adopted a higher wage base, although most states have annual maximums of $20,000 or less, such as New York, where the wage base is $8,500. All states use experience rating to determine the employer's contribution rate.[17] Federal law allows states to experience-rate any employer after one year of experience in the UI program. States use varying formulas

16 The description of experience rating in Unemployment Insurance is largely based on U.S. Department of Labor (2014).

17 Only Alaska, New Jersey, and Pennsylvania require employee contributions for UI.

to determine an employer's prior record of benefit payments.[18] Schedules are then used to convert the results of the state's formula into a tax rate. In most states, a low balance in the state's UI fund triggers a schedule with higher tax rates, and a high balance in the UI fund results in lower rates. In New York, for example, when the UI fund balance is less than 0 percent of payroll, the rates in the schedule range from 0.9 percent to 8.9 percent of payroll, and when the UI fund balance is more than 5 percent of payroll, the rates range from 0.0 percent to 5.9 percent of payroll.[19]

Experience Rating in the WC Program

All state WC programs rely on two levels of experience rating. Industry-level (or for a few classes, occupation-level) experience rating relies on insurance rates for each of the 500 or more insurance classes used in most states. A pure premium rate is calculated for each class based largely on prior benefit payments to workers in that class. In most states, carriers add a loading factor to the pure premium in order to determine an insurance rate per $100 of payroll. These insurance rates vary significantly among classes within each state. For example, the rate for bakeries may be $2 per $100 of payroll while the rate for loggers may be $50 per $100 of payroll. The insurance rate is multiplied by the employer's payroll in that class to determine most of the workers' compensation premium for that employer.[20]

Most employers are only eligible for industry-level experience rating. An employer with a sufficient premium obligation (which varies among states) may also qualify for firm-level experience rating in addition to industry-level experience rating.[21] In Florida, an employer must be experience rated at the firm level if it had at least $10,000 in premiums during the most recent 24 months, or had at least an

---

18 Most states rely on the reserve-ratio formula, which is (contributions minus benefits charged to the employer) /payroll. In most of these states, the contributions and benefits include all past years, and the payroll is the average of the three most recent years. Other states rely on the benefit-ratio formula, which is benefits charged to the employer's covered payroll. In most of these states, the benefits are those charged in the last three years and the payroll is the average of the three most recent years A few states rely on other formulas, such as the Benefit-Wage-Ratio formula.

19 Federal law requires that the maximum tax rate be at least 5.4 percent.

20 Workers' compensation premiums include other charges, such as expense constants Burton (2011, Appendix 22.1).

21 The discussion of firm-level experience rating in WC is largely based on NCCI (2014)

average annual premium of $5,000 in the experience period, which is normally three years. The firm-level experience rating formula places more weight on the frequency of claims than on the severity of claims, on the theory that severity is more likely due to chance. The greater the size of the firm (as measured by premium), the more weight is given to the firm's experience relative to the experience of other firms in the industry. A large bakery with a particularly adverse record of benefit payments may pay $4 per $100 of payroll rather than the classification rate of $2 per $100 of payroll. Conversely, a very safe bakery may pay $0.50 per $100 of payroll.

A very large firm may qualify for a retrospectively-rated insurance policy, in which the premium is based primarily on the firm's own record of benefit payments. In addition, about 25 percent of all workers' compensation benefits are paid by self-insuring employers, which means their WC costs are almost perfectly experience rated.

Comparisons of Experience Rating in UI and WC

This comparison of UI and WC makes clear that the two programs' use of experience rating of employer contributions differs considerably in the following ways: (1) WC relies on industry-level experience rating for most employers, while UI does not. (2) UI requires firm-level experience rating for all employers, regardless of size. Most employers are too small to qualify for firm-level experience rating in WC. (3) UI relies on a relatively unsophisticated experience-rating formula that ignores factors affecting credibility, such as the size of the firm and the occurrence of random events such as catastrophes. The experience-rating formula used in WC considers these factors. (4) UI relies on a combination of constricted definitions of covered payroll with contribution schedules with minimum and maximum rates to produce actual contributions that exceed the expected losses of some employers who pay the minimum rates, and that also result in contributions that are less than the expected losses for some employers who pay the maximum rates. One result is that low-risk employers subsidize high-risk employers in the UI program. There is no such systematic subsidy of high-risk employers in the WC program.

Experience Rating in Workers' Compensation: Theory and Evidence[22]

The two levels of experience rating in WC are designed to promote safety (Burton 2009, 249-250). Industry-level experience rating establishes a premium for each industry that is largely based on prior WC benefit payments by the industry. The resulting differences in labor costs and prices across industries should in theory shift the composition of national consumption towards safer products. We are unaware of any studies that test this theory.

Firm-level experience rating determines the WC premium for each firm above a minimum size by comparing its prior benefits payments to those of other firms in the industry. Firm-level experience rating has been used in WC since the program's origin in the early twentieth century. John R. Commons, a leading economist of that era who helped design the Wisconsin WC program, asserted that experience rating provides economic incentives to employers to get the "safety spirit" that would otherwise be lacking (Burton 2015b, 865). The rudimentary theory is that firms have an incentive to improve safety in order to reduce premiums and remain competitive. Guo and Burton (2010) developed a more comprehensive theory to identify the incentives for experience-rated employers when WC benefits (and as a result premiums) increase:

a) The safety effect – the employer is encouraged to improve workplace safety

b) The underreporting or monitoring effect – the employer is encouraged to resist the reporting and acceptance of claims, which *inter alia* should reduce the prevalence of fraudulent claims

c) The rehabilitation or return-to-work effect – the employer is encouraged to strengthen claims management practices in order to reduce the duration of benefit payments

There are also incentives for workers when workers' compensation benefits are increased:

---

22 We confine our discussion of the effect of experience rating to studies of the WC program. There is also an extensive literature on the effects of experience rating in the UI program. Ehrenberg and Smith (2015, 529) summarize one aspect of this research:

Empirical analysis of the effects of imperfect experience rating on employer behavior suggests that it is substantial. These studies have estimated that unemployment would fall by 10 percent to 33 percent if UI taxes in the United States were perfectly experience rated (so that employers laying off workers would have to pay the full cost of the added UI benefits).

d) The true injury effect – the worker is less concerned about job safety, which results in a greater frequency and severity of injuries

e) The reporting effect – the increase in benefits may induce workers to submit claims they otherwise would not have bothered to submit

f) The duration effect – the increase in benefits may case workers to extend the periods for which they claim benefits

A number of studies of experience rating provide evidence that should help assess the overall effect of experience rating and the relative influence of the six effects of higher benefits (Burton 2015b). Almost without exception, the studies find that experience rating reduces the number of workers' compensation claims. What is unclear, however, is whether the reduction in claims is a result of the safety effect—with fewer actual injuries—or is due to the monitoring effect—with employers denying more claims. The survey of experience-rating studies by Boden (1995) concluded that "research on the safety impacts has not provided a clear answer to whether WC improves workplace safety." In contrast, Thomason (2005) asserted that most (11 of 14) studies he surveyed found that experience rating improves safety and health and concluded: "Taken as a whole, the evidence is quite compelling: experience rating works." A markedly different conclusion was reached by Mansfield, MacEachen, Tompa et al. (2012),[23] who concluded that:

> Although experience rating is intended to stimulate safer workplaces, a growing body of literature reveals that it has not achieved that effect. . . . The absence of a safety effect may arise because employers focus on managing reported claims rather than prevention.

We believe this conclusion overstates the evidence about the failure of experience rating to promote safety. Instead, we agree with the assessment by Butler, Gardner,

---

[23] Mansfield, MacEachen, Tompa et al. (2012) is one of a collection of articles that provide largely negative assessments of experience rating. For example, Tompa, Hogg-Johnson, Amick et al. (2012) conclude that their study of Ontario "suggests that experience rating provides an incentive for secondary prevention, but less so for primary prevention [safety]." The only "good news" for experience rating in this set of articles was provided by Seabury et al.(2012), who found that workers injured at self-insuring employers (who are perfectly experience rated) have significantly improved return-to-work experience for up to five years after the date of injury (the rehabilitation effect).

and Kleinman (2013, 453) based on their review of the literature: "Evidence tends to support the hypotheses that experience rating strengthens firms' economic incentives for safety, but not all research is conclusive." In any case, the issue is not a choice between the safety effect *or* the monitoring effect. As Butler, Gardner, and Kleinman indicated (2013, 454) in reviewing a study by Thomason and Pozzebon (2002), "experience rating causes employers both to improve workplace safety and health and to engage in more aggressive claims management." While we recognize the danger that "aggressive claims management" can morph into employers resisting legitimate claims, we nonetheless conclude that experience rating in WC provides a convincing rationale for the introduction of experience rating into the SSDI program. [24]

Description and Analysis of the Proposal to Experience Rate the SSDI Program

The suggestion to experience-rate SSDI contributions by employers is not new. Burkhauser and Daly (2011, 111) credit Berkowitz and Burton (1970) and Burton and Berkowitz (1971) with "the first systematic set of efficiency arguments for experience rating in the context of WC." Berkowitz and Burton asserted these arguments were applicable to the SSDI program. However, Burkhauser and Daly (2011, 110-111) had enough reservations about evidence on experience rating in WC that they did not recommend immediate implementation of such a major change in SSDI policy. Instead, they recommended that SSA shift its

[24] A study by Guo and Burton (2010) did not explicitly examine the effect of experience rating in workers' compensation but did provide relevant information about the importance of the economic incentives for employers and workers in the workers' compensation program, where experience rating of premiums is an important feature. We relied on yearly observations for each of 46 jurisdictions (including the District of Columbia). A key independent variable was the expected cash benefits prescribed by each state's worker' compensation statute. In some regressions, the dependent variable was the BLS injury rate for the state. We found that the frequency elasticity for cash benefits was not significantly greater than 0 in Period I (1975-1989) or in Period II (1990-1999). This contrasts with some previous studies that found a positive frequency elasticity. One interpretation of these results is that the true injury effect is offset by the safety effect. In other regressions, the dependent variable was incurred cash benefits per 100,000 workers, which are the insurance carriers' estimates of the cash benefits that will actually be paid for injuries that occurred in a particular policy period. We found that the benefit elasticity (the association between expected and actual benefits) was significantly less than 1.0 in both study periods. One interpretation of these results is that the monitoring and rehabilitation effects for employers are stronger than the reporting and duration effects for workers. The results differ from most previous studies' findings of benefit elasticities greater than 1.0.

demonstration funding to test the efficacy of experience rating and other policies that could slow the movement of disabled workers onto the SSDI rolls. Liebman and Smalligan (2013, 3) also recommended several demonstration projects, including one that would provide financial rewards to employers who had fewer employees become eligible for SSDI benefits than predicted based on historical data and information on the current profile of employees. The only empirical study we have seen examining the possible use of experience rating of SSDI is Stapleton, Mann, and Song (2014), which we discuss in the next subsection.

We propose that experience rating for SSDI should consist of seven elements:

(1) SSA would produce industry-level contribution rates calculated as (a) the SSDI benefits paid to workers in the industry during the most recent 10 years with data / (b) covered wages for workers in the industry during the most recent 10 years with data. The industry levels correspond to six-digit North American Industry Classification System codes.

(2) Unless a firm qualifies for firm-level experience rating (as described below), in each industry the employer and employee contributions would each be one-half of the contribution rates calculated in element (1) up to an annual maximum of earnings.[25]

(3) A firm would be subject to mandatory firm-level experience rating if the total of the firm's projected employer and employee contributions under element (2) are at least 50 times the average of the total of projected employer and employee contributions in the firm's industry. (The multiplier of 50 will be adjusted based on experience.)

(4) The mandatory firm-level experience rating would only apply to the employer's contribution.

(5) A firm that qualifies for experience rating under element (3) would have increasing credibility given to its own experience as the size of the firm's total contributions increase. A firm with contributions sufficiently large compared to the average contributions of other employers in the industry would have its contribution rate based entirely on the firm's own experience.

25 Arguably only the employer and not the employee should be required to pay a higher premium in a hazardous industry. This option should be considered during the initial implementation phase of our proposal.

(6) A firm that qualifies for experience rating would have its contribution rate for a given year calculated as the SSDI benefits paid to current or former employees of the firm in the most recent 10 years of data / the covered wages for the firm during the most recent 10 years with data, subject to the credibility rules in element (5).

(7) New hires receiving workers' compensation cash benefits or veteran's benefits within the five years prior to the dates on which they were hired would see their SSDI benefits and wages excluded from the SSDI experience rating formula. The employer would be charged the industry-wide contribution rates for those workers.

The proposal to experience rate SSDI contributions at the industry level for both employees and employers would provide economic incentives to shift production to safety industries. The proposal to experience rate SSDI employer contributions at the firm level provides economic incentives to firms to improve the health and safety of their workers, to provide disabled workers effective medical care and rehabilitation services, and to return the workers to employment. Many employers already have established networks of medical care and rehabilitation providers and return-to-work programs that focus on employees with work-related injuries, and the introduction of experience rating into the SSDI programs will encourage these employers to extend these services to workers disabled by other causes.

Concerns about the Proposal and Responses to Concerns

(1) Concern has been expressed about whether firm-level experience rating for the SSDI program is viable for smaller firms. Stapleton, Mann, and Song (2014) found extremely high variation in relative SSDI claims experience (the proportion of benefits attributed to the employer divided by the taxable wages by the employer) for firms with fewer than 50 employees. However, over half of successful SSDI applicants were from firms that on average were much larger than other firms and that employed nearly three-quarters of all workers. Our experience rating proposal for SSDI is unlike UI—where experience rating is applied to virtually all employers, regardless of size —but instead is like WC, where firm-level experience rating is *not* used for small firms. In essence, our proposal for experience rating of SSDI benefits will rely on the WC approach to credibility and therefore will not experience rate small employers.

(2) Concern has been expressed about lack of a work-related test in the SSDI program, which means that "if a worker is diagnosed with MS, or cancer, unrelated

entirely to the job, the employer [under the proposal] will still be penalized." This objection was anticipated by Berkowitz and Burton (1970, note 20).[26] To restate the response in a somewhat expanded version, our proposal to experience rate employers for SSDI benefits provided to their workers with disabilities applies to three types of the disabilities:

(i) Type one disabilities, which are the results of work-related injuries or diseases for which the employer (a) can help prevent the injuries and diseases and/or (b) can reduce the consequences of the injuries through rehabilitation and return-to-work (RTW) programs

(ii) Type two disabilities, which are the result of injuries or diseases that are not work-related but for which the employer (a) can help prevent the injuries or diseases through wellness programs and employer-supported health care and/or (b) can reduce the consequences of the injuries through rehabilitation and RTW programs

(iii) Type three disabilities, for which the employer (a) cannot help prevent the injuries or diseases and (b) cannot reduce the consequences of the injuries through rehabilitation and RTW programs.

If it is assumed that type three disabilities are distributed randomly among workers, then our proposal in essence reduces to a flat-rate tax on all firms for those SSDI benefits for which a particular employer is not responsible (type three disabilities) plus an experience-rated tax for each firm to finance SSDI benefits for which the employer is at least partially responsible (types one and two disabilities).

---

[26] Berkowitz and Burton (1970, Note 20) opined: "It is possible that the work-related test could be eliminated completely without ignoring any of the objectives of the workmen's disability income system. An employer could be charged for the benefits paid to his disabled workers, whether or not the disabling injuries were work related. This would eliminate any disputes about the cause of the disability. However, if it could be assumed that nonwork-related injuries are distributed randomly among the working population, the system in effect reduces to a flat-rate tax on all businesses to finance benefits for off-the-job injuries and an experience-rated tax on each business to finance work-related injuries. Obviously, questions such as the credibility to be given to each firm's experience would have to be resolved, but this plan would appear to fulfill the accident prevention and cost allocation objectives of the workmen's disability income system."

There are two major advantages of this proposal. First, employers would have financial incentives to reduce the incidence and consequences of type two disabilities, which are incentives that do not exist in the current WC and SSDI programs. And the significant costs of distinguishing between work-related and nonwork-related injuries and diseases would be eliminated.

(3) Concern has also been expressed about whether firm-level experience rating results in increased discrimination against individuals at higher risk of disability, such as job applicants with prior injuries. There are several responses to this concern.

First, the Americans with Disabilities Act "prohibits pre-employment medical examinations and, indeed, all pre-employment inquiries about disabilities. §102(d). Medical examinations are permissible after a conditional offer of employment is made, but only if certain conditions are met. §102(d)(3)" (Willborn et al. 2012). This provision could be strengthened by increasing the contribution rate for SSDI for employers who violate §102(d).

Second, element (7) of our proposal for experience rating of SSDI could be modified to provide even stronger financial incentives for employers to hire workers with prior disabilities that resulted in WC or veterans disability benefits. For example, the wages but not the SSDI benefits of these workers subsequent to their being hired for the new jobs could be used in the experience-rating formula.[27]

Third, WC programs in most states have second-injury funds, which are designed to eliminate discrimination against previously impaired workers by limiting the charges to employers for benefits provided to a worker with a previous injury who experiences a new injury (Larson and Burton 1985). The second-injury funds pay for some or all of the benefits that would not have been incurred but for the preexisting impairments. This WC approach could be adapted for SSDI by excluding from the experience-rating procedure any SSDI benefit payments made to a worker after he or she was hired when the health examination administered by the employer after a conditional job offer revealed a preexisting medical condition that was serious enough to jeopardize the worker's ability to perform

[27] Element (7) could be expanded to include workers who previously received SSDI benefits. For example if a worker who received SSDI benefits based on employment with employer A is subsequently hired by employer B, the wages paid to the worker by employer B, but not any additional SSDI benefits paid to the worker by employer B, would be used in the experience-rating formula to determine the contribution rate for employer B.

the job.[28] One advantage of this approach compared to the approach described in the previous subsection is that it would not be confined to workers who received workers' compensation or veterans' disability benefits.

Implementation of the Proposal: Initial and Ultimate

Initial implementation should require SSA to conduct demonstration projects applicable to (a) firms with large numbers of employees, (b) firms in industries with relatively stable workforces over time as opposed to industries in which workers typically have multiple employers (such as construction), and (c) firms that volunteer to be experience rated (although adverse selection needs to be considered). The initial implementation could bypass the first two elements of the proposal, which involve industry-level experience rating, and proceed directly to the firm-level experience rating in element (3). The ultimate implementation should contain all seven of the elements in our proposal and extend experience rating to all firms that meet the credibility requirement in element (3).

The Dual Advantages of the Experience-Rating Proposal

One effect of experience rating SSDI contributions is that employers would have several financial incentives to directly reduce expenditures on SSDI benefits, namely a) the safety and health effect, b) the underreporting or monitoring effect, and c) the rehabilitation or return-to work effect. These are similar to the effects of experience rating in WC.

An important additional effect of experience rating the SSDI program is that the current incentives for employers to shift costs from WC to SSDI would be reduced. Under the current financing arrangements, an employer benefits financially if benefits are paid by SSDI instead of WC because only WC benefits increase the employer's contributions to these programs. However, if the employer was experience rated for benefits in both the SSDI and WC programs, there would be less incentive for the employer to shift the source of the disability benefit payments to SSDI. In turn, this should reduce efforts by employers to reduce the adequacy and coverage of state WC programs, thus reducing the amount of cost shifting from WC to SSDI discussed earlier.

---

[28] Second Injury Fund requirements for the worker's prior injury necessary for coverage are discussed by Larson and Burton (1985, 124).

PROPOSAL FOUR: FEDERAL STANDARDS FOR STATE WORKERS' COMPENSATION PROGRAMS

The Source of Inadequate WC Benefits: Interstate Competition

The National Commission on State Workmen's Compensation Laws (National Commission) was created by the Occupational Safety and Health Act of 1970 and directed to determine if state WC laws "provide an adequate, prompt, and equitable system of compensation for injury or death arising out of or in the course of employment." The commission, most of whose members were appointed by the Nixon administration, issued a unanimous report (1972, 25) concluding that "State workmen's compensation laws are in general neither adequate nor equitable." Of greater relevance to an understanding of current WC programs is the commission's analysis of a major source of the deficiencies of state programs (1972, 124-25):

> **Competition among States.** The economic system of the United States encourages the forces of efficiency and mobility. These forces tend to drive employers to locate where the environment offers the best prospects for profit. At the same time, many of the programs which governments use to regulate industrialization are designed and applied by states rather the federal government. Any state which seeks to regulate the byproducts of industrialization, such as work accidents, invariably must tax or charge employers to cover the expenses of such regulations. This combination of mobility and regulation poses a dilemma for policymakers in state governments. Each state is forced to consider carefully how it regulate its domestic enterprises because relative restrictive or costly regulation may precipitate the departure of the employers to be regulated or deter the entry of new enterprises.
>
> Can a state have a modern workers' compensation program without driving employers away? Our analysis of the cost of workmen's compensation has convinced us that no state should hesitate to adopt a modern workmen's compensation program. . . .
>
> While the facts dictate that no state should hesitate to improve its workmen's compensation program for fear of losing employers, unfortunately this appears to be an area where emotions too often triumphs over facts. . . . whenever a state legislature contemplates

> an improvement in workers' compensation which will increase insurance costs, the legislators likely will hear claims from some employers that the increase in costs will force a business exodus. It will be virtually impossible for the legislators to know how genuine are these claims. To add to the confusion, certain states have abetted the illusion of the runaway employer by advertising the low costs of workmen's compensation in their jurisdictions.
>
> When the sum of these inhibiting factors is considered, it seems likely that many states have been dissuaded from reform of their workmen's compensation programs because of the specter of the vanishing employer, even if that apparition is a product of fancy not fact. A few states have achieved genuine reform, but most suffer with inadequate laws because of the drag of laws of competing states.

The Solution to Inadequate WC Benefits: Federal Standards

The National Commission made 84 recommendations for improving state WC programs. Of particular relevance to developing a strategy to deal with the deleterious effect of competition among states were the designation of 19 of these recommendations as essential and a recommendation (National Commission 1972, 127) that "compliance of the states should be evaluated on July 1, 1975, and, if necessary, Congress with no further delay in the effective date should guarantee compliance." There were no dissents from this recommendation for federal standards among members of the commission.

Federal standards for WC have not been enacted. The threat of federal intervention probably explains the surge in improvements in WC statutes in the 1970s shown in Figure 2. With the change in the national political environment since 1980, the threat of federal standards diminished in the 1980s and disappeared in subsequent decades. Federal standards for state programs arguably would improve the level of cash benefits and broaden the compensability rules so that less of the costs of work-related injuries and disease would be shifted from WC to SSDI. A starting point for federal standards could be the 19 essential recommendations of the 1972 National Commission.

Concerns about the Proposal and Responses to the Concerns

Burton (2015a) identified several problems with the proposal to enact federal standards for state WC programs in the twenty-first century, which make this an unrealistic approach to help solve the current financial difficulties of SSDI. One of the problems is that the 19 essential recommendations of the 1972 National Commission largely deal with aspects of the program that are relatively easy to quantify, such as the maximum weekly benefit for permanent total disability benefits, which could readily be turned into federal standards. However, the post-1990 developments in WC laws that arguably have resulted in cost shifting to SSDI largely involve changes in compensability rules that are harder to quantify, such as requirements that the major contributing cause (MCC) of a worker's disability must be work related. Writing a federal standard to nullify the MCC provision would be challenging. Another and even more serious obstacle to enactment of federal standards is that he current political environment makes federal standards for state WC laws impossible. As a result of these problems, further discussion of federal standards as a partial solution to the cost shifting from WC to SSDI is unwarranted, despite the considerable virtue of this approach.[29]

CONCLUSIONS

Recapitulation

WC pays for a substantial portion of the costs of work-related disability. However, SSDI also pays for a substantial portion of the costs as a result of cost shifting from WC, which adds to the financial difficulties of the Disability Trust Fund. Some of the cost shifting is a byproduct of the offset provision used to coordinate WC and SSDI benefits. Some of the cost shifting is a result of inadequate WC cash benefits, a problem that appears to have become more serious in recent decades.

Two of our proposals would modify current programs that coordinate WC with federal programs for disabled workers. Proposal One would eliminate the reverse-offset provision for WC and SSDI and strengthen the verification procedure for

---

[29] Commenting on an earlier draft of this paper, Marjorie Baldwin asked: "Would it be feasible to experience rate SSDI by state?" SSA should explore this intriguing possibility as it implements Proposal Three. This variant of experience rating could be an important incentive for states to stop reducing WC coverage and benefits in order to attract employers.

the collection of WC data needed to implement the offset provision. Proposal Two would require that WC settlements not only include sufficient resources for future medical benefits (a current requirement) but also require that WC settlements include sufficient resources for future cash benefits.

Our other two proposals involve more significant changes. Proposal Three requires the SSDI program to be experience rated, which should directly reduce expenditures on SSDI benefits and should indirectly reduce cost shifting from WC to SSDI. Proposal Four would establish federal standards for state WC programs, which would increase the adequacy of WC benefits and thus reduce the amount of work-related disability costs shifted to SSDI. However, we do not recommend implementation of Proposal Four because the approach is currently infeasible.

Initial Implementation

The initial implementation of our proposals would include several components:

- Conducting a national survey with the same questions contained in the 1992 Health and Retirement Survey (HRS) to provide evidence about whether shifting of the costs of work-related injuries and diseases from WC to SSDI has increased over time.
- Eliminating the reverse-offset provisions that currently allow 15 states to reduce WC benefits in order to limit the combined total of SSDI and WC benefits.
- Establishing a coordinated effort of the Social Security Administration (SSA), the National Institute for Occupational Safety and Health (NIOSH), and the Centers for Medicaid and Medicare Services (CMS) to collect data on WC settlements in order to increase the effectiveness of the current offset provision for WC and SSDI benefits.
- Establishing a task force with representatives from SSA, CMS, and other constituencies to develop a unitary plan to require prior approval of both the cash and medical benefits components of WC settlements.
- Establishing mandatory experience rating of employer contributions to SSDI. The implementation could begin with pilot projects.

Acknowledgements

We appreciate the comments on earlier drafts of the study and other assistance from several persons, and we hereby absolve them of any remaining errors:

Marjorie Baldwin, Yonatan Ben-Shalom, Leslie Boden, Richard Burkhauser, Richard Butler, Peter Calderone, Philip de Jong, Jeff Eddinger, Corbin Evans, Marc Goldwein, Nortin Hadler, Douglas Holmes, Andrew Houtenville, Frederick Kilbourne, Greg Krohm, Mike Manley, Dan Meyer, Virginia Reno, Ishita Sengupta, Robert Smith, Emily Spieler, Jennifer Tiedeman, Wayne Vroman, David Wittenburg, and Steve Wurzelbacher.

Discussion of Interaction with Other Programs Proposals

David Wittenburg

This discussion is a summary of the comments made by the discussant at the SSDI Solutions Conference on August 4, 2015 before chapters were made final.

This review summarizes three policy proposals intended to improve the interactions between Social Security Disability Insurance (SSDI) and other programs that serve people with disabilities. A common theme among the three proposals is that each describes a reform that, if properly calibrated, could improve employment outcomes, align incentives for service delivery, and reduce burden on the SSDI trust fund.

Burton and Guo

Workers who experience an injury on the job may qualify for both Workers' Compensation (WC) and SSDI. Burton and Guo motivate their proposal by identifying programmatic disincentives that shift costs from WC to SSDI. As one example, they cite state differences in the calculation of the benefit offset for dual entitlement cases. In most states, SSDI amounts are "offset" in most cases of dual entitlement between WC and SSDI, but 15 states have a "reverse offset" that reduces WC instead of SSDI.[1] Burton and Guo also note that the Social Security Administration (SSA) lacks procedures to ensure WC settlements include enough resources to cover future cash benefits.

Burton and Guo highlight three potential changes to address program fragmentations between WC and SSDI. The first is to simplify the offset

1 The combined value of SSDI and WC are adjusted so that the total value does not exceed 80 percent of the worker's prior wages.

provisions, including elimination of the existing "reverse offset." Second, they propose adjusting the calculation of WC liabilities to cover future benefits to SSDI beneficiaries following the Medicare Secondary Payer Act, which requires WC to cover medical costs in cases where a person is dually eligible for WC and Medicare. Finally, they propose a fundamental change to experience rating for the SSDI trust fund, modeled on WC experience rating.

A fundamental challenge in assessing the benefits and costs of these proposals is that it is difficult to define the overlap between WC and SSDI. For simplicity, consider two cases where the timing and severity of the workplace injury differs. In the first case, a WC claimant with a minor injury who, due to an unrelated impairment, transitions to SSDI several years later indicates no or very limited WC-SSDI program interaction. In a second example, a worker who experiences a severe work injury (e.g., paralysis) and enters SSDI immediately indicates a case where WC costs are being shifted to SSDI. While difficult to quantify the exact overlap, there appear to be opportunities to better align incentives between the WC and SSDI programs, particularly given state differences in the calculation of the offset. Three questions for future consideration include:

1. How should policymakers define and identify the overlap between WC and SSDI?
2. Would combining proposal components (e.g., offset and Medicare Secondary Payer) generate efficiencies, or do the alternative proposals function better independently?
3. How would experience rating be implemented, especially for small firms?

Babbel and Meyer

Babbel and Meyer motivate their proposal by highlighting the limited options for short-term income and work supports for people with disabilities. They argue that group disability insurance is a strong avenue for early intervention that may facilitate return to work. They note that approximately one-third of employers currently have this type of coverage, indicating an opportunity to expand to a much larger share of employers.

Babbel and Meyer propose to expand group disability through an automatic enrollment plan for employers with an "opt-out" arrangement. The opt-out provision would ensure the program is voluntary, while automatic enrollment would substantially expand knowledge and use of group disability plans relative to their current levels. They also suggest a public information campaign to further increase awareness of group disability programs and encourage enrollment.

Three general issues that could affect potential benefits and costs should be considered in expanding group disability plans, especially such an expansion's impact on the SSDI trust fund. First, the proposal does not address existing incentives for insurers to refer people to apply for SSDI when their injuries qualify for both group disability and SSDI. Without such a change, it is not clear that this type of expansion would necessarily lead to a decrease in reliance on SSDI as envisioned if insurers still have strong incentives to facilitate SSDI applications. Second, the demand for group disability plans might be limited for low-wage workers, particularly given their replacement rates in SSDI might be comparable (or higher). Finally, employers who offer these plans might be less likely to hire people with disabilities if these plans induce additional costs for employing people with disabilities. Three questions for future consideration:

1. Can insurer incentives be sharpened in ways to reduce burden on the SSDI trust fund?
2. Would group disability alter firm incentives to hire people with disabilities?
3. Who should pay for the information campaign: government or private industry?

Perriello

Perriello identifies potential gaps in the availability of health and long-term services and supports, such as behavioral health treatments and personal assistant services. He argues these gaps may negatively affect employment among people with disabilities. While some states offer Medicaid Buy-In programs to expand access to these services, nearly all of these programs exclude participation of workers with income above a certain threshold (albeit above the traditional Medicaid threshold), and some states do not have these programs. People with disabilities may also be able to deduct their out-of-pocket impairment-related work expenditures, including those for long-term services and supports, from their federal taxable income, but the usefulness of this provision is limited because it excludes some necessary expenses and because it is a tax deduction rather than a tax credit. The extent to which lack of access to long-term services and supports might impact employment and SSDI participation is unknown, and, as Perriello argues in the paper, difficult to estimate.

Perriello proposes three options to increase access to long-term services and supports among people with disabilities. First, he proposes a national Medicaid Buy-In program that would expand access to these services and supports in all states, with consistent eligibility requirements and coverage options. Second, he proposes the creation of a new program providing long-term support and services coverage to working people with disabilities that would wrap around private health care insurance, which typically does not include such coverage. The combination of the first two options would increase access to these supports for working beneficiaries with a range of incomes above the traditional Medicaid eligibility threshold. Finally, he proposes a new tax credit that would allow individuals to out-of-pocket expenses for additional impairment-related work expenses including long-term services and supports, through a credit on their federal tax returns.

A general issue for the reforms outlined in Perriello is weighing the financial cost of these expansions, which could potentially be large for some states and the federal government, with their benefits. The costs are especially important if they represent new costs to state budgets, which could lead to strong political pushback. To illustrate the potential costs, the Massachusetts Medicaid Buy-In program spent $20.8 million providing personal assistant services (PAS) to workers with disabilities in 2012.[2] It is difficult to assess whether these costs are high relative to their potential benefits for work and SSDI, which are both difficult to estimate. The tax credit Perriello proposes would be relatively cheaper than the aforementioned Medicaid Buy-In expansions. Implementation of a tax credit would also be less of an administrative challenge because it could build on similar provisions already in the tax code. Three policy questions for further consideration include:

1. Is a national Medicaid Buy-In program politically viable?
2. What form should the tax credit take (refundable or nonrefundable)?
3. Is it possible to test the credit as a pilot within state tax systems to assess interest and costs before rolling it out nationally?

[2] See Gettens, John, Denise Hoffman, Alexis Henry. 2015. "Expenditures and Use of Wraparound Health Insurance for Employed People with Disabilities," Mathematica Policy Research, Washington DC.

Summary

Each of the papers outlines an important program interaction or gap in the system serving people with disabilities that is part of a larger issue associated with program fragmentation in the supports offered to this population. A recurring theme in all of the papers is that many existing programs have unintended incentives that divert people toward SSDI as opposed to other options, such as shorter-term supports and employment. A challenge in implementing any of the proposals is the lack of an evidence base on how these reforms might operate, and uncertainty around who would bear the costs of their implementation. A lack of evidence indicates full-scale implementation of any reform could have potentially unknown adverse outcomes. Nonetheless, the gaps identified in the papers suggest a more proactive approach by policymakers to address the general issue of program fragmentation.

Section V

Structural Reforms

12

Transitional Benefits for a Subset of the Social Security Disability Insurance Population

Kim Hildred, Pamela Mazerski, Harold J. Krent, and Jennifer Christian

INTRODUCTION

The Social Security Disability Insurance (SSDI) program presents the Social Security Administration (SSA) with what in essence is a binary choice—either claimants are disabled or not. There is no middle ground. For individuals who receive a favorable determination, benefits continue indefinitely until one of the following events occurs: conversion to retirement benefits, death, medical recovery, or return to work. Only about one-half of 1 percent of beneficiaries leave the rolls annually because of a return to work (SSA 2014b, 128).

This paper addresses the small subset of new beneficiaries who are likely to experience medical recovery. These individuals need cash benefits and other support services as they recover sufficiently to transition back to work.

At the time of the benefit award, nothing turns on whether medical recovery is likely. Although beneficiaries are evaluated and categorized as to the likelihood of medical improvement when benefits are awarded, those with favorable prognoses are not required to actively pursue special rehabilitative or medical services to facilitate their return to work.

Later, through the statutorily required Continuing Disability Review (CDR) process, SSA may determine that beneficiaries have improved medically to the point at which they can resume gainful employment. In fact, each year 6 percent (SSA 2014a) of beneficiaries who undergo a full medical review pursuant to the CDR process are ultimately determined to have medically improved sufficiently that benefits are ceased. Yet when benefits end, these beneficiaries are not provided with medical supports or employment services that would facilitate their return to work. Further, because SSA has been unable to conduct the number of CDRs required each year, the length of time those who have medically improved have been detached from the labor market has increased, making finding work even more difficult.

In contrast, when Congress first considered adding a disability insurance component to the Social Security program, many contemplated a system of transitional benefits (Berkowitz 1987, 61-64) coupled with vocational services designed to get people back on their feet and into the workforce. Arthur Altmeyer, the first head of SSA, strongly advocated combining vocational and rehabilitation services with benefits whenever there was a hope that a claimant could reenter the workforce (Kearney 2005/2006, 5).[1] The 1948 Advisory Council on Social Security similarly recommended that rehabilitation services should be provided to facilitate beneficiaries' return to work[2] (Challenges Facing Social Security 2000). Health, Education, and Welfare (HEW) Secretary Oveta Culp Hobby recommended during the first part of the Eisenhower administration that the trust funds be used to provide *only* rehabilitation services and not cash benefits to those who became disabled (Challenges Facing Social Security 2000): "no accountant can estimate the physical rewards, the sense of independence, pride and usefulness and the relief from family strains which accrue to one of the disabled when he returns to his old job or to a newly learned job suited to his limitations." Assistant Secretary of HEW Roswell Perkins stated on behalf of the administration (Berkowitz 1987) shortly thereafter that "the first line of attack on disability should be rehabilitation, in order that people be restored to useful and productive lives" (Kearney 2005/2006, 1). The goal was to help individuals through a rough patch until they could work again.

Nonetheless, political winds shifted, and a majority in Congress coalesced on a program of permanent disability. The 1956 law that ensued confined disability

1 "Thus, the social insurance disability program he proposed had a threefold purpose: medical care to prevent and cure chronic disease, rehabilitation for workers with chronic impairment, and cash benefits for the chronic invalid" (Kearney 2005/2006).

2 Statement of Edward D. Berkowitz, Ph.D., Professor and Chair, Department of History, George Washington University.

payments to workers who were 50 years or older[3] and presumed permanently disabled, severing the earlier connection between disability payment and rehabilitation services[4] (Berkowitz 1987, 76-78).

Consistent with the SSDI Solutions Initiative to identify practical solutions to improve the SSDI program, this paper encourages lawmakers to revisit the link between rehabilitation services and disability and consider creating transitional benefits for the small subset of beneficiaries whose disability is not in question, but who have conditions expected to improve. SSA would administer a compassionate system of transitional benefits with employment supports with the goal of employment, financial independence, and better quality of life. As Chairman Sam Johnson (R-TX) stated in a February 25 Committee on Ways and Means Subcommittee on Social Security hearing, Congress should "mak[e] the disability insurance system work better, and promot[e] opportunity for those trying to return to work."[5]

THE PROBLEM

The SSDI program is an essential financial safety net for those unable to perform substantial work due to disability, as well as for their families. As often highlighted by Representative Xavier Becerra, Ranking Member of the Committee on Ways and Means Subcommittee on Social Security (Opening Statement 2015) "[t]he eligibility rules are very strict, and only four out of every 10 applicants are found to have impairments which are severe enough to qualify for SSDI. Many disabled Americans do not live long enough to collect retirement benefits—death rates among disabled Social Security recipients are three to six times higher [than] among others their age."

Through its own process of setting so-called diary dates (due dates for planned CDRs), SSA identifies those whose conditions are expected to last more than 12 months but who are expected to medically improve with treatment. Medical Improvement Expected (MIE) diary dates for these cases occur within three

---

3 The Social Security Amendments of 1960, Pub. L. No. 86-778, 74 Stat. 924 (1960), extended disability benefits to workers under age 50.

4 Berkowitz critiques the decision to abandon a focus on rehabilitation services.

5 "Chairman Johnson Lays Out Principles for Disability Insurance Reform." 2015. U.S. House of Representatives Committee on Ways and Means. February 25. Accessed July 9, 2015. http://waysandmeans.house.gov/chairman-johnson-lays-out-principles-for-disability-insurance-reform/.

years or less. Examples include people who were in a catastrophic accidents, had major thoracic, abdominal, or reconstructive musculoskeletal surgeries, or have affective mood disorders—those with impairments arising out of conditions that respond well to medical and/or rehabilitative treatment (GAO 2006). According to data provided by the Office of the Chief Actuary, 2.7 percent of all disabled workers receiving benefits in 2011 had MIE diaries. These individuals need cash benefits and other support services as they recover sufficiently to transition back to work, yet they are not required to pursue the medical or rehabilitation support services they may need upon benefit award.

Further, these individuals face huge employment challenges given the length of time they have already waited for an SSDI award in addition to the length of time before a CDR occurs. And when the CDR occurs and they receive a notice that their benefits will cease because of medical improvement, they are not offered services to help them reenter the labor market with the ability to earn sustainable and substantial earnings.

The Inspector General has reported that 1.3 million CDRs were pending at the end of FY 2013 (SSA OIG 2014c, 3) and the agency conducted more CDRs 10 years ago than it does today (SSAB 2012, 11). According to a recent report (SSAB 2014, 6) to the bipartisan Social Security Advisory Board, "This backlog prevents SSA from taking timely action to discontinue payments to beneficiaries who are no longer eligible, thus causing misuse of program resources. It also harms beneficiaries by delaying return to work efforts, which become more difficult with time. Failure to perform CDRs may also create a misimpression that eligibility is permanent, regardless of disability status."

The problems with CDR determinations run deeper. In conducting CDRs, the touchstone is medical improvement. If the decision supporting the initial disability finding is vague,[6] (SSA OIG 2014a, 4-5) SSA may not be able to determine improvement even if the beneficiary is no longer disabled. SSA and congressional committees have critiqued administrative law judges (ALJ) in particular for writing conclusory decisions granting benefits (Social Security Disability Programs 2012). Worse, when CDRs result in beneficiaries leaving the benefit rolls, these individuals return to the SSDI rolls in substantial numbers. In a study on CDRs, SSA estimated that about 20 percent of former SSDI-only

6 A recent study by SSA's Office of the Inspector General examined 275 sample grant decisions, concluding that 216 of the 275 had "quality" issues and, of those, SSA's Division of Quality (Office of Appellate Operations) remanded half back to ALJs for correction.

workers and about 21 percent of former concurrent workers will return to SSDI within eight years of the cessation decision (Hemmetter and Stegman 2013). While it is conceivable that some returns were due to deteriorating health, it is also conceivable that a portion of those who returned to the program were not prepared to reenter the labor market and could have benefited from services and employment supports.

Moreover, experts increasingly have highlighted other assistance that may benefit those who are expected to medically improve. Jeffrey Liebman and Jack Smalligan in their 2013 paper included the following as one of reason the SSDI program is in need of reform: "First, there is a sizable minority of the beneficiary population who would be better off with a form of assistance that is different from the one they are receiving today. These individuals need assistance that helps them back on their feet and returns them to employment, instead of receiving the current benefit package. . . ."

For those beneficiaries who are able, the value of work cannot be overstated. In his October 1, 2007, letter to the president transmitting the National Council on Disability report entitled, *Empowerment for Americans with Disabilities: Breaking Barriers to Careers and Full Employment,* Chairperson John R. Vaughn summarized the benefits of work for those with disabilities: "There is a direct benefit to expanding employment opportunities for people with disabilities. For employers who are projected to face labor shortages as the baby-boom generation retires, non-employed people with disabilities represent a valuable tool of human resources to help fill those needs. For people with disabilities, employment has not just economic value, but important social and psychological value as well. For government, increased employment of people with disabilities helps increase tax receipts and decrease social expenditures. Finally, as recognized in the passage of the Americans with Disabilities Act, there are societal benefits from greater inclusiveness in mainstream society as the barriers facing people with disabilities are dismantled."

Additionally, in his June 2013 Committee on Ways and Means Subcommittee on Social Security hearing questions for the record response regarding lessons learned from welfare reform, Mark Duggan said, "While the beneficiaries of the two programs differ in many ways and thus the effect of a specific reform may not be the same for the two groups, the results from AFDC/TANF show that simultaneously improving the financial incentive to work while reducing the incentive to remain enrolled can produce substantial changes in behavior that increase employment and improve economic well-being while reducing government expenditures and increasing tax revenues. Reforms to SSDI that incorporate these features and are tailored to the characteristics of program beneficiaries could improve the economic well-being of many individuals with disabilities while reducing program expenditures." Later, in response to a question regarding time-limited benefits, Mr. Duggan added, "One potentially important benefit of such a change is that SSDI awardees who 'just qualified' would have an incentive to further their skills and remain connected to the labor market while on SSDI so that they could make the transition back to work if possible given the evolving nature of their health."

Also, in aiming to prevent people from becoming permanently trapped on disability benefits, an increasing number of Organisation for Economic Co-operation and Development (OECD) countries are restricting new applicants to time-limited or temporary payments (OECD 2010, 113).

DETAILED PROPOSAL

Our proposal for transitional benefits would change the dynamic of disability in four respects:

- First, and most importantly, awarding transitional benefits would ensure that claimants have access to supports and services that will aid them in the medical recovery and work reentry process. That would make it more likely that beneficiaries would successfully recover and make the transition back to work as soon as practicable.
- Second, the fixed length of the benefits award for certain new applicants would send a clear message that they need temporary financial support to aid them during the transitional period while they are coping with their medical problems and recuperating. But, it would also signal the expectation that they will be returning to work.
- Third, beneficiaries receiving transitional benefits would not be subject to any limitation on earned income during the transitional benefit period.
- Finally, should beneficiaries believe they are unable to work at the end of their transitional benefit period, they would have to file a new application and demonstrate that they meet SSA's definition of disability. Under current policy, the agency must schedule the CDRs, collect medical information, and then determine whether to terminate benefits based on the medical improvement review standard.

Proposal

1. Disability Determination Services (DDS) examiners and ALJs would first determine, as they do now, whether a claimant meets the statutory definition of disability.
2. To ensure accuracy and consistency, decision makers would use a newly developed predictive analytics model to determine whether the medical condition is expected to improve.
3. If so, transitional benefits would be awarded for a two- or three-year period. The default length would be specified by the predictive model. The decision maker would have the discretion to expand the transitional period predicted under the model up to the maximum three-year transitional term.
4. As soon as practicable, names and contact information of individuals receiving transitional benefits would be sent to their local community work incentives coordinators under the Work Incentive Planning and Assistance (WIPA) program, modified to prioritize services for transitional beneficiaries, including direct referral to a Ticket to Work service provider.
5. Under a modified Ticket to Work program for transitional beneficiaries, employment network or vocational rehabilitation agency service providers would provide customized services to increase medical and/or functional recovery,[7] if necessary, in order to achieve employment.
6. There would be no cap on earned income during the transitional benefit period to encourage beneficiaries to experiment with gradual or intermittent return to productive paid work activity.

---

[7] Employment networks and state vocational rehabilitation (VR) agencies provide a wide array of services, some of which include services, supports and accommodations that assist in increasing medical and/or functional improvement. According to Section 103(a) of the Rehabilitation Act of 1973, Pub. L. No. 93-112, 87 Stat. 355 (1973), and as amended, VR services are provided for purposes of eligible individuals achieving an employment outcome. Some examples of VR services include; vocational counseling, guidance and referral services; physical and mental restoration services; vocational and other training, including on-the-job training; personal assistance services and job placement services.

Implementation

1. *Predictive Analytical Model*

SSA has experience using predictive modeling in the CDR process. Currently, SSA's predictive model determines which cases with matured medical diaries should undergo full medical reviews. Based on statistical analysis, the model assigns a case a score of low, medium, or high likelihood of benefit cessation (SSA 2015a). Beneficiaries in the low category are sent a questionnaire designed to solicit key information about their medical conditions and recent treatment. Those in the high group are placed in the queue for a full medical review. Beneficiaries in the medium category may receive a mailer or undergo a full medical review based on budgetary and other factors. SSA's existing model considers age, types of impairments, and length of time on the SSDI program to determine statistically who will likely recover.[8]

SSA would need to update the current guidelines used to determine CDR diary designations, given advances in medical treatment since the mid-1990's when the medical improvement expected guidelines were last updated.

The modern approach to data-derived predictive analytics is to have the model continuously self-updating as new data become available. Therefore, we recommend data analytics to devise a model to predict the likelihood of medical recovery by leveraging data in the disability application, electronic medical evidence, and Centers for Medicare and Medicaid Services data.[9] We also recommend the periodic convening of an advisory panel of medical and functional recovery specialists selected for their knowledge of clinical developments in this area for the purpose of updating the medical improvement criteria used by SSA decision makers.

2. *Appeals*

We propose making a DDS or ALJ decision as to transitional benefits non-appealable. Permitting an appeal in this context would undercut the

---

8 Given those correlates, it is doubtful that anyone over 55 would receive transitional benefits. Nonetheless, if the transitional benefits program is successful, everyone found disabled should be able to opt into the transitional benefits track to take advantage of the additional health and vocational advantages.

9 For an excellent proposal on how a data analytics model can be established, see Constantin et al. 2015.

proposal's goal of encouraging the beneficiary to take the steps needed to reenter the workforce instead of waiting for the appeal process to unfold. Congress has precluded appeal in analogous contexts in the past.[10] Moreover, the five-month waiting period would not apply to beneficiaries who file a new application and are awarded benefits immediately after receiving transitional benefits.

3. *Supports*

SSA administers the Work Incentives Planning and Assistance[11] (WIPA) program. The WIPA program emerged out of the Ticket to Work and Self-Sufficiency Act and was created to provide beneficiaries with information about how earnings would affect benefits and about services available to assist with employment reentry (SSA 2015). The WIPA program is implemented through community work incentive coordinators (CWICs) available in each state. In 2006, SSA shifted the focus of the program to provide tailored assistance that included written plans surrounding job options, long-term supports necessary for employment success, and work incentive and benefit counseling expertise. The foundational shift involved integrating CWICs into the vocational services system, as opposed to solely providing benefit counseling (Schimmel 2011).

Under the Ticket to Work program, beneficiaries select an approved service provider called an employment network (EN) (a public or private entity or combination of entities who deliver or coordinate employment support services) (SSA 2012b) or a state vocational rehabilitation (VR) agency to help them obtain and maintain employment. ENs and VR agencies may provide training, vocational rehabilitation, and job placement, among other services. ENs are paid for employment outcomes achieved by the beneficiary. SSA pays state VR agencies for services provided to beneficiaries when those services result in nine months of earnings at the substantial gainful activity level ($1,090/month).

---

10 Congress, for instance, has precluded judicial review of several categories of claims arising under the Medicare Act. See, e.g., 28 U.S.C.A. § 405(h) (WestlawNext through P.L. 114-25 (excluding P.L. 114-18)); see generally United States v. Erika, Inc., 456 U.S. 201 (1982) (upholding preclusion of Medicare claim); Webster v. Doe, 486 U.S. 592 (1988) (upholding preclusion of review, at least of statutory claims, based on CIA Director's decision to terminate an employee.). As under current law, claimants would still be able to appeal DDS or ALJ determinations that otherwise are not considered favorable enough, such as those relating to date of onset or, in a closed period decision, the end date of disability.

11 The WIPA program was originally entitled the Benefits Planning, Assistance, and Outreach in the Ticket to Work and Work Incentives Improvement Act.

Because transitional beneficiaries have great potential to medically improve, we strongly recommend that this group be provided with priority services throughout their transitional benefit period. To conserve resources and for administrative ease, the authors recommend that SSA deliver employment supports and services to transitional beneficiaries through the existing WIPA program in conjunction with the Ticket to Work program and VR agencies. The current process allows SSA through contractor staff to refer beneficiaries to CWICs (Schimmel et al. 2013).

We recommend that transitional beneficiaries receive expedited referral to CWICs and that the CWICs give priority to contacting newly awarded transitional beneficiaries as soon as possible following the benefit award. Early (and continued) contact with an impaired individual is a key concept in the rehabilitation to work process since it permits early action to assist with access to health care and return to work (Waddell and Burton 2004).

CWICs will play a key role by offering information and basic guidance to transitional beneficiaries. Currently, CWICs conduct initial intake interviews and develop work incentive plans. The intake interview for transitional beneficiaries will be modestly expanded to include eliciting beneficiaries' goals and expectations of the timeline for their medical recovery and return to work, along with any plans they have and specific obstacles they foresee along with potential solutions. The CWIC will make use of this information in performing an expanded preliminary assessment of potential service needs, such as physical or mental restoration services, job placement assistance, post-employment job supports, retraining, and rehabilitation technology services. Additionally, the CWIC will: 1) provide information about local ENs and VR agencies so that the individuals can select a provider of their choosing; and 2) facilitate connection to that provider. Since time is of the essence in instilling positive expectations and actually achieving recovery and return to work within the benefit award period, WIPAs will be required to report quarterly on the mean and median interval between notification of award by SSA and the conduct of these initial intake interviews.[12]

CWICs are currently required to be knowledgeable about beneficiary health care options, including Medicaid, Medicaid Buy-in, Medicaid waivers, the Affordable Care Act (ACA), and complex interactions between private health care coverage

[12] The changes to the WIPA interview described in this paragraph are based on Dr. Jennifer Christian's knowledge of the medical and psychological literature as well as common operating practices in outcome-driven private and public sector programs.

and public health care programs. While transitional beneficiaries will be required to meet the current statutory 24-month Medicare waiting period, we recommend that CWICs provide transitional beneficiaries with information about possible eligibility for subsidized coverage under the ACA or Medicaid and refer them to the appropriate agencies to access health care, and that state VR agencies be encouraged to prioritize expenditure of their physical and mental restoration funds on transitional beneficiaries. This will be particularly important so that transitional beneficiaries receive necessary medical treatment.

We believe that, with minor modifications, the existing foundation of the Ticket to Work program, supported by its experienced ENs and VR agencies, will be able to support the needs of transitional beneficiaries. ENs will maintain the flexibility to choose which beneficiaries to accept and maintain their working relationship with. ENs and VR agencies can provide many of the services most commonly needed by transitional beneficiaries, including: career planning; benefits counseling and management; job training advice and assistance; job placement; and post-employment job retention supports to the end of the transition period. The Ticket's current process of allowing ENs and VRs to share outcome payments will especially assist those transitional beneficiaries who need those only a VR agency can provide, such as physical or mental restoration services.

We recommend modifying the Ticket to Work program payment system to ensure that transitional beneficiaries receive necessary services and supports for successful employment reentry and that providers are adequately incentivized both to serve them and find them jobs that pay commensurate or higher wages than transitional beneficiaries received before they were determined to be disabled. We also recommend that a study be conducted to determine the feasibility of amending the Rehabilitation Act to require that transitional beneficiaries be served on a priority basis.

4. *Required Compliance*

Beneficiaries must comply with prescribed treatment to improve their ability to engage in substantial gainful activity. Failure to do so will be grounds for terminating benefits, as is currently the case for any beneficiary who fails to abide by SSA guidelines for regaining the capacity to work.[13] Additionally, transitional beneficiaries must take advantage of Ticket or VR services if needed to facilitate a workforce reattachment.

---

13 See *Need to Follow Prescribed Treatment*, 20 C.F.R. 404.1530 (2015).

5. *Notice of the Termination of Benefits*

SSA should notify transitional beneficiaries in writing six months prior to expiration of benefits, so that beneficiaries may take any needed action, such as seeking supports and services and/or applying for benefits if they believe they are disabled.

Statutory Changes

Congress would amend the Social Security Act to direct the agency (at both the DDS and ALJ levels) to designate a transitional benefits term, wherever appropriate, including modified appeal rights as discussed earlier. Congress would also amend 223 (i) of the Act (Standard of Review for Termination of Disability Benefits) to require: 1) that transitional beneficiaries follow prescribed treatment that would be expected to restore their ability to engage in substantial gainful activity; and 2) to participate if employment supports are needed to return to work.

Additionally, Congress would amend the Social Security Act to allow transitional beneficiaries to work and earn above the substantial gainful activity level for each month during entitlement to transitional benefits without affecting their SSDI benefits. Congress would also amend the Act so that transitional beneficiaries would not be subject to a second five-month waiting period upon a reapplication and benefit award after transitional benefits terminate.

We also advocate either updating SSA regulations to prioritize state VR reimbursement for those beneficiaries receiving transitional benefits, or amending the Rehabilitation Act to require VR agencies to give the highest priority to SSDI beneficiaries receiving transitional benefits (contingent on the results of the study referred to previously). Currently, all SSDI beneficiaries are considered individuals with the most severe disabilities (Hager 2004, 23) for purposes of determining eligibility and order of selection for VR services. Because transitional beneficiaries will have income supports only for a limited time, we recommend they have the highest priority for services necessary to facilitate their reentry into the labor market. All second awards of transitional benefits for an additional period that are due to lack of access to essential VR services should be tracked and reported annually to the states and Congress to aid in budgeting decisions.

INTERMEDIATE STEPS

Although we believe the full implementation of transitional benefits is justified, the following are two intermediate steps that could be considered:

- Commission a study to analyze the CDR process, including longitudinal data on SSDI awardees regarding the diary code assigned, date of award, type of impairment, diary date, date actual CDR conducted and ultimate outcome for a five-year period that would provide baseline data to inform a well-designed transitional benefit program.
- Congress could authorize testing all elements of the transitional benefit program as outlined in the proposal section of the paper. We recommend that a pilot be first conducted in a few states or region. Pilots provide the ability to rigorously test policy changes to work out operational issues on a small scale and provide an opportunity to gather preliminary evidence to determine the merits before implementing a large-scale national demonstration project (Liebman and Smalligan 2012, 2). If preliminary results indicate positive outcomes, then the pilot could be rolled out more broadly to a sample size required to detect the effects of the policy change within a sufficient level of confidence.
- Currently, there is no SSDI demonstration authority available to conduct a transitional benefit test.[14]
- Should Congress reinstate SSDI demonstration authority, pilots and demonstrations of transitional benefits could be conducted several ways. Transitional demonstration projects could be conducted through an interagency arrangement consisting of agencies that touch the SSDI program: Departments of Health and Human Services (Assistant Secretary for Planning and Evaluation, Centers for Medicare and Medicaid Services), Labor (American Job Centers), Education (Vocational Rehabilitation) and SSA. Another option would allow state innovation and experimentation with partnerships among state disability determination services, state vocational rehabilitation agencies and ENs within the state.

---

[14] In 1980, Congress authorized SSA to conduct SSDI demonstration projects to test policy alternatives that would encourage beneficiaries to reenter the labor market. Historically, Congress has granted SSA SSDI demonstration authority on a temporary basis, the last of which expired in 2005. Under such authority, SSA can waive SSDI program eligibility rules and benefit administration for purposes of increasing beneficiary return-to-work rates (GAO 2008).

Such state projects could be funded by nonprofit foundations or by social impact bonds.[15]

- With either option, we would strongly recommend that demonstrations be conducted as randomized controlled trials with a strong experimental design to allow for a rigorous evaluation of a transitional benefits policy. These demonstrations could also provide the opportunity to allow other beneficiaries the option of participating in a transitional benefit program, including possible incentives.

QUESTIONS OR CONCERNS

Objections will be raised by those who oppose the concept of time-limited benefits. However, we believe that establishing transitional benefits for the small subset of beneficiaries whose conditions are expected to improve, combined with employment support services and the ability to earn unlimited amounts during the transitional benefit period, is a compassionate solution that better serves these individuals. And, of course, those who fail to improve as expected during the transitional benefit period will be able to reapply.

With respect to the method for determining which individuals should be able to reenter the workplace in the near future, the proposed predictive analytics model veers away from an individualized determination of future medical improvement. Claims against the government rarely, if ever, are based on probabilistic outcomes. Yet, the massive size of the disability program warrants the probabilistic approach, and it would ensure more consistent outcomes nationally. Moreover, the predictive analytics approach does not rob an individual claimant of his or her ability to argue for disability at a later time: no claim is lost by dint of the predictive analytics. Claimants can refile and argue anew for disability at the end of the transitional term.[16]

---

15 A social impact bond is a funding mechanism that allows government agencies to pay for outcomes. Investors providing the funding for administration of a program and a third-party evaluator determine whether results have been achieved (Costa 2014).

16 The change to transitional benefits would not affect the claimants' ability to attract counsel, which currently almost 80 percent do. The lure of back benefits would assure claimants counsel at the first step—attorney fees would be the same whether claimants ultimately receive full or transitional benefits. As is the case for beneficiaries facing a CDR hearing currently, claimants who receive transitional benefits might struggle to attract counsel should they wish to reapply for benefits at the end of the term, given that there are no back benefits from which to obtain attorney fees. Legislative action would be needed to provide incentive for counsel in either context.

With respect to costs, adoption of the transitional disability concept would impose greater administrative burdens on SSA, which might need to adjudicate more claims because transitional beneficiaries could reapply after their transitional term completes. Moreover, additional individuals might file for SSDI or Supplemental Security Income benefits to take advantage of the transitional supports we recommend. At this point, the costs are speculative, but we are confident that the costs would be eclipsed by the long-term savings to the SSDI trust fund.

First, SSA would face more DDS determinations as some beneficiaries reapply for benefits at the end of their transitional terms. For the sake of discussion, assume that, of the 800,000 decisions or so awarding benefits each year (at the DDS and ALJ levels combined), the agency determines that about 3 percent[17] or 25,000 claimants a year fall within the transitional disability category (Morton 2014, 4). (The agency currently estimates that about 3 percent of beneficiaries carry an MIE diary, although that may shift as the agency's methodology is updated.) If all 25,000 later reapplied for benefits, SSA would over time face a 3 percent increase in applications. The more successful that transitional benefit supports are in helping individuals return to work, the more the number of reapplications would diminish. For example, if only 25 percent of transitional beneficiaries reapplied, the increase in the number of applications would be less than 1 percent.

A transitional term option would have even less impact at the ALJ level, where the hearings are far more expensive because of the court-type procedures followed. Of the 25,000 assumed cases in the worst-case scenario, ALJs would hear only those cases denied by DDS, which—using the current DDS denial rate of 64 percent for the sake of illustration—would reduce the potential pool of ALJ hearings from 25,000 to 11,000. Given that a substantial percentage of beneficiaries who are denied at the DDS level (including at the reconsideration stage) likely will not appeal to an ALJ (SSAB 2012),[18] the expected increase should not be substantial. And, if instead of the worst case scenario of 25,000 transitional beneficiaries reapplying for disability, we assume as before that only 6,000 reapply at the end of the transition period, the number of those who are then denied at the DDS level and appeal to an ALJ would present an insignificant increase in the number of ALJ hearings a year. Moreover, if the claimant was

---

17 SSA, Office of the Actuary.

18 Indeed, a significant number of claimants currently decline to pursue appeals at each stage of the process—at the DDS, ALJ, and agency levels; see, e.g., (Krent and Morris 2013, 76). Krent and Morris note the substantial percentage of claimants who decline to appeal denials at ALJ and Appeals Council levels.

denied at the DDS level and no evidence of new disability was presented, the hearing before the ALJ would be relatively straightforward given that much information concerning the claimant's condition had already been assessed and would be in the record. Finally, over time, there would be an offset because fewer CDR hearings (as currently constituted) would take place. The transitional term would obviate much of the need to schedule hearings for those presently placed on disability but who are expected to recover.

Second, revising the Ticket to Work payment system to accommodate transitional beneficiaries may increase Ticket to Work costs. But since SSA pays employment support service providers only when they successfully assist beneficiaries in securing and maintaining employment at certain earnings levels, overall cost increases should not be significant. We acknowledge that the additional responsibilities outlined earlier for CWICs may require an adjustment in administrative funding for the WIPA program, but believe that the benefits would offset the costs.

Third, some may worry that the more supports SSA offers to transitional beneficiaries to help them recover, the more new applications for disability there will be. We are skeptical. Current law already permits a nine-month trial work period that allows earnings up to any level for SSDI beneficiaries. Moreover, Ticket to Work services are available to beneficiaries today, and individuals would still have to meet the statutory definition of disability. Although we cannot rule out an incentive effect, we doubt that the move to a transitional benefit as proposed would result in a significant increase in additional filings.[19]

In short, the transitional term would increase the number of DDS determinations somewhat, and the number of ALJ hearings even more modestly. The increase in transition services would be manageable.

In contrast, consider that the SSA Inspector General recently estimated that, in light of SSA's backlog of over 1 million CDRs, roughly $2 billion was overspent (SSA OIG 2014b). That estimate addresses only CDRs in the current backlog, and so does not factor in overpayment from future delays.[20] The transitional disability

[19] Nor should there be any concern that DDS or ALJ decision makers in close cases will find more claimants disabled in light of the potential lesser cost to the trust fund arising from designation of a transitory term. Under our proposal, the transition term can only be determined via a computerized system after a finding of disability has already been made, thus taking discretion out of hands of DDS and ALJ decision makers.

[20] A similar estimate was made by the CBO in 1997, see (CBO 1997).

concept would result in a return to work or a new application for disability much sooner than under the current continuing disability review process. In contrast to such savings, the additional process and rehabilitation costs assumed by SSA seem quite modest.

Some may contend that a transitional benefit program would be unnecessary if SSA were to receive additional funding to conduct the statutorily required number of CDRs each year. There are several reasons why additional funding would not solve the issues this paper addresses. As mentioned elsewhere in this paper, SSA has not updated its medical improvement expected criteria for CDR diaries since the early 1990s, which could result in under-identifying individuals likely to medically recover. Additionally, a GAO study (2006) indicated that limitations in SSA's instructions in defining the degree to which improvement meets the required standard poses challenges in determining continuing eligibility. Moreover, the transitional term, unlike the uncertain prospect of a CDR, would put beneficiaries on notice of the pressing need to pursue steps to reenter the workforce. Most importantly, under the current CDR process, beneficiaries determined to have improved lose benefits without the offer of employment supports and services to prepare themselves to reattach to the labor market as provided for in this proposal.

CONCLUSION

According to the Department of Health and Human Services, the 2015 poverty guideline for a household of one is $11,770 per year. The average SSDI benefit at $13,980 a year is only slightly higher than what constitutes the poverty threshold for an individual living alone. We believe individuals with disabilities deserve better outcomes that are consistent with the Americans with Disabilities Act, i.e., inclusion of individuals living with disabilities in all aspects of life, particularly employment.

As mentioned throughout this paper, there is a small subset of individuals who enter the SSDI program and who have medical impairments that are expected to improve. While the CDR process conducts full medical reviews of some of these individuals, benefits are often terminated without the provision of employment supports and services. The crucial safety net of the SSDI program must be preserved for those who cannot work, but services and supports should be provided to those who are able to medically improve and transition from public support to gainful employment and financial independence.

Studies by Mathematica have indicated that age, health, and time on the rolls are characteristics associated with beneficiary work-related activity and employment success (Livermore 2011). The authors believe that limiting time on the rolls for the small subset of SSDI beneficiaries who have a high likelihood of medical improvement, coupled with supports and services aimed at improving health and increasing employment reentry, will result in better economic outcomes and overall improved quality of life for a portion of SSDI beneficiaries.

13

BEYOND ALL OR NOTHING: REFORMING SOCIAL SECURITY DISABILITY INSURANCE TO ENCOURAGE WORK AND WEALTH

Jason J. Fichtner and Jason S. Seligman[1]

INTRODUCTION

Reform of the Social Security Disability Insurance (SSDI) program should be fiscally responsible and socially humane. This chapter proposes a reform that creates a temporary disability award and allows for partial disability awards, to better reflect the reality that disability is not an all-or-nothing condition that precludes work.[2] In our view, administration of a temporary disability award program that allows partial benefits requires mandatory continuing case reviews. Additionally, we explore what role private employers might play in the insurance of disability (directly and through better integration of Americans with Disabilities Act accommodations).[3] Further, we describe a tiered approach to implementing a disability insurance system that allows for temporary and partial disability awards, including pilot project designs allowing for empirical evaluation ahead of any proposed national changes.

---

1 The views in this piece are the authors' and do not necessarily represent the views of the Mercatus Center, the United States Department of Treasury, or the U.S. Government.

2 Even without any changes to eligibility standards, a temporary program that also allows partial disability awards could increase the number of people in the program if those making the determination become more lenient, in turn increasing both the size and cost of the DI program. That recognized, we intend to design a program that mitigates or minimizes any increased enrollment driven by way of a moral hazard problem. To this point, we also offer changes to the financing and delivery of the Continuing Disability Review (CDR) process.

3 For a general example of how employers might play a role, see Autor & Duggan, 2010. http://www.brookings.edu/research/papers/2010/12/disability-insurance-autor

The SSDI program requires reform and improvement in order to ensure it continues to provide a vital safety net for disabled Americans. Due to the impending depletion of the SSDI trust fund in 2016, we believe there is a unique opportunity to redesign the program to better meet the needs of twenty-first century workers and families.[4] The retirement program, Old-Age and Survivors Insurance (OASI), has its own trust fund, which is projected to become insolvent in 2034. On a combined basis, the two trust funds have a projected insolvency date of 2033. Should disability insurance be considered for reform first, anticipating the magnitude and type of potential spillover effect and any subsequent program reforms to Social Security's retirement program will be important.

According to the Social Security Trustees, "Social Security's Disability Insurance (DI) program satisfies neither the Trustees' long-range test of close actuarial balance nor their short-range test of financial adequacy and faces the most immediate financing shortfall of any of the separate trust funds."[5] The OASI and DI trust funds are legally separate because they are designed to serve different purposes and different populations.[6] While historically the financial assets of one trust fund have sometimes supported the other, sharing resources between trust funds is not part of current law (Kollmann 2000).

Merging the two trust funds would have drawbacks. The programs were designed for separate insurance purposes: one insures in case of disability, whereas the other insures against old age and for a surviving spouse. If the two trust funds were combined, future financial or operational problems related to the individual programs might be masked, receive less timely attention, and cause greater fiscal strain before remedial action(s) are taken.

Beyond linking the funds, any stopgap solution for the pending 2016 DI shortfall does nothing to solve the underlying disincentives inherent in the disability program that discourage work, saving, and investment. For those reasons, we maintain that meaningful reforms to the Social Security system are necessary now and should not be delayed.

---

4 This chapter was written prior to the enactment of the Bipartisan Budget Act of 2015, which pushed depletion to 2022.

5 http://ssa.gov/oact/TRSUM/tr14summary.pdf

6 See http://www.ssa.gov/OACT/ProgData/fundFAQ.html#a0=0 and http://ssa.gov/oact/TRSUM/index.html

Our main goals for the program design we offer are: to support improved opportunities for work and saving while lowering public costs and improving the finances of the SSDI program. Under our system of reforms, the SSDI system would encourage and support remaining in the labor force, for those who can. Our design incentivizes the engagement of employers to assist with, and benefit from, these holistic efforts. Working from both the labor supply and demand sides, our reform seeks to increase labor force participation, U.S. productivity, and household income and wealth. Concepts in this chapter do not exclude other reform opportunities and in many cases complement other reform ideas, which will be addressed where appropriate in the chapter.[7] Additionally, by moving to a temporary disability insurance program that allows partial benefit awards, our hope is to also change a growing public and media perception that the SSDI program has moved away from being an insurance program and become a welfare program for the unemployed; one that creates a permanent welfare dependency.[8]

Temporary and Partial Disability Benefits for Workers and the Program

Under the current SSDI program, you are either disabled, or you are not. Neither a person suffering from debilitating pain who is able to work earning above $1,090 a month, nor one who cannot work even part time but who is expected to recover in less than one year is considered "disabled;" and neither person is currently eligible for benefits.[9] This binary all-or-nothing approach to

---

7 One complimentary reform that could also assist in determining the amount of any partial award would be removing or improving vocational grids: http://www.ssab.gov/documents/SocialSecurityDefinitionOfDisability.pdf. Any particular redesign of a grid will become stale over time, so we would emphasize redesigns that dynamically reassess disability employment over industries and occupations.

8 For an example of a popular media story reflecting this type of narrative, see: "Unfit for Work: The Startling Rise of Disability in America," Chana Joffe-Walt. National Public Radio. 2013. Available online: http://apps.npr.org/unfit-for-work/

9 "To be eligible for disability benefits, a person must be unable to engage in substantial gainful activity (SGA). A person who is earning more than a certain monthly amount (net of impairment-related work expenses) is ordinarily considered to be engaging in SGA. The amount of monthly earnings considered as SGA depends on the nature of a person's disability. The Social Security Act specifies a higher SGA amount for statutorily blind individuals; federal regulations specify a lower SGA amount for non-blind individuals. Both SGA amounts generally change with changes in the national average wage index. The monthly SGA amount for statutorily blind individuals for 2015 is $1,820. For non-blind individuals, the monthly substantial gainful activity (SGA) amount for 2015 is $1,090." See: https://www.socialsecurity.gov/oact/cola/sga.html

disability does not reflect the reality that many with disabilities are capable and willing to work. It also raises the stakes for the determination process, because determinations often require somewhat subjective interpretation of applicants at a single moment in time to forecast their ability to work. Further, in line with the concept of *permanent* disability, under the current DI program many who are awarded disability benefits leave the workforce entirely and never return. Although DI payments may be terminated as a result of either a return to the labor force or a reevaluation initiated by the Social Security Administration (SSA), in practice leaving the DI program due to medical improvement or returning to work are relatively rare events.[10]

Temporary and partial disability awards would better afford opportunities for rehabilitation, improving the subsequent quality and productivity of the workforce commensurately. Importantly, as we envision it, the program would require the beneficiary to undergo a disability review after the initial award period expired, in one to two years depending on the initial disabling condition. In sum, both to address challenges faced by the current determination system and to address the systems shortcomings in accommodating temporary and partial disability, we propose considering a design whereby all future initial awards are temporary and some are partial as well.

Though the assessment of ability to work can be difficult, a large and growing literature documents the ability of work capacity, at some level, among disabled applicants and beneficiaries. For example, a review of the literature by Na Yin (2015) "concluded that a nontrivial proportion of disability applicants and beneficiaries are able to work to some extent." Further, Yin (2015) cites several research studies suggesting "that around 20 percent of DI awardees are partially disabled or not disabled, and have residual work capacity."

It is important for us to state up front that the design we envision, whereby all new awards would be temporary, does not mean that awards would expire automatically or could not be continued. Our design is intended to protect beneficiaries and their right to due process by guaranteeing them a timely continuing disability review (CDR) for medical improvement and functional

[10] In December 2013, a total of 10,228,364 people received Social Security disability benefits. In 2013, fully 92,485 beneficiaries (or approximately 1 percent) had their benefits terminated for not continuing to meet the plan's requirements, including medical improvement or earning above the substantial gainful activity amount. See Table 50: http://www.ssa.gov/policy/docs/statcomps/di_asr/2013/sect03f.html

ability to work. A beneficiary's benefits could not be canceled due to inability of SSA to administer timely CDRs. Proper funding of SSA's CDR process is integral to the success of any temporary and partial disability insurance system. In essence, the temporary award system we propose would be similar to the current program if CDRs were properly funded and conducted in a timelier manner. The differences are that we propose a program that would allow for partial awards to enable those that can continue some work to remain attached to the labor force, and we propose that CDRs would occur more frequently. Partial awards could be decreased or increased at each review depending on medical improvement or decline. We point out here that changing the program to make all awards temporary changes the motivation of both the recipient and the CDR administrator. Previously, the CDR model was based loosely on an audit design. In lieu of a review, the recipient is able to keep the award, whether or not he or she remains disabled. Making CDRs mandatory for benefit continuation, the expectations are changed and a signal is sent that SSDI is an insurance program. This shift from an audit framework to an assessment framework for reviews motivates the individual to seek a CDR when eligible, and to begin planning for a return to the workforce when they are not.[11] We believe this assessment framework can be coupled with assistance for those transitioning back to the workforce, or in the case of partial awards, to not leave the workforce entirely.[12]

---

11 Models of this sort are employed in other cases in which skills and capacity are subject to change over time—for example, continuing care retirement communities. While the analogue is by no means perfect, we note that for those who are aging and need to rebalance independent living with assisted care, there is an incentive to start planning. Similarly, those regaining capacity to work would have an incentive to begin planning for a return to the workforce.

12 Another type of temporary and partial award system could involve time-limited benefits where the applicant is awarded benefits for a set period of time only, for example 12-24 months. After such time, a person would have to reapply for benefits if he/she wanted them continued. This would start the entire application process over again. After discussions with congressional staff, SSA employees, advocates for the disabled, and other interested parties—and given the current timeline for a determination, and to have an appeal heard before an administrative law judge—no one thought SSA has the administrative capacity to handle a true time-limited disability insurance program. Under better funding and administrative capacity, such a program could be adopted or pilot tested, but we believe that the mandatory CDR model is better for reasons stated above.

Integrated Employer Engagement in Disability Insurance and Worker Accommodation

We also propose a separate reform to engage employers. This change could take place regardless of whether a temporary or partial disability structure was adopted. It would give employers an expanded role in the disability insurance program. Specifically, employers would pay premiums to cover the first two years of disability payments. A near-term continuation review, roughly one year from initial determination, would evaluate the worker's ability to return to work, either full- or part-time, in line with a short-term disability program. At the two-year mark, those unable to return to work would exit the private system and could transfer to the DI trust fund, depending on the outcome of an SSDI evaluation. SSDI evaluation would begin following the private CDR just mentioned, to make the hand off seamless for those eligible. Besides being independent, the SSDI employment evaluation would be broader, based on the expert advice of medical, technical and vocational experts and including opportunities beyond the previous employer and occupation.

From the perspective of an insurance product, employers would offer relatively short-term disability coverage, while the government would continue to finance long-term disability liabilities. From the perspective of labor force participation and productivity, keeping workers and employers engaged through the shorter term would better allow them to explore any mutual benefit from accommodation and health insurance-financed therapies, relative to work stoppage, potentially enhancing the efficacy of the 1990 Americans with Disabilities Act.

Autor and Duggan (2010) propose experience-rating employer contributions to the system. That rating would be based on the history of employees' disability applications. The goal of experience rating is to remove a potential moral hazard problem. Businesses whose employees exhibit higher instances of disability would not be able to shift those workers to a disability program without direct costs. If an employer is required to cover the first two years of worker disability through private market insurance, the employer may have more incentive to either keep partially disabled workers employed or improve working conditions by way of accommodations that reduce the overall incidence of marginal disability applications and awards.

As we (Fichtner and Seligman) mention in our 2015 paper, such program innovations hold promise in as much as they expand the private system and thereby reduce the burden of retirement system reforms to address disability.

However, employers' motivation to protect experience-rating markups in the public system and avoid two-year claim payouts within their group policies might well create perverse incentives for business. Businesses may choose to avoid exposure to both public and private premium increases by avoiding hiring employees prone to disability claims—including those who might be returning to the workforce following a disability claim. Hence, at this time, we do not support experience rating for a private disability insurance component. As we will discuss later in the chapter, a pilot demonstration could provide evidence on this issue.

By way of both (1) the partial and temporary and (2) the employer engagement reform components, we offer a design that acknowledges the dignity afforded by work, alongside the dignity of exit from the workforce for those who cannot work. Our proposed reforms are intended to be prudent and judicious. In that spirit, we propose providing grant funding to run competing prototype modular demonstration projects. These would be sequenced in a logical order such that outcomes from preliminary projects inform those that follow. Outcomes would be evaluated along a rigorous program time path. We believe that such work should be ongoing with the goal of continually improving the disability insurance programs—a research and development (R&D) function to target more humane and empowering coverage at efficient costs.

The reform we are proposing is close in spirit to one implemented in the Netherlands, which changed its disability program in 2002 to require employers to cover the first two years of disability payments after the onset of a health condition.[13] According to Burkhauser et al. (2013), "These changes effectively meant that during the first two years following a health shock, workers were the responsibility of the firm and not eligible for long-term government-provided disability benefits. During these two years, employers must allow workers receiving sickness benefits to remain with the firm and can only dismiss employees who refuse to cooperate in a reasonable work-resumption plan."

---

13 For more information on the recent history of the Netherlands' disability program and reforms, see: Pierre Koning and Maarten Lindeboom, "The Rise and Fall of Disability Insurance Enrollment in the Netherlands." 2015.

THE PROGRAM – CURRENT DESIGN AND ASSOCIATED CHALLENGES

SSDI, as designed, provides cash benefits for those who cannot work above the SGA amount[14] due to a medical condition expected to last 12 months or longer, or result in death. There are legal definitions of what constitutes "disability" and the program does not currently allow for temporary or partial-disability payments. An applicant is determined to be either fully disabled, or not disabled. Examples of people who fail to be considered "disabled" include: (1) a person suffering from back pain who is able to work only part-time; (2) a person who cannot work even part time but who is expected to recover in six to 10 months and, (3) a person temporarily disabled due to pregnancy.

By contrast, consider two other disability insurance outlets, the private market and the U.S. Department of Veterans Affairs. Private insurers generally offer both short- and long-term disability insurance; these can usually be purchased separately.[15] The Department of Veterans Affairs (VA) offers *partial* disability awards to military veterans, acknowledging that some disabilities limit work entirely while others limit opportunities to a lesser degree.[16] While neither the private market nor the VA covers anywhere near the same percentage of the U.S. population as Social Security, and both types of programs face their own challenges, adoption of the better design elements of each merits consideration. In fact, some of the challenges faced by each type of program result from the inconsistencies across them, which generate an ad-hoc landscape of gaps and redundancies in disability coverage. Harmonization and integration can help to both (1) better define/support markets for insurance coverage and (2) better provide assistance for those suffering as a result of disability.

Structural and Cyclical Challenges to Current Program

A particular challenge regarding disability relates to its relative nature. The U.S. labor market has changed since the SSDI program was introduced. Work has becomes less physical in nature, and traditionally defined disability has become

---

14 See https://www.socialsecurity.gov/oact/cola/sga.html

15 For just one example of a private disability insurance offered by Unum, see: http://www.unum.com/Employees/Benefits/Disability.aspx

16 The Department of Veterans Affairs offers disability compensation in 10 percent increments, based on the level of disability. For more information, see: http://www.benefits.va.gov/COMPENSATION/types-disability.asp

easier to accommodate in the workplace. The reverse is true for mental disabilities. As work has become more analytic and social, mental disabilities weigh heavier on opportunities for employment. This shift has changed the applicant pool and weighs on the determination process. It has resulted in a shift toward mental and musculoskeletal-related conditions which are more challenging to diagnose. This is an issue that affects disability programs in many developed nations (Burkhauser et al. 2013).

Addressing the changing claimant profile, Germany changed their disability program in response to problems similar to those the United States faces. German disability payments are now discounted, such that younger workers find disability less appealing than older workers. Younger workers can be more receptive to retraining, and both workers and firms have longer to recoup the costs of retraining investments. In Figure 1, we can see the evolution of claims for the United States. The German program is depicted in Figure 2. Looking at both, one can see the change in caseload dynamics that emerged in the mid-1990s as Germany began reforms.

Figure 1. Social Security Disability Insurance Awards (per 1,000 insured by diagnosis).

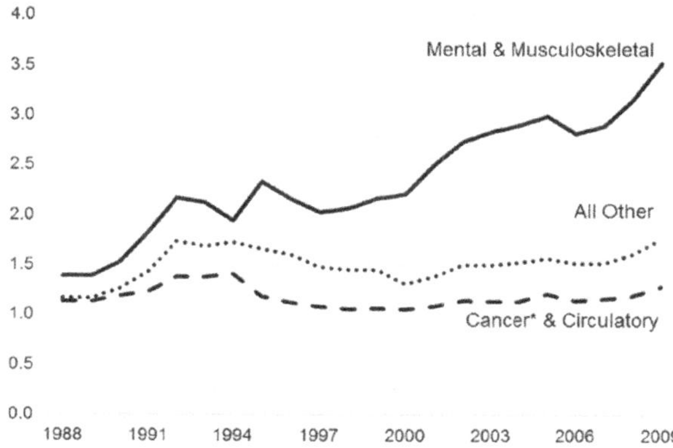

Data Source: Social Security Administration.
Note: *Cancer figures include all awards categorized under neoplastic diseases.
The figure above highlights that mental and musculoskeletal disability awards have been large drivers of growth for the U.S. DI program.

Figure 2. German Disability Awards by Category 1984 – 2012.

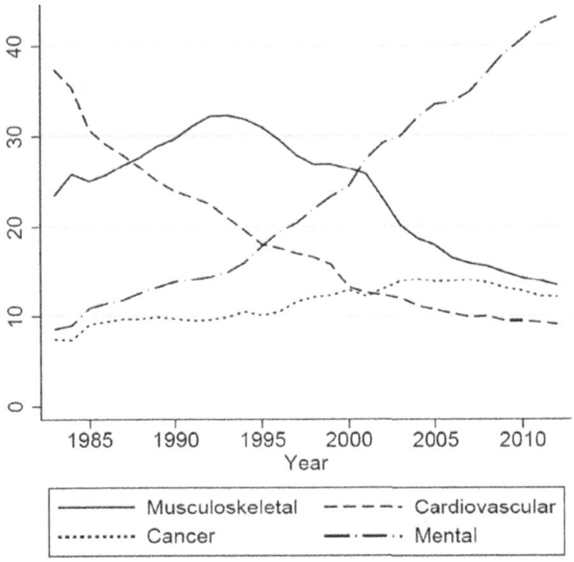

Source: We thank Hendrik Juerges for producing this combined-sex look at German disability awards by ailment and granting us the opportunity to share it here, in this chapter.

The figure above highlights that in Germany, too, mental health awards have driven application. Mental health awards have represented an increasing share of awards, both before and throughout the era associated with the German reform process.

Germany's 1992 reforms were evidently successful at reducing growth in musculoskeletal awards. German reforms were less successful at addressing growth in mental health based awards. As we noted at the onset of this section, some of this may have to do with the changing nature of work.

Germany's reforms are rather blunt regarding claiming and welfare dynamics of workers by age. While we think that motivating younger workers to choose rehabilitation over disability insurance payments is useful for enhancing both personal and societal welfare, the type and degree of disability are important to consider. German reforms treat all young disabled workers equally, regardless of the severity of a disability. Those suffering cancer or cardiovascular ailments at age 30 are treated similar to those for whom a weak back (spine) might otherwise be treated with physical therapy whilst they remain in the workforce.

This brings us to our second point regarding the evolution of German reforms. Broadly speaking, the German social insurance system has faced many of the same challenges as the U.S. system over roughly equivalent timeframes, with modest reforms beginning in 1984 (Boersch-Supan & Juerges 2011), only a year after the U.S. effort of 1983. By 1992, U.S. reforms were acknowledged as inadequate over the long run, prompting further actions in 1994. Those changes generally increased the maximum amount of wages that could be taxed and were especially important for Medicare. In 1992, Germany also began to consider the sustainability of its system, beginning what Boersch-Supan & Juerges (2011) describe as "a 15-year lasting process of reform." By 2007, the German system had been restored to long-term actuarial balance. But the pace of reform was not uniform in its rate of transformation and most of the fiscally meaningful reforms occurred in the period after 2000. This has prompted concern among the authors that the German polis has since entered a state of "backlash." Thus, the German achievement of fiscally sustainability may yet turn out to be temporary.

The German system is, by most accounts, still a good deal more generous than the current U.S. system. We see the parable of German system reforms for the United States as advising the sort of preannounced and slow-moving phase-ins of incremental changes along the lines of the 1983 U.S. reforms. Indeed, as Boersch-Supan & Juerges (2011) document, between 2003 and 2007 some announced changes were accelerated to meet the broad sustainability goal. While reforms still phase-in over relatively long periods, when considered from a behavioral perspective, they took some German voters who value the insurance program by surprise. Negative surprises are never welcome, especially after sacrifices have already been agreed to. The broad message we take away from these efforts is that process matters and that the very best program reforms will work to more effectively improve the welfare of those who rely on the program at some future point. Again, we believe that a long-term commitment to program innovation through a more continual R&D process is likely to be better for the program and for the nation's financing of the program over time.

The disability program is also challenged by issues related to the business cycle. The Great Recession, like other recessions since 1965, dramatically increased the number of disability applications and awards. For many people, the U.S. disability program now serves as an early retirement program, which has resulted in a commensurate increase in public financial burdens.[17] According to Liebman

---

17 Whereas the average age of disabled-worker beneficiaries has increased, from 51.0 in 2002 (US Social Security Administration 2003) to 53.2 in 2012, retirement ages have increased since the turn of the century as well (US Social Security Administration 2013). Providing important information for both structural and cyclical shocks' impacts on disability finance, Benítez-Silva, Disney, and Jiménez-Martín (2010, 1) find that "for a range of countries and

(2015), "...there has been a change in the composition of DI recipients, with more recipients claiming benefits for hard-to-verify impairments and with the program playing an increasingly important role in providing income for low-skilled workers whose economic prospects have stagnated." Against this backdrop of increasing structural and cyclical growth, the (DI) trust fund is stressed and the Social Security trustees now estimate that it will be exhausted in 2016 (Trustees 2015), roughly one year from the publication of this chapter.

Problems and Challenges with Disability Determination

The private market and the VA are two other disability insurance outlets. Private insurers generally offer both short- and long-term DI, which can usually be purchased separately or in tandem.[18] The VA offers partial-disability awards to military veterans, thereby acknowledging that some disabilities completely prohibit the ability to work, whereas others limit opportunities to a lesser degree.[19] The programs take somewhat different approaches to disability determination.

Over time, the private market system has evolved and now often requires the insured to apply to the SSDI program in order to continue receiving awards. A private market determination that requires application to the public system, either following or in tandem to its own determination process, may be challenging for individuals to navigate. At the same time, it is not unreasonable to encourage those entitled to public benefits to seek them. We believe that a reform that integrates private and public insurance could do a great deal to simplify the disability insurance application process, normalize expectations and help facilitate determination for the public system. In short, an integrated private short-term, public long-term program design may both offset increasing costs for the public sector and further standardize a private market for disability insurance.

This is particularly true because the application process for SSDI can be confusing and lengthy, and essentially requires workforce exit for no fewer than five months. Thus, partial and temporary disabilities are not conducive to application for SSDI. Some disabled workers may suffer in jobs past when they should exit the labor force. Uncertainty regarding SSDI eligibility can generate such an outcome

data sets, levels of claims for disability benefits are not simply related to changes in the incidence of health disability in the population and are strongly influenced by prevailing economic conditions."

18 Ibid., http://www.unum.com/Employees/Benefits/Disability.aspx

19 Ibid., http://www.benefits.va.gov/COMPENSATION/types-disability.asp

among workers with low productivity and poor job-market prospects. This is a bad for both (1) workers suffering from abnormally high pain and suffering and (2) employers suffering from abnormally low productivity. The current system does not encourage employers to assist and support a dignified transition from full-time work. Of course, once unemployed for five months, a marginally disabled worker then has a strong incentive to apply for disability rather than seek partial or temporary employment, even when they maintain some work force functioning.

Consider instead a system wherein the employer-sponsored disability insurance plan awarded a short-term award (temporary or otherwise) for an initial period of 12 months. During that period, the policy would make employee contributions to health and retirement benefits, affording the employee an opportunity to continue saving for retirement and to rehabilitate their work-functioning. At month 12, a mandatory review would occur. Should functioning continue to be impaired in the second year, facilitation and support from the private system's determination would be organized to send to SSDI for review at month 18. At month 24, SSDI would determine eligibility for a partial or full award, and the worker would transition from the labor force as appropriate.

Currently, applicants for SSDI can apply either at a Social Security field office (in person or over the phone) or online.[20] Social Security disability claims are initially processed through SSA field offices and then passed on to Disability Determination Services (DDS), which are run by the states but funded by the federal government. Subsequent appeals of unfavorable determinations may be decided by DDS or by an SSA administrative law judge (ALJ), appeals council or, federal court.[21]

Applicants rejected at the DDS level may ask the SSA to reconsider the decision in most states.[22] Almost 90 percent of rejected applicants appealed at the reconsideration stage in 2005, but only 13 percent had the decision overturned and were awarded benefits at that stage of the application process (Autor and Duggan 2010, as reported in Lindner and Burdick 2013). Those applicants who are still rejected have the option of appealing further to an ALJ, appeals council,

---

20 For more information on the determination process, see: http://www.ssa.gov/disability/determination.htm

21 For more information on the appeal process, see: http://www.socialsecurity.gov/pubs/EN-05-10041.pdf

22 See http://www.disabilitysecrets.com/topics/reconsideration-review

and federal court. The waiting time to have a case heard by an ALJ varies by office but can be well over a year.[23] Most denials that reach the ALJ level are reversed; applicants are then awarded benefits.[24] Given the high variation of ALJ decisions and the need for a transparent and equitable decision process, data on judgments are of value. In fact, the SSA makes public data on each judge's overall decision for awards and denials available for those interested in performing this sort of analysis.[25]

A striking discontinuity exists between (a) staying in the workforce and seeking a work accommodation under the 1990 Americans with Disabilities Act (ADA) and (b) exiting the workforce to apply to the SSA disability program. Having presented some basics regarding the program and its growth over time, we now consider DI in the context of the funding of the Social Security system.

Current Program Dynamics - Cyclical and Structural Factors and Impacts of the Great Recession

The financial crisis that began in 2007 resulted in a large unanticipated loss of wealth for millions of people. The U.S. stock market, as measured by the broad Standard & Poor's (S&P) 500 index, lost more than half its value (falling 56.7 percent) from a peak on October 10, 2007, to a trough on March 9, 2009.[26] Housing prices plummeted, and unemployment rose quickly to double-digit rates. Unemployment persisted at elevated rates well into the recovery: unemployment rates for workers ages 55 to 64 averaged 7 percent for the years 2009–2010, compared to 3 percent for the period 2005–2008.[27] Although unemployment has

---

23 See http://www.ssa.gov/appeals/DataSets/01_NetStat_Report.html.

24 The award rate at the ALJ level was 67 percent in FY2010 and 62 percent in FY2011. See: http://oig.ssa.gov/sites/default/files/audit/full/pdf/A-07-12-21234.pdf. For FY2013, the OIG reports the award rate at 56 percent, see: http://oig.ssa.gov/sites/default/files/audit/full/pdf/A-12-13-13084.pdf. For FY2014, SSA reports in an agency budget document the allowance rate was 45 percent. http://www.ssa.gov/budget/FY16Files/2016LAE.pdf (Table 3.27).

25 See http://www.ssa.gov/appeals/DataSets/03_ALJ_Disposition_Data.html.

26 Data are available from Yahoo! Finance. The S&P 500 index value at market close on October 10, 2007, was 1562.47. The index value at market close on March 9, 2009, was 676.53. The National Bureau of Economic Research, the arbiter of the start and end dates of a recession, determined that the recession that began in December 2007 ended in June 2009, roughly coinciding with the peak and trough dates of the S&P 500 index.

27 Bureau of Labor Statistics, Labor Force Statistics from the Current Population Survey, July 2011, http://www.bls.gov/cps/cpsaat1.pdf.

improved, U.S. labor force participation (LFP) has dropped by more than three percentage points, from 66.2 percent to 62.8 percent, as shown in Figure 3.

Figure 3. U.S. Employment to Population Ratio, 1973–2013

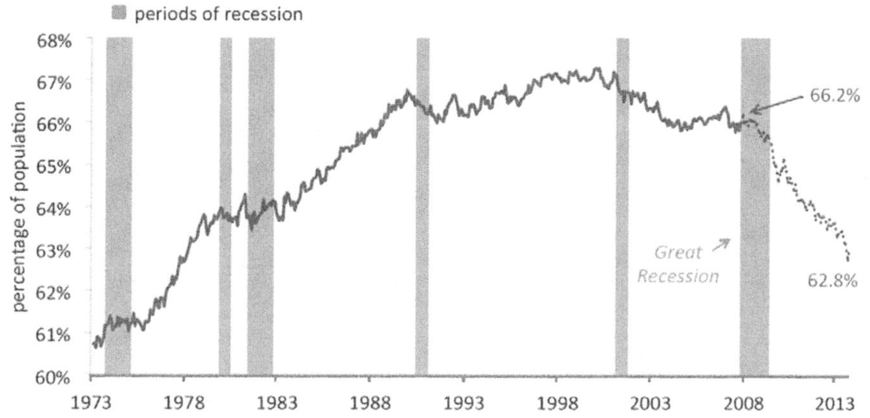

Source: U.S. Bureau of Labor Statistics, http://www.bls.gov/cps/cpsaat1.pdf; National Bureau of Economic Research Business Cycle Dating Committee, http://www.nber.org/cycles/recessions.html.
Note: Data adjusted monthly and seasonally.

Those economic conditions have vastly changed the employment and financial landscape for millions of Americans and appear to have had an impact on the number of people seeking DI payments (Lindner and Burdick 2013). The changes in the stock market, housing market, or labor market clearly do not cause physical disability, but such changes lead to an economic decline and increased unemployment (especially for individuals who might be considered marginally disabled). Such circumstances cause people who find themselves unemployed to have a greater proclivity to characterize themselves as disabled and apply for DI benefits. This process is not unique to the United States; the cyclicality in disability awards is consistent with findings for several countries (Benítez-Silva, Disney, and Jiménez-Martín 2010).

Figure 4. Disability Insurance Applications and Awards per 1,000 Insured Workers, 1965–2011

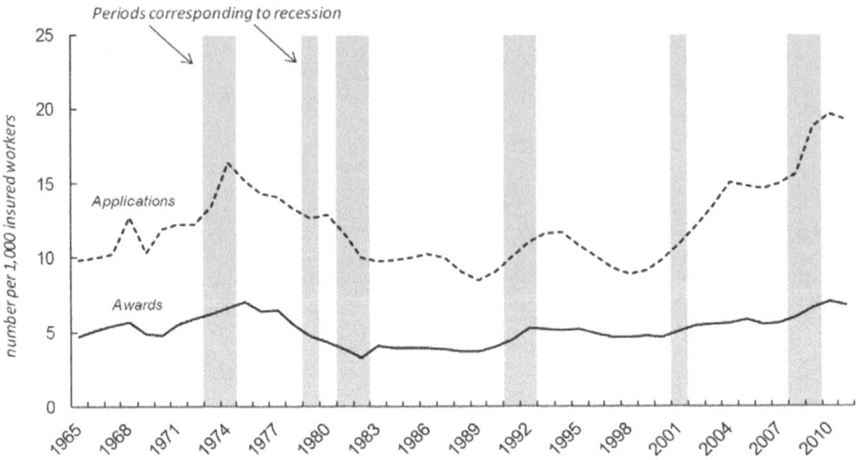

Sources: Social Security Administration, National Bureau of Economic Research Business Cycle Dating Committee, http://www.nber.org/cycles/recessions.html.

Figure 4 details that disability applications and awards are also linked with recessions. The Great Recession is again linked with uniquely high application rates, along with increases in awards. Overall, applications per thousand insured workers are 5.1 percentage points higher during recessions and awards average 2.1 percentage points higher over the 1965–2011 period. Those increases are, respectively, 7.8 and 4.2 times the rates of application and award in non-recessionary times. Lindner and Burdick (2013) suggest that people with moderate disabilities who can work but might find difficulty gaining employment turn to the DI program during economic downturns, possibly as a means of obtaining unemployment insurance—which is not what the SSDI program is designed to cover. To the extent the current design of SSDI is contributing at any rate to the decline in labor force participation, transitioning to a temporary and partial disability insurance system, with an expanded role for private sector disability insurance, could mitigate or reverse this trend.

Social Security, Hardships, and Associated Prospects for Reform

Recessions are depicted as discrete events, but unemployment evolves more continuously. That is also true for the growth of savings in retirement accounts. The value of those assets, in turn, constitutes the basis for most retirement wealth.[28] Thus, considering the influence of unemployment and financial shocks on the Social Security Disability Insurance system in a less discrete fashion makes sense before turning to evaluating how specific plan reforms might impact human and fiscal outcomes—including the social goal of helping able-bodied individuals return to meaningful work.

Although the proportion of the population receiving Social Security retirement benefits has been steadily increasing over time, the disability program has been growing faster. The annual rate of increase in the number of beneficiaries in the retirement program from 1971 to 2011 was 1.6 percent. However, for disabled workers, the rate of growth was 2.2 percent (SSA2012). Disabled beneficiaries include both adults and children. Between 1980 and 2013, spending on SSI and DI benefits grew from 0.7 percent of gross domestic product (GDP) to 1.2 percent of GDP (Liebman and Smalligan 2013). Further, the percentage of working-age Americans receiving SSDI benefits has "increased significantly in recent decades, from 2.2 percent in the late 1970s to 3.6 percent in the years immediately preceding the 2007-2009 recession and 4.6 percent in 2013" (Liebman 2015).

For some time now, research has suggested that the number of applications to the DI program is highly correlated with the unemployment rate (for example, see Rupp and Stapleton 1995). So far, we have discussed cyclical disability application; however, structural changes to the U.S. economy must be considered as well. In particular, the United States has experienced diminished LFP rates, as shown in Figure 5.

[28] Seligman and Wenger (2006) estimate the impact of unemployment on defined contribution retirement savings and find that unemployment is coincident with negative shocks to equities prices, which implies that workers may systematically miss investment opportunities. That might seem to be less the case for disability; an upshot of the situation would be that equity investments might do a better job protecting against disability simply because disability risks and financial risks are not naturally coincident. However, in light of Figure 5 and recent DI application and award increases—as well as the findings of Benítez-Silva, Disney, and Jiménez-Martín (2010) noted earlier—we take seriously the idea of a persistent, countercyclical, boom-bust cycle in disability awards.

Figure 5. U.S. Labor Force Participation over Economic Recoveries Following Recessions, 1973–2013

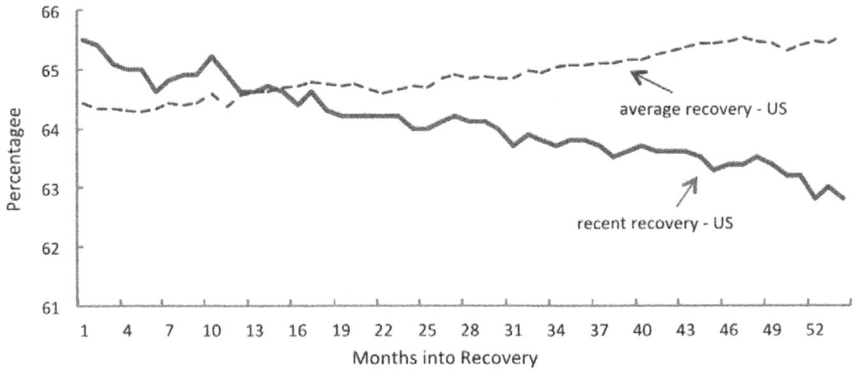

Source: Labor force participation statistics from the Bureau of Labor Statistics (1973–2014); recovery statistics from the National Bureau of Economic Research Business Cycle Dating Committee, http://www.nber.org/cycles/recessions.html.

The DI program is intended to provide income support to individuals with permanent disabilities who cannot work above SGA. However, as discussed previously, some people with marginal disabilities who can work might seek DI benefits during tough economic times when jobs are harder to find, suggesting that some people on DI might be able to work if jobs were available. In fact, the SSA has current programs in place to help return such people to the workforce. Yet, as Autor and Duggan (2010) explain, efforts to return marginally disabled people to the workforce have yielded consistently weak results and have broadly been deemed a failure.

That failure could be partially the result of moral hazard problems inherent in the program. The program may be failing to insure against only permanent disabilities, or the program may inhibit LFP among clients with marginal disabilities—that is to say, those who could benefit from work.

One reason people on DI might hesitate to look for work is that successful transition to the workforce eventually detaches them from the health insurance they likely received through Medicare and Medicaid, especially because few low-wage jobs currently offer such benefits. The health care exchanges established under the Affordable Care Act (ACA) may help to ease those concerns; however, coverage under the ACA typically requires contributions and a failure to purchase the insurance carries a penalty. As described in Hackmann, Kolstad and Kowalski (2015), penalties can be significant—on the order of $1,280 for an individual annually.

Recent work by Blahous (2014) points out that although the ACA creates new fiscal burdens for the federal government, impacts are dependent on states' decisions about whether to expand Medicaid eligibility as allowed under the ACA. Notably, because other social welfare programs vary from one state to another, interactions impacting DI uptake incentives are likely to vary as well. Although health insurance purchased through the exchanges will generally have real costs for the majority of participants, Medicaid requires no premiums or out-of-pocket expenses, which could create an additional incentive to apply when DI benefits are between 100 percent and 138 percent of the federal poverty level. Whether that incentive is enough to motivate additional DI applications in states engaging in the full expansion of Medicaid under the ACA will have to be researched over the next few years.

As stated previously, the proper role for DI is to be an insurance program targeting individuals with physical and mental disabilities that preclude work. Figure 6 documents exits from DI over the period 1992–2012.

The spike in Figure 6 occurs during the Clinton administration and is a result of increased emphasis on case review. The ADA improved accommodation requirements and disabled workers' rights, but it is not associated with any meaningful spike or change in long-term exit trends. A similar spike occurred during the Reagan administration.

Figure 6. Percentage of Social Security Disability Insurance Recipients Leaving the Program for Not Meeting Medical Criteria, 1992–2012

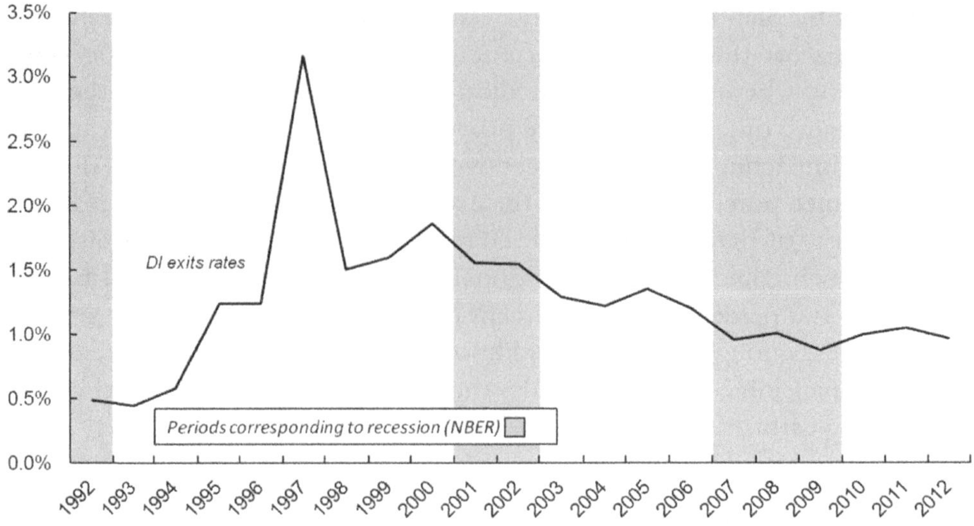

Source: Social Security Administration, National Bureau of Economic Research Business Cycle Dating Committee, http://www.nber.org/cycles/recessions.html.
Note: This figure describes exits related to health over time. Notably, the Americans with Disabilities Act (1990), which worked to improve accommodation for disabled workers, does not seem to be associated with any long-term trend of increased exits.

We note that a well-functioning program would display relatively smooth exits over time. Spikes, if they occurred, would be the result of sudden improvements in therapy or accommodations that improve job prospects. We offer that the increase in exits during either the Clinton or Reagan years was only temporary, and that a longer-term investment in case review would have the opportunity to improve efficacy—including the efficacy of efforts to provide fairness in standards of determination, and of the expectations of participants and those budgeting for the program. Most importantly, an investment in more continuous and thoughtful review would benefit the broad pool of insured individuals who fund and rely on the program's contingent support across their working years.

REFORMING THE SOCIAL SECURITY DISABILITY INSURANCE PROGRAM

Temporary and Partial Disability Awards

In order to reform and improve the SSDI program, temporary disability awards should be the default and partial disability awards allowed to better reflect the reality that disability is not an all-or-nothing condition that precludes work. As previously stated, administration of a temporary disability award program that allows partial benefits requires mandatory continuing case reviews. Additionally, private employers might play an increased role in the insurance of disability (whether directly and/or through better integration of ADA accommodations). Pilot projects to test these proposals are best done at the state level and should be designed to afford for rigorous empirical evaluation.

Well-designed temporary and partial disability awards promise to better afford opportunities for rehabilitation, improving the subsequent quality and productivity of the workforce commensurately. Importantly, the program as we envision it would require the beneficiary to undergo a disability review after the initial time period expired, between a one and two-year period and based on the type of disabling condition. In sum, both to address challenges faced by the current determination system and to address the system's shortcomings in accommodating temporary and partial disability, we propose considering a design whereby all future initial awards are temporary and some are partial.

A natural question arises, *how much should a partial award be?* We suggest that determining the proper amount of any partial award can be done through the pilot program process. While many pilot designs should be considered, we suggest including a baseline pilot program where the partial award is set at 50 percent of the fully eligible award. Under the baseline pilot, someone who doesn't currently qualify for the DI program still would not qualify. Someone who currently qualifies for DI would have the option to participate in a partial award program with broader labor force participation opportunities. The results of the pilot would inform which types of people (based on demographics, education, and medical condition) are most likely to succeed in remaining attached to the labor force. The results, if encouraging, would then be used to design a national program where certain medical conditions might automatically place people into the partial disability award program. Although an overly broad example, medical conditions that meet the current listing for SSA's Compassionate Allowances[29] would receive full benefits, while those awarded benefits for mental and muscular skeletal conditions would be placed into the partial award program. Other pilot program proposals that varied in their partial and temporary design could be compared to this one in terms of residual labor force participation/exit at 6, 12, 18 and 24-month markers.

One alternative might start from the Veterans Affairs standard of consideration, which compensates partial disability in increments of 10 percent.[30] The current SSDI program already computes a residual functional capacity (RFC) to help determine eligibility.[31] RFC could also be used to calculate a range of partial benefit awards. Either way, the results of the initial pilot program as described previously would inform policymakers whether a more varied partial disability award program is possible, and how to design and implement such a program.

As previously stated and stated again here so that there is no confusion, the proposal that all new rewards be temporary does not mean that all awards would expire automatically, or could not be continued without another application. To the contrary, our design is intended to protect beneficiaries and their right to due process by guaranteeing them a timely continuing disability review for medical improvement and functional ability to work. Benefits could not be canceled due to inability of SSA to administer timely CDRs. Proper funding of SSA's CDR process is integral to the success of any temporary and partial disability insurance system.[32] (Proper funding should also protect program participants from unexpected and time-inconsistent surges in case reviews like the one documented in Figure 6.) In essence, the temporary award system we propose would be similar to the current program that exists today if CDRs were properly funded and conducted timely and accurately. The differences are that we now propose a program that allows for partial awards to enable those that can continue some work to remain attached to the labor force, and we propose that CDRs occur on a more frequent schedule. Partial awards could be raised or lowered at each review period depending on medical improvement. And, changing to a program

---

29 See: http://www.ssa.gov/compassionateallowances/ and http://ssa.gov/compassionateallowances/conditions.htm

30 Ibid., http://www.benefits.va.gov/COMPENSATION/types-disability.asp_

31 See: http://www.ssa.gov/OP_Home/cfr20/416/416-0945.htm

32 Since timely and frequent CDRs are an integral part of our proposal, some guarantee of funding for CDRs will be necessary. Such guarantee could include mandatory funding for CDRs or adjustments to discretionary budget caps.

where all awards are temporary, even if in name only, would change expectations and send a signal that SSDI is an insurance program to help those workers who are not able to stay attached to the workforce, without forcing them to leave it entirely.

Figure 7. Reformed Program Design with Mandatory Continuation Review after 12-24 Months

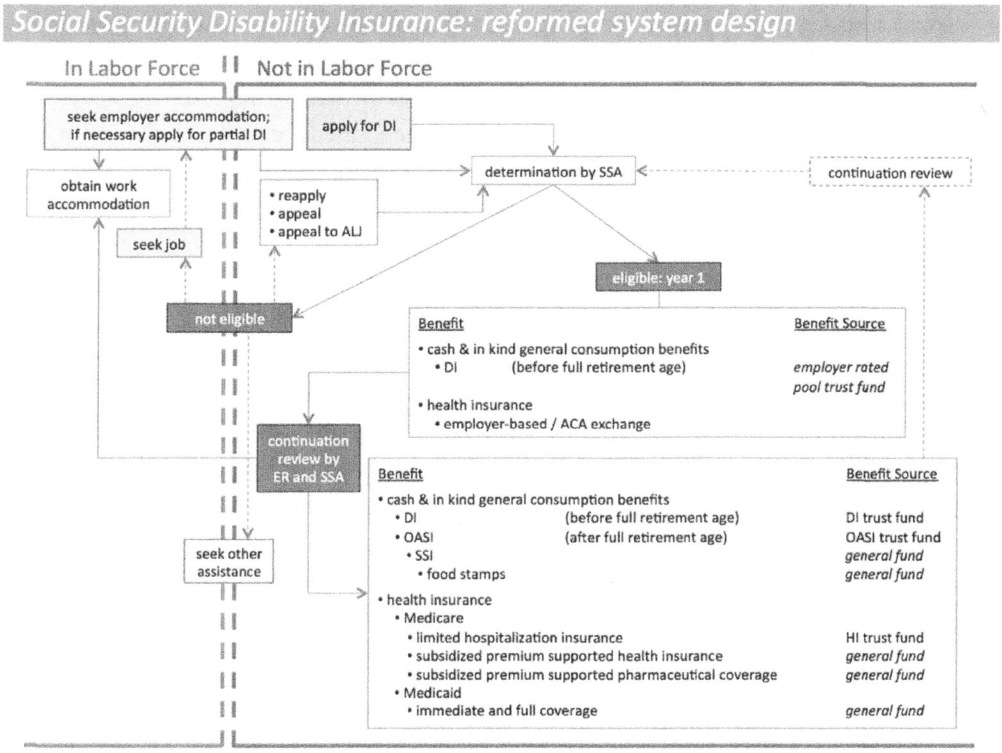

Note: ACA = Affordable Care Act (2009); ALJ = administrative law judge; DI = Disability Insurance; ER = employer (or previous employer); HI = Medicare Part A Hospital Insurance; OASI = Old-Age and Survivors Insurance; SSI = Supplemental Security Insurance.

Another big difference between the proposed system and the current one is the proposed system's integration of the eligibility determination with employers' responsibilities under the ADA to encourage labor force attachment and rehabilitation. Also, the initial DI award would always be temporary, with a mandatory continuation review between 12-24 months. In the proposed system in which the employer would have responsibility for providing private disability insurance coverage, responsibility for continuing disability review would be shared between the employer (or previous employer), denoted "ER"—who would have to provide private DI—and the SSA.[33]

ANALYSIS OF FULL PROPOSAL

Under a reformed system where all new awards are temporary, there's an allowance for partial awards, and employers pay premiums in a private market system to cover the first two years of disability payments, the perverse incentive of the current program to discourage work and labor force attachment would be removed. Employers would have an incentive to assist in evaluating a worker's ability to return to his or her previous position, either full- or part-time. Following a demonstration project, if experience rating can be included in the premium design without adversely impacting near-, partial- and, returning-disabled labor force participation, then experience rated premiums should be included. A potential avenue for such a program would be to scale and tune a credit program that acknowledges the hiring of at-risk and recovering persons. One metric might be developed around firms' investments in accommodation and rehabilitation services. In such a case, the positive experience-rating incentive should be large enough to motivate employers to rehabilitate employees whenever such rehabilitation is useful and humane. At the second-year mark, the time of potential transfer to the DI trust fund, reevaluation should be broader in terms of opportunities for employment outside the employer and occupation previously held.

Allowing for partial awards, whether at the 50 percent level or with a more complex yet flexible partial benefit schedule would provide the proper incentive to workers to remain employed and attached to the labor force in whatever capacity they are functionally able.

Again, conditional on useful and humane employment, the design affords an opportunity to acknowledge the dignity afforded by the ability to work, as well as the dignity of full or partial exit from the workforce in the face of significant suffering resulting from disability. Of course, further research into the costs and benefits of such a system—and the effects that such a system would have on labor force participation—should be conducted using pilot programs.

---

33 Under this basic scheme, individuals with verified medical conditions, for which the impairment is permanent or likely to result in death within 12 months, would receive permanent disability benefits and not be subject to a mandatory one-year review.

Research by Yin (2015) utilizes a life-cycle model to simulate the costs of a partial disability insurance program and estimates that "the (financial) cost of the DI program, calculated as the present value of benefits paid out less the present value of tax paid in, will be lower." However, Yin's research is a simulation model with different levels of partial benefits, not an actual real-world empirical study, further supporting our belief in the need for pilot programs to test the policy reforms proposed in this chapter.

Additionally, research by Burkhauser et al. (2013) on disability program reforms internationally show that "key among the findings based on their successful efforts to reduce their disability recipiency rates is that a substantial share of people who were moving onto the long-term cash transfer disability programs were, with reasonable levels of support, able to find or maintain employment." This is not an indictment of any one disability insurance program, but rather recognition of the continuing progress in helping those with disabilities succeed in the workforce. From a fiscal policy standpoint, getting able-bodied people back into the workforce increases DI and OASI trust fund contributions and reduces likely dependency on public programs. The policy leaves households with better income and better retirement income prospects.

INTERMEDIATE STEPS

People on SSDI can exhibit severe disabilities combined with health conditions that can make daily living difficult, let alone maintaining attachment to the labor force. For those that have residual work capacity, the combination of limited and inadequate evidence upon which to base program design reforms has hindered both the success of past attempts and our ability to offer detailed estimates on program costs/savings or number of persons that would benefit from a national temporary or partial disability program.[34] Therefore, it is necessary to first conduct properly designed pilot programs to gather the proper and necessary evidence to inform further policy designs.

[34] As discussed in Yin (2015), "Since the inception of the DI program, the SSA has implemented a series of policy initiatives to support and increase employment among disability beneficiaries: Trial Work Period, Continuing Disability Reviews, Extended Period of Eligibility, Expanded Availability of Health Care Services, Expedited Benefits, Disability reviews Postponed, Project ABLE, Work Incentives Improvement Act of 1999, Ticket to Work and Self-Sufficiency Program. None of these policy efforts has been particularly successful in promoting work among disability beneficiaries." Page 468.

We recommend pilot demonstration projects to test and evaluate the merits of each of our reform proposals. Long-run resources and infrastructure needed to scale up to national implementation are dependent upon the successful trials of pilot projects. Below, we sketch out two possible pilot designs, one on the individual side and one on the employer side.

On the Individual Side

In perhaps three to five states, we would offer both new entrants and existing (already eligible) SSDI beneficiaries who attempt work the opportunity to participate in a partial disability pilot. These working beneficiaries would be informed that they could stay in the existing current SSDI program or choose to enter the pilot and be guaranteed 50 percent of their benefit each month as long as earnings do not exceed a predetermined level—perhaps $3,500 per month, depending on local cost of living with a benefit offset schedule to protect against any cash-cliff dynamics. Benefit counseling would be available to beneficiaries considering participation and those enrolled in the pilot. Participating states would be chosen based on economic and demographic characteristics in order to design an empirically testable pilot.

Pilot participants would receive CDRs more frequently—at least every year or two, depending on their condition. At these reviews, participants could be switched back to the normal, full benefit if their condition has worsened and significant work effort is no longer possible. Additionally, if a pilot participant experienced a worsening of their condition before this regular review, they could request an expedited, early review to switch back to the standard program rules. As under the current program, if medical improvement occurred to the point where beneficiaries are able to earn above the maximum monthly allowable earnings, they would graduate from the pilot.

Participants would remain attached to the program, however, in case their condition once again worsened and they became eligible to restart program benefits. In other words, a participant in the program who medically improves and is terminated from the SSDI program would not have to go through the regular application process again to resume benefits.

A beneficiary considering this pilot would therefore be faced with a tradeoff. If volunteering for the pilot, the beneficiary would receive a smaller monthly benefit payment than in the regular program—for example 50 percent less—but that benefit amount would not be reduced so long as earnings are less than the maximum allowed (again, for example, $3,500 per month). As an illustrative example, consider a beneficiary that would receive a $1,000 monthly DI benefit under the existing program and ability to earn up to the SGA amount of $1,090 for a maximum monthly income of $2,090. Enrolling in the pilot would cause the beneficiary to forgo $500 of monthly benefit for the ability to earn up to $3,500 in additional income. This yields a maximum monthly income of $4,000; in essence double the amount a beneficiary could earn under the existing program. Further, if the beneficiary who participates in the pilot program medically improves, resulting in termination of benefit payments, the pilot allows for an easier resumption of benefits if the beneficiary's medical condition worsens than if the beneficiary had stayed out of the pilot.

On the Employer Side

Jeffrey Liebman (2015) has proposed a possible pilot to incentivize employers to take on more responsibility for employee disability insurance. Under Liebman's proposal, an employer that reduced the incidence of disability among its workforce by at least 20 percent would be provided a tax credit of an unspecified amount to offset payroll taxes.

From our perspective, a pilot program similar to Liebman's could be constructed in a few select states that would offer firms a tax credit against the cost of premiums for private disability insurance coverage, up to a set amount. In exchange, those on private disability insurance would be precluded from enrolling in public SSDI for some period of time—one to two years. This pilot would test our reform of providing more engagement in disability insurance by employers, as discussed previously in this chapter under the section titled "***Integrated employer engagement in disability insurance and accommodation setting.***" A pilot program along these lines would also allow us to gain better empirical insights into the feasibility of such a reform design at a national level.

Regardless of the pilot or pilots initially implemented, moving to an SSDI program in which all new awards are temporary could be done as a pilot at the state level, or done at the federal level as a national policy change. Either way, we'd suggest that moving to a system of partial benefits definitely be done first as a pilot in states volunteering to participate and selected so that a diverse group of beneficiaries would be covered. A rigorous and well-designed evaluation program is also necessary to properly test and evaluate the pilot programs.

Additionally, though an official scoring of our proposal is outside the scope of this chapter and requires the assistance of the Social Security Administration's Office of the Chief Actuary, an intermediate step would be to start working with SSA to evaluate the costs and savings of these reforms and where inflection points exist that would increase costs or lead to savings.

QUESTIONS OR CONCERNS

During the course of our research, writing, reviewer comments, and discussions with knowledgeable parties, a few questions or concerns have been raised. Where possible, we have addressed those questions in the current version of this chapter. However, some additional questions or concerns may still remain and need addressing.

For example, some on the advisory panel recognized that one of the things our reform proposal tries to do is change the public narrative of the SSDI program. Our proposal to give everyone a temporary benefit designation would, in reality, have little impact on the majority of DI beneficiaries. For example, someone who dies within a 12 to 24-month period after initial award would notice no effective change, nor would someone whose condition isn't expected to improve and doesn't improve. Except for a mandatory and timely CDR, the program would remain permanent for many, consistent with their chronic disability. What the reform to temporary DI would do is attempt to remove the perception that SSDI is *unjustly* permanent. The advisory panel suggested we be upfront about the positive change in public perspective our reform proposal could have. While this change in perception ultimately may or may not happen, we have discussed this throughout the chapter.

Additionally, the question of who receives partial benefits and how much would that benefit be is one that would have to be answered fairly and consistently. Given SSA's current administrative challenges, some have expressed concern about SSA's ability to administer such a program. Our "keep it simple" 50 percent partial benefit proposal was motivated by this comment. We note as well that the program can (and should) be modified based on pilot program findings.

Further related to partial benefit awards, we were asked which medical conditions would trigger partial benefits. Would certain conditions be fast-tracked (muscular skeletal and mental) and would some conditions be excluded automatically? As mentioned in the chapter, the pilot program would start with volunteers, but could eventually be expanded to a mandatory program where all would be initially considered for partial benefits with some conditions automatically receiving full benefits, such as those based on the Compassionate Allowances program or on the vocational grid and residual functional capacity. Also, beneficiaries could go from partial to full, from full to partial, etc. We envision the scope of benefit coverage being fluid in nature. In fact, one of the goals of reform is to move away from the static all-or-nothing DI program as it currently exists.

With respect to the appeal process, as depicted in Figure 7, our reform would still allow appeals. A question has been raised whether someone's initial award could be reduced by a judge on appeal. This is a question that still requires consideration, but the answer is likely yes. We don't want to remove the right to due process. At the same time, however, the goal isn't to provide a perverse incentive to file appeals. This would be the case if there was only upside risk for any award decision. Thus our intuition is that, just as a judge should be able to look at the evidence and increase an award from partial to full, a judge should also be empowered to reduce the level of award.

It is important to again recognize that a temporary designation is not designed to throw people off the DI rolls. The goal of reform is to change the narrative and perception of DI and protect the dignity and opportunity for work. The reform design realizes that some beneficiaries might be able to work more at particular times and then less at other times. We envision a design for DI that is more fluid.

Another concern raised deals with a beneficiary who can work and get partial benefits awarded on day one, but six months out their condition worsens and they're not up for a CDR for another 6-18 months. We have been asked, "What recourse do they have to appeal for full benefits before their scheduled medical review?' From our standpoint, there should be some avenue—perhaps through a caseworker—that the beneficiary could pursue.

With respect to moving to a system with greater involvement by private employers and the private market for disability insurance, it is important to note that this part of the reform design is mutually exclusive and separate from other components of our reform proposal. It can be adopted without changing the current SSDI program to temporary or partial awards, or it can be integrated. Our hope is that the reforms would be integrated so as to improve efficiency. An additional question raised was what happens to people who do not have an employer at the time of disability onset in a system where employers are responsible for the first two years of disability insurance. For a pilot program, this wouldn't be an issue, but for a national program it is a valid concern and one that requires further discussion. An easy answer would be to allow non-employed people to apply directly to the public SSDI program, bypassing the two years of private disability insurance. But this could create a perverse incentive, which in turn might motivate employers to dismiss employees over concern they might soon file for private disability.

Further, our intention is not to expand the definition of disability, but to use a broader definition to allow for earlier intervention by private employers so that longer-term attachment to the labor force is preserved, encouraged and, incentivized. It would be unfortunate if moving to a system where the first two years of disability were covered by private disability insurance only delayed transition to the public SSDI program instead of helping meaningful numbers of those who would benefit from longer attachment to the labor force. The goal of any pilot program is to provide empirical data to help answer these concerns.

Lastly, one of our goals is to improve the disability insurance process by making it less complex. Some of the reform proposal may add complexity to an already complex issue. The Social Security Administration has limited capacity to handle additional workload. We are mindful of this issue and wish to make the process more simple and efficient, while also removing the barriers to work that exist in the current program design. Existing offices in the Social Security Administration may require additional resources to manage new pilot programs, and the continuing R&D function we propose. At all points in the reform process, we assume and encourage full administrative funding.

CONCLUSION

Broadly speaking, the Social Security Disability Insurance program and the retirement program require reform. The DI program is currently fiscally unsustainable in both the short and long run and fails to provide a structure for individuals with disabilities who could return to work (part or full time) and find gainful and dignified employment.

The reforms discussed in this chapter propose changing the DI program to a system where all new awards are temporary, some are partial, and there is a larger role for private employers. Though we only focus on the DI program, we believe that the best opportunities for reforming the social insurance system will be holistic in nature, including the retirement program, and will honor an overarching goal of improving both personal and public finances. We further believe that such designs are feasible. What these proposed reforms require is an incremental design approach with pilot programs, long-term phase-ins and consideration of the roles of each social insurance component, along with a reconsideration of the roles and responsibilities that private insurance, employers, and individuals have in society.

14

Exploring an Alternative Social Security Definition of Disability

Neil Jacobson, Aya Aghabi, Barbara Butz, and Anita Aaron

INTRODUCTION

Since Congress created the Social Security Disability Insurance (SSDI) program in 1956, studies, briefs, and advocates have examined the definition of disability in the Social Security Act in a context of being a barrier to the employment of people with disabilities. "*Securing the Social Contract: Reforming Social Security Disability*" is a recent example of a straightforward discussion on the topic addressed to the President and Congress (National Council on Disability 2015, 1).

The authors acknowledge and applaud the Social Security disability programs' track record of preventing millions of people with disabilities from living in abject poverty or family dependency. At the same time, the current strict definition, tied to an exhaustive and time-consuming application process, has measurably extended time spent away from the workforce, or preparing a return to it.

Systemically prolonging time away from the workforce may be the most cogent reason to evaluate a repurposing of the SSDI program.

We cite the definition of disability for adults in the Social Security Act, in use by both the SSDI and the Supplemental Security Income (SSI) programs: "disability is the inability to do any substantial gainful activity (SGA) by reason of any medically determinable physical or mental impairment which can be expected to result in death or which has lasted or can be expected to last for a continuous period of not less than 12 months."[1] Under this definition, people with disabilities have been required to prove their inability to work at SGA ($1090 per month in 2015) to be eligible for Social Security disability programs. This definition of disability used by the Social Security Administration (SSA) for both the SSDI and SSI disability programs has not kept pace with the changing nature of work, options available for accommodations, and technological supports available to people with disabilities.

In 2006, the Social Security Advisory Board wrote: "At the same time, we believe that the existing definition of disability that emphasizes inability to work does not represent the proper central approach to providing support to persons with significant mental or physical limitations. An overall uniformly applicable and systematic approach needs to be adopted in which the initial focus is on assessing what individuals can do and helping them to obtain the support services, both financial and nonfinancial, that are needed to maintain or increase expectations that return to work (or, as appropriate, starting work) is a realistic possibility. The determination that an individual cannot work should be the option of last resort, not the first option" (Social Security Advisory Board 2006, 1).

The nature of work in the United States has fundamentally changed in the past 60 years since the establishment of the SSDI program and later the SSI program. In 1955, as Congress was shaping the legal framework for the SSDI program, more than 30 percent of American jobs were in manufacturing. Over the next 50 years, that number decreased to 17 percent, while white-collar, service industry, and retail jobs increased substantially (Lee and Mather 2008, 9). The digital age since the 1990s is transforming the workplace for a second time since 1956. Laws including the Americans with Disabilities Act of 1990 (ADA) created accessible transportation and workspace standards, along with requirements for employers to provide reasonable accommodations for people with disabilities. The authors' experiences show that these laws enable many people with disabilities to pursue employment and careers they could not have done before. Likewise, technology and the trend toward virtual offices and online businesses have greatly increased career and employment opportunities for people with disabilities. The authors postulate that as the nature of work changes, so, too, should the definition of disability.

A systemic assumption that people with disabilities are unable to work acts as a disincentive to the employment of people with disabilities. Complex and lengthy

---

[1] 42 U.S.C. § 423, 1382c.

application procedures that apply this construct set up a risk-averse culture after the award of benefits that moves away from seeking employment, or any change that is perceived to jeopardize benefits. While the authors are not benefits planners in the field, we hear regularly from benefits planners that disability beneficiaries are risk averse when it comes to planning employment, with the experience of undergoing the current application process cited as a chief reason for their risk-averse thinking and behavior. While recent beneficiary survey data shows that over 40 percent of Social Security disability beneficiaries want to work, the SSA disability application process supports a prolonged separation of a large group of Americans from productive living (Livermore 2010, 7).

Social Security's systemic definition of disability can foster a culture of low expectations, inhibit early interventions, and cannot integrate well with employers' opportunities to provide accommodations for their employees with disabilities. To encourage the investment in employment of people with disabilities, the authors call for modernizing the definition of disability by eliminating the requirement that people with disabilities prove their inability to work to get the supports they need to enter or re-enter the workforce.

Developing a new construct to replace the phrase "inability to engage in any substantial gainful activity" can lead to a change in the fundamental principles of the SSDI program and, in turn, provide an integrated focus on early intervention. From there, the mission of SSDI could expand from a wage replacement program to a program that safeguards against the high cost of disability and enables workers to connect to work, stay at work, or return to work. The re-purposed SSDI program would work in tandem with braided and blended vocational and other public funding streams.

We want to emphasize the need for a careful development phase where many of the details of the suggestions put forth throughout this paper would be worked on by affected agencies. The section titled "Intermediate Steps – The Development Phase" provides details of this process. We want to emphasize the importance of carefully testing a re-purposed SSDI program. Throughout this paper, we will recommend ways to limit potential exposure until evidence based data is available. We recommend that one or more pilots be conducted before a national rollout of the proposed program.

THE PROBLEM – THE CURRENT SOCIAL SECURITY DEFINITION OF DISABILITY IN THE SSDI PROGRAM

According to the U.S. Census Bureau, in 2010 approximately 56.7 million people (18.7 percent) of the 303.9 million in the civilian noninstitutionalized population had a disability (Brault 2012, 4). Four in every 10 individuals aged 21 to 64 with a disability were employed (41.1 percent), compared to eight in 10 adults without disabilities (79.1 percent) (Brault 2012, 5). Further, 34 percent of people with disabilities live in households with annual incomes of $15,000 or less – a percentage almost three-times higher compared to non-disabled peers (34 percent versus 12 percent, respectively). In addition to limited household income, 59 percent of people with disabilities reported having insufficient resources to live at the poverty level for three months without another means of support, while 37 percent without disabilities report being asset poor (Katz and DeRose 2010, 345).

Much of the social-political progress made by people with disabilities since the 1950s can be attributed to a paradigm shift from the medical model to the independent living and social model framing disability. June Isaacson Kailes has documented a comprehensive comparison of these two paradigms. This shift included a self-identifying conviction from Americans with disabilities that society must be accessible to all people (Kailes 2002).

Surprisingly, in the context of a huge cultural and legislative shift since the 1960s, the employment rates of people with disabilities since enactment of the ADA have not changed significantly. We view the systemic penetration of SSA's definition of disability into the practice and culture surrounding these Americans as an impediment to their economic growth. The definition systematically sets up low expectations of people with disabilities, which influence the unemployment trends of people with disabilities (Social Security Advisory Board 2006, 1). While the Rehabilitation Act of 1973 and the ADA have resulted in greater accessibility and acceptance for those with disabilities, and have changed the entire legal framework for workers with disabilities, they have had little impact on the employment rates of people with disabilities (Jacobson 2013).

By defining the eligibility requirement for benefits as the inability to work and connecting the receipt of disability benefits to a form of compensation for an inability to work, Social Security reinforces the notion that people with disabilities cannot work and need not try. At the least, we posit there are negative effects on the risk management and decision-making environment for significant numbers of SSDI beneficiaries. As the Social Security Advisory Board suggested in their

2006 *Statement on the Supplemental Security Income Program*, "it should be possible to make changes that would simplify that program and at the same time provide stronger work incentive features" (SSAB 2006, 22).

The current monthly stipend is one of the systemic problems with the SSDI program. The SSDI cash benefits are a partial replacement of lost wages associated with long-term impairment. Although SSDI recognizes that there are often additional costs caused by disability and allows beneficiaries to take individual work related expenses into account when calculating earnings, benefits planners report to us that many beneficiaries find these features complex and not worth the effort (SSA 2015a). Another systematic problem is that SSDI does not foster, address, or connect with early intervention strategies. Without early intervention, the opportunities to help employers make accommodations for their employees are often lost. The benefits of early interventions have been well documented (Mitra and Brucker 2004, 159-67). For people who become disabled or whose disability progresses while working, early intervention can reduce time away from the workforce. The sooner employees address and manage their disability, the sooner their environment becomes accessible to their needs, and the sooner they receive services they need the better. It is important for the system that employees acknowledge and address their emerging disability issues promptly so that the employer can make necessary accommodation as quickly as possible and keep the employee working when possible. The proposed new definition of disability promotes and can work with early intervention strategies in play today, including working with employers to make reasonable accommodations that allow more workers to remain employed.

It is acknowledged that there have been studies that argue the current Social Security definition is appropriate and should not change. These studies say the SSDI program and the strict "inability to work" is based on the assumption that only a small subset of individuals with disabilities—those with the most severe limitations—are precluded from work and, therefore, deserving of income replacement, and that it should remain that way. In 2004, the National Academy of Social Insurance issued such a study. That study also said that all other individuals with disabilities can and should work, and that a variety of programs to assist those individuals in working are available (Reno 2004). However, a recent Social Security Advisory Board study stated that, "the current disability programs, though well intentioned, are badly fractured and disjointed. A unifying point of vision, oversight, and management is desperately needed" (SSAB 2006, 32).

To be awarded SSDI, a person with disabilities must show they are not working above SGA. To receive vocational rehabilitation services, a person must show that the vocational services are warranted and likely to improve employment outcomes. To receive services from workforce development agencies, a person must be looking for work or work with the agency on a plan for employment. To have reasonable accommodations that support a person with a disability at work, a person must be employed. With current work incentive programs, vocational rehabilitation programs, workforce development programs, higher education programs for people with disabilities, and supported employment services for people with a developmental disability or mental illness, federal agencies spend billions of dollars annually trying, with mixed results, to improve the employment rate of people with disabilities (Livermore et al. 2011, 6).

Redefining SSDI's definition of disability could pave the way for more people with disabilities to achieve economic success.

As the Social Security Advisory Board wrote in its 2006 report, "The result has been to confirm our belief that a definition based on inability to work collides with the goals of the Americans with Disabilities Act, which proclaimed that the Nation's proper goals regarding individuals with disabilities are to assure equality of opportunity, full participation, independent living, and economic self-sufficiency for such individuals." In this global economy, when employers know they can hire highly qualified and experienced people anywhere in the world, expecting them to hire people with disabilities will only become more difficult. These antiquated constructs are the crux of the problem behind the employment of people with disabilities. The paradigm for the 21st century should shift from perceiving people with disabilities as unable to work to providing people with disabilities the technology and services they need so that they can work and be independent.

Social Security work incentive programs in place over the last few decades to improve the rate of employment for disability beneficiaries have not appreciably changed employment rates for those eligible for them. For example, the Ticket to Work program has been designed to assist recipients to return to work by expanding vocational services available to SSDI and SSI recipients, and providing additional protections to return to work without risking their benefits. Under the Ticket to Work program, vocational services, nonprofits, and other entities can become Employment Networks (ENs). SSDI and SSI beneficiaries receive services from ENs by assigning their Tickets to them (Roberts 2008). A recent study concluded that the number of beneficiaries who were assigned a Ticket to an EN has continued to grow but, as of December 2010, represented only 6.25 percent of work-oriented beneficiaries and only 2.5 percent of all beneficiaries (Prenovitz et al. 2012, 39). In addition, this growth has not been significant. "[Ticket To Work] participation among work-oriented beneficiaries was 6 percent in 2010, 5.6 percent in December 2009, and 5.4 percent in December 2008" (Livermore et al. 2013, 13). The Ticket to Work program is having a limited impact on the employment of people with disabilities. We suggest that a significant reason for this outcome is because it does not address the root of the problem—the definition of disability.

THE PROPOSED SOLUTION

The New Definition of Disability

The Social Security Administration defines disability by saying:[2]

> To meet our definition of disability, you must not be able to engage in any Substantial Gainful Activity (SGA) because of a medically determinable physical or mental impairment(s):
>
> - That is expected to result in death, or
> - That has lasted or is expected to last for a continuous period of at least 12 months.[3]

We recommend that disability should be defined as follows:

> "A disability is a medically determinable physical or mental impairment(s) that has resulted in a substantial impediment to employment and is expected to result in death or has lasted or is expected to last for a continuous period of at least 12 months."

This proposed definition could focus the SSDI program on removing impediments to employment rather than on the inability of beneficiaries to work. It would set an expectation that impediments could be addressed and removed, enabling beneficiaries to stay at work or return to work as soon as possible. The definition would work with constructs that employees should seek assistance from SSDI as

---

2 42 U.S.C. § 423, 1382c.

3 Social Security Ruling 82-53, "Titles II and XVI: Basic Disability Evaluation Guides." http://www.socialsecurity.gov/OP_Home/rulings/di/01/SSR82-53-di-01.html

soon as they experience a substantial impediment to employment and, if possible, not wait until they are unemployed.

The California Department of Rehabilitation defines a substantial impediment to employment as "a physical or mental impairment (in light of attendant medical, psychological, vocational, educational, communication, and other related factors) that hinders an individual from preparing for, entering into, engaging in, or retaining employment consistent with the individual's abilities and capabilities."[4]

The Social Security Administration has experience evaluating induced entry into disability rolls caused by policy changes. In 2010, at SSA's request, the Rand Corporation issued a report suggesting two models for evaluating induced entry. One model is a research design using stated preferences (SP) and the other is a research design using past policy (PP) changes in a simple structural framework (Maestas et al. 2010). These models can be modified to incorporate policy changes suggested arising from the proposed redefinition of disability. Executing one of these models during the Development Phase would enhance the accuracy of the proposed cost-benefit analysis.

To avoid the induced entry of new applicants because of changes in the program, SSDI may decide to restrict eligibility to applicants categorized as "most significantly disabled" on the Level of Significance of Disability. Most Significantly Disabled is defined by California statute as an eligible individual who has a serious limitation in terms of an employment outcome in at least four functional capacity areas.[5] It is recognized that changing Social Security's definition of disability will require regulatory changes regarding eligibility determinations. These changes should be defined during the development phase.

Implications of the New Definition

Under the current definition, SSDI provides a cash benefit that partially replaces lost wages, Medicare after two years of cash benefits, and access to the Ticket to Work program.

Integrated with the proposed definition, two stages of SSDI would be available to SSDI beneficiaries. The first stage would provide Coordinated Employment Services; the second stage would be a cash benefit that offsets the high cost of

---

4 CCR Title 9 Section 2027.

5 CCR §7051(a)(5)(C).

disability. This model is similar to one proposed by the Social Security Advisory Board in 2006. The new definition of disability together with the two new stages of SSDI is what we believe will significantly improve the employment rate for people with disabilities.

Coordinated Employment Services would support the SSDI beneficiary Individualized Career Plan (ICP), created, monitored, and maintained with professional services from a career coach. The ICP describes tasks to be accomplished to stay at work or return to work. These tasks may include:

- Completing a rehabilitation program
- Finishing a school, training or retraining program
- Assessing and modifying the workplace environment
- Obtaining benefit and financial planning services
- Acquiring self-employment and business start-up services

Many, if not all, of these services are available to people with disabilities today. There is, however, no formal coordination of these services. Systematically there are few if any federal requirements to coordinate these services. The proposed new definition of disability implicitly calls for such expectation and coordination to be established. This can be accomplished through a collaborative effort among federal agencies, including SSA and the Departments of Health and Human Services, Education and Labor. How these agencies will collaborate would be defined and agreed upon during the development phase. One precedent for this type of collaboration is in the PROMISE program and other efforts targeted to SSI youth (Thompson and Barnes 2007, 13-4). The administrative responsibility for Coordinated Employment Services should be with the SSDI program since that is where most people go when their disabilities impede their employment.

We acknowledge that some beneficiaries do not work and will not be able to work even with more readily available supports. For beneficiaries unable to work, the ICP would indicate that fact, along with providing a date similar to current SSDI regulations, if any, when the situation should be re-evaluated. Except perhaps meeting briefly with a career coach, these beneficiaries should experience no change from the current SSDI program.

We emphasize that only the coordination of services is being added. Career coaches will help participants navigate their way through existing services. It is not suggested that services be consolidated or centralized. With proper collaborative agreements, the costs, eligibility and administration of these services would be shared with each agency contributing through a blended and braided approach.

With the new definition of disability, the SSDI eligibility criteria would change. A person would be eligible for SSDI and Medicare if the person has earned at least 40 Social Security work credits, 20 of which were earned in the last 10 years, and is considered disabled under the new definition. The applicant with enough work credits may still be employed and qualify for services (SSA 2015b).

The new definition of disability does not use the concept of "substantial gainful activity." In lieu of defining the monthly cash stipend as a replacement of lost income, it should be seen as an offset for the high cost of disability. The cost of disability is often quite substantial and has been well documented. In 2008, Livermore, Stapleton and O'Toole reported the average federal expenditure for people with disabilities who were receiving SSI and/or SSDI was $27,100. This was 261 percent greater than the 2008 federal poverty level (Livermore et al. 2011, 8).[6] It is acknowledged that this includes Medicaid and Medicare expenditures. Given that the high cost of disability is often health care related, e.g. Personal Assistant Services, including Medicare and Medicaid expenditure is appropriate. Another report states, "There is little disagreement with the idea that disability imposes extra costs on individuals and their households, above and beyond the often negative effect on the individual's earnings" (Stapleton et al. 2008, 8).

The formula for determining the amount of the insured individual's monthly benefit could remain the same as it is today. To begin receiving cash benefits, SSDI beneficiaries should meet the same criteria as today, thus avoiding the woodwork effect and focusing attention on Coordinated Employment Services. Cash stipends should be viewed as temporary benefits rather than lifelong payments by beneficiaries able to return to work. The purpose of the stipend (offsetting the high cost of living versus wage replacement) is just as important, if not more so, than how the amount of the stipend was derived.

A person would continue to qualify for SSDI until they were no longer disabled as per the new definition of disability, or until they reached retirement age or died. Recognizing that at some earnings level a person with a disability should be able to afford the high cost of his/her disability, beneficiaries should keep their

---

6 Gina Livermore, David Stapleton and Meghan O'Toole, "Federal Expenditure for Working Age People with Disabilities in Fiscal Year 2008." [2002] http://www.researchondisability.org/docs/sos-2012-presentations/3a-federal-disability-expenditures.pdf?sfvrsn=2

full federal stipend until their total earnings plus stipend exceeds 250 percent of the federal poverty level. After reaching that earning level, stipends would be reduced by $1 for every $3 earned. Earnings would be reevaluated annually. Participants experiencing intermittent unemployment could request earnings re-evaluations more frequently. Stipends are to offset the high costs of disability.

This new way of determining continuing eligibility for cash stipends should significantly enable and entice SSDI beneficiaries to return to work and result in cost savings for SSDI. During the development phase, the earnings limit for receiving cash stipends might change based on cost-benefit analysis findings and consensus of affected agencies and advocates.

Pilot projects with a sunset date should be conducted in up to five states to learn how to implement and fine-tune the effectiveness of Coordinated Employment Services and a new cash stipend program. Pilots would also test the accuracy of the costs and savings projections and new sets of work and benefits rules.

Pilot participants would be ineligible for current SSDI work incentive programs. Complexity is in itself a work disincentive, and today's SSDI work incentive programs are extremely complex. Beneficiaries need rules that are simple to understand, such as the ones suggested here (SSAB 2006, 10).

Predicted Benefits

Providing Coordinated Employment Services to people with disabilities while they still have connections to the workforce and their career would be a major benefit. Instead of waiting months after being unemployed, beneficiaries would receive needed services as soon as they know their disabilities cause an impediment to employment meeting the new definition. And instead of having to navigate the maze of siloed services available to them today, with the help of a career coach, an ICP would be developed that to clearly outline the tasks they need to perform to return to work and/or stay at work. Rather than seeing SSDI as a replacement for lost wages, beneficiaries would see SSDI as a coordination program that helps them to return to work and/or stay at work, as well as assisting them with their high cost of disability. Coordinated Employment Services should be outsourced to vocational rehabilitation agencies, independent living centers, employment networks and other authorized vendors.

Another predicted benefit is that employers would view SSDI as the go-to program to learn how to retain valuable employees facing impediments to employment caused by disability. Today, an overwhelming number of service providers exist to which employers can turn. As such, viewing SSDI not only as the place to pay FICA taxes but also as the single point of entry for Coordinated Employment Services would be of great benefit to employers.

Knowing there are real expectations for beneficiaries to return to work and/or stay at work is another benefit of these proposed changes. Career coaches would work with beneficiaries to meet their ICP objectives. Furthermore, eliminating the complex set of work incentive reporting requirements would better enable beneficiaries to focus on their careers.

Implementing blended, braided, and streamlined Coordinated Employment Services should result in substantial savings for the federal and state governments. Undeniably, the most complex and most critical aspect of implementing this new definition of disability will be determining how the multitude of employment services that exist today can be coordinated. 'The National Collaborative on Workforce and Disability (2006) describes in its January 2006 *InfoBrief* paper the importance of blended and braided services and funding in areas such as mentoring, employer outreach and internships that has proven to be successful.

Allowing more disability beneficiaries to reduce their time spent away from the workforce should result in savings for the SSDI Trust Fund. An economic impact study (that is beyond the scope of this paper) should analyze how many more beneficiaries would need to return to work in order to achieve cost neutrality. The economic impact study combined with the cost-benefit analysis and pilots will be the true indicators of net savings. Dr. Kevin Hollenbeck, senior economist at the W.E. Upjohn Institute, estimates that the economic significance of 10 percent of people with disabilities staying at work or returning to work is about $25 billion (Hollenbeck 2015).

Perhaps most importantly, we expect a significant increase in the number of employed people with disabilities that will dramatically improve the American workplace fiscally and culturally, and set new international standards in the process.

Why Now?

2015 is the 25th anniversary of the Americans with Disabilities Act. We are celebrating the progress people with disabilities have achieved since its passage, while also recognizing that employment is the area that has shown the least amount of progress. The time has come to remove work disincentives (Harkin 2014).

The Achieving a Better Life Experience (ABLE) Act, passed with bipartisan support in 2014, demonstrates that Congress recognizes that the costs of living with a disability can be significant. The ABLE Act will provide new tax vehicles to save and accumulate funds to pay for these extra expenses (Vennochi 2015).

The Employment First initiatives in most states today provide major cultural and systemic opportunities for employment. Employment First, with some of its roots in the U.S. Supreme Court *Olmstead* decision, has become an evolving, national set of policies to facilitate the full inclusion of people with the most significant disabilities into the workplace and the community (U.S. Department of Labor 2015). In the Employment First initiative, community-based, integrated employment is the first option for employment services for youth and adults with significant disabilities (U.S. Department of Labor 2015). This initiative, like so many others, will not succeed until and unless people with disabilities can focus on their careers instead of focusing on keeping their government subsidy.

Several states have already adopted a definition of disability similar to the one proposed in this paper. The New York State Human Rights Law, which is used to determine who gets disability employment services, defines disability as follows:

> The term "disability" means
>
> > (a) a physical, mental or medical impairment resulting from anatomical, physiological, genetic or neurological conditions which prevents the exercise of a normal bodily function or is demonstrable by medically accepted clinical or laboratory diagnostic techniques or
> >
> > (b) a record of such an impairment or
> >
> > (c) a condition regarded by others as such an impairment.[7]

Another example is the way California defines disability for state programs including Medi-Cal: "a physical or mental impairment, or perceived impairment, that substantially limits one or more of the major life activities of such a person, or is perceived as limiting one or more such activities" (California Health Advocates 2014).

---

7 N.Y. Exec. Law §§ 290-301. http://www.dhr.state.ny.us/doc/hrl.pdf_

ANALYSIS OF THE IMPACT OF PROPOSED CHANGES

The authors posit that the paper's changes will have a measurable fiscal impact on the lives of individuals with disabilities, the communities in which they live, and the resources available to Social Security and the federal government. While there are short-term modernization costs in transition and pilot project phases, we anticipate that for everyone who prolongs their separation date from the workforce, or does not leave work entirely, or returns to the workplace early after a disability onset, the savings to the Social Security Trust Fund, health care costs, and the overall tax base will be substantial over time (Hall and Kurth 2013). As Dr. Kevin Hollenbeck (2015), senior economist at the W.E. Upjohn Institute, said, "Almost any policy that results in more retention/re-employment is going to pass benefit-cost test."

Perceived advantages of the new definition include:

- Establishing an expectation that workers with disabilities will maintain their attachment to the workforce or return to the workforce more quickly after the onset of a disability.
- Minimizing fear of poverty resulting from disability and loss of connectivity to the workforce.
- Creating a national system of coordinated services with blended and braided funding that will support individuals in their effort to maintain a workforce connection.
- Creating a more simple and straightforward system that will serve and support workers with disabilities and will not serve as an impediment to a continued workforce connection.

The current system asks individuals to "prove they cannot work" as opposed to expecting individuals to maintain their current work through analysis of job requirements and identifications of needed accommodations, or by helping them return to work after a break caused by the onset of disability through provision of timely, coordinated services and supports.

Our proposal prioritizes work as the goal for people with disabilities who can work and understands that individuals may need distinct services and supports to achieve this goal. We posit that many beneficiaries would choose to access a system that would assist them financially, as they worked to identify their new level of abilities, and develop an ICP to use those abilities and keep their connection to work and career.

Of note, these are foundation values and objectives of the private sector's disability management models. The key elements of this service approach reflect the best practices of the private sector in their disability management programs. As noted in an article from AskEARN (2013), "An effective disability management program reduces the human and financial costs associated with absence, disability, health care, return to work, and worker's compensation claims and ensures that organizations are able to retain diverse, knowledgeable and experienced employees."

Receiving early Coordinated Employment Services, viewing the cash stipend as temporary and the increased earning allowance make this approach attractive to the newly disabled worker, as it causes the least interruptions. Research shows that the length of time away from work is a determining factor both in the individual's sense of attachment to work and in their belief that they can work after an interruption caused by a disabling condition (SSAB 2006, 17).

Efforts to simplify the system and its expectations will greatly improve the interaction between the system and individuals with disabilities. It shifts the dialogue from requiring proving an inability to work before assistance can be provided, to focusing on what a person with a disability can do, even if his/her abilities have changed (SSAB 2006, 22). This philosophy aligns with a strong career-planning focus and the acquisition of coordinated services from existing service sources to create a program of temporary benefits to replace lost income during what should be a re-evaluation and re-training period. The program shift and realignment would create a program that:

- Focuses on work capacity, not incapacity
- Helps the worker with a disability evaluate the current level of ability and use the information to create an ICP that provides necessary services and supports to assist the individual's ability to continue to work or return to work with minimal disruption.

The authors believe the impact of this proposal is substantial at all levels and will achieve an improvement in the life of the individual, reduced human service costs, and an increase in taxes paid in the community. It will also lead to a long-term fiscal benefit, as in this model, workers with disabilities who can work will either not access SSDI or will use SSDI as a support while preparing for the next period of employment.

INTERMEDIATE STEPS – THE DEVELOPMENT PHASE

Reasonable, attainable, and measurable goals are critical to success. First, it is necessary to develop processes and procedures for creating and maintaining ICPs, which will include coaching, counseling and employment support services. Definition of the roles of career coaches must occur. The qualifications and responsibilities of career coaches must be detailed. How career coaches will monitor ICPs by working on case management, coaching, and supporting disability beneficiaries to assist them in achieving their career goals through federally approved agencies and organizations must be agreed upon. For participants unable to work, there must be a straightforward way for the ICP to indicate that fact, along with a date, if any, when the situation should be reevaluated. Coordinated Employment Services are necessary to "facilitate rehabilitation and employment by coordinating and integrating the various sources of assistance and support that are now inconsistently provided by multiple uncoordinated programs" (SSAB 2006, 11).

Another important intermediate step is defining and obtaining agreements for the provision of blended and braided services. As the new definition of disability is adopted and people with disabilities are expected to work, there will be a higher demand for supportive employment services and vocational rehabilitation programs. Federal agencies including SSA and the Departments of Health and Human Services, Education, and Labor will need to work collaboratively to develop a funding, implementation and oversight plan. There is a precedent for this type of collaboration in the federal Department of Education PROMISE grants and other efforts targeted to SSI youth (Thompson and Barnes 2007, 13-14).

Projected costs from all participating agencies must be considered in conducting a cost-benefit analysis to show empirically that our expectation of the effects of redefining disability is correct and the solutions are feasible. An actuarial study could include the impact of increased numbers of people with disabilities becoming employed, the effect on federal and state taxes, possible reduced public health care utilization, and other identified markers.

In addition, in order for states to pilot the new definition of disability and the consequential policy and program changes, waivers from Social Security will be needed not only to test the new definition but also to waive restrictions regarding Substantial Gainful Activities, asset limits, suspension of current work incentive programs, etc.

During the development phase, it needs to be determined how many SSDI beneficiaries need to return to work in order to make the program sustainable. In order to do this, a true cross-agency cost-benefit analysis must be performed, as well as a true economic impact report.

Finally, it is important to obtain support from the disability community, the rehabilitation community, the business community, affected government agencies, and legislators. In order for the new definition of disability to result in the significant improvements we are aiming for in employment for people with disabilities, upfront consensus and cooperation from many communities and agencies is required.

EXPECTED DOWNSIDE OF NEW DEFINITION AND PROPOSED MITIGATION

In this section, we discuss possible adverse effects, implementation challenges, and unintended consequences of changing the definition of disability, as well as how they may be addressed.

A significant concern is that costs may increase, when a goal of the program is to reduce expense. Although it may appear that new employment services are being added, it should be emphasized that most, if not all, the services are available today. Coordinating existing services and promoting the expectation that providing Coordinated Employment Services will enable many more participants to return to work/stay at work and will not increase costs. It may also appear that costs will rise as a result of raising the limit at which participants stop receiving their cash stipend. But so few participants currently leave the rolls that the proposed changes will improve this issue, allowing people to successfully return to work.

For those receiving a cash stipend, the proposal calls for a gross earning plus stipend disregard of 250 percent of the federal poverty level, followed by a $1 reduction for every $3 earned. Earnings should be analyzed annually unless a pilot participant requests more frequent reviews. This approach, together with Coordinated Employment Services, should further encourage and enable participants' return to work or stay at work. Our proposal suggests that during pilots, current SSDI work incentive programs be suspended. This will result in a much less complex system as well as cost savings. A true cross-agency, cost-benefit analysis must be performed before pilots begin to determine how many participants must stay at work or return to work in order to achieve cost neutrality and financial sustainability.

Another commonly expressed concern is that redefining disability will negatively affect people with disabilities who are unable to work. We acknowledge that although the proposed definition is based on a belief that people with disabilities can work when provided the proper environment and support services, some people with disabilities cannot. Neither the language of the proposed definition nor the parameters of the program reforms should result in disparaging treatment or benefit decreases for people with disabilities who cannot work. Their SSDI experience should be unchanged.

Recognizing that many excellent ideas and proposals have been presented over the past few decades promising to significantly improve current programs and policies, what makes this proposal different? The main difference is the proposed change in the base definition of what disability is and what SSDI represents. Instead of trying to find and fix "low-hanging fruit," a major overhaul of the entire system is required. Rather than adding another complex program to an already complex system, significant simplification is needed. In order to achieve success, we must blend and braid existing employment services in a coordinated fashion with the high expectation that these services will truly lead people with disabilities to employment. Another important difference is that a cross-agency, cost-benefit analysis and an economic impact report is requested in order to set measurable, attainable goals with which to determine program success. Most importantly, a real buy-in from the disability community, the rehabilitation community, the business community, and all affected government must be obtained before pilots begin, with the expectation that continual improvements to the program will be made.

CONCLUSION

We believe that changing the definition of disability by removing reference to the phrase "inability to engage in substantial gainful activity" will lead to a positive shift in the fundamental principles of SSDI and markedly improve the focus on early intervention. As a result, the mission of SSDI will change from a wage replacement program to one that safeguards against the high cost of disability, while enabling insured workers to connect to work, stay at work, or return to work.

The current definition of disability does not adequately address the high cost of disability; the current monthly stipend is a partial replacement of lost wages. The current SSDI program makes it difficult and complex for beneficiaries to account for additional costs incurred by their disability.

This paper's proposed definition of disability would enable employees to work with employers to make reasonable accommodations that may allow a worker to remain employed for longer periods of time, which could reduce fiscal stress on SSDI.

In summary, the paper defines disability as follows: "A disability is a medically determinable physical or mental impairment(s) that has resulted in a substantial impediment to employment, is expected to result in death or has lasted or is expected to last for a continuous period of at least 12 months."

Along with the new definition of disability, there would be new eligibility criteria. A person would be eligible for SSDI and Medicare if the applicant has earned the required work credits within the required period in accordance with current rules, and the person is found disabled per the new definition.

With the proposed definition, two provisions via SSDI would be available to disability beneficiaries. The first is providing Coordinated Employment Services; the second is a cash benefit that offsets the high cost of disability. Advantages and objectives of the new definition include:

- Raising the expectation that workers with disabilities will maintain their attachment to the workforce, and/or return to the workforce more quickly after the onset of a disability;
- Reducing fear of poverty resulting from disability and loss of connectivity to the workforce;
- Creating a national system of coordinated services with blended and braided funding to support individuals in their efforts to maintain a workforce connection; and,
- Establishing a more straightforward, purposeful system to serve and support workers with disabilities and reducing prolonged periods of time away from the workforce.

Discussion of Structural Reform Proposals

Art Spencer

This discussion is a summary of the comments made by the discussant at the SSDI Solutions Conference on August 4, 2015 before chapters were made final.

In reading these papers, I was struck by the similar themes presented by authors who approached their task from very different organizational perspectives. It is clear that the arguments presented here have merit for further discussion and elaboration. It is also clear that these papers could be combined into one without harm to any of the individual core arguments. Likely this hypothetical single paper would be made stronger than any of the three.

Some of the similar themes within the three papers include an emphasis on Social Security Disability Insurance (SSDI) as a temporary income replacement, otherwise known as "transitional benefits," that would lead to beneficiaries returning to work, and an emphasis on Continuing Disability Reviews (CDRs). They also all provide support to maintain applicant ties to the workplace and shorten the time removed from work while applying for SSDI, allow beneficiaries to work without a limit on earnings (as they medically improve and engage in rehabilitation), and recognize the need to "pilot" their proposed changes to create the final operational processes. Underlying these changes are a strong belief that most beneficiaries can work, especially with appropriate workplace accommodation and support, and that therefore we should focus on work capacity rather than incapacity.

Nonetheless, and certainly as expected, there are unique approaches within these three papers. But as said above, I believe these differences could be resolved into strengths with additional discussion and deliberation. Some of the different approaches to the problem presented include the questions of whether some benefits should be "partial" as well as temporary, whether the employer should directly finance the first years of benefits, what is the impact of unemployment and economic shocks on SSDI applications, whether all benefits should be temporary or temporary only for a small subset of beneficiaries, and whether the temporary designation should be appealable. Another approach asked whether the definition of disability ought to be modified to remove the tie to the ability to work.

Given that the title of this panel is "Structural Reforms," significant changes to operational processes would be likely if these ideas were implemented.[1] Change, of course, is rarely easy, often resisted, and generally requires one to be adept at changing horses in the middle of a stream. That said, I present some cautions and reminders if we move forward.

First, program and administrative costs and savings are two separate entities. Saving program monies does not increase the funding available to administer the program. And a great idea cannot be implemented without needed resources, even if that requires finding additional resources. Second, there is the issue of operational realities. A complex program is more expensive to run. For example, suggesting the Veteran Affairs (VA) Department's benefits program as a model for SSDI may forget recent VA history with backlogs, costs, and never-ending appeals. Third, when looking at temporary disability alternatives, we need to remember to review the programs in Rhode Island, New York, New Jersey, California, and Hawaii as well as private or employer-based disability insurance, to see their effect on the population. Fourth, please use caution when suggesting that Residual Functional Capacity (RFC) is a good model for an individualized functional assessment; many believe that it is an imperfect system that warrants additional scrutiny. Additionally, we should generally use caution when assuming decision-maker compliance. Training, oversight and a robust quality review process at every appeal level must be an ongoing priority to ensure fairness and correct decisions, and care must be taken when deciding what administrative decisions are or are not appealable.

It also appears that significant inter-agency cooperation and collaboration is an integral part of these papers, perhaps more than should be expected given our bureaucratic reality. The Social Security Administration's research suggests that many beneficiaries attempt a return to work, but most don't work very long, and few maintain substantial gainful activity. And while the focus here is on

---

1 There is also agreement that statutory and regulatory changes would be required, but my focus here will be on operational issues that will needed to be addressed in order to make these ideas live.

SSDI, perhaps the Supplemental Security Income (SSI) program should also be modified to match any changes incorporated into SSDI, since the two are interconnected as supports for people with disabilities.

Additionally, these papers appropriately assume, and would even require, beneficiary cooperation in medical and vocational improvement efforts. But what if beneficiaries did not cooperate fully? And this begs the question, while certainly a bigger issue than SSDI, is the "real" issue: What should be the economic safety net for all Americans?

As reiterated over and over again at the conference, we may have the opportunity now to propose significant changes to the SSDI program, changes that must protect the economic safety net for current and future beneficiaries, yet changes that emphasize the value and benefit of work for individuals, families, and society. These papers present a framework for continuing discussion and debate to reach those goals.

Section VI

International Comparisons and Long-Term Solvency

15

Approaches to Assisting Working-Aged People with Disabilities: Insights from Around the World

Robert Haveman

INTRODUCTION

A 2003 report from the Organisation for Economic Co-operation and Development (OECD), *Transforming Disability into Ability,* concluded that sickness and disability policies in the member states were afflicted with serious efficiency and equity problems requiring fundamental and comprehensive reform (OECD 2003). The 2010 OECD report, *Sickness, Disability, and Work: Breaking the Barriers,* indicated that in the intervening years, several countries had made efforts to reform their disability and sickness policies (OECD 2010). While evaluation results are not definitive, there is evidence that these efforts have achieved some success in reducing the growth in benefit recipiency rates, and encouraging rehabilitation and continued work.

In the next section, I present some background on the size and characteristics of the population of workers with disabilities across developed countries. They are older and have less education, far less contact with the labor market, and a relatively low economic position.

The third section discusses the overall structure of policy targeted on the working-age disabled population in six Western, developed nations. This overview describes overall policy structure from the bottom tier of social minimum support policies to the third tier of disability and old-age pensions. The nature of disability-related income support programs in each country is described. The basic characteristics of the income support programs targeted on workers with disabilities in those countries are presented in some detail. For each country, the percentage of the working-age population receiving disability income support benefits is shown, as well as the percentage of each nation's Gross Domestic Product (GDP) spent on income support and sickness benefits for workers with disabilities.

The fourth section of the paper describes in broad-brush terms the nature of the changes in disability policy that have been made in several Western developed nations. The fifth section presents a country-by-country analysis of the nature of policy revisions over the past several decades in the six countries on which we have concentrated.

The sixth section draws lessons from these reform efforts of other nations for the United States, and the final section concludes.

BACKGROUND ON THE DISABLED WORKING-AGE POPULATION

In spite of differences in the definition of working-age disability, the general characteristics of the disabled population are similar. Those individuals tend to be older than the average working-age person and have less education. For example, the percentage of the working-age population with less than a high school degree is substantially higher among the disabled than it is among the able-bodied (OECD 2010). For both of these reasons, the average employment rate for persons with disabilities tends to be lower than that for the able-bodied working-age population.[1] Consistent with this, their incomes are lower as well.[2] Because of differences in the generosity of the social welfare systems, poverty rates across countries vary widely. While Sweden and the Netherlands have achieved relatively equal rates of poverty across households both with and without a disabled person, countries with less generous social program benefits have not.

1 Across the OECD countries, the employment rates of people with disabilities were about 40 percent compared with about 75 percent for people without disability. Across these nations, about 25 percent of employed disabled people work part-time, while only about 13 percent of working nondisabled people work part-time. Across OECD nations, the unemployment rate for people with disabilities is about twice that as for those without (OECD 2010).

2 In most OECD countries, working-age households with a disabled person have a significantly higher risk of *relative* income poverty than do other households. Across OECD countries, the poverty rate for households with a person with a disability is about 22 percent, compared with 14 percent for other households (OECD 2010).

It should be emphasized, however, that the outcomes of those with disabilities reflect both basic underlying conditions that lead to a lack of work capability and their behavioral responses to incentives created by existing policies. Without a clear counterfactual, it is difficult to ascertain how these employment and economic well-being characteristics would be altered should policy be changed. Our cross-national approach is one way to attempt to observe changes in behavior/economic well-being in response to a policy change. However, even with this approach, establishing a clear counterfactual is not straightforward; a variety of other economic and policy changes may occur simultaneously with changes in disability policy. In sum, two things seem clear: first, there are real and meaningful differences in economic status and well-being between those with and without disabilities, and, second, that policies directed at people with disabilities may affect behavior and hence these observed characteristics.

Interpreting these conclusions regarding the economic position of people with disabilities is difficult, as countries vary in terms of how they interpret the concept of work disability. To identify this group and observe their characteristics—and hence the choice of policies designed to protect and support them—requires both a definition of disability and a performance norm or standard. From an economic point of view, individuals of working age with disabilities are those with physical or mental characteristics that limit normal daily activities or result in a substantial decrease in work productivity. In order to establish a clear definition, it is necessary to establish a performance norm or standard—just how much must a person be constrained or fall short of being able to fully undertake normal daily activities or to be productive at work in order to be classified as disabled? Different nations have chosen different characteristics to be used in establishing disabled status, as well as different performance norms and standards to which performance shortfalls are compared. As a result, the rates of working-age disability vary widely across countries, as do their characteristics.

THE STRUCTURE OF POLICY ASSISTING DISABLED WORKERS IN SEVERAL WESTERN NATIONS

Overview

Virtually all Western developed nations have a complex set of policies that provide protection to workers with disabilities. As Burkhauser, Daly, and Ziebarth (2015) have discussed, most countries provide this protection in tiers, which vary across the countries. As they have noted, the first tier typically provides universal, long-term, needs-based cash transfers designed to guarantee a minimum level of income support to families headed by a working-age person. The second tier supports the income of those able and expected to work, but who are temporarily unemployed. The amount of support provided tends to be based on the level of past work and earnings; the benefits are time-limited and in some cases related to household needs. The third tier provides income support to those who are aged, sick and disabled. These programs can either be needs-based or based on past earnings. Since recipients of sickness benefits are viewed as temporarily unable to work, support is generally time-limited. Disability pension benefits are reserved for those who are not expected to be employed; hence, support is not time-limited. The generosity of disability pension benefits tends to be greater than the support available in tiers one and two.[3]

All industrialized nations have third-tier, pension-type programs that provide financial assistance to working-age individuals with disabilities. Governments face a difficult balancing act in designing their disability benefits programs. They want to ensure that people who cannot work because of their health do not fall into poverty, while at the same time not creating undue incentives for the healthy to retire early by offering generous benefits.

In all nations, in order to secure benefits, workers are required to meet established eligibility standards concerning the extent of the disabling condition and the implication of the condition for successful participation in the labor market. The benefits from these disability pension programs offset the income loss due to the inability of the worker to engage in full-time work.

I have chosen a set of Western, developed countries to illustrate these patterns; they include the Federal Republic of Germany, the Netherlands, Sweden, Australia, the United Kingdom, and the United States. Brief descriptions of the basic characteristics of the income support programs targeted on workers with disabilities are presented in the next part.

A review of the disability-related programs across these countries reveals the following:

- Most of these nations have a first-tier universal needs-based cash transfer program providing social minimum income support to all working-age citizens. For some of the nations, such basic income support is limited

[3] Burkhauser, Daly, and Ziebarth (2015) provide a more full-bodied discussion of the typical three-tier structure of social protection policies.

to people with specific characteristics; for example, in the United States, minimum income support through the Supplemental Security Income program (SSI) is available to the aged and people with disabilities who do not qualify for pension-type benefits or in conjunction with pension-type benefits for the severely poor.

- All of the nations have a cash income support program providing assistance to workers who become unemployed. Typically, these unemployment benefit programs are funded by a payroll tax paid by both workers and employers. The generosity of the benefits varies widely among the countries, as does the period of time for which support is available.
- The extent and generosity of sickness benefits varies widely across the nations. All of the countries except the United States offer some form of sickness benefit.[4] In most of the countries, receipt of sickness benefits is a gateway to the receipt of disability pension benefits.
- All of the countries have well-developed and long-standing disability pension programs that provide income support to working-age people with serious health conditions. Some of the nations (e.g., the United States) provide support only to workers who are totally disabled, while other nations provide support to workers who are totally and partially disabled. The benefit levels (relative to average wages) vary substantially across these programs.
- All of these nations have well-defined rules that determine whether applicants for support are eligible for public full-and partial disability-related income support. The stringency of these rules varies substantially across the nations, as does their application.

Table 1 indicates the substantial variation in the disability and sickness income support programs across the six countries. For each country, the percentage of the working-age and the older (ages 60-64 years) population receiving disability and sickness benefits is shown in column 2. The percentage of the working-age population that receives disability benefits varies from a low of 3 percent in Germany to about 7.5 percent in Sweden (Burkhauser, Daly, and Ziebarth 2015; Burkhauser et al. 2014).[5] Column 3 gives some insight into the extent to which older working-age people (ages 50-64) are receiving benefits from the disability

4 The United States does not have a general public sickness benefit program but provides paid sick leave to government employees.

5 Statistics on the percentage of the working-age population receiving benefits are from Burkhauser, Daly, and Ziebarth (2015) and Burkhauser et al. (2014).

insurance (DI) program in their country. The percentage of older workers—those aged 50-64—receiving disability benefits is substantially greater than the overall percentages. While about 21.5 percent of the people in this age range receive DI benefits in Sweden, only about 7.5 percent of these older working-age people receive DI benefits in Germany.[6] In the United States, about 10 percent of people of these ages receive disability benefits. Column 4 shows the level of public spending (as a percentage of GDP) devoted to disability-related programs across the countries. Expenditures on disability-related benefits, including sickness benefits, ranges from a low of 1.4 percent of GDP in the United States to 2.9 percent of GDP in the Netherlands.[7] Finally, column 5 shows the growth rate of overall disability pension recipiency across a selection of these countries. The 3.1 percent growth rate for the United States is the highest among the countries shown.[8]

---

6 Data on the percentage of the population aged 50-64 receiving disability benefits taken from Figure 2.A1.2., page 72 of OECD (2010).

7 Data on the percentage of GDP spent on sickness and disability cash benefits is from the OECD Statistics Library, accessed on September 2, 2015.

8 The growth rates were calculated from statistics in the OECD Statistics Library. (See also OECD [2010, figs. 1.1-1.7].)

Table 1: The Disabled Population Receiving Disability Benefits and the Level of Public Spending on Disability-Related Programs				
Country	Percent of working-age population receiving disability benefits	Percent of population aged 50-64 receiving disability benefits	Disability-related public expenditures as a percentage of GDP (2011)	Average Annual Growth in disability benefit recipiency: 1970-final
Federal Republic of Germany	3 percent	7.5 percent	1.3 percent (sickness benefits = 0.3 percent)	-0.93 percent
The Netherlands	6 percent (other disability-related benefits = 2 percent)	15.1 percent	2.9 percent (sickness benefits = 0.9 percent)	2.69 percent
Sweden	7.5 percent	21.5 percent	2.2 percent (sickness benefits = 0.7 percent)	2.30 percent
Australia	5.3 percent	11.5 percent	2.1 percent (sickness benefits = 0.6 percent)	NA
United Kingdom	6 percent	12.0 percent	2.0 percent (sickness benefits = 0.1 percent)	2.08 percent
United States	4.8 percent	10.1 percent	1.4 percent (sickness benefits = 0.2 percent)	3.10 percent

Disability-Related Support Programs in Six Developed, Western Economies

In this subsection, I briefly describe the disability-related income support programs in each of these countries, emphasizing the basic characteristics of the income support programs targeted on workers with disabilities.[9]

Federal Republic of Germany

As do other European nations, Germany provides a social minimum income to all citizens through a universal needs-based cash transfer program. Benefits are funded out of general revenues. In general, beneficiaries of the first tier program

9 Most of these nations also have programs, often tied to the income support programs, which emphasize work, and are designed to encourage and facilitate the labor market connections of the disabled worker. The country-specific descriptions that follow emphasize the disability-related income support programs.

are considered to be able to work. Benefit levels are set nationally and vary based on household size and composition (Burkhauser, Daly, and Ziebarth 2015).

Germany also provides second- and third-tier benefits. Benefits targeted on workers temporarily not working are provided through an unemployment insurance (UI) program funded by a payroll tax; support is available to workers who have been employed for at least 24 months prior to applying. Unemployed workers under the age of 50 are paid benefits for up to 12 months. The duration of benefits for workers older than age 50 increases in steps up to the maximum level of 24 months, which is reached at age 58. Earnings replacement rates vary from 60 percent to 67 percent (SSA 2014; Burkhauser, Daly, and Ziebarth 2015).

Third-tier benefits in Germany include the sickness benefits program, the Statutory Old-Age Pension Scheme (OAP) and the Work Disability Pension (WDP) for both partially and totally disabled workers. Full- or part-time employees who become unfit for work due to sickness, have 100 percent of their net wages paid by their employer for six weeks. If the sickness spell continues, workers are evaluated for access to long-term sickness benefits that replace 70 percent of net wages for an additional 78 weeks during a period of three years.[10]

The WDP disability pension program pays benefits to workers who have paid into the system during their work life. Similar to UI, employers and employees are each subject to a payroll tax—9.45 percent of the monthly gross wage up to the social insurance contribution ceiling. In 2014, total WDP benefits paid per month were about €11 billion, or about 4 percent of total OAP/WDP spending (Burkhauser, Daly, and Ziebarth 2015).

The entry into the disability pension program is typically through the receipt of sickness benefits. Upon the exhaustion of sickness benefits, workers can apply for WDP benefits. They must present documentation of continued health problems that require them to work less than six hours per day. If it is determined that they are able work between three and six hours per day, they receive partial disability benefits. If the worker is able to work no more than three hours per day, he/she is awarded a full disability pension (Burkhauser, Daly, and Ziebarth 2015; OECD 2010; SSA 2014).

---

[10] See Burkhauser, Daly, and Ziebarth (2015) for a discussion of the benefit programs in the three tiers.

There are about 80,000 partial WDP beneficiaries; their annual average cash benefit equals about €6,000. There are nearly 1.3 million full WDP beneficiaries and their average annual benefit received is about €8,700 (Burkhauser, Daly, and Ziebarth 2015; OECD 2010; SSA 2015). WDP beneficiaries total about 3 percent of the working-age population. OECD estimates that, in 2011, public spending on incapacity was 1.3 percent of GDP (OECD 2015).

The Netherlands

As in Germany, the Netherlands has a social minimum benefit program for disabled adults with little or no work history. This categorical disability-based welfare program is not means tested. The Netherlands also offers social insurance programs that protect workers against lost labor earnings if disabled.

The Dutch sickness benefit program mandates that employers provide 70 percent wage replacement to employees too sick to work for up to two years. Collective bargaining agreements often raise the replacement rate to 100 percent (Burkhauser et al. 2014).

The main disability benefit program (WAO/WIA) distinguishes between fully and partially disabled workers.[11] Those who are fully disabled receive guaranteed income until age 65; the benefits paid to the partially disabled depend upon their work history and level of incapacity as determined by medical providers. Fully disabled workers covered by the program have 75 percent of their daily wage covered by public benefits. The programs are supported by employer contributions (Burkhauser et al. 2014; Prinz and Tompson 2009; Van Sonsbeek and Gradus 2011; OECD 2010; SSA 2014).

Currently, about 6 percent of the working-age population, or about 650,000 people, receives disability pension benefits. When all disability related programs are taken into account, the percentage increases to about 8 percent, or about 850,000 individuals. OECD estimates that public spending on incapacity was 2.9 percent of GDP in 2011 (OECD 2015).

Sweden

---

[11] A worker is judged to be fully and permanently disabled if his/her earning capacity is less than 20 percent of former earnings. Partial disability benefits are paid to workers younger than age 65 with assessed disabilities prohibit them from earning 79 percent of former earnings.

As in Germany and the Netherlands, Sweden has a three-tier social benefit structure. At the base is a public and universal needs-based cash transfer program providing a social minimum income guarantee to all residents. Applicants are required to specify the reason for seeking support; disability, parental needs, or old age are all options.

The second tier of the income support system is the unemployment insurance benefits program. The mandatory component of the program is supported by employers and replaces a minimum fraction of wages for covered workers for at least six months. A voluntary unemployment insurance program also exists and covers most workers; benefits in this program reflect negotiations between firms and trade unions. Swedish residents can also privately purchase unemployment insurance.

The third tier of income support benefits in Sweden includes national social insurance programs providing pensions for retired and disabled workers. These programs are financed by statutory employer and employee contributions. Collectively bargained occupational-based insurance and pension programs supported by employers are also available to many Swedish workers. Sickness benefits are available for the first 14 days of illness, with a doctor's approval. Workers are required to periodically document their health problems.

Two forms of disability income support are available to those judged by program administrators to have permanent reductions in work capacity. The first is a universally guaranteed pension which provides assistance to all those residing in Sweden; the second provides an earnings related pension in which benefits depend on weeks of work and past earnings (Burkhauser, Daly, and Ziebarth 2015; OECD 2010).

About 450,000 people receive a disability-related pension, which is about 7.5 percent of the working-age population. OECD estimates that public spending on incapacity was 2.2 percent of GDP in 2011(OECD 2015).

Australia

Australia has a sickness benefit program, the Sickness Allowance program. To be eligible, a worker must be judged unable to work or study full-time because of a temporary medical condition, illness, or injury. Eligibility also requires a job to return to; if a full-time student is on public support, the applicant must return to full-time study upon recovery. The program covers Australian citizens between age 21 and the pension age.

Australia's disability income support program—the Disability Support Pension (DSP)—is basically a universal, means-tested guaranteed income benefit program available to all workers with disabilities over the age of 16. As such, it is both a tier one benefit program and a disability pension program. An eligible worker must be determined to have a physical, intellectual, or psychiatric impairment with a severe impact on his/her ability to function. Severity is determined as an inability to work at least 15 hours per week in a minimum-wage job for at least two years.

The benefits provided do not reflect past earnings, and benefits are available even if the worker has not contributed to the funds that support benefit payments. Hence, the Australian program is not a typical social insurance program. Benefits in the program exceed those in the welfare and unemployment insurance programs. Overall, benefits are substantially less generous than those in Sweden, the Netherlands, or Germany (Burkhauser, Daly, and Ziebarth 2015; OECD 2010; SSA 2015).

Recipients total about 5.3 percent of the working age population. OECD estimates that public spending on incapacity was 2.1 percent of GDP in 2011 (OECD 2015).

United Kingdom

Great Britain, like the other European countries, provides first-tier benefits through its universal, needs-based income support program, the Supplementary Benefits program. The central program in the second tier is the Unemployment Benefit program for those expected to work.

Starting in the 1970s, Great Britain established the third-tier Invalidity Benefit program (IVB) designed to provide social insurance-type benefits to working-age people with disabilities. Workers with sufficient social insurance contributions (made while employed) whose physical or mental health condition kept them from working in their usual occupation were deemed eligible for income support through the IVB program. They established eligibility via their family doctor, who certified the nature of their condition. If they met these conditions they first received a Sickness Benefit (which lasted for 28 weeks) through the IVB, followed by IVB disabled worker payments. The income support payments exceeded the benefits paid in the unemployment insurance program. In addition, some recipients with long work histories were provided an additional subsidy related to the level of their market earnings. Even for these workers, the replacement rate was lower than those in the other western-European programs (Burkhauser et al. 2014; OECD 2010; SSA 2015).

Workers with insufficient contributions to the social insurance program who established eligibility for disability income support had their social insurance contributions paid by the IVB program, and were then provided lower, first-tier Supplementary Benefits payments.

This basic program structure, though modified over time in several ways,[12] stood until 2008. In 2008, the Employment and Support Allowance (ESA) program replaced the disability pension program that had evolved from the IVB program. Like the original IVB program, the ESA also provided a social insurance-type benefit for those with sufficiently long work histories and means-tested benefits for those without sufficient work history. However, the process of establishing eligibility for benefits was greatly tightened, and the emphasis was directed toward work-related activities. In the new work assessment program, workers must be judged to have "limited capacity to work" based upon a numerical scoring system, i.e. scoring 15 or more points on a points-based assessment of physical and mental capabilities.[13]

OECD estimates that public spending on incapacity was 2 percent of GDP in 2011. About 6 percent of the working age population receives disability-related income support. Over 1.8 million people are benefit recipients (OECD 2015).

United States

Unlike the European countries, the United States has neither a universal needs-based cash transfer program nor a mandated sickness benefit program. The nation's only long-term needs-based cash transfer program is the Supplemental Security Income (SSI) program, which is limited to the aged, disabled adults, and parents of disabled children. The Temporary Assistance for Needy Families (TANF) program is the successor to the Aid to Families with Dependent Children

12 For example, in 1995 the IVB program was replaced by the Invalidity Benefits program (IB). This change reduced the level of income support, raised the bar for establishing ability to work, and tightened the process through which eligibility was determined.

13 See Morris (2015) for a detailed description of this process. See also Adam, Bozio, and Emmerson (2010).

(AFDC) program and provides needs-based cash transfers to single mothers at a benefit level lower than the SSI program. Support is limited to five years, and efforts to secure employment are required.

The second tier of benefit programs in the United States includes unemployment insurance which provides wage replacement for 26 weeks (which is often extended during recessionary periods, reaching 99 weeks after the onset of the Great Recession).

The Social Security Old-Age and Survivors' Insurance retirement (OASI) and disability (SSDI) programs constitute the third tier of benefits, and provide social insurance benefits to workers who have contributed to the programs over their working lives through payment of Social Security taxes. To qualify for OASI and SSDI benefits, workers must have accumulated quarters of coverage representing substantial attachment to the work force. Benefits paid are based on past earnings and are higher than the benefits guaranteed by the SSI aged and disability programs.

The SSDI program provides benefits to workers who meet a federal disability standard. State-based administrative evaluators and adjudicators make a determination of eligibility. Eligibility requires that a worker be "unable to perform any substantial gainful activity on any job in the economy for at least one year." The United States has no disability-related program that provides support in case of a partially disabling condition (Burkhauser, Daly, and Ziebarth 2015; OECD 2010; SSA 2014; Burkhauser et al. 2014).

In 2011, 10.6 million people collected SSDI benefits, up from 7.2 million in 2002. The share of the US working-age (ages 25-64) population receiving SSDI benefits stood at about 4.8 percent. In 2013, the average monthly disability payment was $1,146, or about $14,000 per year.[14] OECD estimates that public spending on incapacity was 1.4 percent of GDP in 2011 (OECD 2015).

RECENT TRENDS IN DISABILITY POLICY ACROSS SELECTED DEVELOPED COUNTRIES

The structure of public support provided to working-age people with disabilities varies widely across nations. These different approaches reflect different values

[14] http://ssa.gov/policy/docs/statcomps/di_asr/2013/sect01b.html Accessed September 1, 2015.

and disparate assessments of the economic gains and costs assigned to alternative approaches to assisting the population with disabilities.

For example, public policies supporting people with disabilities are used to provide better economic outcomes for these people. Income support and rehabilitation policies are the natural responses to this desire to help people with disabilities. However, cash transfer programs, like income replacement programs, also produce work disincentives and impose increased costs on the rest of the economy. These costs lead to initiatives that would correct the market distortions, such as measures to reduce the private costs of hiring people with disabilities and to increase the possibility that people with disabilities would find and hold a job. Proposals for direct job creation programs, such as employment subsidies, the subsidization of private sector efforts to adapt workplaces, and quotas for hiring people with disabilities reflect this emphasis. An equal access rationale supports antidiscrimination laws for workers with disabilities designed to guarantee equal access to employment, education, and mobility.

The nations with the most comprehensive approach to the population with disabilities—Denmark, the Netherlands, Switzerland, Finland, Germany, Norway, and Sweden—tend to have universal benefit programs that provide generous financial support. These nations also tend to have a relatively low threshold for determining the presence of disabling conditions, though such thresholds have been increasing in recent years. Most of these countries also tend to have a broad, accessible employment integration policy with a strong focus on rehabilitation.

A second set of countries, including the United States, Canada, United Kingdom, Japan, Korea, Australia, and New Zealand, also have an extensive set of programs supporting people with disabilities. However, the benefits paid are relatively low and the criteria for establishing disability tend to be rather strict. For example, in assessing the work capacity of applicants for benefits, authorities may assess an individual's capabilities relative to *any* job rather that the applicant's usual occupation. Rehabilitation efforts tend to be modest and direct incentives to work are evident in only some of the countries.

Many of the nations have programs that are intermediate to those in the first two categories in terms of generosity, eligibility leniency, and rehabilitation. In general, the policies that characterize this set of countries—including Austria,

Belgium, Hungary, France, Luxembourg, Ireland, Italy, and Spain—also tend to have fewer work incentives and more limited coverage of the population.[15]

In this section, we present an overview of recent efforts to reform public policy toward people with disabilities across these OECD nations, recognizing the wide disparities in their policy approaches toward working-age people with disabilities.[16] In the next section, we discuss the nature of these policy changes in a selection of Western, developed economies, including Germany, Sweden, the Netherlands, Australia, the United Kingdom, and the United States.

Over the past decade, reform in disability pension programs has taken many forms, but in most cases policy changes have been concentrated on disability pension policies. These changes have focused on reducing the rate of disability beneficiary status while simultaneously encouraging continued labor market work for those with disabilities. While nations have sought to attain these goals in different ways, two major thrusts have dominated policy changes:

1. Creating incentives to encourage rehabilitation, accommodation, and continued employment.
2. Tightening both the level of and access to disability pension benefits.

Employment and Rehabilitation Measures

Over past decades, nearly all developed countries have established policies designed to encourage people with disabilities to remain in or re-enter the workforce. Most of these policies are tied to disability benefit program reform. Vocational rehabilitation efforts seek to restore and develop the skills and capabilities of people with disabilities increasing their productivity and participation in the workforce (OECD 2010).

Early rehabilitation efforts have played an important role in Germany, Sweden, the Netherlands, and the United Kingdom. Sweden has imposed workplace accommodation requirements on employers, also for new job applicants. In

---

[15] These categories of policy approaches to people with disabilities rest upon distinctions made in OECD (2010, 88). There these approaches were referred to as the 'Social Democratic model', the 'Liberal model', and the 'Corporatist model'.

[16] The discussion of the various reform measures across countries in this section draws heavily from OECD (2010, 78-84). Discussion of reforms in a more limited set of countries is found in Burkhauser, Daly, and Ziebarth (2015) and Burkhauser et al. (2014).

the Netherlands, employers are required to undertake efforts to reintegrate sick employees into the workplace. In line with their obligation to provide sickness benefits for two years (described above), employers are also responsible for retraining over this period (OECD 2010). Other countries have also emphasized early rehabilitation efforts. In Austria, provision for vocational rehabilitation became compulsory in 1996; claims for disability benefits are treated as an application for rehabilitation. Hungary, too, has introduced a "rehabilitation-before-benefit" principle, allowing workers with disabilities to transition into the disability benefit program only if there is no potential for rehabilitation. Switzerland has gone a step further, and is moving towards a rehabilitation-instead-of-benefits principle, requiring applicants to fulfill explicit rehabilitation obligations before receiving benefits, with sanctions for noncompliance. Several countries, including Sweden and the United Kingdom, have brought forward the assessment process to ensure that rehabilitation is much closer to disability onset (when return to work is more likely).

Several countries have focused on ***strengthening employer incentives*** to keep sick people or people with disabilities in work. Both the Netherlands and Sweden have merged their sickness and disability programs, since a key driver of beneficiary inflows was from workers who take extended sick leave. As described above, employers in the Netherlands pay sickness benefits for up to two years, and a third year of benefit support is required if it is found that insufficient efforts have been made to reintegrate sick workers into the workforce. In some countries including the Netherlands, Finland, Canada, and Switzerland, employer contributions to social insurance depend upon the number of their workers that lodge disability claims ("experience rating"), providing a strong an incentive for employers to maintain and rehabilitate workers with disabilities.

The focus on controlling access to disability benefits through receiving sickness benefits has also led to ***stricter sickness absence monitoring*** in a number of countries. Danish municipalities have been given increased incentive to rigorously monitor worker absence because of sickness and to introduce early intervention efforts. Spain has established an agency charged with monitoring absence rates, and thereby reducing them. Both the Netherlands and Sweden have provided general practitioners with detailed medical guidelines to be used in granting sick-leave certificates. These measures seek to ensure that sick workers return to work as soon as feasible (OECD 2010).

Other countries including the Netherlands have ***turned partial benefits into work payments*** rather than passive income support. In 2006, the Netherlands instituted an employer-based wage supplement for workers with partial work capacity if they work a sufficient number of hours. The objective of the wage subsidy is to change labor costs in favor of workers with disabilities, so as to increase the demand for them. Several countries including Belgium and Denmark have abolished partial benefit schemes due to their high costs, and instead provide an in-work subsidy which covers the difference between the wage a person was receiving before the onset of disability and their new wage. Denmark subsidizes the wages of workers with disabilities who are not able to perform their work under normal conditions; the subsidies are available only after rehabilitation efforts have been exhausted (OECD 2010). Others, such as Australia, Germany, the United Kingdom, and Norway have also sought to link disability and other benefit programs with work requirements, encouraging the enforcement of such requirements.

Many countries, including the United Kingdom and Germany, have also ***increased the emphasis on work capacity in addition to medical injury in the eligibility determination process***. Since 2003, Denmark began assessing a person's functional capabilities and the tasks the person can perform in determining eligibility for income support.

Tightening Benefit Compensation Policy

A number of developed countries have reduced the access to benefits in recent decades, but few countries have actually reduced benefit payments; the Netherlands and Denmark are exceptions. Access to benefits by new applicants has been restricted through tighter eligibility criteria or more rigorous application of them. A focus of these efforts is increasing the effectiveness of the monitoring of the sickness absence phase, which often leads to the receipt of long-term disability benefits.

One way to restrict access to disability benefits is to ***increase the minimum level of incapacity*** required to gain eligibility for benefits. Australia (along with the Netherlands, Italy, and Luxembourg) has followed this strategy. In Australia, eligibility was changed by increasing from 15 to 30 the number of hours per week that the partially disabled worker was capable of working. In the Netherlands, the minimum earnings capacity loss necessary to qualify for disability benefits was increased from 15 percent to 35 percent.

Another approach has been to ***centralize medical assessment***, assigning responsibility for assessing capability to government agencies instead of family doctors. The goal is to make medical assessments more objective by reducing the reliance on judgments by a diverse range of family medical practitioners. The United Kingdom has embraced this approach most strongly. Spain, New Zealand, and Switzerland have recently tightened the application of medical assessments by assigning the responsibility for disability determination to personnel employed by the public sector rather than the doctors of benefit applicants (OECD 2010).

Other countries have introduced ***more stringent vocational criteria*** into the determinations process, often by expanding the range of jobs taken into account in determining eligibility. The Netherlands, for example, requires applicants to demonstrate that they are unable to do any theoretically available job in order to receive benefits. The United Kingdom also moved to assess work capacity based on an applicant's ability to do any work, rather than just their usual occupation. Germany implemented such a change for younger workers, but insured workers older than 40 years have their capabilities compared to the norms of their own occupations.

There has also been a shift toward ***providing temporary, rather than permanent benefits***. Germany (as well as Austria and Poland) has moved from a situation where benefits were permanent (with no robust reassessment) to making them temporary, except in the case of a full disability. In Poland, benefits are awarded for a three-year period, after which recipients must reapply and be reassessed. In practice, moving to a temporary benefits system requires some form of reassessment after a set period of time; countries have adopted quite different approaches to handling this reassessment.

A number of countries have attempted to ***increase the work incentives*** for disability benefit recipients. In the United Kingdom, for example, a special working tax credit and a temporary earnings subsidy were introduced to increase the take-home earnings of labor market work. Similarly, the Netherlands offers a wage subsidy for partially or temporarily disabled people who perform market work. Other countries have increased work incentives by enabling people with disabilities to combine work and disability benefit receipt, often through an "earnings disregard" benefit structure. The Nordic countries (Sweden, Norway, Denmark, Finland) and Canada enable workers with disabilities to put their awarded benefit on hold while they try to succeed in employment; no reassessment is required to return to benefit status.

Improving Institutional Arrangements

In several countries, the expansion of employment measures has been accompanied by changes in the structure of service provision. Financing mechanisms have also been strengthened by providing incentives to public authorities and service providers for encouraging work by those with disabilities (OECD 2010).

Some countries have moved toward a ***one-stop-shop model*** for benefit and service provision for people with a disability. In Australia, one agency determines disability payment eligibility and provides benefit payments for disability and unemployment, along with a range of government support services. A new customer-oriented UK agency coordinates employment arrangements and benefits advice for people of working age. New Zealand and Norway have also attempted to move toward this coordinated model in which income support and employment assistance is provided by a single agency.

In a related policy change, some countries have attempted to provide ***stronger incentives for benefit authorities*** to assist those with partial work capacity to become employed. Denmark, for example, pays higher reimbursement rates to local governments (which are responsible for employment support and benefit grants) if they provide effective employment supports; the hope is that with the higher rates, local governments will have an interest in avoiding benefit payments. In a similar but less developed way, Dutch municipalities are rewarded if they can demonstrate improved utilization of the work-related programs available to their clients.

A more recent development in some countries—Australia, the Netherlands, and the United Kingdom, for example—is a shift toward ***outcome-based funding*** of employment services. With such a policy, service providers are reimbursed only for the actual employment or participation outcomes delivered (OECD 2010).

DISABILITY POLICY REFORMS IN SELECTED DEVELOPED COUNTRIES

This section describes the nature of recent changes in disability policy in five developed nations—Germany, Sweden, the Netherlands, Australia, and the United Kingdom. Germany, Sweden, and the Netherlands have been characterized by OECD as conforming to a Social Democratic model; Australia and the United

Kingdom are thought of as conforming to the Liberal model.[17] These countries have been the focus of our earlier discussion of disability policy in the third section. These country-specific descriptions draw heavily from Burkhauser, Daly, and Ziebarth 2015; Burkhauser et al. 2014; and OECD 2010.

Germany

Germany, like most European nations, has a needs-based program of assistance that provides a guaranteed minimum income to all citizens. Benefit levels are set nationally and vary based on household size and composition. Beneficiaries are considered to be able to work at least three hours per day and are counted as part of the workforce. Beginning in 2004, the program imposed job search and job training requirements on beneficiaries.

As described in the third section, Germany also has a generous unemployment benefits program paying benefits for up to 12 months with extensive work experience (up to 24 months for workers who are at least 50 years old when becoming unemployed). Benefits range from 60 to 67 percent of average monthly wage earnings over the prior year.

Workers in Germany are also eligible for sickness benefits that pay between 70 and 100 percent of their net wages. Those benefits are provided by employers, and receiving the sickness benefit is often the first step toward receipt of a disability pension.

As discussed in the third section, partially and totally disabled workers who have contributed to the payroll tax supporting the program during their working life are covered by the Statutory Old-Age Pension Scheme (OAP) and the Work Disability Pension (WDP).

Starting in the early-1970s, policy changes to expand eligibility for WDP benefits resulted in an increase in the prevalence of disability pension receipt. As a result, during this period Germany had among the highest recipiency rates of any of the countries shown in Table 1. One reason for this higher rate was a change in WDP rules in 1969 that allowed partially disabled workers to receive full WDP benefits if they could demonstrate an inability to find a job. Further expansions in 1972 extended coverage to housewives and the self-employed and allowed workers with disabilities to transition to the retirement program at age 62 without

[17] See OECD (2010, 88).

an actuarial reduction in benefits. Both of these measures contributed to the rapid growth in disability recipiency throughout the 1970s. By 1984, 5.8 percent of the working-age population received disability pensions.

After 1984, in response to the rise in beneficiaries and program cost, Germany tightened the criteria for gaining coverage. The number of years of market work experience required to gain coverage was increased, reducing access to program benefits for women not working in the paid labor market.

Additional changes were made in the 1990s and 2000s. In 1996, caps on the earnings of WDP beneficiaries were introduced to reduce the inflow of (primarily male) workers into the program by about one-half. In 2001, another round of structural WDP changes occurred, principally an increase in the standard for being declared "work limited" from the occupation in the last job (or a job comparable to it) to being unable to work in any available job. WDP changes in 2004 continued to focus on reducing the flow of new recipients into the program, largely by promoting worker accommodation on the job. Employers were required to provide reintegration to the job in the case of a work-limiting impairment. The goal was to keep impaired workers on the job and off the WDP roles.

In sum, the early expansion of coverage and generosity of the German program resulted in both a high level of recipiency and rapid program growth. Subsequent reforms limited access, made benefits less attractive, and mandated that employers undertake reintegration activities. These changes resulted in a decrease in disability benefit recipiency rates over the past four decades.

^ ^ ^

Prior to reform efforts beginning in the 1980s, Germany had one of the most generous and inclusive sickness and disability benefit systems among the countries studied; recipiency rates were high and rising. In response, a series of restrictive reforms were introduced, including:

- The number of years of required market work was increased to gain coverage (reducing access to previously covered nonworkers including housewives) (mid-1980s)
- A cap on the earnings of disability pension recipients was imposed (reducing substantially the number of new male recipients) (mid-1990s)

- Eligibility for coverage was tightened (from being work-limited in the last or comparable job to any job in the economy); employers were required to provide rehabilitation and reintegration services for workers experiencing work limitation (early and mid-2000s)

The Netherlands

As in most northern European nations, one disability pension system supports the income of workers with health impairments while a second program provides minimum benefits for those with insufficient work history. The Dutch disability pension program (WAO/WIA) provides benefits for both partially and fully disabled workers. The benefits provided are related to the extent of lost earnings due to the health impairment. Conversely, the welfare-type program targeting people with disabilities without sufficient work history provides a social minimum level of income support. The Dutch disability pension program grew rapidly over the decade of the 1970s, largely because of a high level of wage replacement. The Dutch sickness benefit program—the gateway to the receipt of disability benefits—covers up to 80 percent of lost earnings for up to a year. In addition, sick workers received additional income support through agreements bargained with their employers. After receiving a year of sickness benefits, workers whose health kept them from working in a job consistent with their training or experience were eligible to receive disability pension benefits. Benefits paid to those viewed as fully disabled were equal to 80 percent of their net earnings; those who were partially disabled received benefits commensurate with their impairment with a minimum of 15 percent of wage replacement (Burkhauser, Daly, and Ziebarth 2015).

Legal developments also contributed to the rapid growth. In the 1970s, court decisions required those responsible for evaluating disability status to find that discrimination caused the absence of work for those found to be partially disabled. As a result of these rulings, it became standard practice to classify partially disabled workers without employment as being fully disabled. Those rulings effectively eliminated the designation of partial disability. The combination of relatively high benefit payments and the effective elimination of partial disability benefits explained the high (11 percent) growth rate of disability recipiency in the Netherlands during the 1970s (Burkhauser, Daly, and Ziebarth 2015). This rapid growth in recipiency and costs led to changes in the Dutch disability pension system in the early 1980s. By the mid-1980s, the level of benefits relative to wages was reduced from 80 percent to 70 percent. Although the "discrimination rule" was eliminated, most of those granted a disability pension were awarded full benefits. Moreover, the percentage of applicants denied benefits remained low. The rate of growth in recipiency and cost was lower in the 1980s than in the 1970s (Burkhauser, Daly, and Ziebarth 2015). In recent years, the Netherlands has reoriented its approach to sickness and disability income support by placing more responsibility on firms. In 1994, eligibility criteria were further tightened. Firms were required to cover the sickness benefits of workers for the first six weeks; in 1996 this was extended to one year, and in the early-2000s to two years. In addition, firms were required to follow rather fixed procedures in assisting the rehabilitation or accommodation of workers. This deliberate shift toward employer responsibility for accommodation and rehabilitation relieved the demands on the disability pension program.

In 2002, a third phase of reforms was initiated in Holland. The disability pension program (WAO) was replaced in 2004 by a new scheme—the Work and Income Act (WIA). Work rather than benefit receipt was viewed as the norm and even greater incentives were provided both workers and firms to provide accommodation and rehabilitation to workers with health limitations. These changes represented a fundamental change in Dutch disability policy (Burkhauser, Daly, and Ziebarth 2015).

With these work-orientation mandates in place, workers with limitations had to wait for two years before applying for a disability pension. Upon application, they were required to provide detailed documentation of efforts to gain employment during the prior two years. The rate of benefit denial increased, and employers continued to be responsible for the worker's support until a job was found or the application accepted. Requirements designed to stem the high rate of benefit recipiency were complemented by other changes. A pay-as-you-go rate was imposed on employers to support the disability pension program. In addition, employers were required to pay premiums in support of the first 10 years of benefit receipt based on their experience in employing workers with disabilities.[18] The partial disability program also required employer support, although employers could avoid this cost if they enrolled their workers in a private disability insurance program (Burkhauser, Daly, and Ziebarth 2015).

Because of these reforms, the Dutch disability system is increasingly viewed as an example for other countries to follow. Researchers suggest that by 2040, these

18 After 10 years, the uniform pay-as-you-go rates that cover the fully and permanently disabled and the stock of current beneficiaries under the old system also cover the partial disability program.

post-2002 policy changes will reduce the number of disability pension recipients by nearly 1 million (van Sonsbeek and Gradus 2011).

^ ^ ^

In recent decades, disability benefit reform in the Netherlands has been triggered by concern over the high and rising disability recipiency rates in the 1970s and early 1980s. The major reforms occurred at three different times and consisted of the following:

- Reduction in replacement rates from 80 percent to 70 percent; attempted tightening of eligibility criterion (mid-1980s)
- Continued tightening of eligibility criteria; assignment to employers of responsibility for first year of sick pay in order to encourage efforts to provide continued employment to workers with illness and other limitations (mid-1990s)
- Employer responsibility for sick pay increased from one to two years; a prescribed list of rehabilitation and accommodation requirements stipulated for firms to provide employee assistance in returning to work or finding a new job; workers required to document their work efforts in order to claim disability benefits after two years on sickness benefits; employers required to pay for the full disability program through a uniform premium payment and for the partial disability program through experience-rated premiums (mid-2000s)

Sweden

As described previously, Sweden, like most European nations, has a base universal means-tested income support program providing an indexed social minimum income floor. Benefits are uniform across the nation and indexed.

Sweden's second-tier program supports covered workers who have lost their jobs or are temporarily laid off. The mandatory part of the program relies on employer payments and replaces a fraction of lost wages. There is also a voluntary unemployment benefits program that is the result of union-firm negotiations. At least six months of income support is provided.

Finally, Sweden has both sickness benefits and a disability benefits programs. Workers with sufficient work history are covered by both programs, which are financed by employer and employee contributions. In addition, many private firms contribute to occupational programs providing disability coverage for employees.

During the 1970s, the Swedish disability pension program grew rapidly, in part due to the attraction of generous benefits and the ease of access to benefits. For example, the sickness benefit program had an earnings replacement rate of about 90 percent for workers experiencing a loss of work capacity of at least 25 percent.

After one year of receipt of sickness benefits, employees experiencing a loss of work capacity greater than 50 percent are able to apply for long-term disability pension benefits. In addition to receiving income support, rehabilitation and vocational training services are provided to workers aged less than 60 years. The earnings replacement rate in the disability benefits program is similar to the generous benefits provided by the sickness program.

During the 1970s, it became possible for a worker to receive disability income support if unemployed for more than one year. In effect, the disability benefit program became a long-term unemployment insurance program offering generous benefits. This change, together with the high earnings replacement rate and the ease of gaining access to benefits, led to continued rapid growth in disability benefit recipiency through the 1980s and into the early 1990s recession.

In the early-1990s, policymakers made adjustments designed to slow the growth of disability program costs and recipients. Employers were first required to pay sickness benefits for the first two weeks of absence from work due to illness; subsequent changes further increased employer costs for worker sickness absence. Moreover, the threshold for gaining access to benefit receipt was increased. In part due to these changes, the size of disability roles stabilized until the 1990s.

In the early 2000s, the reforms begun in the 1990s were accelerated. Taken as a package, these policy changes reflected the decision that public support for work would replace income support in lieu of work. As a first step, the sickness and disability programs were merged in 2003. The screening process was standardized between the two programs, and rehabilitation and vocational training to promote participation in work prior to cash benefit receipt was emphasized. This merger also required that vocational and rehabilitation experts become involved early in the process in an effort to reduce the rate of initial application for long-term disability benefits. Receipt of sickness benefits was limited to one year, and reevaluation of recipients was done every six months. Employers were mandated to cooperate with disability program administrators in creating rehabilitation and training programs. These efforts to emphasize work rather than income support and to tighten access to benefits led to reductions in the prevalence of both sickness and disability benefit receipt.

Further reforms designed to curb increases in sickness and disability program recipiency and costs were undertaken within the past decade. These reforms continued the emphasis on work rather than income support in lieu of work. Additional work incentives were provided to workers with health conditions at the same time that employers were required to accelerate the development of rehabilitation and training plans. Periodic reevaluation of benefit recipients was pursued and the generosity of sickness benefits awarded to those who should have—but did not—return to work. As a result of these changes, increasing numbers of sickness benefit recipients returned to work, and the average time spent in receipt of benefits was reduced.

^ ^ ^

Sweden has undertaken a series of reforms designed to reduce growth in the disability recipiency rate. Many of these changes did not take place until after the turn of the century. There is evidence that these changes reduced beneficiary inflows into the program, and increased return to work for new sickness program entrants. Reforms included:

- The replacement rate in the sickness benefit program was reduced, employers were made responsible for covering the early months of sickness benefits, and the threshold eligibility criteria was increased (1990s)
- The sickness and disability benefit systems were merged in an effort to break the connection between sick absence volumes and inflows onto the disability benefits; work support, rather than income support without work became the driving principle. In addition, the screening process in the two programs was standardized and vocational and rehabilitation personnel became involved earlier. Sickness benefits cease after one year, and beneficiaries are evaluated for work ability after six months of absence from work (early-2000s)
- Employers were required to document the types of accommodation they made for workers; new deadlines for provision of rehabilitation services were set; the extent of work capacity was regularly evaluated while sickness benefits were received; sickness benefit payments for those who should—but did not—return to work were reduced; assessments

of work capacity were performed after 3, 6, and 12 months of sickness benefit receipt (late-2000s)

Australia

Australia's disability income support program—the Disability Support Pension (DSP)—provides a guaranteed minimum income for eligible people with disabilities; the income guarantee exceeds that in the nation's welfare and unemployment benefit programs, but by European standards the replacement rate is not high. Nonetheless, the DSP program is susceptible to substantial growth, as disability benefits tend to exceed those paid in other programs. That the concept of disability on which access to benefits is based is not tightly defined may also encourage growth in both recipients and costs.

While there have been some changes since 1970 in the DSP formula for determining benefits, benefit levels relative to average wages have remained quite constant. However, since 1993, DSP benefits to lower-income workers with disabilities have become somewhat more generous relative to earnings, the minimum wage and other income support payments (e.g., unemployment benefits). However, these changes in program generosity seem insufficient to explain the growth in disability recipiency that has been experienced.

Another candidate to explain the increasing recipiency rate is the pattern of changes in disability eligibility criteria. Research evidence suggests that more rigorous eligibility rules which placed greater emphasis on medical factors rather than socioeconomic considerations explains the small decrease in the number of DSP recipients between 1980 and 1982. However, after 1982 the eligibility criteria were again relaxed (Cai and Gregory 2003).

The most significant increase in the DSP recipiency rate occurred in the 1990s. In the midst of the serious recession in the early 1990s, the DSP eligibility criterion was relaxed. The standard for determining eligibility was decreased from an 85 percent impairment standard to about 25 percent impairment. As a result, the emphasis of the DSP program tended toward a long-term partial disability program rather than a program providing support for workers who were totally disabled. DSP officials were required to determine whether a worker with some disabling conditions (25 percent or less) became unemployed due to the impairments or because of poor macroeconomic conditions.

In the absence of a substantial increase in benefits, it is likely that the large increase in the DSP recipiency rate during the early 1990s is due to this change in the eligibility criterion. DSP provided a higher permanent income floor than benefits in the base welfare program, but with no work requirement.

As the Australian economy expanded after the recession in the early 1990s, growth in DSP recipiency rates slowed. Although Australia did not experience a significant slowdown during the 2001 and 2008 worldwide recessions, DSP recipiency increased during both recessionary periods. Indeed, since 2008, DSP recipiency rates have tended upward despite: a) a major tightening in the eligibility criterion in 2006 (which effectively increased the impairment standard from 25 percent to about 62 percent), and b) abolition of partial disability benefits requiring those with partial work capacity to seek income support through regular unemployment benefits requiring beneficiaries to be actively seeking work. Research studies suggest that the growth in DSP benefit levels relative to both the minimum wage and social minimum benefits in the welfare program explains this growth. The studies also note the role played by the introduction of verifiable job search and participation in active labor market programs requirements in the unemployment and lone parents benefits programs. Those requirements made DSP benefits an increasingly appealing alternative (Cai and Gregory 2003; McVicar and Wilkins 2013). Over the period from 1993 to 2011, receipt of public income support benefits other than DSP by people with a disability fell, while the DSP recipiency rate rose.

^ ^ ^

Over the years, Australia has also made a number of changes to the disability pension program, only a few of which were designed to slow the growth of disability recipiency; these included tightening eligibility criterion and shifting partially disabled recipients onto the unemployment rolls. Several policy changes, however, have encouraged access to disability pension benefits. As a result, since 1970, the growth in Australia's disability recipiency rate was the largest among the countries studied, save for the United States.

United Kingdom

Over the past four decades, the United Kingdom has substantially changed its social insurance and social welfare cash transfer programs. In 1971, basic minimum benefits were provided through the Supplementary Benefit program. The Unemployment Benefit program provided somewhat higher benefits for those expected to work. Between 1971 and 1995, the Invalidity Benefit (IVB) program was the primary source of income support for working age people with disabilities (Burkhauser et al. 2014). People of working age who suffered ill health or were disabled and hence found unable to work in their usual occupation (as determined by the family doctor) and who had sufficient work history were eligible, first for Sickness Benefit (the first 28 weeks) and then for IVB. For longer-duration recipients, IVB paid a benefit which was more generous than unemployment benefits. However, the disability benefit replacement rates paid were considerably below those in northern European countries including Sweden or the Netherlands. These policies existed throughout the 1970s and early 1980s, when the disability recipiency rate grew steadily.

A number of major changes in the 1980s contributed both positively and negatively to IVB recipiency rates. The introduction of Statutory Sick Pay in 1983 required that employers pay the first eight weeks of sickness benefits; in 1986, that was extended to 28 weeks. The resulting shift of costs to employers likely reduced many short-duration claims for sickness benefits. And, because receipt of sickness benefits is an access route to disability pension payments, this change also had a negative effect on IVB benefit claims.

Recessions in the early 1980s and early 1990s and the rapid shift from heavy industry towards services during the same period acted to increase disability recipiency. The growth in the IVB program in the late 1980s and early 1990s suggests that it served as a form of hidden employment. Unemployed workers with health-related impairments who faced a depressed labor market tended to apply for IVB benefits after they exhausted their support from the unemployment benefit program (Burkhauser et al. 2014).

In the late-1980s, long-term unemployment benefits claimants were required to have work-focused interviews, reducing the attractiveness of this source of public support. Studies suggest that moves from unemployment benefit support to IVB resulted in an increase in disability recipiency rates. At the same time, it became possible for those who claimed social minimum welfare benefits on grounds of disability to receive a higher benefit than those claiming support on other grounds. Those claiming benefits because of disability were counted in the disability recipiency rate, which also contributed to the increase (OECD 2010).

By the mid-1990s, the growth in disability recipiency rates slowed. At that time, the IVB program was replaced by the Incapacity Benefit (IB) program. The new program (IB) was less generous than IVB, and tightened eligibility requirements.

Government doctors rather than family doctors were assigned responsibility for medical screening. The threshold to gain benefits through the screening was also raised; a claimant now had to be assessed as unable to perform work of any sort, rather than work in their usual occupation. Further, in 1999 a form of means test was introduced for new claimants with substantial private pension income (even though they had a sufficient work history). At about the same time, the requirements for receiving unemployment benefits were tightened, and generosity was reduced. Both of these factors contributed to the slower growth in the costs and recipients of disability benefits.

In the mid-2000s, a new set of work-first reforms was introduced in order to further reduce inflows to the disability benefit rolls and to increase outflows. They made it mandatory for those who claimed disability-based support to attend work-focused interviews designed to steer at least some recipients back into the labor market. This move was supported by the introduction of a bonus paid for return to employment and the provision of additional in-work health support for those who did find work. Finally, medical assessments were now made earlier into the IB claim. Evaluation evidence suggests that these changes contributed to reduced disability recipiency rates (OECD 2010; Adam, Bozio, and Emmerson 2010).

Indeed, the number of disability recipients has continued to decline since the mid-2000s, in spite of the high unemployment that accompanied the 2008 financial crisis. Additional IB reforms undertaken in recent years supported this trend. In 2008, the Employment and Support Allowance (ESA) program replaced the IB program. This program provided both an insurance-based pension benefit for workers with disabilities with sufficient work history and a means-tested social assistance benefit for those without. The disabled worker program included a new tougher Work Capability Assessment, with relatively few exemptions. Engaging in a work-related activity was required for all but those who were disabled; benefits for about one quarter of beneficiaries were available only if they complied with this requirement. Also, payment of a higher benefit for longer-duration claims was abandoned. These changes decreased the role of disability income support programs as an alternative to unemployment benefits. Finally, between 2009 and 2013, the eligibility of existing IB recipients was reassessed using the new and more rigorous eligibility standards. As a result, many recipients have been judged ineligible, leading to both appeals (many of which were successful) and migration onto the unemployment benefits program.

^ ^ ^

In summary, the United Kingdom has undertaken several policy changes designed to reduce the growth of disability recipiency rates. These included:

- Additional employer responsibility for sickness benefits was required (mid-1980s)
- Benefit generosity was reduced and the medical requirements necessary to gain benefit eligibility were tightened; assessments are to be done by program doctors rather than family doctors (1995)
- Disability benefit claimants were required to attend work-focused interviews designed to encourage reemployment; a "back-to-work" bonus payment was introduced; medical assessments were required earlier in the period of benefit receipt, occurring at three months into the claim rather than six months (mid-2000s)
- Applicants were assessed on the basis of their capacity to carry out any work rather than being employed in their usual occupation; work-related activities were required for all but severely disabled (late-2000s).

LESSONS FROM ABROAD FOR IMPROVING THE U.S. DISABILITY SYSTEM

As our review has shown, countries have adopted several reforms to their disability pension systems in order to better manage the number of recipients and the costs of the programs. Overall, the results in terms of restraining the recipient rolls and the costs have been mixed. Although rigorous evaluations are scarce, the evidence suggests that slowing the inflow of people with disabilities onto the rolls is much more successful than efforts to wean recipients off the rolls and back into the labor market.

In many of the countries studied, but not in the United States, two disability program characteristics exist that facilitate management of the caseload. These are: a) a public sickness benefits program (which typically serves as the gateway into disability pension receipt), and b) support provided to people who are partially disabled (as opposed to totally and permanently disabled, as in the United States). As a result, early intervention (e.g., rehabilitation and reintegration) and stricter monitoring of work absence through the sickness benefits program are not available in the United States. Because SSDI requires total and permanent disability, the conversion of partial disability benefits into payments for work is also not possible.

Across the countries studied, a number of options to better manage the disability pension caseload—aside from reforms to the public sickness benefit programs—have been pursued; these include:

- The introduction of more stringent vocational criteria into the eligibility determination process, e.g., in determining ability to work, moving from reference to jobs in the worker's own occupation or jobs for which the worker has been trained to all jobs in the economy.
- The centralization of disability assessment. Instead of relying on an applicant's own doctors, responsibility for assessing capability has been assigned to government agencies. The goal is to make medical assessments more objective and consistent over applicants.
- Increasing the emphasis on work capacity itself relative to medical conditions in the eligibility determination process. (For example, in the US system, a physical and mental Listing of Impairments has been established to identify conditions considered sufficiently severe to prevent an individual from performing any gainful activity.)
- Changing the emphasis in the disability pension program toward a "rehabilitation before benefits" model involving the requirement that benefit applicants have undertaken rehabilitation efforts, as well as requiring employers to pursue workplace accommodation.
- Substituting for the current uniform payroll tax obligations an arrangement in which employer contributions to social insurance depend upon the number of their workers that apply for disability benefits ("experience rating").
- Limiting the duration of disability pension payments to a fixed period (say, three years), with the need to reapply and reestablish eligibility after that period in order to continue benefit receipt.
- Increasing work incentives for benefit recipients through wage or employment subsidies or disregarding earnings in calculating benefits for recipients who combine work and disability benefit receipt.

These policies—and evidence regarding their effectiveness—lead to two basic lessons for reform of the US SSDI program. The first lesson is that *being classified as "disabled" does not mean that productive activity is impossible.* Efforts to reform SSDI need to seriously consider the available options for promoting work and labor force participation of potential benefit applicants. The second lesson is that *provision of strong pro-work incentives to workers, employers, and SSDI officials responsible for eligibility determination is likely to increase the share of people with disabilities that remain in the workforce.* Incentives are able to induce desirable behaviors, and the challenge is to craft a set of incentives for all parties that promote continued work and labor force participation of people with disabilities, rather than having them rely on pension benefits as their primary income source. Given these overarching lessons, the trick is to identify a set of policy changes consistent with them that could manage the rolls, while not imposing large costs on people with disabilities. If such policies can be developed, the flow of new beneficiaries is likely to be reduced—a much more productive path than attempting to reduce the existing stock of beneficiaries.

CONCLUSION

This paper has presented an international comparison of disability pension policies and has drawn lessons from the international experience that might inform policy toward people with disabilities in the United States. After presenting background information on the size and characteristics of working-age people with disabilities in selected Western countries, the basic structure of disability policy in these countries is described. The nature of policy among these countries varies from those with universal and generous benefits and relatively low hurdles for accessing benefits to those with relatively low benefit levels, strict criteria for accessing support, and relatively low rehabilitation efforts.

The paper then presents a full-bodied discussion of the nature of disability policy reform in the countries studied. Reforms to benefit structures, eligibility criteria, rehabilitation and employment efforts, and a variety of institutional arrangements are described. Finally, the paper has drawn lessons for the United States from the reform efforts of these other nations. The basic lesson from these international efforts is that it is possible to achieve a responsible balance between providing support to people with disabilities and creating incentives for people with physical and mental health problems to remain active labor force participants. Having disabling conditions does not require the foregoing of productive labor market work.

16

Options to Address SSDI's Financial Shortfall

Marc Goldwein and Edward Lorenzen

INTRODUCTION

The Social Security Disability Insurance (SSDI) program provides a vital source of income for most of its 11 million beneficiaries, and it is an important source of income security for the more than 150 million workers currently insured by the program. Yet the SSDI program faces a significant medium and long-term funding gap, even after accounting for the temporary reallocation of payroll taxes included in the Bipartisan Budget Act of 2015.

In 2014 alone, the SSDI program spent over $30 billion more on benefits than it collected in dedicated revenue—which is the equivalent of roughly 0.55 percent of taxable payroll; for context, the dedicated payroll tax for SSDI is typically 1.8 percent of payroll (Trustees 2015). According to the Social Security Trustees (2015), this gap between spending and revenues will persist, declining to just above 0.2 percent of payroll by 2030, remaining relatively stable through 2040, and then rising to more than 0.4 percent by the early 2080s.

As a result of this imbalance, the program is expected to deplete its trust fund reserves by 2022 (Goss 2015), at which point only 85 percent of scheduled benefits could be paid. Over the next 75 years, the SSDI trust fund faces a shortfall of roughly 0.26 percent of taxable payroll based on projections from the Social Security Trustees (2015) and 0.67 percent based on projections from the Congressional Budget Office (CBO 2015).

Figure 1: Social Security Disability Insurance Revenue and Benefits (Percent of Payroll)

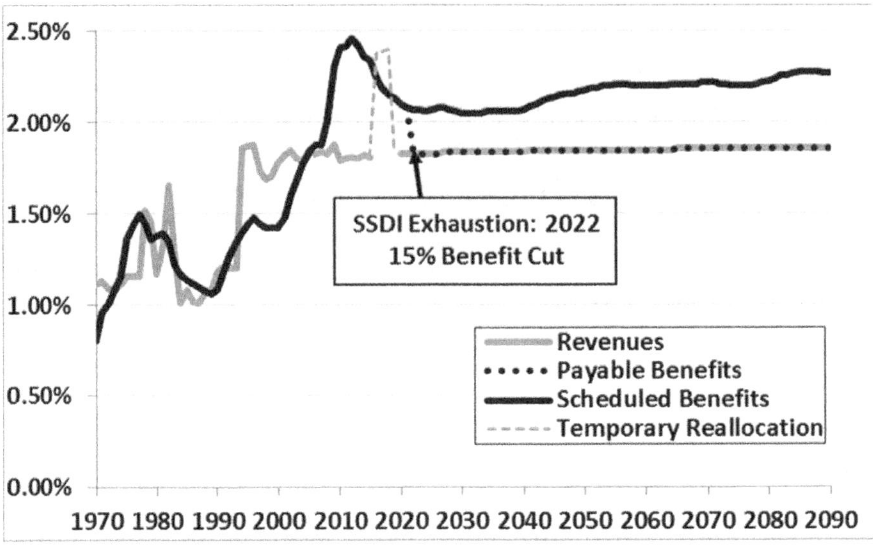

Source: 2015 Social Security Trustees' Report & authors' calculations.

Ultimately, policymakers must address SSDI's funding gap by increasing dedicated revenue, reducing program costs, diverting funds into the program from other sources, or some combination of the three. Closing a 0.26 percent of payroll shortfall would be the equivalent of reducing all new and future benefits by 15 percent, increasing dedicated taxes by 14 percent, or diverting enough funds from the old-age program to increase its actuarial imbalance by 10 percent.

In this paper, we put forward concrete policy options which could help to close this imbalance.

UNDERSTANDING THE SSDI FUNDING GAP

Although we will not put forward any recommendations in this paper, careful study of the financial issues surrounding the SSDI program makes at least a few findings clear.

First, even with the reallocation it will be extremely difficult to avoid trust fund depletion without directing new money into the trust fund. The Bipartisan Budget Act is projected to have extended the life of the trust fund to 2022 (Goss 2015), which is too little time for the most plausible changes in benefits or eligibility to be sufficiently phased in. As a result, either new revenue or some type of direct or indirect transfer or reallocation from the old-age trust fund will likely be necessary, at least in the near-term.

Second, the SSDI program faces a structural gap between spending and revenue—not simply a temporary shortfall. Although the current deficit is projected to subside in the coming years, it is not likely to disappear. Based on estimates from the Social Security Trustees (2015) and factoring in the Bipartisan Budget Act of 2015, policymakers will ultimately need to increase revenue, reduce spending, or divert resources into the program equal to almost 0.3 percent of payroll for long-term solvency. CBO (2015) estimates a gap closer to almost 0.7 percent of payroll.

Third, policymakers cannot count on improvements to the SSDI program, promising as they may be, to close the entirety of its financial shortfall. This book contains a dozen sets of proposals with the potential to improve SSDI in areas such as early intervention and work supports, program administration, interaction with other programs, and structural reforms. Although these and other proposals can make the SSDI program more efficient and effective, the savings they generate are mostly modest, long-term, or highly uncertain. Indeed, many of these proposals require upfront investments that would initially increase costs.

And finally, SSDI's financial gap would ideally be closed as part of comprehensive Social Security reform that also addresses the Old-Age and Survivors' Insurance (OASI) program. After all, the old-age and disability programs share a common benefits formula and tax base, a number of interactions, and a common cost growth driver in the form of an aging population. Addressing the finances of the two programs together would also allow for much better targeting and many more tradeoffs because the full Social Security population is much larger and more diverse than the SSDI population.

Short of comprehensive reform, however, policymakers must identify changes to avoid SSDI trust fund depletion before 2022, and those changes should preferably improve the long-term finances of the program. These changes could take a variety of forms, ranging from diverting existing resources to SSDI to increasing tax revenue to changing benefit levels, structure, or eligibility rules.

In this paper, we identify a variety of options which could improve SSDI's long-term financial state. Our list is not exhaustive, but it is meant to give a sense of the types of choices available. We focus mainly on options with significant direct financial impacts rather than on those that may indirectly impact costs by changing award decisions or through behavioral effects (though many of the options we discuss may also influence behavior). We do not include options that would generally be applied both to SSDI and OASI such as a change to the Primary Insurance Amount (PIA) formula.

Importantly, we take no view on which of these options are better or worse than other options, nor on the question of whether any of these options should be adopted in the near-term or later in conjunction with comprehensive reform.

A SUMMARY OF OPTIONS TO IMPROVE SSDI'S FINANCES

The summary tables below list many of the options discussed in this chapter to improve the solvency of the SSDI program. The table also measures the 75-year financial impact of these provisions, measured as a share of taxable payroll. By this measure, a combination of changes which reduced the shortfall by above 0.26 percent of payroll would make SSDI solvent (at least on average) over the next 75 years.

Importantly, estimates are based on the full impact of the provisions on the OASDI program, which means a portion of the savings or some costs may actually accrue to the retirement program rather than the SSDI program. No estimates include costs or savings outside of the Social Security program, though both may exist. Most estimates are rough numbers provided generously by the Social Security Chief Actuary. Where we have provided our own estimates, numbers are marked with an asterisk (*). All estimates are based on benefit and revenue projections from the Social Security Trustees, rather than CBO. Estimates marked with a caret (^) indicate that it would produce savings or costs less than 0.005 percent of payroll.

Figure 2: Options to Increase SSDI Income and Resources (with effects on OASI when applicable)

	75-Year Actuarial Impact on SSDI (Percent of Payroll)	75-Year Actuarial Impact on OASI (Percent of Payroll)
Social Security Disability Insurance (SSDI) 75-Year Shortfall	-0.26%*	n/a
Direct Funds Into the SSDI Trust Fund		
Reallocate the payroll tax from OASI to SSDI to extend the SSDI trust fund for five years (until 2027)	+0.02%*	-0.02%*
Reallocate the payroll tax from OASI to SSDI to equalize the trust funds (extends until 2034)	+0.05%*	-0.05%*
Reallocate the payroll tax to achieve 75-year solvency (extends until 2090)	+0.28%*	-0.28%*
Allocate taxation of Social Security benefits proportionally	+0.07%*	-0.07%*
Allocate all taxation of SSDI benefits to SSDI, none to Medicare	+0.04%	^
Transfer $120 billion from the OASI fund to the SSDI fund in 2022, extending the SSDI fund for five years	+0.02%*	-0.02%*
Transfer $250 billion from the OASI fund to the SSDI fund in 2022, equalizing the funds' depletion dates	+0.05%*	-0.05%*
Allow interfund borrowing between OASI & SSDI	varies	varies
Merge the OASI and SSDI trust funds	n/a	
Increase SSDI Revenue (Options Begin in 2019)		
Increase the SSDI payroll tax rate from 1.8% to 2.1%	+0.28%*	+0.01%*
Eliminate SSDI taxable maximum	+0.34%*	^
Eliminate SSDI taxable maximum for employers only	+0.17%*	^
Cover all newly-hired state & local workers under SSDI	+0.01%	^
"Experience rate" the payroll tax	varies	varies

Figure 3: Options to Reduce SSDI Costs

	75-Year Actuarial Impact on OASDI (Percent of Payroll)
Social Security Disability Insurance (SSDI) 75-Year Shortfall	-0.26%*
Modify SSDI Eligibility	
Require applicants to have worked 5 of the last 8 years (instead of 5/10)	+0.12%
Require applicants to have worked 4 of the last 6 years (instead of 5/10)	+0.16%
Only count quarters of coverage with earnings above SGA	+0.13%
Redefine SGA to be the lesser of an individual's AIME & current SGA	+0.01%
Raise "grid" age thresholds with NRA increase & index to age longevity	+0.01%
Raise "grid" age thresholds as outlined in Sen. Tom Coburn's 2011 proposal	+0.04%
Modify Relationship between SSDI and Earliest Eligibility Age	
Convert SSDI beneficiaries to OASI at age 62 (instead of age 66, headed to 67) & apply actuarial reduction for early retirement	+0.50%
Freeze current relationship between EEA & NRA at 4-year difference	+0.18%
Restore relationship between EEA & NRA to 3-year difference	+0.32%
Limit SSDI eligibility to workers who become disabled before age 62 & phase down benefits for those who apply between age 53 and 61, converting to OASI at NRA[1]	+0.13%
Improve Program Administration and Interactions	
Expand CDIs nationwide & enact various anti-fraud policies	^
Reduce SSDI/Unemployment Insurance "Double-Dipping"	+0.01%
Reform & simplify Workers' Compensation offset and close loopholes	+0.01%
Restore reconsideration in prototype states	+0.01%
Close the record to submit evidence one week before ALJ hearings	+0.01%
Eliminate the "controlling weight standard" for medical evidence	+0.02%
Include a government representative at ALJ hearings	^
Other Savings Options	
Reduce maximum period of retroactive benefits from 12 to 6 months	+0.02%
Pay retroactive benefits at half the level of future benefits	+0.02%
Increase waiting period between onset and eligibility from 5 to 6 months	+0.02%
Increasing waiting period between onset and eligibility to 1 year	+0.13%
Fully eliminate dropout years	+0.15%*

1 If converted to OASI at the EEA instead of the NRA, the estimated impact on SSDI would be +0.45 percent of payroll with the net effect on OASDI of +0.13 percent.

Figure 4: Options to Expand SSDI Benefits

	75-Year Actuarial Impact on OASDI (Percent of Payroll)
Social Security Disability Insurance (SSDI) 75-Year Shortfall	-0.26%
Benefit Expansions	
Eliminate the waiting period	-0.09%
Require applicants to have worked 4 of the last 10 years (instead of 5)	-0.10%
Allow those age 60 and above to qualify for reduced benefits without meeting the recency of work requirements	+0.01%
Allow SSDI beneficiaries to enroll in Medicare immediately	-0.02%
Establish a poverty-level minimum benefit for SSDI beneficiaries	-0.07-0.03%
Reduce an individual's SSDI benefits by $1 for every $2 the individual earns above SGA for all beneficiaries to avoid "cash cliff"	-0.04%
Reduce an individual's SSDI benefits by $1 for every $2 the individual earns beginning at the first dollar	^
Eliminate the payroll tax for SSDI beneficiaries who return to work	-0.01%

OPTIONS FOR DIRECTING FUNDS INTO THE SSDI TRUST FUND

One way to improve the financial strength of the SSDI program would involve directing money currently dedicated to some other government purpose into the SSDI trust fund. A number of options exist for policymakers to enact such a change, including "reallocation" of payroll tax revenue from the old-age program and interfund borrowing or transfers, among others.

Regardless of which option policymakers choose, specific design choices will require policymakers to decide how many years they intend to extend the solvency of the trust fund, as well as whether or not they intend to "offset" any loss of funds. Box 1 of this paper provides an illustrative list of tax and spending options which could be used to offset a reallocation or transfer from the old-age trust fund.

Below are a number of options to direct funds into the SSDI trust fund:

Reallocation of the Payroll Tax

One option to improve SSDI's finances would be to reallocate part of the payroll tax from the Social Security old-age trust fund to the disability insurance trust fund.

Under current law, the SSDI trust fund is generally financed primarily from a 1.8 percent payroll tax, while the OASI trust fund is financed with a 10.6 percent payroll tax. The combined 12.4 percent tax is split evenly between employer and employee, and it applies to a worker's first $118,500 of wages (indexed to average wage growth).

The Bipartisan Budget Act of 2015 temporarily reallocated 0.57 percent of the payroll tax from the OASI trust fund to the SSDI trust fund for the years 2016, 2017, and 2018. This reallocation delayed the projected depletion date of the SSDI trust fund from 2016 to 2022, while the OASI trust fund is estimated to remain solvent through 2035 (Trustees 2015; Goss 2015).

To further extend the life of the SSDI trust fund, policymakers could enact an additional reallocation beyond 2018. The size and length of a reallocation would depend in part on how long policymakers want to extend the solvency of the SSDI trust fund.

For example, a five-year extension and reallocation beginning in 2022 would require shifting an average of about 0.22 percent of the payroll tax into the SSDI program, the equivalent of 0.02 percent of payroll over 75 years. That reallocation could be further extended through 2034 in order to align the reserve depletion date of the two trust funds, at a 75-year cost to the OASI program of 0.05 percent of payroll.

The program could be made solvent over 75 years by reallocating 0.30 percent of payroll into the SSDI program permanently beginning in 2022, the equivalent of 0.28 percent of payroll over 75 years. Other options are also possible.

Figure 5: Reallocation Options (as a percentage of payroll, starting in 2022)

Trust Fund Extension	5 years (Extends to 2027)	12 years (Extends to 2034)	Permanent (Extends to 2090)
Average annual reallocation	0.22%	0.22%	0.30%
75-year actuarial impact on OASI	-0.02%	-0.05%	-0.28%

Source: Authors' estimates based on the 2015 Social Security Trustees' Report.

Reallocation of Other Revenue Streams

Although both Social Security programs and the Medicare Hospital Insurance program are funded mainly from the payroll tax, a small portion of all three programs is funded from the partial income taxation of Social Security benefits. Specifically, Social Security beneficiaries who make above $25,000 (or $32,000 for married couples) must count 50 percent of their Social Security benefits as income for tax purposes. Revenue from taxation of retirement benefits is currently dedicated to the OASI trust fund, and taxation of disability benefits is dedicated to the SSDI trust fund. In 2014, the two trust funds received roughly $28 billion and $2 billion, respectively, in income tax revenue (Trustees 2015). An additional 35 percent of benefits are taxable for individuals making above $34,000 per year (or $44,000 for married couples), with the additional funds dedicated to the Medicare Hospital Insurance trust fund.

In place of the current practice, a larger portion of revenue from taxation of benefits could be allocated to the SSDI trust fund. For example, revenue from taxation of Social Security benefits could be split proportionally to the payroll tax allocation between the programs, rather than based on which benefit is taxed. That would improve the financial state of the SSDI program (and worsen the state of the OASI program) by about 0.07 percent of payroll over 75 years. Alternatively (or additionally), taxation of SSDI benefits currently dedicated to Medicare could instead be dedicated to the SSDI program—a change that would divert the equivalent of about 0.04 percent of payroll.

Trust Fund Transfer

Rather than dedicating a stream of revenue to the SSDI trust fund, policymakers could enact a one-time transfer of funds into the system. Based on estimates from the Trustees, a five-year extension of trust fund solvency (from 2022 to 2027) would require a roughly $120 billion immediate transfer, and an extension through 2034 (from 2022) would require a roughly $250 billion transfer. This transfer could be paid from the OASI trust fund—in which case it would in many ways resemble reallocation—or from another source.

Interfund Borrowing

As an alternative to transferring the money on a permanent basis, policymakers could allow the SSDI fund to borrow from OASI or other funds on a temporary basis. Borrowing authority would allow the SSDI program to continue to pay benefits as needed by drawing from the old-age trust fund, with the expectation that the SSDI fund would ultimately pay back these borrowed funds with interest. Policymakers could allow for unlimited borrowing authority, could limit the dollar amount SSDI could borrow, or could allow borrowing through a certain date. Policymakers could also schedule a loan repayment plan, allow the trust fund to pay interest only, or allow the loan to be rolled over into perpetuity.

Merge the Trust Funds

Rather than shifting resources between the SSDI and OASI trust funds, policymakers could merge the two into a single Social Security Trust Fund. Such a move would allow SSDI and the old-age program to draw from a common pool of resources (funded mainly with the 12.4 percent Social Security payroll tax), and the reserve depletion of those two programs would by definition come at the same time—2034 according to the Trustees (2015) and 2029 according to CBO (2015).

Adjust Responsibilities of SSDI and OASI for Older SSDI Beneficiaries

While the options described here would increase the amount of money that goes into the SSDI trust fund by reducing revenue going elsewhere, it is also possible to reduce the money being drawn from the trust fund.

SSDI provides full benefits for recipients until they reach the normal retirement age—currently 66 and scheduled to increase to 67. At that point, the old-age program pays full benefits. One alternative would be for the OASI program to begin paying for benefits at age 65, as it did prior to the recent increase in the normal retirement age.

Another alternative would be to make the OASI trust fund responsible for a portion of benefits beginning at age 62—the equivalent of what it would have paid in reduced benefits to an early retiree—with the SSDI program responsible for the "top off" to full benefits. Beneficiaries would be paid through a single check. This change could (but need not) be offset in future years by continuing that division of payments beyond the normal retirement age.

Box 1. Illustrative Options to Offset Reallocation

Assuming policymakers divert resources from the old-age trust fund to the SSDI trust fund—through reallocation or other means—doing so would modestly worsen the finances of the old-age trust fund. For example, we estimate that a reallocation of resources to extend the SSDI trust fund depletion date by one year would increase the 75-year actuarial shortfall of the old-age trust fund by about 0.01 percent of payroll. A diversion that lines up the depletion dates of the trust funds to 2034, on the other hand, would increase the 75-year shortfall by 0.08 percent of payroll, based on our estimates.

One option to avoid increasing the shortfall of the old-age trust fund would be to offset the loss over 75 years with modest adjustments to the old-age program or revenue base. The following table offers a number of illustrative options:

	75-Year Actuarial Impact on OASI as a Percent of Payroll *(SSDI Impact, when significant)*
Funding Options	
Extension to 2027 (from 2022; five-year extension)	-0.02%(*+0.02%*)*
Extension to 2034 (to equalize depletion dates)	-0.05% (*+0.05%*)*
Extension to 2090 (to achieve 75-year solvency)	-0.28% (*+0.28%*)*
Revenue Offset Options	
Improve collection of pension information from states and localities	+0.01%
Reform and rationalize Windfall Elimination Provision (WEP) and Government Pension Offset (GPO)	+0.08%
Eliminate the Retirement Earnings Test	+0.01%
Stop benefit payments for felons with outstanding arrest warrants	+0.01%*
Repeal "RIB-LIM" floor on widow(er)s benefits	+0.03%*
Reduce top PIA bend point from 15% to 14%	+0.03%*
Increase retirement age from 67 to 67 and 1 month	+0.03%*
Eliminate student exemptions from the payroll tax	+0.02%*
Repeal payroll tax exemptions for foreign workers	+0.01%*
Equalize FICA and SECA rates	+0.01%*
Close "John Edwards/Newt Gingrich" tax loophole	+0.02%*
Increase certainty with respect to worker classification	+0.01%*
Repeal deductibility of cafeteria plans	+0.17% (*+0.03%*)
Cover newly hired state and local workers	+0.14% (*+0.01%*)
Raise Taxable Maximum by 2 percent	+0.02%*

Source: * indicates that the estimate is the authors' calculations based on existing CBO, OMB, and Social Security Trustee data. Otherwise, data is based on estimates from the Social Security Chief Actuary.

OPTIONS FOR INCREASING SSDI REVENUE

Another way to improve the financial strength of the SSDI program would involve increasing the total amount of tax revenue raised and dedicated to the SSDI program. Currently, SSDI is funded primarily by 1.8 percent of the payroll tax (split between employers and employees) on up to $118,500 of wage income.

Below are a number of options to increase revenue going into the SSDI trust fund:

Raise the Payroll Tax Rate

Raising the 1.8 percent payroll tax rate would be one option to strengthen the financial state of the SSDI program. An increase of 0.3 percent beginning in 2019, divided evenly between employer and employee, would be enough to avoid trust fund depletion and achieve 75-year solvency (with a few years of negative balance) based on projections from the Social Security Trustees' report (2015). In other words, the total SSDI payroll tax rate would need to rise from 1.8 percent of payroll to about 2.1 percent of payroll, and the combined Social Security payroll tax rate from 12.4 percent of payroll to about 12.7 percent. A somewhat larger increase would be needed to ensure "sustainable solvency" over 75 years or to achieve solvency by CBO estimates, while a somewhat smaller increase would be needed if it were combined with other options.

Raise the Taxable Maximum

The Social Security payroll tax—for both OASI and SSDI—currently applies to a worker's first $118,500 of wages, a threshold indexed annually with average wage growth. Income above that threshold is not subject to the Social Security payroll tax, nor is it incorporated into benefit calculations. Many Social Security reform proposals would increase or eliminate this "taxable maximum," but it is also possible to raise this threshold for the SSDI payroll tax only.

Fully eliminating the SSDI taxable maximum starting in 2019 without additional benefit credits, therefore imposing an additional 1.8 percent tax on income above $118,500, would improve the financial state of the SSDI program by 0.34 percent of payroll. In other words, this would more than fully eliminate SSDI's 75-year shortfall as estimated by the Trustees and close most of the gap in the 75th year. Obviously, providing SSDI beneficiaries with additional benefits for income above the current taxable maximum would reduce the amount of savings this change would produce, and so, too, would increasing but not eliminating the SSDI taxable maximum.

A variation on this policy would eliminate the taxable maximum for the employer only, effectively increasing the payroll tax on income above the current maximum by 0.9 percent. Coincidentally, a 0.9 payroll surtax is already imposed on high-income workers (on the employee side) for Medicare, and the two taxes could be streamlined as part of this change. In total, this option would reduce the SSDI 75-year shortfall by 0.17 percent of payroll.

Cover All Newly Hired State and Local Workers under SSDI

About one quarter of state and local workers are not covered by Social Security and are instead covered by pensions and disability insurance offered at the state and local level. Although a number of proposals would fully extend Social Security coverage (including payroll tax contributions) from that population, one option is to extend only SSDI coverage. Under this option, all newly hired state and local workers would begin paying a 1.8 percent payroll tax (split between employer and employee) and would become eligible to apply for and receive SSDI. At the normal retirement age, these workers would be paid from their state and local pensions (or from Social Security to the extent they had enough covered work) under current law.

This policy change would improve the state of the SSDI trust fund by about 0.01 percent of payroll, or somewhat more if enacted in concert with other revenue or benefit changes.

"Experience Rate" the Payroll Tax

When it comes to private insurance, Workers' Compensation, and unemployment insurance, employers generally pay a variable rate depending on the likelihood that their employees will end up relying on insurance benefits (and the degree to which they will). Companies that have dismissed a greater proportion of workers in the past generally pay a higher unemployment insurance payroll tax rate than companies with higher retention rates.

This principle could be applied to SSDI by "experience rating" the 0.9 percent payroll tax that employers pay to the SSDI trust fund. Under this model, the tax rate would go up for some companies and down for others. Depending on design specifics, this policy could increase, reduce, or maintain current revenue collection. To the extent this change incentivized employers to retain and support workers with the potential of otherwise entering the SSDI program, experience rating could also reduce program costs.

MODIFY SSDI ELIGIBILITY

In order to reduce the costs of the SSDI program, one option is to make eligibility criteria stricter and therefore reduce the number of new entrants. Many of the options to slow the growth in the SSDI rolls would focus on changing program administration, modifying incentives, encouraging early intervention, or changing the standards by which one is determined to have a disability. Below are a number of options that instead focus on the mechanical and objective criteria of eligibility:

Modify the Recency of Work Rules

In order to receive SSDI benefits, an individual must generally have worked at least five of the 10 years prior to becoming disabled (fewer years are required for those under age 31). This recency-of-work test is used to determine whether an individual is "insured" and therefore eligible for benefits as a result of their employment record. One option to reduce eligibility would be to tighten this standard. Requiring an individual to have worked five of the past eight years would reduce total Social Security costs by 0.12 percent of payroll over 75 years, with most of the savings accruing to the SSDI program. A requirement of four of the last six years would reduce costs by 0.16 percent of payroll. Other combinations would also be possible.

Conform the Levels for Substantial Gainful Activity (SGA) and Quarters of Coverage

To become eligible for SSDI benefits, an individual must have worked for a minimum number of quarters of coverage, as defined by quarters in which the person made at least $1,220 (indexed to wage growth). At the same time, to be considered disabled for the purposes of SSDI, an individual generally must be unable to perform Substantial Gainful Activity (SGA) as defined by earning $1,090 *per month* (indexed to wage growth). One result of these two rules is that a person effectively needs to have earned only about $5,000 per year to be considered an eligible worker but a much higher amount of above $13,000 per year to be considered able to engage in substantial work.

Conforming these two numbers would reduce eligibility for the program. For example, changing the definition of quarters of coverage to count only earnings above SGA (about $3,270 per quarter) would reduce the cost of the program by 0.13 percent of payroll over 75 years. Alternatively, policymakers could redefine SGA to be the lesser of current law levels or an individual's average indexed monthly earnings (AIME)—essentially making someone ineligible if he or she can earn what they did prior to having the disability. That would reduce the cost of the program by 0.01 percent of payroll over 75 years.

Modify the Medical-Vocational Guidelines

If an individual has a condition that is not already on the list of pre-checked disabilities that qualify for SSDI benefits, SSA will use a "grid" system called Medical-Vocational Guidelines in order to determine whether their disability limits their ability to participate in the national economy. These grids take into account an applicant's age, education level, Residual Functional Capacity (their capacity to engage in work), work history, and skills. These grids are organized by age level. Disability Determination Services (DDS) agencies use these grids to determine if a condition meets the statutory definition of disability without being one of the medically listed impairments that qualify for benefits.

These grids could be modified in any number of ways, but one option would be to change the age ranges associated with different vocational factors. The thresholds for less restrictive factors are currently ages 45, 50, 55, and 60. Increasing these ages by one year as Social Security's normal retirement age (NRA) rises from 66 to 67, and then indexing them to growing life expectancy, would save about 0.01 percent of payroll over 75 years. Increasing the age 50 threshold to 58, the age 55 threshold to 61, and the top threshold to the EEA as outlined in Sen. Tom Coburn's 2011 proposal would save about 0.04 percent of payroll. Other options are also possible, including changes to the various criteria underlying the grids themselves or even repealing the grids altogether.

MODIFY RELATIONSHIP BETWEEN SSDI AND THE EARLIEST ELIGIBILITY AGE

Those who enter the SSDI program receive benefits comparable to what they would have received under Social Security from working their entire career and retiring at the NRA. Moreover, once they reach the NRA—currently 66 and headed to 67—their SSDI benefits are "converted" to a retirement benefit that continues to be paid out at the same level. By comparison, those who retire prior to the NRA receive a smaller benefit. For example, workers retiring at the earliest eligible age (EEA) of 62 receive 25 percent less than they would if they retired at the NRA or received SSDI benefits. That gap will widen to 30 percent as the NRA rises to 67. Importantly, because workers can apply for SSDI up until the NRA, this creates a situation where two workers exiting the labor force at the same age could receive very different levels of benefits depending on whether they enter the disability or old-age program. A number of options would adjust the relationship between the SSDI program and the old-age program, particularly as it relates to the EEA.

Convert Disabled Workers to Retired Status at the EEA

Currently, SSDI beneficiaries collect benefits from the SSDI trust fund up until they reach the NRA and then "convert" to retired status in order to receive the identical level of benefits paid from the old-age trust fund. One option to reduce costs for the SSDI program would be to convert a worker to retired status at the EEA of 62, at which point their benefits would be paid from the old-age trust fund. This change would reduce SSDI's actuarial shortfall but would increase the shortfall of the old-age trust fund by a similar amount. To avoid this cost shift and reduce overall costs, a worker's benefits could be actuarially reduced to EEA levels—either gradually or all at once—when they convert to retired worker status. If the reduction was applied immediately, it would save about 0.50 percent of payroll. A more modest version of this policy might simply reduce or freeze cost of living adjustments (COLAs) between the EEA and the NRA.

Freeze the Current Relationship Between SSDI and EEA Level Benefits

Currently, SSDI benefits are paid at a level comparable to collecting at the NRA of 66, whereas EEA-level benefits for those retiring at age 62 are about 25 percent lower. As the NRA rises to 67, this gap will widen, and EEA-level benefits will be about 30 percent lower than SSDI-level benefits. To prevent this gap from growing, one option is to freeze the relationship between SSDI and the EEA so that SSDI benefits are always comparable in size to a worker retiring at age 66—four years after the EEA—even as the NRA rises to 67. This change would reduce Social Security's total actuarial shortfall by about 0.18 percent of payroll, with the distribution of that reduction between the old-age and disability trust funds dependent on when a worker is assumed to "convert" to old-age benefits. Another version of this policy would gradually *restore* the relationship between SSDI and the EEA that existed when the NRA was 65, ultimately calculating

SSDI benefits as comparable to a worker retiring three years after the EEA. This policy would likely save about 0.32 percent of payroll.

Eliminate SSDI Eligibility Starting at Age 62

Individuals between the EEA of 62 and the NRA of 66 (approaching 67) may be eligible for either old-age benefits or disability benefits. Because retirement benefits at the EEA are 25 (approaching 30) percent smaller than disability benefits, there may be an incentive for early retirees to apply for the more generous and therefore more costly SSDI benefits. One option to address this concern would be to limit SSDI to workers who become disabled prior to age 62 and require those 62 and over to apply for the old-age program. To avoid a "cliff effect," where potential benefits drop substantially between a 61-year-old disabled worker and 62-year-old disabled worker, policymakers could begin to phase down the value of initial benefits at some earlier age. Enacting this policy with a phase-down beginning at age 53 and converting to the OASI program at the NRA, for example, would generate savings for the Social Security program of about 0.13 percent of payroll. The same overall savings would be achieved if SSDI beneficiaries converted to OASI at the EEA, but it would save SSDI about 0.45 percent of payroll (and there would be a 0.32 percent of payroll cost to the OASI trust fund).

A slightly more modest version of this policy would limit eligibility (with or without a phase-in) to some age between the EEA and NRA. Allowing application until age 63, for example, would ensure no change in Medicare eligibility, which is currently available two years after the onset of a disability or at age 65. A much more modest alternative would be to disallow applications above the current NRA of 66 even as it rises to 67, or to restrict seniors from *applying* for SSDI benefits once they reach the NRA of 67 (which a beneficiary might do in order to collect retroactive benefits).

Provide a Hybrid Old-Age/Disability Benefit for Those Applying after the EEA

As explained above, workers with disabilities who are above the age of 62 (the current EEA) can apply for full SSDI benefits and are also eligible to collect reduced old-age benefits. Rather than allowing workers to collect one or the other, one option would be to pay older workers with disabilities a hybrid of the two benefits based on age relative to the EEA and NRA. For example, a worker who becomes eligible for SSDI benefits at age 63—assuming an EEA of 62 and an NRA of 67—would receive four-fifths of his or her benefits in the form of an unreduced SSDI benefit and the other fifth as an actuarially-reduced old-age benefit. The proportion of benefits paid as unreduced SSDI benefits would go up for younger applicants and down for older applicants. Under this policy, each trust fund would be responsible for its share of the benefit (although recipients would receive only one check), and at the NRA the recipient would convert to retired status—with benefits continued at the same level—as under current law.

IMPROVE PROGRAM ADMINISTRATION AND INTERACTIONS

Although large, unambiguous programmatic savings will generally require changes to benefit levels or eligibility, some reductions in spending can be achieved by improving the determination and adjudication process, strengthening program integrity, or addressing interactions with other programs. Dozens, if not hundreds, of ideas exist to improve the overall administration of the program—some of which are featured in this book. In this section, we focus on a few sets of options that have generally been scored by the Chief Actuary or others as saving money.

Reduce SSDI Fraud

Although fraud is not a major cost driver in the SSDI program, the fraud that does exist imposes an unnecessary cost on the trust fund. Though not always easy to find, fraud has been identified at times from actions of SSDI recipients, their attorneys, physicians, judges, and others. A large number of ideas have been put forward to help reduce fraud. Some ideas include: increasing penalties for involvement in fraud; improving data sharing and matching; excluding evidence from sanctioned sources; focusing on judges, lawyers, and doctors with unusually high award-rates for cases they are involved in; clarifying to beneficiaries the need to fully report earnings and the penalties of failing to do so; and using predictive analytics to better identify fraud. Funding and requiring expanded fraud investigations—particularly Cooperative Disability Investigations (CDIs) between SSA and local law enforcement that currently exist in over half the states—can also help reduce fraud. While these and other antifraud measures can help to improve the overall integrity of the program, the total direct savings are likely to be modest—likely less than 0.005 percent of payroll. The Bipartisan Budget Act of 2015 included many of the most commonly proposed ideas, including expansion of CDIs to all 50 states and territories as well as smaller measures like increasing civil monetary penalties and creating new felony classifications for committing Social Security fraud.

Increase and Improve Continuing Disability Reviews (CDRs)

Under current law, SSDI recipients are supposed to receive regular Continuing Disability Reviews (CDR) to determine whether they remain eligible for the program. Based on likelihood of recovery, recipients are supposed to be reviewed either every 6 to 18 months, 3 years, or 5 to 7 years for medical improvement (often by mail but sometimes with a full review) and are also reviewed regularly for earnings. Those with significant medical improvement or earnings above the SGA amount (about $13,000 per year) are removed from the program. However, CDRs are often not conducted on time, and a significant backlog currently exists. CDRs may also not be conducted efficiently.

According to the Chief Actuary, every dollar we spend on CDRs yields $8 to $12 dollars in current and future savings to federal government programs by removing recovered workers from the SSDI rolls (SSAB 2014, 21). Some have argued to make this funding mandatory (rather than appropriated every year) and somewhat fungible between years in order to better assure these savings materialize.

In addition to or instead of more funding, a number of changes could be made to the CDR process. One option would be to eliminate the current "medical improvement review standard" (MIRS) and require CDRs to determine level of disability rather than level of improvement. Short of this, existing MIRS exceptions under current law could be strengthened, clarified, and used more regularly and consistently. Other options include moving to more individualized "diaries" to determine when someone should receive a CDR, to widen the criteria for conducting "risk-based CDRs," to increase the number of in-person (as opposed to via mail) CDRs, or to improve wage and medical status reporting and data collection. An aggressive set of reforms to how CDRs are conducted would likely result in additional though likely relatively modest programmatic savings.

Reduce Concurrent Payments with Other Programs

Under current law, SSDI recipients may simultaneously receive cash benefits from other government programs. In many cases, these concurrent receipts are by design, but in other cases this might not be so. For example, a small number of disabled workers have concurrently claimed SSDI benefits and unemployment insurance (UI) benefits, even though the former is for individuals who cannot work and the latter for individuals who are between jobs and looking for work.

This "double-dip" could be addressed in a number of ways, though all existing proposals would save about 0.01 percent of payroll.

Workers' Compensation (WC)—a benefit provided for workplace-related injuries and disabilities—has a very significant overlap with SSDI. Under current law, beneficiaries who collect both are limited to a combined SSDI-WC benefit equal to 80 percent of their pre-disability earnings. Generally, the "offset" for excessive benefits comes in the form of lower SSDI benefits, though in 15 states it comes in the form of lower WC benefits. Critics argue the current offset is confusing, can be avoided in part or in whole through a number of loopholes, and is sometimes not applied due to lack of data. Simplifying the offset, improving data reporting, and closing various WC loopholes would likely save a modest amount of money—perhaps about 0.01 percent of payroll. Policymakers could also eliminate the "reverse offset" so that reductions always apply to SSDI rather than WC.

In addition to these two programs, it may be possible to save money by addressing interactions or concurrent receipts with a number of other programs including SSI, military benefits, certain retirement programs, or even private disability insurance.

Reform the Determination and Adjudication Process

A huge number of changes could be made to the SSDI determination process as well as the rules and procedures on evidence and hearings, particularly when it comes to administrative law judge (ALJ) hearings. We will not make an effort here to list the many changes that could improve accuracy and in some cases save money. Instead, we will focus on a few that have been estimated by the Chief Actuary to improve solvency by a significant degree (above 0.01 percent of payroll).

The Chief Actuary estimates that restoring the first appeals step of reconsideration in all states (reconsideration does not exist in 10 states), for example, will save about 0.01 percent of payroll. Closing the record to submit evidence (and keeping it closed) one week before an ALJ hearing would save 0.01 percent of payroll. Eliminating the "controlling weight" for treating physicians—which gives priority to medical opinions submitted by an applicant's own doctor in the event that evidence might conflict between two medical sources[1]—would save 0.02 percent of payroll.

A number of other changes may also produce significant trust fund savings, however no estimates are currently available.

OTHER SAVINGS OPTIONS

Besides the options described here, a number of other policy changes could reduce the cost of the SSDI program. Several of those options are discussed below:

Modify Retroactive Benefits

SSDI recipients can receive up to one year in retroactive benefits for disabilities that were onset prior to approval of their SSDI application excluding the mandatory five-month waiting period. These benefits are paid in the form of a lump-sum check issued after a recipient is determined to be eligible for benefits.

To cut the cost of the program, policymakers could reduce the size or length of retroactive benefits. As one example, reducing the maximum period of retroactive benefits in half to six months would save about 0.02 percent of payroll over 75 years. An alternative policy of paying retroactive benefits up to 12 months but only at half the level of future benefits could also save 0.02 percent of payroll.

Without reducing retroactive benefits, it may also be possible to generate some near-term savings and/or administrative savings by paying retroactive benefits in a worker's next Social Security check or spread out over future checks rather than as soon as eligibility for retroactive benefits is determined.

Increase the SSDI Waiting Period

SSDI has a five-month waiting period between when a person becomes disabled and when they become eligible for benefits. Extending that waiting period would reduce costs to the program by reducing the number of months SSDI would have to pay beneficiaries, and in some cases by discouraging beneficiaries to apply in the first place.

---

1 See 20 CFR § 404.1527.

Extending the waiting period from five to six months, as it was prior to 1972, would reduce the program's 75 year shortfall by about 0.02 percent of payroll. Further extending the waiting period to a full year would reduce the shortfall by about 0.13 percent of payroll.

Reduce Dropout Years

Like the old-age program, SSDI benefits are computed using an individual's AIME. For an applicant age 62 or older, benefits are technically calculated based on 40 years of earnings – but the five lowest years (often years with zero earnings) are dropped out so only 35 years remain. Younger SSDI applications receive fewer "drop-out years," proportionally reduced depending on their elapsed years since 21 through the year before they first become eligible for SSDI benefits. This is known as the "one-for-five" rule, where an applicant will have one year dropped from AIME calculation for every five years that have passed since they turned 21 (Moulta-Ali 2014).

Reducing the number of dropout years would reduce the cost of SSDI by incorporating more low- and zero-earning years into average income calculations, thereby reducing benefit levels.

For example, fully eliminating the dropout years would likely reduce Social Security's 75-year shortfall by about 0.15 percent of payroll, with some of those savings accruing to the SSDI program, and some to the old-age trust fund ("converted" benefits at the normal retirement age would be lower as a result of this change).[2] A smaller reduction in the number of dropout years would generate smaller savings.

Time Limit Benefits

Although SSDI benefits are not intended to be permanent, under current law they continue automatically unless a person voluntarily returns to work or is removed from the program due to earnings or improvement identified through a CDR. One way to reduce program costs would be to make some or all benefits temporary and to require SSDI recipients to reapply (generally on a fast-tracked basis) if they remain disabled.

---

2 Authors' estimates based on information provided by the Social Security Administration's Chief Actuary.

According to the Chief Actuary, making *all* benefits temporary—lasting between two and five years depending on the likelihood of medical improvement—would save about 0.10 percent of payroll. A much more modest proposal to make benefits temporary for only the small subset of beneficiaries for whom medical recovery is expected would save closer to 0.01 percent of payroll.

BENEFIT EXPANSIONS

In addition to options that would reduce or eliminate the SSDI program's financial shortfall, a number of options exist that could improve the overall generosity of SSDI or related programs. Some of those options are discussed below:

Reduce (or Eliminate) the Waiting Period

As explained in the previous section, SSDI currently has a five-month waiting period between when a person first becomes disabled and when they become eligible for benefits. One option would be to reduce the length of that waiting period and therefore reduce the number of months a person will have had to be considered disabled before receiving benefits. As an example, policymakers could fully eliminate the waiting period at a cost of 0.09 percent of payroll over 75 years. Retaining but shortening the waiting period would cost less.

Loosen the Recency of Work Requirement for Some or All Applicants

As explained in the eligibility section, SSDI beneficiaries generally are required to have worked five of the previous 10 years before the onset of a disability. One option to increase the number of workers eligible for SSDI would be to require fewer recent years of work. For example, reducing the recency of work requirement so beneficiaries only needed to work four of the previous 10 years instead of five would cost about 0.10 percent of payroll over 75 years. Any of a number of other combinations would also be possible.

A modified version of this policy would be to maintain the recency of work requirement for most SSDI applicants, but allow those age 60 and above to qualify for reduced benefits without meeting the recency of work requirements. More specifically, this policy would provide those recipients with benefits equal to those provided at Social Security's EEA of 62, which are currently about 25 percent lower (and scheduled to be 30 percent lower) than normal benefits. This change would cost about 0.01 percent of payroll over 75 years.

Allow SSDI Beneficiaries to Enroll in Medicare Immediately

Under current law, SSDI beneficiaries are generally eligible to enroll in the Medicare program prior to the normal eligibility age of 65. However, eligibility for Medicare does not begin until two years after eligibility for SSDI, creating a waiting period during which individuals have to rely on private insurance or Medicaid, or else go uninsured. One option would be to reduce or eliminate this waiting period and instead offer Medicare benefits as soon as an individual begins receiving SSDI payments (or retroactively to the beginning of the eligibility period). The Medicare waiting period could be reduced or eliminated for all beneficiaries, or just for those without access to affordable health coverage. In 2008, CBO (2008) estimated this change could cost between $3 billion and $13 billion per year, or the equivalent of about 0.04 to 0.15 percent of payroll. Since then, the enactment of the Affordable Care Act, which now offers Medicaid or subsidized insurance exchange coverage to many workers with disabilities during the Medicare waiting period, has likely dramatically reduced the cost of this proposal. The impact on the SSDI program itself is also unclear, since better health coverage might make return-to-work more likely, but faster health coverage might increase the attractiveness of the SSDI benefit and therefore total enrollment in the program. According to the Chief Actuary, this policy would increase the size of the shortfall by 0.02 percent of payroll.

Establish a Special Minimum Benefit for SSDI Beneficiaries

Despite receiving SSDI benefits, about one in five SSDI beneficiaries live at or below the poverty line (White House 2015). At $14,000, the average SSDI benefit is large enough to keep an individual out of poverty (about $12,000 for an individual) even without other income. However, many SSDI beneficiaries receive benefits below this average—with about one-third receiving less than $11,000 per year—and not all of them collect Supplemental Security Income (SSI) to make up the difference. One option would be to set a "minimum benefit" for workers with disabilities. Ensuring all primary SSDI benefits at least equal the poverty line would cost about 0.03 percent of payroll over 75 years, or 0.07 percent if that minimum benefit were indexed to wage growth. Those costs would be incurred to both the SSDI and old-age programs, though a portion would be offset with savings to the SSI program.

Eliminate "Cash Cliff" and Provide Partial Benefits Above the Current SGA

Currently, workers who earn above the SGA level—generally about $1,100 per month this year—risk losing their SSDI benefits. Although an SSDI beneficiary may attempt to work at such levels for nine months without penalty under a "trial work period," after that time their cash benefits will be discontinued. Although SSDI has several mechanisms to encourage work—including a three-year period when a beneficiary can return to SSDI without having to reapply and a seven-year period when they can continue to receive publicly funded Medicare benefits—the loss of cash benefits immediately above SGA creates a "cash cliff" that might discourage additional work effort for some beneficiaries.

One option to address this cash cliff is to reduce benefits gradually as earnings increase rather than all at once after earnings exceed the SGA. For example, the Social Security Administration has tested benefit offset policies that would reduce an individual's SSDI benefits by $1 for every $2 the individual earns above SGA. Applying this offset to all SSDI beneficiaries above SGA, while also eliminating the trial work period, would cost about 0.04 percent of payroll. Applying this benefits offset beginning at or near an individual's first dollar of earnings would be roughly cost-neutral. Other thresholds, offset levels, and parameters are also possible.

Reduce or Eliminate the Payroll Tax for SSDI Beneficiaries Who Return to Work

Almost all workers, including those with disabilities, pay a 12.4 percent Social Security tax split evenly between employer and employee. One option to encourage SSDI beneficiaries to reenter the labor force, encourage employers to hire these workers, and increase take-home pay for those workers would be to reduce the payroll tax for those who were on the SSDI program. Such a payroll tax reduction could be made available for current and past SSDI recipients, or only for those no longer receiving cash benefits; it could be applied to the entire 12.4 percent Social Security payroll tax or only the 1.8 percent SSDI payroll tax; and it could be offered to employers, employees, or both. According to the Chief Actuary, this proposal would cost about 0.01 percent of payroll.

CONCLUSION

In the near term, some diversion of resources into the SSDI trust fund will be necessary to avoid trust fund depletion. If those funds come from the OASI trust fund, however, it will worsen the already weak financial state of that program. And to the extent this diversion of resources is temporary—even if long-term—lawmakers will need to shore up the financial state of both programs.

Ideally, the next step after addressing SSDI's near-term funding gap would be to pursue comprehensive Social Security reform that addresses the finances of the OASI and SSDI programs simultaneously. In that case, financial improvements to the SSDI program such as the ones described here could be part of a much larger package that ultimately brings total Social Security spending and revenue in line. Alternatively, each trust fund could be addressed separately, in which case the options in this chapter will be that much more important to maintaining the solvency of the SSDI program.

Reforming SSDI should be about far more than addressing its finances. It should be about improving the many aspects of the program, and related supports, for those with disabilities and for society more broadly. As lawmakers continue to pursue these improvements, they should also ensure the financial solvency and sustainability of both the SSDI program and Social Security as a whole.

Acknowledgements

The authors would like to thank Chief Actuary Stephen C. Goss, the staff at the Social Security Administration's Office of the Chief Actuary, and the staff of the Committee for a Responsible Federal Budget for their help in calculating estimates. We would also like to thank Joyce Manchester for her helpful advice and input on this draft.

References

Seizing the Opportunity: Ideas for Improving Disability Programs

Jim McCrery and Earl Pomeroy

Bailey, Michelle Stegman, and Jeffrey Hemmeter. 2015. "Characteristics of Noninstitutionalized DI and SSI Program Participants, 2013 Update." Social Security Administration Research and Statistics Note No. 2015-02 (September).

Bipartisan Policy Center (BPC). 2015. "Improve the SSDI Program and Address the Impending Trust Fund Depletion: Consensus Recommendations of BPC's Disability Insurance Working Group." Bipartisan Policy Center. Available at http://bipartisanpolicy.org/wp-content/uploads/2015/08/BPC-Economy-SSDI-Program.pdf.

Democratic Staff of the Committee on Ways and Means Subcommittee on Social Security (W&M). 2015. "Cooperative Disability Investigation Units." U.S. House of Representatives Committee on Ways and Means Subcommittee on Social Security. Available at http://democrats.waysandmeans.house.gov/sites/democrats.waysandmeans.house.gov/files/documents/CDI%20one%20pager.pdf.

Coburn, Tom. 2014. Protecting Social Security Disability Act of 2014. Introduced in the 113th Congress (December). Available at https://web.archive.org/web/20141231021843/http://www.coburn.senate.gov/public//index.cfm?a=Files.Serve&File_id=c0a4e044-f7c7-454a-96ca-53e3a077e0cc.

Government Accountability Office (GAO). 2004. "Social Security Administration: More Effort Needed to Address Consistency of Disability Decisions." Report to the Chairman, Subcommittee on Social Security, Committee on Ways and Means, House of Representatives. Available at http://www.gao.gov/assets/250/243276.pdf.

Krent, Harold J., and Scott Morris. 2013. "Achieving Greater Consistency in Social Security Disability Adjudication: An Empirical Study and Suggested Reforms." Administrative Conference of the United

States (April 3). Available at https://www.acus.gov/sites/default/files/documents/Achieving_Greater_Consistency_Final_Report_4-3-2013_clean.pdf.

Lankford, James, and Jackie Speier. 2014. Letter to Social Security Administration Acting Commissioner Carolyn W. Colvin (April 8). Available at https://oversight.house.gov/wp-content/uploads/2014/04/2014-04-08-Lankford-Speier-to-Colvin-SSA-SSDI-SSI-federal-disability-programs.pdf.

Lorenzen, Ed. 2015. Testimony before the Committee on Ways and Means Subcommittee on Social Security. Committee for a Responsible Federal Budget (February 25). Available at http://crfb.org/document/ed-lorenzen-testimony-disability-insurance-solvency-subcommittee-social-security.

Social Security Administration (SSA). 2015. "Annual Statistical Report on the Social Security Disability Insurance Program, 2014." Social Security Administration Research, Statistics, & Policy Analysis. December. Accessed December 7, 2015. Available at http://www.ssa.gov/policy/docs/statcomps/di_asr/index.html.

______. 2015a. "Annual Statistical Supplement to the Social Security Bulletin, 2014." Social Security Administration Research, Statistics, & Policy Analysis. April. Accessed September 30, 2015. Available at http://www.ssa.gov/policy/docs/statcomps/di_asr/index.html.

______. 2015b. "SSA's FY 2015 Actual Performance." Social Security Administration website. Accessed December 7, 2015. Available at https://www.ssa.gov/budget/FY15Files/2015ActualPerformance.pdf.

______. 2015c. "Improper Payments Information Detailed Report." The Social Security Administration's Agency Final Report for Fiscal Year 2015. Available at http://www.ssa.gov/finance/2015/Improper%20Payments.pdf.

______. 2015d. "Limitation on Administrative Expenses." Social Security Administrative FY 2016 Budget Estimates and Related Information. Available at http://www.ssa.gov/budget/FY16Files/2016LAE.pdf.

Social Security Administration Office of the Inspector General (SSA OIG). 2015. "Cooperative Disability Investigations (CDI)." Social Security Administration website. Accessed October 12, 2015. Available at http://oig.ssa.gov/cooperative-disability-investigations-cdi.

______. 2015a. "Fiscal Year 2015 Inspector General Statement on The Social Security Administration's Major Management and Performance Challenges." Social Security Administration (November).

Accessed December 7, 2015. Available at http://oig.ssa.gov/audits-and-investigations/audit-reports/A-02-16-50118.
______. 2012. "Oversight of Administrative Law Judge Workload Trends." Social Security Administration (February). Available at http://oig.ssa.gov/sites/default/files/audit/full/pdf/A-12-11-01138_0.pdf.
Social Security Advisory Board (SSAB). 2014. "2014 Disability Policy Panel: Continuing Disability Reviews." Social Security Advisory Board Disability Policy Panel. Available at http://ssab.gov/Portals/0/Documents/2014_DPP_Report_Final.pdf.
______. 2006. "Improving the Social Security Administration's Hearing Process." Social Security Advisory Board (September). Available at http://ssab.gov/Portals/0/documents/HearingProcess.pdf.
Social Security Board of Trustees (Trustees). 2015. The 2015 Annual Report of the Board of Trustees of the Federal Old-Age and Survivors Insurance and Federal Disability Insurance Trust Funds. Washington: U.S. Government Publishing Office.
White House Office of Management and Budget (President's budget). 2015. Budget of the United States Government, Fiscal Year 2016. Available at https://www.whitehouse.gov/omb/budget/Overview.

An Overview of Social Security Disability Insurance (SSDI)
Patricia Owens

Autor, David H. 2011. "The Unsustainable Rise of the Disability Rolls in the United States: Causes, Consequences, and Policy Options." *NBER Working Paper* No. 17697.
Autor, David H., and Mark G. Duggan. 2006. "The Growth in the Social Security Disability Rolls: A Fiscal Crisis Unfolding." *Journal of Economic Perspectives* 20 (3): 71-96.
Autor, David H., and Mark G. Duggan. 2003. "The Rise in the Disability Rolls and the Decline in Unemployment." *Quarterly Journal of Economics*: 157-205.
Bailey, Michelle Stegman, and Jeffrey Hemmeter. 2014. "Characteristics of Noninstitutionalized DI and SSI Program Participants, 2010 Update." *Research and Statistics Note* 2014-02.
Colvin, Carolyn W. 2012. "Statement of Carolyn W. Colvin, Deputy Commissioner, Social Security Administration, before the House Committee on Ways and Means, Subcommittee on Social Security." Social Security Administration website. January 24. Accessed

September 1, 2015. Available at http://www.ssa.gov/legislation/testimony_012412.html.

Congressional Budget Office (CBO). 2015. The 2015 Long-Term Budget Outlook. Washington: Congressional Budget Office.

______. 2012. Policy Options for the Social Security Disability Insurance Program. Washington: Congressional Budget Office.

Goss, Steven C. 2014. "The Foreseen Trend in the Cost of Disability Insurance Benefits." Testimony to the Senate Committee on Finance, Social Security Administration. Available at http://www.ssa.gov/OACT/testimony/SenateFinance_20140724.pdf.

______. 2015. Estimate of the Effects on the OASI and DI Trust Funds of enacting the provisions of Title VIII of H.R. 1314, the "Bipartisan Budget Act of 2015," introduced on October 27, 2015 by Representative John Boehner. Available at https://www.ssa.gov/OACT/solvency/JBoehner_20151027.pdf

Government Accountability Office (GAO). 2008. Federal Disability Programs: More Strategic Coordination Could Help Overcome Challenges to Needed Transformation. Report to the Ranking Member, Subcommittee on Oversight of Government Management, the Federal Workforce, and the District of Columbia, Committee on Homeland Security and Governmental Affairs, U.S. Senate, Washington: Government Accountability Office.

______. 2010a. Social Security Reform: Raising the Retirement Ages Would Have Implications for Older Workers and SSA Disability Rolls. GAO-11-125, Washington: Government Accountability Office.

______. 2010b. Actions That Could Increase Work Participation For Adults With Disabilities. GAO-10-812SP Highlights of a forum, Washington: Government Accountability Office.

______. 2014. Review of Concurrent Receipt of Department of Defense Retirement, Department of Veterans Affairs Disability Compensation, and Social Security Disability Insurance. GAO-14-854R Disability Compensation, Washington: Government Accountability Office.

______. 2015. Improving and Modernizing Federal Disability Programs. GAO-15-290 High-Risk Series: An Update, Washington: Government Accountability Office.

Kearney, John R. 2005/2006. Social Security and the "D" in OASDI: The History of a Federal Program Insuring Earners Against Disability. August. Accessed September 1, 2015. Available at http://www.ssa.gov/policy/docs/ssb/v66n3/v66n3p1.html.

Livermore, Gina, Arif Mamun, Jody Schimmel, and Sarah Prenovitz. 2013. Executive Summary of the Seventh Ticket to Work Evaluation Report. Final Report, Washington: Mathematica Policy Research.

Livermore, Gina, David Wittenburg, and David Neumark. 2014. "Finding Alternatives to Disability Benefit Receipt." *IZA Journal of Labor Policy* 3 (14).

Morton, William R. 2014. Primer on Disability Benefits: Social Security Disability Insurance (SSDI) and Supplemental Security Income (SSI). Congressional Research Service.

Rajnes, David. 2012. "'Fast-track' Strategies in Long-Term Public Disability Programs Around the World." *Social Security Bulletin* (February): 79-108. Available at http://www.ssa.gov/policy/docs/ssb/v72n1/v72n1p79.html.

Reno, Virginia, Cecili Thompson Williams, and Ishita Sengupta. 2003/2004. "Workers' Compensation, Social Security Disability Insurance, and the Offset: A Fact Sheet." *Social Security Bulletin* 65 (4).

Rondinelli, Robert D (AMA). 2008. AMA Guides to the Evaluation of Permanent Impairment, Sixth Edition. American Medical Association.

Ruffing, Kathy. 2014. "How Much of the Growth in Disability Insurance Stems From Demographic Changes?" Washington: Center on Budget and Policy Priorities. Available at http://www.cbpp.org/research/how-much-of-the-growth-in-disability-insurance-stems-from-demographic-changes.

Rupp, Kalman. 2012. "Factors Affecting Initial Disability Allowance Rates for the Disability Insurance and Supplemental Security Income Programs: The Role of the Demographic and Diagnostic Composition of Applicants and Local Labor Market Conditions." *Social Security Bulletin* 72 (4).

Social Security Administration (SSA). 2011. "FY 2012 Limitation on Administrative Expenses - FY 2010 Disability Workload." Social Security Administration Budget Estimates and Related Information - Historical Data. March. Accessed September 15, 2015. Available at http://www.socialsecurity.gov/budget/hist/FY2012/2012LAE.pdf.

______. 2012. "FY 2013 Limitation on Administrative Expenses - FY 2011 Disability Workload." Social Security Administration Budget Estimates and Related Information - Historical Data. February. Accessed September 17, 2015. Available at http://www.socialsecurity.gov/budget/hist/FY2013/2013LAE.pdf.

______. 2013. "FY 2014 Administrative Expenses - FY 2012 Disability Workload." Social Security Administration Budget Estimates And Related Information. April. Accessed September 17, 2015. Available at http://www.ssa.gov/budget/FY14Files/2014AE.pdf.

______. 2014a. "Annual Statistical Supplement of the Social Security Disability Insurance Program, 2013." Social Security Administration Research, Statistics, & Policy Analysis. December. Accessed September 17, 2015. Available at http://www.ssa.gov/policy/docs/statcomps/di_asr/index.html.

______. 2014b. "FY 2015 Limitation on Administrative Expenses - FY 2013 Disability Workload." Social Security Administration Budget Estimates And Related Information. March. Accessed September 17, 2015. Available at http://www.ssa.gov/budget/FY15Files/2015LAE.pdf.

______. 2015a. Quarter of Coverage. Accessed September 1, 2015. Available at https://www.socialsecurity.gov/oact/cola/QC.html.

______. 2015b. Substantial Gainful Activity. Accessed September 1, 2015. Available atwww.socialsecurity.gov/OACT/COLA/sga.html.

______. 2015c. Monthly Statistical Snapshot, July 2015. August. Accessed September 17, 2015. Available at http://www.ssa.gov/policy/docs/quickfacts/stat_snapshot/index.html?number#table2.

______. 2015d. Hearings Held In-Person or Via Video Conferencing Report. Falls Church: Office of Disability Adjudication and Review. Available at http://www.socialsecurity.gov/appeals/DataSets/06_Hearings_Held_InPerson_Video_Report.html.

______. 2015e. "FY 2016 Limitation on Administrative Expenses - FY 2014 Disability Workload." Social Security Administration Budget Estimates and Related Information. February. Accessed September 17, 2015. Available at http://www.ssa.gov/budget/FY16Files/2016LAE.pdf.

______. 2015f. 2015 Red Book: A Summary Guide to Employment Supports for Persons with Disabilities Under the Social Security Disability Insurance and Supplemental Security Income Programs.

______. 2015g. Annual Statistical Supplement to the Social Security Bulletin, 2014. Washington, April.

Social Security Advisory Board (SSAB). 2015. "The Single Decision Maker Pilot: A 16 Year Flight and Still No Clear Landing." Social Security Advisory Board website. June. Accessed September 1, 2015. Available at http://ssab.gov/Portals/0/Reports/SDM_Final.pdf.

Social Security Board of Trustees. 2015. The 2015 Annual Report of the Board of Trustees of the Federal Old-Age and Survivors Insurance and Federal Disability Insurance Trust Funds. Washington: U.S. Government Publishing Office.

Wixon, Bernard, and Alexander Strand. 2013. "Identifying SSA's Sequential Disability Determination Steps Using Administrative Data." *Research and Statistics Note* No. 2013-01 (June). Available at http://www.ssa.gov/policy/docs/rsnotes/rsn2013-01.html.

The Employment/Eligibility Service System: A New Gateway for Employment Supports and Social Security Disability Benefits
David Stapleton, Yonatan Ben-Shalom, and David Mann

American College of Occupational & Environmental Medicine. 2006. "Preventing Needless Work Disability by Helping People Stay Employed." *Journal of Occupational and Environmental Medicine* 48: 972–87.

Autor, David, Mark Duggan, and Jonathan Gruber. 2014. "Moral Hazard and Claims Deterrence in Private Disability Insurance." *American Economic Journal: Applied Economics* 6: 110–41.

Autor, David H., Nicole Maestas, Kathleen J. Mullen, and Alexander Strand. 2015. "Does Delay Cause Decay? The Effect of Administrative Decision Time on the Labor Force Participation and Earnings of Disability Applicants." NBER Working Paper w20840. Cambridge, MA: National Bureau of Economic Research.

Ben-Shalom, Yonatan. 2015. "Assessing the Costs and Benefits of Return-to-Work Programs." Washington, DC: Mathematica Policy Research.

Ben-Shalom, Yonatan, and Arif Mamun. 2013. "Return-to-Work Outcomes Among Social Security Disability Insurance Program Beneficiaries." Washington, DC: Mathematica Policy Research.

Block, Frank, Jeffrey Lubbers, and Paul Verkuil. 2014. "The Social Security Administration's New Disability Adjudication Rules: A Significant and Promising Reform." Cornell Law Review 92: 234–47.

Boden, Leslie I. 2005. "Running on Empty: Families, Time, and Workplace Injuries." *American Journal of Public Health* 95:1894–97.

Bureau of Labor Statistics. 2014. "Table 1. Number, Median Days Away From Work, and Incidence Rate for Nonfatal Occupational Injuries and Illnesses Involving Days Away from Work by Ownership, Industry, Musculoskeletal Disorders, and Event or Exposure." In *Nonfatal Occupational Injuries and Illnesses Requiring Days Away From Work, 2013.*

Washington, DC: Bureau of Labor Statistics. Available at http://www.bls.gov/news.releas /osh2.t01.htm.

Burkhauser, Richard V., Mary C. Daly, Duncan McVicar, and Roger Wilkins. 2014. "Disability Benefit Growth and Disability Reform in the US: Lessons from Other OECD Nations." *IZA Journal of Labor Policy* 3: 1–30.

Burton, John F. 2007. "Workers' Compensation in the United States: A Primer." *Perspectives on Work* 11: 23–25.

Cody, Scott, and Andrew Asher. 2014. "Smarter, Better, Faster: The Potential for Predictive Analytics and Rapid Cycle Evaluation to Improve Program Development and Outcomes." In *Policies to Address Poverty in America*, edited by Melissa S. Kearney, and Benjamin H. Harris. Washington, DC: The Hamilton Project.

Franche, R., K. Cullen, J. Clarke, E. Irvin, S. Sinclair, and J. Frank. 2005. "Workplace-Based Return-to-Work Interventions: A Systematic Review of the Quantitative Literature." *Journal of Occupational Rehabilitation* 15: 607–31.

Fraker, Thomas, Arif Mamun, and Lori Timmins. 2015. "The Youth Transition Demonstration: Three-Year Impacts of Services and Work Incentives on Youth with Disabilities." Mathematica Issue Brief. Washington, DC: Mathematica Policy Research.

Fraker, Thomas, Erik Carter, Todd Honeycutt, Jacqueline Kauff, Gina Livermore, and Arif Mamun. 2014. "Promoting Readiness of Minors in SSI (PROMISE) Evaluation Design Report." Washington, DC: Center for Studying Disability Policy, Mathematica Policy Research.

French, Eric, and Jae Song. 2014. "The Effect of Disability Insurance Receipt on Labor Supply." *American Economic Journal: Economic Policy* 6: 291–337.

Government Accountability Office (GAO). 2004. "Social Security Administration: More Effort Needed to Assess Consistency of Disability Decisions." Washington, DC: Government Accountability Office.

______. 2012. "Modernizing SSA Disability Programs: Progress Made, but Key Efforts Warrant More Management Focus." Washington, DC: Government Accountability Office.

Hullegie, Patrick, and Pierre Koning. 2014. "Employee Health and Employer Incentives." Amsterdam: VU University Amsterdam. Available at www.hha.dk/nat/larss/CAFE2014 /PHullegie.pdf.

Joffe-Walt, Chana. 2013. "Unfit for Work: The Startling Rise of Disability in America." Available at http://apps.npr.org/unfit-for-work/. Accessed June 9, 2015.

Kornfeld, Robert, and Kalman Rupp. 2000. "Net Effects of the Project NetWork Return-to-Work Case Management Experiment on Participant Earnings, Benefit Receipt, and Other Outcomes." *Social Security Bulletin* 63: 12–33.

Liebman, Jeffrey B., and Jack A. Smalligan. 2013. "An Evidence-Based Path to Disability Insurance Reform." Washington, DC: The Hamilton Project, Brookings Institution.

Liu, Su, and David C. Stapleton. 2011. "Longitudinal Statistics on Work Activity and Use of Employment Supports for New Social Security Disability Insurance Beneficiaries." *Social Security Bulletin* 71: 35–60.

MacDonald, Bryon, and Megan O'Neill. 2006. "Being American: The Way Out of Poverty." Berkeley, CA: World Institute on Disability.

Maestas, Nicole, Kathleen J. Mullen, and Alexander Strand. 2013. "Does Disability Insurance Receipt Discourage Work? Using Examiner Assignment to Estimate Causal Effects of SSDI Receipt." *American Economic Review* 103: 1797–829.

Mann, David R., and David C. Stapleton. 2011. "Fiscal Austerity and the Transition to Twenty-First Century Disability Policy: A Road Map." Washington, DC: Mathematica Policy Research.

Mann, David R., David C. Stapleton, and Jeanette de Richemond. 2014. "Vocational Factors in the Social Security Disability Determination Process: A Literature Review." Washington, DC: Mathematica Policy Research.

Monaco, Kristen. 2015. "Disability Insurance Plans: Trends in Employee Access and Employer Costs." *Beyond the Numbers: Pay & Benefits*, vol. 4, no. 4. Washington, DC: U.S. Bureau of Labor Statistics.

Muijzer, Anna, Johan W. Groothoff, W.E.L. de Boer, Jan H.B. Geertzen, and Sandra Brouwer. 2010. "The Assessment of Efforts to Return to Work in the European Union." *The European Journal of Public Health* 20: 689–94.

Rehabilitation Services Administration. 2014. "Rehabilitation Services Administration: Annual Report for Fiscal Year 2012." Washington, DC: RSA.

Riley, Gerald F., and Kalman Rupp. 2015. "Cumulative Expenditures Under the DI, SSI, Medicare, and Medicaid Programs for a Cohort of Disabled Working-Age Adults." *Health Services Research* 50: 514–36.

Schimmel, Jody, and David C. Stapleton. 2012. "The Financial Repercussions of New Work-Limiting Health Conditions for Older Workers." *Inquiry* 49: 345–54.

Social Security Administration (SSA). 2011. "FY2012 President's Budget: Key Tables." Baltimore, MD: SSA, February 2011. Available at http://www.socialsecurity.gov/budget/hist/FY2012/2012KeyTables.pdf. Accessed March 19, 2015.

_______. 2014. "Annual Statistical Report on the Social Security Disability Insurance Program, 2013." Baltimore, MD: Social Security Administration.

Social Security Advisory Board (SSAB). 2006. "A Disability System for the 21st Century." Washington, DC: Social Security Advisory Board.

Stapleton, David C. 2012. "Testimony for Hearing on Securing the Future of the Social Security Disability Insurance Program." U.S. House of Representatives Committee on Ways and Means, Subcommittee on Social Security, Washington, DC: Mathematica Policy Research, September 14.

Stapleton, David C., Richard V. Burkhauser, Peiyun She, Robert Weathers, and Gina A. Livermore. 2009. "Income Security for Workers: A Stressed Support System in Need of Innovation." *Journal of Disability Policy Studies* 19: 204–20.

Stapleton, David C., David R. Mann, and Jae Song. 2015. "Firm-Level Early Intervention Incentives: Which Recent Employers of Disability Program Entrants Would Pay More?" Washington, DC: Mathematica Policy Research.

Stapleton, David C., and Frank H. Martin. 2012. "Vocational Rehabilitation on the Road to Social Security Disability: Longitudinal Statistics from Matched Administrative Data." Working Paper 2012-269. Ann Arbor, MI: Michigan Retirement Research Center.

Sullivan, Michael J.L., and Heather Adams. 2010. "Psychosocial Treatment Techniques to Augment the Impact of Physiotherapy Interventions for Low Back Pain." *Physiotherapy Canada* 63: 180–89.

Von Wachter, Till, Jae Song, and Joyce Manchester. 2011. "Trends in Employment and Earnings of Allowed and Rejected Applicants to the Social Security Disability Insurance Program." *American Economic Review* 101: 3308–329.

Waddell, Gordon, A. Kim Burton, and Nicholas A.S. Kendall. 2008. "Vocational Rehabilitation: What Works, for Whom, and When?" London: Department for Work and Pensions.

Wickizer, Thomas M., Gary Franklin, Deborah Fulton-Kehoe, Jeremy Gluck, Robert Mootz, Terri Smith-Weller, and Roy Plaeger-Brockway. 2011. "Improving Quality, Preventing Disability and Reducing Costs in Workers' Compensation Healthcare: A Population-Based Intervention Study." *Medical Care* 49: 1105–111.

World Health Organization (WHO). 2002. "Towards a Common Language for Functioning, Disability, and Health: ICF." Geneva, Switzerland: World Health Organization.

A Community-Focused Health & Work Service (HWS)

Jennifer Christian, Thomas Wickizer, and A. Kim Burton

Abásolo, Lydia, Margarita Blanco, Javier Bachiller, Gloria Candelas, Paz Collado, Cristina Lajas, Marcelino Revenga, Patricia Ricci, Pablo Lázaro, Maria Dolores Aguilar, Emilio Vargas, Benjamín Fernández-Gutiérrez, César Hernández-García, Loreto Carmona, and Juan A. Jover. 2005. "A Health System Program to Reduce Work Disability Related to Musculoskeletal Disorders." *Annals of Internal Medicine* 143: 404-414.

American College of Occupational and Environmental Medicine (ACOEM). 2010. "Cornerstones of Disability Prevention and Management." Chapter 5, *ACOEM Practice Guidelines*, American College of Occupational & Environmental Medicine 2010.

______. 2006. "Preventing Needless Work Disability by Helping People Stay Employed." Guidance Statement, 2006.

Arends, Iris, Jac JL van der Klink, Willem van Rhenen, Michiel R de Boer, and Ute Bültmann. 2014. "Predictors of recurrent sickness absence among workers having returned to work after sick leave due to common mental disorders." *Scandinavian Journal of Work, Environment, & Health* 40(2): 195–202. doi:10.5271/sjweh.3384

Aurbach, Robert. 2014. "Breaking the Web of Needless Disability." *Work* 48(4):591-607 (ISSN: 1875-9270).

Autor, David H. 2011. "The Unsustainable Rise of Disability Rolls in the United States: Causes, Consequences and Policy Options." MIT, National Bureau of Economic Research, November 2011.

Bernacki, Edward J., Xuguang Tao, and Larry Yuspeh. 2010. "The Impact of Cost Intensive Physicians on Workers' Compensation." *Journal of Occupational & Environmental Medicine* 52(1): 22-8.

Black, Carol M. 2008. "Working for a Healthier Tomorrow: Summary of Evidence Submitted, Dame Carol Black's Review of the Health of Britain's Working Age Population." The Stationery Office.

Black, Carol M., and David Frost. 2011. "Health at Work: An Independent Review of Sickness Absence." Presented to Parliament by the Secretary of State for Work and Pensions. The Stationery Office.

Boos, Norbert, Rico Rieder, Volker Schade, Kevin F. Spratt, Norbert Semmer, and Max Aebi. 1995. "Volvo Award in clinical science: The diagnostic accuracy of MRI, work perception, and psychosocial factors in identifying symptomatic disc herniations." Spine – 1995; 20:2613-2625.

Bowling, Maddy. 2000. "The 'Halo Effect': Measuring the Power of Intangibles in Workers' Compensation." *Journal of Workers Compensation*, Fall 2000.

Burton, A. Kim, Nick Kendall, Serena McCluskey, and Pauline Dibben. 2013. "Telephonic Support to Facilitate Return to Work: What Works, How, and When?" UK Department of Work and Pensions, 2013.

Caruso, Garson M. 2013. "Biopsychosocial Considerations in Unnecessary Work Disability." *Psychological Injury and Law* 6: 164-182.

Charbonneau Andrea, William Bruning, Teresa Titus-Howard, Edward Ellerbeck, Jeff Whittle, Sandra Hall, Jan Campbell, Susan Crain Lewis, and Stuart Munro. 2005. The Community Initiative on Depression: Report from a Multiphase Work Site Depression Intervention. *Journal of Occupational & Environmental Medicine* 47(1): 60-67.

Cheadle, Allen, Gary Franklin, Carl Wolfhagen, James Savarino, P.Y. Liu, Charles Salley, and Marcia Weaver. 1994. "Factors influencing the duration of work-related disability: a population-based study of Washington State workers' compensation." *American Journal of Public Health*. 1994 February; 84(2): 190–196.

Christian, Jennifer. 2009 "Introduction to the New Work Disability Prevention Paradigm." 60 Summits Project, 2009.

Cornelius, L.R., J.J.L. van der Klink, J.W. Groothoff, and S. Brouwer. 2011. "Prognostic factors of long term disability due to mental disorders: A systematic review." *Journal of Occupational Rehabilitation* 21 (2): 259–274.

Darlow, B., B.M. Fullen, S. Dean, D.A. Hurley, G.D. Baxter, and A. Dowell. 2011. "The association between healthcare professional attitudes and beliefs and the attitudes and beliefs, clinical management and outcomes of patients with low back pain: A systematic review." European Journal of Pain 16: 3-17. DOI: 10.1016/j.ejpain 2011.06.006.

Dartmouth Institute for Health Policy and Clinical Practice. 2008. "Tracking the Care of Patients with Severe Chronic Illness." Dartmouth Institute for Health Policy and Clinical Practice, 2008.

DeWitt, Marcia, and The Guilford Group, Ltd of Baltimore, MD. 1995. Graph with data from a 1995 study of employees of a large company with workers compensation claims showing the decreasing likelihood of ever returning to work by increasing weeks of work disability, in *Workers' Compensation Newsletter*, 1995.

Deyo, Richard A. 2013. "Real Help and Red Herrings in Spinal Imaging." *New England Journal of Medicine* 368;11: 1056-1058. March 14, 2013.

DMEC - Disability Management Employer Coalition. 2015. Conference brochure. Employer-speakers discuss their own company's best practices and success stories. Available at: http:www.dmec.org.

Feinberg, Steven D., Robert J. Gatchel, Steven Stanos, Rachel Feinberg, and Valerie Johnson-Montieth. 2013 "Interdisciplinary Functional Restoration and Pain Programs" in *Treatment of Chronic Pain by Medical, Interventional, and Integrative Approaches*, Chapter 82. American Academy of Pain Medicine, 2013. DOI 10.1007/978-1-4614-1560_82

Franklin, Gary M., and Kathryn Mueller. 2015. Letter to NIOSH, February 15, 2015. ACOEM Public Comments: http://www.acoem.org/PrioritizingSecondaryPrevention_NIOSH.aspx.

Franklin, Gary M., Bert D. Stover, Judith A. Turner, Deborah Fulton-Kehoe, and Thomas M. Wickizer. 2008. "Early Opioid Prescription and Subsequent Disability Among Workers With Back Injuries: The Disability Risk Identification Study Cohort." *Spine* 33(2): 199-204. doi:10.1097/BRS.0b013e318160455c.

Franklin, Gary M., Judith A. Turner, Thomas M. Wickizer, Deborah Fulton-Kehoe, and Robert D. Mootz. 2013. "Disability Prevention." *Encyclopedia of Pain*: 628-31.

Franklin, Gary M., Thomas M. Wickizer, Norma B. Coe, and Deborah Fulton-Kehoe. 2014. "Workers' Compensation: Poor Quality Health Care and the Growing Disability Problem in the United States." *American Journal of Industrial Medicine* 58: 245-251. doi:10.1002/ajim.22399

Global Burden of Disease Study 2013 Collaborators. 2015. "Global, regional and national incidence, prevalence, and years living with disability for 301 acute and chronic diseases and injuries in 188 countries, 1990-2013: a systematic analysis for the Global Burden of Disease Study 2013". *The Lancet* June 7, 2015. DOI: http://dx.doi.org/10.1016/S0140-6736(15)60692-4

Habeck, Rochelle V., H. Allan Hunt, and Brett VanTol. 1998. "Workplace Factors Associated With Preventing and Managing Work Disability." Rehabilitation Counseling Bulletin 42(2) (December): 98-143.

Harris, Ashley M., E. John Orav, David W. Bates, and Arthur J. Barsky. 2008. "Somatization increases disability independent of comorbidity." *Journal of General Internal Medicine* 24: 155-161.

Hashemi, Lobat, Barbara S. Webster, Edward A. Clancy, and Ernest Volinn. 1997. "Length of Disability and Cost of Workers' Compensation Low Back Claims." *Journal of Occupational and Environmental Medicine* 39(10): 937-45.

Hill, Jonathan C., Kate M. Dunn, Chris J. Main, and Elaine M. Hay. 2010. "Subgrouping low back pain: A comparison of the STarT Back Tool with the Örebro Musculoskeletal Pain Screening Questionnaire." *European Journal of Pain* 14(1):83-9.

Hillage, Jim. 2012. "Evaluation of the Fit for Work Service pilots: first year report." Department of Work and Pensions, Research Report 792.

Iles, Ross Anthony, Mary Wyatt, and G. Pransky 2012. "Multi-Faceted Case Management: Reducing Compensation costs of Musculoskeletal work Injuries in Australia." *Journal of Occupational Rehabilitation* 22(4). DOI: 10.1007/x10926-012-9364-2

Institute of Medicine (IOM). 2001. "Crossing the Quality Chasm: A New Health System for the 21st Century." National Academy Press.

IBI-Integrated Benefits Institute. 2015. "Low Back Pain: A Major Employer Uses Guidelines to Manage Quality, Costs and Outcomes." William Bunn, MD, Harris Allen, PhD, Michael Erdil, MD. Recorded webinar presentation. Available at https://www.ibiweb.org/research-resources/detail/low-back-pain-a-major-employer-uses-guidelines-to-manage-quality-costs-outc.

Johnson, David, and Tim Fry. 2002. "Factors Affecting Return to Work after Injury: A study for the Victorian WorkCover Authority." Melbourne: Melbourne Institute of Applied Economic and Social Research.

Kendall, Nicholas A.S., A. Kim Burton, Chris J. Main, and Paul J. Watson. 2009. "Tackling musculoskeletal problems: a guide for the clinic and workplace – identifying obstacles using the psychosocial flags framework." London, The Stationery Office.

Krause, Niklas, and David R. Ragland. 1994. "Occupational disability due to low back pain: A new interdisciplinary classification based on a phase model of disability." *Spine* 19:1011-1020.

Kroenke, Kurt, Jingwei Wu, Matthew J. Bair, Erin E. Krebs, Teresa M. Damush, and Wanzhu Tu. 2011. "Reciprocal Relationship Between Pain and Depression: A 12-Month Longitudinal Analysis in Primary Care". *The Journal of Pain* 12 (9) (September): 964-73.

Lagerveld, Suzanne E., Roland W.B. Blonk, Veerle Brenninkmeijer, Leoniek Wijingaards-de Meij, and Wilmar B. Schaufeli. 2012. "Work-Focused Treatment of Common Mental Disorders and Return to Work: A Comparative Outcome Study." *Journal of Occupational Health Psychology* 17 (2) (April): 220-34. doi: 10.1037/a0027049

Leopold, Ronald S. 2003. *A year in the life of a million American workers*. MetLife Group Disability: 17-20.

Lerner, Debra, David A. Adler, William H. Rogers, Hong Chang, Annabel Greenhill, Elina Cymerman, and Francisca Azocar. 2015. "A Randomized Clinical Trial of a Telephone Depression Intervention to Reduce Employee Presenteeism and Absenteeism." *Psychiatric Services* 66 (6): 570-77. dx.doi.org/10.1176/appi.ps.201400350

Loisel, Patrick, Lucien Abenhaim, Pierre Durand, John M. Esdaile, Samy Suissa, Lise Gosselin, Robert Simard, Jean Turcotte, and Jacques Lemaire. 1997. "A population-based, randomized clinical trial on back pain management." *Spine* 22 (24): 2911-2918.

Loisel, Patrick, and Johannes Anema, Eds. 2013. *Handbook of Work Disability Prevention: Prevention and Management*. Springer, New York.

Lötters, Freek and Alex Burdorf. 2006. "Prognostic factors for duration of sickness absence due to musculoskeletal disorders." *Clinical Journal of Pain* 22 (2): 212-21.

Mahmud, Mohammed A., Barbara S. Webster, Theodore K. Courtney, Simon Matz, James A. Tacci, and David C. Christiani. 2000. "Clinical Management and the Duration of Disability for Work-Related Low Back Pain." *Journal of Occupational & Environmental Medicine* 42 (12) (December): 1178-1187.

Martin, Brook I., Judith A. Turner, Sohail K. Mirza, Michael J. Lee, Bryan A. Comstock, and Richard A. Deyo. 2009. "Trends in health care expenditures, utilization, and health status among US adults with spine problems, 1997–2006." *Spine* 34 (19): 2077-84.

McLaren, Christopher F., Robert T. Reville, and Seth A. Seabury. 2010. "How effective are employer return to work programs?" Rand Corporation, prepared for the California Commission on Health, Safety and Workers' Compensation. Working paper series WR-745-CHSWC. http://www.rand.org/content/dam/rand/pubs/working_papers/2010/RAND_WR745.pdf

Melloh, Markus, Achim Elfering, Carmen Egli Presland, Christoph Roeder, T. Barz, Cornelia Rolli Salathé, Oezguer Tamcan, Urs Mueller, and Jean-Claude Theis. 2009. "Identification of prognostic factors for chronicity in patients with low back pain: a review of screening instruments." *International Orthopaedics* 33 (2) (April): 301-13. DOI: 10.1007/s00264-008-07078/.

Mitchell, Kenneth. 2012. "The Return to Work Dividend: Protecting Productivity. Stay-at-Work and Back-to-Work Strategies: Lessons from the Private Sector." Testimony to the U.S. Senate Committee on Health, Education, Labor and Pensions, March 22. Available at http://www.help.senate.gov/imo/media/doc/Mitchell6.pdf.

Nicholas, Michael K., Steven J. Linton, Paul J. Watson, and Chris J. Main. 2011. "Early identification and management of psychological risk factors ("yellow flags") in patients with low back pain: a reappraisal." *Journal of the American Physical Therapy Association* 91: 737–53.

Nguyen, Trang H., David C. Randolph, James Talmage, Paul Succop, and Russell Travis. 2011. "Long-term outcomes of lumbar fusion among workers' compensation subjects." *Spine* 36 (4): 320-31.

National Institute of Mental Health. 2015. "Any Anxiety Disorder Among Adults." Accessed on September 10, 2015. Available at http://www.nimh.nih.gov/health/statistics/prevalence/any-anxiety-disorder-among-adults.shtml.

National Institute for Occupational Safety and Health (NIOSH). 2015. "Disability Prevention Research: A Look to the Future." May 29, 2015. Featured speakers Kathryn Mueller and Gary Franklin. U.S. Centers for Disease Control and Prevention. Webinar recording available at https://nioshtwh.adobeconnect.com/p9law27cnd3/.

Rumack, Eric. 2015. Graph based on 1987 Ontario Canada Workers Compensation Board report. Accessed on September 10, 2015. Available at www.occupationalphysician.ca/history.html.

Schultz, Izabela Z., Anna W. Stowell, Michael Feuerstein, and Robert J. Gatchel. 2007. "Models of Return to Work for Musculoskeletal Disorders." *Journal of Occupational Rehabilitation* 17: 327-52. DOI 10.1007/s10926-007-9071-6.

Shaw, William S., Silje E. Reme, Glenn Pransky, Mary Jane Woiszwillo, Ivan Steenstra, and Steven J. Linton. 2013. "The Pain Recovery Inventory of Concerns and Expectations: A Psychosocial Screening Instrument to Identify Intervention Needs Among Patients at Elevated Risk of Back Disability." *Journal of Occupational and Environmental Medicine* 55 (8): 885-94.

Social Security Administration (SSA). 2013. "Annual Statistical Report on the Social Security Disability Insurance Program, 2013" Available at http://www.ssa.gov/policy/docs/statcomps/di_asr/2013/sect03.html.

Sullivan, Michael J.L., Michael Feuerstein, Robert Gatchel, Steven J. Linton, and Glenn Pransky. 2005 "Integrating Psychosocial and Behavioral Interventions to Achieve Optimal Rehabilitation outcomes." *Journal of Occupational Rehabilitation* 15 (4): 475-89. DOI: 10.1007/s10926-005-8029-9.

Steinbrecher, Natalie, Stephanie Koerber, Dirk Frieser, and Wolfgang Hiller. 2011. "The Prevalence of Medically Unexplained Symptoms in Primary Care." *Psychosomatics* 52: 263-71.

Strully, Kate W. 2009. "Job Loss and Health in the U.S. Labor Market." *Demography* 46 (2): 221–46.

Turner, Judith A., Gary Franklin, Deborah Fulton-Kehoe, Lianne Sheppard, Bert Stover, Rae Wu, Jeremy V. Gluck, and Thomas M. Wickizer. 2008. "ISSLS prize winner: Early predictors for chronic work disability: A prospective, population-based study of workers with back injuries." *Spine* 33: 2809-18.

Unum. 2015. "Employer Spotlight: Tyson Foods." Accessed on September 10, 2015. Available at http://www.unum.com/Employers/UnumDifference/EmployerSpotlight.aspx.

U.S. Burden of Disease Collaborators. 2013. "The State of US Health, 1990-2010: Burden of Diseases, Injuries, and Risk Factors." *Journal of the American Medical Association* 310 (6): 591-606. doi:10.1001/jama.2013.13805.

Waddell, Gordon, and A. Kim Burton. 2006. *Is work good for your health and well-being?* United Kingdom. The Stationery Office.

Waddell, Gordon, and Mansel Aylward. 2009. *Models of Sickness and Disability Applied to Common Health Problems.* Royal Society of Medicine Press.

Waddell, Gordon, A. Kim Burton, and Mansel Aylward. 2008. "A Biopsychosocial Model of Sickness and Disability." *The Guidelines Newsletter*, AMA (May/June).

Waddell, Gordon, and A. Kim Burton. 2004. *Concepts of Rehabilitation for the Management of Common Health Problems*. United Kingdom. The Stationery Office.

Waddell, Gordon, A. Kim Burton, and Chris J. Main. 2001. *Screening to Identify People at Risk of Longterm Incapacity for Work: a Conceptual and Scientific Review*. Royal Society of Medicine Press.

Wickizer, Thomas M., Gary Franklin, Deborah Fulton-Kehoe, Jeremy Gluck, Robert Mootz, Terri Smith-Weller, and Roy Plaeger-Brockway. 2011. "Improving quality, preventing disability and reducing costs in workers' compensation healthcare: a population-based intervention study." *Medical Care* 49 (12): 1105-11.

Wickizer, Thomas M., Gary M. Franklin, Robert D. Mootz, Deborah Fulton-Kehoe, Roy Plaeger-Brockway, Diana Drylie, Judith A. Turner, and Terri Smith-Weller. 2004. "A communitywide intervention to improve outcomes and reduce disability among injured workers in Washington State." *The Milbank Quarterly* 82 (3): 547-67.

Wickizer, Thomas M., Gary M. Franklin, and Deborah Fulton-Kehoe. 2015. "Evaluation of a System Intervention that Achieved the Triple Aim." Presentation at the 2015 AcademyHealth Annual Research Meeting, Minneapolis (June).

Wickizer, Thomas M., Gary Franklin, Deborah Fulton-Kehoe, Judith A. Turner, Robert Mootz, and Terri Smith-Weller. 2004. "Patient satisfaction, treatment experience, and disability outcomes in a population-based cohort of injured workers in Washington State: implications for quality improvement." *Health Services Research* 39 (4 Pt 1): 727-48.

Wickizer, Thomas M., Gary Franklin, Roy Plaeger-Brockway, and Robert D. Mootz. 2007. "Improving the quality of workers' compensation health care delivery: the Washington State Occupational Health Services Project." *The Milbank Quarterly* 79 (1): 5-33.

Using Transitional Jobs to Increase Employment of SSDI Applicants and Beneficiaries

Julie Kerksick, David Riemer, and Conor Williams

Center for Studying Disability Policy (CSDP). 2015. "CSDP Forum: Early Findings from the Benefit Offset National Demonstration (BOND)." Webinar featuring Howard Rolston, Stephen Bell, David Stapleton, and Susan Wischke. Mathematica Policy Research (February 26). Available at http://www.mathematica-mpr.com/video/csdp-forum-bond-february-2015.

Davis, Angela, and Timothy Rupinski. 2013. "Evaluation of the Transitional Jobs Demonstration Program." Wisconsin Department of Children and Families (September). Available at http://dcf.wisconsin.gov/w2/pdf/tjdp_final_evaluation.pdf.

DeNavas-Walt, Carmen and Bernadette D. Proctor. 2014. "Income and Poverty in the United States: 2013," U.S. Census Bureau, Current Population Reports (September): 60-249. Available at http://www.census.gov/content/dam/Census/library/publications/2014/demo/p60-249.pdf.

Donosky, Lea. 1986. "Sweeping Tax Overhaul Now the Law." The Chicago Tribune (October 23). Accessed on September 11, 2015. Available at http://articles.chicagotribune.com/1986-10-23/news/8603190911_1_tax-code-tax-reform-tax-bills-next-year.

Huston, Aletha, Cynthia Miller, Lashawn Richburg-Hayes, Greg Duncan, Carolyn Eldred, Thomas S. Weisner, Edward D. Lowe, Vonnie McLoyd, Danielle Crosby, Marika N. Ripke, and Cindy Redcross. 2003. "New Hope for Families and Children: Five-Year Results of a Program to Reduce Poverty and Reform Welfare." MDRC (June). Available at http://www.mdrc.org/publication/new-hope-families-and-children.

Internal Revenue Service (IRS). 2014. "EITC Income Limits, Maximum Credit Amounts, and Tax Law Updates." Available at http://www.irs.gov/Individuals/EITC-Income-Limits,-Maximum-Credit--Amounts-and-Tax-Law-Updates.

Lippold, Kye. 2015. "Reducing Poverty in the United States." Urban Institute (February) Available at http://www.urban.org/research/publication/reducing-poverty-united-states.

Maestas, Nicole, Kathleen J. Mullen and Alexander Strand. 2010. "Does Disability Insurance Receipt Discourage Work? Using Examiner Assignment to Estimate the Causal Effects of SSDI Receipt," University of Michigan Retirement Research Center, Working Paper 2010-241. Available at http://www.mrrc.isr.umich.edu/publications/papers/pdf/ wp241.pdf.

Mamun, Arif, Paul O'Leary, David C. Wittenburg, and Jesse Gregory. 2011. "Employment Among Social Security Disability Program Beneficiaries, 1996–2007." Social Security Bulletin 71 (3): 11–34. Available at http:// www.ssa.gov/policy/docs/ssb/v71n3/v71n3p11.pdf.

Marzahl, David, and Dylan Bellisle. 2014. "Chicago Earned Income Tax Credit (EITC) Periodic Payment Pilot: Interim Report." Center for Economic Progress (December 18). Available at http://www.

economicprogress.org/sites/economicprogress.org/files/chi_periodicearnedincometaxcredit_1.pdf.

McGarry, Kathleen, and Jonathan Skinner. 2012. "The Importance of Private and Government Safety Nets: A Comparison of Approved and Denied SSDI Applicants." National Bureau of Economic Research, Retirement Research Center (September). Available at http://www.nber.org/aging/rrc/papers/orrc12-14.executive_summary.pdf.

National Employment Law Project (NELP). 2012. "The Low Wage Recovery and Growing Income Inequality." Data Brief (August). Available at http:/www.nelp.org/content/uploads/2015/03/LowWageRecovery2012.pdf.

National Transitional Jobs Network website, www.ntjn.org, per Steve Holt, holtsolutions.net.

Organization for Economic Cooperation and Development (OECD). 2010. *Sickness, Disability and Work: Breaking the Barriers: A Synthesis of Findings across OECD Countries*. OECD Publishing, Paris. DOI: http://dx.doi.org/10.1787/9789264088856-en.

Pavetti, LaDonna, Liz Schott, and Elizabeth Lower-Basch. 2011. "Creating Subsidized Employment Opportunities for Low-Income Parents: The Legacy of the TANF Emergency Fund," Center on Budget and Policy Priorities and Center for Law and Social Responsibility (February 16). Available at http://www.cbpp.org/files/2-16-11tanf.pdf.

Rampell, Catherine. 2012. "Majority of New Jobs Pay Low Wages, Study Finds." *The New York Times* (August 30). Accessed on September 11, 2015. Available at http://www.nytimes.com/2012/08/31/business/majority-of-new-jobs-pay-low-wages-study-finds.html.

Roder, Anne, and Mark Elliott. 2013. "Stimulating Opportunity: An Evaluation of ARRA-Funded Subsidized Employment Programs." Economic Mobility Corporation (September): 51. Available at http://economicmobilitycorp.org/uploads/stimulating-opportunity-full-report.pdf.

Social Security Administration (SSA). 2014. "Annual Statistical Report on the Social Security Disability Program, 2013." Available at http://ssa.gov/policy/docs/statcomps/di_asr/2013/.

Vallas, Rebecca, and Shawn Fremstad. 2015. "Social Security Disability Insurance: A Bedrock of Security for American Workers," Center for American Progress. Available at https://cdn.americanprogress.org/wp-content/uploads/2015/06/SSDI_update-brief-6.16.pdf.

Wisconsin Department of Children and Families. 2013. "Quarterly Report on Transitional Jobs Demonstration." Available at http://legis.wisconsin.gov/lfb/jfc/reports/Documents/2013_01_31_DCF%20Report%20to%20JFC%20on%20Transitional%20Jobs%20Demonstration%20Project.pdf.

Wright, Debra, Gina Livermore, Denise Hoffman, Eric Grau, and Maura Bardos. 2012. "2010 National Beneficiary Survey: Methodology and Descriptive Statistics Final Report." Mathematica Policy Research Center for Studying Disability Policy (April 2). Available at http://www.ssa.gov/disabilityresearch/documents/NBS%20stats%20methods%20508.pdf.

Wright, Debra, Gina Livermore, Denise Hoffman, Eric Grau, and Maura Bardos. 2012. "2010 National Beneficiary Survey: Methodology and Descriptive Statistics Final Report." Mathematica Policy Research Center for Studying Disability Policy (April 2). Available at http://www.ssa.gov/disabilityresearch/documents/NBS%20stats%20methods%20508.pdf.

Social Security Disability Adjudicative Reform: Ending the Reconsideration Stage of SSDI Adjudication after Sixteen Years of Testing and Enhancing Initial Stage Record Development

Jon C. Dubin

Bertoni, Daniel. 2007. "Social Security Disability: Better Planning, Management, and Evaluation Could Help Address Backlogs." GAO-08-40. U.S. Government Accountability Office. Available at http://www.gao.gov/products/GAO-08-40.

Barnett v. Bowen, 665 F. Supp. 1096 (D. Vt. 1987).

Blasi, Gary L. 1988. "Litigation Strategies for Addressing Bureaucratic Disentitlement." N.Y.U Review of Law and Social Change 16: 591.

Bloch, Frank S., Jeffrey S. Lubbers, and Paul R. Verkuil. 2007. "The Social Security Administration's New Disability Adjudication Rules: A Significant and Promising Reform." Cornell Law Review 92 (2): 237.

Bowen v. City of New York, 476 U.S. 467 (1986).

Browning v. Colvin, 766 F.3d 702 (7th Cir. 2104).

Califano v. White, 435 U.S. 908 (1978).

Carrow, Milton M. 1994. "A Tortuous Road to Bureaucratic Fairness: Righting the Social Security Claims Process." *Administrative Law Review* 46: 297.

Cunningham v. Astrue, 360 Fed. Appx. 606 (6th Cir. 2010).

Dubin, Jon C. 2011. "The Labor Market Side of Disability Benefits Law and Policy." *Southern California Review of Law and Social Justice* 20: 1.

Dubin, Jon C., and Robert E. Rains. 2012. "Scapegoating Social Security Disability Claimants (and The Judges Who Evaluate Them)." *Advance: J. ACS Issue Groups* 6:109.

Frey v. Bowen, 816 F.2d 508 (10th Cir. 1986).

Gellhorn, Gay. 1995. "Disability and Welfare Reform: Keep the Supplemental Security Income Program but Reengineer the Disability Determination Process." *Fordham Urban Law Journal* 22(4): 961.

Heckler v. Day, 467 U.S. 107 (1983).

Herrmann v. Colvin, 772 F.3d 1110 (7th Cir. 2014).

Koch, Jr., Charles H., and David L. Koplow. 1990. "The Fourth Bite Of the Apple: A Study of the Operation and Utility of the Social Security Administration's Appeals Council." *Florida State University Law Review* 17: 199.

Krauser v. Astrue, 638 F.3d 1324 (10th Cir. 2011).

Kubitschek, Carolyn A., and Jon C. Dubin. 2015. *Social Security Disability: Law and Procedure in Federal Court.* Thomson Reuters.

Laird v. Stidwell, 969 F. Supp. 1167 (D. Iowa 1997).

Lipsky, Michael. 1984. "Bureaucratic Disentitlement in Social Welfare Programs." *Social Service Review* 58 (1): 3.

Mason v. Shalala, 994 F.2d 1058 (3d Cir. 1993).

Mashaw, Jerry L. 1984. *Bureaucratic Justice: Managing Social Security Disability Claims.* Yale University Press.

Mashaw, Jerry L., Charles L. Goetz, Frank I. Goodman, Warren F. Schwartz, Paul R. Verkuil, and Milton M. Carrow. 1978. *Social Security Hearings and Appeals: A Study of the Social Security Administration Hearing System.* Lexington Books.

McCarthy v. Madigan, 503 U.S. 140 (1992).

Moore, Christine M. 1994. "SSA Disability Adjudication in Crisis!" *Judges Journal* 33:2.

Pierce, Richard J. 2011. "What Should We Do About Social Security Appeals?" *Regulation* 34 (3). Available at http://papers.ssrn.com/sol3/papers.cfm?abstract_id=1956016.

Rains, Robert E. 2007. "A Response to Bloch, Lubbers & Verkuil's the Social Security Administration's New Disability Adjudication Rules: A Cause for Optimism... And Concern." *Cornell Law Review* 92 (2): 250.

Ralph v. Colvin, 2015 U.S. Dist. LEXIS 61083 (M.D. Pa. 2015).

Robinson, Robert E. 2002a. Social Security Disability: Disappointing Results from SSA's Efforts to Improve the Disability Claims Process Warrant Immediate Attention. GAO-02-322. U.S. Government Accountability Office. Available at http://www.gpo.gov/fdsys/

pkg/GAOREPORTS-GAO-02-322/html/GAOREPORTS-GAO-02-322.htm.

______. 2002b. SSA and VA Disability Programs: Re-Examination of Disability Criteria Needed to Help Ensure Program Integrity. GAO-02-597. U.S Government Accountability Office. Available at http://www.gao.gov/products/GAO-02-597.

Sims v. Apfel, 530 U.S. 103 (2000).

Social Security Administration (SSA). 2010a. "2011 Budget Overview." Available at http://www.socialsecurity.gov/budget/hist/FY2011/2011BudgetOverview.pdf.

______. 2010b. "Social Security Testimony before Congress." Available at http://www.ssa.gov/legislation/testimony_042710.html.

______. 2010c. "Joint Hearing on the Social Security Disability Claims Backlog." Available at http://oig.ssa.gov/sites/default/files/04272010testimony.txt.

______. 2013. "Programs Operation Manual System." Available at https://secure.ssa.gov/poms.nsf/lnx/0412005020.

______. 2014. "Programs Operations Manual System." Available at https://secure.ssa.gov/apps10/poms.nsf/lnx/0427001001.

______. 2015a. "Disability Determination Process." Accessed August 20. Available at http://www.ssa.gov/disability/determination.htm.

______. 2015b. *FY 2016 Congressional Justification.* FY 2014 Disability Workload. Accessed August 20. Available at http://www.ssa.gov/budget/FY16Files/2016FCJ.pdf.

______. 2015c. *FY 2016 President's Budget.* Accessed August 20. Available at http://www.ssa.gov/budget/FY16Files/2016KT.pdf.

______. 2015d. "Medical/Professional Relations." Accessed August 20. Available at http://www.ssa.gov/disability/professionals/bluebook/general-info.htm.

______. 2015e. "Occupational Information System Project." Accessed August 20. Available at http://www.socialsecurity.gov/disabilityresearch/occupational_info_systems.html.

Social Security Advisory Board (SSAB). 2008. *Clearing the Disability Backlog-Giving the Social Security Administration the Resources it needs to provide the Benefit Workers Have Earned.* Committee on Ways and Means, U.S. House of Representatives. Available at http://www.ssab.gov/portals/0/documents/schieberwaysandmeans042308.pdf.

______. 2015. *The Single Decision Maker Pilot: A 16-Year Flight and Still No Clear Landing.* Available at http://www.ssab.gov/Portals/0/Homepage/SDM_final_508.pdf?ver=2015-07-19-120603-710.

Tippins, Nancy T., and Margaret L. Hilton, eds. 2010. *A Database for a Changing Economy: Review of the Occupational Information Network (O*NET).* Washington D.C., The National Academy Press. Available at http://www.nap.edu/openbook.php?record_id=12814&page=R1.

Traver, David F. 2009. *Social Security Disability Advocate's Handbook.* James Publishing.

U.S. Department of Labor (DOL). 1991. *Dictionary Of Occupational Titles (DOT) Revised.* 4th ed.

Voigt v. Colvin, 781 F.3d 871 (7th Cir. 2015).

White v. Mathews, 434 F. Supp. 1252 (D. Conn. 1976).

Wittenberg, David, Gordon Steinagle, Shane Frost, and Ron Fine. 2012. *An Assessment of Consultant Examination (CE) Processes, Content, and Quality: Findings from the CE Review Data, Final Report.* Available at http://www.ssa.gov/disabilityresearch/documents/CE Report 2.pdf.

Social Security: Restructuring Disability Adjudication

David W. Engel, Dale Glendening and Jeffrey S. Wolfe

Administrative Conference of the United States (ACUS). 1987. "A New Role for the Social Security Appeals Council." Recommendation 87-7 (December).

Clermont, *Kevin, M. 2009. Federal Rules of Civil Procedure.* 1 Foundation Press, Rev. ed.

Coquillette, Daniel R. 2014. *Federal Rules of Civil Procedure, Rule 1, Scope and Purpose* 1. Moore's Federal Practice-Civil.

Farenthold, David A. 2014. "The Social Security Office of Judges Who Hear Appeals for Disability Benefits is 990,399 Cases Behind." *Washington Post* (October 18). Accessed September 20, 2015. Available at http://www.washingtonpost.com/wp-srv/special/national/breaking-points/#backlog.

Fuller, Lon. 1971. "The Adversary System." In *Talks on American Law*, edited by Harold Berman. New York: Vintage Books.

Government Accountability Office (GAO). 2014. "Social Security Disability Benefits, Agency Could Improve Oversight of Representatives Providing Disability Advocacy Services." GAO Report No. 15-62 (December). Accessed September 17, 2015. Available at http://www.gao.gov/assets/670/667284.pdf.

Hedeen, Timothy. 2011. "Remodeling the Multi-Door Courthouse to Fit the Forum to the Folks: How Screening and Preparation Will Enhance ADR." *Marquette Law Review* 95: 941.

Kessler, Gladys, and Linda J. Finkelstein. 1988. "Evolution of a Multi-Door Courthouse." *Catholic University Law Review* 37: 577.

Paletta, Damian, and Dionne Searcey. 2011. "Two Lawyers Strike Gold in U.S. Disability System." *Wall Street Journal* (December 22). Accessed September 20, 2015. Available at http://www.wsj.com/articles/SB10001424052970203518404577096632862007046.

Social Security Administration (SSA). 2015. Hearings, Appeals and Litigation Law Manual (HALLEX). Accessed September 20, 2015. Available at http://www.ssa.gov/OP_Home/hallex/hallex.html.

Social Security Administration Office of the General Counsel. 2015. "Mission Statement." Office of General Counsel, Social Security Administration. Accessed September 20, 2015. Available at http://www.ssa. gov/org/orgogc.htm.

Social Security Administration Office of the Inspector General (SSA OIG). 2007. "Claimant Representatives Barred From Practicing Before the Social Security Administration." Report No. A-12-07-17057 (September). Accessed September 17, 2015. Available at http://oig.ssa.gov/sites/default/files/audit/full/html/A-12-07-17057.html.

______. 2010. "Hearing Request Dismissals." Report No. A-07-10-21049 (July). Accessed September 18, 2015. Available at http://oig.ssa.gov/sites/ default/files/audit/summary/html/A-07-10-21049.html.

______. 2011. "The Office of Disability Adjudication and Review's Hearings Backlog and Processing Times." Report No. A-12-11-21192. Social Security Administration, accessed September 17, 2015. Available at http://oig.ssa.gov/sites/default/files/audit/full/pdf/A-12-11-21192.pdf.

______. 2012a. "Current and Expanded Use of Video Hearings." Report No. A-05-12-21287 (June). Accessed September 17, 2015. Available at http://oig.ssa.gov/sites/ default/files/audit/summary/pdf/Summary%2021287.pdf.

______. 2012b. "The Social Security Administration's Review of Administrative Law Judges' Decisions." Report No. A-07-12-21234 (March). Accessed September 18, 2015. Available at http://oig.ssa.gov/sites/default/files/audit/full/pdf/A-07-12-21234.pdf.

______. 2013. "Effects of the Senior Attorney Adjudicator Program on Hearing Workloads." Report No. A-12-13-23002 (June). Accessed September 17, 2015. Available at http://oig.ssa.gov/audits-and-investigations/audit-reports/a-12-13-23002.

______. 2014. "Subsequent Appellate Actions on Denials Issued by Low-Allowance Administrative Law Judges." Report No.

A-12-13-13084 (July). Accessed September 17, 2015. Available at http://oig.ssa.gov/sites/default/files/audit/full/pdf/A-12-13-13084.pdf.

______. 2015a. "Reduce the Hearings Backlog and Prevent its Recurrence". Accessed September 20, 2015. Available at http://oig.ssa.gov/audits-and-investigations/top-ssa-management-issues/social-security-disability-hearings-backlog.

______. 2015b. "Informational Report - Agency Payments to Claimant's Representatives." Report No. A-05-15-15017 (July). Accessed September 17, 2015. Available at http://oig.ssa.gov/sites/default/files/audit/full/pdf/A-05-15-15017.pdf.

Social Security Administration Official Website. 2015. "Age Distribution of Pending Hearings FY2008 – FY2015." Accessed September 5, 2015, from: http://ssa.gov/appeals/#a0=0.

Social Security Board. 1941. 1940 Report, reprinted, in Monograph of the Attorney General's Committee on Administrative Procedure, Part 3, Senate Doc. No. 10, 77th Cong., 1st Sess. 37, 46 App.

Thibaut, John, Laurens Walker, and E. Allan Lind. 1972. "Adversary presentation and bias in legal decisionmaking." *Harvard Law Review* 86: 386, 393.

Verkuil, Paul R. 1978. "The Emerging Concept of Administrative Procedure." *Columbia Law Review*: 258-329.

Viles, Robert M. 1968. "Social Security Administration Versus the Lawyers... and Poor People Too." *Mississippi Law Journal* 40: 24, 40-41.

Wolfe, Jeffrey S. 2009. "Times They Are a Changin': A New Jurisprudence for Social Security." *Journal of the National Association of Administrative Law Judiciary* 29: 515, 529.

Wolfe, Jeffrey S., and David W. Engel. 2013. "Restoring Social Security Disability's Purpose." *Regulation* 36: 46.

Data-Driven Solutions for Improving the Continuing Disability Review Process

Alex Constantin, Julia Porcino, Chunxiao Zhou, and John Collins

Centers for Medicare and Medicaid Services. 2013. *Workers' Compensation Medicare Set-Aside Arrangement (WCMSA) Reference Guide* (March).

Centers for Medicare and Medicaid Services. 2010. *Modernizing CMS computer and data systems to support improvements in care delivery* (December).

Government Accountability Office (GAO). 2007. SSA has taken steps to address conflicting court decisions, but needs to manage data better on the increasing number of remands.

______. 2014. SSA could take steps to improve its assessment of continued eligibility.

Highsmith, Jim. 2004. *Agile Project Management: Creating Innovative Products*. Redwood City, CA, USA: Addison Wesley Longman Publishing Co., Inc.

House Committee on Oversight and Government Reform Subcommittee on Energy Policy, Health Care and Entitlements. 2014. *Examining Ways the Social Security Administration Can Improve the Disability Review Process: Hearing Before the House Committee on Oversight and Government Reform Subcommittee on Energy Policy, Health Care and Entitlements*. 113th Cong. 1 (statement of Marianna LaCanfora, Acting Deputy Commissioner for Retirement and Disability Policy, Social Security Administration).

Pokorny, Jaroslav. 2011. *NoSQL databases: A step to database scalability in web environment*. In Proceedings of the 13th International Conference on Information Integration and Web-based Applications and Services, iiWAS '11: 278–83.

Social Security Administration (SSA). 2011. *Compilation of the Social Security Laws: Including the Social Security Act, as Amended, and Related Enactments Through January 1, 2011*. Social Security Administration.

______. 2012. DI 280001.003 - An overview of processing continuing disability review (CDR) mailer forms SSA-455 and SSA-455-OCR-SM.

______. 2014. Annual report on continuing disability reviews, fiscal year 2012.

Social Security Administration Office of the Inspector General (SSA OIG). 2010. *Full Medical Continuing Disability Reviews*. Social Security Administration (March).

______. 2014a. *Full Medical Continuing Disability Review Cessations Reversed at the Reconsideration Level of Appeal*. Social Security Administration (April).

______. 2014b. *The Medical Improvement Review Standard During Continuing Disability Reviews*. Social Security Administration (May).

______. 2014c. *The Social Security Administration's Ability to Prevent and Detect Disability Fraud*. Social Security Administration (September).

Social Security Advisory Board (SSAB). 2014. "2014 Disability Policy Panel: Continuing Disability Reviews." Washington D.C.: Social Security Advisory Board. Available at http://ssab.gov/Portals/0/Documents/2014_DPP_Report_Final.pdf.

Veterans Benefits Administration. 2013. Department of Veterans Affairs (VA) Strategic Plan to Eliminate the Compensation Claims Backlog. US Department of Veterans Affairs (January).

Expanding Private Disability Insurance Coverage to Help the SSDI Program
David F. Babbel and Mark F. Meyer

Advisory Council on Employee Welfare and Pension Benefit Plans, Report to the Honorable Hilda A. Solis, United States Secretary of Labor. 2012. *Managing Disability Risks in an Environment of Individual Responsibility.*

Autor, David, Amitabh Chandra, and Mark Duggan. 2011. "Public Health Expenditures on the Working Age Disabled: Assessing Medicare and Medicaid Utilization of SSDI and SSI Recipients." NBER Retirement Research Center Paper No. NB 09-08 (September).

Autor, David, Nicole Maestas, Kathleen Mullen and Alexander Strand. 2011. "Does Delay Cause Decay? The Effect of Administrative Decision Time on the Labor Force Participation and Earnings of Disability Applicants." University of Michigan Retirement Research Center Working Paper WP 2011-258. A shortened version of this paper was presented at the 14th Annual Joint Conference of the Retirement Research Consortium, August 2-3, 2012, Washington, DC.

Babbel, David F., Jaime Cuevas Dermody, Miguel Herce, Mark F. Meyer, and Navendu Vasavada. 2011. *Financial Security for Working Americans: An Economic Analysis of Insurance Products in Workplace Benefits Programs.* UNUM/CRA.

Babbel, David F., and Mark F. Meyer. 2013. *Private Disability Insurance and Return-to-Work: Cost Savings to SSDI and Other Federal Programs.* AHIP.

Ben-Shalom, Yonatan, and Arif A. Mamum. 2015. "Return-to-Work Outcomes Among Social Security Disability Insurance Program Beneficiaries." *Journal of Disability Policy Studies.* 26.

Bardos, Maura, Hannah Burak, and Yonatan Ben-Shalom. 2015. *Assessing the Costs and Benefits of Return-to-Work Programs.* Mathematica Center for Studying Disability Policy.

Bureau of Labor Statistics (BLS). 2015. *Occupational Employment and Wage* May 2014. http://www.bls.gov/news.release/pdf/ocwage.pdf

______. September 2014. *National Compensation Survey:* Employee Benefits in the United States, March 2014. Bulletin 2776.

______. January 2014, *Occupational Outlook Handbook.* http://www.bls.gov/ooh/

______. January 22, 2014, *Usual Weekly Earnings of Wage and Salary Workers, Fourth Quarter 2013.*

Consumer Federation of America and Unum. 2015. "The Role of Disability Insurance for Small Employers."

______. 2012. "Employee Knowledge and Attitudes about Employer-Provided Disability Insurance."

Council for Disability Awareness. 2014a. *2014 Long Term Disability Claims Review.*

______. 2014b. *2014 Consumer Disability Awareness Study, America's Income Protection Picture.*

______. 2013. *2013 Long Term Disability Claims Review.*

______. 2012. *2012 Long Term Disability Claims Review.*

DeNavas-Walt, Carmen, Bernadette D. Proctor, and Jessica C. Smith. 2013. U.S. Census Bureau, Current Population Reports, P60-245, *Income, Poverty, and Health Insurance Coverage in the United States: 2012.* USGPO.

Employee Benefit Research Institute. 2009. *Fundamentals of Employee Benefit Programs, 6th Ed.*

GenRe Research. 2014. *U.S. Group Disability and Group Term Life Market Survey, Summary of 2013 Results.*

______. 2012. *Disability Fact Book, 7th Ed., 2013-2014.*

Internal Revenue Service. 2015. "Life Insurance & Disability Insurance Proceeds," http://www.irs.gov/Help-&-Resources/Tools-&-FAQs/FAQs-for-Individuals/Frequently-Asked-Tax-Questions-&-Answers/Interest,-Dividends,-Other-Types-of-Income/Life-Insurance-&-Disability-Insurance-Proceeds/Life-Insurance-&-Disability-Insurance-Proceeds-1.

LIMRA. 2015. "Keeping Up With the Times."

Liu, Su, and David Stapleton. 2011. "Longitudinal Statistics on Work Activity and Use of Employment Supports for New Social Security Disability Insurance Beneficiaries." *Social Security Bulletin* 71.

Maestas, Nicole, Kathleen J. Mullen and Alexander Strand. 2013. "Does Disability Insurance Receipt Discourage Work? Using Examiner Assignment to Estimate Causal Effects of SSDI Receipt." *American Economic Review* 103:1797–1829.

Milliman, Inc. 2007. *Survey of Rehabilitation and Return-to-Work Practices among U.S. Disability Carriers.*

______. 2005. *Impact of Disability Insurance Policy Mandates Proposed by the California Department of Insurance.*

O'Leary, Paul, Gina A. Livermore, and David C. Stapleton. 2011. "Employment of Individuals in the Social Security Disability Programs." *Social Security Bulletin* 71:1-10.

O'Neill, John, Arif A. Mamun, Elizabeth Potamites, Fong Chan, and Elizabeth da Silva Cordoso. 2015. "Return to Work of Disability Insurance Beneficiaries Who Do and Do Not Access State Vocational Rehabilitation Agency Services," *Journal of Disability Policy Studies* 26.

Plan Sponsor Council of America. 2014. *57th Annual Survey of Profit Sharing and 401(k) Plans.*

______. 2012. *55th Annual Survey of Profit Sharing and 401(k) Plans.*

______. 2010. *53rd Annual Survey of Profit Sharing and 401(k) Plans.*

______. 2008. *51st Annual Survey of Profit Sharing and 401(k) Plans.*

Schimmel, Jody, and David C. Stapleton. 2011. "Disability Benefits Suspended or Terminated Because of Work" *Social Security Bulletin* 71.

Social Security Administration (SSA). 2015a. *Budget Estimates and Related Information, Technical Materials, Limitation on Administrative Expenses,* http://www.ssa.gov/budget/FY16Files/2016LAE.pdf.

______. 2015b. *OASDI and SSI Program Rates & Limits, 2015.*

______. 2014. *Annual Statistical Report on the Social Security Disability Insurance Program, 2013,* SSA Publication No. 13-11826.

Social Security Administration, Office of the Inspector General. 2011. *Audit Report: Overall Disability Claim Times for 2009.*

______. 2015. *Audit Report: Performance Indicator Audit: Minimize Average Wait Time for Initial Disability Claims.*

Social Security and Medicare Boards of Trustees. 2015. *Status of the Social Security and Medicare Programs, A Summary of the 2014 Annual Social Security and Medicare Trust Fund Reports.*

Society of Actuaries. 2009. 2008 *Long Term Disability Experience Study Report.*

______. 2011. *2008 Group Long Term Disability Experience Table Report.*

Society for Human Resource Management. 2011. "401(k) Plans Add Features to Drive Participation and Savings."

U.S. Department of Agriculture, Food and Nutrition Service. 2014. *Characteristics of Supplemental Nutrition Assistance Program Households: Fiscal Year 2013,* Report No. SNAP-14-CHAR.

U.S. Department of Health & Human Services, Centers for Medicare & Medicaid Services, Office of the Actuary. 2013. *2013 Actuarial Report on the Financial Outlook for Medicaid.*

Vanguard. 2014. *How America Saves 2014.*

Ensuring Access to Long-Term Services and Supports for People with Disabilities and Chronic Conditions

Mark Perriello

American Psychological Association (APA). 2015. "Disability and Socioeconomic Status." Accessed on September 8, 2015. Available at http://www.apa.org/pi/ses/resources/publications/factsheet-disability.aspx.

Bureau of Labor Statistics (BLS). 2015. "Table A-6. Employment status of the civilian population by sex, age, and disability status, not seasonally adjusted." U.S. Department of Labor (January). Available at http://www.bls.gov/news.release/empsit.t06.htm.

Chapman, Shawna L., Jean P. Hall, and Janice M. Moore. 2013. "Health Care Access Affects Attitudes About Health Outcomes and Decisions to Apply for Social Security Disability Benefits." *Journal of Disability Policy Studies* 24 (2): 113-21.

Congressional Research Service (CRS). 2013. "Health Policy Essentials: Medicaid, CHIP, and Long-Term Services and Supports (LTSS)." Fundamentals Briefing (March 15). Available at http://www.nhpf.org/library/details.cfm/2918.

Favreault, Melissa M., Richard W. Johnson, and Karen E. Smith. 2013. "How Important is Social Security Disability Insurance to U.S. Workers?" Urban Institute (June 21). Available at http://www.urban.org/research/publication/how-important-social-security-disability-insurance-us-workers.

Gavin, Brigitte, Marci McCoy-Roth, and Vasudha Gidugu. 2011. "Review of studies regarding the Medicaid Buy In Program." Boston University Sargent College, Center for Psychiatric Rehabilitation. Available at http://www.bu.edu/drrk/research-syntheses/psychiatric-disabilities/medicaid-buy-in/.

Internal Revenue Service (IRS). 2014. *Publication 529 (2014), Miscellaneous Deductions*. Internal Revenue Service. Available at http://www.irs.gov/publications/p529/.

Kearney, John R. 2005/2006. "Social Security and the 'D' in OASDI: The History of a Federal Program Insuring Earners Against Disability." *Social Security Bulletin* 66 (3).

Kehn, Matthew, Sarah Croake, and Jody Schimmel. 2010. *A Government Performance and Results (GPRA) Report: The Status of the Medicaid Infrastructure Grants Program as of 12/31/09*. Mathematica Policy Research (December 30). Available at http://www.mathematica-mpr.com/~/media/publications/PDFs/disability/GPRA_09.pdf.

Medicaid and CHIP Payment Access Commission (MACPAC). 2014. "Medicaid's Role in Providing Assistance with Long-Term Services and Supports." *Report to the Congress on Medicaid and CHIP* (June). Available at https://www.macpac.gov/wp content/uploads/2015/01/Medicaids_Role_in_Providing_Assistance_with_Long-Term_Services_and_Supports.pdf.

National Council on Disability (NCD). 2015. "Securing the Social Contract: Reforming Social Security Disability." National Council on Disability (January 29). Available at https://www.ncd.gov/rawmedia_repository/b01bc342_353d_4b08_ba4b_7f0edfb0dd68.pdf.

StatsRRTC – The Research and Training Center on Disability Statistics and Demographics. 2014a. "Section 4: Poverty." Annual Disability Statistics Compendium. Accessed on September 8, 2015. Available at http://disabilitycompendium.org/compendium-statistics/poverty.

______. 2014b. "Section 12: Vocational Rehabilitation." Annual Disability Statistics Compendium. Accessed on September 8, 2015. Available at http://disabilitycompendium.org/compendium-statistics/vocational-rehabilitation.

UMass Medical School's Center for Health Law and Economics and Office of Long-Term Support Studies (UMass). 2010. Securing the Future. Report of the Massachusetts Long-Term Care Financing Advisory Committee (November). Available at http://www.mass.gov/eohhs/docs/eohhs/ltc/ma-ltcf-full.pdf.

Vallas, Rebecca, Shawn Fremstad, and Lisa Ekman. 2015. "A Fair Shot for Workers with Disabilities." Center for American Progress (January 28). Available at https://cdn.americanprogress.org/wp-content/uploads/2015/01/WorkersDisabilities.pdf.

Whalen, Denise, Gilbert Gimm, Henry Ireys, Boyd Gilman, and Sarah Croake. 2012. "Demonstration to Maintain Independence and Employment (DMIE) Final Report." Mathematica Policy Research (February 13). Available at http://www.mathematica mpr.com/~/media/publications/PDFs/disability/dmie_final.pdf

Improving the Interaction Between the SSDI and Workers' Compensation Programs

John F. Burton and Xuguang Guo

Altomare, Valerie. 2009. "Challenges in Implementing Workers' Compensation (WC) and Public Disability Benefit (PDB) Offset." PowerPoint Presentation to Research Seminar on *Implications of Developments in*

Workers' Compensation for Social Security Disability Insurance co-sponsored by the Social Security Administration and the National Academy of Social Insurance. Available at https://www.nasi.org/civicrm/event/infro?reset+=1&id=7.

Berkowitz, Monroe, and John F. Burton Jr. 1970. "The Income Maintenance Objective in Workmen's Compensation" *Industrial and Labor Relations Review*, Vol. 24 (October): 13-31.

______. 1987. *Permanent Disability Benefits in Workers' Compensation*. Kalamazoo, MI: W.E. Upjohn Institute for Employment Research.

Boden, Leslie I. 1995. "Creating Economic Incentives: Lessons from Workers' Compensation Systems", in *Proceedings of the Forty-Seventh Annual Meeting*, Madison, WI: Industrial Relations Research Association.

Boden, Leslie I., Robert T. Reville and Jeff Biddle. 2005. "The Adequacy of Workers' Compensation Cash Benefits", in Karen Roberts, John F. Burton, Jr. and Matthew M. Bodah, (eds), *Workplace Injuries and Diseases: Prevention and Compensation: Essays in Honor of Terry Thomason*, Kalamazoo, MI: W.E. Upjohn Institute for Employment Research: 37-68.

Burkhauser, Richard V., and Mary C. Daly. 2011. *The Declining Work and Welfare of People with Disabilities*. Washington, DC: The AEI Press.

Burton, John F. Jr. 2005. "Permanent Partial Disability Benefits", in Karen Roberts, John F. Burton, Jr. and Matthew M. Bodah (eds), *Workplace Injuries and Diseases: Prevention and Compensation: Essays in Honor of Terry Thomason*, Kalamazoo, MI: W.E. Upjohn Institute for Employment Research: 69-116.

______. 2009. "Workers' Compensation," in Kenneth G. Dau-Schmidt, Seth D. Harris, and Orly Lobel, *Labor and Employment Law and Economics*, Northampton, MA: Edward Elgar Publishing. 235-274.

______. 2011. "Workers' Compensation," in Jerry S. Rosenberg, ed. *The Handbook of Employee Benefits, Seventh Edition*. New York: McGraw-Hill: 575-611.

______. 2012. "Comments on the Prepared Statement of Gregory Krohm." *IAIABC Journal*, Vol. 49, No. 1: 48-55.

______. 2015a. "Should There Be a 21st Century National Commission on State Workers' Compensation Laws?" *IAIABC Journal*, Vol. 51, No.1: 11-38.

______. 2015b. "Economics of Safety." In *International Encyclopedia of the Social and Behavioral Sciences, 2md Edition*, ed. James D. Wright. Oxford, England: Elsevier Ltd.

Burton, John F. Jr. and Monroe Berkowitz. 1971. "Objectives Other Than Income Maintenance for Workmen's Compensation." *Journal of Risk and Insurance*, Vol. 38, No. 3: 343-45.

Butler, Richard J., Harold H. Gardner, and Nathan L. Kleinman. 2013. "Workers' Compensation: Occupational Injury Insurance's Influence on the Workplace," in Georges Dionne (ed), *Handbook of Insurance* (Second Edition): New York: Springer-Vertag.

Centers for Medicare & Medicaid Services (CMS). 2015. *Workers' Compensation Medicare Set-Aside Arrangements (WCMSA) Reference Guide.* (COBR-Q1-2015-v). Washington, DC: Department of Health and Human Services, Center for Medicare & Medicaid Services.

Colvin, Carolyn W. 2015. *FY 2016 Budget Overview: A Message from the [Acting] Commissioner.* Washington, DC: Social Security Administration.

Ehrenberg, Ronald G., and Robert S. Smith. 2015. *Modern Labor Economics: Theory and Public Policy* (Twelfth Edition). Boston: Prentice-Hall.

Government Accounting Office. 2001. *Workers' Compensation: Action Needed to Reduce Payment Errors in SSA Disability and Other Programs.* (GAO-01-367). Washington, DC: Government Accounting Office.

Government Accountability Office (GAO). 2015. *Disability Insurance: Actions Needed to Help Prevent Potential Overpayments to Individuals Receiving Concurrent Federal Workers' Compensation.* (GAO-15-531). Washington, DC: Government Accountability Office.

Grabell, Michael, and Howard Berkes. 2015. *The Demolition of Workers' Compensation.* ProPublica and NPR. Available at http://www.propublica.org/article/the-demolition-of-workers-compensation.

Guo, Xuguang (Steve), and John F. Burton Jr. 2010. "Workers' Compensation: Recent Developments in Moral Hazard and Benefit Payments." *Industrial and Labor Relations Review* 63 (2): 340-55.

______. 2012. "The Growth in Applications for Social Security Disability Insurance." *Social Security Bulletin* 72 (3): 69-88.

Hunt, Allan H. 2004. *Adequacy of Earnings Replacement in Workers' Compensation Programs.* Kalamazoo, MI: W.E. Upjohn Institute for Employment Research.

Larson, Lex. 2015. *Larson's Workers' Compensation, Desk Edition.* New Providence, NJ: Matthew Bender.

Larson, Lloyd, and John F. Burton Jr. 1985. "Special Funds in Workers' Compensation." In John D. Worrall and David Appel, eds. *Workers' Compensation Benefits: Adequacy, Equity, and Efficiency.* Ithaca, NY: ILR Press.

Leigh, J. Paul, and James P. Marcin. 2012. "Workers' Compensation Benefits and Shifting Costs of Occupational Injury and Illness." *Journal of Occupational and Environmental Medicine* 54 (4): 445-50.

Liebman, Jeffery B., and Jack A. Smalligan. 2013. Proposal 4: *An Evidence-Based Path to Disability Insurance Reform.* Washington, DC: The Hamilton Project and Brookings Institution. Available at: http://www.brookings.edu/~/media/research/files/papers/2013/02/thp-budget-papers/thp_15waysfedbudget_prop4.pdf.

Mansfield, Liz, MacEachen, Ellen, Tompa, Emile, Kalcevich, Christina, Endicott, Marion, and Mi, Natalie Yeung. 2012. "A Critical Review of Literature on Experience Rating in Workers' Compensation Systems." *Policy and Practice in Health and Safety* 1: 3-25.

McInerney, Melisa, and Kosali Simon. 2012. "The Effect of State Workers' Compensation Program Changes on the Use of Federal Social Security Disability Insurance." *Industrial Relations* 51 (1): 57-88.

National Commission on State Workmen's Compensation Laws (National Commission). 1972. *The Report of the National Commission on State Workmen's Compensation Laws.* Washington, DC: Government Printing Office. Available at www.workerscompresources.com.

National Council on Compensation Insurance (NCCI). 2014. *ABCs of Experience Rating.* Boca Raton, FL: National Council on Compensation Insurance

______. 2015. *Annual Statistical Bulletin: 2015 Edition* (and earlier editions). Boca Raton, FL: National Council on Compensation Insurance.

National Institute for Occupational Safety and Health (NISOH). 2014. *Current Projects: Center for Workers' Compensation Studies* (CWCS). Atlanta, GA: National Institute for Occupational Safety and Health, Centers for Disease Control and Prevention, Center for Workers' Compensation Studies.

O'Leary, Paulo, Leslie I. Boden, Seth A. Seabury, Al Ozonoff, and Ethan Scherer. 2012. "Workplace Injuries and the Take-Up of Social Security Disability Benefits." *Social Security Bulletin* 72 (3): 1-17.

Rauner, Bruce. 2015. *The Illinois Turnaround.* Available at https://www2.Illinois.gov/gov/Pages/default.aspx.

Reville, Robert T., and Robert F. Schoeni. 2003/2004. "The Fraction of Disability Caused at Work." *Social Security Bulletin* 65 (4): 31-7.

Robinson, Thomas A. 2013. "Oklahoma Commentary" In Thomas A. Robinson and Robin E. Kobayashi, eds. *Workers' Compensation Emerging Issues Analysis, 2013 Edition.* New Providence, NJ: LexisNexis: 154-164.

Savych, Bogdan. 2012. *Return to Work after a Lump-Sum Settlement.* WC-12-21. Cambridge, MA: Workers Compensation Research Institute.

Seabury, Seth A., McLaren, Christopher F., Reville, Robert, Neuhauser, Frank, and Mendeloff, John. 2012. "Workers' compensation experience rating and return to work." *Policy and Practice in Health and Safety* 1, 97-115

Sengupta, Ishita, Virginia Reno, and John F. Burton, Jr. 2011. *Workers' Compensation: Benefits, Coverage, and Costs, 2009.* Washington, DC: National Academy of Social Insurance.

Sengupta, Ishita, Marjorie Baldwin, and Virginia Reno. 2014. *Workers' Compensation: Benefits, Coverage, and Costs, 2012.* Washington, DC: National Academy of Social Insurance.

Sengupta, Ishita, and Marjorie Baldwin. 2015. *Workers' Compensation: Benefits, Coverage, and Costs, 2013.* Washington, DC: National Academy of Social Insurance.

Spieler, Emily A., and John F. Burton, Jr. 2012. "The Lack of Correspondence Between Work-Related Disability and Receipt of Workers' Compensation Benefits." *American Journal of Industrial Medicine* 55: 487-505.

Stapleton, David, David R. Mann, and Jae Song. 2014. "Firm-Level Early Incentives: Which Recent Employers of Disability Program Entrants Would Pay More?" Paper presented to the 2nd Annual Meeting of the Disability Research Consortium.

Tanabe, Ramona P. 2014. *Workers' Compensation Laws as of January 1, 2014.* Cambridge, MA: Workers' Compensation Research Institute.

Thomason, Terry. 2005. "Economic Incentives and Workplace Safety." in Karen Roberts, John F. Burton, Jr. and Matthew M. Bodah (eds), *Workplace Injuries and Diseases: Prevention and Compensation: Essays in Honor of Terry Thomason*, Kalamazoo, MI: W.E. Upjohn Institute for Employment Research: 9-35.

Thomason, Terry, and John F. Burton Jr. 1993. "Economic Effects of Workers' Compensation in the United States: Private Insurance and the Administration of Compensation Claims." *Journal of Labor Economics* 11 (1, Part 2): S1-S37.

______. "The Effects of Changes in the Oregon Workers' Compensation Program on Employees' Benefits and Employers' Costs" *Workers' Compensation Policy Review* 1 (4): 7-23. Available at www.workerscompresources.com.

Thomason, Terry and Silvana Pozzebon. 2002. "Determinant of Firm Workplace Health and Safety and Claims Management Practices." *Industrial and Labor Relations Review* 55 (2): 286-307.

Tompa, Emile, Hogg-Johnson, Shelia, Amick, Benjamin C, Wang, Ying, Shen, Enquig, Mustard, Cam, and Robson, Lynda. (2012). "Financial incentives in workers' compensation: an analysis of the experience-rating programme in Ontario, Canada." *Policy and Practice in Health and Safety* 1: 117-37

Torrey, David B. 2007. "Compromise Settlements under State Workers' Compensation Acts: Law, Policy, Practice, and Ten Years of the Pennsylvania Experience." *Widener Law Journal* 16: 199-469.

______. 2015. Editor. *The Centennial of the Pennsylvania Workers' Compensation Act.* Harrisburg, PA: Workers' Compensation Section, Pennsylvania Bar Association.

U.S. Department of Labor. 2014. *Comparison of State Unemployment Insurance Laws.* Washington, DC: U.S. Department of Labor, Employment and Training Administration.

Willborn, Steven L., Stewart J. Schwab, John F. Burton, Jr., and Gillian L.L. Lester. 2012. *Employment Law: Cases and Materials, Fifth Edition.* New Providence, NJ: LexisNexis.

Transitional Benefits for a Subset of the Social Security Disability Insurance Population

Kim Hildred, Pam Mazerski, Harold Krent, and Jennifer Christian

Berkowitz, Edward D. 1987. *Disabled Policy: America's Programs for the Handicapped.* New York: Cambridge University Press.

Burkhauser, Richard V., and Mary C. Daly. 2011. *The Declining Work and Welfare of People With Disabilities: What Went Wrong and a Strategy for Change.* Washington, D.C.: AEI Press.

Congressional Budget Office (CBO). 1997. Time-Limiting Federal Disability Benefits. CBO Memorandum. Washington, D.C.: Congressional Budget Office. Available at http://www.cbo.gov/sites/default/files/1997doc02-entire.pdf.

Challenges Facing Social Security Disability Programs in the 21st Century: Hearing Before the Subcomm. on Social Security of the Comm. On Ways and Means. 106th Cong. 35 (2000) (statement of Edward D. Berkowitz, Ph.D., Professor and Chair, Department of History, George Washington University).

Constantin, Alexandra, Julia Porcino, John Collins, and Chunxiao Zhou. 2015. "Data Driven Solutions for Improving the Continuing Disability Review Process," Paper presented at The McCrery-Pomeroy SSDI

Solutions Conference, Washington, D.C., August 4. Available at http://ssdisolutions.org/sites/default/files/cdr_presentation_7_31.pdf.

Costa, Kristina. 2014. "Fact Sheet: Social Impact Bonds in the United States." Washington, D.C.: Center for American Progress. Available at https://www.americanprogress.org/wp-content/uploads/2014/02/SocialImpactBonds3.pdf.

Government Accountability Office (GAO). 1996. Social Security Disability: Improvements Needed to Continuing Disability Review Process. Washington, D.C.: US Government Accountability Office. Available at http://www.gao.gov/assets/230/223379.pdf.

______. 2008. Social Security Disability: Management Controls Needed to Strengthen Demonstration Projects. Washington, D.C.: US Government Accountability Office. Available at http://www.gao.gov/assets/290/281904.pdf.

______. 2006. Social Security Disability Programs: Clearer Guidance Could Help SSA Apply the Medical Improvement Standard More Consistently. Washington, D.C.: US Government Accountability Office. Available at http://www.gao.gov/assets/260/252268.pdf.

Hager, Ronald M. 2004. "Order of Selection for Vocational Rehabilitation Services: An Option for State VR Agencies Who Cannot Serve All Eligible Individuals." Policy and Practice Brief 23. Ithaca, N.Y.: Employment and Disability Institute School of Industrial and Labor Relations Cornell University.

Hemmeter, Jeffrey, and Michelle Stegman. 2013. "Subsequent Program Participation of Former Social Security Disability Insurance Beneficiaries and Supplement Security Income Recipients Whose Eligibility Ceased Because of Medical Improvement," *Social Security Bulletin* 73 (2): 1-38.

Kearney, John R. 2005/2006. "Social Security and the 'D' in OASDI: The History of a Federal Program Insuring Earners Against Disability." Social Security Bulletin 66 (3): 1-27.

Krent, Harold J., and Scott Morris. 2013. "Achieving Greater Consistency in Social Security Disability Adjudication: An Empirical Study and Suggested Reforms." Washington, D.C.: Administrative Conference of the United States, 2013. Available at https://www.acus.gov/sites/default/files/documents/Achieving_Greater_Consistency_Final_Report_4-3-2013_clean.pdf.

Liebman, Jeffrey B., and Jack A. Smalligan. 2013. "Proposal 4: An Evidence-Based Path to Disability Insurance Reform." In 15 Ways to Rethink the Federal Budget, ed. Michael Greenstone, Max Harris, Karen Li, Adam Looney, and Jeremy Patashnik. Washington, D.C.: The Brookings Institution. Available at http://www.hamiltonproject.org/papers/15_ways_to_rethink_the_federal_budget/.

______. 2012. "An Evidence-Based Path to Disability Insurance Reform," 2, September, Permission to cite granted by authors.

Livermore, Gina A. 2011. "Social Security Disability Beneficiaries with Work-Related Goals and Expectations," Social Security Bulletin 71 (3).

Morton, William R. 2014. Primer on Disability Benefits: Social Security Disability Insurance (SSDI) and Supplemental Security Income (SSI). Washington, D.C.: Congressional Research Service. Available at https://www.fas.org/sgp/crs/misc/RL32279.pdf.

National Council on Disability. 2007. Empowerment for Americans with Disabilities: Breaking Barriers to Careers and Full Employment. Washington, D.C.: National Council on Disability. Available at https://www.ncd.gov/rawmedia_repository/d87db786_9053_49c2_8032_092dddde6752.pdf.

Opening Statement Before the Subcommittee On Social Security of the Committee On Ways and Means. 114th Cong. (2015) (statement of Xavier Becerra, Ranking Member).

Organisation for Economic Co-operation and Development (OECD). 2010. *Sickness, Disability and Work: Breaking Barriers; A Synthesis of Findings Across OECD Countries. Paris: OECD*. Available at http://ec.europa.eu/health/mental_health/eu_compass/reports_studies/disability_synthesis_2010_en.pdf.

Questions for the Record Response before the Subcommittee On Social Security of the Committee On Ways and Means. 113th Cong. (2013) (responses by Mark Duggan, Professor and Chair, Business Economics and Public Policy Department, Wharton University of Pennsylvania). Available at https://perma.cc/KN6R-EUE4. (URL archived).

Schimmel, Jody, Sarah Prenovitz, Gina Livermore, Alex Brice. 2013. Evaluation of the Work Incentives Planning and Assistance (WIPA) Program in 2011: Beneficiaries Served, Services Provided, and Program Costs Final Report (Washington, D.C.: Mathematica Policy Research), 3. Available at http://socialsecurity.gov/disabilityresearch/documents/WIPA%20Report%204%20Final.pdf.

Schimmel, Jody, Allison Roche, and Gina Livermore. 2011. Evaluation of the Recent Experience of the Work Incentives Planning and Assistance (WIPA) Program: Beneficiaries Served, Services Provided, and

Program Costs. Washington, D.C.: Mathematica Policy Research. Available at http://www.mathematica mpr.com/~/media/publications/PDFs/disability/WIPA_update.pdf.

Social Security Disability Programs: Improving the Quality of Benefit Award Decisions: Minority Staff Report: Permanent Subcommittee on Investigations. 112th Cong. (2012).

Social Security Administration (SSA). 2012a. Annual Report of Continuing Disability Reviews: Fiscal Year 2010. Baltimore: Social Security Administration. Available at http://www.socialsecurity.gov/legislation/FY%202010%20CDR%20Report.pdf.

______. 2014a. Annual Report of Continuing Disability Reviews: Fiscal Year 2012. Baltimore: Social Security Administration. Available at http://www.ssa.gov/legislation/FY%202012%20CDR%20Report.pdf.

______. 2014b. Annual Statistical Report on the Social Security Disability Insurance Program, 2013. Baltimore: Social Security Administration, published December. Available at http://www.socialsecurity.gov/policy/docs/statcomps/di_asr/2013/di_asr13.pdf.

______. 2012b. Employment Networks in Social Security's Ticket to Work Program. Baltimore: Social Security Administration. Available at http://www.ssa.gov/pubs/EN-05-10065.pdf.

______. 2015a. "Program Operations Manual System--DI 40502.001: Processing Center Instructions for the Continuing Disability Review Mailer Forms SSA-455 and SSA-455-OCR-SM." February 20. Available at https://secure.ssa.gov/poms.nsf/lnx/0440502001#a.

______. 2015b. "Work Incentives Planning and Assistance." Accessed July 17. Available at http://www.ssa.gov/work/WIPA.html.

Social Security Advisory Board (SSAB). 2012. Aspects of Disability Decision Making: Data and Materials. Washington, D.C.: Social Security Advisory Board. Available at http://www.aadpr.org/pdf_files/Data_and_Materials_2012.pdf.

______. 2014. "2014 Disability Policy Panel: Continuing Disability Reviews." Washington D.C.: Social Security Advisory Board. Available at http://ssab.gov/Portals/0/Documents/2014_DPP_Report_Final.pdf.

Social Security Administration Office of the Inspector General (SSA OIG). 2014a. Administrative Law Judges with Both High Disposition and High Allowance Rates, A-12-14-24092. Baltimore: Social Security Administration Office of the Inspector General. Available at http://oig.ssa.gov/sites/default/files/audit/full/pdf/A-12-14-24092_0.pdf.

______. 2014b. Audit Work Plan: Fiscal Year 2015. Baltimore: Social Security Administration Office of the Inspector General. Available at http://

oig.ssa.gov/sites/default/files/audit/full/pdf/FY%202015%20 Audit%20Plan.pdf.

______. 2014c. Fiscal Year 2014 Inspector General Statement on the Social Security Administration's Major Management and Performance Challenges. A-01-15-15038. Baltimore: Social Security Administration Office of the Inspector General. Available at http://oig.ssa.gov/sites/default/files/audit/summary/pdf/Summary%2015038_0.pdf.

Waddell, Gordon, and A. Kim Burton. 2004. Concepts of Rehabilitation for the Management of Common Health Problems. London: TSO. Available at https://www.gov.uk/government/uploads/system/uploads/attachment_data/file/208968/hwwb-concepts-of-rehabilitation.pdf.

Beyond All Or Nothing: Reforming Social Security Disability Insurance To Encourage Work And Wealth

Jason J. Fichtner and Jason S. Seligman

Autor, David H., and Mark G. Duggan. 2010. *Supporting Work: A Proposal for Modernizing the U.S. Disability Insurance System.* Washington, DC: Center for American Progress and the Hamilton Project.

Benítez-Silva, Hugo, Richard Disney, and Sergi Jiménez-Martín. 2010. "Disability, Capacity for Work and the Business Cycle: An International Perspective." *Economic Policy* 25 (63): 483–536.

Blahous, Charles P. 2014. "Medicaid under the Affordable Care Act." In The Economics of Medicaid, edited by Jason J. Fichtner, 83–98. Arlington, VA: Mercatus Center at George Mason University.

Boersch-Supan, A. H. & Juerges, H. (2011). "Disability, Pension Reform and Early Retirement in Germany" NBER Working Paper, 17079.

Bureau of Labor Statistics. 2010. *Issues in Labor Statistics*, Summary 10-04. Available at www.bls.gov/opub/ils//summary_10_04/older_workers.htm.

______. 2011. *Labor Force Statistics from the Current Population Survey.* Available at http://www.bls.gov/cps/cpsaat1.pdf.

Burkhauser, Richard V., and Mary Daly. 2011. *The Declining Work and Welfare of People with Disabilities.* Washington, DC: American Enterprise Institute Press.

______. 2012. "Social Security Disability Insurance: Time for Fundamental Change." *Journal of Public Policy Analysis and Management* 31 (2): 454–61.

Burkhauser, Richard V., Mary C. Daly, Duncan McVicar, and Roger Wilkins. 2013. "Disability Benefit Growth and Disability Reform in the U.S.:

Lessons from Other OECD Nations." Working Paper 2013-40, Federal Reserve Bank of San Francisco, San Francisco, CA. Available at http://www.frbsf.org/economic-research/files/wp2013-40.pdf.

Chan, Sewin, and Anne H. Stevens. 2001. "Job Loss and Employment Patterns of Older Workers." *Journal of Labor Economics* 19 (2): 484–521.

Congressional Research Service (CRS). 2007. *CRS Report for Congress, Unemployment and Older Workers*. Washington, DC.

Daly, Mary C., Brian T. Lucking, and Jonathon Schwabish. 2013. "Explaining the Rapid Growth in the Social Security Disability Rolls." *Disability Policy Watch*, March 22, 2013. Available at http://www.frbsf.org/economic-research/files/explaining-disability-growth.pdf.

DeCesaro, Anne, and Jeffrey Hemmeter. 2008. "Characteristics of Noninstitutionalized DI and SSI Program Participants." U.S. Social Security Administration, Washington, DC. Available at http://www.ssa.gov/policy/ docs/rsnotes/rsn2008-02.html.

Domenici. P., A. Rivlin, and Debt Reduction Task Force. 2010. *Restoring America's Future: Reviving the Economy, Cutting Spending and Debt, and Creating a Simple, Pro-growth Tax System*. Washington, DC: Bipartisan Policy Center.

Employee Benefit Research Institute and Mathew Greenwald and Associates Inc. 2007. *Retirement Confidence Survey*. Available at http://www.ebri.org/surveys/rcs/2007.

______. 2011. *Retirement Confidence Survey*. Available at http://www.ebri.org/surveys/rcs/2011.

Fichtner, Jason J. 2014. "Medicaid's Budgetary Impact: The Federal Side of the Budget Equation." In *The Economics of Medicaid: Assessing the Costs and Consequences*, edited by Jason J. Fichtner, 49–82. Arlington, VA: Mercatus Center at George Mason University.

Fichtner, Jason J., and Jason S. Seligman. 2015. "Saving Social Security Disability Insurance: Reforms Within the Context of Holistic Social Security Reform." Mercatus Working Paper. Arlington, VA: Mercatus Center at George Mason University.

______. 2014. "Public Disability Insurance Programs in the Context of Pension Reforms." In *Pensions: Policies, New Reforms and Current Challenges*, edited by Thom Reilly, 167–86. New York: NOVA Press.

Glick, Reuven, and Kevin J. Lansing. 2011. "Consumers and the Economy, Part I: Household Credit and Personal Saving." FRBSF Economic Letter No. 2011-01, Federal Reserve Board of San Francisco, San Francisco, CA.

Greenspan Commission. 1983. "Report of the Bi-partisan National Commission on Social Security Reform." Historical report of the U.S. Social Security Administration, Washington, DC. http://www.ssa.gov/history/reports/gspan.html.

Hackmann, Martin B., Jonathan T. Kolstad, and Amanda E. Kowalski. 2015. "Adverse Selection and an Individual Mandate: When Theory Meets Practice" *The American Economic Review* 105(3): 1030-1066.

Health and Retirement Study. 1992–2010 wave data files. Public use dataset. Produced and distributed by the University of Michigan with funding from the National Institute on Aging (grant number NIA U01AG009740). Ann Arbor, MI.

Hurd, Michael D., and Susann Rohwedder. 2010. "The Effects of the Economic Crisis on the Older Population." MRRC Working Paper No. 2010-231, Retirement Research Center, University of Michigan, Ann Arbor, MI.

Joffe-Walt, Chana. 2013. "Unfit for Work: The Startling Rise of Disability in America." *Planet Money Blog*. National Public Radio, March 22, 2013. Available at http://apps.npr.org/unfit-for-work.

Kollmann, Geoffrey. 2000. "Social Security: Summary of Major Changes in the Cash Benefits Program." CRS Legislative Histories 2. Washington, DC: U.S. Social Security Administration. Available at http://www.ssa.gov/history/reports/crsleghist2.html.

Koning, Pierre, and Maarten Lindeboom. 2015. "The Rise and Fall of Disability Insurance Enrollment in the Netherlands." *Journal of Economic Perspectives* 29(2): 151-172.

Liebman, Jeffry B. 2015. "Understanding the Increase in Disability Insurance Benefit Receipt in the United States." *Journal of Economic Perspectives* 29(2): 123-150.

Liebman, Jeffrey B., and Jack A. Smalligan. 2013. "An Evidence-Based Path to Disability Insurance Reform." Hamilton Project policy proposal, Brookings Institute, Washington, DC.

Lindner, Stephan, and Clark Burdick. 2013. "Characteristics and Employment of Applicants for Social Security Disability Insurance over the Business Cycle." CRR Working Paper 2013-11, Center for Retirement Research, Boston College, Chestnut Hills, MA.

Mann, David, and David Stapleton. 2012. "A Roadmap to a 21st-Century Disability Policy." Issue Brief 12-01, Center for Studying Disability Policy, Mathematica Policy Research, Princeton, NJ.

Moynihan, Daniel P., Richard Parsons, and the President's Commission to Strengthen Social Security. 2001. *Strengthening Social Security and*

Creating Personal Wealth for All Americans: Report of the President's Commission. Washington, DC: U.S. Government Printing Office.

Mueller, Andreas I., Jesse Rothstein, and Till M. von Wachter. 2013. "Unemployment Insurance and Disability Insurance in the Great Recession." NBER Working Paper 19672. Cambridge, MA.

RAND HRS Data, Version L. 2011. Produced by the RAND Center for the Study of Aging, with funding from the National Institute on Aging and the Social Security Administration. Santa Monica, CA.

Reno, Virginia, and Ekman L. 2012. "Social Security Disability Insurance: Essential Protection When Work Incapacity Strikes." *Journal of Public Policy Analysis and Management* 31 (2): 461–69.

Rix, Sara E. 2002. "Update on the Older Worker: 2002." Data Digest 88, AARP Public Policy Institute, Washington, DC.

Rupp, Kalman, and David Stapleton. 1995. "Determinants of the Growth in Social Security Administration's Disability Programs—an Overview." *Social Security Bulletin* 58 (4): 43–70.

Seligman, Jason S. 2014. "Involuntary Retirement, U.S. Social Security Program Participation and the Great Recession." *Public Finance and Management* 14 (3): 329–56.

Seligman, Jason S., and Jeffrey B. Wenger. 2006. "Asynchronous Risk: Unemployment, Equity Markets, and Retirement Savings." *Journal of Pension Economics and Finance* 5 (3): 237–55.

Shapiro, Matthew D. 2010. "The Effects of the Financial Crisis on the Well-Being of Older Americans: Evidence from the Cognitive Economics Study." MRRC Working Paper No. 228, Retirement Research Center, University of Michigan, Ann Arbor, MI.

Social Security Administration (SSA). 2003. "Fast Facts and Figures about Social Security, 2002." SSA Publication No. 13-11785, August 2003. U.S. Social Security Administration, Washington, DC.

______. 2012. "Fast Facts and Figures about Social Security, 2012." SSA Publication No. 13-11785. August 2012. U.S. Social Security Administration, Washington, DC.

______. 2013. "Fast Facts and Figures about Social Security, 2013." SSA Publication No. 13-11785. August 2013. U.S. Social Security Administration, Washington, DC.

______. 2014. "Understanding the Benefits." SSA Publication No. 05-10024, U.S. Social Security Administration, Washington, DC.

Social Security Board of Trustees (Trustees). 2015. The 2015 Annual Report of the Board of Trustees of the Federal Old-Age and Survivors

Insurance and Federal Disability Insurance Trust Funds. Washington: U.S. Government Publishing Office.

Solis, Hilda L., and Keith Hall. 2010. "National Compensation Survey: Employee Benefits in the United States, March 2010." Bulletin 2731, Bureau of Labor Statistics, U.S. Department of Labor, Washington, DC.

Warshawsky, Mark J. and Ross A. Marchand. 2015. "Modernizing the SSDI Eligibility Criteria: A Reform Proposal That Eliminates the Outdated Medical-Vocational Grid." Mercatus Working Paper. Arlington, VA: Mercatus Center at George Mason University.

Yin, Na. 2015. "Partial Benefits in the Social Security Disability Insurance Program." *The Journal of Risk and Insurance*. 82(2). 463-504.

Exploring an Alternative Social Security Definition of Disability
Neil Jacobson, Barbara Butz, Anita Shafer Aaron, and Aya Aghabi

AskEARN. 2013. "Disability Management Programs." Last modified September 10, 2013. Available at http://askearn.org/refdesk/Diversity_Goals/Disability_Management.

Brault, Matthew W. 2012. "Americans With Disabilities: 2010." *Current Population Reports*, July. Available at http://www.census.gov/prod/2012pubs/p70-131.pdf.

California Health Advocates. 2014. "Glossary." December 9. Available at http://cahealthadvocates.org/glossary/index.html.

Hall, Jean P., and Noelle K. Kurth. 2013. "Kansas Medicaid Buy-In Participants Continue to Earn More and Cost Less." *Working Healthy Policy Brief* 14.

Harkin, Tom. 2014. "Harkin Statement on Equal Employment Opportunity Commission Nominees." Speech, Senate Committee on Health, Education, Labor & Pensions Hearing on Two Equal Employment Opportunity Commission (EEOC) Nominees, Washington, D.C., November 13. Available at http://www.help.senate.gov/ranking/newsroom/press/harkin-statement-on-equal-employment-opportunity-commission-nominees.

Hollenbeck, Kevin. 2015. "Job Retention/Re-employment for Workers Who Experience Productivity Loss." Lecture, SAW/RTW Policy Collaborative Webinar, W.E. Upjohn Institute for Employment Research, May 20. Available at https://econsys.adobeconnect.com/_a968322745/p1qsoe82kzk/?launcher=false&fcsContent=true&pbMode=normal.

Jacobson, Neil. 2013. "Neil Jacobson: Labor Day No Holiday for Many People with Disabilities." *The Wichita Eagle*. September 2. Available at http://www.kansas.com/opinion/opn-columns-blogs/article1121805.html.

Kailes, June Isaacson. 2002. "Independent Living and Traditional Paradigms*." June Isaacson Kailes. http://www.jik.com/ilcpara.html#INDEPENDENT_LIVING_AND_TRADITIONAL.

Katz, Elaine, and Rodger DeRose. 2010. "The ADA 20 Years Later: The 2010 Survey of Americans with Disabilities." *The Journal of Spinal Cord Medicine* 33.

Lee, Marlene A., and Mark Mather. 2008. "U.S. Labor Force Trends." *Population Bulletin* 63. Available at http://www.prb.org/pdf08/63.2uslabor.pdf.

Livermore, Gina, Arif Mamun, Jody Schimmel, and Sarah Prenovitz. 2013. *Executive Summary of the Seventh Ticket to Work Evaluation Report*. June 30. Available at http://www.disabilitypolicyresearch.org/~/media/publications/pdfs/disability/es_7th_ttw_rpt.pdf.

Livermore, Gina. 2010. "Longitudinal Employment Outcomes for Social Security Disability Beneficiaries with Work Goals and Expectations." Speech, Center for Studying Disability Policy Research Forum, Washington, DC May 19. Available at http://www.mathematica-mpr.com/~/media/publications/pdfs/disability/csdp_may2010_forum_livermore.pdf.

Livermore, Gina, Meghan O'Toole, and David Stapleton. 2011. "Federal Expenditures for Working-Age People with Disabilities in Fiscal Year 2008." *Mathematica Policy Research*. Available at http://www.mathematica-mpr.com/~/media/publications/pdfs/disability/fedspend_livermore_20110608.pdf.

Maestas, Nicole, Kathleen J. Mullen, and Gema Zamarro. 2010. "Research Designs for Estimating Induced Entry into the SSDI Program Resulting from a Benefit Offset." Santa Monica: *RAND Labor and Population*. Available at http://www.rand.org/content/dam/rand/pubs/technical_reports/2010/RAND_TR908.pdf.

Mitra, Sophie, and Debra Brucker. 2004. "The Early Intervention Project: An Innovative Initiative to Return Disability Insurance Applicants to Work." *Journal of Disability Policy Studies* 3: 159-67.

National Collaborative on Workforce and Disability for Youth. 2006. "Blending and Braiding Funds and Resources: The Intermediary as Facilitator." *National Collaborative on Workforce and Disability (NCWD) InfoBrief* 16. Available at http://www.ncwd-youth.info/information-brief-18.

National Council on Disability. 2015. "Securing the Social Contract: Reforming Social Security Disability." Report. Washington, D.C.:

National Council on Disability. Available at http://www.ncd.gov/publications/2015/01292015/.

Prenovitz, Sarah, Maura Bardos, and Bonnie O'Day. 2012. "Ticket to Work After the Release of the 2008 Revised Regulations: Progress and Prospects." Report. Center for Studying Disability Policy. Available at http://socialsecurity.gov/disabilityresearch/documents/FINAL%20Revised%20Regulations.pdf.

Reno, Virginia. 2004. "Social Security as Part of an Integrated National Disability Policy Is Social Security Definition Out of Sync?"" *National Academy of Social Insurance*. Available at https://www.nasi.org/sites/default/files/research/Testimony_to_the_Social_Security_Advisory_Board.pdf.

Research and Training Center on Community Living at the University of Minnesota. 2014. "Employment First Across the Nation: Progress on the Policy Front." *Policy Research Brief* 24.

Roberts, Joel. 2008. "Social Security Disability: Ticket to Work Program | Disability Secrets." Disability Secrets. Available at http://www.disabilitysecrets.com/dnewsblog/2008/01/social-security-ticket-to-work-program.html.

Social Security Administration (SSA). 2015a. *2015 Red Book*. SSA Publication No. 64-030. Washington, D.C.: Available at http://www.ssa.gov/redbook/documents/TheRedBook2015.pdf.

______. 2015b. "Disability Planner: How You Qualify For Disability Benefits." Accessed July 13, 2015. http://www.ssa.gov/planners/disability/dqualify.html.

Social Security Advisory Board (SSAB). 2006. "A Disability System for the 21st Century." Washington, DC: Social Security Advisory Board. Available at http://www.ssab.gov/documents/disability-system-21st.pdf.

Stapleton, David, Ali Protik, and Christal Stone. 2008. "Review of International Evidence on the Cost of Disability." Report no. 542. Norwich: Department for Work and Pensions. Available at http://www.mathematica-mpr.com/~/media/publications/PDFs/disability/international_evidence_cost.pdf.

Thompson, Secretary Tommy G., and Governor Roy E. Barnes. 2007. *Beyond NCLB: Fulfilling the Promise to Our Nation's Children*. Publication. Washington, D.C.: Aspen Institute. Available at https://www.aucd.org/docs/Aspen%20Commission%20on%20NCLB.pdf.

U.S. Department of Labor Office of Disability Employment Policy. 2015. "Employment First." Accessed July 12, 2015. Available at http://www.dol.gov/odep/topics/EmploymentFirst.htm.

Vennochi, Joan. 2015. "A Disabilities Act, Long in Planning, Is Finally Law." *The Boston Globe*, January 4. Available at http://www.bostonglobe.com/opinion/2015/01/02/the-able-act-finally-allows-savings-for-people-with-disabilities/q60mNy4MMazxG2omrXGUWO/story.html.

Approaches to Assisting Working-Aged People with Disabilities: Insights from Around the World
Robert Haveman

Adam, Stuart, Antoine Bozio, and Carl Emmerson. 2010. "Reforming Disability Insurance in the UK: Evaluation of the Pathways to Work Programme." Institute for Fiscal Studies, London.

Autor, David, and Mark Duggan. 2003. "The Rise in the Disability Rolls and the Decline in Unemployment." *Quarterly Journal of Economics* 118 (February): 157–206.

Blomberg, Renee. 2013. "Who Is Granted Disability Benefit in Sweden? Description of Risk Factors and the Effect of the 2008 Law Reform." Master's thesis in Mathematical Statistics, Royal Institute of Technology, School of Engineering Sciences, Stockholm, Sweden.

Cai, Lixin, and Robert Gregory. 2002–03. "Inflows, Outflows and the Growth of the Disability Support Pension (DSP) Program." *Australian Social Policy* 121–43.

Burkhauser, Richard, Mary C. Daly, Duncan McVicar, and Roger Wilkins. 2014. "Disability Benefit Growth and Disability Reform in the US: Lessons from Other OECD Nations." *IZA Journal of Labor Policy* 3 (4): 1–30.

Burkhauser, Richard, Mary C. Daly, and Nicholas Ziebarth. 2015. "Protecting Working-Age People with Disabilities: Lessons from Four Industrialized Nations." Unpublished working paper.

Haveman, Robert H., Victor Halberstadt, and Richard Burkhauser. 1984. *Public Policy toward Disabled Workers: Cross National Analyses of Economic Impacts*. Ithaca, NY: Cornell University Press.

McVicar, Duncan, and Roger Wilkins. 2013. "Explaining the Growth in the Number of Recipients of the Disability Support Pension in Australia." *Australian Economic Review* 46 (3): 345–56.

Morris, Zachary A. 2015. "Disability Benefit Reform in Great Britain from the Perspective of the United States." *International Social Security Review* 68 (1): 47–67.

Organisation for Economic Co-operation and Development (OECD). 2010. *Sickness, Disability and Work: Breaking the Barriers: A Synthesis of Findings across OECD Countries*. OECD Publishing, Paris. DOI: http://dx.doi.org/10.1787/9789264088856-en

______. 2003. *Transforming Disability into Ability. Paris, France*. Available at http://www.virk.is/static/files/4_disability%20to%20ability.pdf. Accessed August 1, 2015.

______. 2015. Statistics Library. *Public expenditure on disability and sickness cash benefits, in % GDP*. Available at http://stats.oecd.org/index.aspx?queryid=33415. Accessed September 2, 2015.

Prinz, Christopher, and William Tompson. 2009. "Sickness and Disability Benefit Programmes: What Is Driving Policy Convergence?" *International Social Security Review*, Special Issue: Policy Learning and Social Protection 62 (October/December): 41–61.

Social Security Administration (SSA). 2014. *Social Security Programs throughout the World: Europe*, 2014. SSA Publication No. 13-11801. Washington, DC. Available at http://www.ssa.gov/policy/docs/progdesc/ssptw/2014-2015/europe/ssptw14europe.pdf. Accessed September 1, 2015.

Van Sonsbeek, Jan-Maarten, and Raymond Gradus. 2011. "Estimating the Effects of Recent Disability Reforms in the Netherlands." Tinbergen Institute Discussion Paper 2011-121/3. Amsterdam, NL: Tinbergen Institute. Available at http://papers.tinbergen.nl/11121.pdf. Accessed August 1, 2015.

Options to Address SSDI's Financial Shortfall
Marc Goldwein and Edward Lorenzen

Congressional Budget Office (CBO). 2015. CBO's 2015 Long-Term Projections for Social Security: Additional Information. Available at https://www.cbo.gov/publication/51047.

______. 2008. "Budget Options, Volume 1: Health Care." (December) Available at https://www.cbo.gov/sites/default/files/110th-congress-2007-2008/reports/12-18-healthoptions.pdf.

Goss, Steven C. 2015. Estimate of the Effects on the OASI and DI Trust Funds of enacting the provisions of Title VIII of H.R. 1314, the "Bipartisan Budget Act of 2015," introduced on October 27, 2015 by Representative John Boehner. Available at https://www.ssa.gov/OACT/solvency/JBoehner_20151027.pdf

Moulta-Ali, Umar. 2014. "Social Security Disability Insurance: Becoming Insured, Calculating Benefit Payments, and the Effect of Dropout Year Provisions." Congressional Research Service (January 24). Available at http://greenbook.waysandmeans.house.gov/sites/greenbook.waysandmeans.house.gov/files/R43370_gb.pdf.

Social Security Advisory Board (SSAB). 2014. "2014 Disability Policy Panel: Continuing Disability Reviews." Social Security Advisory Board Disability Policy Panel. Available at http://ssab.gov/Portals/0/Documents/2014_DPP_Report_Final.pdf.Social Security Board of Trustees (Trustees). 2015. The 2015 Annual Report of the Board of Trustees of the Federal Old-Age and Survivors' Insurance and Federal Disability Insurance Trust Funds. Washington: U.S. Government Publishing Office.

Social Security Board of Trustees (Trustees). 2015. The 2015 Annual Report of the Board of Trustees of the Federal Old-Age and Survivors' Insurance and Federal Disability Insurance Trust Funds. Washington: U.S. Government Publishing Office.

The White House (White House). 2015. "Social Security Disability Insurance: A Lifeline for American Workers and Families." *The White House Blog* (July). Available at https://www.whitehouse.gov/sites/default/files/docs/ssdi_national_report_7-17-2015.pdf.

List of Contributors

Authors

Anita Aaron, Executive Director, World Institute on Disability.

Aya Aghabi, Communications Director, Abilicorp.

David Babbel, Senior Advisor & Practice Leader of Insurance Economics, Charles River Associates. Professor Emeritus, Wharton School, University of Pennsylvania.

Yonatan Ben-Shalom, Senior Researcher, Mathematica Center for Studying Disability Policy.

John Burton, Professor Emeritus, Rutgers University School of Management and Labor Relations. Professor Emeritus, Cornell University School of Industrial and Labor Relations.

A. Kim Burton, Honorary Fellow of Faculty of Occupational Medicine, University of Huddersfield. Freelance Occupational Health Researcher.

Barbara Butz, President & CEO, PolicyWorks.

Jennifer Christian, President, Webility Corporation.

John Collins, Assistant Research Professor, George Mason Department of Rehabilitation Science. Consultant, National Institutes of Health.

Alex Constantin, Statistician, National Institutes of Health.

Jon Dubin, Professor of Law, Alfred C. Clapp Public Service Scholar & Associate Dean for Clinical Education, Rutgers School of Law-Newark.

David Engel, Hearing Office Chief Administrative Law Judge, Office of Disability Adjudication and Review, Social Security Administration.

Jason Fichtner, Senior Research Fellow, Mercatus Center at George Mason University.

Dale Glendening, Administrative Law Judge, Office of Disability Adjudication and Review, Social Security Administration.

Marc Goldwein, Senior Vice President & Senior Policy Director, Committee for a Responsible Federal Budget.

Xuguang (Steve) Guo, Assistant Professor of Management, Cal Poly Pomona.

Robert Haveman, Professor Emeritus of Economics and Public Affairs and Research Associate, Institute for Research on Poverty, University of Wisconsin-Madison.

Kim Hildred, President, Hildred Consulting, LLC.

Neil Jacobson, Founder & CEO, Abilicorp.

Julie Kerksick, Senior Policy Advocate, Community Advocates Public Policy Institute.

Harold Krent, Dean & Professor, IIT Chicago-Kent College of Law.

Edward Lorenzen, Senior Advisor, Committee for a Responsible Federal Budget.

David Mann, Senior Researcher, Mathematica Center for Studying Disability Policy

Pamela Mazerski, Independent Consultant, Former SSA Associate Commissioner.

Mark Meyer, Vice President, Practice Co-Leader of Insurance Economics, Charles River Associates.

Patricia Owens, former Associate U.S. Commissioner for Disability, Social Security Administration.

Mark Perriello, Disability Advocate.

Julia Porcino, Mathematician & Computer Programmer in Epidemiology and Biostatistics, National Institutes of Health Clinical Center.

David Riemer, Senior Fellow, Community Advocates Public Policy Institute.

Jason Seligman, Office of Economic Policy, U.S. Department of Treasury.

David Stapleton, Director, Mathematica Center for Studying Disability Policy.

Thomas Wickizer, Stephen F. Loebs Distinguished Professor of Health Services Management and Policy & Chair of the Division of Health Services Management and Policy, The Ohio State University College of Public Health.

Conor Williams, Economic Policy Analyst, Community Advocates Public Policy Institute.

Jeffrey Wolfe, Administrative Law Judge, Office of Disability Adjudication and Review, Social Security Administration.

Chunxiao Zhou, Senior Statistician, National Institutes of Health. Senior Statistician, IMPAQ International, LLC.

Conference Discussants

Lisa D. Ekman, President, Ekman Advocates for Progress, LLC.

Margaret Malone, Former Staff Director of the Social Security Advisory Board and Special Advisor for Disability to the Commissioner of Social Security.

Art Spencer, Former Associate Commissioner for Disability Programs, Social Security Administration.

David Wittenburg, Director of Health Research, Mathematica Policy Research.

Project Staff

This project is supported by staff from the Committee for a Responsible Federal Budget.

Mike Murphy, Chief of Staff and Director of Strategic Initiatives. Project Director.

Marc Goldwein, Senior Vice President and Senior Policy Director.

Edward Lorenzen, Senior Advisor.

Corbin Evans, Legislative Associate.

Chris Towner, Program Associate.

David Barnes, Consultant.

Special thanks to Alexandra de Filippo, Erich Hartman, and Walker Irving for their contributions.

About the Initiative Co-Chairs

Jim McCrery

Former Congressman Jim McCrery served as a member of the U.S. House of Representatives for nearly 21 years representing Louisiana. He was a member of the Ways and Means Committee from 1993 through 2008, serving as a ranking member from 2007-2008. Previously, he was Chairman of the Social Security and the Select Revenue Measures Subcommittees.

As ranking member of the Ways and Means Committee, Congressman McCrery worked closely with Chairman Rangel and other Democratic members to craft bipartisan approaches on health care and trade matters. As a member of the Health Subcommittee for 14 years, Mr. McCrery helped draft and pass a number of major health care bills, including the Balanced Budget Act of 1997 and the Medicare Prescription Drug, Improvement, and Modernization Act of 2003.

While Congressman McCrery is widely acknowledged as being well-versed on policy issues, he also understands the political side of Washington, having served for ten years on the executive committee of the National Republican Congressional Committee (NRCC).

Former Congressman Jim McCrery is currently a partner with Capitol Counsel LLC, where he counsels clients on tax, trade, and health care issues.

Earl Pomeroy

Former Congressman Earl Pomeroy represented his home state of North Dakota for 18 years as the state's lone member of the U.S. House of Representatives and eight years as Insurance Commissioner.

As a Congressman, Mr. Pomeroy served on the Ways and Means and Agriculture Committees, including as Chairman of the Social Security Subcommittee. In keeping with his insurance regulatory experience, he was a leader in health, pension and group insurance issues. In Congress, Mr. Pomeroy had a reputation for centrist practical approaches to public policy issues and a willingness to work in a bipartisan fashion.

As Insurance Commissioner, Mr. Pomeroy served as President of the National Association of Insurance Commissioners, where he advanced a program of minimum standards for financial regulation by state insurance departments, which is still operative today. As Commissioner, he chaired a number of health insurance committees, including small group market reform and standardization of Medicare supplement policies.

Mr. Pomeroy is currently an attorney at Alston & Bird law firm, where he is a member of the health policy group.

Made in the USA
Coppell, TX
05 November 2026

11299177R00302